THE BIBLE IN ITS WORLD

David Noel Freedman, *General Editor*
Astrid B. Beck, *Associate Editor*

THE BIBLE IN ITS WORLD series offers an in-depth view of significant aspects of the biblical world. Reflecting current advances in scholarship, these volumes provide insights into the context of the Bible. Individual studies apply up-to-date historical, literary, cultural, and theological methods and techniques to enhance understanding of the biblical texts and their setting. Among the topics addressed are archaeology, geography, anthropology, history, linguistics, and religion as they apply to the Hebrew Bible/Old Testament, Apocrypha/Deutero-canonicals, and New Testament.

Contributors to THE BIBLE IN ITS WORLD are among the foremost authorities in their respective fields worldwide and represent a broad range of religious and institutional affiliations. Authors are charged to offer fresh interpretations that are scholarly, responsible, and engaging. Accessible to serious general readers and scholars alike, THE BIBLE IN ITS WORLD series will interest anyone who seeks a deeper understanding of the Bible and its world.

David's Secret Demons

MESSIAH
MURDERER
TRAITOR
KING

Baruch Halpern

WILLIAM B. EERDMANS PUBLISHING COMPANY
GRAND RAPIDS, MICHIGAN / CAMBRIDGE, U.K.

© 2001 Wm. B. Eerdmans Publishing Co.

Wm. B. Eerdmans Publishing Co.
255 Jefferson Ave. S.E., Grand Rapids, Michigan 49503 /
P.O. Box 163, Cambridge CB3 9PU U.K.
www.eerdmans.com

Paperback edition 2004

Printed in the United States of America

09 08 07 06 05 04   9 8 7 6 5 4 3

Library of Congress Cataloging-in-Publication Data

Halpern, Baruch.
David's secred demons: messiah, murderer, traitor, king / Baruch Halpern.
p.   cm.   — (The Bible in its world)
Includes bibliographical references and index.
ISBN 0-8028-2797-7 (pbk. : alk. paper)
1. Bible. O.T. Samuel — Criticism, interpretation, etc. 2. David, King of Israel.
I. Title.   II. Series.

BS580.D3 H26 2001
222 .4067 — dc21

00-069198

To Aunt Claire,
for the whoops of horror it occasioned

Contents

PART II: PENETRATING THE TEXTUAL VEIL

PART III: DEFINING DAVID'S EMPIRE

PART IV: A HISTORICAL OVERTURE TO DAVID'S CAREER

PART V: A LIFE OF DAVID

APPENDIX

Acknowledgments

This study has been so long in the making, and those who have influenced it are so numerous, that thanking them all individually would double the length of the book. The students who decorated various courses about David's kingdom and ancient history-writing with their insights and incisive questions, and with their enthusiasm, have shaped this volume more than they will know, and it is certainly beyond my capacity to repay them. My colleagues, at York University in Toronto, at Penn State, at the University of Heidelberg and the Hochschule for Jewish Studies in Heidelberg, on the Megiddo Expedition, and elsewhere, have made substantial contributions. And finally, my friends and especially my family, have been inspirational. All of them patiently permitted me to squirrel myself away with Winston in order to complete this project, but offered release in its most difficult stages.

Two institutions have supported the writing of this book. The College of the Liberal Arts at Penn State has helped in every way, including a leave and a sabbatical, to see it through. The Gold Family Foundation has supported the writing with a generous grant. In addition, the Israel Exploration Society and Dr. Joseph Aviram have been very kind in permitting reproduction of materials for this volume from the *Israel Exploration Journal*. The maps in the volume come courtesy of Philip J. Kolb and Adam C. Hegedus, Horizon Media Solutions. The indices were prepared by Jonathan David.

I am also grateful to Doubleday-Anchor, for allowing me to write this book as a prelude to a history of Israel for the Anchor Bible Reference Library. My subject editor for that volume is happily also the editor for this one — David Noel Freedman, to whom I am profoundly indebted for encouragement, for many ideas and for extraordinary patience. To Allen Myers, the supervising editor at Eerdmans, sincere thanks. Thanks also to Klaas Wolterstorff, the Production Manager at Eerdmans, and to Judith Dekel, of the Tel-Aviv University Institute of Archaeology, for all their hard work on the archaeological figures.

My gurus in the field of archaeology deserve special thanks: Bill Dever, Israel Finkelstein, Sy Gitin, Jack Holladay, Alex Joffe, Larry Stager, and David Ussishkin. Israel, David, and I co-direct the Megiddo Expedition and frequently discuss the implications of the archaeological evidence for the history of the period. Despite this, they and the other scholars mentioned here have put a clumsy historian through a long and arduous curriculum that permits at least some of our disagreements to be serious. There are very few scholars whose gentle patience is so expansive, whose pedagogy is so talented, whose sense of humor so effectively pillories ineptitude, and who are as much fun to sit and talk with as this group.

Special thanks to Josh, Ami, and Lew for everything, and for encouragement that included the drastic measure of reading much of the first draft and making invaluable suggestions for improvement.

Preface

First impressions matter.

When we take in a news story, in the daily paper, in a magazine, on radio or television, we start from the assumption that it is true. We believe it from the beginning. We suspend disbelief. This is why panic ensued from the Orson Welles Mercury Theater broadcast of *War of the Worlds.* It is why Mark Twain had to scotch by telegram the news of his death. It is why most of the electorate actually believes what one or another politician says.

There is a reason for this. We have evolved to receive instruction from our parents and from our society. The instruction takes the form of rules of behavior, rules of expression, and rules of identity and thought. We have also evolved, perhaps more recently, to revolt against that instruction in adolescence. That revolt, too, must have its sociobiological function, perhaps in permitting us to test our instruction, test the narrative we have received, and thus improve it as we hand it on to another generation.

Still, the principle of belief remains. It holds most consistently among children and students, who trust almost anything they are told. No matter how critically we approach an ancient text, then, we are more or less indentured to it.

In the case of the first kings of ancient Israel, Saul appears to us as an abortion, a failure. Few people even recognize the name of Ishbaal, Saul's son and successor. David and Solomon preside over an empire. What we are reading is a text stemming from circles close to David and Solomon, and most readers accept its claims. More important, they accept its evaluation of David and Solomon. The framework of historical narrative confines our imagination of events.

Yet it was David's agenda, as we shall see, systematically to root out Saul's family. And it is the agenda of the apology for David to portray Saul's failures and to efface the memory of his son, Ishbaal. The bias of the source is patent.

Might we suspect that the party faction behind David's homicidal policy in the case of Saul's family also underlies the reports of our text? Would it be enough to eradicate the line if one did not also reduce its achievements to the negligible? How did the politics of David's time shape what we read in our reports about him?

These are the sorts of questions this book addresses.

To escape the framework of the historical narrative, we need only imagine the events from a political and ideological position opposite that of the text. Our only direct information about David, in the books of Samuel, essentially presents him as a hero. The present book is therefore a glimpse of David as his enemies saw him. To the extent that those enemies were right in their view, it is also a glimpse of how his closest associates saw him.

The resulting picture is not a pretty one. But the fact that it produces a recognizably human David — not the brilliant literary creation in Samuel, but a flesh-and-blood man — indicates that the portrait of David in the Bible was aimed at answering the accusations I attribute to his enemies here — whether those accusations were shouted, whispered, or merely anticipated by the author of Samuel. The David of this book is in a sense the opposite of the David of Samuel. He is the anti-David or, by implication, the anti-Messiah.

To contemplate David as his enemies saw him is to understand why the book of Samuel takes the form that it does. Much of Samuel goes to defend David against his enemies' picture of him, for Samuel was written for David's successor, Solomon, and transmitted by the kings of the dynasty he founded. This shows, against the drift of much contemporary scholarship, that David was an important historical agent. But the other aim that the present undertaking realizes is to give voice to David's opponents.

Contemporary literary theorists seem forever to be talking about the "marginalized" and the "oppressed," and pretending to represent them. But there is nothing marginal about those with the power to express their views, for they at least have the opportunity to persuade others. The truly marginal are those who are not even suffered to speak. And the most marginal of all are those who have passed, silent, from history.

David's enemies fall into this category. As a result we have only one version of his career. In the absence of a competing narrative from antiquity, it falls to us to construct one based on his dynasty's narrative. In so doing, we allow the silent to speak. We permit the people unable to express their own views in the text to do so in our imagination. We recover a perspective that has otherwise vanished from our record. We do not complete the evidence, but we augment it with new testimony.

Enemies tend to be irrational, even downright paranoid, about one another, which is why David liquidated Saul's family. So the historical David belongs somewhere on the continuum between the propaganda written about him under Solomon and the view from the opposite side. In this book, the reader will find, first, a summary of Solomon's presentation. Then comes a defense of the other side. At that juncture, the reader can position David anywhere on the spectrum between the two.

This leaves the matters of David's character and achievements ambiguous. However, it does have the merit of establishing his reality, his historicity. His enemies viewed him as moderns tend to portray their foes. His son, and perhaps his "wife" Bathsheba, responded to the charges. No one went around demonizing King Arthur, and it would be difficult to reconstruct coherent charges against Abraham to which the text of Genesis replies. However damning this treatment may be, it has the merit of establishing that David existed, and reigned. In contrast, the biblical version, in the books of Samuel, presents a man who never did exist, a ruler altogether too good to be true.

A few notes are in order regarding conventions employed in this book. First, the name of the chief Israelite god (yes, there were others, including his consort, Ashtoret) is written with the letters y-h-w-h in the Bible and in inscriptions. This is the term usually translated LORD in English-language Bibles, or Jehovah in others. In popular pronunciation in the period of the Israelite kingdoms, it probably sounded more or less like Yau (*yow!*) or Yaui. But this is not sure. In scholarly journals, it is often represented simply by the four consonants of the Bible: YHWH. To make the text less difficult to read, however, I have spelled this name as Yahweh (except when reporting Hebrew words).

Second, the judge, prophet, and priest Samuel also lends his name to the books of 1 and 2 Samuel. Scholars, using professional shorthand, tend to refer to both as "Samuel." They leave it to their colleagues to discern which is meant. I have tried to distinguish the two here, and particularly to identify the man, Samuel, as a person where that figure is intended. But in some contexts where the meaning seems unambiguous to me, I have used "Samuel," alone, to refer to the biblical record.

Third, I have not addressed the reality of the numbers of warriors or other people in the ancient texts. Generally, scholars agree that numbers of warriors fielded in biblical texts tend to be, but are not always, exaggerated. The Bible, after all, is a transmitted text, and some of it was transmitted orally for a considerable time before being committed to writing. In oral transmission, especially, exaggeration is almost inevitable — it is a trope of expression. A considerable controversy rages over almost every number related in Assyrian and Egyptian royal inscriptions — pertaining to warriors, captives, even quantities of tribute. In my view, the numbers in inscriptions tend to be reliable in magnitude, but this rule is far from being unbroken. Archaeology affords a little control (not as much as is often claimed) on population figures, but this is based entirely on hypothetical coefficients of density for inhabited areas (25 or 50 persons per dunam in towns). Beyond this, however, numbers range from garrisons of 25 soldiers to control major ports in the 14th century B.C.E., to an army of 10 thousand Greeks cutting a swath through all of western Asia in the 4th century, to armies in the tens of thousands in between. More specific reliable numbers are rare. Probably, King Ahab of Israel led about 15 thousand troops to a battle in central Syria in 853. That is an expeditionary force, and cannot represent the extent of the Israelite army. In the mid-8th century, Israel seems to have had a population of free adult male heads of households exceeding 60 thousand. But such figures are in any case merely limits beyond which it would be imprudent to follow textual claims. Each case involving numbers must be evaluated on its own merits.

Finally, the word "god" is a common, not proper noun. There are Greek gods, Norse gods, sports gods. Jupiter was a high god for the Romans. Most writers capitalize the term when referring to their own Gods, and observant Jews even write "G-d" in order to avoid committing what they think is a name to print. I have tried to achieve some consistency on this point, but ask the reader's indulgence in interpreting the alternation. In this book, at the request of the series editor, "David's God" is the high god, Yahweh, but "the pharaoh's god" is merely one of several. This seems unfair to the pharaoh, but then, the pharaoh is unlikely to buy a copy of the book.

Abbreviations

AASOR	Annual of the American Schools of Oriental Research
AB	Anchor Bible
ABD	*Anchor Bible Dictionary,* ed. D. N. Freedman
ABL	*Assyrian and Babylonian Letters Belonging to the Kouyunjik Collections of the British Museum*
ADAJ	*Annual of the Department of Antiquities of Jordan*
AfO	*Archiv für Orientforschung*
ANEP	*The Ancient Near East in Pictures,* ed. J. B. Pritchard
AOS	American Oriental Series
ARAB	D. D. Luckenbill, *Ancient Records of Assyria and Babylonia*
ARE	*Ancient Records of Egypt,* ed. J. H. Breasted
AS	Assyriological Studies
ASOR	American Schools of Oriental Research
BA	*Biblical Archaeologist*
BAR	*Biblical Archaeology Review*
BASOR	*Bulletin of the American Schools of Oriental Research*
BeO	*Bibbia e Oriente*
Bibl	*Biblica*
BibOr	Biblica et orientalia
BN	*Biblische Notizen*
BR	*Bible Review*
BWANT	Beiträge zur Wissenschaft vom Alten und Neuen Testament
BZAW	Beihefte zur *ZAW*
CAH	*Cambridge Ancient History*
CBQ	*Catholic Biblical Quarterly*
Chr	Chronicler

ConBOT	Coniectanea biblica, Old Testament
DMOA	Documenta et Monumenta Orientis Antiqui
DtrH	Deuteronomistic History
EA	El Amarna text
EHAT	Exegetisches Handbuch zum Alten Testament
ErIsr	*Eretz Israel*
FAT	Forschungen zum Alten Testament
HAR	*Hebrew Annual Review*
HS	*Hebrew Studies*
HSM	Harvard Semitic Monographs
HSS	Harvard Semitic Studies
Herm	Hermeneia
HUCA	*Hebrew Union College Annual*
ICC	International Critical Commentary
ICK	*Inscriptions Cunéiformes de Kültepe*, ed. B. Hrozný
IEJ	*Israel Exploration Journal*
JAOS	*Journal of the American Oriental Society*
JBL	*Journal of Biblical Literature*
JCS	*Journal of Cuneiform Studies*
JNES	*Journal of Near Eastern Studies*
JQR	*Jewish Quarterly Review*
JSOT	*Journal for the Study of the Old Testament*
JTS	*Journal of Theological Studies*
K.	Tablets in the Kouyunjik collection of the British Museum
KAI	H. Donner and W. Rollig, *Kanaanäische und aramäische Inschriften*
LAS	S. Parpola, *Letters from Assyrian Scholars*
LXX	Septuagint
MDB	*Le Monde de la Bible*
MDOG	*Mitteilungen der Deutschen Orient-Gesellschaft*
NEA	*Near Eastern Archaeology*
NEAEHL	*New Encyclopedia of Archaeological Excavation in the Holy Land*, ed. E. Stern
OBO	Orbis biblicus et orientalis
OIP	Oriental Institute Publication
Or	*Orientalia*
OTL	Old Testament Library
OTS	Oudtestamentische Studiën
PRU	*Le Palais royal d'Ugarit*
Qad	*Qadmoniot*
QR	Qumran
RB	*Revue biblique*
RIMA	The Royal Inscriptions of Mesopotamia, Assyrian Periods
RLA	*Reallexikon der Assyriologie*, ed. E. Ebeling–B. Meissner

RSO	*Rivista degli studi orientali*
SAA	State Archives of Assyria
SBLDS	Society of Biblical Literature Dissertation Series
SBLMS	Society of Biblical Literature Monograph Series
SBLSBS	Society of Biblical Literature Sources for Biblical Study
SBLTT	Society of Biblical Literature Texts and Translations
SBT	Studies in Biblical Theology
SEL	*Studi epigrafici e linguistici*
SHANE	Studies in the History of the Ancient Near East
SLA	R. H. Pfeiffer, *State Letters of Assyria*
SS	Studi semitici
Sup	Supplement
TA	*Tel Aviv*
TynBul	*Tyndale Bulletin*
UF	*Ugarit-Forschungen*
VAB	*Vorderasiatische Bibliothek*
VT	*Vetus Testamentum*
WO	*Die Welt des Orients*
ZA	*Zeitschrift für Assyriologie*
ZABR	*Zeitschrift für Altorientalische und Biblische Rechtsgeschichte*
ZAW	*Zeitschrift für die alttestamentliche Wissenschaft*
ZDPV	*Zeitschrift des Deutschen Palästina-Vereins*

Ancient Writings

Josephus
Ag. Ap.	*Against Apion*
Ant.	*Antiquities of the Jews*
P.An.	Papyrus Anastasi I

PART I

DAVID IN WRITING

CHAPTER 1

The Surprising David

The Gregorian calendar calls the year A.D. 2000 the 2000th Year of the Lord *(annus domini)* or the 2000th year C.E. (of the Common Era), depending on one's sensibilities. Thousands of celebrants planned travel for the year well in advance, many of them learning only later that 2000 C.E. was the end of the 2nd millennium of the Gregorian calendar, not the start of the 3rd. In Gregorian reckoning, there was no Year 0. Hence the year 1000 was the 1000th year in the calendar, the last year of the 1st millennium. January 1, 2001 marked the start of the new millennium.

The Year 1 in this calendar is defined as that of the birth of Jesus, thought by Christians to be the Messiah, the anointed son of God. But the claim that Jesus is the Messiah, the claim that he is the son of the Jewish God, depends on his linear descent from David. There is no direct juxtaposition of Jesus with Moses, and no implication in the Jewish or Christian traditions that Moses's descendants would somehow redeem humanity. Likewise, no gospel text stresses Jesus's connections with the patriarchs of Genesis, such as Abraham. Instead, the emphasis is on the connection to David, because the messianic hopes of the Jews, near the turn of the era (1 C.E., not 0), focused principally on figures of Davidic ancestry. (There are other messianic figures in the Dead Sea Scrolls, but these do not figure in mainstream Jewish tradition.)

In biblical and later Jewish tradition, David is not a lawgiver. Though a great king, though a conqueror, he is far from being a saint, or even demonstratively pious. Yet his is the line that is elected by Yahweh, Israel's God. In a nonconfessional view, this means that the kings of David's dynasty, who ruled the state of Judah after the division of the kingdom in 932 B.C.E. (Before the Common Era), claimed

3

that their God had promised them eternal kingship. The truth of this claim cannot be evaluated by historians. Its longevity, however; its acceptance in Judaism, in Christianity; its survival in the West are remarkable phenomena. The idea of a messiah, of a Millennium with a capital M, revolves around David.

For this longevity, whatever the claims of the dynasty, we must accord credit to the picture of David himself. Some of this picture comes from later reflections on that king, including the idea that he composed a large number of biblical psalms. Some of it, such as the report on David's combat with Goliath, or on his relations with Saul, is of indeterminate age, though it is older than the pietistic view of David propagated in Chronicles, for example, or in the usual interpretation of Psalms.[1] But a great deal of what the books of Samuel and the first chapters of 1 Kings have to say about David is contemporary, or very nearly contemporary, with that king, in the 10th century B.C.E.

Strangely, it is not in the texts in which he is most saintly that David's image captivates readers and even worshippers. The historical David appears in the books of 1 and 2 Samuel, and dies in the 2nd chapter of 1 Kings. He is, the text tells us, promised eternal kingship in Israel. He is, the text tells us, Yahweh's elect, the fulfillment of all Yahweh's promises to the patriarchs about Israel's land and nationhood. These properties exalt him, make him crucial to Jesus's genealogy. But even if we were to regard these claims as somehow independent of his dynasty, as true, they would not account for David's appeal in the history of Western literature and culture.

Moses, to be sure, is portrayed in art, film, and novels. Jesus has been endlessly portrayed. But the novelists, artists, and filmmakers are almost uniform in presenting the Moses that a confessional audience expects, the Jesus that redeems the world. There are exceptions, including film satires — Monty Python's amusingly adolescent *Life of Brian*, Luis Bunuel's superbly sardonic *The Milky Way*. And in novels, excellent, earthy explorations of Jesus as a person are not uncommon, as Nikos Kazantzakis's *Last Temptation of Christ* and Robert Graves's *King Jesus*. Still, the imagining even of Jesus is almost always devotional, however it may humanize him.

David is another story. He is, like Moses or Jesus, the subject of "Classic Comics" portrayals. In these, the story of his fight with Goliath is foregrounded, and misrepresented, as it is in the tradition: David is the underdog, relying on faith. This is probably the only time that David exhibits the transcendent devotion that marks him as a man (or, rather, boy) of faith.

---

1. For a unique study of this view, and discussion of David as psalmist, see A. M. Cooper, "The Life and Times of King David According to the Book of Psalms," in *The Poet and the Historian*, ed. Richard Elliott Friedman. HSS 26 (Chico: Scholars Press, 1983), 117-31.

But David is far from being a redemptive figure even in the tradition. True, Moses can be represented as a man tortured by doubt about his own endurance and greatness, as a punishingly resentful man of flashing anger. David, however, is presented differently. His story invites more earthy, steamy treatments. Even in unembarrassedly partisan hagiographies, movies such as Gregory Peck's *David and Bathsheba* or Richard Gere's *King David* mix in human violence, murder, warfare, sex, and court politics in a more realistic way than any film about Jesus or Moses has ever done. *Absalom and Ahitophel* reflects on David emotionally in such a way as to concretize a suicidal agony unknown even in Moses's deepest despair.

Novels about David sometimes present him with the reverence accorded other iconic biblical characters. In a work like Disraeli's *David Alroy* ("David the King"), his persona is even combined with that of Joshua in an intricate celebration of military imperialism. *Absalom, Absalom* evokes him as an evil parental archetype, manipulative, cruel, yet almost as a counterpart of Job, suffering, however guilty, pulsations of unmerited pain.

Both the promise of David's youth and the flaws of his maturity imprint themselves on the imagination of writers. No novel about the Bible is so accomplished in the historical art as Stefan Heym's brilliant *The King David Report*: in a profound comment both on ancient Israel and on life behind the Iron Curtain, Heym shows how a state in control of reporting on itself, in control of the media for propagating history, twists, airbrushes, and sanitizes the seamy aspects of its past. Like Heym's exposé, satires also tend to deconstruct the text, to penetrate to a reality behind the veil of representation, and to present David in a less favorable or less saintly light. This is clear from the disappointing satirical theodicy of Joseph Heller, *God Knows,* in which David reports discovering after experimenting with various techniques that it was easiest to collect foreskins from the Philistines, as a bride-price for Saul's daughter, "if you killed them first." Heller too attacks the image of David that has become his icon, and inspired Michelangelo's iconic statue: the warranty of his divine election, the fight against Goliath. The poor oaf "didn't stand a chance."

What is it about David? Why does he, of all the figures in the Bible, attract such treatment — treatment that is at once irreverent *and* serious, treatment that punctures his apparent holiness, heroism, and honesty? The answer is that the text itself invites such an approach. 1 and 2 Samuel furnish a circumstantial character history whose complexity makes even the most sophisticated ancient biography seem like a cartoon in comparison. Samuel takes its reader through the protagonist's evolution from shepherd, to courtier, to therapon — Patrocles to the Achilles of King Saul's son, Jonathan. He flees into exile, is transformed into a bandit, then mercenary, statesman, leader, king, victor, conqueror, and ruler. The author of 2 Samuel traces the growth of an independence of the law, a personal lust, born in David's days as an exile in the wilderness, but cultivated in power, that results in adultery and murder. He documents the disintegration of the royal family, internecine intrigue and revolt, and imputes to David's lawlessness a Lear-like status in his dotage. At the end, he is a weak, yet still violent and vengeful old man, unable to hold his own either in politics or in bed.

David, in a word, is human, fully, four-dimensionally, recognizably human. He grows, he learns, he travails, he triumphs, and he suffers immeasurable tragedy and loss. He is the first human being in world literature.

There is more. David is almost, or perhaps more than, a Shakespearean character. Even at the height of his career, he is not a religious symbol, but the embodiment of worldly success. At the nadir of his fortunes, he embodies the fragility of achievement, the importance of the right life rather than a high station. But at almost all times, he is a *secular* icon — a character so extraordinary and yet so very human, so realistically fallible, that the innocent reader almost inevitably empathizes with him. His deeds are divorced from miracle, his relationships are with other people, whether friend or foe, rather than with his God. Heller erred in imagining David reviewing his life in dialogue with his God, rather than humans. The reasons for David's behavior and even the consequences of his behavior remain always on a purely human, and often unconventional, level.

In basing his relationships on personal and political foundations, in banishing supernatural intervention and sometimes even instruction from the arena of social activity, David is a consummate revolutionary. Subtly but repeatedly, he sets traditional assumptions and practices on their ear. The great genius of his portrayal is not merely that it is convincing: it is that his nature, his individuality, drives his behavior at every crucial juncture in the story. David is not just the first human in literature, he is the first true individual, the first modern human.

Nowhere is this principle better exemplified than in the story of David's combat with Goliath (1 Sam. 17), and nowhere is it clearer how the imposition of our own cultural values in interpretation can veil the text's real meaning.

Two problems with the story should be mentioned. First, the oldest translation of the text, the "Old Greek" version of the Septuagint, probably from the 3rd century B.C.E., lacks much of the text present in the Hebrew. Some scholars believe that the Hebrew text is a combination of two stories, one of which was incorporated only after the 3rd century. But this is probably incorrect.[2] In

---

2. See Emanuel Tov, "The Composition of 1 Samuel 16–18 in the Light of the Septuagint Version," in *Empirical Models for Biblical Criticism,* ed. Jeffrey H. Tigay (Philadelphia: University of Pennsylvania Press, 1985), 97-130; Alexander Rofé, "The Battle of David and

1 Samuel, David has already been attached to Saul's court when the Goliath story begins. But several verses in the story presume that David and Saul are strangers (when Saul asks, 'Who is that boy?' for example, and Abner does *not* respond, 'I don't know, but he's always around when we need him'). The omissions in the Greek contain all of the verses suggesting that David was unknown to Saul when the confrontation with Goliath took place. So it looks as though the Greek text was harmonizing apparent contradictions.[3] In any case, the omissions do not materially affect the shape of the story.

Second, there is still another tradition about Goliath's death. Materials appended at the end of 2 Samuel describe the achievements of David's heroes. Among them is the verse, 2 Sam. 21:19:

> There was another battle in Gob with the Philistines, and Elhanan son of Yaare Orgim from Bethlehem smote Goliath the Gittite, the shaft of whose spear was like a weaver's beam.

The name of Elhanan's father has been garbled — Orgim means "weavers" and has been mistakenly copied from the description of Goliath's weaponry. The parallel text in Chronicles and the Old Greek translation recognize the word as a scribal error and suppress it. The only other Elhanan and the only other Bethlehemite in the lists of David's heroes is "Elhanan ben-Dodo from Bethlehem" (2 Sam. 23:24). He was probably originally listed as Goliath's killer.

Two texts reconcile the entry about Elhanan with the narrative of Goliath's death in 1 Samuel. The Targum, the translation of the Bible into Aramaic, identifies Elhanan as David, seeing as both are from Bethlehem (Targ. to 2 Sam. 21:19). But why then list Elhanan among David's heroes? And why, as the medieval commentator David Kimhi asks, do the killings occur in different places? Elhanan kills Goliath at Gob, whereas David in 1 Samuel kills him at Socho or Ephes Dammim.

A second text, in Chronicles, says that Elhanan slew Lahmi, Goliath's brother (1 Chr. 20:5). But Goliath's brother's name reflects a misreading of

Goliath: Folklore, Theology, Eschatology," in *Judaic Perspectives on Ancient Israel,* ed. Jacob Neusner, Baruch A. Levine, and Ernest S. Frerichs (Philadelphia: Fortress, 1987), 117-51; Walter Dietrich, "Die Erzählung von David und Goliat in I Sam 17," *ZAW* 108 (1996): 172-91.

3. The same applies to the material omitted by the Greek in 1 Sam. 18:17-19 (and probably 21c), where Saul reneges on the promise of his daughter Merab's hand in marriage that he makes in 17:25 (not in the Old Greek). By way of contrast, the pluses in the Hebrew text do not have the character of apologetic expansions, but reflect a contradictory version of the story.

Lahmi *('et laḥmî)* for (Elhanan) "the Bethlehemite" *(bēt hallaḥmî)* in Samuel. Chronicles has either emended the text or seized opportunistically on a scribal error to produce a brother of Goliath and resolve the conflicting claims. The Jewish historian Flavius Josephus, writing late in the 1st century C.E. *(Ant.* 7.302), simply omits the name of Goliath in connection with Elhanan, whom he identifies as David's relative (as both are from Bethlehem). We could also resort to a fourth harmonization, namely that there were two "Goliaths from Gath, the shafts of whose spears were like weavers' beams." With that eminent biblical scholar, Samuel Langhorne Clemens, then, we might suggest that David did not kill Goliath, but another man of the same name.

The harmonizations in Chronicles, the Targum, and Josephus all reflect a concern with history. All differ with our texts. To say David was Elhanan, or that Elhanan slew Goliath's brother, or even that there were two Goliaths, is to dissent from Samuel. Omitting Goliath's name in the note about Elhanan is no less a critical historical decision. Most likely, storytellers displaced the deed from the otherwise obscure Elhanan onto the more famous character, David. This displacement was facilitated by the facts that Elhanan was from Bethlehem, and that his father's name, Dodo *(d-d-w),* resembled David's name *(d-w-d).* But more was involved. The story as it was told was invaluable for delineating David's character.

1 Sam. 17 can be epitomized as follows:

Inland from Azekah, on the edge of the flat coastal plain bordering the hill country of Judah, the Israelites and Philistines drew up on the slopes of the Wadi Elah. From the Philistine lines a warrior stepped forth, Goliath by name, from Gath. The eminent Dead Sea scroll scholar, Patrick Skehan, remarked on discovering from a scroll of Samuel that Goliath was "only" 6 ft. 5 in. in height that the villain could not even play center in basketball.[4] He wore a helmet, and a cuirass of bronze plates, weighing more than 110 lb. He wore greaves to protect his legs and a bronze sword strapped across his back. The shaft of his spear was "like a weaver's beam." The last phrase refers not to the shaft's weight, but to a rope wrapped around the butt to serve as a handle: the spear Goliath carried was a thrusting weapon, not a ballistic one, with a 15-lb. iron tip.

Goliath challenged Israel to field a warrior against him in single combat, and Saul and all Israel were afraid.

David was either the king's minstrel or a boy dispatched from Bethlehem by his father with victuals for his older, veteran, brothers. He volunteered to take on

---

4. In a letter to Frank Moore Cross. Actually, if the text were using the long cubit, Goliath would remain 8 ft. tall. In either case, during the transmission of the Massoretic (or traditional) Hebrew text, Goliath enjoyed a late growth spurt.

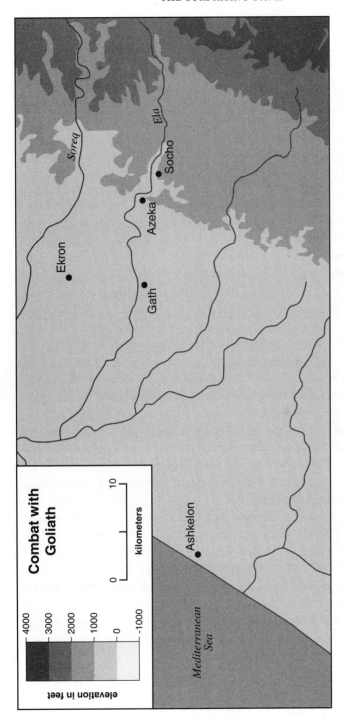

Combat with Goliath

elevation in feet

4000
3000
2000
1000
0
-1000

kilometers

0   10

Soreq

Ela

Socho

Azeka

Ekron

Gath

Ashkelon

Mediterranean
Sea

Map 1.1

Goliath. Saul said, "You cannot go to this Philistine, to fight with him, for you are a stripling, and he has been a man of war since his youth." David's immortal reply:

> Your servant was a shepherd for his father, and when the lion or the bear came and bore off a sheep from the flock, I would go out after it, and smite it, and snatch its prey from its mouth, and it would rise up against me and I would grasp its beard and smite it and slay it. Your servant has smitten the lion and the bear, and this uncircumcised Philistine will be as one of them, for he has taunted the alignments of the Living God.

David donned Saul's armor, but found the outfit too awkward, too restricting. So he advanced in mufti. Carrying his staff, he loaded his pouch with a few smooth stones for his sling. The Philistine saw him — a mere youth — and protested, contemptuously, "Am I a dog that you come against me with sticks?" David retorted, "You come against me with a sword, a spear, and a scimitar, but I come against you in the name of Yahweh of Hosts." And as the Philistine drew near, David slung a stone and smote the Philistine on the forehead [or: on the greave, kneecapping him],[5] and ran forward, and drew the Philistine's sword, and lopped off his head.

This story has sufficient resonance in the canons of our culture that one need not dwell on the cast traditional readers have given it. David is a mere youth, we are told at least twice. He is without armor, or even shield. Goliath towers menacingly, and is protected by an impressive array of armor and a shield-bearer. David has only a staff and sling: he advances against Goliath with mere sticks, implements for controlling dogs. Goliath has a spear, a thrusting sword, and some third weapon, perhaps a scimitar. David reposes his faith in God, and it is through God's agency that a stone, propelled from the shepherd's sling, knocks the giant down. The battle is a victory of the delicate little amateur over the battle-hardened titan.

All this, on the surface of the presentation, has registered in popular reflection. Yet early commentators already express some curiosity about the traditional interpretation. Kimhi, an astute student of language, draws our attention to the action in 1 Sam. 17:41-48, when the battle begins: V. 41, "The Philistine drew ever nearer to David, with his shield-bearer before him." V. 42, "and the Philistine saw David, and belittled him." V. 44, "And the Philistine said to David, 'Come to me, and I will give your flesh to the birds of the heaven and the beasts of the field.'" V. 48, "When the Philistine arose, and went and drew near to meet David. . . ." Why, asked Kimhi, does it take Goliath so long to get near

---

5. For the kneecapping of Goliath, see Ariela Deem, "'. . . And the Stone Sank into His Forehead': A Short Note on 1 Samuel XVII 49," *VT* 28 (1978): 349-51.

David? Why does he need to invite David to approach him? The answer, once the question is asked, is clear — the Philistine is weighed down under a ton of metal, and any mobility lies on David's side. Josephus makes the same observation: "Still, the Philistine, the load of his armor impeding a more rapid advance, gradually approached David" (*Ant.* 6.188).

This observation is crucial, and it is remarkable that Josephus and Kimhi, despite making it, adhere to a pietistic interpretation of the chapter. Is David trusting in his God, as he claims, or avenging an insult to him? In antiquity, arms fell into three divisions: heavy infantry — in our case Goliath; cavalry, which in our case is absent; and light infantry. Light infantry were projectile warriors, archers, slingers, javelin hurlers.

Think of these arms in terms of the game "paper, scissors, rock." In formation, heavy infantry could withstand cavalry or chariotry by the use of pikes. The cavalry protected the heavy infantry against flanking sorties, operating best against light infantry. The light infantry were skirmishers, picking off heavy infantry with their projectiles, but vulnerable to the cavalry. Light infantry, if protected by the heavy infantry, could also help withstand enemy cavalry. But by their nature, light infantry were at a premium in hilly terrain, such as the Israelite highlands, where cavalry did not operate. For, unaided, the heavy infantry could never catch up with the light infantry. Only cavalry or one's own light infantry could clear the field of these projectile warriors. This is why the Athenian expedition to Sicily failed in the Peloponnesian War: Thucydides describes at length how Athens's heavy infantry was decimated in the mountains by local light infantry, principally using the sling.

This is all the background one needs in order to understand the profoundest commentary ever written on the duel with Goliath. The following excerpt comes from Mr. Clemens's novel, *A Connecticut Yankee in King Arthur's Court:*

> The Yankee was in "the simplest and comfortablest of gymnast costumes," his opponent in full armor. Sir Sagramour set out to chase him down.
>
> Says the Yankee, "Why, he hadn't any show in the world at that; it was a game of tag, with all the advantages on my side; I whirled out of his path with ease whenever I chose, and once I slapped him on the back as I went to the rear." The hunt went on.
>
> When the combatants retired to the ends of the lists, the Yankee "slipped my lasso from the horn of the saddle. . . . This time you should have seen him come! It was a business trip, sure . . . when the space between us had narrowed. . . . I sent the snaky spirals of the rope a-cleaving through the air, then darted aside and faced about and brought my

trained animal to a halt with all his feet braced under him for a surge. The next moment the rope sprang taut and yanked Sir Sagramour out of the saddle!"

No tactic could more eloquently express the relationship of the light-armored to the heavy-armored infantryman. Here, a light cavalryman surprises the Arthurian knight, just as the uncatchable David catches Goliath unawares.

His rope-a-dope tactics bring the Yankee successive victories in the joust. But his rival, Merlin, steals his lariat. This leads to the last stage in the duel. Sir Sagramour is back, and refuses the Yankee leave to borrow Launcelot's weapons. Each takes his place. Twain's narrative takes up:

> "It seemed as if the king could not take heart to give the signal. But at last he lifted his hand, the clear note of the bugle followed, Sir Sagramour's long blade described a flashing curve in the air, and it was superb to see him come. I sat still. On he came. I did not move. People got so excited that they shouted to me, 'Fly, fly! Save thyself! This is murther!'
>
> "I never budged so much as an inch, till that thundering apparition had got within fifteen paces of me; then I snatched a dragoon revolver out of my holster, there was a flash and a roar, and the revolver was back in the holster before anybody could tell what had happened.
>
> "Here was a riderless horse plunging by, and yonder lay Sir Sagramour, stone dead."

If the first part of the story whimsically transposes David's freedom of maneuver into Arthur's court, this second part is even more sardonic. With the knight charging down on him, apparently defenseless, the Yankee pulls out his pistol and guns him down. The suddenness, and the incongruity, are funny. But they are also fair comment on David's duel with Goliath.

Twain's point is simple. Goliath and all the other participants in the battle expected a close-quarter contest between two champions. This is why Saul tries to outfit David in a suit of armor. It is also why Goliath continually invites the unarmored, uncatchable David to draw near. The "rules of the game" dictated that the combatants should close. David declines to abide by the rules, and fights from outside the ring.

Goliath never thought that he was challenging the artillery. Yet up turns David, naked of all armor, carrying a shepherd's staff. And suddenly, the shot from the sling penetrates Goliath's defenses and decks him. Heller's treatment of the incident, in *God Knows*, is similar. David refuses to fight by Marquis of

Queensberry rules. This is a blow below the belt, a sucker punch, a man with a howitzer mowing down a peasant with a pitchfork.

In popular understanding, David's achievement is miraculous. The defenseless waif, with faith in God, overpowers the maleficent ogre: this is Jack and the Beanstalk, Hansel and Gretel, Tom Sawyer and Injun Joe. But military history stamps another aspect on the business — and suggests that David had Goliath at a disadvantage. The narrator certainly stands on David's piety, but the nature of that piety is his pride. He does not so much rely on Yahweh as avenge an insult to Yahweh's dignity. Goliath has taunted the alignments of the Living God and has to pay.

The magnification of David's achievement — as though he stood no chance against his heavy-weighted opponent — enhances our hero's renown. By way of contrast, it would be no credit to Goliath that he chewed up an unarmed shepherd. Anyway, all the dramatization goes to reinforce the view that David was the underdog — to highlight the courage and faith of the future king.

And David *would* be the underdog, had he accepted combat on traditional terms. The narrative thus demonstrates that the element of surprise, the ruse, is critical for leveraging skills into victory. This is also the point of Twain's notion that David may as well have pulled out a sten gun, that Goliath never stood a chance.

This reading reverses the values of the usual interpretation. Specifically, Twain and Heller deny that David was in any imminent danger. At the start of the action, Samuel implies that Goliath was invulnerable. With Kimhi, Twain says David was uncatchable, and this is precisely what Samuel says as well. For Twain, David is modern man, rejecting the mindless, medieval ritualized combat of the Philistines: the fates of nations cannot depend on single combat, for the fates of nations are too important to scruple about the rules of sport. Combat is not a matter of personal honor, but of national destiny. So far, the 19th-century liberal, who hoped the costs of real warfare would bring an end to all warfare.

But Twain's take on the story is a perfectly accurate interpretation of Samuel. David begins his career as a musician playing the lyre for Saul. In the Goliath episode, he moves on to reject the etiquette of social relations shared by all around him. This is the pattern that will persist throughout his history. He is not just Yahweh's elect: he is Yahweh's avenger. He is not just destined for greatness: he shapes his greatness by a complete disregard for orthodoxy.

This is a beginning for understanding the literary portrayal of David. His modernity, his rejection of conventional behavior and thought, will come up again and again. In the discussion that follows, the story of 1 and 2 Samuel will be reviewed, and the development of David's character over time — in the narrative — underscored.

CHAPTER 2

David's History in the Books of Samuel

What we read in 1 and 2 Samuel is only a profile of David. It is not a statue in the round, not a full relief, not even a frontal view of his face. Instead. we see the sides of him that an apologist was interested in our seeing. Or rather, we see the sides that an audience, long ago, was intended to see. David as we have him is a literary character, and those scholars who claim that the character in the narrative never existed cannot really be blamed for their skepticism. He never did exist precisely and only as the narrative specifies. Indeed, all historical characters have an existence beyond what is recorded about them. Most have lives different from what is recorded about them.

The molds on which the presentation of David's career and character were modeled can have come from only two sources.[1] The first was the Israelite idea of the "hero." The second was biographies of other kings who founded dynasties — that is, usurpers. Concerning these, there was considerable literature by the time even the earliest parts of 2 Samuel were written down, let alone the latest parts of 1 Samuel, which are even more shrouded in the veils of oral tradition, legend, and the narrative logic of monarchic Israelite elite authors.

---

1. For the nature of such modeling, including emulation by the historical actors themselves, see Victor W. Turner, *Dramas, Fields, and Metaphors* (Ithaca: Cornell University Press, 1974).

14

A. The Stage Set

The story begins in a period when Israel remains without a king, unlike its neighbors in Philistia, Ammon, and Edom. Yahweh, Israel's God, previously administered Israel through the medium of leaders raised on an occasional basis, called "judges." The book of 1 Samuel, however, opens with Israel settled in the central hill country of Canaan under the leadership of the priests of Shiloh and their patriarch, Eli. At the time in question, historically, Israelites south of the tribe of Ephraim were probably all lumped together as belonging to the tribe of Benjamin, whose center was north of Jerusalem.[2]

These priests have custody of the ark. But Yahweh rejects their leadership, and the Philistines capture the ark. By means of a plague, Yahweh then induces the Philistines to return the ark to the town of Qiryath-Yearim, south of Israel's territory, just north of Jerusalem. (Qiryath-Yearim lies in the territory of the "Gibeonites.") Some years later, the prophet Samuel, who was raised at Shiloh, assumes the reins of government and defeats the Philistines, recapturing the territories lost under his predecessors, down to the edge of the coastal plain, where the Philistines dominate.

From this point forward, from 1 Sam. 8 to 2 Sam. 1, two parallel narratives have been combined into the present text.[3] These narratives, called A and B for convenience' sake, conflict from time to time, but are for the most part complementary. Their primary divergence concerns the introduction of the monarchy into Israel.

In one version (B), in Samuel's senescence, Yahweh and the people adjudge his children corrupt. The people — concerned with the onslaught of Nahash, king of Ammon, against the Israelites in Transjordan[4] — therefore demand constitutional change. They insist on introducing a monarchy to prevent Samuel's sons from coming to power. Samuel warns them that a king's imposts will impoverish them, and alter their status from that of free men to subjects. Both Samuel and Yahweh regard the demand for a monarchy as a rejection of the di-

---

2. Judah and Simeon were distinguished from Benjamin only in the 10th century B.C.E. See below, Chapter 15 D.

3. For scholarly reconstructions of the A and B sources in 1-2 Samuel, see Baruch Halpern, *The Constitution of the Monarchy in Israel.* HSM 25 (Chico: Scholars, 1981), 149-74; Richard Elliott Friedman, *The Hidden Book in the Bible* (San Francisco: HarperCollins, 1998), 12.

4. See Frank M. Cross, "The Ammonite Oppression of the Tribes of Gad and Reuben: Missing Verses from 1 Samuel 11 Found in 4QSamuel[a]," in *History, Historiography and Interpretation,* ed. Hayim Tadmor and Moshe Weinfeld (Jerusalem: Magnes, 1983), 148-58.

vine order. But Yahweh nevertheless bestows his blessing on the monarchy, on the condition that the king remain subject to Yahweh's law.

The first king is Saul, from Benjamin, the southernmost Israelite tribe. Yahweh nominates him by means of the lot, a form of oracle. Once Saul is nominated, the Israelites acclaim him king. This becomes the dominant pattern for legitimating kingship in Israel: "God proposes, man disposes." Yahweh nominates the candidate, and the governed consent to the choice.

Saul's first task is to defend the town of Jabesh Gilead, to which the Transjordanian Israelites have fled, and which Nahash has invested. Saul relieves the siege and scatters the Ammonite aggressors. In a public acknowledgment that the victory betokens Yahweh's benevolence, Saul crosses the river into Cisjordan on the triumphant march home, and Samuel and the people confirm his kingship ("renew the monarchy") in Gilgal.

Saul's second campaign is directed against Amaleq, the enemy who attacked during Israel's wanderings in the desert after the Exodus. Samuel commissions Saul to conduct a Holy War against them, leaving no man, woman, child, or beast alive. However, Saul spares the cattle and the king. Samuel therefore denounces him, declares that Yahweh has rejected him, and promises that the kingship will pass to another line.

In the parallel narrative (A), it is Yahweh who takes the initiative in introducing kingship. Saul and his aide are scouring the countryside, searching for errant asses belonging to Saul's father. Despairing of success, they happen on a settlement where a seer is presiding over a local festival, probably celebrating ancestors. The seer is Samuel, who has had a divine revelation: he is to anoint Saul as king-designate over Israel and commission him to fight against the Philistines. Samuel promises Saul the accomplishment of several predictions as confirmation that his designation originates with Yahweh. Thereafter, Saul is to take military action ("do what comes to hand") against a Philistine garrison at Gibeah ("hill"), in the hills of Benjamin north of Jerusalem. And Saul is to meet Samuel in a week's time in Gilgal, to muster the Israelites at large against the Philistines.

All goes well, until Saul arrives in Gilgal. He waits, and waits, and his army begins slowly to melt away from the camp, yet Samuel does not turn up. Finally, to stop the desertion, Saul conducts the necessary sacrifices himself. At this point, Samuel suddenly appears, condemns him, and withdraws from him Yahweh's election. Nevertheless, Jonathan, Saul's son, surprises the Philistines in their camp, and in the resulting rout the Israelites sweep the Philistines out of the eastern sector of the Ayyalon Pass, the east-west route through the hills north of Jerusalem.

Unfortunately, the victory is not more decisive and leaves the Philistines in possession of the western part of the Ayyalon Pass. The text explains why. After

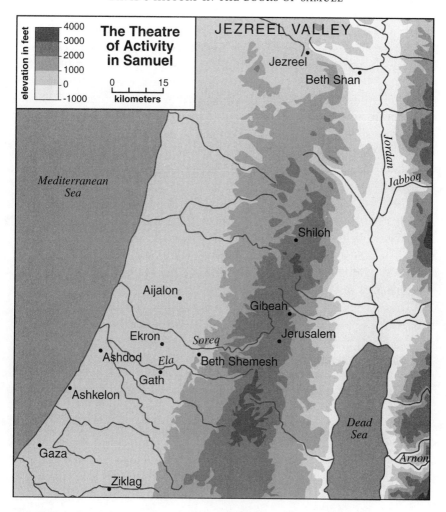

Map 2.1

Jonathan's surprise assault, Saul vows to Yahweh that no Israelite would touch food before sundown — a form of abstinence intended to attract Yahweh's favor. Jonathan, unaware of the oath, unwittingly violates it. A later divination ritual determines that it was Jonathan's violation that prevented complete subjection of the Philistines. (Reports on such divinatory rituals are common in 1-2 Samuel, and rare in later texts.) However, the triumph is sufficient to secure Saul's personal position as king, and he subsequently goes on to fight Ammon, Moab, Edom, and the kingdom of Zobah in the Beqaʿ Valley between the Anti-Lebanon mountain chain in southern Syria and the Lebanon mountain chain on the Phoenician coast.

These two versions share features. Kingship is introduced by Samuel. Saul is the first king-designate, chosen to contend against Israel's enemies. He wins his inaugural battle, but a cultic faux pas — sparing the Amaleqite king, or sacrificing before Samuel's arrival at Gilgal — leads Samuel to repudiate him. Though he continues as Yahweh's elected king, the reader is assured from the start that Saul will not establish a dynasty.

The two versions also manifest differences, although neither is sympathetic to Saul. The first version (B) focuses on the constitutional transition, the second (A) on the person of Saul. The B version holds that Saul was elected by the entire nation, whereas the A version makes no such claim, suggesting rather that he "captured" the kingship, after his divine designation, by dint of arms. The B version is the only text in the ancient Near East to describe the introduction of kingship to a society as a human political decision.

The B version implies that the populace had universally, legally acquiesced in the introduction of the monarchy, making the institution unarguable. The A version claims that Yahweh simply proclaimed the monarchy, which is a less deft form of legitimation. Most tellingly, the B version stands in a continuum with the earlier reports on Samuel's wars. It maintains that Saul's first battles were against the Ammonites and Amaleqites, peoples on Israel's periphery. It denies Saul credit for driving the Philistines out of the hills north of Jerusalem, confining his activity to Israel's peripheries. There, his initial actions defended, rather than expanded, Israelite territory. The second version (A) holds that Saul fought Philistine elements that had established themselves in the heart of Israel's central hill country.

B. Introducing David

In both sources, it is at this juncture that David, youngest son of Jesse, enters the story. In the B source, Samuel seeks him out in Bethlehem as an unassuming but attractive youth. Samuel anoints him to be king after Saul. David's election as a youth mirrors a common motif in royal literature from the ancient world. He is the seventh son of Jesse, the child who tends the sheep, an unemployable, in 1 Sam. 16:1-13. Samuel, who is there to elect him, can hardly believe that the others are not Yahweh's choices. The tableau concretizes the ritual humility of the Israelite leader. Until one is singled out by Yahweh, one is a youth (Solomon, Gideon) and weak (Rehoboam, David in 2 Sam. 2), an outcast (Jephthah, Jeremiah), incapable of action or speech (Moses, Ezekiel, Isaiah), someone of low status (Jotham's bramble in Judg. 9; Saul in 1 Sam. 9:16).

Saul, meanwhile, begins to suffer bouts of psychological disturbance, and David enters the court as the musician whose strains soothe him. Next comes the Goliath episode, on the border between Judah and the Philistine plain, where David by bold confidence in his capacity for combat — and for rewriting its rules — earns his stripes as a warrior and the promise of Saul's daughter in marriage. David's confrontation, naked of all armor, with an invincible titan is the equivalent of Oedipus's contest with the Sphinx — the overcoming of a monster in the career of a hero. By this point, in both sources, David has been introduced into the court.

David's first military assignment in Saul's court is as Jonathan's armorbearer.[5] Here begins a relationship of keen importance. Gradually, Jonathan and David become allies to the point at which Jonathan, the lawful heir to the throne, recognizes that David has been elected by Yahweh to succeed Saul. Saul, meanwhile, appoints David to command a brigade and commits a daughter to him in marriage. David's martial success, however, and perhaps his undisguised confidence, excite Saul's envy. The ditty, "Saul has slain his thousands, David his myriads," sends Saul into a flight of fury. He repeatedly tries to kill David, who repeatedly escapes the attacks. Some of the duplication arises from the combination of parallel sources, but the point is, and often the words are, the same in both. In any case, Saul requires that David collect Philistine foreskins as a brideprice for his daughter Michal, in the hope that David will be killed in the process of collecting it. David probably kills the victims before collecting the foreskins. (Had Heller been at the top of his form, his David would have tried persuasion and inducements before force.)

Ultimately, David deserts the court without leave, abetted in one of the sources (A) by Jonathan.[6] David flees to Nob, probably a Gibeonite town, like

5. 1 Sam. 18:4 probably reflects an originally more limited claim of this nature.

6. That David is not free to leave the court in 1 Sam. 20 is reminiscent of the practice recorded in the 14th-century Amarna archive of kings detaining foreign emissaries, as in EA 3; 4; 7; 28; 29; 33; 59:14. Is David portrayed as a sort of ambassador from Bethlehem? In

the one housing the ark. He fools the priests of the town into thinking he is on a mission for the crown. They give him food and Goliath's sword. Saul lays waste to the town: his servant, Doeg the Edomite, kills every man, woman, child, and beast in it. The slaughter propels the surviving descendant of Eli, priest of Shiloh, into David's camp. Abiathar, Eli's scion, would become David's divination specialist.

From Nob, David flees to Achish, king of Gath, to sue for asylum. The Philistines of Gath, however, quote the ditty that had enraged Saul. David therefore feigns madness, allowing the spittle to dribble down his face, in order to be ejected rather than killed. This story, from the A source, is significant. It denies that David had worked for the Philistines, a point that the B source, and the text as it has been assembled as a whole, concede. But the A source does relate that David placed his parents in the hands of the king of Moab for safekeeping, and returned to Judah only when instructed to do so by the prophet Gad.

At this point, in both sources, David gathers a band of desperadoes and lives as a bandit chief in the wilderness of Judah. Thus, during his youth, after his rise in the court, David is a fugitive. The same story is told of King Idrimi of Alalakh in Syria, some centuries earlier.[7] The idea of a bandit figure reaching the throne is not dissimilar from the story of Jephthah in Judg. 11 or the Moses myth as well. However, Idrimi claims to be of royal stock, where David does not.[8] As in the case of Saul, Yahweh has elected a lowly vessel to elevate to power.

Saul pursues David, and falls providentially within his reach. Though David's subordinates urge him to take advantage of the opportunity, David offers Saul no harm, and Saul departs, recognizing, as Jonathan had done earlier, that David was Yahweh's elected successor to the kingship. David's banditry, however, is a crucial element in his later character development. While he remains spotless to this point, his henchmen here evince a violent streak. For them, the fury of enmity overrides decorum. It obliterates the sense of proportion that should dictate a response to provocation. They would not stop short of regicide itself in pursuing a grudge, if not restrained by David's piety.

David himself soon almost succumbs to the outlaw ethic of his subordi-

---

the world of Amarna, at least, his treatment might lead us to think of Jesse as "the man of Bethlehem."

7. For the parallels with Idrimi, see, for example, Michael C. Astour, *Hittite History and the Absolute Chronology of the Bronze Age* (Partille: Paul Åströms, 1989).

8. The myth of the birth of Sargon, first attested in the 7th century, mimics features of the Moses birth legend, but does not include life as a fugitive before Sargon achieves kingship.

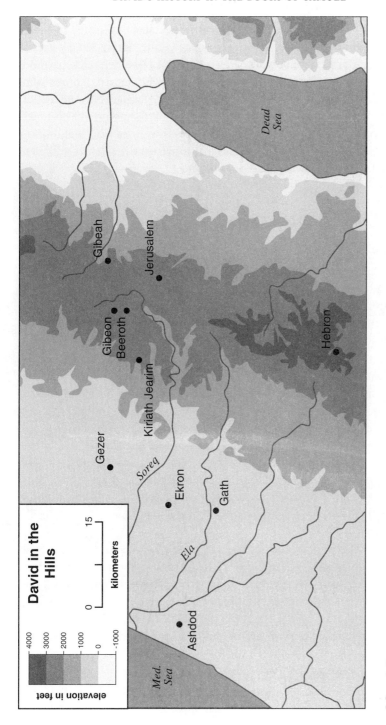

David in the
Hills

elevation in feet

4000
3000
2000
1000
0
-1000

0   15
kilometers

Dead
Sea

Gibeah

Jerusalem

Gibeon
Beeroth

Hebron

Kiriath Jearim

Gezer

Soreq

Ekron

Gath

Ela

Ashdod

Med.
Sea

Map 2.2

nates. 1 Sam. 25 finds him extorting payment from Nabal of Carmel, a gentleman in the wilderness of Judah. David is working a protection racket. His claim is that he has refrained from preying on Nabal's sheep. Nabal refuses to pay, and David angrily declaims his intention to kill Nabal. David's reprieve comes from a stranger: Nabal's wife Abigail begs David for mercy. Her plea puts the matter in its proper perspective, and David complies with it. But the world he occupies lends itself to violence not required by the circumstances, violence out of proportion to the provocation. Meanwhile, Nabal conveniently collapses and dies. David collects Abigail and proceeds on his way.

C. Saul's Death

At this point, the A source cuts to the eve of Saul's final battle, against "the Philistines" in the Jezreel Valley. Saul had banished mediums. But he asks the "witch" (really, medium) of Ein-Dor to summon Samuel's specter to furnish counsel. David's royal predecessor — Saul in this case, Ishbaal in others — is once again convicted of impiety, and his dynasty consigned to the dustbin of history. He is also soundly defeated, because of divine disfavor. The Philistines hound him, then wound him in battle, and kill his three sons. Saul takes his own life. The Philistines dismember him, and hack his head from his body. The head they send on tour through their own cities. They hang his blood-soaked torso, and those of his sons, from the city wall of Beth Shan as public trophies. They display his weapons in Ashtarot, in Transjordan.

The author of the A source could have blamed Saul's death on his violation of the treaty with Gibeon (below), but 2 Samuel uses that episode only as an explanation of David's later purge of Saul's descendants. Instead, we get two connections to the cult — disobeying Samuel, twice; failing to fulfil the requirements of the Holy War, once; plus necromancy (seeking oracles from the dead), after banning it.

This latter charge makes sense only if the intention was to claim that Saul outlawed necromancers, but hypocritically had recourse to them himself. It is thus a defense of necromancy. This story predates Deuteronomy, a text of the 7th century, since Deuteronomy suppresses necromancy. It may be that, like the Chronicler, later editors of our account thought the problem was the consultation, not the policy of suppression. But the real problem is the hypocrisy. This story comes from a time when the suppression was undreamt of in Jerusalem, as it was to Isaiah (ca. 700). The story as it stands condemns Saul's policy on the necromancers, and as such portrays Samuel as in a sense taking revenge.

The B source tells a different story about Saul's last days. Here, David successfully defects to the Philistines (for a year and four months). He becomes the chief of the bodyguard of Achish, king of Gath. He is the ruler of Ziklag, a town subordinate to Gath. David has made the transition to abandoning his true ethnic loyalty. At least on the face of things, he is a traitor.

As Achish's subordinate, David raids the peoples occupying Israel's peripheries, including the Amaleqites in the south and either the Geshurites or the otherwise unidentified Gerizzites.[9] All the while, he gives his Philistine master to understand that his raids were focused on Judah, not Judah's enemies. Now, the text claims, David was practiced not just in banditry or in extortion — in the case of Nabal — but in deception as well. David is not the first double agent in world literature. Others are represented in the inscriptions of Ramses II (1304-1237).[10] But he is the first to be presented as a protagonist rather than a villain.

The B source version of David's involvement with Saul's final battle is complex. David accompanies his Philistine master, Achish of Gath, to the Philistine staging point for the thrust into the Jezreel Valley. Saul draws up his forces at the site of Jezreel, near Mount Gilboa on the eastern end of the Valley. However, the other Philistine kings doubt David's reliability: is this not, they ask, the David of whom it was said, "Saul has slain his thousands, and David his myriads"? Achish mournfully dismisses David, professing complete confidence in his loyal, blameless subaltern. The narrative leaves us in some doubt as to whether David's service was in fact wholehearted, and whether he would have taken the field against the Israelites on behalf of the Philistines. Overtly, his practice of raiding elements on the borders of Judah would seem to suggest he would have defected to the Israelite side. On the other hand, Achish's confidence in him is unbounded: Achish has made David responsible for guarding his person. And David protests his loyalty, pleading to join Achish in battle. The suspicions of

9. Qere Gezerites. Josh. 13:2-3 probably associates Geshurites with Philistia on the basis of the reference in 1 Sam. 27:8. The opponents may in fact be the denizens of Gezer here.

10. This represents the high chronology for Egyptian kings. An alternative, low chronology (1279-1212) for Ramses II, is offered in Edward F. Wente, "Ramesses II," *ABD* 5:618-20. The dating is as yet dependent on lunar eclipse data, and as lunar eclipses are frequent, the real dates are indeterminate. If, as Egyptian sources indicate, Thutmosis III came to the throne about two centuries before Ramses II, then the transition from Middle Bronze to Late Bronze culture in Syro-Palestine occasioned by the invasions of Thutmosis III and his immediate predecessors cannot helpfully be down-dated into the late 15th century. The higher chronology is preferable on the basis of the archaeological data as they must be interpreted through the lens of texts.

the other Philistine monarchs thus rescue David from betraying either his countrymen, the Israelites, or his adopted protector.[11]

David returns to his own town, Ziklag, only to discover that the Amaleqites have raided the settlement and carried off all those whom he has left behind. As a result, while the Philistines and Israelites fight in the Jezreel Valley, he is chasing down the captors of his dependents along the Wadi Besor in the south. Luckily, he catches and defeats the aggressors, and recovers his people and property as well as taking other booty from Amaleq. In this context, David introduces a new order: in dividing booty, both the fighters and the guards at home are to share. "They also serve who only stand and wait."

On his return to Ziklag, therefore, David distributes booty to all of Judah's population as far north as Hebron. This is an extension of the same principle. It is also a transparent attempt to curry favor. In other words, David introduces the principle of community, and of redistribution. His position is statist, and more modern than the rough individualism of the premonarchic era.

While David is careering around Judah's southern periphery, the Philistines and Saul lock arms in combat. The Philistines prevail, killing Saul's sons, and chasing Saul down, finally, on the high ground of Gilboa. There, in the A version, Saul entreats his armor-bearer to kill him. The latter refuses, so Saul falls on his own sword. The Israelites flee, and the Philistines occupy their former settlements, both across the valley and across the Jordan.

Saul's decapitation and the exhibition of his head and torso have a rough parallel in the suppression of restiveness earlier in the 11th century by the Assyrian king Tiglath-Pileser I: "Their heads I cut off, beside their cities like grain piles I stacked them."[12] A tomb at Lachish (T. 120), after the Assyrian army reduced the town in 701, also contained skulls — 1500 of them — stacked separately from corpses. These heads may also have been left on display for a time to demonstrate Assyria's ferocity.

In light of such atrocities, it is especially heroic that the inhabitants of Jabesh Gilead, in Transjordan, abduct Saul's corpse and the corpses of his three sons — Jonathan, Abinadab and Malkishua — from Beth Shan. The men of Jabesh accord Saul's family a funerary pyre in Jabesh. Saul had saved them from Nahash, king of Ammon, whose condition for their submission was that he put out their right eyes.

11. In the A source, the ditty ("Saul has slain his thousands, David his myriads") saves David from working for the Philistines at all, despite his interest in defecting. It thus saves him from himself. In the B source, it rescues him from participating in a battle against Saul.

12. RIMA 2.A.0.87.1:81f.

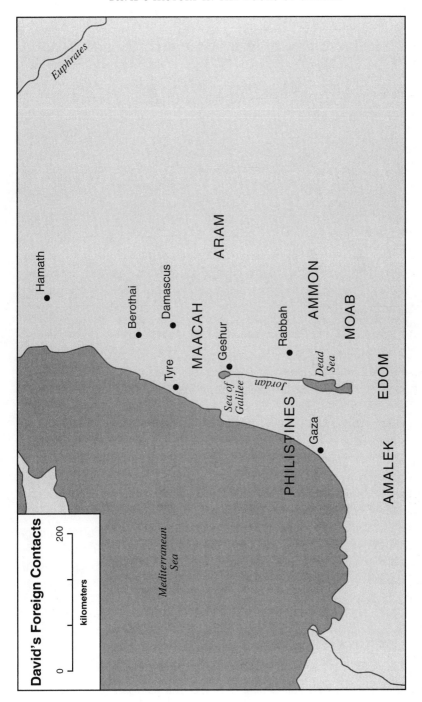

Map 2.3

25

The B version of Saul's death differs from A. In the first instance, the action remains with David, so that Saul's death is reported only indirectly. The account claims that David returned to Ziklag, and chased Amaleqites for three days. Then a runner appears from Saul's camp, to announce the defeat at Jezreel. The messenger, himself an Amaleqite, claims that Saul turned to him, on Mount Gilboa, to beg for release from life. The Amaleqite obliged the already-wounded king, and brought his crown and armlet to David. After fasting and mourning for Saul and Jonathan all the way until evening, David executes the Amaleqite for killing "the anointed of Yahweh." He also composes and sings the famous lament, "How are the mighty fallen," as a memorial for Saul and Jonathan. (The elegy omits the names of Saul's other sons.)

Thus the B source does not relate Saul's death in direct narrative, as does the A source. It announces Saul's death in the Amaleqite's report to David. The reader learns of it as David does, and immediately learns how David avenges the death. Here, David again stands up against regicide, whatever the circumstances. And yet, Saul's killer rushes straightaway to David, a bearer of good news. David is the direct beneficiary, who will shortly establish a breakaway kingdom, for himself, in Judah. David is unconventional. He avenges and mourns his enemies.

D. The Civil War

After learning of Saul's death in the B source, David asks Yahweh whether to proceed to a highland village in Judah. Yahweh tells him to go to Hebron; "the men of Judah" anoint him to be king. David's election implies a hereditary sinecure, just as in the patriarchal narratives of Genesis. Like land, election to office is "granted." The idea is exemplified also in the protest by a king of Jerusalem in the 14th century to the pharaoh Amenhotep III, namely, that neither his father nor his mother,[13] but the strong arm of the pharaoh, placed him on his (hereditary) throne. Generally, grants involve hereditary rights.[14] So, David's election, by Yahweh and by Judah, is for one time only. It thereafter implies dynastic continuity.

David's enthronement does not imply a secession by Judah from Saul's

---

13. Note the direct reference to matrilinear claims on the throne.

14. See latterly Gary N. Knoppers, "Ancient Near Eastern Royal Grants and the Davidic Covenant: A Parallel?" *JAOS* 116 (1996): 670-97. See also Tomoo Ishida, *The Royal Dynasties in Ancient Israel: A Study on the Formation and Development of Royal-Dynastic Ideology.* BZAW 142 (Berlin: de Gruyter, 1977).

kingdom. In continuity with the B source, it has the implication that Judah was never a part of that kingdom. Jerusalem had not, in either the A or the B source, fallen to Saul. The B source does not relate that Saul attacked Nob or any other Gibeonite town north of Jerusalem — and 2 Samuel relates this only obliquely, as we shall see. And the B source does not claim that Saul cleared any Philistine elements from the Ayyalon Pass. Judah thus remains separate from Israel in the B source until David becomes king of both.

Ensconced at Hebron, David learns that the men of Jabesh Gilead had buried Saul, and he sends an embassy asking them to support his kingship. The text implies, but does not say, that he would have received support had not Saul's chief-of-staff, Abner, moved Saul's son Ishbaal to Transjordan and crowned him there. The minimum claim that the text makes is that David tried to establish diplomatic relations with the Israelites in Gilead, Saul's most ardent supporters.

From this point forward, only one source reports on David's history. Either the A or the B source leaves off. Or perhaps the A and B versions represent alternative introductions — prequels — to the story of David's kingship. In any case, starting with 2 Sam. 2 there are no more duplicate narratives, or duplicate explanations of circumstances (as with Saul's death) in the text. At the same juncture, starting with 2 Sam. 2 the level of political reportage rises to a height paralleled in antiquity only by Thucydides. It differs from Thucydides and his epigones in devoting the sort of attention to women, family, and personal motivations and frailties that characterizes the work of Herodotus — themes that would not attract treatment again until the imperial era in Rome.

After Saul's death, Saul's general Abner enthrones Saul's surviving son, Ishbaal, over Israel, other than Judah. Abner takes him across the river to Mahanaim for the coronation. Perhaps Abner had Ishbaal reenact Saul's enthronement by crossing the Jordan back to Gilgal, but this is not recorded. Ishbaal claims kingship over "Gilead, 'the Ashurite' (probably Galilee), Jezreel and Ephraim and Manasseh." The text locates his court in Mahanaim, in Transjordan, suggesting, subtly and deceptively, that he did not really control Cisjordanian territory. The immediate consequence of Ishbaal's coronation is described by Samuel as a civil war.

David comes to the throne in Hebron and starts the civil war in 2 Sam. 2. 2 Sam. 3 begins with a notice of protracted warfare between "the house of Saul and the house of David." The first verse of the chapter — the house of David was on the wax, that of Saul was on the wane — is a summary of all that follows until David's elevation over Israel in 2 Sam. 5:1-3. The narrator next takes the opportunity to insert an enumeration of the six sons born to David "in Hebron" (2 Sam. 3:2-5). One of them, Absalom, is the grandson of the king of Geshur, in the Golan, so David has scored a diplomatic coup.

27

The point here is threefold: First, the war was a long one, taking the six-and-a-half years David spent ruling from Hebron — he produced one son per year. Second, the house of David was, as the start of the chapter claims (2 Sam. 3:1), on the wax, not just in its military fortunes but also in its physical size. And third, the issue of dynasty, of children, of succession, of the accumulation of appropriate wives, is intimately connected with the successful establishment of a breakaway petty state independent of the court of Saul, or in this instance, of Ishbaal.

The extended civil war is the subject as well of 2 Sam. 3:6: Abner controlled the house of Saul. The term "house of Saul" designates the dynasty, since the representative of the current generation is not Saul, but Ishbaal. The implication is not that Abner's ascendance took place *after* David's sons were born, but rather that it persisted from Ishbaal's coronation throughout the six-year period of conflict. Thus to some extent, the order of the narrative is not chronological.

Only one battle of the civil war is described (2 Sam. 2:12-32). Abner's army meets that of Joab, David's general, at Gibeon. Gibeon was the central town of an ethnic group, the Hivvites, north of Jerusalem. The Hivvites, or Gibeonites, also inhabited Qiryath-Yearim, the home of the ark in the period, and Beeroth. In the initial encounter, 12 champions from each side pair off and plunge their swords into one another by "the pool of Gibeon." A general engagement ensues, in which "the servants of David" prevail.

Joab and his brothers, Abishai and Asahel, pursue the fleeing Israelites. Asahel, swift as a gazelle, dogs Abner. Abner repeatedly warns him off, asking how he could possibly face Joab if he smites Asahel, but Asahel persists. Finally, with Asahel on his heels, Abner strikes back unexpectedly with the butt of his spear. The butt penetrates Asahel's breastplate ("fifth rib") and erupts through the back of his torso. The spectacle of Asahel's corpse brings the Judahites up short, but the pursuit continues down the steppe east of Gibeon, in the direction of the Jordan Valley, until the evening. Finally, Abner asks Joab to desist, and the latter agrees. Abner makes for Mahanaim and Joab for Hebron after burying Asahel, on the way, in his father's tomb in Bethlehem.

More interesting is the treatment of Abner: this figure is responsible for Ishbaal's enthronement over Israel (2 Sam. 2:8-9). As noted, he sustained the house of Saul during the civil war (3:6), an unusual claim in that he was not the king, Ishbaal. But the author reports in 3:7 that Ishbaal asked Abner, "Why did you enter unto the concubine of my father?" Biblical Hebrew has two words for "why," and Ishbaal uses the neutral one, rather than the negative one.[15] All the

15. The neutral term is *maddû[a]*, the negative one *lāmâ*. The latter often has the meaning "lest" ("why should you die?" = lest you die), "don't" or "you ought not have

same, the question represents a grave accusation. Solomon will execute his brother Adonijah because the latter approaches Bathsheba to request David's nurse/consort as a sort of consolation prize for losing the throne to Solomon. Absalom will violate David's wives and concubines in front of all Israel. His purpose is to show that the break with his father is irrevocable. At the same time, the deed represents Yahweh's punishment of David, according to the narrator, for his adultery with Bathsheba — despite the fact that Yahweh had given David Saul's "women." So, relations with royal concubines in Samuel represent a claim on the throne. The act is freighted with significance, and with danger.

The author neither confirms nor denies the truth of Ishbaal's allegation about Abner's affair with Saul's concubine, Rizpah, daughter of Ayyah. Ishbaal has in effect accused Abner of laying stake to the throne. Abner reacts violently to the aspersion on his loyalty, the last straw. Angrily, he promises to accomplish Yahweh's promise to make David king "over Israel and over Judah from Dan to Beersheba" (2 Sam. 3:8-10). Ishbaal, paralyzed by fear, does not reply to the tirade (3:11). But it is of some moment that Abner's evidence of his own innocence is in fact that "I have not traduced you into the power of David" (3:8). The reader is left in the air as to whether Abner's loyalty extends to respect for the inviolability of Saul's harem. The continuation of the account discusses *David's* dispute over one of Saul's women — David recovers Saul's daughter Michal. This subject may have inspired our narrator to claim that a dispute over another of Saul's women alienated Abner from Ishbaal.

Abner initiates relations with David. David's condition for treating with Abner is that Abner bring with him Saul's daughter Michal, formerly betrothed to him. David demands the same concession of Ishbaal. Ishbaal then actually remits Michal, taking her from her husband to Bahurim, a center of Saul's clan, just east of Jerusalem. From Bahurim, Abner accompanies her to David's court at Hebron (3:13-16, 20). In the interim, the narrator explains that Abner's plan was to throw Israel's support behind David, against Ishbaal (3:9-10, 12-13, 17-19). Ishbaal's acquiescence in the extradition of Michal, even if motivated by moral paralysis, is the acknowledgment of David's right to the woman, and through her, to the throne. In fact, it can only have been a part of the peace deal

---

done" ("why have you disturbed me" = "you shouldn't have disturbed me"). See generally, Alfred Jepsen, "Warum? Eine lexikalische und theologische Studie," in *Das ferne und nahe Wort*, ed. Fritz Maass. Festschrift L. Rost. BZAW 105 (Berlin: Töpelmann, 1967), 106-13; Ronald T. Hyman, "Fielding 'Why' Questions in Genesis," *HAR* 11 (1987): 173-83. Cf. James Barr, "'Why?' in Biblical Hebrew," *JTS* 36 (1985): 1-33; Toyozo W. Nakarai, "*Lmh* and *Mduʿ* in the TANAK," *HS* 23 (1982): 45-50.

between Ishbaal and David that was meant to free each of them to conduct campaigns in other areas.

The narrator's claim, thus, is that Abner was the mainstay of northern independence, and that his death led to Israel's collapse into David's bosom. He claims further that David was formerly betrothed to Michal, adding the detail that the brideprice was 100 Philistine foreskins. This claim jibes with 1 Sam. 18:25-29, and could be harmonized with 1 Sam. 17:25. The implication is that David has a right to recover Michal from her husband.

Abner, now, with 20 retainers in tow, delivers Michal to David in Hebron, capital of Judah. He promises David kingship over Israel, and departs in peace. Under the circumstances, David has no reason to massacre Abner's peace party. Abner had not only broken with Ishbaal, and swung Israelite support behind David. He had even produced Michal as a token of his good faith. Politics and murder, but also sex, are the building blocks of the presentation.

However, Joab, who has been out on a raid, learns after the fact that David has entertained Abner. Coming to Hebron, Abner knew that Joab would seek to avenge the death of his brother Asahel. Abner relied on David's safe-passage to restrain Joab from indulging in a vendetta. Joab, however, interprets Abner's mission as one of espionage. Joab recalls Abner to Hebron. He takes him aside in the town gate, and strikes him treacherously in his breastplate ("fifth rib").

David himself leads the mourning for his erstwhile enemy, Abner, and instructs Joab and his men to join in. He composes a lament over Abner, follows the funerary bier, entombs him in Hebron, and refuses food all the way to sunset. But David declares publicly — while cursing Joab — that he himself is powerless to oppose Joab and Abishai, the brothers of Asahel. Joab here gives vent to the tendency toward murder that David had held under control when Saul was in his power. David no longer prevents his subordinate from, or punishes him for, behaving with wanton savagery, in the manner of a murderer.

But the real stroke of literary genius is the claim that Abner was the main power in the north. The only evidence for this is the narrator's assertion. Why magnify Abner above the king, Ishbaal? On the one hand, the portrait furnishes evidence that Abner's counterpart, Joab, might also act independently of his own sovereign — in the case of Abner's murder, for example. But more immediately, Abner's magnification makes it plausible that he could have translated northern support to David when he decided to betray Ishbaal. In effect, Ishbaal and Abner both support David rather than supporting one another.

Further, David did not even invite Abner's defection: it was precipitated by Ishbaal's accusation that Abner was plotting to seize the throne. Given Abner's power, and his manifest selflessness in acknowledging David's divine right to be king, this allegation is clearly untrue. Ishbaal, like his paranoid father, is seeing phantasms, whatever the truth of his belief that Abner had had relations with Rizpah, Saul's concubine. The importance of hidden meanings is a theme of 2 Samuel: David will miss them later, when Nathan and then the Wise Woman of Tekoa come to him with parables masquerading as judicial cases. David is also deceived as to the implications when he hears the news of Absalom's murdering Amnon. During the lead-up to Absalom's revolt itself, he consistently misses the significance of his own behavior. One might also argue that the narrator means to say that he misses the implications of Joab's providential murders. In any case, it is only as the Absalom revolt winds down that David too, in the narrative, begins to perceive aright.

The news of Abner's death demoralizes Ishbaal, and all Israel. Just at this juncture, two Hivvites, whose congeners Saul had expelled from the Gibeonite settlement of Beeroth, sneak into Ishbaal's palace during the afternoon siesta masquerading as tributaries. They murder the king in his sleep and decapitate him. Like Saul's Amaleqite killer, they bring a token of their deed to David — in this case Ishbaal's head. As in the case of Saul, David executes the assassins, for killing a "righteous man," that is, an innocent man; the text is careful not to call him "the anointed."

Again, here David is the beneficiary of an assassination, of his chief rival, and again by killers who assume that he will reward their action. Instead, he rejects the tactic of regicide, and avenges and mourns his foe. He decapitates, dismembers, and displays the corpses of Ishbaal's killers — at the "pool *(brkh)* in Hebron" (2 Sam. 4:12). The pool in Hebron is the site where the civil war ends, just as it began at the pool in Gibeon. And oddly enough, David's dismembering the corpses of Ishbaal's killers mimics the Philistines' treatment of Saul's corpse. In that sense he repays the insult to Saul — and implies that the Gibeonites are allies of the Philistines. All the same, his dismembering Ishbaal's killers is extraordinary. Once in the case of Saul, twice in the civil war, his allies or subordinates act on his behalf, outside the law. He remains inactive in the case of his subordinates, who were, as he himself was, in the wilderness. He punishes his erstwhile allies and mourns their victims. Yet in some sense, the killers were merely carrying out Yahweh's rejection of Saul and his dynasty.

E. Building the Israelite State

After Ishbaal's death, a delegation of Israelite "elders" offer David kingship over Israel. David marches on Jerusalem. Jerusalem's non-Israelite (Jebusite) inhabitants jeer at him with the taunt that he will as soon capture Jerusalem as he will eliminate the blind and the lame. He takes the town by direct assault. And the blind and lame are banned, later, from the temple[16] — so that David fulfills, in a sense, the terms of the Jebusite challenge.

Jerusalem is the royal city of David's kingdom, the place where his younger children are born. In ensconcing David there, the text implies that he was the king who introduced the principle of a capital city into an Israel formerly consisting only of agrarian villages and bazaar towns. David creates, the text will claim, a regular administrative apparatus, and even a state cult in the capital: his models, no matter how he adapts them, can only be those of neighboring city-states.

And the Israelite state now assumes a form recognizable to those neighbors. The occupation of the historic capital of the southern hills leads Hiram of Tyre to take notice: Hiram sends his greetings and congratulations on David's new position. After each of David's coronations, in Hebron and in Jerusalem, David wins a battle, is described as "on the wax," and begets sons. Thus, the author of 2 Samuel marks off both coronations with signs of divine favor and prosperity.

The taking of Jerusalem and proclamation of David's sovereignty over Israel also send a message that invites assault by Philistine elements. These David defeats, in two engagements in the vicinity of the new capital. In the first engagement, he captures the Philistines' icons, just as the Philistines themselves had once captured the ark. (2 Sam. 5:21 leaves the identity of the icons unclear.[17]) In the second battle, David routs the Philistine force from Geba, in Benjamin north of Jerusalem, all the way to the boundary of the city-state Gezer, sitting on the coastal plain at the mouth of the Ayyalon Pass. David, therefore, is assigned credit for clearing the central hill country of Philistines, including the western part of the pass Saul had failed to capture.

This claim stands in continuity both with the A source (in which Saul clears the eastern part of the pass), and with the B source, in which Samuel clears the whole of the hill country, in 1 Samuel. In the B source, the implication is that the Philistines had reasserted control of the hills north of Jerusalem during Saul's and Ishbaal's reigns. They then assaulted David once he had been made king of Israel. In continuity with A, the implication is that David completed the task at which Saul had merely made a beginning. But in either case, the result of the action around Jerusalem in 2 Sam. 5:17-25 is that David secures the hill country as the hinterland of his capital to the end of the Ayyalon Pass: Gezer is the western border of the kingdom.

---

16. See S. M. Olyan, "'Anyone Blind or Lame Shall Not Enter the House': On the Interpretation of Second Samuel 5:8b," *CBQ* 60 (1998): 218-27.

17. See below, Chapter 18 B, for a suggestion.

Immediately thereafter, David gathers all the Israelites under arms — 30 thousand, says the text — to repatriate the ark from Qiryath-Yearim, here called Baala. The attempt is a debacle, resulting in the death of a non-Levite who handles the object. The ark is therefore resident for three months in a way-station, "the house of Obed Edom, the Gittite." In a second attempt, David succeeds in bringing the ark to his new capital. He celebrates its entry with a tremendous feast, like that Solomon would lay on at the dedication of the temple, or like that of the Assyrian Assurnasirpal a century later. During the festivities, however, Saul's daughter Michal espies David cavorting with less circumspection than enthusiasm before the ark, perhaps doing cartwheels in an era before the invention of underwear. As Michal reproaches David with his shamelessness, he retorts that he would gladly abase himself before the lowliest handmaids in Israel in the service of Yahweh. He consigns her to chastity thereafter, in the harem. Yet his pledge of abasement foreshadows the punitive service he must perform for Yahweh in the course of Absalom's revolt.

On installing the ark in a new tent in Jerusalem, David offers to build Yahweh a temple of cedar in the city,[18] and initially his prophet, Nathan, approves. Nathan soon returns, however, with an injunction against constructing the edifice. Yahweh has replied that he has always wandered from place to place, and never requested a temple. But he promises that David's son will take the throne, and that the dynasty will endure forever. Yahweh also accepts the principle of fixing his residence in a temple, which David's son is to build.[19] He reserves to himself only the option of punishing temporarily wayward scions of the royal line.

There follows in 2 Sam. 8 a summary account of David's various conquests.

18. Note the reference to a house of cedars built for Sin in Harran in the 7th century: LAS 117 (ABL 923; SLA 248; K. 2701a). Marduk-šum-usur relates: "Assur in a dream called the king my lord's grandfather a Sage. The king, lord of kings, is the scion of a Sage and Adapa. Your wisdom surpasses the Apsu (the sweet water on which the earth floats) and all master craft. When the king my lord's father went to the land Egypt, in the region of the town Harran he built a temple of cedar. . . . (The moon-god) Sin was kneeling before a staff. Two crowns were placed on (his) head. . . . The god Mercury stood in his presence. The king my lord's father entered, placed [a crown] on (his) head. 'You will go to countries . . . you will conquer.' He went to Egypt, he conquered. The rest of the lands that have not submitted to Assur and Sin, the king the lord of kings will conquer." Is Sin related to the god on the stela from Beth Saida? See Monika Bernett and Othmar Keel, *Mond, Stier und Kult am Stadttor: Die Stele von Betsaida (et-Tell).* OBO 161 (Fribourg: University of Fribourg, 1998).

19. 2 Sam. 7. See Frank M. Cross, *Canaanite Myth and Hebrew Epic* (Cambridge, Mass.: Harvard University Press, 1973), 229-65; latterly David Vanderhooft, "Dwelling Beneath the Sacred Place: A Proposal for Reading 2 Samuel 7:10," *JBL* 118 (1999): 625-33.

He defeats "the Philistines" and takes from them the enigmatic "Meteg Ha-Ammah." He smites Moab, killing two thirds of his captives and reducing the rest to vassalage. He confronts Hadadezer, son of Rehob, king of Aram Zobah, when he goes to erect a stela on "the River," a text usually interpreted to imply that David reached the Euphrates on the border between Syria and Mesopotamia (modern Iraq). Indeed, many manuscripts make this identification explicit by adding the word "Euphrates" in 2 Sam. 8:3. David also defeats the allies who come to Hadadezer's aid from Damascus, installing garrisons in Damascus. Toi, king of Hamath, a powerful city-state in central Syria, on the southern Orontes River north of Zobah, sends lavish gifts. And David also takes booty from Aram, Moab, Ammon, Philistia, and Amaleq. He garrisons the entire territory of Edom.

F. David and Bathsheba

The next textual movement begins in 2 Sam. 9. Here, David seeks out the sole remaining descendant of Saul. The heir to the line is called Mephiboshet in 2 Samuel (as 9:6), Meribbaal in 1 Chr. 8:34 and 9:40, and Mephibaal in the Old Greek translation of Samuel. The alternation between Merib- and Mephi- at the start of the name is difficult to explain. The alternation between -boshet and -baal at the end of the name has a parallel in the treatment of Saul's successor in Israel — Ishbaal in Chronicles, Ishboshet in Kings. Here, Saul's grandson will be referred to as Mephibaal.[20]

Mephibaal, a son of Jonathan, has been lame in both legs from his infancy. David generously assigns Saul's estates to Mephibaal. The steward Ziba and his 15 sons and 20 slaves are to work the land to provide Mephibaal with food and drink. Mephibaal himself is to dwell, with his son Micah, in David's palace and to eat at the royal table "like one of the king's sons." Mephibaal has been residing in the house of Machir, son of Ammiel, in the town of Lo-Debar; Lo-Debar

---

20. Heb. *ba'al* is the sobriquet, "master, owner," of a god. Sometimes the god in question is Yahweh, sometimes other figures. Most scholars theorize that to avoid the implication that Saul's sons were named for a god other than Yahweh, such as Hadad, scribes altered names and substituted the term *bōšet*, "shame." For a recent defense of the latter term as a divine epithet, see Gordon J. Hamilton, "New Evidence for the Authenticity of *bšt* in Hebrew Personal Names and for Its Use as a Divine Epithet in Biblical Texts," *CBQ* 60 (1998): 228-50. The term appears to signify a divinity in Amorite names of the mid-2nd millennium. It would not be surprising were it related to the name of the Egyptian god Bastet. Indeed, since *s bstt*, "son of Bastet," becomes a royal epithet in Egypt starting with the 21st Dynasty, the name Ishboshet ('*šbšt*) may even represent an attempt to curry favor in Tanis. (Egyp. *s* and Can. *š* are often interchanged.)

is in northern Gilead (Israelite Transjordan). David relocates him in Jerusalem. This isolated incident paves the way for a more complex narrative, beginning in 2 Sam. 10.

All this while, Nahash, Saul's early antagonist at Jabesh Gilead (1 Sam. 11), has remained king in Ammon and has been David's ally. On his death, David dispatches a delegation to extend condolences to Nahash's son and heir, Hanun. Hanun's advisers, however, much like David's when Abner came to Hebron, insist that the Israelite envoys have come only to spy on the capital. Their response — and their restraint in comparison with Joab is telling — is to humiliate the legation by shaving off half of their beards, and cutting off half their clothing. (David allows the messengers to remain in Jericho, at the Jordan, until their beards grow back.) The shaving of the hair here foreshadows what is to come in the case of Absalom, whose hair is his physical glory and also the physical cause of his undoing.

Hanun of Ammon summons the Arameans of southern Syria to his aid. His allies are the House of Rehob (a dynasty), Zobah (a country), the king of Maacah (a dynasty), and Ish Tob (unclear, but probably a vassal of Zobah). Confronted with the rebuff of his ambassadors and with the introduction of Aramean forces as a *casus belli*, David dispatches Joab and his brother Abishai against Ammon. Joab drives back the Arameans, and the Ammonites flee from Abishai's brigade into the capital. The Aramean leader, King Hadadezer of Zobah, then summons help from "Aram that is across the river." At this point David leads an assault that defeats and disperses them. The Arameans sue for peace as vassals.

After the battle, "at the turn of the year, at the time when kings go forth (to war)," David perversely stays at home and sends Joab to reduce Rabbah, the capital of Ammon. While all the warriors but the king are away, David, walking along the palace parapet, spots the "very beautiful" Bathsheba, daughter of Eliam (or Ammiel), the wife of Uriah the Hittite, as she is bathing. The celebrated incident ensues. David fetches Bathsheba to the palace. He and she have intercourse just at the time of her ritual cleansing from a period, probably a week into her menstrual cycle.

Bathsheba misses her next period. She informs David of the fact, and David summons Uriah from Rabbat Ammon. David interviews Uriah at the palace. He urges Uriah to go home to sleep with his wife, even gets him drunk — all, it seems, to cover up David's adultery. Uriah, however, steadfastly refuses to indulge himself, on the grounds that the army and the ark are in the field.[21] The

---

21. See Michael M. Homan, "Booths or Succoth? A Response to Yigael Yadin," *JBL* 118 (1999): 691-97.

point is not that Uriah is declining special privileges. Rather, intercourse would render him ritually unclean for combat. Uriah's interest in propriety and ritual correctness contrasts with David's adoption, in the episode, of the attitude of a scofflaw and, eventually, bandit.

Unable to provide real cover for his adultery, David chooses to kill Uriah, rather than take the consequences. Bill Cosby used to describe the football tactics of his *alma mater,* Temple University, against the larger, fiercer team from Hofstra. Cosby was a running back, and the only play that Temple employed against Hofstra was "Cosby up the middle, and the rest of the team off the field." David calls that play. He sends Uriah to Joab with a message instructing the general to send Uriah into the fiercest point of line combat and abandon him in a retreat. Joab accordingly orders an assault on the city, Rabbat Ammon, and stations Uriah in the van.

In his report on the incident, Joab instructs his messenger how to reply if the king reprimands him for taking casualties in a direct assault on a fortified city. In the event of such a reprimand, the messenger is to state that Uriah, too, died in the assault. On hearing the full version of the news, David calmly speaks of the accidents of war.[22] David has now sunk to or even below the level of his subordinates in earlier narratives: as king, he has become, in the end, the outlaw he once represented without incurring guilt. He has murdered not an enemy, nor even a former enemy, but a loyal and upstanding subordinate. He has claimed that subordinate's wife. Nor does the husband simply drop dead at a convenient moment, as Abigail's husband had done earlier: David has usurped the role of Yahweh, by providing, violently, for himself. The stench of corruption cleaves to him, personally, rather than wafting up only from those around him.[23]

Yahweh is furious. The prophet Nathan confronts David, and traps him into pronouncing the death sentence — and a fourfold restitution — for his own crime by disguising it as a different case. Nathan pronounces Yahweh's judgment: David has committed adultery. He has killed an innocent man. In consequence, an "intimate" will sleep with David's wives in public. The "sword will not depart" from his house. And the son of David's adultery is to die.

Here, the story teases us with another glimpse of David's modernity. Bathsheba's son sickens, in accordance with Nathan's prediction. During the child's illness, David bewails the child so fervidly that his servants (the "elders

---

22. For the text, P. Kyle McCarter, *II Samuel.* AB 9 (Garden City: Doubleday, 1984), 282-83.

23. See Leo G. Perdue, "'Is There Anyone Left of the House of Saul . . . ?' Ambiguity and the Characterization of David in the Succession Narrative," *JSOT* 30 (1984): 67-84.

of his house") fear to inform him of the child's death. But when he senses from their consternation that the infant has died, David abandons his apotropaic fast and prostration in sackcloth, and resumes his normal life, taking food and beverage. He reasons, "After all, I shall be going to join the child, not he returning to join me." Death is irreversible, and it is only during the period when Yahweh might be persuaded to reverse his judgment that a ritual of abasement is profitable. The behavior confounds David's attendants. It represents, however, a practical approach to the question of petitions to God: after the child's death, mourning, or petitioning, would be pointless, as the decision could not be reversed (2 Sam. 12:15-23).

In contrast to David, Bathsheba contritely mourns her husband properly. Only after the period of mourning ends does she move to the palace, before the birth of the doomed son. After the son's death, David comforts her, and begets the son he calls Solomon (Nathan, possibly on his enthronement, calls him Jedediah). And Joab, having penetrated the city, summons David to complete the conquest of the Ammonite capital, Rabbah. David dons the 70-pound gold crown of the Ammonite state god Milcom, or perhaps of the king of Ammon. He subjects the population of Rabbah to forced labor, bringing the episode to a temporary, unbalanced close.

The death of the first son, some critics have suggested, lays to rest the suspicion that Solomon was the offspring of the illicit union between David and Bathsheba.[24] However, Solomon's very name, probably meaning "his replacement" or "[the God] made good his loss," suggests another interpretation: Solomon is named to commemorate not the condemned son's, but Uriah's death.[25] In fact, then, the death of the first son David fathered on Uriah leaves the reader in no doubt that Solomon, whose paternity would otherwise be clouded, is certainly David's son. In the same way, the description of Bathsheba purifying herself from her period before her tryst with the king shows that the first son was David's, not Uriah's.

There are various ways to model the implications for David's character.

---

24. As T. N. D. Mettinger, *King and Messiah: The Civil and Sacral Legitimation of the Israelite Kings.* ConBOT 8 (Lund: Gleerup, 1976), 30. Mettinger also points out that the punishment of the child exonerates the rest of the dynasty for David's adultery.

25. So, incisively, Timo Veijola, "Salomo — der erstgeborene Bathsebas," *VTSup* 30 (1979): 230-50, esp. 236-37. Some names with the element *šlm* might refer to the god of the sunset, Shalem, known from Ugaritic myth of the 13th century. This is probably the case with the name Jerusalem (perhaps, "May Shalem provide an oracle"). However, such names as Shelemiah ("Yahweh has provided compensation") and Shelumiel ("God is my compensation") indicate that in Israelite personal names, the element *šlm* denotes replacement or recompense.

Saul M. Olyan has pointed out that the text portrays the reversal of the standard mourning ritual.[26] David mourns his son before death, in an effort to fend off the impending death, rather than allowing the death to set off the cycle of mourning. In this way, he turns the ritual from a reaction into an agency of its own. The implication, as noted, is that David has a very practical take: ritual is useful only insofar as it is efficacious, or potentially efficacious, in achieving the aims of the performer.[27] But at the same time, one might doubt the king's sincerity in the performance of the ritual — that's that, he says at the end, dusting himself off on the way to the lunch buffet, no point carrying on any further. The incident exposes the contradictions in David's character: he mourns his enemies demonstratively, but not those to whom he is loyal. Or, one might take him to be the first "modern" character in the text: he accepts the universe, and subscribes to the Lockean dictum that the earth is for the living.

And yet, this is not all that the text encodes. In the first instance, there is the comparison to his later treatment of Absalom. Absalom dies in the course of David's divine punishment for the adultery and murder that led to the infant's birth and death. Yet on Absalom's death, the king is seemingly inconsolable. For, the text maintains, in mourning Absalom, David was anything but practical. His ululation demoralized the army and dismayed all his partisans. It is Joab who has to set him right and have him address his troops. Joab, who kills Uriah only on David's order rather than on his own initiative, has now become the moral compass in his relationship with David, rather than the other way around.

The contrast between the mourning for the infant and the mourning for Absalom may have ramifications, too, for the reader's reflection on the various rituals of mourning in which David indulges throughout 2 Samuel. His first act of mourning is for Saul and Jonathan; the second is for Abner; the third, in effect, is for Ishbaal. It is difficult to be sure that the author of the text is calling the sincerity, as distinct from the utility, of these incidents into question, the more so as we encounter them all before reading about the death of Bathsheba's son in 2 Sam. 12. One is certainly tempted, however, to take them, along with the mourning of Absalom, to be matters of practical political necessity, of public relations work.

---

26. Saul M. Olyan, "Honor, Shame, and Covenant Relations in Ancient Israel and Its Environment," *JBL* 115 (1997): 201-18, esp. 208-9.

27. See Johannes Pedersen, *Israel, Its Life and Culture* III-IV (London: Oxford University Press, 1940), 457, for the classic formulation of this view, which begins from the reversal of the mourning customs. For a review of scholarship on the issue, see Veijola, *VTSup* 30 (1979): 241-43.

The second textual connection established here is to the death of David's firstborn, Amnon, soon to be murdered at Absalom's hand. David leaves off mourning for Amnon, and sets his heart on Absalom instead. In this instance, the Lockean axiom — the earth is for the living — again comes into play: Burke's much more traditional idea that life is a partnership between the living, the dead, and those unborn is not in view.

G. Absalom's Coup

From this point begins the account of Absalom's revolt, which fulfills the divine curse pronounced against David because of his adultery and murder of Uriah. As we shall see, all the events in it have two causes — a divine cause, which is obscure to the actors, and the actors' own human motivations. The story begins in 2 Sam. 13:1 with these words:

> It was so, afterward: Absalom, son of David, had a lovely sister. Her name was Tamar. And Amnon, son of David, loved her. And Amnon was in distress to the point of making himself ill over Tamar, his sister, for she was a virgin, and it baffled him how to get to her (lit., do anything to her).

Like Abigail before Nabal's death, like Rizpah at Ishbaal's court, and especially like Bathsheba before Uriah's death, Tamar is fetching, but unavailable. David's fling with his underling's wife precipitates an assault on his own women, just as Nathan had predicted.

Amnon's cousin devises a conceit to get Tamar, Absalom's full sister, as-signed to Amnon's residence. Amnon feigns illness. David, taken in by false ap-pearances, orders Tamar to feed him. Amnon entices her into his bedchamber, then rapes her, despite her plea that he ask the king for her hand. After the rape, Amnon ejects her from his domicile and bolts the door behind her. Tamar goes wailing on her way, heaping ash on her head, rending her "coat of many colors" (really, a full-length gown),[28] the ensign of virgin daughters of the king. Strik-ingly, Amnon's behavior is the inverse of David's relations with Saul's daughter Michal. Amnon rapes the king's daughter and then rejects her, where David had betrothed himself to the king's daughter, then attempted to recover her when she was taken away. Amnon's behavior is the opposite too of the behavior of Shechem in Gen. 34: the Hivvite rapist of Dinah, Jacob's daughter, afterward begs for her hand in marriage.

28. See McCarter, 325.

39

David, though angry, does not act. His inaction has been interpreted variously, but it is perhaps best understood as a result of his own status: as an adulterer himself, he is not in a position to take appropriate measures to punish his eldest son (see further below, Chapter 21). Previously, he failed to discipline Joab and Abishai for suggesting Saul's murder and committing the murder of Abner. Now he arrives at the point of tolerating criminal behavior by his own son. His inaction, rooted in his character, is crucial to the unfolding of David's punishment for his adultery with Bathsheba. In legal terms, David merits the death sentence for adultery and for murder. Amnon should, legally, make good his violation of Tamar by wedding her or paying damages to her father. But as he is the son of the same father, no proper resolution of his case is possible.

But Absalom sees his way to a resolution. Absalom's relationship to Tamar after Amnon violates her mirrors that of Nergal and Ereshkigal in the ancient myth of that name. The woman is raped, and is to be either married or avenged. Neither marriage nor punishment eventuates. Two years later, Absalom seeks permission from David to invite his brothers to a festival to celebrate the shearing of his sheep in Baal Hazor. (The verse in which Absalom first takes the initiative thus refers to cutting hair.) David declines to come, but bestows his blessing on the enterprise. All of Absalom's brothers attend. Once again, David has been taken in by a son's deceit, oblivious to the reality behind the appearance. Absalom waits until Amnon has imbibed enough wine. Then his retainers stab the rapist to death. Amnon suffers the penalty paid by all the men of Shechem in the story of Dinah's rape in Gen. 34.

The assembled princes of the royal family flee to Jerusalem. While they are en route, reports reach the capital that Absalom has slaughtered all his brothers. David rends his clothes and stretches out on the ground. But the "very wise" cousin who advised Amnon how to rape Tamar understands that only Amnon was targeted.[29] He penetrates beyond the rumor to the reality. David recovers from his panic. In reality, his mourning for his sons is futile. Yet it also has a desirable result: only one has been murdered after all. At the arrival of the other sons, they and the king sit and weep together.

Absalom, meanwhile, flees to the kingdom of Geshur on the Golan, where his maternal grandfather is king. There he remains for a period of three years. David now is reconciled to the death of Amnon — he is the ultimate pragmatist, after all, who here exhibits exactly the properties he evinced in connection with the death of Bathsheba's bastard son. His heart begins to go out to the survivor, Absalom. In sum, he not only tolerates cutthroats, and eventually suc-

---

29. Is "rumor" in 13:30 *(šmw'h)* a pun on the adviser's patronym in v. 32 *(šm'h)?*

cumbs to their ethic, he fosters and then abets them. Absalom, after all, was driven to murder Amnon by David's failure to punish Amnon, or to compel him to marry the victim of his rape. David's increasing lawlessness begets lawlessness directed against his family.

Three years after Absalom's flight, Joab, knowing that David yearns for his son, commissions a "wise woman" from Tekoa, in southeastern Judah, to approach David. She claims that her two sons fought, and that her kinsmen want to execute the survivor. David extracts a waiver from the Wise Woman, holding him morally harmless for the survivor's bloodguilt, partly to avoid another surprise like the one Nathan had summarized with the words, "You are the man!" (2 Sam. 14:5-11). He then pardons the killer, again because it is in his nature: the woman's plight has rekindled his instinct that a living child is dearer and more important than a dead one. Not one hair of her son's head will fall to the ground, he promises, invoking Yahweh as guarantor of his oath. Her son is a stand-in for Absalom. In the end, Absalom's hair does not touch the ground.

The Wise Woman declares that David has acted as Yahweh's agent (angel) in the matter — and urges him to pardon his own exiled son. Though divining Joab's part in the imposture, David complies. Says the woman, David is as wise as an agent (angel) of Yahweh. He allows Joab to trick him into restoring Absalom to Israel. Indeed, David is doing Yahweh's work, arranging for his own punishment. For the fourth time, he connives with Yahweh by being hoodwinked by people in order to suffer his just deserts — and he will continue to do so.[30] Shrewdly, the Wise Woman expresses the hope that David's decision will lead to "respite" or "rest." For David, it will lead to the opposite, complete unrest, and yet Absalom's repatriation will also balance his sin and lead to respite in Solomon's day (2 Sam. 14:17; 1 Kgs. 5:4[Heb. 18]).

Absalom thus returns to Jerusalem. But David keeps him under house arrest, isolated from the court, for another two years. Here, the text pauses, to describe Absalom as perfect in loveliness: the motif brings him into favorable comparison with David himself, with Tamar, and later with his brother

30. David collaborates in his punishment: by pronouncing the death sentence when Nathan fools him by disguising the identity of the killer and victim; by sending Tamar to Amnon when the latter feigns illness; when Absalom fools him, by keeping silent and then pretending nothing is amiss, into sending all the sons to Absalom's feast; when Joab's plan and the Wise Woman of Tekoa's imposture of a suppliant fool him into allowing Absalom's return home; and when Absalom fools him into thinking that he means to go to Hebron to worship, rather than revolt. One could argue that David's inaction after Amnon's rape, or abandonment of Jerusalem, also contributed, but the motif of deception seems to underline what the narrator thinks of as the cruxes in the action.

Adonijah. Especially his hair was lush, and its periodic cuttings weighed 5 pounds. He had three sons, and a daughter named Tamar.[31]

At the end of two years under house arrest in Jerusalem, Absalom has his slaves put Joab's barley field to the torch in order to attract enough attention to be reintroduced to the palace compound. (The word for barley is related to that for hair.) The indignant Joab confronts Absalom, who demands that David either rehabilitate or execute him.

David welcomes Absalom back into the bosom of the court. The dead son is forgotten. "Will the sword consume forever?" Abner had asked Joab. "The sword will not depart from your house," Nathan had told David. David's bent is against allowing hatred to rage. He has a forgiving disposition, merciful rather than punitive. For David, what is past is dead, and what is dead is past. The earth is for the living.

Yet the past is not dead for normal people, nor is it for Absalom. David has clasped a viper to his breast. Absalom begins to campaign actively to win the hearts of all Israel. He appropriates a retinue for himself, achieving a level of display that leaves no doubt as to his exalted station.

The proximate cause of the Absalom revolt is his campaigning at the "hand," or outer extension, of the gate in front of Jerusalem. The nature of that campaigning is not usually understood. The text says,

> Absalom acquired a chariot and horses, and fifty men as Runners before him. And Absalom rose early, and stood on the "hand" of the road. So that every man who had a lawsuit to come to the king for judgment, Absalom hailed him, and said, "What town are you from?" And he'd say, "Your servant is from one of the tribes of Israel." So Absalom would say to him, "Look, your cause is good and justified, but you have no one from the king to hear you." Absalom would say, "If only I were made judge in the land, and every man who has a lawsuit for judgment would come to me so that I could award him judgment." And when the man would draw near to bow to him, he would send forth his hand and grasp him and kiss him. And Absalom acted in this manner to all Israel who would come for judgment to the king, and Absalom stole the heart of the men of Israel. (2 Sam. 15:1-6)

Absalom, striking for his hair and physique, promises each man individually that he would find in his favor — like a politician attempting to please competing constituencies, implies the text. And although he was perfectly transparent

---

31. 2 Sam. 14:27. On the relation of this text to 18:18, in which Absalom claims he has no son, see below, Chapter 22 B.

about it, the Israelites never recognized what he was doing, namely, laying the groundwork for a coup that could only end in disappointment for his supporters. Again, David was oblivious, as when Amnon requested Tamar's services or Absalom arranged his sheep-shearing feast. Again, there is a double meaning — Absalom's overt versus covert reasons for telling people what he did. The hidden agenda is central to this segment of David's biography.

After four years more, 11 years after the rape of Tamar, Absalom asks permission from his father to go to Hebron to fulfill the vow he made in exile. The oblivious David again accedes to the request. The vow was that on his repatriation Absalom would "serve Yahweh." The nature of the service to Yahweh?

On arriving in Hebron, Absalom dispatches agents throughout Israel.[32] These, at his signal, rally the population with the cry, "Absalom reigns in Hebron!" — an acclamation of his kingship. The success of this stratagem impels David to abandon Jerusalem, ostensibly to spare the city. There, he leaves 10 concubines in charge of the palace.[33] The scene of his withdrawal is sad and extended. With him come his officials and the Cherethites, and Pelethites, and the Gittites, 600 men who came from Gath under his command,[34] namely, the Philistine force he commanded at Ziklag. David offers the Gittites the chance to remain and join "the king," Absalom, as they are not Israelites, but they elect personal loyalty over their official position.

The priests, Zadoq and Abiathar, along with all the Levites, march the ark out of the city and set it up to squire the people in their retreat across the Qidron Brook eastward. David orders them to return with the ark to the capital. About a century earlier, Tiglath-Pileser I, king of Assyria, furnishes a description of people fleeing with their gods — that is, the icons of their gods — to avoid allowing them to be taken captive: "To save their lives, they picked up

32. Note the pluperfect *yaqtul* in 15:10: Absalom went to Hebron having already sent agents around the country to respond to his phony acclamation in Hebron with support. There is some question in what contexts the *yaqtul* can represent a pluperfect. See C. John Collins, "The wayyiqtol as 'Pluperfect': When and Why?" *TynBul* 46 (1995): 117-40. However, there may be a diachronic element in the choice of *qatala* or *yaqtul* in this capacity.

33. Note the locution *nšym plgšm* in 15:16. The only biblical parallel is in the singular in Judg. 19:1, 27. The latter is probably derivative, but it is striking that the story in Judg. 19–21 links Jabesh Gilead to Gibeah. *Plgš* is spelled defectively in Samuel, with one exception. In its other attestations, it is *plene* except in one occurrence.

34. Note the locution *b*ʾ*w brglw* (with defective spelling) in 15:16-18, with semantic parallels only in Exod. 11:8; Judg. 5:15; 8:5; 1 Kgs. 20:10, but not in the text interpreting Judg. 5, namely the prose narrative in Judg. 4. Cf. *lrgl* in Gen. 30:30; 33:14; Deut. 11:6; 1 Sam. 25:42; 2 Kgs. 3:9; Hab. 3:5.

their gods and goods and flew like birds to the crags of the high hills."[35] This was a common strategy in antiquity. The capture of a god could be interpreted by rebel elements to mean that the gods had abandoned the ruling dynasty out of anger. Yet David intentionally permits the ark to fall into Absalom's hands.

The cost of David's decision is that Yahweh appears to be electing Absalom as king (the people having acclaimed him). David's characteristically unconventional logic: if Yahweh looks favorably on him, Yahweh will restore him to the palace. As a pragmatist, David takes no stock in the symbolic; he does not care for appearances. And suddenly, he is again himself in this respect. His barb to Zadoq is, "Are you a seer?" the implication being that no human agency can foresee David's death or return.[36] Even oracles, without Yahweh's consent, can be of no assistance. David acknowledges that Yahweh has abandoned him, and that possession of the symbol, the mere appearance, the ark, is worthless unless the hidden reality of Yahweh's favor corresponds to its possession.

The ploy of sending the ark back has a practical side. It leaves David with partisans and runners in the capital. The priests, Zadoq and Abiathar, are to inform him of Absalom's plans. As specialists in divination, they would naturally be consulted in connection with any fateful decision. By leaving them to swear fealty to Absalom, David in effect creates a situation in which the priests have two masters, in which the very sacral center of the kingdom is double-dealing. Here, for the first time since Amnon raped Tamar, the duplicity is directed against Absalom's interests.

As David retreats across the Qidron Valley and up the Mount of Olives, bareheaded and barefoot, he calls on Yahweh to confound the counsel of Absalom's adviser, Ahitophel of Giloh. Just as he reaches the crest of the Mount of Olives, "where one prostrates oneself to God(s)," Hushai crosses his path. David now recognizes the providential hand behind the human appearances, especially as the signal comes at a shrine. He seizes on Hushai as the answer to his prayer: Hushai is to confound Ahitophel's counsel, and report the transactions of Absalom's inner circle to the priests. He too is a double agent, David's under-

35. The site of the flight is in Kummuh (Commagene). See for comment Morton Cogan, *Imperialism and Religion*. SBLMS 19 (Missoula: Scholars, 1974), 30-34. For the text, RIMA 2.87.1.ii.36-42.

36. 2 Sam. 15:27. The independent use of the locution "seer," which is paralleled only in Isa. 30 and 1 Sam. 9:9, the latter with an explanatory gloss, the former in parallel to a more common term, again suggests the antiquity of our prose text here. Note further that Zadoq is accompanied by Levites (2 Sam. 15:24), not descendants of Aaron. The text is thus far older than Chronicles. Note also the words *wyṣqw* ("they stationed," or "presented") the ark of the God. There is a possible pun on Zadoq's name here. Further, Abiathar stays by the ark until the exodus from Jerusalem is complete.

cover man in Absalom's court (2 Sam. 15:31-37). David is suddenly in tune with the hidden messages of Yahweh.

On his way from the Mount of Olives down through the steppe to the Jordan, David is met with supplies by Ziba, the steward of Jonathan's son Mephibaal. Mephibaal, the steward claims, has remained in Jerusalem expecting to be restored to his ancestral throne. David immediately transfers Saul's estates to the steward.

Bahurim, the ancestral village of Saul's clan, lay just east of the Mount of Olives on the road to the Jordan. There, a kinsman of Saul named Shimei curses and throws stones at David, calling him "Man of Blood, and Man of Belial" (the latter means "wastrel, hellion"). "Yahweh has requited you for all the blood of the House of Saul . . ." (2 Sam. 16:5-8). Abishai, Joab's brother, offers to execute Shimei. David prudently prohibits the killing. He thus returns to the policy of his youth, when he forbade his subordinates to kill Saul. In the case of Shimei, David reasons that Yahweh may have ordained the taunting as part of his own humiliation. Hoping in extremis for mercy from Yahweh in exchange for bearing his punishment, he now applies the brakes to the spiraling cycle of violence that has hitherto raged about him. He now perceives the reality underlying events.

As David and his loyalists arrive at the Jordan, Absalom convenes his advisers in the capital he has now occupied. Hushai approaches Absalom: "Long live the king, long live the king," he declares. This is the only occasion on which the formula, used for acclaiming kings, is repeated. The repetition might be a copying error, as the Greek translations omit it. But the repetition does subtly reflect the fact that the country now has two legally installed kings. Hushai is not exactly stuttering in panic, but signaling the ambiguity of the situation.[37]

Absalom taxes Hushai with abandoning his "intimate," David. In response, Hushai professes his loyalty, ambiguously, to "him whom Yahweh and this people and all the men of Israel have chosen; his will I be and with him will I dwell." Absalom takes this to be a description of himself, rather than of his father. Then comes "And second, to whom will I do service? Not before his son?" The irony and duplicity here are particularly delicious. The profession of loyalty to the son is phrased as a question rather than a commitment. But Hushai means that he will serve David, while fooling Absalom into thinking he has changed sides.

Thus, in 2 Sam. 16:19, Hushai informs Absalom, "As I served before your father, so I will be before you." This is a clear double entendre, since the implication of the words, taken literally, is that Hushai will continue to serve David as he had done before. David had instructed Hushai to prevaricate, to tell Absa-

---

37. David Noel Freedman, in correspondence, 9 May 2000.

lom, "I am your servant, O king! I was your servant from of old, and now I am your servant." Hushai, however, skillfully reformulates the presentation. He tells the truth, or rather, does not tell a lie, about his loyalties. Hushai's language indicates a consciousness that two meanings can be encoded in a single statement. Yet it is natural that Absalom apprehends the avowal as a statement that Hushai will be loyal to him whom he serves. Absalom expects Hushai, in sum, to continue to serve without a hidden agenda, a second intention.

This sense of double entendre, or of received versus transmitted message, is how the author constructs double causation not for the actors, but for the reader. There are human as well as divine reasons for Absalom's revolt and its outcome. Still, the message of complementary causation is delivered without overt divine action being narrated, so it is the reader who must divine the providential character of the events.

At this juncture, Ahitophel instructs Absalom to sleep with his father's concubines so as to demonstrate his commitment to the uprising. Absalom pitches a tent on the palace roof. There, in the sight of the assembled populace, he enters the presence of his father's women. This is the explicit fulfillment of part of Nathan's curse on David for the Uriah and Bathsheba affair. The text drily glosses it, "The counsel of Ahitophel, which he dispensed in those days, was as though one had asked for a divine oracle" (2 Sam. 16:20-23). Ahitophel, like David, Absalom, Hushai, and even Shimei and Joab, is Yahweh's implement in shaping the course of events by which David is chastised.

Ahitophel urges pursuit of David with the 12 thousand troops immediately available. He persuades Absalom and all the elders of Israel — the deliberative body responsible for presenting resolutions to the people. Absalom then summons Hushai to comment on the plan. And Hushai persuades Absalom and "all the men of Israel" — the body entrusted with making decisions — to assemble the whole tribal muster of Israel before risking battle, so as to enjoy an insurmountable numerical advantage and prevent David's engaging in hit-and-run guerilla tactics.[38] Glosses the author, "Yahweh had ordained that the good advice of Ahitophel be confounded in order that Yahweh should bring evil on Absalom" (2 Sam. 17:14). Only here does the historian explicitly describe Yahweh's role in the political process. The text confirms that Hushai's appearance "where one bows down to God(s)" was Yahweh's answer to David's prayer.

---

38. Ironically, all Israel votes to assemble the rest of Israel. The deliberative body, or elders, meet in all likelihood indoors, while the "men of Israel" probably meet outdoors, in line with the protocol outlined in Baruch Halpern, *The First Historians: The Hebrew Bible and History* (San Francisco: Harper & Row, 1988), ch. 3. What is interesting is the democratic organization of Absalom's supporters.

Here, again, a concern with rumor crops up. First comes the misconstruction of Absalom's murder of Amnon as an attempt at revolution, in 2 Sam. 14:29-33, mentioned above. This turns out to be an exaggeration at the time, though it foreshadows Absalom's assault on the royal family in the succeeding action. The second text addressing the issue comes with Hushai's argument in 2 Sam. 17:11 that all Israel must be mustered to confront David: after all, a rumor of an initial victory by David over Absalom's army, growing greater as it travels, would otherwise demoralize all Israel. Again stressing that all of Israel took Absalom's side, this text presents Hushai's case against immediate pursuit of David.

A reader might suspect a hidden message to Absalom even in this reasoned counsel: can one trust the courtiers who take Absalom's side to fight against David? If not, one must muster the entire country to prevent defections to David's side. Still, this bracketing with rumor indicates an understanding of the impact of news on the hearer, who overreacts, misinterprets the reality which the words reflect. In sum, words — even truthful words — can be and are deceptive; they have two sides. This is both an unusually honest (and virtuoso) exposure of the scribal ethic about composition and a key to understanding how an inner circle was meant to understand the text.

Linked to the claim of human misapprehension is the use of complementary causation — divine and human — in the narrative. The essential property of complementary causation is that human actors pursue their aims for good and sufficient personal reasons. Thus, Joseph's brothers are driven to criminality by their jealousy at Joseph's preferential treatment, or by the very dreams that augur his eminence. They sell him into slavery, or leave him to die at the bottom of a cistern — depending on the version of the story one examines. Joseph claims that dreams are correctly deciphered not by him, but by God, that it is God who has played a trick on Benjamin (when it was Joseph who did so), and so on. Finally, it becomes clear, Joseph's elevation and the brothers' reaction to it are both part of a divine plan to rescue Israel from famine in Canaan, and indeed to rescue Egypt from famine. All is well, and all is forgiven, by the last episodes of the Joseph story (see Chapter 21).

Likewise, Amnon rapes Tamar because he is taken with her. He discards her because, having satisfied himself with her, he has no further desire for her. Absalom schemes to murder Amnon out of revenge, because David has dallied in exacting retribution. Joab engineers his return, through the intervention of the Wise Woman of Tekoa. The latter implies that the king is like the agent (angel) of God. And he *is* Yahweh's agent insofar as he forgives Absalom and thus sets off dramatic momentum, toward a climax. He is also like God, ironically, in seeing that there is a human hand behind the Wise Woman's implication that he should repatriate Absalom. But he does not see that Joab, seemingly acting on his behalf, is also an agent of divine will.

In this drama, then, David's sin precipitates divine intervention. But the intervention takes the form of human actors reacting naturally to the circumstances into which they are put, and it is the sum of their actions that accomplishes Yahweh's ends. The implication is that the autonomy of the personalities involved is in some measure compromised, that their behavior, like that of the pharaoh whose heart is hardened, is not altogether their own. Instead, they are pawns in a very complex interaction of moral-political economy, without, however, their being in a position to disavow responsibility for their actions.

This has implications for David's character, and indeed for the understanding of human character generally in the books of Samuel.[39] The self is not always self-contained, in these texts. Nor is it without internal conflict. The latter is exemplified by David's ambivalence over Tamar's suffering and Absalom's rehabilitation and, later, killing. He sits by after Absalom's sister is raped, not forcing the perpetrator to marry her as required in Exod. 22:16-17(15-16) and in normal Near Eastern usage — rather as he disavows any responsibility, including for punishment, when Joab commits political murders. He forgives Absalom for murder. Admittedly, the murder was a reaction to Amnon's provocation. Still, even at the end, David does not want Absalom killed, although only through Absalom's death can David's own life be secure. The divided self of the actors in the dynastic drama is, as noted, shared with the Joseph story in Genesis, but not with the literature of the 7th century and later. In the theology or psychological theory of later sources from Judah, the individual is precisely defined as indivisible, and therefore completely morally liable for his or her deeds.

The course of the revolt continues. Absalom and all the men of Israel having accepted Hushai's counsel, Zadoq and Abiathar dispatch their sons to inform David of the decision. The two runners elude capture in Bahurim, where the wife of a man, probably Ziba or one of his dependents, hides them in a cistern.[40] Ahitophel, meanwhile, despairing at the rejection of his advice, hangs himself in his home.

39. Marvin DuBois calls my attention to this issue, citing J.-P Vernant, *L'individu dans la cité* (1987), 32, unavailable to me, to the effect that archaic and classical Greeks experienced their selves as neither delimited nor unified; and he cites Fränkel's portrayal of Homeric man as "ein offenes Kraftfeld."

40. The woman tells the pursuers that Jonathan and Ahimaaz had "crossed the water container," diverting them with a truth which they misinterpret: they had, in a sense, crossed (over to) the water container. Even the woman in Bahurim has twin audiences. The sentient reader is the insider, the casual reader the outsider. The word for "container" is *Michal*, identical with the name of the daughter of Saul.

David arrives at last at the fortified town of Mahanaim in central Transjordan, formerly Ishbaal's stronghold. There, David receives support and supplies from three Transjordanian allies: Shobi, son of Nahash, from Rabbah, the capital of Ammon, the king whom David installed as a vassal there; Machir, son of Ammiel, from Lo-Debar, the former host of Jonathan's son Mephibaal; and Barzillai, not explicitly identified as Saul's brother-in-law, from Rogelim. David assigns command of the center of his army to Joab, and of the wings to Abishai, Joab's brother, and to Ittay, the chief of the Gittites. The army insist that David remain in the town rather than taking the field.[41]

Absalom and his commander, Amasa, Joab's maternal cousin, cross the Jordan for a confrontation. David publicly instructs his three brigadiers not to kill Absalom.[42] David's professional army meets the Israelites in "the forest of Ephraim." They win a decisive victory, killing 20 thousand Israelites and scattering them so that the forest "eats up" more of the muster than does the sword — the image is of a rout and loss of command control and coordination on the Israelite side.

Absalom, renowned for his glorious hair, rides his mule into the forest. The mule is the vehicle on which Absalom's brothers fled him (2 Sam. 13:29), and on which Solomon rides to his coronation. Absalom's mule, however, leaves him eaten by the forest. The rebel's hair becomes tangled in the limb of an oak (Heb. "Goddess"). As he hangs from it — suspended in an indeterminate state, between heaven and earth, not a hair falling to the ground — Joab orders a subordinate to kill him. The aide refuses, having heard David's charge, and fearing that Joab will scapegoat him for the killing. This drives home the point that David really ordered his men to take Absalom alive. However, after Joab strikes the first three darts into Absalom, his 10 armor-bearers finish the job, then bury Absalom in a grave they mark with large stones. Absalom's other monument, "the monument of Absalom" in the King's Valley, outside Jerusalem, is one that he built because he had no son to perpetuate his name.[43]

Finally, Joab has executed a victim against David's explicit orders. And the execution is in fact just. It is a mark of the reversal of moral roles that the narrative does not censure Joab for this killing. Instead, it presents a mirror image of

41. The parallel to 2 Sam. 18:2b-3 is found in the list of David's heroes (21:17), placed in the context of a Goliath-like Philistine bearing down on David. The locution differs, but the sentiment is the same.
42. David's locution, that his commanders are to *l't* ("go easy on") Absalom in 2 Sam. 18:5, calls to mind the use of the same term in 19:5, where David covers (*l't*) his face to mourn for Absalom. In the text, Joab fulfilled his order in a double entendre. Similar double meanings involve the terms *rgl* and *mṣ'* in the text.
43. 2 Sam. 18:18. See above, n. 31.

the killing of Uriah, when Joab feared the consequences of taking the measures necessary to strike the victim down. There, David orders the murder; here, David orders prescission from the execution of a traitor and killer. There, Joab wrongly obeys the command; here, he rightly countermands it. In both cases, Joab remains the killer.

Israel then flees "to its tents," and Joab's runners carry the news of the victory, and of Absalom's death, to David at Mahanaim. David's first concern is with Absalom's safety. Learning of his death, David takes himself to the upper story of the city gate and wails. The ululation depresses the army, and it is Joab who must brace David to emerge and congratulate his soldiery on their achievement.

Next begins the campaign for David's re-election. Pragmatists in the countryside recognize that Absalom's death makes David the only candidate for the throne. David also sends Zadoq and Abiathar to encourage the tribesmen of Judah to recognize his sovereignty before the Israelites do. He promises that Absalom's general, Amasa, will replace Joab as his army chief — the equivalent would be Lincoln or Johnson appointing Robert E. Lee Secretary of the Army after the Civil War.

These concessions induce the Judahites to embrace David's sovereignty again. As they arrive at the Jordan, Shimei, the kinsman of Saul, comes as well, with a hundred Benjaminites. Also present is Ziba, the steward of Mephibaal, to squire David across the river. David again restrains Abishai from executing Shimei. Across the river, Mephibaal arrives and relates that his steward had prevented him from leaving Jerusalem with David. Mephibaal's unkempt appearance, the evidence he hoped for David's restoration, might formerly have been presented to Absalom as Mephibaal's self-abasement in hope of Yahweh's vengeance on the murderer of his family. But it is the narrator who says Mephibaal hadn't done his feet, done his moustache, or laundered his clothes until the king should come in peace. Not only does the narrator take Mephibaal's side, then, but he also adduces Mephibaal's untrimmed, unwashed hair — the contrast is to Absalom's hair — as evidence of innocence. But, says Mephibaal, David is "like an agent of the God,"[44] whose judgment Mephibaal will accept. Da-

44. 2 Sam. 19:27(28). The phrase also occurs in 14:17, 20. But in 1 Sam. 29:9 Achish paves the way for it by declaring that David is like an emissary of God. In late texts, prophets are referred to as "angels" or emissaries: Hag. 1:13; 2 Chr. 36:15, 16; Ps. 103:20; Job 4:18; perhaps Isa. 44:26; Ps. 91:11; cf. Mal. 2:7 (priests). A royal figure is also juxtaposed with Yahweh in oath formulae, as 1 Sam. 20:3; 25:26; 2 Sam. 15:21 and perhaps the original of 11:11. These texts have a derivative in Zech. 12:8, which predicts that the lowest of Jerusalem's inhabitants "will be like David, and the House of David will be like a God, like the angel of Yahweh before them." This seems to conflate the literature on David

vid, therefore, cuts Saul's estate in half, restoring half of it from the servant to the master, doing the least injustice to each.

David also asks Barzillai to accompany him to the court in Jerusalem. The latter begs off on the basis of his age. So David takes Barzillai's son in his stead, to reward his service.[45] He insists on having a hostage from Transjordan, despite the support he receives there.

On the way to Jerusalem, David, having crossed the river like Saul after his defeat of the Ammonites, and perhaps like Ishbaal after his enthronement in Mahanaim, stops at Gilgal. There he receives the acclamation both of Judah and of the Israelites. The ceremony recalls Saul's coronation in the B source in 1 Samuel. Israel and Judah, however, here compete to restore David to the throne. Saul was merely the darling of Israel.

The story of the revolt, and David's rehabilitation, has an epilogue. A wastrel Benjaminite, Sheba son of Bichri, calls for a revolt against David.

> He blew the ram's horn and said, "We have no lot in David, nor have we an ancestral portion in the son of Jesse." And all the men of Israel defected from David after Sheba. (2 Sam. 20:1-2)

David returns to Jerusalem, and arranges for the concubines defiled by Absalom to occupy their own harem: "They were sequestered to the day of their death in living widowhood" — like Michal's earlier fate. He then instructs Amasa, Absalom's general, to assemble the muster of Judah, within three days. This is just after the Judahites have returned home from supporting Absalom's cause. Understandably, Amasa is unable to meet the deadline.

David tells Abishai, Joab's brother, that Sheba's revolt will do more harm than Absalom's, and orders him to pursue Sheba with the professional army —

---

with Exod. 4:16; 7:1; 14:19. Other texts juxtaposing God and a leader include Lev. 19:32; Exod. 22:28; 1 Kgs. 21:10, 13; Isa. 8:21 (cursing a leader and God; cf. Lev. 24:10-23; Job 2:9); Zeph. 1:5; 2 Kgs. 2:2, 4, 6; 4:30 (swearing by a leader and God); Prov. 24:21; and in a different sense, 2 Chr. 19:11. For a dedication "To (the) baal and to Padi" incised on a store jar in a temple at Eqron, see Seymour Gitin and Mordechai Cogan, "A New Type of Dedicatory Inscription from Ekron," *IEJ* 49 (1999): 193-202. Gitin and Cogan cite Neo-Assyrian parallels, denying that the oaths by God and king in biblical texts are comparable to a dedication. However, several of the texts cited refer to reviling God and leader, which suggests certain requirements for offerings to them. And Judg. 7:18, 20 depicts the dedication of a battle "to Yahweh and to Gideon," a man who will thereafter be offered kingship. Old Babylonian oath formulae are not materially different.

45. A direct parallel occurs in EA 137:27ff., where Rib-Addi begs Akhenaten to take his son as a substitute for himself, too old to travel to Egypt. Amarna (and Taanach Letter) kinglets seem to prefer sending relations to see the pharaoh rather than going themselves.

"Joab, and the Cherethites and Pelethites and all the warriors."[46] This force links up with Amasa at Gibeon. There, Joab greets Amasa, gripping his beard with his right hand to deliver a kiss. But Amasa misses the movement of Joab's left hand. Joab strikes with his sword at Amasa's breastplate ("fifth rib"), and Amasa's guts cascade to the ground. Having executed Absalom, Joab has now returned to being the born killer he was during David's early career.

The nauseating sight of Amasa rolling around in his own gore stops the newly-mustered men of Judah short. So Joab's lieutenant covers Amasa and pushes him into a ditch, and the muster of Judah follows Joab. The rebel Sheba takes refuge at the furthest extremity of Israelite territory or perhaps just beyond, in the town of Abel, in the dynastic fief of the House of Maacah. Joab invests the city and a "wise woman" negotiates for the town. Rather than surrender, the people of Abel lop off Sheba's head and hurl it over the wall to Joab. Joab then assumes the position of head of the army, while Benaiah son of Jehoiada becomes head of the professional soldiery.

Between the conclusion of the story of Sheba, and of the murder of Amasa, and the conclusion of the story of David, there appear several appendices. Of these, two are lists of the accomplishments of David's "heroes," his most decorated military underlings, or brief anecdotes about their accomplishments.[47]

Two of the appendices are narratives. One story tells of a famine. An oracle of Yahweh indicates that the famine was occasioned by Saul's violation of Israel's treaty with the Gibeonites, or Hivvites north of Jerusalem. To expunge the guilt, David hands all but one of Saul's lineal descendants over to the Gibeonites, who hang them. The other narrative concerns David's acquisition of the future site of the temple.

David's story closes in 1 Kgs. 1–2. Old and frail, David is unable to experience warmth without cuddling the lovely Abishag, who nevertheless remains a virgin. Meanwhile, David's heir apparent, Adonijah, proclaims himself king. Joab takes Adonijah's side, though he did not take Absalom's side. So too do Abiathar the priest and all the other sons of the king. Nathan and Bathsheba, however, intervene and remind the king of his promise, hitherto unreported, to place Bathsheba's son Solomon on the throne. David sends Zadok, Nathan, and Benaiah, head of the royal bodyguard, to enthrone Solomon. Adonijah's supporters, including all other sons of the king plus Joab and Abiathar, scatter.

46. The start of the list is probably corrupt. See McCarter.

47. For the argument to read not "the Thirty" but "officers," see Nadav Na'aman, "The List of David's Officers (šālîšîm)," VT 38 (1988): 71-79. This is almost surely right, and it is possible that "the Three" is also in origin a term for a specific military office.

Adonijah himself takes refuge in the sanctuary of Yahweh until Solomon promises not to kill him.

The dying David then instructs Solomon to observe the will of Yahweh. He also urges Solomon to kill Joab, for murdering Abner and Amasa, and thus spilling the blood of war when there was peace. He commends the sons of Barzillai for their support during the Absalom uprising. (They seem from later evidence to have been rewarded with an appointment as priests.) And he asks Solomon to kill Shimei, whom he himself had sworn not to kill. Solomon accomplishes the killings, but by entrapping the victims rather than acting unilaterally. David, finally, expires, having learned and imparted the lesson to his son, how to eliminate enemies without incurring guilt. Solomon also executes Adonijah, but only after the latter has given provocation. A more detailed examination of Solomon's Terror is supplied at the end of the book.

The narrative of David's career is one of the great accomplishments of Israel's culture. The picture it paints of the king has imprinted itself on all of subsequent Western culture. It owes, perhaps, a debt to Idrimi, a king of Alalakh who details in his autobiography his time among the bandits of the steppe. It probably reflects influence, direct or indirect, from the inscriptions of Tiglath-Pileser I, the Assyrian king slightly older than David who constructed an empire, at least in literature. But its portrayal of the character and tribulations of the king is an original. From youth to dotage, it follows David as a human being, never fearing to underscore shortcomings, nor to stress peculiarities.

PART II

PENETRATING THE TEXTUAL VEIL

CHAPTER 3

Dating 2 Samuel

How is a historian to understand the literary presentation of David? Was he innocent of all the murders on which the story concentrates? Did he conquer all the territory from Egypt to the Euphrates, as interpreters have inferred from the time of early Israel until the present? Did he subjugate the Philistines, as almost all commentators agree? Was he as accommodating of the Israelites — and as popular among them — as the text suggests? Was he as careful as the text suggests to construct a kingdom that adhered to Israelite tradition? How did he advance, how did he corrupt, the constitution of the Israelite state?

The basic question is, why do we have *this* text? What was its purpose? Who wrote it? The answer to the riddle is straightforward: most of David's story was written during Solomon's reign, and the object was both to glorify the founder of the dynasty and to advance Solomon's political position. The historical evidence for this position — against other scholarly views that the story was composed three, or five, centuries later — will emerge *en passant* in the following discussion. The present chapter deals with hard evidence that limits the dating of 2 Samuel or of the sources it uses. Some of the evidence is a bit *recherché,* and readers uninterested in the details should move on directly to Chapter 4.

The overwhelming preponderance of the reliable evidence tells us that the text is early. Certainly, it was earlier than Judah's exile to Babylon in 586 B.C.E. The royal court, in other words, was still functioning when the text was written, and thus its records were still available. One indication comes from references to evanescent realia. For example, from archaeological sites before the Exile, excavators recover weights marked as the amount *pym.* This term occurs in

1 Sam. 13:21, but is unattested in the period after Judah's exile.[1] Similarly, inscriptions attest the same Canaanite month names that we find in the older sources in the Pentateuch (JE) and 1 Kgs. 6–8.[2] But these names were no longer in use in the literature of the 7th century, and Babylonian month names supplanted them completely in the postexilic period.

Likewise, the layout of houses presupposed by the text reflects the architectural tradition of the preexilic period, not the architecture of the subsequent Restoration in the Persian period. And the text also assumes the legitimacy of multiple shrines for sacrifice — a point that enabled the great Swiss biblicist W. M. L. de Wette to show that it was older than the book of Deuteronomy. These details are authentic. They are also incidental to the author's point. Lest we suspect our authors of archaizing for atmosphere, the distribution of such references is more important than any one of them. The references that must be preexilic are concentrated in texts that on other grounds have normally been understood to be relatively early.[3]

---

1. This observation stems from William G. Dever, in conversation. For the inscriptions, see Graham I. Davies, *Ancient Hebrew Inscriptions* (Cambridge: Cambridge University Press, 1991), 108.021; 023; 054.

2. The old Canaanite month names that appear in the Bible are the second month, Ziv (1 Kgs. 6:1, 37); the seventh month, Ethanim (8:2); the eighth month, Bul (6:38); the first month, Abib (Exod. 13:4; 23:15; 34:18 *bis;* derivatively, Deut. 16:1 *bis*). Bul and Ethanim appear in other sources as well. Months are also numbered rather than named, specifically in Kings and Jeremiah, as well as P and Ezekiel, and Ezra, Haggai, and Zechariah, which suggested to Julian Morgenstern ("The Three Calendars of Ancient Israel," *HUCA* 1 [1924]: 13-78) a second stage of calendrical terminology. The third terminology was that of the Babylonian calendar, which characterizes postexilic works: Ezra and 1 Esdras, Nehemiah, Zechariah, Esther, and 1-2 Maccabees (the Jerusalem Talmud actually commemorates the adoption of the terminology during the Restoration in *Roš Haš.* 1.56d). The shift from the first to the second (numbered months) terminology might be ideological in character, if not an attempt to mediate records of trade and other traffic with Mesopotamia on the basis of abstract mensal equations, emptied of historical cultural content. If ideological reaction is involved, it is in the transition away from traditional culture documented for the 7th century, on which see Baruch Halpern, "Sybil, or the Two Nations: Archaism, Kinship, Alienation, and the Elite Redefinition of Traditional Culture in Judah in the 8th-7th Centuries B.C.E.," in *The Study of the Ancient Near East in the 21st Century: The William Foxwell Albright Centennial Conference,* ed. Jerrold S. Cooper and Glenn M. Schwartz (Winona Lake: Eisenbrauns, 1996), 291-338.

3. Aside from weights, dimensions, building techniques, and architectural configurations all figure in the question. On texts presupposing the layout of a four-room house, of the preexilic variety, see Halpern, *The First Historians,* ch. 3; on gates, "Eli's Death and the Israelite Gate: A Philological-Architectural Correlation," *ErIsr* 26 (1999): 52*-63*. This goes for purely philological data about cultural configurations as well: thus, the gloss in

Like house forms, the shape of Solomon's temple as described in 1 Kgs. 6–7 has ample correlates in the ground. The form described is of one long room, divided into three sacred spaces. Along the outside walls of the temple are three tiers of administrative office space. All the parallels to this layout stem from the 18th to the 8th centuries, as William G. Dever has shown. In addition, most of the temple appurtenances described in Kings have their strongest parallels in the Iron Age. The temple would have been a genuine anachronism after the 8th century, and the biblical claim of its belonging to the 10th century is entirely plausible.[4]

There is also linguistic evidence. In the main, this shows conclusively that the text was written before the 6th century, when Babylon exiled the population of Judah. Orthography, or spelling, is a key index. Before the Exile, for the most part, Israelite orthography was "defective" — with few vowels represented except at the ends of words.[5] After the Exile, "plene" spelling, which used consonants such as *h, w* and *y* to represent vowels in medial position, inside words, was far more common. Later spellings — of the plene variety — dominate in

---

1 Sam. 9:9 about prophets formerly being called seers *(r'h)* suggests a late monarchic date. By way of contrast, 2 Sam. 15:27 probably uses the term "seer" in its technical sense without elaboration or explanation. The only other text to use the participle as a substantive having to do with mantic perception is Isa. 30:10, and there as a parallel in elevated prose or poetry with the common technical designation, *ḥōzeh*, and, indeed, perhaps as a sort of pun. In any case, whether the term was "live" at the time of Isaiah or not, it certainly was not common when the gloss was inserted, nor does it appear in any properly Deuteronomistic literature or in postexilic texts. The Samuel usage is no later than the 8th century.

4. See William G. Dever, "Monumental Architecture in Ancient Israel in the Period of the United Monarchy," in *Studies in the Period of David and Solomon and Other Essays*, ed. Tomoo Ishida (Winona Lake: Eisenbrauns, 1982), 269-306; also "Archaeology and the 'Age of Solomon': A Case-Study in Archaeology and Historiography," in *The Age of Solomon*, ed. Lowell K. Handy. SHANE 11 (Leiden: Brill, 1997), 217-51; further, his trenchant comments in "Archaeology, Ideology, and the Quest for an 'Ancient' or 'Biblical' Israel," *NEA* 61 (1998): 39-52; Amihai Mazar, "Temples of the Middle and Late Bronze Ages and the Iron Age," in *The Architecture of Ancient Israel*, ed. Aharon Kempinski and Ronny Reich (Jerusalem: Israel Exploration Society, 1992); Lawrence E. Stager, "Jerusalem and the Garden of Eden," *ErIsr* 26 (1999): 183*-94*. See recently John Monson, "The New 'Ain Dara Temple. Closest Solomonic Parallel," *BAR* 26/3 (2000): 20-35, 67; Ali Abu-Assaf, *Der Tempel von 'Ain Dara*. Damaszener Forschungen 3 (Mainz: Philipp von Zabern, 1990).

5. This judgment is based on inscriptions with clear archaeological provenances. For purposes of establishing orthographic typology, inscriptions purchased in the antiquities market, in the absence of overwhelming evidence of authenticity, should not be taken into consideration.

our text, because scribes "corrected" spelling as they recopied scrolls, so that many Dead Sea Scroll manuscripts, for example, have very late orthography.

This means that plene spellings, with internal vowel letters, are demonstrably late. In the case of biblical books, the spelling may have been updated by late copyists. But defective spellings indicate a preexilic date. The concentration of such defective spellings in the books of Samuel is extraordinary. The old spellings point to a starting point before the 6th century for the transmission of the text. No Israelite composing a text in the 5th century would have written "you were" *(hāyyîtā)* as *hyt* (the -y- is a consonant), rather than as *hyyt* (the first -y- is a consonant, the second a vowel) or even *hyyth* (the -h on the end is also a vowel). The number of defective spellings in 2 Samuel, even at Qumran, around the turn of the era, is remarkable. The contrast is to other works in the Former Prophets.[6]

One example will do duty for the data as a whole. In 2 Sam. 23, two verses have extraordinary defective spellings: "after him," in Hebrew, is otherwise always spelled "after" + -*yw* (him); in 2 Sam. 23, the spelling is "after" + -*w*, something never seen after the 7th century in inscriptions, or even in biblical texts.[7] The contrast to postexilic works is even starker. The statistical evaluation of this phenomenon, detailed by Francis I. Andersen and A. Dean Forbes, is not yet settled; but the distribution, again, suggests an early date.[8] Similar defective spellings characterize 2 Samuel throughout.

Likewise, the spelling of foreign names in 2 Samuel reflects a repertoire of sounds no longer present in later materials. The phonemes — basic sounds in a language — that were unstable in antiquity are not unlike those that are unstable today. English, for example, represents two phonemes by the letters *th*. One is the *th* with which the words "thank" and "think" begin; it can be pronounced without the use of the vocal chords, unvoiced. The other phoneme is the *th* with

---

6. Theme vowels, e.g., such as those of the prefix conjugation in the hiphil, are often not marked before plural endings.

7. At issue is the 3rd masculine singular suffix on a plural stem. 2 Sam. 23:9, 11 have *'ḥrw* for the expected *'ḥryw*, which is one of the most uniformly plene orthographies in late Biblical Hebrew (but defective in the preexilic Siloam inscription and Lachish letters). Further cases of this omission of *y* in this form include 1 Sam. 18:14: *drkw;* 21:12: *b'lpw,* *brbbtw;* 26:11: *mr'štw;* 2 Sam. 1:11: *bgdw;* 13:34: *'ynw;* 15:18: *brglw,* which is plene in 15:16, 17; 16:8: *tḥtw;* 18:17: *'ḥlw* = 2 Kgs. 14:12; 2 Sam. 18:18: *bḥyw* (also, in the same verse, *'t mṣbt* — the noun in the absolute elsewhere only in Isa. 6:13 — for the later *'t hmṣbh);* 2 Sam. 20:8: *'lw;* 24:14: *rḥmw.* There are at least 23 cases of this particular defective spelling in Samuel, more per word than in any other source.

8. Francis I. Andersen and A. Dean Forbes, *Spelling in the Hebrew Bible.* BibOr 41 (Rome: Pontifical Biblical Institute, 1986), e.g., 4-5, 183-85, 229.

which the word "there" begins; it is pronounced with voicing. The unvoiced *th* ("thank") becomes a /t/ sound in some New York City (Bronx and Brooklyn) dialects ("tanks, pal"); the voiced *th* ("there") becomes a /d/ sound ("ovuh dere, pal"). The New York City dialects treat these sounds exactly as Western Aramaic — the language of ancient Syria — treated them, from the 7th century forward, and as Eastern Aramaic treated them slightly earlier. Starting in the 7th century, and regularly from the 6th century, Aramaic texts spell the unvoiced *th* ("think") with a /t/, the voiced *th* ("there") with a /d/. Other sounds seem to shift roughly at the same time.[9]

The spelling of some foreign (Aramaic) names in Samuel and in the account of Solomon's reign points to an early date. An example is the letter *zayin*, English *z*, in the name of Rezon, founder of the independent kingdom of Damascus. This name was originally Raδyanu, with an *edh* emphatic. (*Edh* alone is like /th/ as in "there." *Edh* emphatic is the sound expressed explosively through

---

9. We actually know the transition points, which fall in the 7th century: Jer. 10:11 is a key text for this purpose. One word there, *ʾrδ, "earth," appears twice, with different reflexes for the third radical. In the first occurrence, the reflex is the standard Old Aramaic form, /q/; in the second, it is the Eastern (and Imperial) Aramaic reflex, /ʿ/. 4QJer[b] attests the second form. One might argue either that the first occurrence represents archaizing or the survival of a frozen formula in a clause about creation ("heaven and earth"), and that the second occurrence, in a freer compositional context, is contemporary. Or, one might argue that the second occurrence has been updated in the transmission. It is, however, hard to imagine that one would be updated, the other not, so the contextual difference is a better explanation. Tending to confirm this inference is the presence in the relative pronoun of a phoneme, */d/, which is realized orthographically not on the Old Aramaic model /z/, but on the Eastern and Imperial Aramaic model, /d/. What this suggests is that the transition to the Imperial phonology was at latest contemporary with Jeremiah, in whose time frozen remnants of the earlier phonetic realizations remained. These are not, however, the rule in Aramaic itself. Further, the Saqqara papyrus, from king Adon of Eqron in the late 7th century, still employs the old orthography. So the filtering of the change to Judah in the 7th century is probably a product of Babylonian, that is Eastern, influence.

Now, there is some argument that Jer. 10, or some parts of it (not, usually, including v. 11), is late. This is improbable, in fact (Baruch Halpern, "The New Names of Isaiah 62:4: Jeremiah's Reception in the Restoration and the Politics of 'Third Isaiah,'" *JBL* 117 [1998]: 623-43; Benjamin D. Sommer, *A Prophet Reads Scripture: Allusion in Isaiah 40–66* [Stanford: Stanford University Press, 1998]; "New Light on the Composition of Jeremiah," *CBQ* 61 [1999]: 646-66). But were one to excise ch. 10 or part of it, the implication would be to concede that the rest of the text is early, i.e., 7th-6th century. And this would mean that other references in Jeremiah, to P and D and Dtr, e.g., attest the antiquity of all that literature. Once we remove the text from the Persian era, the whole minimalist case falls apart. On this, see below, Chapter 4.

the side of the mouth, by forcing air between the tongue, at the side of the mouth, and the maxillary teeth against which it is held.) In the West Semitic ("Phoenician") alphabet, there is no separate sign for this sound, or even for simple *edh*. Normally, Hebrew represents *edh* emphatic with the letter *ṣādê* (ṣ, now pronounced /ts/). Old Aramaic represented it with the letter *qôp*, English *q*, while later Aramaic employed the letter *'ayin*, a guttural sound not employed in contemporary Western languages. The completely irregular reflex of *edh* emphatic in /z/, in the name Rezon, stems from a time when the rules for representing foreign sounds had not yet been fixed in Hebrew. The same name, Raẟyanu, appears in texts of the 8th century as Reṣin, with a *ṣādê* for the *edh* emphatic, and the *edh* emphatic is represented as *ṣādê* and as *qôp* in the book of Isaiah. "Rezon" is a very early writing of the name indeed.[10]

Other spellings have less specific temporal implications,[11] but place Sam-

10. See below, Chapter 22, for another unstable rendering of *edh* emphatic in the 10th century. The occurrences in Isaiah come in Isa. 28, on which see Baruch Halpern, "'The Excremental Vision'. The Doomed Priests of Doom in Isaiah 28," *HAR* 10 (1986): 109-21, and in his references to Assyria as the *qw qw* people, mocking their realization of the phoneme.

11. The name Rezin is rendered with a *ṣādê* in Isaiah and 2 Kings, the standard Iron Age reflex in Hebrew (*ḥa* in the annals of Tiglath-Pileser III; normally, /q/ in Old Aramaic, *'ayin* in Eastern and Imperial Aramaic (for /ǵ/), which is the realization reflected by Tiglath-Pileser). Importantly, the king of Zobah in Samuel is Hadadezer. The same name (*hdd'dr*) of another king, of Damascus, in the inscriptions of Shalmaneser III in the 9th century, is realized as Adad-idri, that is, with /d/ rather than /z/. Likewise, the name of the town, Hazarikku, is realized as Hadarikka in Assyrian from the 9th century forward, and Hadrach in Zechariah, representing the Eastern and Imperial phonology respectively. Hezyon, the grandfather of Ben-Hadad ben-Tabrimmon, king of Damascus in 1 Kgs. 15:18, has been thought to reflect the same phoneme (/ḏ/), based on the appearance of a later king, Hadianu, in Assyrian records. On the other hand, Toi, king of Hamath in Samuel, has a name that was originally *t'y*. In the normal old Aramaic phonology, it would appear as *š'y;* but the /t/ would seem to fit with the Assyrian trend rather than the Aramaic/ Israelite. This may be deceptive, as the discussion of the phonotactics of the name Ittay, below, indicates. See further Chapter 9, n. 1.

Another point in the onomastica is that of Philistia, for instance Goliath of Gath. Goliath appears not just in the displacement upward of 1 Sam. 17 but also in 2 Sam. 21:19, which I have endeavored to explain elsewhere as one inspiration of an effort to portray David as sovereign over Gath (on which see Chapters 1 and 19). Goliath's name is 3 f. sg. *qatala* G from the verb *gly* (= "DN [fem.] revealed"), and is not Hebrew, which would render this form as *gālĕtâ* (except possibly as an archaism): *galayat* > *galât* > *galâ* = 3 m. sg., with correction for contrast following (for an argument to philological conditioning, see W. Randall Garr, *Dialect Geography of Syria-Palestine, 1000-586 B.C.E.* [Philadelphia: University of Pennsylvania Press, 1985], 60-61). Phoenician preserves *-t*, but not in the 3 f. sg. *qatala* (i.e.,

uel and JE before the late 7th century. The contrast is to P, probably Jeremiah, and especially Ezra-Nehemiah and Zechariah, all of which share the late phonology. One might argue that terms in JE and Samuel are archaic names incorporated in later narratives. But the other texts — P, Jeremiah, Ezra — should also have such archaic names, if they are roughly contemporary, spelled in an archaic way. As Avi Hurvitz has shown, too, Aramaic influences, and especially clear Aramaic loanwords and calques, are far more frequent in texts dated after

---

Standard Phoenician, and later Byblian: Garr, 125-26), so the name is not one we would anticipate. Yet the *-t* is preserved into the 7th century in the Eqron inscriptions in *'šrt,* Heb. Ashera. This is an authentically Philistine name, of the preexilic era, for in the postexilic period the population of Philistia is in fact a mix of Aramean and Phoenician whose onomasticon is pure Phoenician.

The name of Achish of Gath in David's time is identical with that of a later king, the author of the Tel Miqne inscription, *'kyš,* Assyrian I-ka-u-su, possibly Akhaios (Joseph Naveh, "Achish-Ikausu in the Light of the Ekron Dedication," *BASOR* 310 [1998]: 35-37), and certainly not Anchises. But the name is again preexilic, with no resonance for the postexilic period whatever. In fact, Gath is probably not occupied, or at least not strategically significant, in the 7th century and plays no real role in our literature after Hazael's campaign in the late 9th century, except to be dominated successively by Ashdod and by Assyria under Sargon II. See below, Chapters 7, 18, 21, and generally William M. Schniedewind, "The Geopolitical History of Philistine Gath," *BASOR* 309 (1998): 69-77. For the Tel Miqne stela, see S. Gitin, T. Dothan, and J. Naveh, "A Royal Dedicatory Inscription from Ekron," *IEJ* 47 (1997): 1-16.

The name of Ittay the Gittite also deserves remark. If it is parallel, as we think, to Jesse, Eshbaal (son of Saul), and Ittobaal of Tyre (Hebrew Ethbaal), it is based on **'t,* "there is," and a divine name represented here by a hypocoristicon. If so, the rendition of the phoneme deserves special remark, as it is different from the rendition of the same phoneme in the name of Asherah herself, Tel Miqne's *'šrt,* in later Philistia. Possibly, Ethbaal, father of Jezebel, was named "with Baal," or "Baal is with him," so that Ittay could be "with (DN)." Josephus's vocalization (Ittobaal) is older, suggesting MT is defective: "DN is with him" also jibes with the Assyrian version, Tuba'il, but even then onomastic parallels are not plentiful. It is best, then, to take this and the rendition of Ethbaal's name in Kings as evidence of continuing phonemic instability, in the case of *t,* at least, into the 9th century, a situation that is not surprising in light of Assyrian realizations, and that is certainly consistent with the reportage on the Shibboleth incident (*šblt* versus *tblt*). A related phenomenon is the name of Adriel, son of Barzillai in Gilead. This name reflects the verb *'dr,* but employs the Aramaic phonology which seems to have characterized Gilead's dialect.

Two other allegedly Gittite names are Obed-Edom and Sippay (2 Sam. 21:18, *sap;* this is from 1 Chr. 20:4). The former is just not a name we run into. The latter is probably not even Semitic, despite a possible association with *swp.*

For the names of David's heroes, see below, n. 20.

the exile of 587 than before it.[12] In other words, Samuel is either older than the 7th century or incorporates sources older than the 7th century.

There is further evidence from language. It is very likely that the poems 2 Samuel attributes to David, especially David's laments over Saul and Abner and his "last words," are of great antiquity, older certainly than the written prophecy of the 7th century, and probably older than that of the 8th. But evidence of this variety is less dependable than that from other sources. A full-scale investigation of the syntax and grammar of 1 and 2 Samuel would probably be rewarding. Until then, the appearance of such features as the enclitic marking direct discourse in Canaanite Akkadian of the Late Bronze Age, the particle -*mi*,[13] cannot with confidence be called conclusive evidence of antiquity. Unusual syntactical features, shared with Late Bronze Canaanite Akkadian, such as conditional clauses marked not with "if" but with "and" or "and, lo,"[14] also suggest that the text is older than the frameworks in Joshua, Judges, and the rest of Kings, which stem from the 8th and 7th centuries. More certainly, they prove that Samuel is older than the prose of the postexilic era. Still, without a definitive diachronic history of Hebrew syntax, no firm specific conclusions can be drawn from the data.

In addition, the topography of the texts can be an invaluable index. Some of the evidence is inner-textual. In Samuel and 1 Kgs. 2, David's relations with the House of Saul revolve around Bahurim, just east of Jerusalem en route to the Jordan. This is also Shimei's home, so when Solomon adjures Shimei not to cross the Wadi Qidron out of Jerusalem, he is telling him not to go home. And when Shimei goes west to Gath to extradite his runaway slaves, his path does not cross the Qidron. Solomon, however, executes him for leaving town, not heading homeward. The relationship here is nuanced, yet neither the Joshua toponym lists, from the 8th-7th century, nor the postexilic ones mention Bahurim, although some pilgrim accounts do furnish locations for it.[15] The lo-

---

12. Hurvitz, "The Historical Quest for 'Ancient Israel' and the Linguistic Evidence of the Hebrew Bible: Some Methodological Observations," *VT* 47 (1997): 301-15; also "Hebrew and Aramaic in the Biblical Period — the Problem of 'Aramaisms' in the Linguistic Research of the Bible," in *Studies in Hebrew and Jewish Languages,* ed. M. Bar-Asher. Festschrift S. Morag (Jerusalem: Bialik Institute, 1986), 79-94; cf. also Baruch Levine, "The Pronoun 'ש' in Biblical Hebrew in the Light of Ancient Epigraphy," *ErIsr* 18 (1985): 147-52.

13. 2 Sam. 18:12. Cf. also *mh* in 18:22, 23, probably reflecting the same particle.

14. 2 Sam. 18:12, 13. Note also the less common forms of impersonal construction in Samuel using the 3 m. sg. active *yaqtulu* for habitual actions, which are strongly represented in JE, less so in later documents, and virtually absent in the postexilic period.

15. See Aubrey Stewart and Sir C. W. Wilson, *Of the Holy Places Visited by Antoninus Martyr (Circ. 560-570 A.D.)* (London: Palestine Pilgrims' Text Society, 1896), 13-14, ch.

cation of Saul's family tomb, Zela in Benjamin, appears in a different form in Josh. 18:28. The city Nob, destroyed with its priests by Saul, does not appear in Joshua, though its location was apparently still recalled around 700 (Isa. 10:32). The suggestion is that Samuel is in fact older than the materials in Joshua.

One can easily extend this sort of analysis. Thus, the list of David's champions in 2 Sam. 21 and 23 associates most of the warriors with a kin group or a settlement. But many of the place-names connected with David's heroes do not appear in later literature, from the 8th century into the 5th. And some of the kin groups mentioned do not reflect the genealogical structure of Judah and Benjamin as this was ratified in subsequent preexilic sources such as J and P. Three to six of the warriors bear the designation "Hararite," or "mountain man" — they came from the undeveloped upland backwoods of Judah, in all likelihood, and had no defined place in the political economy of Israel. Not dissimilarly, Saul's clan in 1 Sam. 9:1 (Bekorat or Aphiah) and 10:21 (Matri) does not appear as such in later descriptions of the genealogy of Benjamin.

Almost all of David's other warriors and the actors in 1 and 2 Samuel stem from southern Benjamin or southern Judah (see Map 3.1, p. 66). The books of Samuel thus suggest that there were settlers in the Negev and in the vicinity of Jerusalem, but few elements attached themselves to David from the hills of Judah or the Shephelah — the piedmont between the hills and the coast. This fits the archaeological situation of the 10th and earlier centuries. It is inconceivable that an author writing later than the 9th century — or, as we shall see, even the early 9th century — would have invented such a distribution. The Shephelah was from that time forward heavily populated, and the hills were brimming in the 8th century.

Further, the presence of "mountain men" means that Judah contained ter-

---

XVI: "Ascending the rising ground in the neighbourhood of Jerusalem, not far from Jerusalem itself, we came to Bahurim. Turning back thence, towards the left, we came to the villages of the Mount of Olives, to Bethany, to the tomb of Lazarus. . . ." In a note, Stewart and Wilson state that "Antoninus is the only pilgrim who mentions Bahurim, which Tobler identifies with Khurbet el Murassas, on the left-hand side of the road going up to Jerusalem from Jericho. If, however, Antoninus followed the Roman Road, Bahurim must have been near El 'Aisâwîyeh." See, however, Aubrey Stewart and C. R. Conder, *Burchard of Mount Sion. A.D. 1280* (London: Palestine Pilgrims' Text Society, 1896), 63: four leagues west of Jericho lay Adummim. Two leagues west of Adummim, Bahurim stood on a high hill. Two bowshots west of Bahurim was Bethany. As an index of scale, in this latter work, Jerusalem is 13 leagues from Joppa, 7 from Jericho, 2 from Bethlehem, and 8 from Hebron. This places Bahurim on the Jericho road a seventh of the way from Jerusalem to Jericho. On the location of Bahurim, and an argument to its identity with Nob, see Wolfgang Zwickel, "Bahurim und Nob," *BN* 61 (1992): 84-93.

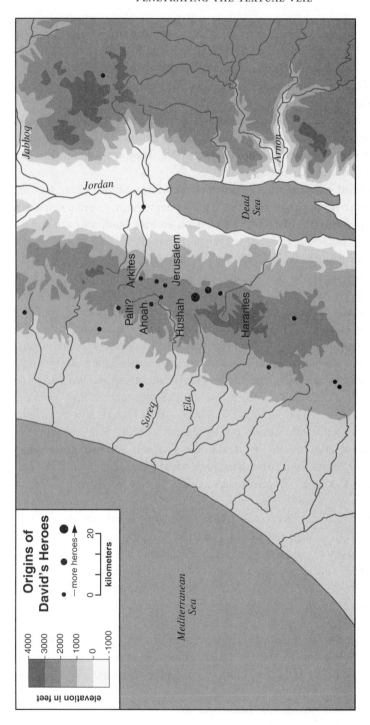

map 3.1

ritory, in the hills, that was not integrated into any systematized kinship system or genealogy. The region around Hebron, and especially between it and Jerusalem, was thus called simply "the mountains" rather than being associated with particular kin groups. Not much later, Judah was divided much more neatly into territories — "clans" and sections of clans. The portrait in Samuel fits with the survey evidence for the 10th century, which indicates that the hills of Judah were virtually devoid of permanent settlement up to David's time. These particulars date Samuel early (see below, Chapter 14). They are not something to be dismissed without explanation.

A third point is the question of how our texts imagine their contemporary landscape in the south, where exploitation and demography were particularly labile. What pattern of settlement, and of the use of the land, does the text reflect? Settlement patterns were the key to dating the list of Judah's settlements in the book of Joshua — the list includes towns that were not founded until the 7th century. But 2 Samuel posits a distribution of Negev settlement that conforms to the archaeology of the 10th century, and not to that of later centuries. The settlements cluster in the central Negev, in the high desert south of Beersheba. Archaeologically, these sites are found in surveys, and they exhibit the form of way-stations for caravan traffic probably administered by a state which is based elsewhere. They are implicated in the exploitation of the southern trade routes, involving spices and drugs. These settlements would not be tolerated by competing power centers, such as the city-states of the Philistines on the coast, unless they were under Philistine control or protected from the Philistines by a center like the one at Jerusalem.[16]

In addition, after Solomon's death, the pharaoh Shishaq campaigned against Philistia, Judah, and Israel. Kings records the campaign insofar as it affected Judah (1 Kgs. 14:25-27), claiming he came more or less directly to Jerusalem. And Shishaq left an itinerary on the walls of a temple in Thebes, confirming that he marched up the northern Shephelah and straight over to Jerusalem. In his record, however, a large number of sites in Judah appear far from the rest of his march, precisely in the central Negev. In other words, the presuppositions of Samuel about the landscape of Judah (and of Kings about the southern trade — with the Queen of Sheba) and the facts as reflected archaeologically and in a contemporary inscription coincide. Yet such a general picture of the pattern of occupation in the period could not survive long unless written — folk memory of peripheral settlement *clusters* does not extend over a long period of abandonment. After Shishaq, the Negev was almost empty of settlement until the 7th century. More important, the focus of the 7th-century settlement was, for rea-

16. Further discussion below, in Chapters 22-23.

sons very logical at the time, in the eastern, not the central, Negev. The indication of reliance on information from the 10th century could not be clearer.

By the same token, 1 Sam. 27:6 claims that Ziklag remained subordinate to the kings of Judah at the time of the writing of Samuel. Ziklag lay in the hinterland of Gath. (It is often identified with Tell es-Sharia near Tel Haror on the southern coastal plain, but a Shephelah location is just as possible.) In 701, the Assyrian king Sennacherib reassigned western Judah to the Philistine cities of the time. Of these, Gath is the only one not mentioned, probably because it had been incorporated into the territory of Eqron — the alternative being that it was subject to Ashdod or Ashkelon, which in light of the politics of the time seems improbable. If Gath's hinterland belonged to a Philistine town after 701, Ziklag could not have belonged to kings of Judah before the mid-7th century. It may not even have been inhabited in the 9th-8th centuries. Further argument from the conception of the borders of Israel will be offered in later chapters.

Similar points can be made about the human landscape. Only in connection with David's reign does Israelite historiography furnish us with lists of military officers and anecdotes about their feats of courage (2 Sam. 21; 23). In the account of David's army, the text distinguishes among professional troops, mercenaries, and the regular army. The professionals are the royal guard, the standing army of the king. They are augmented by mercenaries from abroad. These are soldiers who train together regularly, even combining arms such as the light and heavy infantry. Conversely, the regular army is the muster of all free, landed adult males of fighting age from the general population. These are weekend soldiers, comparable to the National Guard in the United States, but less well drilled in the art of coordinated fighting. This is why the forest "consumed" more than the sword in the Absalom revolt: the tribal levies, the occasional soldiers, found military maneuver and communications daunting. They were useful as cannon fodder to absorb charges against the heavy infantry, or for pursuing fleeing enemies, but lacked the discipline and the practice to make an effective offensive force against professionals. Hushai's advice was calculated to bring elements prone to panic into Absalom's battle plan against David.

In connection with David, the conception of the royal guard, and the terminology for it, is different than in connection with subsequent kings: David is served professionally by Israelites, and by the Cherethites, and Pelethites, and a contingent of Gittites (from Gath of the Philistines). Joab's armor bearers are a Gibeonite, from Beeroth, and possibly an Ammonite. The last few warriors mentioned in the list of David's officers are apparently foreign. After David's death, the Cherethites, Pelethites, Gittites, and other foreigners disappear from view in our texts, even though it is a certainty that later kings employed mercenaries.

Nor is David's military cabinet structured like that under Solomon, let alone those under later kings. Joab, for example, commands the regular army during David's reign; Abishai and later Benaiah command the professional soldiery. Under Solomon, there is no clear replacement for Joab. And Solomon's officialdom is more highly developed than David's, as H. Michael Niemann has shown.[17]

Finally, it is implausible that later denizens of Judah would imagine their king as having been in the service of a king of Gath. By the late 9th century, Gath was at best a minor site, and by the 8th a dependency either of Judah or of Ashdod, and then of Assyria. In the 7th century, it was probably no longer settled (see Chapters 7, 18). It does not appear in literature from after the Babylonian exile of 587. The notion that an Israelite king might have risen from the rank of a Gittite vassal does not stem from an era of Israelite power and Philistine decline.

All this serves to limit the date of the text. For the most part, it places 2 Samuel, for example, no later than the 9th century, since the text reflects memories of the 10th century — and it is the connection through Shishaq's list to the archaeology of the Negev that permits this specificity. Were the Negev continually exploited, or were there no Shishaq text to guarantee the 10th-century date of the central Negev settlements, this would all be in the realm of dispute. But the exclusion of the hills of Judah from a developed genealogy of Judah also coincides with the archaeological evidence there. The linguistic evidence yields only a rougher date, in the 8th century or earlier.

It will not much advance the case for an early dating to focus on Samuel's vocabulary. This is the standard form of argument in Biblical Studies. And Samuel is rich in unusual vocabulary and unusual phrases, not found in later texts. All the same, authors use different words for different reasons. There are differences in style, differences in nuance, differences in ideology, differences in defining the meanings of words, and differences in content. As Gary Rendsburg has suggested, there are also differences in dialect — he argues for geographical difference, and one can add the variation caused by social distinctions such as education or economic status and even subject matter.[18]

17. H. Michael Niemann, *Herrschaft, Königtum und Staat: Skizzen zur soziokulturellen Entwicklung im monarchischen Israel.* FAT 6 (Tübingen: Mohr, 1993). On the professional soldiery, contrast "runners" in the accounts of Rehoboam and Joash of Judah, and the "Urbi" hired by Hezekiah according to Sennacherib's annals.

18. See e.g. Gary A. Rendsburg, "Israelian Hebrew Features in Genesis 49," *MAARAV* 8 (1992): 161-70; "Morphological Evidence for Regional Dialects in Ancient Hebrew," in *Linguistics and Biblical Hebrew*, ed. Walter R. Bodine (Winona Lake: Eisenbrauns, 1992), 65-88; *Linguistic Evidence for the Northern Origin of Selected Psalms.* SBLMS 43 (Atlanta:

Sorting out all these variables is beyond the patience of most scholars, including myself. So discussions in the professional literature tend to be impressionistic rather than comprehensive. Some of the diction in Samuel probably implies that the text is earlier than the literature of the prophets of the 8th-7th centuries.[19] Still, the grammar of the text, never carefully examined on its own, likely suggests an early date. And the names of people in the book certainly do not conform to the patterns of personal names found in the 8th-7th centuries.[20]

Scholars, 1990); "The Northern Origin of 'The Last Words of David' (2 Sam 23,1-7)," *Bibl* 69 (1988): 113-21; "Additional Notes on 'The Last Words of David' (2 Sam 23,1-7)," *Bibl* 70 (1989): 403-8.

19. Thus, the niphal of *ḥšb* plus the preposition *'l* means "is ascribed to," instead of *'l* being adversative, "is reckoned against," as in other texts (2 Sam. 4:2). The usage is not Deuteronomistic, though the phrase occurs in P. Samuel employs other locutions not paralleled inside the Deuteronomistic corpus — e.g., *hikkîr* occurring as an intransitive verb. To this usage, there is an arguable, but not in my mind palpable, parallel in Neh. 6:12. For other peculiarities, there are likely synchronic explanations: *mašûaḥ melek*, in 2 Sam. 3:39, instead of the usage *mšḥ lmlk* with the preposition, as in 2:7; 5:3 and 1 Sam. 9:16; 10:1, but this may well be a function of the passive::active contrast in voice; also, *l' hyth mhmlk lhmyt*, "it was not from the king to kill" (2 Sam. 3:37), with a parallel construction of the infinitive as appositive to an impersonal feminine subject in Josh. 11:20, among other texts.

Note that Samuel reports on "tyrants of the Philistines" as *srny* (1 Sam. 5:8, 11; 6:4, 12, 16, 18; 7:7; 29:2, 6, 7; 1 Chr. 12:19[20]) and as *śry* (1 Sam. 18:30; 29:3, 4, 9; this is the title assumed by Achish of Eqron). The former usage occurs in 8th-7th century contexts in Joshua (13:3) and Judges (3:3; 16:5, 8, 18, 23, 27, 30). But in the late 7th century, Jeremiah (25:20) speaks of the "kings" *(mlky)* of the land of the Philistines, and J (Gen. 26:1, 8; 9th-8th century) has a "king *(mlk)* of the Philistines."

Note in 2 Sam. 15:32 the impersonal masculine singular verb without a subject ("where [one] prostrates himself to god[s]"). This usage is not unparalleled in Samuel. Third person masculine singular active *yaqtulu* impersonals are rare in describing habitual action outside of J and Samuel.

Another unusual form occurs in 2 Sam. 23:10: *wh'm yšbw*, "and the people returned." Here we have an unconverted *yaqtul* in subject-verb-object syntax, where we should expect a *qatala*.

The use of the verb *prṣ b-* with the meaning "to insist, press" is restricted to 1 Sam. 28:23; 2 Sam. 13:25, 27; and 2 Kgs. 5:23. The verb with this meaning in other texts is *pṣr* as in Gen. 19:3, 9; 33:11; Judg. 19:7; 2 Kgs. 2:17; 5:16. The last reference suggests a scribal error reversing the last two letters of the verb in 2 Kgs. 5:23.

20. It has been the practice of the profession to take names, like grammar, as a synchronic corpus. It is true that the onomasticon has no diachronic external correlative, in the way that landscape clearly does. But there is an abundance of onomastic data for the 8th-7th centuries and for the Persian era. Though the diachronic trends in this corpus are

Other data also suggest that Samuel has early sources, although they do not show that Samuel was written just after David's time. Namely, the web of references to Israelite kings in foreign inscriptions, and to foreign kings, always in just the right order, in the books of Kings. I have detailed these references elsewhere,[21] and will mention only the early ones here. First, the Tel Dan inscription, from the late 9th century, calls Judah the "House of David," suggesting the early general acknowledgment that David founded the dynasty there. Second, Kings mentions Shishaq as attacking Judah just after Solomon's death, which corresponds with his inscriptional record — though the inscription does include Israel as well. Shishaq's inscription may even mention "the highlands of

---

not grammatical, the control sample is large enough now to permit us to evaluate more than the theophorics.

A few cases will serve to indicate the nature of the evidence. The name Nahray in 2 Sam. 23:37 derives from the Ugaritic term Anḫaru, Assyrian naḫiru. This is a Middle Assyrian term only.

Likewise, the names Hushai and yaḥūš, the latter found on a bronze arrowhead in archaic script, of the 11th-9th centuries (Frank M. Cross, "Newly Discovered Arrowheads of the Eleventh Century B.C.E.," *Israel Museum Journal* 10 [1992]: 57-62, esp. 61). The root ḥwš is not attested/common in the onomasticon of Iron IIB-C. Similarly, the arrowheads inscribed Maharan, parallel to David's hero Maharay (Cross), among other arrowheads with archaic names (see André Lemaire, "Nouvelle pointe de flèche inscrite proto phénicienne," *SEL* 7 [1989]: 53-56; Robert Deutsch and Michael Heltzer, *New Epigraphic Evidence from the Biblical Period* [Tel Aviv: Archaeological Center, 1995], 18-19). Note, however, the contrary juxtaposition in *Maher Shallal Hash Baz* in Isa. 8! See further Robert Deutsch and Michael Heltzer, *Forty New Ancient West Semitic Inscriptions* (Tel Aviv: Archaeological Center, 1994), 16; Frank M. Cross, "A Note on a Recently Published Arrowhead," *IEJ* 45 (1995): 188-89, on an arrowhead inscribed ḥṣ kty mšl 'bdy. Kty here, "the Kittite," suggests someone from Kition, a Phoenician town on Cyprus from the 10th century on. 'Abdon may be the Tyrian town ascribed to Asher until Solomon's day (Josh. 21:30; 1 Chr. 6:74[59]). The term mšl, for "ruler," would be suspicious here, except that Achish of Eqron in the 7th century does not call himself "king," mlk, but śr of Eqron; but the key point is that the name kty is not dissimilar in its implications of geographic origin from that of David's mercenaries, the krty and the plty.

Finally, a very low proportion of the names in 2 Samuel is Yahwistic — the key exceptions being Jonathan, Saul's son; Benaiah son of Jehoiada, with father *and* son bearing Yahwistic names; Adonijah, David's son; and Uriah, the Hittite! This is not true in later periods, including as witnessed in the epigraphic onomasticon of the late preexilic or postexilic eras.

21. Baruch Halpern, "Erasing History — The Minimalist Assault on Ancient Israel," *BR* 11/6 (1995): 26-35, 47. See further Gary N. Knoppers, "The Vanishing Solomon: The Disappearance of the United Monarchy from Recent Histories of Ancient Israel," *JBL* 16 (1997): 19-44.

David," a point that makes sense in light of evidence adduced below, in Chapters 22-23, to the effect that David garrisoned the central Negev. Third, an Assyrian king, Shalmaneser III, mentions both Ahab of Israel in the mid-9th century and his father Omri as the founder of Ahab's dynasty in Israel. Shalmaneser also mentions Jehu, later, as in Kings. His inscriptions, along with the Tel Dan stela, bear out the sequence of kings in Israel, Judah, and Damascus from Ahab through to Jehu. The Dan stela shows that Kings correctly dates the coup of Hazael in Damascus before the accession of Jehu in Israel, and it shows that other reportage in Kings on Jehu's coup is accurate (Chapter 22). Even the king of Moab — a country best described as the back side of the moon — in this era is correctly recollected in both Kings and a contemporary inscription.[22]

In other words, the political coverage of the 9th century is meticulous in Kings. There was no discontinuity between the 10th century and the 9th century in the royal courts of Israel and Judah. It follows that the accounts of the 10th century should be reasonably trustworthy — not as to the spin the sources place on the events, nor indeed as to particular details. Still, as in the 9th century, our account should be based on records that are reasonably robust about major events, such as the succession to the throne, the when and where of campaigns, and the other major upheavals of the period. Samuel, in other words, is a very good place to start in analyzing the early history of Israel.

22. Tel Dan in Avraham Biran and Joseph Naveh, "An Aramaic Stele Fragment from Tel Dan," *IEJ* 43 (1993): 81-98; "The Tel Dan Inscription: A New Fragment," *IEJ* 45 (1995): 1-18. For further citations, Halpern, *BR* 11/6 (1995): 26-35, 47; Knoppers, *JBL* 16 (1997): 19-44.

CHAPTER 4

King David, Serial Killer

A. The Portrayal of David and the Date of 2 Samuel

To reconstruct David, one has mainly to understand the books of Samuel and especially the intentions that shaped them. Samuel was later incorporated into the Israelite canon, then into Judaism and Christianity. Given David's status in those traditions, this history indicates that Samuel for the most part represents an apology on David's behalf. But the perspective it adopts is not uncritical — in fact, it condemns David as an adulterer and murderer late in his career. What issues, precisely, occupy the book's attention? In other words, what were the concerns about David that Samuel was formulated to address?

The same question has broader implications, both for the dating of the text and for the existence and nature of the early Israelite monarchy. This holds in part because Samuel is extraordinary in providing a narrative about the formation of the state. State literatures in the Near East tend to promote the view that kingship was, in the words of one Mesopotamian text, "lowered from heaven." Kingship always was.

But one question before us is the very historicity of the United Monarchy. In recent years, numerous books have directly or indirectly questioned the existence of David and Solomon.[1] These works have been written from literary, ar-

---

1. John Van Seters, *In Search of History* (1983; repr. Winona Lake: Eisenbrauns, 1997); *Prologue to History: The Yahwist as Historian in Genesis* (Louisville: Westminster John Knox, 1992); Thomas L. Thompson, *Early History of the Israelite People: From the Written and Archaeological Sources.* SHANE 4 (Leiden: Brill, 1992); Philip R. Davies, *In Search of*

chaeological, anthropological, and philosophical perspectives. What many of them share is a "minimalist" approach that denies the presence of an Israelite state until Assyrian inscriptions, starting in the year 853, attest a kingship of Ahab, and shortly after attest that his father, Omri, founded the dynasty and that Jehu overthrew it.

The historicity of the United Monarchy has been the hot historical topic in Biblical Studies for almost a decade. Scholars reject the historicity of the patriarchs, despair of reconstructing an exodus from Egypt. They deny that the Israelites conquered Canaan *en masse*. They feel that the "period of the judges" is illuminated, if at all, only in fragments: no real history of the period can rely on the texts about it, as opposed to the archaeology. Now their skepticism — in the instance of the minimalists — has butted up against the United Monarchy. And yet, it is the United Monarchy, in some form, rather than Omri, that enjoys the earliest attestation of a figure in external sources.

We no longer need debate the existence of a David, now that the Tel Dan stela — and, according to some scholars, the Mesha stela[2] — shows that Judah's dynastic name was "the House of David" already in the 9th century. The revisionists do debate it. But to ask whether David was invented wholecloth not only ignores the early date of the material, and all the evidence that will be addressed below. It also, ultimately, is dull.[3] The real question among historians is whether David constructed an empire, which was then administered, and lost, by his son Solomon. While the archaeological evidence for a central state has been called into question more than once,[4] the easiest evidence to dismiss is that of the biblical text. Nor does a critical disposition toward the archaeology rule David's activity out of court — it merely limits the way in which one re-

---

"Ancient Israel." JSOTSup 148 (Sheffield: Sheffield Academic, 1992); James W. Flanagan, *David's Social Drama: A Hologram of Israel's Early Iron Age*. JSOTSup 73 (Sheffield: Almond, 1988); David W. Jamieson-Drake, *Scribes and Schools in Monarchic Judah: A Socio-Archeological Approach*. JSOTSup 109 (Sheffield: Almond, 1991). See for further bibliography and response, William G. Dever, "Archaeology, Urbanism, and the Rise of the Israelite State," in *Urbanism in Antiquity: From Mesopotamia to Crete*, ed. Walter E. Aufrecht, Neil A. Mirau, and Steven W. Gauley. JSOTSup 244 (Sheffield: JSOT, 1997), 172-93; "Archaeology and the 'Age of Solomon.'"

2. KAI 181:31, as read by Émile Puech, "La stèle araméenne de Dan: Bar Hadad II et la coalition des Omrides et de la maison de David," *RB* 101 (1994): 215-41, esp. 227; André Lemaire, "'House of David' Restored in Moabite Inscription," *BAR* 20/3 (1994): 30-37. The traces in the photograph fit Lemaire's reading, but the syntax seems peculiar at this stage. An alternative proposed by Nadav Na'aman is reviewed below, Chapter 23.

3. See Hans M. Barstad, "History and the Hebrew Bible," in *Can a "History of Israel" Be Written?* ed. Lester L. Grabbe. JSOTSup 245 (Sheffield: JSOT, 1997), 37-64.

4. Especially by Flanagan, *David's Social Drama*.

constructs it. So, a critical overture to the books of Samuel — an overture intended to explain their contents in detail, not merely to scoff at them — becomes crucial. What does such an approach imply about the early existence of the Israelite state?

The figure of David was as firmly imprinted on the identity of Judah's elite as the Tel Dan stela would suggest. Over and over the books of Kings hold him up as a standard for royal conduct and as the ancestral guarantor of divine favor for Judah's capital city. He becomes the author of many Psalms. In the books of Chronicles, in the postexilic era, probably in the 5th century B.C.E., he is ever *more* important. He plans and prepares for the building of the temple, down to the appointment of its officiants. David is Jerusalem's claim to sovereignty over all Israel, not just Judah. Yet the David of Samuel, and especially of 2 Samuel, is not the plaster saint of later memory and messianism. In 2 Samuel, as we have seen, David is a human being.

Scholarly literature on the date and purpose of Samuel has laid waste to forests. But the field today is split. Is 2 Samuel early, even roughly contemporary with the events it describes?[5] Or is it, as some critics claim, a late, fictional concoction?[6] What are the nature and purpose of Samuel — and thus its origin? And how does knowledge of Samuel's nature and purpose enable us to reconstruct David's career, not exactly as the text presents it, but against the background of the social and political situation that evoked the portrait? Philip R. Davies has written that it is a "ruse" to understand ancient persons or events in ways that vary from our reports about them, rather than deny their existence *tout court*.[7] In the field of history, this "ruse" is called "reconstruction."

A fertile approach to reconstructing David is that of P. Kyle McCarter.[8] What strikes a historian on reading the text of Samuel is that so many key actors die violently. Samuel spends a lot of time defending the principal architect of Israelite identity in Judah against what seem to be allegations raised against

5. This was the consensus from the early 19th century roughly until the 1970s. As noted, it was actions described in Samuel, especially, that enabled W. M. L. de Wette to ascertain that the theology of the Deuteronomic reform had not always been programmatic for Israelite cultic practice.

6. E.g., van Seters, *In Search of History,* 249-91; Davies, *In Search of "Ancient Israel";* Thompson. For a devastating response to van Seters's approach, see Richard E. Friedman, *The Hidden Book in the Bible,* 350-78, especially in regard to the antiquity of J.

7. Philip R. Davies, "Introduction," in *The Origins of the Ancient Israelite States,* ed. Volkmar Fritz and Davies. JSOTSup 228 (Sheffield: Sheffield Academic, 1996), 15.

8. P. Kyle McCarter, Jr., *II Samuel;* see also "The Apology of David," *JBL* 99 (1980): 489-504; cf. also especially James C. VanderKam, "Davidic Complicity in the Deaths of Abner and Eshbaal: A Historical and Redactional Study," *JBL* 99 (1980): 521-39.

him by contemporary opponents. Most of the clearest allegations concern murders. As McCarter observes, the author of the text thus evinces political concerns that had to be dead horses, even forgotten horses, within a generation of David's death. For this reason, one should give credence — not unqualified, but nevertheless credence — to many claims that Samuel makes.

In his treatment of David's apology, McCarter identifies the following killings, not as those for which David is responsible, but as those of which he was accused: Saul and Jonathan, who were dismembered by Philistines after the battle of Jezreel; Abner, who was stabbed under the armor by Joab and Abishai during an otherwise friendly consultation; Ishbaal, stabbed in the chest and decapitated by Gibeonites;[9] Uriah, killed in warfare by Ammonites, but on Joab's order; Amnon, David's eldest son, murdered by his third son, Absalom, by repeated stabbing during a festival; Absalom, stabbed time and again by Joab and his armor-bearers with thrusting sticks; and Amasa, also stabbed in the chest during a kiss of greeting, by Joab.

This is not all the fun in the book. In addition to these cases, Nabal, the husband of David's second wife, expires naturally, but suddenly, and at an extremely convenient time. Abner kills Asahel, Joab's brother, in battle, by thrusting the butt of his spear into his chest (2 Sam. 2:23). David is avowedly responsible for: hanging seven other Saulides; killing an Amaleqite who claims to have killed Saul and brings Saul's regalia in token thereof; killing and dismembering the Gibeonites who assassinated Ishbaal and brought David his head (2 Sam. 4:12). The people of Abel decapitate Sheba and hurl his head over the wall at Joab's insistence. Finally, Benaiah kills Adonijah (1 Kgs. 2:13-25), Joab (2:28-35), and Shimei (2:36-44) on Solomon's order. These are just the highlights. If all this is factitious, we have an author who rolled Hamlet and Richard III into one, the ancient equivalent of Thomas Harris, with the explicit intention of *concealing* the existence of Hannibal Lector. It is strong evidence that David is historical, but equally strong evidence that he was unsavory. So when "minimalists" compare his image to that of King Arthur, differences are immediately apparent: Arthurian legend does not convict him as a murderer, and does not spend most of its time apologizing for the fact that his enemies keep dying violently.

9. 2 Sam. 3:27, 30; 4:6-8.

B. Ten Little Indians

Case 1: Nabal

The apology that alibis David for these killings is ham-fisted. But can we reconstruct history from it? David's first providential death is that of Nabal (1 Sam. 25). Abigail has pleaded with David not to kill the man, when he conveniently drops dead of natural causes. This is how David acquires his second wife, who brings him a substantial estate in the hinterland of Judah, but plays no further role in the narrative. Did Abigail murder her husband to defect to David? One cannot help but think of the occasional topos of the murder suspect who comes to believe that the death of all who cross him or her is a divine judgment. This is the basis of the plot in one of Agatha Christie's novels.[10] A predictable psychological variation would be the beneficiary of violent or providential death who takes on the role of agent after a time. Is Abigail David's catalyst? The case is hard to call.

The literary position of the Abigail account, however, deserves attention. In the B source, it comes just before David refrains from killing Saul, when the latter is completely at his mercy (1 Sam. 26). Chastened by Abigail's confession of Nabal's wickedness, David next spares the life even of his own most lethal enemy. The sparing of Saul not only indicates David's innocence in that king's death, it deflects suspicion from David's contact with Nabal. At least the suspicion that contemporaries accused David of Nabal's murder is justified — and the narrative tells them that Nabal's last contact was not with David, whom he never met personally, but with Abigail. If the accusation was whispered among the tribesmen of southern Judah, the literary account would redirect it onto Abigail herself, even while defending her. This double insulation of David is certainly suggestive; and the failure of any sons of Abigail to figure in the story of the succession to the throne may be related to the strategy of the text: Abigail seems to have been relegated to a secondary political status in David's court. More likely, however, the disappearance of Abigail's sons has to do with the fact that one of them, Amasa, was probably the general of Absalom's rebel army.[11]

---

10. Readers curious to know which should consult "The Web Companion to Agatha Christie." It would be unfair to spoil the riddle for those who have not encountered the book.

11. See below, Chapter 22; and Jon D. Levenson and Baruch Halpern, "The Political Import of David's Marriages," *JBL* 99 (1980): 507-18.

Case 2: Saul and His Sons at Gilboa

For Saul's death, with his three sons, at Gilboa, the agents of death are the Philistines. At the time, the Philistines were David's allies. So Samuel distances David from the battle of Gilboa, or Jezreel. Both sources (1 Sam. 24; 26) maintain that David had Saul completely in his power, but rejected the urging of subordinates to kill him. David thereby earned Saul's forgiveness and in one case his blessing on David's succession to the throne. This improbable sequence smacks of unusually optimistic partisanship.

In addition, one source (A) denies that David *ever* worked for the Philistines (1 Sam. 21:10-15[11-16]). The other (B) stresses: (1) that Saul's persecution drove David to join the Philistines; (2) that David told his overlord, Achish of Gath, he was raiding Judah when he was really raiding desert camps; (3) that David joined the Philistines at the staging zone for their thrust into the Jezreel, but was detailed to the rear as bodyguard for Achish;[12] and (4) that the other tyrants feared duplicity, and cited the snippet, "Saul has slain his thousands, and David his myriads," so that Achish sent him back home. In addition, (5) during the battle, David was off in the south chasing Amaleqites who had raided Ziklag in his absence; (6) when he learned from an Amaleqite, who brought him Saul's regalia, that Saul was dead, and at Saul's request by the Amaleqite's own hand, David killed Saul's killer; and (7) David composed a lament to mourn Saul's and Jonathan's deaths publicly (1 Sam. 24–2 Sam. 1).

Protest? This is a dissertation of denial! But the alibi doesn't even completely remove David from the battle: it admits he was in the Philistine camp, arrayed for war. It concedes that he was a trusted vassal of Achish, who did fight in the battle. It documents not that David killed Saul, but that the accusation that he helped the Philistines to victory had real sting.

A text in Chronicles, five centuries later, illustrates how profoundly embarrassing even this version of events proved to be. 1 Chr. 12:20-21 relates that

> From Manasseh, there defected to David when he came with the Philistines against Saul to battle — and he didn't help them, for in council the tyrants of the Philistines sent him away, saying, "He will defect against our interest to his master, Saul" — When he went to Ziklag, there defected to him from Manasseh [names of recruits follow]

---

12. 1 Sam. 29:2, to the rear; as a bodyguard, 28:1-2. On the Israelite model of David's era, the bodyguard was unlikely to see frontline action except in the case of a rout in one or another direction. But in other places, and at other times in Israel, the royal guard were front-line shock troops.

There is an epanalepsis, or rhetorical repetition, here: "from Manasseh, there defected to him, when he came to battle" to "when he went to Ziklag, there defected to him from Manasseh. . . ." The information between the two is explanatory: David didn't actually fight Saul, it was only when he returned to Ziklag that these Manassites joined him, while the battle was raging. A scribe has added the qualification, that David did not fight. The original text probably reported that Manassites joined David at Apheq. The source cannot have reached the author of Chronicles in this form, but the awkward reformulation indicates typical Israelite respect for the source, which could instead have been recast as, "And in Ziklag, after the death of Saul, there came to him. . . ." Instead, the text mentions defections at the time of the battle of Jezreel! It probably originally mentioned defections just *before* the battle.

David was at the front. But the mythmaking machinery of the text portrays him as the great slayer of Philistines in his youth: "Is this not David, servant of Saul the king of Israel. . . . Is this not David of whom they chant with flutes, saying, 'Saul has smitten his thousands, and David his myriads'?" (1 Sam. 29:3, 5). Is the story of David's attachment to Saul's court true, or merely a political convenience — balancing and especially justifying his later attachment to Philistia? We shall probably never know, but we should certainly entertain the question.

In the text, David winds up with Saul's regalia: Saul's Amaleqite killer brings it to him (2 Sam. 1). McCarter takes this to be the source of the accusation of complicity in Saul's death. In other words, the text explains how David came to be in physical possession of Saul's crown. The story may be pure invention, foreshadowing David's succession by endowing him with the symbols of kingship. But if not, McCarter must be right.

Even more significant is the complexity of David's alibi for Saul's death. It is *not* the claim of the B source that David went home from the staging area for the battle: during the battle itself, he was careering around the Negev. Why does the account remove David from Ziklag? Why does it have him all but annihilate the Amaleqites he meets during the time of the battle of Jezreel (1 Sam. 30)?

The text not only explains how David came into possession of Saul's regalia, it also explains why he was *not to be found in Ziklag* at the time of Saul's death, despite having been sent home from the battlefield. Had he been in the field, he would have been in the rear, as Achish's bodyguard. And, had he been at the front, he would not have killed Saul, as he had previously demonstrated by sparing that king. All this is curiously reminiscent of the triple defense employed by Earl Rogers in a murder trial: his client was not present on the scene of the crime; if the client was present, he did not commit the murder; and, if he did commit the murder, he was insane at the time.

The claims that David never attacked Israelites when working for the

Philistines, but annihilated his non-Israelite opponents and sent booty to Judah, reinforce the same message.[13] They effectively deny — as in the A source — that David worked for the Philistines at all. They certainly deny that David was capable of working against Israelite interests. This raises the question not just of David's complicity in Saul's defeat and death, but of his relationship with Philistia both before and during his reign.

To put it differently, the text *admits* that David worked for the Philistines. It admits that he was the trusted lieutenant of Achish of Gath. It admits that Achish adjudged him so worthy as to bestow on him the captaincy of an outlying Gittite settlement. It admits that from this base he conducted raids and forays the results of which pleased his Philistine liege lord. It admits in fact that David stood in the royal bodyguard of Gath — a position, in the Near East, affording him easy access to the king, and control of a considerable force of elite soldiers. It admits that he offered Achish, the Philistine king, no harm whatever — so much so that whereas Saul pursues David, Achish merely commends him. It admits that, in his position as royal bodyguard, policing the regular forces of Gath from the center of their command, rather than harmlessly lounging in the rear, David formed up his troops and presented himself at the staging area for the battle of Jezreel. It goes so far as to claim that he protested his dismissal from the battle of Jezreel. It admits, too, that he was absent from his home at the time of the fatal confrontation. It admits that he never confronted Philistines at all, except in the central hills around Jerusalem — long after he was allegedly king of Judah in Hebron. It admits that he came into possession of Saul's crown and other royal insignia stripped at the end of the battle of Jezreel. The text effectively concedes all the most damaging information one could conceive, in order to rescue David from a single suspicion: that he was instrumental in the defeat and death of Saul. So much admission, for so small, and yet so exquisite, a denial.

Consider the following principle: where the author of an ancient text puts himself to the considerable trouble of denying an accusation explicitly, then the historian owes him, at a minimum, the courtesy of taking the accusation seriously. Second Samuel offers a laboratory course in denial. Unlike modern journalism, or antiquarian literature even in ancient times, three of its facets demand attention: what it alleges; what it denies; and what subjects it cools in the refreshing shadow of its silence. In this chapter, our concern is principally with denial, in the political realm, while silence is addressed in connection with its treatment of David's achievements. Denial and silence are the twin engines of the text's most important nuances. What is explicit is perspicuous, is there to

13. 1 Sam. 27:8-12; 30:26-31.

lead the reader. What is unsaid is penumbral, constituting the gray area between what the author dare not and what he cannot say. What is denied, however, throws the author's deepest concerns into sharp relief, defining the character of the explicit remarks in the book.

Case 3: Ishbaal

In this light, Saul's death deserves comparison to that of his successor. If Saul's killers were Philistines, or an Amaleqite, Ishbaal's assassins were Gibeonites, belonging to the ethnic group the Hivvites. They were residents of the town of Beeroth. The Hivvite population of Beeroth had been expelled and, along with other Gibeonites, persecuted by Saul. The assassins, having dispatched the new king, race to David in Hebron — just as the Amaleqite who killed Saul had done. Ishbaal's killers deliver up the king's head, David being already in possession of the crown. As in Saul's case, David strings the killers up. He also cuts off their arms and legs and displays their torsos by the Pool in Hebron (see further Chapter 17).

Notably, instead of sending it back for burial, David keeps Ishbaal's head with Abner's remains in Hebron, away from the house of Saul (2 Sam. 4:6-8, 12). The significance of retaining control over corpses was not lost on David, who never repatriated the remains of Saul and Jonathan from Jabesh Gilead until *after* he had wiped out Saul's remaining descendants, Mephibaal being the sole exception. Only in 2 Sam. 21:12-14 are the male heirs executed at Gibeon, and Saul and Jonathan removed to the tomb of Saul's father, Kish. As Mephibaal was confined to Jerusalem, David effectively prevented the development of a royal ancestral cult at Saul's tomb or, in fact, a tomb specific to the head of the dynasty. It is not reported that he ever removed either Ishbaal's head or Abner's remains to the dynastic tomb.

In the aftermath of Ishbaal's assassination, the northern kingdom falls into David's lap. If David commissioned the killing, or even solicited tenders on a contract, his killing the assassins is standard mob-style procedure. The text *admits* that the death was providential for David — it is as providential, we read, as Saul's death (2 Sam. 4:9-10).

Note the formulation of David's speech:

As Yahweh lives, who redeemed my life from all trouble, when the one who told me, 'Lo, Saul is dead,' — and he thought himself an herald of glad tidings — I seized him and slew him in Ziklag, which is how I rewarded him for glad tidings. But when wicked men have slain an inno-

81

cent man in his house on his bed, must I not now seek his bloodguilt from your hands, and expunge you from the land?

Yahweh has indeed redeemed David's life from trouble, both by killing Saul and by killing Ishbaal, without David's involvement.[14]

Anyone familiar with contemporary paranoia about public life — in an age of abundant journalistic monitoring and information — will recognize that David's political opponents *must* have accused him of Ishbaal's murder. The punishment of the killers, like Saul's Amaleqite not significant political players, indicates that he understood the danger that he would indeed be accused. What is more, the killers are Gibeonites, who, we shall see, were David's allies. Chances are, David commissioned the hit.

Case 4: Abner

Just before Ishbaal's murder, Abner's death is a tidy little bonus. Abner was Warwick to Ishbaal's Edward IV, claims the text. He was Ishbaal's second-in-command. The text describes a quarrel between the two, over Abner's alleged relations with one of Saul's concubines (2 Sam. 3:7-11). Yet, in 1 Kgs. 2, Solomon executes his brother Adonijah for *asking* for one of David's concubines. "Ask for him the kingship," he tells Bathsheba, the alleged intermediary of the request, then dispatches the reliable Benaiah to execute him. Each text assumes that relations with a concubine establish a claim on the throne. How believable is this in either instance? As we shall see, it is part of the patterned strategies of exculpation that repeatedly characterize this author's work.

Abner is alienated by Ishbaal's accusation. He then acquires Michal, Saul's daughter (2 Sam. 3:13-16), on Ishbaal's order, and brings her, *with 20 atten-*

---

14. 2 Sam. 4:9-11. Note the response to the incurred bloodguilt: it must be driven out of the land. This is usually thought to be Deuteronomic language, but Deuteronomy speaks only of expunging evil *(r')* from "your midst" or "from Israel," or of expunging "innocent blood" *(dm nqy)* "from Israel" (Deut. 19:13), or "from your midst" (21:9). References outside ritual contexts (Deut. 26:13, 14) are found in 13:5[6]; 17:7; 19:19; 21:21; 22:21, 24; 24:7 ("from your midst"); 17:12; 22:22 ("from Israel"). Usage in Kings in Deuteronomistic contexts is "burn/drive 'after' you" (or "the last of you"? 1 Kgs. 14:10; 16:3; 21:21) or just "burn/drive out" (2 Kgs. 23:24). In the last instance, the context may imply "from the land," but this is explicit outside of 2 Sam. 4:11 only in 1 Kgs. 22:46, in the evaluation of Jehoshaphat; 2 Chr. 19:3 (a speech to Jehoshaphat in part inspired by the report in Kings). The point is that in 2 Sam. 4:11; 1 Kgs. 22:46, the land is what is polluted and must be cleansed, whereas in Deuteronomy it is the covenant community that is affected. In most cases in Kings, the question of what is polluted is not addressed.

dants, to an allegedly secret assignation in Hebron. At this feast, he promises to dump Ishbaal and translate Israelite support to David. Abner departs in peace, an ally. But he had earlier killed Joab's brother Asahel in open battle. And Joab, without David's knowledge (3:26), therefore exacts vengeance.

The story of the assignation occupies 11 verses (2 Sam. 3:17-27). It requires twelve verses to exculpate David. In them, David declares his innocence, curses the house of Joab's otherwise unnamed father, proclaims mourning, conducts a state funeral, elegizes Abner, eulogizes Abner, fasts all the way to sunset, and, the narrator says, persuades all Israel of his innocence. It was not the king's idea to kill Abner. Rather, Joab and Abishai bushwacked Abner for killing Asahel.[15]

The exculpation is longer than the story. But the story, too, is apology: it carefully and categorically denies that David had a motive for the murder. Abner delivered Michal, giving David a claim on the throne, although with Ishbaal's connivance. He campaigned for David among the Israelite elders. He promised to make David king. But Joab gummed up the works: he pursued his vendetta even though Abner had killed Asahel in open battle, and reluctantly at that. Joab, we later learn explicitly, shed the blood of war within the framework of a peaceful relationship. Yet Joab suffers only David's curse: there is no non-verbal reprisal for the murder. The elaborate apparatus of defenses indicates that this murder, like that of Ishbaal, was a live issue when this text — and probably Joab — were framed.[16]

Even highly critical readers, such as Gösta Ahlström,[17] take this story at face value. Abner was a fellow that David had every reason to protect. But it is very easy to imagine — and it is a certainty that many ancients did — that a crafty and unctuous David lured Abner to Hebron for a peace conference. Offering Abner traditional hospitality, safe conduct, and promises of accommo-

---

15. Some scholars argue that 2 Sam. 3:30 is secondary, based on the allegation that Abishai played no role in the murder of Abner. This is specious reasoning: Joab plunged the knife in, but someone else must have occupied or restrained Abner's 20 retainers (3:20). Or possibly slaughtered them. This verse is absolutely critical, because it clearly indicates that Abner killed Asahel *in battle* — just as 2 Sam. 2 has him repeatedly warn Asahel before killing him — to make a simple point: Joab killed someone with whom he was in an alliance, with whom he was at peace; Abner, who killed in battle, should have been exempt from blood vengeance. Note the contrast in 3:30: in MT, Joab and Abishai *hrgw*, whereas Abner *hmyt* — here apparently marking a difference between killing in alliance/peace and in war. The theme that Abner left David "in peace/in alliance" in vv. 21, 22, 23 assumes importance in the account of Joab's death.

16. See McCarter, *II Samuel*, 120-22.

17. *A History of Ancient Palestine*. JSOTSup 146 (Sheffield: Sheffield Academic, 1993), 465.

dation, or even submission, David turned on him and killed him. This is the technique later employed by Absalom against Amnon — the forgive-and-forget banquet followed by homicide. Lethal deception ran in the family.

The concession of Michal might seem to speak against this possibility — the more so in that the author of 2 Sam. 3 adduces it as evidence of the situation. However, it is likely that David made diplomatic recognition a condition of his submission to Ishbaal. In this case, he will have demanded, in token of his special status, that he be permitted to marry the king's sister. In exchange, he must have promised a treasure — including, perhaps, a harvest of Philistine foreskins — for the princess.

The promise of submission led naturally to the dispatching of a peace delegation. Abner's group of 20 retainers, on the face of things, resembles such a delegation far more than it does some secret conspiracy. To be sure, 2 Samuel maintains that Abner had already declaimed his traitorous intentions publicly at court; but one would think that were Ishbaal powerless to oppose Abner, the latter would have seized the throne himself. Indeed, the most suspicious element of the entire story is the claim that *Ishbaal* ordered the sending of Michal to David's court. The text actually claims that he connived with Abner at his own dethronement, yet remained David's opponent after Abner's death. David's request for Michal was couched in terms of submission or alliance, not defiance. Only in such a case would Ishbaal's acquiescence serve a political purpose.

Case 5: Saul's Other Descendants

David's next kills are by inspiration. In 2 Sam. 21 Yahweh inflicts a famine on the land. In response to David's petition, Yahweh lets out that the famine was his way of punishing (David's!) Israel for Saul's violation of a divinely guaranteed treaty: Saul had attacked the Gibeonites. The Gibeonites, to satisfy the wrong, demand seven of Saul's male heirs in retribution, and hang them — two sons by Rizpah bat-Ayya, and five grandsons by Saul's eldest daughter.[18] The

18. McCarter (*II Samuel, ad loc.*) is certainly right that the point of 2 Sam. 6:22-23 is that Michal remained childless to the day of her death because David broke off relations with her and in effect imprisoned her. So the sister in 2 Sam. 21:8, who is married to Ad/zriel son of Barzillai the Meholatite (1 Sam. 18:19), not Paltiel ben-Laish (2 Sam. 3:15), must be Merab. Barzillai the Meholatite is probably identical with Barzillai from Rogelim in Gilead. Abel Meholah was right on the Jordan (1 Kgs. 4:12; Judg. 7:22). Another option is to derive this Barzillai from the Manassite clan of Mahlah. Note not just that the taking of Mephibaal to court is related before the Absalom revolt, but that the disposition of

Gibeonites had now learned to kill Saul's scions only on official pretexts, and the seven males were a sort of compensation for the martyrdom of Ishbaal's assassins. David spares Mephibaal, Jonathan's lame son, and brings him to court permanently — a safe place, betimes, for the lone Saulide heir.[19] David generously left Mephibaal half of Saul's estates in a Solomonic decision after Absalom's revolt.[20]

The killing of Saul's descendants sparked accusations in David's time. Remarkably, one accusation is preserved. As David abandoned Jerusalem at the start of the Absalom revolt, Shimei, a member of Saul's clan, reviled him, calling, "Go, go, Man of Blood, and Hellion. Yahweh has requited you all the bloodguilt of the house of Saul, whom you succeeded . . ." (2 Sam. 16:7-8). Man of Blood, an epithet levied against Lincoln by American southerners during the Civil War, is a peculiarly compelling phrase. It implies bloodguilt, that is, designates the object of the opprobrium as a murderer. And the text concurs that David was a Man of Blood — but, it claims, the blood on his hands was that of Uriah, first husband of Solomon's mother.[21]

Shimei charges that David manipulated the results of oracles so as to rid himself of potential rallying points for resistance. There is direct textual linkage in that the story of the killings at Gibeon begins by reference to Saul's house's

---

Mephibaal's (i.e., all of Saul's — 2 Sam. 9:7) estates is decided immediately afterward. Thus the killings must predate the revolt.

19. The submission of 2 Sam. 9:1-6 is that Mephibaal is the sole remaining male Saulide with whom David can "act in good faith for the sake of Jonathan." Jonathan's lame son is in the house of Machir ben-Ammiel in Lo Debar. Mephibaal's relocation to the court precedes the Absalom revolt, since it is on the basis of his failure to evacuate Jerusalem that David strips him of half of Saul's estates.

20. 2 Sam. 9 presents Ziba as an old retainer of Saul, with 15 sons and a large staff. Regardless whether this was the case, or whether David assigned a stooge of his own to be steward, Ziba obviously found common interests with David. Kickbacks to David were undoubtedly part of this mix — explicitly, in terms of Mephibaal's maintenance at court, but no doubt above and beyond it. See below, Chapter 21.

21. Solomon explains to Hiram in 1 Kgs. 5:3-4(17-18) that David did not build the temple because he was constantly occupied with war; the issue there is one of time, and Solomon, now at peace, is able to undertake the project. The interpretation of the passage is that David was at peace in 2 Sam. 7:1, and had time to move the ark, but next came his conquests (2 Sam. 8). In 1 Chr. 22:7-8, David tells Solomon that Yhwh had refused him (David) permission to build the temple because he had spilled much blood and fought many wars. In this interpretation, which plays on the similarity between Solomon's name and the word šālôm, "peace, harmony," the refusal of permission in 2 Sam. 7 (1 Chr. 17) stemmed from the fact that David was a warrior. But even here, the refusal comes ahead of Uriah's murder.

bloodguilt: For Shimei, David is "the man of bloodguilt," responsible for "all the blood of the house of Saul." In 2 Sam. 21:1, Yahweh announces, "To Saul and to his house there is bloodguilt" because he killed the Gibeonites.[22] But Shimei does not say, "Yahweh has requited you for all the blood of the house of Saul which YOU spilled," as distinct from anyone else. He says, "Yahweh has requited you for ALL the blood of the house of Saul."

McCarter accordingly includes in Shimei's accusation Saul and his sons at Gilboa, Abner, Ishbaal, and the seven grandchildren.[23] David even demanded the separation of Saul's daughter Michal from her husband before condemning her to celibacy and executing her sister's children. He thus controlled the *production* of Saulides. And, one might add, a curious piece of narrative legerdemain concerns Jonathan's lame son, Mephibaal: the steward, Ziba, accuses Mephibaal, *at the time of Absalom's revolt,* of expecting a restoration to his "father's" — Saul's — throne. Though Mephibaal's lameness and appearance later expose this claim as opportunistic, the author intends that the reader, like David, should believe it at the time (2 Sam. 16:1-4; 19:24-30[25-31]). In other words, the reader is to understand, or is perhaps expected to bring the understanding to the textual table, that the fate the Saulides suffered at David's hands was a very live issue indeed at the time of the Absalom revolt, late in the reign.

Overall, in the aftermath of the battle of Gilboa, David can be said to have adopted a policy of systematic extermination toward the house of Saul, rather like Henry VII knocking off Plantagenets and scapegoating Richard III, or like Dennis Price knocking off Alec Guinness 17 times in *Kind Hearts and Coronets.* David even retained Ishbaal's head and Abner's corpse in Hebron, and he repatriated the bodies of Saul and Jonathan from the men of Jabesh Gilead — who stole them from Beth Shan (Stratum VI) — only on the deaths of all the other heirs (2 Sam. 21:12-14). But David carefully preserved Mephibaal's life, confining him instead to the court and stripping him of his estates; and he refrained from killing his accuser, Shimei. Characteristically, he shows remarkable forbearance toward this foe, publicly restraining Abishai, and his brother Joab no doubt, from killing him both before and after his victory (2 Sam. 16:5-13; 19:22-23): Joab and Abishai had taken the lead in attacking Saulides since the

---

22. 'îš had-dāmîm, kōl dĕmê bêt-šā'ûl, 2 Sam. 16:7-8; 'el šā'ûl wĕ-'el bêtô dāmîm, 2 Sam. 21:1. The linkage is concrete, and the difference in authority is that the narrator has Shimei speaking in 16:7-8, but Yahweh speaking in 21:1. Saul was the one who incurred bloodguilt, not David. However, it must have been somewhat galling to David that Shimei's accusation had the matter out in the open, and it is almost possible to believe that David let him live in order to disprove the allegation, then asked Solomon to murder him, as the text claims.

23. McCarter, *II Samuel, ad loc.*

episode when Saul himself lay in David's power (1 Sam. 26:8). With Mephibaal and Shimei, the moderate, merciful David maintained a token hostage and his accuser to show that there was nothing to the accusation. This is one more alibi.

Now, although the Saulides are for the most part disposed of before the time of the Absalom revolt, theirs are not the only deaths of which David is accused or from which he is exculpated. Uriah's murder is conceded by the text, and taken to be the cause of Absalom's revolt. The latter also has a proximate cause, namely, Amnon's rape of Tamar.

Case 6: Amnon

Amnon was David's eldest son, borne by Ahinoam from Jezreel (2 Sam. 3:2). Two women bear this name: Saul's wife (1 Sam. 14:50) and David's. Yahweh also tells David through Nathan, "I gave you your master's house and your master's women to your bosom" (2 Sam. 12:8). So there is a good chance that David's first wife was Saul's wife first.[24] There are also two Jezreels — one in Israel, the later winter capital of Ahab and Jezebel (as 2 Kgs. 10:1; Hos. 1:4) and scene of Saul's last battle (1 Sam. 29:11), and one in Judah. A 7th-century text, Josh. 15:56, attests the occupation of the site in Judah, but there is no indication it was occupied before that time.[25] Likely, Ahinoam came from the northern Jezreel, on the eastern side of the Jezreel Valley under Mount Gilboa. The chances are that she was either Saul's wife or associated with the group from which Saul had taken his wife.

Here, again, is a providence for David. The rapist, Amnon, is the heir presumptive, representing the most prosperous ambitions of an important political constituency. The ravaged sister's grandfather is a foreign kinglet, Talmay king of Geshur, useful for threatening northern Israel (2 Sam. 3:3). Further, if the rapist was borne by Saul's former wife, his removal eliminates the last vestiges of Saul's legacy from the succession — it is a part of David's extermination of the Saulide line. Possibly, David instigated the rape: after all, Jonadab, David's nephew, counseled Amnon, yet thereafter remained in good odor in court,

---

24. See Levenson and Halpern, 507-18.

25. On the date of Josh. 15, see among others Albrecht Alt, "Judas Gaue unter Josia," *Kleine Schriften zur Geschichte des Volkes Israels* 2 (Munich: Beck, 1953), 276-88; Frank Moore Cross, Jr., and George Ernest Wright, "The Boundary and Province Lists of the Kingdom of Judah," *JBL* 75 (1956): 202-26; Zekharyah Kallai, *Historical Geography of the Bible* (Jerusalem: Magnes, 1986), 115-24, 334-97. Alt's position has been repeatedly vindicated by excavations and by surveys (notably, excavations at Ein Gedi, Tel 'Ira, Ḥorvat 'Uza; surveys by Rudolf Cohen, William G. Dever).

according to the text (2 Sam. 13:3-5, 32-33). Provocateur or free agent? His continued good standing inclines one to the former interpretation. Even more providential: the avenger is next in line for the succession.[26]

David is immobile. Absalom models himself on David's murder of Abner, and after two years invites his brothers to a feast, at which he murders Amnon (2 Sam. 13:23-29). David's alibi is that he first believes Absalom has killed all his brothers and then mourns Amnon demonstratively (2 Sam. 13:30-36). But, as noted above, David takes no stock in the dead. Absence makes his heart grow forgetful, especially if the removal was intended from the first as a part of the extermination of contenders for the throne connected to the House of Saul.

Unlike Joab, and unlike the killers of Saul and Ishbaal, Absalom flees. For murder inside groups, expulsion is a common custom. It is attested in the Bible, where Cain, Simeon, and Levi are all landless because they have killed — allies. The adoptive Egyptian, Moses, also flees into the wilderness after killing a member of his own putative group. In other cultures, the fugitive is repatriated after a period of some years.[27]

26. The best list of David's early offspring seems to be that in 2 Sam. 3:2-5, which enumerates the eldest sons of six wives in order to imply that Solomon would be the eldest surviving son of the seventh. This list is duplicated in 1 Chr. 3:1-4, but 3:5 lists Solomon last among four sons of "Bath-Shua" = Bathsheba, daughter of Ammiel, then enumerates nine more sons before excluding sons of concubines and mentioning Tamar. Chronicles has duplicated the list of 2 Sam. 5:14-16, taking the children of 5:14 (achronologically) as those of Bathshua/Bathsheba. The list in Samuel has no such implications, as 2 Sam. 5:13 makes clear. The variant on Bathsheba's name in Chronicles may be exegetical, drawing a connection to Gen. 38 (vv. 2 and 6, the latter involving a Tamar). Or it may be intended to avoid connecting her with the Sibitti, or Seven Gods, to which the element -Sheba ties her. It is possible that the element baal, in the names of the Saulides Ishbaal and Meribaal (here, Mephibaal) in Chronicles, but -boshet in Samuel, is also intended to link Saul to (the) baal. See Gordon J. Hamilton, *CBQ* 60 (1998): 228-50.

27. See Emrys L. Peters, "Some Structural Aspects of the Feud among the Camel-Herding Bedouin of Cyrenaica," *Africa* 37 (1967): 261-82. Cf. Oedipus' *miasma* at Thebes. But note also that Moses returns from the wilderness on the death of the king, and that killers resident in "cities of refuge" can return to their holdings after the death of a high priest in the legal theory of P (Num. 35:9-34; cf. Deut. 19:1-13, which probably contemplates such a return after legal proceedings in the town of origin). The stories about Cain, Simeon, and Levi are etiologies for a nomadic lifestyle, nomads being identified in this culture with those who have been driven, for one or another reason, from the settled lands. See latterly, Eckart Otto, "Gewaltvermeidung und -überwindung in Recht und Religion Israels," in *Dramatische Erlösungslehre*, ed. J. Niewiadomski and W. Palaver (Innsbruck: Tyrolia, 1992), 97-117, esp. 98-99, with further citations and discussion. Otto goes on to observe (100) that the legal strategy of the Covenant Code is to impose death sanctions within the family (Exod. 21:12, 15-17), and this is also indicated by the speech of the Wise

Absalom spends three years with his grandfather, the king of Geshur (2 Sam. 13:38). But Geshur, in the southern Golan, was within the ambit of David's domination or, certainly, menace, by the late part of his reign. He held northern Transjordan before Absalom's revolt. Absalom could have been extradited readily enough. And who is the agent of Absalom's repatriation? Joab. Joab "tricks" David into letting the lad come home, even though David is alive to the deception (2 Sam. 14:1-23). David does not readmit Absalom to the court for a period of two more years (2 Sam. 14:24, 28); but Joab, who previously had refused to intercede with David (14:29), does a complete turn-about after Absalom torches his crops, and the rehabilitation is complete (14:30-33).

This looks like a put-up job. David had a problem, which Absalom solved. Absalom took the consequences and returned to court — the return greased by Joab. Yet if there was a deal between David and Absalom, it probably involved assurances that vengeance would bring Absalom nearer the crown. And, after five years, Absalom may have found matters at court different from when he left: our grandson of a foreign kinglet may have faced some pretty stiff fraternal opposition. And any commitments that David may have made either before Amnon's death or at the time of Absalom's repatriation were very likely undone by the time of the revolt.

Case 7: Absalom

Absalom's death is as straightforward as Amnon's. David charges his commanders in hearing of the troops not to harm his son, and sends them into battle against him (2 Sam. 18:5). Joab kills Absalom nonetheless, while Absalom is hanging helpless by his hair in a tree — his hair not falling to the ground

---

Woman of Tekoa in 2 Sam. 14:5-7, where the typical expectation is that fratricide will be punished by death. So one of the causes of the Absalom revolt in the mind of the author of 2 Samuel is David's willingness to take a humanitarian — noncentral — view of crime within a family. However, the indications are that the culture was less than monolithic in this respect, and that the legislation of the Covenant Code regarding the family reflects the interests of the state. Note especially the regulations regarding refuge starting in Exod. 21:13. The same statist ideology presumably underlies 2 Samuel, which, however, portrays David's decision as essentially compassionate and familial. Note Bernard Williams, *Shame and Necessity* (Berkeley: University of California Press, 1994), arguing that the earliest Greek literary texts presuppose inevitable conflict between human behavior that would later be regarded as "ethical" and the actual nature of the universe. 2 Samuel would seem to present a parallel instance.

(2 Sam. 18:9-15). David mourns publicly (2 Sam. 19:1[2]), as in the case of the Saulide victims. And, Joab remains on the general staff.

One need not go so far as to say, though it is amusing to insinuate, that David *intended* to drive Absalom to revolt. For the result of that uprising was to establish the total superiority of David's professional army over the tribal levies.[28] But whatever David's conscious intentions, it is easy enough to see how Absalom might come to rebel. And it is also easy to see how the man of action, who acquitted the family honor, might score points particularly with the state hierarchy, which seems to have stood behind him.

At any rate, David's public insistence that Absalom be spared is of a piece, literarily, with his refusal to kill Saul, his mourning of Saul, Jonathan, Ishbaal, and Abner, and his inability to punish Joab, Amnon, or, in the end, Absalom after Amnon's death. In constructing a character for him, the author of the apology permits all the alibis and explanations to interlace in a network of mutual support: if David could not kill Saul, how could he kill Absalom? One might argue David's public instruction to the brigade commanders that they spare Absalom is an authentic report, for the text claims that the entire force heard the admonition. But even if so, what is omitted is any charge that David may have communicated to his commanders privately. He did not want to see Absalom, whose popularity far exceeded his own, survive the day.

Case 8: Amasa

The case of Amasa is perhaps the clearest assassination in which David is implicated. Amasa, the military commander in the Absalom revolt, is also David's nephew, and quite possibly his step-son.[29] This is an important indication that

28. And in a way, this is how David created Solomon: he left a legacy of military domination that enabled Solomon to stage an instant coup d'état, and then cement his grip with a set of bloody murders. See Halpern, *The Constitution of the Monarchy,* 242-44; "The Uneasy Compromise: Israel between League and Monarchy," in *Traditions in Transformation: Turning-Points in Biblical Faith,* ed. Halpern and Jon D. Levenson. Festschrift Frank Moore Cross (Winona Lake: Eisenbrauns, 1981), 59-96, esp. 91-95.

29. It is often overlooked that Amasa must also have been a senior officer under David, and was a member of the royal family, being the son of Joab's aunt, David's sister, and probably wife, Abigail. 1 Chronicles places Amasa in David's army, possibly on this basis, in 12:18(19). On Amasa's father, Yitra the "Israelite" or "Jezreelite" (not "Ishmaelite"), and his likely identity with Abigail's first husband, Nabal, see Levenson and Halpern. 1 Chr. 2:17 identifies Amasa's father as an Ishmaelite, while MT of 2 Sam. 17:25 has him as an Israelite, and the versions there either as an Israelite (most versions), an Ishmaelite (G^A and

even within the royal family and the professional army, the revolt was not confined to Absalom. After his victory, in a concession to the rebels, David installs Amasa in Joab's place as commander of the tribal armies (2 Sam. 19:13-14[14-15]).

Immediately after demobilization, however, the revolt of Sheba ben-Bichri breaks out. David gives Amasa three days to remobilize the weekend soldiers of Judah whom he commands. But the muster of the tribe has just gone home, defeated. *Mirabile dictu,* Amasa misses the deadline. There was no hope of the troops obeying an immediate summons to renewed service in short order. If anything, they would have suspected treachery on David's part merely at being called up. The predictably dilatory response is, however, convenient for David. The king dispatches the standing army, under Abishai. These slouch north to Gibeon — where David hanged Saul's heirs — to rendezvous with Amasa. Joab takes this worthy aside for a kiss, and with his left hand thrusts a dagger into his belly (2 Sam. 20:1-13).

Again, David stands to benefit. He has just suffered the humiliation of appointing a rebel general his commander-in-chief. And the revolt during which Amasa is killed turns out to consist of one miserable flea, a man without a following, who takes refuge in a town on Israel's remote northern border, probably in a neighboring kingdom at the time. Sheba's head is unceremoniously lobbed over the wall of Abel of the House of Maacah to the waiting Joab, while the town, without opening its gate, professes its Israelite identity (this is perhaps the story of its annexation). Surely, Sheba was the sorriest revolutionary in history. As McCarter has pointed out, the apology, again, blames Amasa's death on Joab, whom David did not even send — it was Abishai who called him.[30] Now, David may have forgotten that Joab had just killed Absalom, and that Abishai was Joab's brother, and had been complicit in Abner's murder. Circumstantial evidence, as Pudd'nhead Wilson's calendar remarks, can be misleading. Joab returns to the general staff. The citizens of Judah, Absalom's partisans, must have held the unshakeable conviction that David ordered the murder.

The repeated exculpation of David for complicity in providential deaths indicates that accusations were contemporary.[31] Even today, in the Manichaean political universe we tend to inhabit, our opponents represent the children of

---

others), or a Jezreelite (one Old Greek witness, several miniscules, G[M], and probably others). 1 Chr. 12:18(19), however, names him as a Benjaminite recruit to David's cause, presupposing that the father was an Israelite. This may be derivative. See 2 Sam. 20:4-12; 1 Kgs. 2:32; possibly 1 Chr. 15:24 = 6:25, 34(10, 20).

30. McCarter, *II Samuel,* 432.

31. See esp. Vanderkam; McCarter, *JBL* 99 (1980): 489-504.

darkness. With the exception of Gerald Ford, no American president in living memory wasn't evil incarnate to somebody. And even Ford had his Squeaky Fromme. In the early 1990s, the weekly journal *MacLeans* reported that fewer Canadians (12%) supported their then prime minister, Brian Mulroney, than believed that Elvis Presley was alive (17%), a decade after his death. Moving from paranoid demonization of the Other — which establishes that our texts are early — to historical reconstruction presents some difficulties, but the general pattern suggests that murder was an implement of choice in David's strategy for the construction of ethnicity. And the role of states-in-formation in the imposition of ethnicity is more complex and varied than the best theories of state-formation allow.

The *modi operandi* are limited: Joab removes Abner, Absalom, Amasa, Sheba, and, on David's orders, Uriah. He never suffers sanction, except for a three-day-long demotion under Amasa — by the time the army reaches Abel, he is in charge of it again. Three times the killers are aliens: the Philistines kill Saul and three of his sons, and Gibeonites kill the others. Once the killer is David's son. It is convenient for David if somebody dies, and somebody else kills him. This holds for Nabal (natural death), Saul and his three sons (killer: Philistines), Abner (killer: Joab), Ishbaal (killer: Gibeonites [from Beeroth]), Saul's heirs (killer: Gibeonites), Uriah (killer: Joab), Amnon (killer: Absalom), Absalom (killer: Joab), Amasa (killer: Joab), and Sheba (killer: Abel Maacah acting for Joab). Three deaths (Abner, Uriah, Adonijah) involve fallings-out over married women, plus a fourth if we include Abigail and Nabal. Three times the killers are themselves killed — the assassins of Saul and of Ishbaal, and Absalom, killer of Amnon. In the cases of Saul and Jonathan, Abner, Amnon, and Absalom, David leads public mourning. David has emotional or blood bonds with several victims — Jonathan, Amnon, Absalom, Amasa, and Joab. He has a contract with (not on) Abner. He refrained from killing Saul when he had the chance, as well as Shimei. And he is never on the scene of a murder at all: he is present only at the executions of the Amaleqite who killed Saul, and of the Beerothites who killed Ishbaal, for which he explicitly claims credit.

Case 9: Uriah

It is instructive to compare with the others the one case in which the narrative concedes, or rather asserts, that David murdered, the story of Uriah. Uriah's absence from his marital bed — and David's taking his place on it — have created a situation in which Bathsheba's adultery is bound to become apparent. The narrator then assumes that readers will agree: it is therefore necessary that Uriah die. This presupposes that the punishment for adultery, once discovered, is death; that the punishment could not be avoided by the payment of an indemnity; and that David did not wish to flout the law.

This last seems awfully unlikely. David's general lawlessness was well known to his subordinates. Even if he acted out the alibis the texts describe, his partisans can only have been fooled by willful collusion in believing them. In addition, David could always have blamed Bathsheba's son on some underling, or a convenient foreigner. If, for some strange reason, he lacked the stomach for casting the blame on some innocent party — in this one case — he still had other options. The Middle Assyrian Laws allow for the payment of indemnities, or even forgiveness by the wronged husband, in cases of adultery. David could thus have forced Uriah to demand only symbolic reparation. Oddly enough, the one case in which the text proclaims David's guilt is implausible. But the presentation is nonetheless revealing.

Compelled to kill Uriah, David uses the victim himself as the unwitting bearer of the order that he be killed. Through Uriah, David secretly instructs Joab to arrange a setback in battle. In this, Uriah is not the only casualty: David deliberately sacrifices a number of warriors, and exposes others, who survive, to mortal danger, in order to rid himself of the victim of his own appetites. Joab, even under written instruction, fears a rebuke for adopting the inept tactic necessitated by his objective. He instructs the messenger of defeat to mention to David that Uriah died in the foray. And David, immediately, forgets the dead, as is his nature: "The sword," he says, "consumes randomly."

David wants a man dead. He secretly tells Joab to kill him. Joab has him killed at the hands of enemy warriors. The pattern is precisely the same as in the other cases, except that here the secret communication between David and Joab, and the reasons for David's machinations, are exposed — by divine revelation. The source takes considerable pains, here, to assert that David was indeed a killer. So it must have an interest in the concession.[32] His alleged victim, however, is a man of little political importance, apparently without children, a foreigner, employed as a mercenary rather than situated in a lineage. Uriah's name is qualified only by his ethnic affiliation without even the name of his father as a mark of identity, and he is not a scion of Saul's. It is only from other

---

32. Standard procedure among critics is either to regard the story of Uriah as the start of a "Succession Narrative" that is different in origin from the "History of David's Rise" or to excise the story as "secondary" — a late insertion. This recourse reflects a lack of clarity as to the agenda of 2 Samuel, on which see below, Chapter 22. The text makes sense *only* shortly after David's time.

texts that we can infer that Uriah's wife was Ahitophel's granddaughter (see below, Chapter 22).

It was particularly important that Joab engineer the death of Uriah. The author of Samuel intended to expose the irony in Joab's role in bringing on the Absalom revolt, the punishment for David's adultery with Bathsheba. He particularly meant to justify Joab's execution by Solomon. The technique that the author ascribes to David in this case is exactly the one that David's opponents, who numbered most of the population of Cisjordan, must have imagined in the others. Yet note the differences. Politically, Uriah's is the least motivated, and thus least obvious, of David's murders. The sword consumes randomly in battle, so the stratagem is an undetectable method of killing. Uriah himself carried the order for his death, so no one other than David and Joab were privy to it.

Probably, the story, down to the account of the adultery, is untrue. But false or true, it attributes a subtlety, a professionalism, to David that is remarkable. So long as David and Joab kept silent, divine revelation was the only possible means of exposure. For real certainty, in this case, could not follow from a coincidence of an affair between David and Bathsheba and the subsequent death of Uriah. It looks as though David has been framed for Uriah's death, while he is alibied for all the others. Why? An answer is offered at the end of the discussion, in Chapter 22.

C. The Apology and the Absalom Revolt

This question, and the patterns of the killings, lead to another question: why is the Absalom story told as it is? It exonerates David of Amasa's murder, and justifies the execution of Sheba. It also acquits David of proximate responsibility for the uprising.

Still, on balance, the account advertises the justice of Absalom's lost cause. First, Absalom is Yahweh's tool for fulfilling the curse David brought upon himself: Absalom's career is David's punishment for adultery and murder. Second, Absalom is the wronged party in the instance of his sister's rape. He avenges this atrocity with the only means at his disposal, and nevertheless must endure the punishment normally accorded a murderer, rather than an executioner.

Third, the entire nation rises with Absalom, and regards David as a "man of blood" for his treatment of the house of Saul. He is viewed as a thug. Fourth, the apology in Samuel claims that David was not merely reluctant to see Absalom dead, but adamant that the rebel be spared. Fifth, David actually promises to appoint, and for a few days does appoint, Absalom's chief of staff to be his own secretary of the army.

This explains why the promise of dynasty in 2 Sam. 7 is postponed from David, with the charter for building a temple, onto his successor. 2 Samuel claims that, after the dynastic charter, David merited death for killing Uriah. Only the terms of the charter prevented Yahweh from rejecting his dynasty. Later texts, in Kings and Psalms, take the opposite view: it was David's merit that trumped Solomon's sins; "for the sake of ('my servant') David," Yahweh preserves the dynasty in Judah. In comparison, 2 Samuel goes out of its way to stress David's defects.

Absalom's revolt is Yahweh's way of punishing David for Uriah's death. It is to underscore this point that the text identifies David as Yahweh's agent when he contributes to the process and relents about Absalom's exile. This is also why Ahitophel's advice, that Absalom sleep with his father's wives on the palace roof, also leads to the caesura comparing Ahitophel to a divine oracle. It is certainly extraordinary for any dynasty to concede that a revolt it successfully suppressed was ordained by its god. The case may even be unique.

Near Eastern royal literature attributes defeats to divine anger: Mesha of Moab maintains that Israel had conquered Moab, before he liberated it, because the Moabite god Chemosh was "angry with the land." Amos and the classical prophets attribute Israelite defeats to Yahweh's anger. But delegitimating one's own dynasty, even temporarily, is a remarkable tactic of persuasion: only a usurper like Solomon, who pushed aside and then executed the heir expected by "all Israel" to sit on the throne (1 Kgs. 2:15), would adopt it. The tactic is a call for allies from among the antagonists of the establishment.

If the revolt was Yahweh's doing, the participants, as Yahweh's instruments, bear no guilt for their treason. This element of the apology, like the others, is conciliatory. Indeed, the appointment of Amasa, albeit fleeting, the promise to spare Shimei, and the claim that David campaigned actively in other ways for re-election by both Judah and Israel after his victory, indicate that the policy of conciliation was initiated from the time of the revolt. Even the reasons for the rebellion are obscured — Absalom made extravagant campaign promises, is what we read.[33] But the real grievances are not articulated, except to be dismissed in the rest of the history: David murdered Saul's heirs, David's opponents claimed. We can, however, depend on the fact that an even more gruesome history of bullying and bloodshed underlies the united opposition of the population of Cisjordan to David personally, not necessarily to his dynasty — the uprising is led by his son, and the troops are commanded by his nephew.

---

33. 2 Sam. 15:1-6. This is almost certainly a code for a promise of lowering popular obligations to the state, or ending corruption, or placing both administration and the means of corruption in the hands of the lineage structures. See further below, Chapter 21.

The suppression of the grievances from the literary account, like the portrayal of the revolt as divinely inspired, stems from the strategy of reconciliation. The apology is irrelevant at any significant remove from Solomon's reign. And this coincides with Hayim Tadmor's piquant observation that this sort of elaborate royal apology tends to arise early in the reigns of kings whose mothers were heavily involved in a contested succession.[34]

Another pattern confirms this argument. For all the political deaths, David is furnished with an alibi. The list includes Nabal, Saul, and Jonathan,[35] Abner, Ishbaal, Absalom, Amasa. And a famine and Yahweh's oracle forced his hand with the rest of the House of Saul. His behavior in all these cases is woven together with the character stamped upon him by the author of the apology: his unconventionality, his forbearance toward foes, validates his every political alibi. The man who does not mourn after the death of the son of his adultery is extravagantly demonstrative whenever an enemy, including his rebel son Absalom, dies. In other words, David's alleged unconventionality is the counterspin to claims he was a monster.

The flip side of the pattern is more important. The killings for which David *is* made responsible, in which his character shifts, are two executions, of Shimei and of Joab, undertaken by Solomon. The narrator convicts him of one murder only: that of Uriah, the first husband of Solomon's mother. Some of David's killings alibi him for other murders. Indeed, Joab's death also confirms David's alibis in three killings: it avenges not just the Saulide, Abner, and the rebel commander Amasa, but, implicitly, the rebel icon Absalom. However, the killings that might be described as elective are all tied up with Solomon. For the murder of Uriah, too, David attempts first to alibi his adultery, then to alibi the murder, but is found out by mantic means. For the executions of Shimei and Joab, he is vindicated by dint of personal inaction. Again, David kills for Solomon, only.

What is surprising here is that Solomon should have generated conciliatory

---

34. Hayim Tadmor, "Autobiographical Apology in the Royal Assyrian Literature," in Tadmor and Moshe Weinfeld, *History, Historiography and Interpretation*, 36-57, esp. 54-57. Tadmor is surely wrong, however, to entertain the possibility that the apology is a Davidic document, inasmuch as the exculpation of David for doing Saulides dirty continues through the Absalom revolt — to his decision to award half Mephibaal's estates to Ziba — and even into Solomon's reign, when that king finally gives both Joab and Shimei what for. See further below. The image of David projected in the apology — the image mainly of a victim — is not what David himself would have liked. Far more likely is Stefan Heym's intuition, in *The King David Report* (New York: Putnam, 1973), that the apology is Solomon's work. On the chronological issues, see Chapter 13.

35. A second alibi is furnished in 1 Sam. 21:11-15(12-16): the rumor that David had been a vassal of Achish of Gath was false!

apology. David spent his career, on the face of the presentation, hiding responsibility for his actions. He did not build a temple or an imposing capital. He did
not murder his slain political opponents. All of 2 Samuel is his Broadway Alibi.
David operated, at surface level, according to traditional restraints on the exercise of power. Solomon *projected* power through display, from the imposition
of governors over districts of Israel to the press-gang construction of the temple and palace and of fortresses throughout the country. Solomon executed
Adonijah for asking for possession of David's concubine Abishag. He confined
Shimei, killing him on David's orders for violating his parole. He banished
Abiathar. And, in a very significant episode, he condemned Joab for murdering
Amasa and Abner.

This last action speaks volumes about the apology in 2 Samuel. David had
told Solomon, the text claims, "You know what Joab did to the two officers of
the armies of Israel, to Abner son of Ner and to Amasa son of Yeter, that he slew
them and introduced the blood of war in *šālôm* ('in shalom,' 'in peace,' or 'in alliance'). . . . Don't send his grey head to hell in *šālôm*," i.e., peacefully (1 Kgs.
2:5-6).

The manner in which Solomon yields to his father's bidding is telling. Unlike David, Solomon does not initiate violence, but uses it as a weapon of justice
in reaction to provocation — to restore balance. Joab, "who took the part of
Adonijah, though he did not Absalom's" (1 Kgs. 2:28), dictates his own death
even in the sanctuary of Yahweh's tent. Bidden by Benaiah to emerge, so that
Benaiah can strike him down, Joab stymies his executioner, "No, I will die here"
(1 Kgs. 2:30); "'Do as he says,' says the king. . . ." So Benaiah goes back and kills
him (1 Kgs. 2:31-35).[36]

Abner's death in 2 Sam. 3 links directly to this text. Three times 2 Sam. 3
stresses that Abner was in *šālôm* with David (vv. 21-23). It also explicitly points
out that it was because of a deed of Abner in battle, or war-time, the slaying of
Asahel, that Joab and Abishai killed him. In other words, the "sons of Zeruiah"
took vengeance inappropriately: they avenged a battlefield death in time of
peace.[37] Because Joab had killed one with whom he was in alliance (harmony),

---

36. On the nature of Joab's death in the narrative, see Halpern, *The First Historians*,
146: "Solomon is passive even in carnage. . . ." Note that Exod. 21:14 provides for the removal of a homicide from refuge at an altar. This custom is not invoked in justification of
Solomon's decision, whose justice thus depends wholly on Joab's unwitting consent. The
law is later than David's time. See below, Chapter 22.

37. Peace may mean alliance here. These same texts present the solution to the problem of Huldah's oracle in 2 Kgs. 22:15-20 that Josiah would die "in peace": the exilic editor
of Kings reports that Josiah fought Neco, who was assaulting the king of Assyria; the implication is that Josiah was Neco's ally, the opposite of the historical record, which was still

David later instructs Solomon: don't send his grey locks to Sheol in peace (harmony). Thus 1 Kgs. 2:5-6 very much pick up the thread of 2 Sam. 3, both explicitly and implicitly, contrasting killing in peace with killing in battle.

This connection, and the justification of Shimei's execution, make it clear that 2 Samuel was geared to conclude in the account of Solomon's reign. As related above, Solomon tells Shimei not to cross the eastern boundary of Jerusalem, in the direction of the Saulide center of Bahurim. When his slaves escape westward, to Gath, he goes to extradite them from King Achish. Solomon kills him for leaving the town at all.

It does not take much in the way of imagination to realize that the slaves' escape, and their choice of Gath as a refuge, are convenient for Solomon. The king of Gath is David's old sovereign, Achish, or less probably, a grandson named for him (1 Kgs. 2:39-40). Shimei's unimpeded journey to Gath indicates that relations remained warm, and that he expected extradition to be simple. The episode has the marks of staging, again, both the flight and the refuge having probably been arranged by Solomon. It would not be surprising, assuming that any slaves escaped at all, if Solomon killed them at the end of the tirade he directs at Shimei (1 Kgs. 2:41-46). In that case, Benaiah, Solomon's hatchet man, will silently have added two notches to his sword.

The account of Solomon's accession culminates in 1 Kgs. 5. Here, Hiram of Tyre, whose diplomatic mission marks David's "arrival" as a king, acknowledges Solomon's legitimacy. Solomon, or the author of his account, made Joab the chief agent for the violent deaths in David's reign. This alone does not imply the writing of 2 Samuel in the first years of Solomon's reign. But the framework of interpretation that the apology draws on was probably the child of that era.

Solomon could not execute David for these murders. His killing of Joab was partisan, since Joab backed the "usurper" Adonijah for the throne. But Solomon could present Joab's execution as that of the trigger-man for all those violent deaths and, paradigmatically, those of Abner and Amasa — north and south. Ridding himself at once of an adversary and of someone who could relate the truth about David, Solomon remade his father as the political victim of Joab and others, except where he, Solomon, was the beneficiary or agent of the

---

known, e.g., to the Chronicler, to Herodotus, and to Josephus. The reason for the reversal in Kings is to infer an ironic fulfillment of Huldah's oracle: Josiah died at the hand of one with whom he was "at peace" — in alliance. See Baruch Halpern and David S. Vanderhooft, "The Editions of Kings in the 7th-6th Centuries B.C.E.," *HUCA* 62 (1991): 221-29; Halpern, "Why Manasseh Is Blamed for the Babylonian Exile: The Evolution of a Biblical Tradition," *VT* 48 (1998): 473-514.

murder. Solomon was the despot David dreamed of being, and his apology sheltered David from the reputation that his adversaries imposed on him — of the devious, rather than the put-upon, politician, whose enemies made a habit of waking up dead.

Why is Solomon, who settles old and new accounts draconically, concerned that David should not have done so? Why is he concerned with reconciliation when in year 24 of his reign, on the accession of Shishaq, he will pillage the north — sell the tribe of Asher — to secure the south?[38] The strategy of conciliation in the south, especially in the royal family — about the deaths of Absalom and Amasa — reflects a policy of co-option, of setting Judah apart, always a part of Solomon's administrative strategy. But central is the chronology: early in his reign, Solomon made Absalom's daughter the chief wife of Rehoboam, who would bear his successor.[39] Rehoboam was a child at the time, but the war wounds had not healed.

This is also why Rehoboam, son of an Ammonite princess, was made Solomon's heir: Ammonite collaboration was central to David's victory, and was a stick to the carrot of co-option for the north. The Solomonic schism, the secession of Israel from Judah now so vividly attested in the Tel Dan stela, was already on the horizon, and all the detail about the actors in Samuel reflects the early Solomon's policy of smoothing relations rather than the later policy of abandoning the north. Later, when Solomon had consolidated his hold on all the organs of the state, imposed his stamp from above on the Israelite landscape, the velvet glove could be doffed from the mailed fist. All this is explored in Chapter 22.

The point is, 2 Samuel is early, and very much in earnest — for after the loss of the north, and after the passage of years, much of its detail would surely have been omitted, as it was later in Chronicles. It concerns itself with accusations that David murdered his way to the throne, accusations not suddenly in-

38. Baruch Halpern, "Sectionalism and the Schism," *JBL* 93 (1974): 519-32. See below, Chapter 21.

39. Josephus *Ant.* 7.190: Rehoboam married Absalom's daughter. A Greek plus to 2 Sam. 14:27 is much the same. But in *Ant.* 8.249 Maacah, mother of Abijah, is the daughter not of Absalom himself but of Absalom's daughter Tamar. The adjustment probably arises because Kings reports the name of Asa's (queen-)mother as Maacah as well, and some source regarded this as a contradiction — that Rehoboam fathered Abijah by Maacah, then Abijah fathered Asa by her. In fact, it is more likely that Maacah continued in the role of queen-mother (not biological mother) after the brief reign of Abijah. But *Ant.* 8.249 is a brilliant harmonization! It probably stems from Josephus's *Vorlage*, as it doesn't appear already in the earlier treatment, just in the later. On the chronology of Rehoboam's marriage, see below, Chapter 13.

vented in a late period. Its portrait of Israel's struggle to unseat David is actuated by an intention to rally elites hostile to David to Solomon's side.[40] Second Samuel alibis David for his murders, and frames him for Uriah's death, which is the cause of Absalom's revolt. We know that Samuel is accurate because it is nothing but lies.

This conclusion brings us to the question of epistemology. The foregoing is a very textual overture to some historical issues. And that is the point. Historians, if they exercise their imagination at all — and history without imagination is dead history, or, to be explicit, is philology masquerading as history — can invert the obvious implications of textual data.

Sir Ronald Syme revolutionized the study of ancient Rome by taking the history of his subject from the Antonine, not Augustan, perspective.[41] The task of the ancient historian, of any historian, is in the end to recognize and reconstruct the cacophonous constructions of historical realities, the competing and merely alternative narratives, the possible alternative narratives that were or in some cases might have been pertinent to the historical agents, the human beings, involved in historical transactions. It is the historian's burden to elect his or her own narrative that includes, privileges, excludes, or repudiates elements of all those agents' voices.

History is not necessarily accurate, though it must strive to be accurate and correct in the proportions it ascribes to causal factors. Intentional disregard for evidence, intentional inaccuracy or imagination on the basis of no evidence, distinguishes romance, or historical fiction, or even fraudulent history, from real history. Thus, even though Theodor Mommsen's *Römische Geschichte* is shot through with judgments and allegations from which contemporary historians differ, it remains a work of history. Similarly, in the foregoing account, I have presented David as a serial murderer. Other scholars might differ, and might even attribute my own predilections to a contemporary Western obsession with serial killers.[42] Neither my own work nor such a riposte would fall outside the category of history, even though the two would be contradictory.

The text, like the artifact, encodes intention. But the intention of the text is to lead the reader in a particular direction. So contemplation of the alternative

---

40. See esp. Tomoo Ishida's studies, "Adonijah the Son of Haggith and His Supporters," in *The Future of Biblical Studies — the Hebrew Scriptures,* ed. Richard Elliott Friedman and H. G. M. Williamson (Atlanta: Scholars, 1987), 165-87; "The Story of Abner's Murder: A Problem Posed by the Solomonic Apologist," *ErIsr* 23 (1993): 109*-13*.

41. Ronald Syme, *The Roman Revolution* (1939, repr. Oxford: Oxford University Press, 1960), 1.

42. See Philip Jenkins, *Using Murder: The Social Construction of Serial Homicide* (New York: de Gruyter, 1994), esp. 57-78.

possibilities demands that a historian invert the values and claims of the text and propose alternative scenarios, for which there is no other evidence. Epistemologically, history can be reduced almost to the level of philology, but oddly, what we know, what we really *know,* is the least interesting part of the field and the easiest to master. R. G. Collingwood even dismissively distinguishes the "chronicle" from the "history": the former is the Thomas Gradgrind "facts, facts, facts" reduction of all that is human in the latter. History is an art, and what is really important is what we can surmise, but never know. The preceding account admits of no archaeological verification whatever. But it furnishes a perspective unrepresented in our texts, and that is what history is for: done properly, it gives voice to those who do not speak in our texts, who have not left ideologically charged records, who have not successfully manipulated the technologies of persuasion at a temporal remove. Properly undertaken, the art of history is casting light into the dark. It is imagination based on evidence.

And imagination does advance our knowledge, as in other fields of scholarship. In the first instance, it is inconceivable that the alibis of Samuel could have been written much after David's day. A hundred years later, Amasa, Abner, Shimei would not only have been lost to living memory, but almost surely devoid of political resonance. The justification of Joab's execution would no longer have been necessary at all (and Chronicles omits the whole episode of Adonijah and its consequences). How do we know this? By imagining the concerns of the audience the text addresses.

Even in the reign of Rehoboam, one would expect an apology to exonerate Solomon totally. There would be no coup d'etat. There would also be no apology for the murders of northerners. These were, after all, beyond Rehoboam's borders, and those of all his successors.

Nor is it conceivable that the text is a later forgery, a satire meant to inspire suspicion that David was a serial killer. The linguistic and geographic data contradict the theory. And, in addition, no Near Eastern political tract exhibits such a subtle sensibility: as in the case of Uriah, an opponent of David would accuse him outright of having caused every death in the political realm during his career, and of being a Philistine agent throughout it. Both of these accusations would have rung true — the second is explored below, in Part V.

Nor is it remotely possible, as those who deny David's role in founding a Judahite dynasty in the 10th century would claim, that the text projected an imaginary dynasty founder back several centuries in time. We have ample documentation of how usurpers legitimated themselves in the ancient world. No new dynasty in the 8th century would have invented two centuries of very mottled prehistory, when the net result could only have been to make itself the object of universal derision. The most common technique for justifying the seizure of power is to admit to usurpation, but then explain that a god elected a new king because one's predecessors were weak, sinful, or corrupt. This is exactly what Samuel does in claiming that Saul was unfit for Yahweh's charisma. To an extent 1 Kgs. 1–2 employ the same technique, in order to justify Solomon's military coup. But Kings and Samuel put the action in the 10th century, where the Tel Dan stela shows it must belong.

Indeed, the books of Kings get all sorts of foreign and indigenous figures in the right sequences, in the right places, at the right times. Starting in the 6th century with Jehoiachin and Nebuchadrezzar, we have external attestation of large numbers of Judahites and foreigners mentioned in Kings and Jeremiah. Among these are Neco, Gemaryahu son of Shaphan, Manasseh, Esarhaddon, Hezekiah, Sennacherib, Sargon, Ahaz, Shalmaneser V, Rezin of Damascus, Hoshea, Tiglath-Pileser III, Pekah, Menahem, Uzziah, Joash of Israel, Ben-Hadad son of Hazael, Jehu, Hazael, Mesha, probably Ahaziah of Judah and Jehoram of Israel, Ahab, Ittobaal of Tyre, Omri, Hadadezer (misremembered as Ben-Hadad, who is later), Shishaq, Hiram of Tyre, and now David. This is quite a list — all based on correlation to external sources — on its own. Since the Jerusalem temple was standing when Kings was written down, it is highly improbable that the authors of Kings got the builder's name wrong. Yet he was not the dynastic founder, David, attested at Tel Dan. This, of itself, is extraordinary, and is again not a feature that would characterize an invented history.

In the end, attacks on the reality of David are unrealistic. They demand a level of certainty — philological certainty — of which the epistemology of history is incapable in all times and at all places, for example, proof that Napoleon's tomb is a fraud and that the crowned heads of Europe together invented him as an excuse to mobilize armies and raise taxes, or that somebody invented our Solomon or our David — murderers both — in order to legitimate a dynasty that first raised its head in 8th-century Jerusalem. It is an error in historical work to hold in doctrinaire fashion with the detailed claims of texts, without attempting to understand the views of those not represented in them. And texts can err in their assumptions as well. But when it comes to a general assumption that the texts *share* with their audiences, an assumption of which they don't need to convince folks, then alternative possibilities have such a diminished probability that they hardly register as blips on the historical horizon. This is a problem of practical historical epistemology. Perhaps, in the end, it is like the bumblebee or the curve ball: it can't be done in theory, but it works just dandy, thanks. A text that addresses the sorts of accusations with which Samuel is concerned is perhaps the best evidence of David's activity, and of the nature of Israelite society at the time.

Was David the maniac that his opponents accused him of being? And if so, how did he succeed in becoming a nearly universal icon of piety, decorum, and success? In the next chapters, we will examine the texts relating to David's foreign wars, in an effort to reconstruct the exterior contours of his kingdom and in a further attempt to discern the technologies of history-writing that were put to use in the account of his life. At the end of that process, we shall stand in a somewhat better position to address the internal history of his reign.

PART III

DEFINING DAVID'S EMPIRE

CHAPTER 5

How to Take Up What Kings Set Down

A. History, the Public Form of Memory

Philosophers and even the occasional reflective historian sometimes take up the question, what is history? Among students of the ancient Near East, Jan Huizinga's formulation has gained a certain currency: "History is the intellectual form in which a civilization renders account to itself about its past."[1] History on this account is the organization and presentation of some aspect of the past.

This definition is serviceable because it is so broad. But people of one "civilization" can write the history of another. Further, there is a sense in which any *record*, any representation meant publicly to preserve memory, even of the present, should also be brought under the same umbrella. When (En)mebara(ge)si left his name and title, king of Kish, on stone bowls, it may have been his intention to establish ownership. Given the limited number of people who could read or even see the text, it seems more likely that what he left was in fact a record, specifically a record of production. But when Pabilgagi, king of Umma, inscribed a statuette for Enlil, with his own name and title, it is more likely that he expected to project a record of both into the future.[2] Indeed, even paleolithic

---

1. "A Definition of the Concept of History," in *Philosophy and History: Essays Presented to Ernst Cassirer,* ed. Raymond Klibansky and H. J. Paton (New York: Harper, 1963), 9; picked up in Near Eastern Studies first by W. W. Hallo, "Assyrian Historiography Revisited," *ErIsr* 14 (1978): 1-7; thereafter John Van Seters, *In Search of History,* 1.

2. For the texts, see Jerrold S. Cooper, *Sumerian and Akkadian Royal Inscriptions,* 1:

cave-paintings, whatever their motivation in superstition, were intended to provide a stable representation of animals seen in the past but presumed to exist in the present.

History cannot be described accurately — and the task is to describe it, not to define it — without reference to a time beyond the past. History is always written, recording is always done, not for the present, except in its grossest form, but for the future. Only in that context can the recording of events, indeed, even the researching of them, be understood as a purposive activity. Why is it that history is written by the victors, after all? It is because down the line, after it has been written, the victors, the *survivors,* have adopted the version they have adopted. It was Charles Fort who observed that "the survival of the fittest" predicated that the fittest were those who survived: the idea boiled down to the survival of the survivors. "History is written by the victors" is another way of saying that history is written by the historians whose work survives.

As noted in Chapter 4, R. G. Collingwood distinguished between chronicling — maintaining records — and historiography. The historian was a researcher, ascertaining information that was not available at the start of his or her inquiry, information of which he or she was formerly ignorant. The chronicler, by way of contrast, simply recorded facts. This is the difference, ideologically if not in practice, between a Herodotus, asking after customs and backgrounds, and a Thucydides, who maintains that only facts borne out by eyewitnesses merit scrutiny. Thucydides portrays himself as a journalist or chronicler, a role much beloved by those who believe that history should be a branch of philology.[3] In fact, his editorialization abounds. He frequently resorts to the reconstruction of motivations and events. He embellishes, confessedly on some occasions, and undoubtedly in other cases. He is too good a historian, and far too full of himself, to be a chronicler.

And yet, not to exclude the maintenance of records, like chronicles, gener-

---

Presargonic Inscriptions. AOS Translation Series 1 (New Haven: American Oriental Society, 1986), 18 Ki.1; 91-92 Um.1.

3. See R. G. Collingwood, *The Idea of History* (Oxford: Clarendon, 1946), 11-13. On Herodotean antiquarianism and the Thucydidean school of contemporary history only, see esp. Arnaldo Momigliano, "The Place of Herodotus in the History of Historiography," *History* 43 (1958): 1-13, repr. in *Studies in Historiography* (London: Weidenfeld & Nicolson, 1966), 127-42. The inclusive definition is thus more descriptive of the true range of historical writing. In regularly contrasting true "history" with "scissors-and-paste" history, what Collingwood was mainly concerned to exclude from the genre was not the chronicle so much as the florilegium, i.e., the uncritical parroting of "authorities," into which category the medieval chronicle often fits. Even he would probably have recognized the value of record-keeping as a provision for later research.

ally from the genre of historiography, it is perhaps an error to demand that historical writing be intellectually coherent — aimed at answering particular questions. As a reader, one might hope for coherence, and coherence is certainly something we expect of narrative history or biography, as we do of all other forms of literary fiction. But the astute user of records, the professional researcher, hopes instead for complexity, even diffuseness. It would have been delightful, for example, had the archaeologists of the early part of this century anticipated that scholars would be asking different questions today, and collected soils and skeletal materials: they would have had to do so without integrating them into a coherent intellectual program. It would be equally useful had we the equivalent of newspapers — even just the advertising in them — from the ancient world.[4]

Historians must try to reconstitute the sort of unbiased sample of sources that existed before some ancient colleague organized it, and selected what was germane to prove his thesis. One of the great advantages that accrues to historians making use of the biblical testimony is the incorporation of so much source material into it, material that is often at cross-purposes with the compilation into which it is fit. Similarly, the multiplicity of voices in the Bible, the books of various prophets, poets, and historians, makes it much easier to arrive at a critical historical verdict than in the case of the relatively seamless work of a Thucydides.

So far, the issue is the production of history. What of the consumption of history? As a document or even a piece of evidence, a historical record is always a part of the present in which it is under examination. And in that sense, remains at an archaeological site or a text unearthed after five millennia or the latest entry in the History Book Club are all the same. So it is an error to distinguish between the production and the consumption of history in the stark way that philosophers historically have done. Henri Bergson argued that time is in fact becoming, duration. Einstein, when Bergson wrote, had already abolished

---

4. A study detailing the origins and development of commercial advertisement in premodern societies would be a considerable service to the historical profession. To be sure, royal monuments functioned in part in this capacity; but, living as we do in a society in which almost any surface or medium is annexed for the purpose of peddling, our ignorance about ancient equivalents — the commercial role of shape, surface-treatment, and decoration on pottery, for example — is a lacuna that is very hard to explain. However, see e.g., Alexander H. Joffe, "Alcohol and Social Complexity in Ancient Western Asia," *Current Anthropology* 39 (1998): 297-322; Jonathan C. Edmondson, "*Instrumenta Imperii:* Law and Imperialism in Republican Rome," in *Law, Politics and Society in the Ancient Mediterranean World,* ed. Baruch Halpern and Deborah W. Hobson (Sheffield: Sheffield Academic, 1993), 156-92.

the idea of time as sequence, as something that could be understood in spatial terms — there is, for example, no such thing as a "point" in time, an indivisible moment that can be isolated from the time around it.

Unlike Kubla Khan's garden, no period of time can be "with walls and towers girded round." One cannot, for example, logically take a snapshot of the universe, since the speed of light dictates that the snapshot will capture distant galaxies only as they were, not as they are. Though less obviously, the same is true in human affairs. The implication is that the past is not gone, but is incapsulated in the present.[5] So too, by extension, is the contemplation, and thus the construction, of the past. Earlier constructions of the past remain with us now, however we may amend them. The projection of memory into the future is, oddly enough, dialectical: to focus only on the projection, without consideration of the future reception, is to miss out on half the dialectic.

Bergson also argued that life forms were the only things in the universe that defied entropy. In doing so, they represented a macroscopic manifestation of subatomic indeterminacy, of the randomizing element in physics. From his viewpoint, what enabled us to reverse the principle of entropy was that our senses evolved in the way they did in order to maximize our capacity to accumulate fuel.[6] We see doorways, for example, as empty, and walls as solid, instead of perceiving them accurately as looser and denser configurations of molecules. The reason is, this stops us running into walls. Our senses, in other words, evolved to organize the world in such a way as to facilitate our life in it — and particularly hunting, the counter-entropic collection of fuel. Even David Hume conceded, after completely demolishing our epistemology even about the present, that it made a difference whether he left his house by the door or the window.[7] Bergson, without endeavoring to prove the proposition, was able to explain how it was so. We may not be able to prove, with Boolean logic, that our perception is accurate, and in many instances it is not. But the very history of the evolution of the species shows that our sense perception is, statistically, reliable.

In the same way, history is the story that we have evolved to tell ourselves, at the level of biological rather than atomic perception. It is the most conve-

---

5. Henri Bergson, *Creative Evolution* (New York: Holt, 1911); the term "incapsulated" is from R. G. Collingwood, *An Autobiography* (1939, repr. Oxford: Oxford University Press, 1978), 98 (see 97-99). While the latter makes no reference to the former, the connection is sufficiently narrow to demand an inference of direct influence.

6. Bergson, *Creative Evolution*.

7. David Hume, *Dialogues Concerning Natural Religion*. Library of Liberal Arts 174 (Indianapolis: Bobbs-Merrill, 1962).

nient and efficient method of organizing and transmitting certain types of knowledge.

History is the way we organize our understanding of the world as it has been. It is a counter-entropic tool for the construction of identity. In the individual, it takes the form of memory, permitting adaptation to local conditions. But in the community, it is the basis of cohesion. It is the building block of band behavior. So Huizinga's definition captures its most essential feature, if not its range.

In addition, using the same historical knowledge on which we base our individual and communal identities, we project our experiences and the estimated efficacy of our responses to them, into future situations. It is no coincidence that the earliest rationalizers of historical presentation in Greece drew the conclusion that their work could guide future policies.[8] Memory, after all, is the school of hard knocks, from which we learn to trust or not to trust, to act or to temporize. History as it is practiced is only the reduction of memory about human intention, either living or latent, at a public level. It is the public form of memory.

This description is broader than Huizinga's, even if we suppose him to have meant a culture, rather than "a civilization."[9] It includes a bewildering variety of forms, even purely literary forms, a multiplicity of which existed already in the Bronze Age.[10] But there are important parallels among them. To take just the most obvious implements, Egyptian tomb biographies contrast with sometimes telegraphic royal inscriptions, but find parallels in Mesopotamian *narû* literature. Poems celebrating Ramses II's Battle of Qadesh or his son Merneptah's Libyan campaign differ from the annals and display inscriptions that

8. See, e.g., Thucydides 1.22; Polybius; on the Hittite Old Kingdom annals, probably the closest analogy to 2 Samuel, see Harry A. Hoffner, Jr., "Histories and Historians of the Ancient Near East: The Hittites," *Or* 49 (1980): 283-332.

9. So the critique of Van Seters, *In Search of History,* 1 n. 2: Van Seters argues (against Huizinga's intention in the essay) that the term "civilization" implies that Huizinga meant that history was only a comprehensive national record, from the start to the present, of a whole civilization, not a mere culture, and thus that anything earlier than Herodotus was to be excluded; however, anyone engaged in writing is part of some "civilization." Nor is it patent that there was no such effort earlier than Herodotus: the Deuteronomistic History, after all, is typically dated to the 7th-6th centuries.

10. For categories of historiography, see Van Seters, *In Search of History;* Donald B. Redford, *Pharaonic King-Lists, Annals, and Daybooks* (Mississauga: Benben, 1986); A. Kirk Grayson, "Histories and Historians of the Ancient Near East: Assyria and Babylonia," *Or* 49 (1980): 140-94; Hoffner, *Or* 49 (1980): 283-332; Hayim Tadmor and Moshe Weinfeld, *History, Historiography and Interpretation;* F. M. Fales, ed., *Assyrian Royal Inscriptions: New Horizons in Literary, Ideological, and Historical Analysis.* Orientis Antiqui Collectio 17 (Rome: Istituto per l'Oriente, 1981), to name just a few.

dominate the Mesopotamian theater, but resemble poetic epics concerning Tukulti-Ninurta and Tiglath-Pileser I. Hittite court records, such as the Deeds of Šuppiluliuma and the Annals of Muršili, make very extensive use of diplomatic correspondence and direct dialogue, often out of their proper time. In many respects, they resemble Samuel and Kings more than anything in Mesopotamia. But they undergo the same transition, from memoirs to demarcated annals, reporting on each year in sequence, that occurs in Assyria under Tiglath-Pileser I. This is not to mention other documents often not considered historiographic, such as treaty prologues, prologues to law codes, legal documents such as contracts, deeds, boundary markers, dedication inscriptions, and the like, let alone chronological records such as king lists and lists of the names of years. The parallel developments in a variety of cultures suggest that historical techniques, like other technologies from the paleolithic onward, spread rapidly from place to place.

How are we to apply all this to biblical history writing, specifically to the stories about David in Samuel? In the first instance, we must understand the intention dictating the projection of the past into the future. In the second, we must understand how previous constructions of the past, and particularly the techniques for constructing the past, were employed by the author of our materials. Examination of these questions will establish that the scribes responsible for Samuel employed both old and recently developed methods for the presentation of historical information.

Consideration of the same questions will also, curiously enough, confirm the conclusions of Chapters 3 and 4 that the composition of Samuel cannot be placed later than the 9th century, and probably should be dated in the 10th century, shortly after David's death. But most of all, contemplation of the evidence in this framework permits the development of basic rules of interpretation of historical documents from royal contexts.

Historical recitation is an adaptive method of defining community: this is by definition true where the recitation survives through scribal transmission, through the activity of a community, as in the case of David. The means of defining community for the elite with unmediated access to the texts were presumably different from the techniques used to define community for those whose access was indirect. This division of audiences has practical implications that will occupy us in the following chapters.

Briefly, the historian must tell a version of the truth. This version must present a particularly fine face to an outsider audience, with indirect access, manipulating the emotions of that audience as the author intends to do. But the version the historian produces must also not so outrage the audience of insiders as to have them rolling in the aisles with laughter (see below, Section C).

B. The Image of the King in Royal Propaganda

It has long been clear that biblical historiography, in the books of Kings at least, participated in the historical Republic of Letters characterizing the ancient Near East of its time. As early as 1934, J. A. Montgomery argued that certain phrases in Kings come from Israelite annals compiled during the reigns of the kings whom they described.[11] Many scholars have followed his lead.

Montgomery thought that the phrase "then" or "at that time" in Kings, common in the Assyrian record, reflected an origin in annals. However, in large measure, these phrases permit a segue from one to another topic without an implication of chronological sequence (although they could have such implications as well — it is the ambiguity that makes them so useful).[12] So the phrases

11. J. A. Montgomery, "Archival Data in the Book of Kings," *JBL* 53 (1934): 46-52; for further, similar bibliography, see Baruch Halpern, *The First Historians,* 237 n. 19.

12. See Hayim Tadmor, "History and Ideology in the Assyrian Royal Inscriptions," in Fales, *Assyrian Royal Inscriptions,* 13-33; Baruch Halpern, "A Historiographic Commentary on Ezra 1–6 — Achronological Narrative and Dual Chronology in Israelite Historiography," in *The Hebrew Bible and Its Interpreters,* ed. William H. Propp, Halpern, and David Noel Freedman (Winona Lake: Eisenbrauns, 1990), 81-142; David A. Glatt, *Chronological Displacement in Biblical and Related Literatures.* SBLDS 139 (Atlanta: Scholars, 1993). An example of consecution may be the "then" in 2 Kgs. 12:18. If consecutive in function, it would imply a date for Hazael's depredations in Judah after 819 (Joash's 23rd year — 12:6[7]). This is a chronology that would allow Hazael time to recoup from his devastating defeats at the hand of Shalmaneser III in the 830s, then to dominate Israel before reaching the coast during the reign of Jehoahaz. It would accord with 2 Kgs. 10:32-33, which attribute the loss of Transjordan to Hazael during Jehu's reign, and 13:3, 7, which speak of complete vassalship to Hazael under Jehoahaz. If this "then" is consecutive, our understanding of the stela from Tel Dan would be equally enhanced. As indicated in passing below, the stela is not attributable to Hazael, yet recounts his "achievement" of 841, the deaths of Joram of Israel and Ahaziah of Judah. Both were victims, in fact, of Jehu, if the account of 2 Kgs. 9 is to be credited. For a parallel, note the claim of Shalmaneser III to have killed, or alternatively that for fear of his approaching the locals killed, the king of the Balih region: Ernst Michel, "Ein neuentdeckter Annalen-Text Salmanassars III," *WO* 1/6 (1952), 464:2:20-21; "Die Assur-Texte Salmanassars III (858-824). 7. Fortsetzung," *WO* 2/2 (1955), 149:54-55 (Black Obelisk): Year 6: cities of Balih kill Giammu, lord of their cities. In the Kurkh Monolith, it is the "nobles" who killed Giammu: D. D. Luckenbill, *Ancient Records of Assyria and Babylonia* (Chicago: University of Chicago Press, 1926), 610; on the Calah bull-colossi, it is the (people) of the region: Luckenbill, 646. In the Marmorplatte, however, Shalmaneser claims to have killed him: Ernst Michel, "Die Assur-Texte Salmanassars III. (858-824). 6. Fortsetzung," *WO* 2/1 (1954), 32:13-14, or at least the (ambiguous) logogram leaves that impression. On the Tel Dan stela, see the collection of articles edited by Frederick H. Cryer (forthcoming).

signal a relationship to the genre of display inscriptions, which are organized by topic or geography rather than by chronological sequence.[13] A topical order of reportage permitted the writers to punch home themes by building them to a crescendo, and to veil temporary setbacks which a king later overcame. The display model was always a powerful implement in the propaganda tool kit of Near Eastern kings.

In Kings, the closest connections to display inscriptions concentrate in the report on Solomon's reign. The literary sequence there is thematic, not chronological,[14] but the intention is to create an illusion of chronological sequence.[15] That is why the revolt of Hadad, in Edom, inspired by (unexaggerated) reports of David's demise, is related at the end of Solomon's reign. However slow the post, it is unlikely that news of David's death reached Egypt only after 30 years. Likewise, Rezin's revolt is a result of Solomon's senile apostasy. Yet Rezin's military career began at latest in the middle of David's reign, and must have concluded during the first half of Solomon's (see below). The historian here understands that revolt was early. He claims either that success came late, or that the revolt itself was proleptic punishment for Solomon's later sins.

The structure of the account of Solomon conforms to expectations. The image of Solomon as king also reflects a contemporary vision. What is a king supposed to be? In different eras, there are different answers. Solomon's image conforms to the images projected by antecedent and contemporary kings in the Near East. The chronological window for the presentation runs from the 11th to the 9th century, and no later.

Kings portrays Solomon as a natural philosopher:

13. Particularly in the pioneering work of Hayim Tadmor, "The Campaigns of Sargon II of Assur: A Chronological-Historical Study," *JCS* 12 (1958): 22-40, 77-100; "The Inscriptions of Nabunaid: Historical Arrangement," in Hans G. Güterbock and Thorkild Jacobsen, eds, *Studies in Honor of Benno Landsberger on his 75th Birthday.* AS 17 (Chicago: Oriental Institute, 1965), 351-63. See further examples (including Tadmor's "History and Ideology") in Fales, *Assyrian Royal Inscriptions.*

14. See Julius Wellhausen, in Friedrich Bleek, *Einleitung in das Alte Testament,* 4th ed. (Berlin: Reimer, 1878), 239-40; Albert Šanda, *Die Bücher der Könige übersetzt und erklärt.* EHAT 9/1 (Münster: Aschendorff, 1911), 326-27; Martin Noth, *Überlieferungsgeschichtliche Studien* (Tübingen: Niemeyer, 1943), 66-67 n. 3.

15. See Halpern, *First Historians,* 152-53; Gary N. Knoppers, *Two Nations under God: The Deuteronomistic History of Solomon and the Dual Monarchies* 1: *The Reign of Solomon and the Rise of Jeroboam.* HSM 52 (Atlanta: Scholars, 1993), 162-63. Incidentally, Ahijah's oracle in ch. 11 is placed *after* the revolts of Rezon and Hadad close to Solomon's 24th year; Halpern, *JBL* 93 (1974): 519-32. One might almost take it as a *reading* of those events.

Solomon's wisdom waxed greater than the wisdom of all the sons of the East/Antiquity, and than all the wisdom of Egypt.[16] He was wiser than any Man, than Ethan the Ezrahite, and Heman and Kalkol and Darda' the sons of Mahol. . . . And he spoke three thousand proverbs, and his songs were one thousand and five. And he spoke of the trees, from the cedar that is on Mount Lebanon unto the hyssop that comes out on the wall, and he spoke of the wild beasts and of the birds and of the lizards (?) and of the fish. (1 Kgs. 4:30-33[5:10-13])

This is the wisdom for which both Hiram (1 Kgs. 5:7[21]) and the Queen of Sheba (10:1ff.) congratulate him.

1 Kings also represents Solomon as an importer of exotic woods (5:8-10[22-24]; 10:11-12), spices (10:10), and animals, as well as goods:

For the king had a fleet of Tarshish in the sea with Hiram's fleet. Once in three years the fleet of Tarshish would arrive, bearing gold and silver, ivories and apes and *tkyym* (baboons? peacocks?). (1 Kgs. 10:22; cf. v. 25)

The word for "ivories," *šenhabbîm*, is not otherwise used in biblical and Mesopotamian sources, which employ *šin(n)- (piri)*, "tooth (of elephant)." Instead, it probably combines the two elements of that designation in a foreign dialect. Similarly, the *tkyym* (baboons or peacocks) imported here and the *'lmgym* wood of 1 Kgs. 10:11-12 cannot be identified with confidence precisely because they were so exotic. The wood is a variety never reported to have been imported again (or perhaps before). Thus, not only are the commodities themselves rare, even the vocabulary describing them is unexampled in later materials.

This presentation coincides with the portrait of the Assyrian king in the Middle Assyrian era. Starting in the late 12th or early 11th century, the king in Assyria portrays himself as a hunter of all sorts of animals and fish[17] and a

16. The reference to Egypt, which is likely in the first instance to the great monuments of the Bronze Age, especially the pyramids and Sphinx, suggests that the element of antiquity is of moment here, and that the term *bny qdm*, "easterners" or "primordials," may refer to antediluvians.

17. A. Kirk Grayson, *Assyrian Rulers of the Early First Millennium* b.c. *I.* RIMA 2 (Toronto: University of Toronto Press, 1991), hereafter cited as RIMA 2: Tiglath-Pileser I 1.vi.55-84; 3:21-25; 4:67-71; 1001:12'-14'; Assur-bel-kala 1(89):r. 8'-11'; 2.iii:29'-35'; possibly, 3(94):7'-9'; 7.iv.2-13, 22-26; Assur-Dan II 1(135):68-72; Adad-Nirari II 2(154):122-125; Tukulti-Ninurta II 5(173):45-46, (175):80-82, (178):134f.; Assurnasirpal II 1(215f.). iii:48f.; 2(226):40-42; 30(291):84-91; 95(350); for Shalmaneser III, see below.

breeder of exotic animals.[18] Among the herds bred are elephants, lions, wild bulls, deer, ibex, monkeys, lions, ostriches, wild asses, bears, panthers, and others. These kings also present themselves as cultivators of exotic plants and trees.[19]

The first Assyrian king to perfect this image was Tiglath-Pileser I, whose reign began in 1114. Tiglath-Pileser reached the Mediterreanean in the Phoenician theater, and may have placed his stamp on local culture, as the references to him in this treatment indicate. Alternatively, he may himself have been influenced by Western culture in the same period. Regardless, he projected the image of the king as natural philosopher, and as naturalist, an image that endured for 200 years in Assyria and that had resonance in the West.

Tiglath-Pileser was the first king of Assyria to collect carnivores. He left a legacy in royal annals particularly in regard to the hunt. Thus, Shalmaneser III, in the 9th century, presents the hunt as the coda of the Year 22 edition of his annals, which close with the campaign of Year 16:

> Ninurta and Nergal, who love (my) priesthood, bestowed on me the wild animals of the field and summoned me to accomplish hunting. I killed 373 wild bulls, 399 lions, from my open chariot with my heroic attack. 23 elephants I cast down in traps.[20]

The inclusion of the hunt in the annals distracts the reader from the reports of campaigning. In the hunt, the king demonstrates his physical skills, whereas in battle, he is more a chess master than a combatant.

In a later annals version, Shalmaneser claims that in Year 17, on his return from the Amanus Mountains in northwestern Syria, he killed 63 mighty wild bulls with magnificent horns, and captured four alive.[21] This report of a hunt during the course of a campaign occurs right where the hunt does as a coda in the annals from Year 22. So, the summary statement about the hunt, which ear-

18. RIMA 2: Tiglath-Pileser I 1.vii.4-10; 4:27-28; perhaps 1001(72):7'-8', 14'; probably Assur-bel-kala 1.9-11; 7.iv.13-22, 26-34; (as statuary trophies, Tiglath-Pileser I 4:67-71; Assur-bel-kala 7.v.16-19); Adad-Nirari II 2(154):125-127: herds of elephants, lions, wild bulls, deer, ibex, wild asses and ostriches; Tukulti-Ninurta II 5(175):81-82 (ostriches, deer); Assurnasirpal II 1(215f.).iii:48f. (wild bulls, ostriches); 2(226):30-38 (monkeys, lions, wild bulls, elephants, ostriches, wild asses, deer, bears, panthers, and others); 30(291-92): 91-100 (likewise); 77. The motif of the zoo apparently begins with Assur-bel-kala.

19. RIMA 2: Tiglath-Pileser I 1.vii.17-27; probably 1001.9'-11'. Assurnasirpal II, probably, RIMA 2.A.0.101.30(290):36-52.

20. Michel, *WO* 1/6 (1952), 454-74, 472: IV:40–474: IV:48. RIMA 3 A.0.102. 6.iv.40-44 (and additional elements of the complex to line 48).

21. At Zuqarri. Michel, *WO* 2/1 (1954), 27-45: III:37-45. RIMA 3 A.0.102.10.iii.37-45.

lier closed an edition of the annals, was later integrated into the description of a campaign not covered in the previous edition: what formerly was the end of the Year 22 annals — an update of all the hunting to Year 22, now appears in the middle of a latter annals version. But the Year 22 annals enumerate only the animals Shalmaneser killed. His "bag" of 373 bulls leaves 310 unaccounted for in the later edition. The later version adds, for Year 19, a trip to the Amanus range for lumber, on the return from which Shalmaneser killed 10 wild bulls with magnificent horns and two calves.[22] Its record indicates that the Year 22 annals had collapsed all his hunting into a summary, as we would otherwise surmise.

In Assyria, then, the ideal king is a hunter. But he is also a breeder. The image of the king as naturalist had roots in the Bronze Age. The premier case is Hatshepsut's expedition to Punt. The hunting of elephants by Thutmosis II and by Hatshepsut's son, Thutmosis III, is also relevant. But in the Iron Age, and in Asia, the ideal first took root as a subject for public celebration in the inscriptions of Tiglath-Pileser I (1114-1076). It persisted as a theme of royal propaganda into the 9th century.

African simians were in particular demand. These were obtained as prestige items in the exchange of royal gifts that went along with diplomatic relations. The same holds for Solomon in 1 Kgs. 10:22. Thus, in Assyria, Assur-bel-kala (1073-1056) reports proudly:

> A large female monkey *(pa-gu-ta* GAL-*ta)*, a crocodile *(nam-su-ḫa)* and a "man of the river" (LÚ ÍD, often thought to be a hippopotamus), creatures of the Great Sea, the king of Egypt sent.[23]

But other exotic animals were also collected.[24] The king became, in royal propaganda, a zoologist. He became a specialist in animal taxonomy. His job was to collect trophies and stud specimens for breeding at home. The hunt was, for the first time, not purely a demonstration of prowess but an economic asset. Exploration was now a component of the royal mission.

Tiglath-Pileser was also the Assyrian king who made the transition from the pure display inscription to true annals — year by year accounts of his activity, proceeding chronologically. In this new form, the annals, he assigned the

---

22. Again at the town, Zuqarri. Michel, "Assur-Texte," *WO* 2/1 (1954), 40: IV:19-22. RIMA 3 A.0.102.10.iv.19-22.

23. Assur-bel-kala: RIMA 2.104.iv:29-30; Adad-Nirari II, 150:48; Assurnasirpal emphatically: 2(226):30-31; 30(292):98-100. For representations of simians, see A. Hamoto, *Der Affe in der altorientalischen Kunst.* Forschungen zur Anthropologie und Religionsgeschichte 28 (Münster, 1995).

24. As the captured *burhiš* of Tiglath-Pileser I: RIMA 2.44:69-70; 57:13'-15'.

hunt and his activities as a naturalist a separate segment in the peroration. He also began a tradition of mentioning in the annals the king's killing of a *naḫiru*, a sea-creature known to the inhabitants of the Phoenician coast, between Arvad and Sumur, as a sea horse and capable of producing "ivory." It is not clear what a *naḫiru* was, though paleozoologists suggest it was a sperm whale. But other sea creatures, including other cetaceans, come into consideration; were it not for the reference to "ivory," a large porpoise would suit the description. In fact, "marine mammal" may be as far as the taxonomic implication of the word goes. Regardless, the animal is a deep-sea inhabitant.[25]

Tiglath-Pileser relates:

> I rode in boats of the Arvadites, and overcame the six-hour journey from the town, Arvad, which is in the midst of the sea, to the town, Sumur (Samuri), of the land, Amurru. I killed a *naḫiru*, which they call a horse of the sea, in the midst of the sea.[26]

Tiglath-Pileser replicated the *naḫiru* in basalt for his palace, to commemorate the achievement.[27] This report, in a display inscription, is included in the course of a campaign. Usually, in the annals a segment, separated from reports on campaigns, is set aside for the hunt and animal husbandry. For Assur-bel-kala (1073-1056), the *naḫiru* hunt belonged together with the rest of the separate report on the hunt and the breeding of animals in the annals' peroration.[28]

Assur-Dan II (934-912) and Adad-Nirari II (911-891) continued the practice of including the hunt and husbandry in a coda at the end of the annals, though neither claims to have hunted the *naḫiru*.[29] Adad-Nirari II claims to have gotten his "large female monkey and small female monkey" as a gift not from Egypt but from Bit-Adini. He reports their receipt as part of the relevant campaign.[30] This

---

25. On the *naḫiru*, see Paula Wapnish, "Towards Establishing a Conceptual Basis for Animal Categories in Archaeology," in *Methods in the Mediterranean: Historical and Archaeological Views on Texts and Archaeology,* ed. David B. Small. Mnemosyne 135 (Leiden: Brill, 1995), 233-73, esp. 250-72: Ugaritic *Anḫr* = *naḫiru* etymologically, but they may not be the same, the former meaning dolphin or monk seal, the latter meaning sperm whale.

26. RIMA 2.37:21-25. The ivory is attested under Assurnasirpal II: RIMA 2:226:30. The name of the animal may mean "snorter" and suggests the presence of a blow-hole of some sort.

27. RIMA 2.44:67-69; 46:11'-14'; probably 57:11'-13'. So also Assur-bel-kala and Assurnasirpal II, the latter in RIMA 2.228:58f.; 302:9-10.

28. RIMA 2.103.iv:2-3 in the context of iv:1-33.

29. Assur-Dan II: RIMA 2.1(135):68-72. Adad-Nirari: RIMA 2.A.0.99.2(154):122-127.

30. RIMA 2.99.2(150):48.

indicates that the Anatolian states on Assyria's border, along the Euphrates at Carchemish, were also collecting simians at the time. Apparently, coastal sites, including those in Phoenicia and Philistia, were doing the same.[31] Assurnasirpal II (883-859) likewise claims to have received domesticated (formerly wild) bulls and domesticated elephants as tribute.[32] Into this pattern, the claims concerning Solomon fit closely chronologically as well as thematically. Phoenician kings, Philistine kings, anyone who was anyone throughout the Near East, were assembling collections of exotic animals. At the start of the 1st millennium, the ideal king enriched his culture by the introduction of animals fit for breeding and display.

Tukulti-Ninurta II (890-884) likewise reports hunting animals and collecting live specimens in the course of a campaign, in the vicinity of Hindanu, near the bend of the central Euphrates.[33] He also devotes a separate segment to the hunt in the peroration of his royal annals.[34] Importantly, he does not indicate that he is breeding animals in the peroration: the hunt has (again) become the quintessential royal occupation (other than conquest and construction). For Tukulti-Ninurta II it is the mark of the king's ability to control nature.

It is an important departure, then, that the hunt is absent from the peroration of the annals of Assurnasirpal II: it appears, instead, integrated into the course of his campaigns along with the capture of live beasts:

> At that time, I smote forty strong bison on the opposite bank of the Euphrates. I took eight living bison into captivity. I smote twenty ostriches. I took twenty live ostriches into captivity.[35]

Even in a display inscription, he relates that he collected female monkeys from the Phoenician coast and formed herds of monkeys, lions, and other beasts in connection with the course of a campaign. He also received the ivory of *naḫirus* from cities on the Phoenician coast, though he did not hunt them personally. His other tribute includes:

31. For an 11th- or 10th-century baboon statuette at Tel Miqneh, see Trude Dothan, "The Arrival of the Sea Peoples: Cultural Diversity in Early Iron Age Canaan," in *Recent Excavations in Israel: Studies in Iron Age Archaeology*, ed. Seymour Gitin and William G. Dever. AASOR 49 (Winona Lake: Eisenbrauns, 1989), 11 and fig. 1.9. On Phoenicia, see below (regarding Assurnasirpal II). The interest in simians was clearly widespread.

32. RIMA 2 A.0.102 77.

33. Tukulti-Ninurta II: RIMA 2.100.5(175):79-82, killing ostriches and deer and taking their young captive. The importation of animals to Hindanu signifies imitation of Babylonian perquisites in the region in the 9th-8th centuries.

34. Tukulti-Ninurta II: RIMA 2.A.0.100.5(178):134-35.

35. Assurnasirpal II: RIMA 2.A.0.101.1(215f).iii:48-49.

large female simians and small female simians. . . . I carried them to my land, Asshur. In the city, Calah, I very successfully bred their bands. I displayed them to all the people of my land. Exercising my arm and agitating my mind, I took fifteen strong lions from the mountains and forests into captivity. I carried off fifty cubs. In the city, Calah, and the palaces of my land I cast them into cages. I bred their cubs very successfully.[36]

The succeeding text enumerates bison (probably zebu), elephants, lions, ostriches, monkeys, onagers, two kinds of deer, bears, panthers (or leopards), and two other types of animals, possibly including tigers (or panthers). Assurnasirpal bred and displayed all of them as exotic animals. In the display inscription, what follows is an injunction to future generations to preserve the animals of this impressive zoological collection. Only then does Assurnasirpal boast of his prowess in hunting bulls, lions, and elephants.[37]

An early annals edition of Shalmaneser III, quoted above, places the hunt in its apparent peroration; even here, no report of the king's cultivation of herds or plants occurs. Later editions integrate the hunt into a particular campaign and then drop it altogether.[38] So for Shalmaneser, the breeding motif never occurs. Neither the Black Obelisk inscription nor the Kurkh Monolith repeats these motifs, although the Black Obelisk does feature a clear pictorial depiction of captive elephants and monkeys — it transfers the topos of the collection and breeding of exotic animals from the realm of narrated report to that of the visual. Subsequent kings completely drop the motif from their annals. All the same, the hunt itself recurs in later Assyrian palace reliefs and among the Persians.[39] It becomes a feature of the reliefs rather than of the texts.

36. Assurnasirpal II: RIMA 2.A.0.101.2(226):30-35. The receipt of the monkeys along with that of elephants and camels is displayed in a relief.
37. RIMA 2.A.0.101.2(226):35-39, with the hunt in a summary, 226:40-42, but succeeded (227:43-51) by another campaign report, indicating it belongs geographically to the regions between the Phoenician coast and Assyria, namely northern Syria, as is true of the other kings in whose inscriptions it can be located; 30(291-92):84-101 is closer to being a peroration in another display.
38. Michel, WO 1/6 (1952), 472: IV:40–474: IV:48; WO 2/1 (1954), 27-45: Year 17, III:42-45; Year 19, 40: IV:19-22. The appearance of the hunt in the middle of the annals of Shalmaneser, however, may reflect the existence of an earlier annals edition ending with the campaign of which the hunt report is the coda.
39. For apes, e.g., see Hamoto. For the Assyrian hunt, E. Weissert, "Royal Hunt and Royal Triumph in a Prism Fragment of Ashurbanipal (82-5-22,2)," in Assyria 1995, ed. Simo Parpola and Robert M. Whiting (Helsinki: Neo-Assyrian Text Corpus Project, 1997), 339-58. Note also the following text describing a ritual: ABL 366 (82-5-22, 96); SLA 215

Kings continued to build zoos and parks, with imported trees and animals.[40] In the 7th century, the Assyrian king Assurbanipal produced reliefs depicting not just the obligatory lion hunt, but also tame lions, and lions paired in a royal garden.[41] An 8th-century relief from Karatepe, too, depicts a monkey beneath a banquet table.[42] Though it disappears from the annals, the motif survives in building inscriptions, which mention such parks.[43] In this light, the story of the judicial murder of the Israelite Naboth, allegedly by Jezebel, the wife of King Ahab, takes on another complexion: it is not just unlikely but unbelievable that the "garden" with which Ahab reportedly replaced Naboth's vineyard was anything like a "vegetable garden" at all (1 Kgs. 21:2); rather, it was another royal park to be filled with exotic imports. All the same, the motif drops out of the central literature of royal self-presentation, the annals and displays. By the mid-9th century, the institution of the zoological garden had lost its novelty, and the breeding of exotic animals had so progressed that kings could no longer claim to be adding new accessions to the collections.

From Tiglath-Pileser I to Shalmaneser III, the hunt is a fixture of Assyrian royal propaganda. From Tiglath-Pileser to Assurnasirpal II, the breeding of animals is a similar fixture. All the same, the last Assyrian king to emphasize herd-breeding in his annals' peroration stems from the early 10th century. The motif occurs into the 9th century, but is not central to the king's image after the 10th.

Late Middle and early Neo-Assyrian royal historiography also manifests a special concern with aggregated totals of horses and chariots the king accumulates. Tiglath-Pileser I relates that he brought the numbers of chariots in As-

---

coordinates the sacred marriage of Nabu and Tashmetum (cf. ABL 113; SLA 216) with an expedition a week later:

> On 11 Iyyar, Nabu will go out, exercise *(ipaššar)* his feet, go to the park *(ambassi)*.
> He will kill bison. Then he will dwell in his habitation and bless the king.

40. Lawrence E. Stager, in conversation, suggests that biblical references to cedar and cedar groves in Jerusalem, and physical remains of boxwood in Jerusalem, reflect the practice of royal gardening in the city. For the boxwood, see Alon de Groot and Donald T. Ariel, eds., *Excavations at the City of David Directed by Yigal Shiloh*, 3: *Stratigraphical, Environmental and Other Reports*. Qedem 33 (Jerusalem: Hebrew University Institute of Archaeology, 1992), 107-8, with the locus assigned to the 7th-6th centuries (Stratum 10B). For further discussion of the garden motif, see Stephanie Dalley, "Nineveh, Babylon and the Hanging Gardens: Cuneiform and Classical Sources Reconciled," *Iraq* 56 (1994): 45-58.

41. See R. D. Barnett, *Sculptures from the North Palace of Ashurbanipal at Nineveh (668-627 B.C.)* (London: British Museum, 1976), pl. XIV, XV, in addition to multiple hunting reliefs, including hunts of onagers and of gazelles.

42. *ANEP,* 849.

43. An example is RIMA 2.A.0.87.10(55):71-75 (Tiglath-Pileser I).

syria's service to a new high point, that he annexed land and population, giving the people contentment by satisfying their material needs. Assur-Dan II boasts of repatriating the Assyrians who had been driven away from their homes by Aramean invaders, of building palaces in the provinces of his land, of accumulating grain and disposing of horse teams, for the army. Adad-Nirari II relates his construction of palaces in his provincial districts, his accumulation of grain, and his disposal of chariotry teams, following the formula of Assur-Dan II. And Tukulti-Ninurta II counts 2702 horses in his chariotry contingent, claiming that this was the highest number ever. He boasts of building the provincial palaces, accumulating grain, and annexing land and population.[44]

Again to put this into context, in Shalmaneser III's Year 22 annals, a typical text is as follows:

> I directed plows in the lands of my country. Grain and fodder I made more plentiful than before, I poured out. Yoked horse teams of 2002 chariots and 5542 cavalrymen I attached to the forces of my country.[45]

At the end of another text, from his 20th year, Shalmaneser claims:

> 2001 chariots, 5242 horsemen, I attached to the forces of my land.[46]

The numbers clearly represent claims meant to be identical. Between Year 20 and Year 22, the numbers had simply mounted by one chariot and 300 horsemen. In other words, these totals reflect acquisitions until the time of the compilation of the annals editions. This sort of summary seems to be absent in later royal inscriptions. The capture of horses and chariots is related instead in reports of individual campaigns.

This theme is articulated concerning Solomon, His trade in horses is attested in 1 Kgs. 4:26(5:6); 10:25-29. And Tiglath-Pileser's and his successors' concern with agriculture, prosperity, and contentment[47] is another theme shared with 1 Kgs. 3-10. The motif of satiety is common in Semitic royal in-

---

44. The texts just cited are RIMA 2.27.ii:28-35; 72:6'; A.0.98.1:60-67; A.0.99.2:121; A.0.100.5:130f.

45. Michel, WO 1/6 (1952), 454-74, 472: IV:40–474: IV:48.

46. Michel, WO 2/1 (1954), 27-45, 44: left edge. RIMA 3 A.0.102.10: left edge.2b. We also have records of the purchase of horses outside of annals. For a purchase of 2000 at Ugarit, at the end of the Late Bronze Age, see PRU II 27-28.

47. E.g., Tiglath-Pileser I, RIMA 2.A.0.87.1.vi:85-vii:35; Assur-Dan II, 98.1:64-67; Adad-Nirari II, 99.2:120; Tukulti-Ninurta II, 100.5:132; Assurnasirpal II, 101.30:78-83. Probably related is Mesha's insistence that he "added (bovines) to the land" and his reference to sheep: KAI 181:29, 31.

scriptions. Another shared motif is that of the feast, prominent both in the account of Solomon's temple dedication and in the report of the dedication of Calah by Assurnasirpal II.[48] We have already had occasion to mention the dedicatory feast in connection with David's installation of the ark in Jerusalem.

These motifs did not disappear after the 11th century: they climax in one sense in the inscriptions of Assurnasirpal II. But inscriptions of the 10th and early 9th centuries no longer showcase them or bundle them together as earlier texts do. Thus, the theme of plenty recurs in inscriptions especially of Assurbanipal but even of Esarhaddon.[49] But the rest of the Middle Assyrian complex is missing. Nor does the issue of prosperity occupy the key place it does in Middle Assyrian texts, even in the Aramaic inscriptions of the 9th and 8th centuries.[50]

All these motifs are largely absent from accounts of biblical kings later than Solomon. It looks as though the royal ideal, particularly of the king as naturalist, reflected in 1 Kgs. 3-10 stems squarely from the late Middle and early Neo-Assyrian milieu.

Later, in Chronicles, written in the 5th century, Solomon is far less a natural philosopher.[51] Yet the ideal of the king as natural philosopher is also preserved for the 10th century in Tyrian annals reported by Menander of Ephesus. The source alleged that Hiram, contemporary mainly with Solomon, exchanged riddles and proverbs with Solomon; this tradition is elaborated in Dius,[52] with a distinctly pro-Tyrian twist. Here is another claim that a monarch contemporary with Middle Assyrian culture was a philosopher. This is not evidence that our texts about Solomon are from the 10th century. But either the texts or their sources faithfully mirror the royal ideals of that time.

In the next chapters, we shall see that aspects of the presentation of David also conform to certain conventions both of the display inscription and of the techniques of royal propaganda from the Middle Assyrian period. David too

---

48. RIMA 2.101.30(292f.):102-154. See further A. Finet, "Le Banquet de Kalah offert par le roi d'Assyrie Ašurnasirpal II (883-859)," in *Banquets d'Orient*, ed. Rika Gyselen. Res Orientales 4 (Bures-sur-Yvette: Groupe pour l'Étude de la Civilisation du Moyen-Orient, 1992), 31-44; see also D. Collon, "Banquets in the Art of the Ancient Near East," Gyselen, 23-30, with bibliography; and for some literary representations, H. L. J. Vanstiphout, "The Banquet Scene in the Mesopotamian Debate Poems," Gyselen, 9-22; R. D. Barnett, "Asshurbanipal's Feast," *ErIsr* 18 (1985): 1*-6*.

49. See, e.g., P. Gerardi, "Prism Fragments from Sippar: New Esarhaddon Inscriptions," *Iraq* 55 (1993): 122 iv 2'-8'.

50. As KAI 24; 26.

51. The observation is that of Gary Knoppers, in correspondence.

52. Menander in Josephus *Ag. Ap.* 1.120; Dius in *Ag. Ap.* 1.114-15.

captures chariots, for example. More important, the types of interpretation demanded by Assyrian annals and displays are also productive when brought to bear on the biblical texts that most resemble those inscriptions in form. This is an argument for dating the biblical texts. It is more persuasively an argument about the nature of their composition.

C. The Tiglath-Pileser Principle

The Assyrian propaganda implements that serve as vehicles for presenting the royal ideal also deconstruct themselves. Their inconsistencies permitted scholars to unravel the genre of display inscriptions from that of annals: sequence in the display inscriptions, again, is not necessarily chronological; their form of organization is commonly geographic. The flexibility afforded by nonchronological organization enables scribes to provide the most favorable report possible about the king's prowess.

Even in annals that detail the events of each year after those of the preceding, a similar strategy of presentation can often be discerned. Thus, when Sennacherib, king of Assyria, describes his campaign to the West in 701, his report for the year ends with the submission and tribute of Hezekiah, king of Judah. In the course of his campaign, he claims to have met and defeated an Egyptian expeditionary force. However, the confrontation with Egypt may in fact have been the last significant episode in his adventure, before his return home: the rearrangement of the sequence in the narrative permitted him to mask the fact that the battle so weakened him as to compel his withdrawal. Inside a year's account, thus, the annals remain thematic in organization.

In early Assyrian annals, elements of the display inscription remain. There are pauses in the action, for example, in which the author of the text inserts royal epithets — just as display inscriptions consist of a sort of titulary into which references to campaigning are inserted. Early annals also intersperse summary statements between campaigns or even parts of campaigns, where later annals confine them to the end of the text. In one such summary statement in his annals, Tiglath-Pileser claims to have pursued Ahlamu Arameans across the Euphrates 28 times, including twice in one year.[53] The claim somewhat deflates his boast of having conducted a successful campaign from Suhu to Carchemish in a single day.[54] It even deflates itself: an enemy against whom

---

53. RIMA 2.A.0.87.4.34-36. Text 3:29ff. provides a parallel claim, with the number of crossings missing.

54. RIMA 2.A.0.87(Tiglath-Pileser I).1.v.48-50; 2.28-29; 13(59):4'-6'.

one successfully campaigns 28 times is either attacked in tiny bands or is pursuing a strategy of attrition and testing Assyria's attention span. In this light, it is hardly surprising that Arameans made inroads into Assyria at least toward the latter part of Tiglath-Pileser's reign.[55]

Another locution invites comment. Of the reconquered Shubaru, Tiglath-Pileser writes,

> I imposed the heavy yoke of my dominion . . . so that annually they send tribute and tax to my city Assur into my presence.[56]

The emphasis here is on the resumption of lapsed payment. But the formulation is applied to no other subject people. It distinguishes the Shubaru from other vassals. What property is it that marks them off? They behave with unique punctiliousness toward the king. They send tribute annually to Assur, without Tiglath-Pileser even having to go to the Shubaru to collect it!

On close inspection, Tiglath-Pileser's inscriptions differentiate among classes of conquered peoples. First, there are peoples whose towns he loots and burns. Second, on some peoples whose towns he loots and burns, he additionally imposes his yoke. On some of the latter class, he also imposes tribute *(biltu u madattu)*. However, a third class consists of those on whom he imposes tribute without looting and burning towns, including those who submit to him voluntarily (i.e., under duress). Fourth, there are peoples from whom he annexes persons or territory. The modern reader may look askance on some of Tiglath-Pileser's claims — Tiglath-Pileser likely parsed any gift from a foreign king as a token of submission. Yet there is truth in the record as well as spin. Tiglath-Pileser's detailed statements prescind at times from claiming the opponents submitted formally. They admit he was not able to reduce all opponents to the same degree of subjugation.

And yet, here is one of Tiglath-Pileser's summary statements:

> Total: from my accession year to my fifth year, I conquered 42 lands. . . . I brought them under a single authority, took their hostages, imposed tribute and tax on them.

---

55. J. N. Postgate, *AfO* 32 (1985): 95-101. Postgate assumes that a chronicle text (A. Kirk Grayson, *Assyrian and Babylonian Chronicles* [Locust Valley: Augustin, 1970], 189:2-7 or 10-11) refers to a situation after the early part of Tiglath-Pileser's reign. But this is not certain, particularly as the campaign to Katmuhu which succeeds these lines (189:13), coming as it does after the death of Marduk-nadin-ahhe, represents a third foray into that area.

56. RIMA 2.A.0.87.1.ii.90-96.

That is, it is in the nature of the genre that the author distinguishes the various treatments he metes out in the detailed accounts of his campaigns, but blurs the distinctions in the summary accounts. In a similar vein, Tiglath-Pileser claims to have conquered and ravished "the land of Katmuhu in its entirety" (1.i.91-92). Yet he concedes that within the space of a year or two, he had to return, and conquer all the cities of the region, annexing it (1.iii.7-31). A later text (4:22-23) makes no mention of this double appearance. And it would appear that a still later campaign was necessary.[57]

In Assyrian royal inscriptions, then, the torching of a grain field is the conquest of a whole territory beyond it. A looting raid becomes a claim of perpetual sovereignty. But this does not mean that campaigns can be confected. The technique is that of putting extreme spin on real events.

Interpreting such literature demands only a simple rule, the Tiglath-Pileser principle. The question is, what is the minimum the king might have done to lay claim to the achievements he publishes? Looting a town? He shoplifted a toothbrush from the local drug store. Ravaging the countryside? Perhaps he trampled crops near a farmstead. Receiving submission from distant kings in lands one hasn't invaded? A delegation arrived to inaugurate diplomatic relations. Each small mark of prestige becomes the evidence for a grand triumph.

Not long ago, a candidate for the American presidency claimed to have "invented the Internet." He didn't, but he had promoted it a little. The point is, such figures cannot make claims without any basis in fact, risible assertions, lest they invite mockery, as that inventor of the Internet did. But it is always a temptation to paint one's achievements in the best of all possible lights. To correct for this tendency, one has merely to imagine what insignificant action would produce the claim that "I conquered Egypt" (a raid on a border station in the Sinai). The same political hermeneutic applies reasonably well today.

The Tiglath-Pileser principle applies to biblical historiography that draws on written sources. To take just one example, 2 Kings relates that Hezekiah defeated the Philistines "unto Gaza and its territories, from watchtower to fortified town" (2 Kgs. 18:8). The text probably stems from a record left by Hezekiah's court. The action was part of his revolt against Sennacherib, king of Assyria, who invaded in 701.

The text in Kings is easy to interpret. In 701, Hezekiah and his partners, Egypt and Sidon, instigated a coup in Ashkelon, on Gaza's border. Ashkelon thus became a partner in the revolt against Assyria. Meanwhile, Hezekiah took the town of Timnah from Padi of Eqron, another Philistine city. He likely in-

---

57. If the chronicle at Grayson, *Assyrian and Babylonian Chronicles,* 189, is placing a Katmuhu campaign after the death of Marduk-nadin-ahhe.

corporated Philistine Gath into his realm, Gath being the other inland Philistine city-state.[58] So 2 Kgs. 18:8 records Hezekiah's successes, including the revolt in Ashkelon, up to but not including Gaza's territory. It does not say "up to Ashkelon."

Hezekiah probably campaigned no further than Eqron. So a minimal text would have claimed he bested his foes "up to Eqron." Instead, the writer chose to maximize the area covered: Hezekiah "defeated the Philistines unto Gaza," which means he controlled Ashkelon, bordering on Gaza's hinterland. By making the statement in a rubric too, the writer neglected to mention that all this territory was lost in 701. Hezekiah's military activity thus seems to extend from Judah across Gath, Eqron, and Ashkelon to encompass Gaza, when it probably embraced Eqron alone. Yet all of Philistia up to the territory of Gaza was collaborating with him. And the account rightly prescinds from claiming Hezekiah conquered Gaza, although it deliberately invites a naïve reader to infer such a victory. Comically, a contemporary king of Ashkelon could have made almost the same claim as 2 Kgs. 18:8 makes for Hezekiah: he subdued all the territory from Gaza to Samaria. There would in fact be no real conflict between this and the claims about Hezekiah.

The Tiglath-Pileser principle applies as well to some texts that do not stem from sources. Most of these cases are found in the Deuteronomistic History, the final form of the books of Deuteronomy, Joshua, Judges, Samuel, and Kings, from the reign of Josiah of Judah (640-609). The book of Joshua self-consciously employs the techniques of maximizing spin familiar from royal inscriptions. In Josh. 10-11, for example, Joshua's army fights two field battles, one in the south, in the Ayyalon Pass, and one in the north, at Merom, probably in the region of Mount Tabor. A series of sieges follows each battle. In the south, Joshua beleaguers five towns in the hill country of Judah. In the north, he reduces and burns a larger number.

The text of Joshua distinguishes carefully and deliberately between campaigns in which foes are defeated, cases in which territory is "conquered (lkd)," and cases in which the territory is annexed or indigenous populations "supplanted (yrš, C)." For example, none of the northern cities is resettled by the Is-

---

58. This will have been an earlier development were it to prove out that Nadav Na'aman is right to restore Gath as the name of the town mentioned in the "Letter to God" discussed in his study; "Sennacherib's 'Letter to God' on His Campaign to Judah," *BASOR* 214 (1974): 25-39. In any event, Gath plays no role as an independent city-state in any source after the 9th century. Perhaps the reason is that Hazael's depredations there led to its incorporation into a neighboring territorial unit in the 8th century. If the identification of Gath with Tel Haror is correct, however, as proposed by Stager, it is less likely that Na'aman's restoration is correct. On Gath, see below, Chapters 7 and 18.

raelites. But at the end of the southern campaign, a summary of the action statement claims that Joshua "conquered" all the territories from Qadesh Barnea in the south to Gaza in the west to Gibeon in the north (Josh. 10:41-42). At the end of the northern campaign, the conquest is of all the territory promised Israel by Yahweh (11:23; 21:43). This presumably includes land far to the north of the tribes' actual settlement, even reaching the Euphrates (Josh. 1:3-4; Deut. 11:24).

There is no conflict here with the claim that, even after Joshua's campaigns, lands remained to be "annexed"/"supplanted" (Josh. 13:1-6; Judg. 1). A conquest of a part of the promised territory is the theoretical subjection of it all. This is why, for example, the summary statement at the end of the southern campaign in Josh. 10:41-42 can claim that Joshua conquered territory including the Philistine plain, explicitly including Gaza, but 11:22 can concede that the "Anaqim" were not rooted out of Philistine territory as they were from "the hills . . . from all the hill country of Judah and from all the hill country of Israel" (v. 21).[59] (The Anaqim, in the theory of the Deuteronomistic History, were instead rooted out by the Philistines.)

The individual victories metonymically represent the larger conquest (as Josh. 12). The summary statements (Josh. 10:40-43; 11:16-20) suggest this by conflating categories of martial success. The technique is that of royal inscriptions, and has close parallels in Tiglath-Pileser's summaries. This is how the court scribes fashioned their account of Hezekiah's reign, presumably, in that case from a source.[60] The court scribes knew just how to magnify Joshua's achievements without contradicting their accounts of later developments.

The spin in Near Eastern royal historiography (negative spin, when texts indict predecessors) reflects the social circumstances in which the texts were produced. The king was footing the bill, so his achievements are set out with enthusiasm. But the scribes also present the king as embodying the royal ideal of the time (as the king defined it). And the work reflects assumptions as to its readership.

In antiquity, even when rising in the 8th and 7th centuries, rates of literacy were low. And many texts, most famously the 6th-century Behistun Inscription of Darius I, were inaccessible to the public. So some scholars assume that texts were not disseminated. Given a low literacy rate, however, the texts' inaccessibility is irrelevant: royal inscriptions could not be widely read even if mounted

---

59. On the distinction, and the lack of contradiction, see generally Baruch Halpern, "Settlement of Canaan," *ABD* 5.1124-25.

60. Gary Knoppers offers as another, accurate, parallel Mesha's claim that "Israel has perished, perished eternally" when he had encountered only the elements in Transjordan.

on billboards. But their propagandistic aims indicate that the texts were indeed disseminated. The audiences that kings targeted were, at a minimum, the officialdom and army, but even more probably the citizenry of major communities. The texts must have been read or summarized at public events, and this informal means of dissemination may have been more effective than writing. That is, the outsider audience was almost wholly illiterate, while the insider audience had a higher literacy rate.

Still, peculiarities remain. No historical text, and no myth, in the ancient Near East is said to have an author. The first authors of biblical texts are the prophets: Amos, Hosea, then Hezekiah's prophets, in 701, Micah and Isaiah. In these cases, the texts are attributed to individuals for purposes of establishing the texts' authority. Amos and Hosea, in particular, can be cited as having personally predicted the fall of Israel. Micah and Isaiah can be said to have foreseen the Assyrian devastation of Judah. But in Mesopotamia, textual composition is so anonymous that even astronomical advances have no authors, although the Greeks *were* able to name particular Babylonians who invented techniques of analysis. Likewise, in Israel, historiographic texts are purely anonymous.

The inverse is true in Greece. Starting with Homer, we have virtually no texts without a personal ascription. Philosophical works, poetic works, and historical works are all attributed to specific authors. Why the contrast? What is the difference between Greek and Near Eastern authorship or composition? Essentially, Greek texts are all open to public dispute. They are unambiguously partisan, and unambiguously controvertible as a result. From the start, authors attack Homer. Philosophers attack their contemporaries and predecessors. There is no hint that the revision of earlier thought is a private matter, inside of a collective tradition. The conflicts are individual and open.

Near Eastern texts, by way of contrast, are composed by a collective establishment. That authors are not identified is one signal. Another is that Near Eastern myths and historical texts correct antecedent texts without explicitly referring to them. Thus, Gen. 1, the creation story in which Israel's God is infallible, corrects Gen. 2–3, in which Yahweh, creating humans, errs: it is not good that the man should be by himself, for example; or, having determined to make a mate for the man, Yahweh fails to reproduce him from the clay, and engenders animals instead in error. There is no reference in Gen. 1 to Gen. 2–3. Instead, the correction is quiet, indirect.[61]

The adjustments, in the Near East, occur within a tradition. The unity of the tradition is unquestioned. This is in fact no different from the discussions

---

61. On the correction of JE by P, see Richard E. Friedman, *The Exile and Biblical Narrative*. HSM 22 (Chico: Scholars, 1981), 81-132.

that take place within the traditions of Catholicism and of Orthodox Judaism. The elite has a sense of collaboration, a sense of collective identity. This dichotomizes the audience of public documents, such as royal inscriptions.

On the one hand, general audiences heard the inscriptions. Texts describing the king's accomplishments are primarily directed externally — the unlettered reader will take the claims of the text at face value. For such readers, the conquest of 42 lands is understood to mean the enduring subjugation of 42 complete and independent political authorities. Tiglath-Pileser routed the Ahlamu Arameans 28 times — in massive exercises in line combat.

On the other hand, the expectation is that the insider audience, the elite, will analyze the language in detail. The insiders understood the conventions used to amplify achievement. The reason was, army officers and administrative officials knew how foreign relations stood, where the borders were, at the military and at the diplomatic level. Egregious falsification would leave the disgruntled placed to ridicule the king. So the spin, or rhetorical exaggeration, had to be applied within a framework of linguistic conventions that insiders understood and accepted. In other words, members of the elite had to understand how to discount the spin. And once they knew how to do so, they could be expected, unlike David (see below, Part V), but like Solomon threatening to cleave a baby in half, to see through the embellishments of others.

One has almost to imagine the insiders applauding the cleverness of the authors who, without falsification, imply the glory and grandeur of their king's accomplishments. And, the more clever the authors were at the deed, the more deafening the applause. The plaudits are for the persuasion of the outsider audience, consisting not just of people at large, but also of posterity. The object was to be a part of the community whose liege entered the club of "great kings."

For the elite, Tiglath-Pileser's 28 encounters with the Arameans include cases where Assyrians on the west bank of the Euphrates threw stones at two pastoralists with a few sheep. The conquests of the 42 lands are of very different characters: only in one instance was Tiglath-Pileser able to collect tribute without visiting the vanquished territory. In some territories, the conquest consisted of an unsuccessful attempt to set fire to an outlying farmstead.

Mesopotamian royal inscriptions regularly make use of the verb *dâku*, "to kill," as a description of the king's dealings with enemy armies or indeed enemy kings or leaders. Sometimes the meaning of the verb is literal, but far more often it means "to defeat," which is often an optimistic assessment of the results of a battle. Kings who have been "killed" live to fight another day. The metaphoric "killing" — used to describe victory in American sport and even triumphs in the theater — is understood by the elite reader to be the striking of a blow, by the common reader to be either the achievement of victory or an actual killing.

In sum, all Near Eastern royal literature is written for a bifurcated audience: the contrast in audiences is that of insider to outsider.

As with Hezekiah's conquest "unto Gaza and its territories," the conventions of royal literature are sometimes transparent. This transparency often arises from the texts themselves. So Tiglath-Pileser's detailed campaign reports contrast with the summaries of his career. It is not that his scribes were unsophisticated, or foolish. On the contrary, their transparency ensured that the elite would understand that their writing deliberately gave the king's work epic dimensions, translating bloody combat into the realm, or at least the language, of the sacred.[62]

As the tradition of historical composition developed, the conventions grew more sophisticated, in the same way that advertising on television, billboards, and computers has grown more sophisticated in the last 50 years. Royal inscriptions were precisely a form of advertising. It is for this reason that they put the best possible face on their "product," namely the king, without however falling into the trap of risibility. Like Samuel, the texts needed to be both honest and deceitful at the same time, to turn defeat into victory in the field, without political consequences, and victory in the field into conquest.

So the principle of minimal interpretation — not minimalism — has abiding application. This is why Joshua and Judg. 1 distinguish "conquest" from the supplanting of inhabitants in conquered territories: in the theory they perpetrate, the territory between Joshua's northernmost and southernmost battles (Josh. 10–11) was all conquered. But only in the highlands did Israel root out previous inhabitants. The book of Joshua is primarily a Deuteronomistic product — stemming either from the time of Hezekiah (700) or that of Josiah (620). Judg. 1 is a document placed into the history of the Former Prophets by a Josianic editor. Both were written by scribes familiar with the canons of royal historiography.[63]

These lessons apply not just to the account of Solomon's reign, but to that

---

62. For a lucid articulation of the application of the same principle to the New Testament by David Friedrich Strauss starting in the 1830s, see Roy A. Harrisville and Walter Sundberg, *The Bible in Modern Culture: Theology and Historical-Critical Method from Spinoza to Käsemann* (Grand Rapids: Wm. B. Eerdmans, 1995), 96-110. Note that the genre of apocalyptic literature is the ultimate reduction of the principle of insider::outsider literary orientation, excluding the outsider almost totally.

63. On the dating of Judg. 1, see Halpern, *The First Historians,* 121-43; further below, Chapter 22D. Joshua may in large measure belong to the edition of the national history composed under Hezekiah. For bibliography and the history of scholarship, see Erik Eynikel, *The Reform of King Josiah, and the Composition of the Deuteronomistic History.* OTS 33 (Leiden: Brill, 1996).

of David as well. For reasons reviewed above, it seems to me that the majority of scholars have been right to derive 2 Samuel, at least, from the late 10th century.[64] If so, the lessons of Assyrian historiography may expose Samuel's purpose and, again, its antiquity.

This is perfectly straightforward. If the text was meant to vilify David and delegitimate Solomon or the dynasty, the author will have refrained from placing David's achievements in the best possible light (and this is how the text handles Saul's achievements). If the text was written late, as a legitimation of the dynasty, then the claims about David's and Solomon's achievements should be unambiguously grandiose; at a minimum, the explicit claims about his conquests should be identical with the views of those achievements current in later eras — in Chronicles, for example. (In fact, the text was written early, as a legitimation of Solomon, and supplemented late, with an appendix blaming Solomon for the loss of rule over Israel.) The Tiglath-Pileser principle thus offers itself as an intriguing measure of the timbre of 2 Samuel. Its adoption as a tool of analysis should expose the nature of our text.

---

64. Rehoboam's marriage to Absalom's daughter and Solomon's to an Ammonite princess (see below) both tend to confirm the narrative in its own time: there is no later manipulation of such formulary data, as the forms of the names go to show (Baruch Halpern and David S. Vanderhooft, *HUCA* 62 [1991]: 197-99). See further the arguments regarding 2 Samuel below. I should add that in source critical terms, 2 Samuel continues one of two strands of continuous narrative present in 1 Samuel, so the literary source as we now have it probably stretches back to about 1 Sam. 8, if not earlier. See further Friedman, *The Hidden Book in the Bible*.

CHAPTER 6

Reading David's Conquests

Testing the principle of minimal interpretation on 2 Samuel is a daunting prospect, because the narrative is so complex. We have the civil war, the so-called ark narrative and dynastic charter, and the list of conquests in 2 Sam. 8. Inside the Succession Narrative, one has not just the narrative itself, but the Ammonite war in 2 Sam. 10 and 12, where it frames the Uriah story. In addition, the lists and appendices in 2 Sam. 20–24 interrupt the Succession Narrative, possibly to mark the passage of time between the end of Absalom's revolt and Solomon's accession. The narrative ends shortly after David's death, with Solomon's establishment on the throne.

The Succession Narrative — the most brilliant historical narrative of antiquity — dominates the book. But the other materials contribute to the character of the package. All the human interaction makes the historical interpretation of the text on the lines of the Tiglath-Pileser principle potentially controversial — like the question of which individuals David really did murder. However, a clear test case is available. This is the concentrated compilation of David's conquests, or military actions. All, or almost all, of these are gathered together in a single chapter, 2 Sam. 8.

The question of who "inserted" this document is not a primary concern here. However, the results of this study make it clear that it was a part of the original edition of 2 Samuel, long before the consolidation of Israel's historical literature in the Deuteronomistic History — the books of Deuteronomy, Joshua, Judges, Samuel, and Kings. Nothing suggests that the author of the Deuteronomistic History had a hand in shaping the chapter, or in shaping the content of 2 Samuel outside of the programmatic chapter furnishing the dynastic charter, 2 Sam. 7. All the same, 2 Sam. 8 is artfully contextualized in the over-all historiographic continuum, whether by the Deuteronomistic Historian or by the original author of 2 Samuel:

In the chapters leading up to 2 Sam. 8, David has become king of Judah, in Hebron, where Yahweh directed him to go. He has unified Israel and Judah by force under his authority, and has become king of a united Israel with the Isra-elites acknowledging his divine election. He has conquered his capital and re-pulsed two Philistine counterattacks.

David has also brought the ark into Jerusalem, from the Gibeonite town of Qiryath-Yearim. Yahweh's adoption of David as custodian of the ark leads Da-vid to offer the God a temple. In exchange, Yahweh promises David "a great name" (2 Sam. 7:9) and an eternal dynasty. The *foreign* wars of 2 Sam. 8 pro-duce the "great name" paronomastically in the form of a "name" (8:3, 13), that is, a royal monument. Too, the chapter establishes his reputation, his "name," as a conqueror. The chapter summarizes the concrete successes that prove David enjoys divine favor as king of Israel.

The concentration of the accounts of David's foreign wars in 2 Sam. 8, in other words, responds to (or is anticipated by) the "dynastic charter" of 2 Sam. 7.[1] The "dynastic charter" itself is elicited by the repatriation of the ark in 2 Sam. 6 and David's urge to initiate temple-building. (The construction of a temple in the ancient Near East was a royal prerogative expressing divine elec-tion of the king's dynasty.) 2 Sam. 8 is the proof of David's pudding: Yahweh re-ally did intend, through him, to perfect the program of conquest promised originally in Joshua.

The chapter, in sum, is placed thematically. What is to follow it is the Suc-cession Narrative proper, with its focus on the Absalom Revolt and David's sons. 2 Sam. 8 is the capstone of the narrative of David's royal career. We should therefore suspect that some of the campaigns it reports are out of sequence.

There are several challenges in dealing with the chapter. First, the organiza-tion of the chapter's contents too is thematic, rather than chronological, as P. Kyle McCarter, among many others, recognizes.[2] In this respect, it partakes of the character of the display inscription. Still, placing the action in its proper time and place is made difficult by the chapter's disregard for chronological order.

Second, the introduction to the chapter deliberately places it after the tak-ing of Jerusalem: "And it was afterward thus: David smote the Philistines."[3]

---

1. So my colleague, Gary Knoppers, in correspondence.

2. *II Samuel*, 251.

3. 2 Sam. 8:1. This phrase belongs to the original edition of 2 Samuel, as we shall see (below, Chapter 7).

This seemingly means that the events recorded in 2 Sam. 8 were later than the moving of the ark, and for the most part this is probably the case. It also implies that the battle in which David subdues the Philistines at the beginning of 2 Sam. 8 (vv. 1-2) was unrelated to earlier battles with them. Yet the only narrative we have regarding the Philistines' conflict with David is located before the ark's transfer, in 2 Sam. 5.[4] This difficulty is dealt with in Chapter 7 below.

Third, 2 Sam. 8:3 refers to a battle against Hadadezer of Aram Zobah:

> David smote Hadadezer son of Rehob king of Zobah when he went to erect his stela ("hand") at the River.

Here, 2 Sam. 8 summarizes events that are related in detail two chapters later (in 2 Sam. 10) in the run-up to the Bathsheba story. It thus functions as a summary chapter, like the display inscription genre, rather than an independent and chronological historical narrative.

Fourth, 2 Sam. 8:12 refers to booty that David took and dedicated to Yahweh, presumably in the shrine for the ark:

> from Aram and from Moab and from the sons of Ammon, and from Philistines, and from Amaleq, and from the spoil of Hadadezer son of Rehob king of Zobah.

The booty from Ammon, and from Hadadezer, could not have been collected until after the events of chs. 10–12, when Ammon became David's tributary, and when he defeated Hadadezer. In other words, this narrative is explicitly out of its time: 2 Sam. 8 is in fact a summary of David's achievements. At the same time, the chapter partly conceals this fact. It does not include the conquest of Jerusalem, for example, and thus betray that it sums up conquests from earlier as well as later. The way it now reads, it implies that David subjected Ammon, and Zobah as well, early on. So the "later" encounters in 2 Sam. 10–12 seem to represent a revolt by those entities.

Outside of 2 Sam. 5, when David first occupies Jerusalem, and 2 Sam. 8:1-2, reports of conflict with the Philistines are confined to the appendices to 2 Samuel. Thus, in 2 Sam. 21:15-22, there are four contests with the "Yelidim of the

---

4. 5:17-21, 22-25. On the placement of these texts between 2 Sam. 6:11 and 6:12ff. in Chronicles, see Baruch Halpern, "Sacred History and Ideology: Chronicles' Thematic Structure — Indications of an Earlier Source," in *The Creation of Sacred Literature: Composition and Redaction of the Biblical Text*, ed. Richard E. Friedman. Near Eastern Studies 22 (Berkeley: University of California Press, 1981), 36-37; "A Historiographic Commentary on Ezra 1-6," 131; David A. Glatt, *Chronological Displacement*, 58-60. Should the second engagement in fact be placed chronologically after the movement of the ark to Jerusalem?

Rapha" *(ylydy hrph),* those born to the Rapha. This is probably the designation of a military guild, perhaps at Gath (21:22). In the first battle, David tires. One of the Yelidim, armed almost exactly like Goliath in 1 Sam. 17, is about to strike him down. Abishai, however, kills the Philistine, and David's men prohibit him from further participation on the field of battle:

> If you no longer go forth with us to battle, you will not extinguish the "lamp" of Israel (2 Sam. 21:17).[5]

The army's insistence that David remain at Mahanaim during the Absalom revolt has its background in this account.

The second conflict, in 2 Sam. 21:18, relates that Sibchai smote Sap, one of the "Yelidim of the Rapha," at Gob (the location is corrupt, or an early form of spelling). The third confrontation, in 2 Sam. 21:19, is at Gob, between Elhanan, son of Yaare Orgim, and Goliath the Gittite, the staff of whose spear was like a weaver's beam. In the fourth confrontation, a Philistine champion with six digits on each limb, challenges Israel, and Jonathan, son of Shimei, the brother of David kills him. (Jonathan is the brother of Jonadab, Amnon's instigator.)

In these accounts, one sees the building blocks of the Goliath story: the armament, the spear like a weaver's beam, the stature of Goliath, his name. Still further along, we will encounter the location of the story and the course of the combat. These stories give the impression of war with and victories over Gath. By placing them in an appendix, at the end of David's story, the author of Samuel insinuates that David came into conflict with Gath late in his reign.

Several more notices, of the same ilk, appear in 2 Sam. 23:9-17. The first concerns Elazar son of Dodo, the Ahohite. At Epes Dammim, the scene of the Goliath story in 1 Sam. 17, he leads a rout on the field, with the Israelites behind him stripping the corpses.[6] In the second notice, Shamma son of Agee the Harari ("mountain man") reverses an Israelite flight in a barley field. And in the third, David is at Adullam while a Philistine army camps by Jerusalem, before Bethlehem, and a Philistine garrison sits in Bethlehem. David longs for water from the cistern in the Bethlehem gate. So three of his heroes break through the Philistine camp, draw water, and bring it to David. He, however, pours the water out as a libation to Yahweh, refusing to drink it himself:

---

5. The text can be parsed, as here, as an unmarked conditional clause, and thus is probably early. It can, however, be interpreted as a pair of coordinated hortative clauses.

6. Read 2 Sam. 23:9 with 1 Chr. 11:13a.

Yahweh forfend that I should do this! (Should I drink) the blood of men who went at the risk of their lives?[7]

This last story is the basis of the double narrative in 1 Sam. 24 and 26 in which David refuses the urgings of his subordinates to kill Saul, even though he has him in his power. "Yahweh forfend," says he, "that I should do this thing."[8]

The annotations in the appendices in 2 Sam. 21 and 23 about David's heroes thus form the basis of some of the narratives in 1 Samuel. Indeed, another story has it that Benaiah, Solomon's hatchet man, entered combat against an Egyptian armed only with a staff — shades of David in the Goliath story yet again. Benaiah stole the Egyptian's spear, as David stripped Goliath of his sword. Benaiah killed the Egyptian with the Egyptian's own weapon, as David cut Goliath's head off with Goliath's sword.

Just before the story of Benaiah's confrontation with the Egyptian is a note to the effect that he killed two Moabite Ariels (the meaning of the latter term is uncertain, but see Chapter 23). Presumably, this encounter belongs to the time of David's campaign against Moab — from which he collects tribute in 2 Sam. 8. Likewise, the raid David's heroes stage on the Philistines at Bethlehem can only derive from a period early in David's kingship, or before it. In other words, the appendices, like 2 Sam. 8, do not respect chronological sequence. Nor do they claim to do so, as they celebrate the deeds of David's warriors.

Overall, David fights the Philistines in the vicinity of Jerusalem shortly after he conquers his new capital, in 2 Sam. 5. Otherwise, traditions of conflict with Philistines are retrojected into David's youth or confined to the appendices to 2 Samuel. These traditions, however, belong to the period of Jerusalem's conquest, or perhaps describe events that occurred even earlier. Yet the notices come at the end of the book, and are not placed in any chronological context whatever. It looks, on the face of it, as though this was a strategy on the part of the author to imply that there were wars with Philistines after the earliest part of David's reign. There is not the faintest hint of such conflict in the detailed descriptions themselves: the summaries, thus, in 2 Sam. 8 and in the appendices, serve to condition the reader's understanding, as in Josh. 10–11 and in the inscriptions of Tiglath-Pileser.

In sum, 2 Sam. 8 employs the conventions of display inscriptions. Indeed, 2 Sam. 8 punctuates the reports of conquest by interlarding them with statements that David was saved by Yahweh or made temple donations or was just.[9]

---

7. There are locutions peculiar to older texts here: Yahweh forfend, *ḥnh* in the sense of "camp" (Samuel, Ps. 68:10[11]), *maṣṣāb*, as garrison, and note *bqʿ* + *b*.

8. See Baruch Halpern, *The First Historians,* 62-65.

9. 2 Sam. 8:6b, 10-11, 15.

This technique is reminiscent of Tiglath-Pileser's annals with their intermittent titulary or characterization of the king in between reports of campaigns. There are additional parallels in Egyptian texts of the Late Bronze Age, which presumably furnished the inspiration for Tiglath-Pileser.

Given the conformity of 2 Sam. 8 to the conventions of the display inscription, and given the use made by the author of 2 Samuel of the technique of thematic, rather than chronological, organization, 2 Sam. 8:4 deserves renewed attention. In this verse, David takes horses and chariots from Hadadezer, the king of Rehob:

> David captured from him one thousand chariots, and seven hundred horsemen, and twenty thousand foot soldiers, and David hamstrung all the chariot teams, leaving of them one hundred chariot teams.[10]

The hamstringing of Aramean chariot horses is usually explained in one of two ways. Possibly, David could not integrate the chariot arm into the Israelite order of battle, so that the horses were simply surplus.[11] Conversely, one could construe the hamstringing as a literary reference to the Law of the King, which prohibits the king to multiply horses:

> Only, he must not multiply horses for himself, and he must not cause the people to return to Egypt in order to multiply horses, for Yahweh has said to you, "You shall not continue to return on this way any more." He must not multiply wives for himself, that his heart not go astray. . . . (Deut. 17:16-17)

It is almost certain that the destruction of captured Canaanite horses by Joshua, in Josh. 11:9, is a reflex of this text. Hence some scholars argue that David's action in 2 Sam. 8 stems from a Deuteronomistic editor in the 7th century who wanted to underline David's piety.[12]

If historical, as the indices of the antiquity of 2 Sam. 8 will suggest, the hamstringing was certainly intended to prevent the horses' being used again as chariot horses. But the alternative, of killing the beasts, was logically preferable to allowing useless animals to graze. Solomon was later in the horse-trading

---

10. Possibly, "a thousand chariots and seven thousand horsemen" with McCarter, *II Samuel*, 244, but this is not material to the point here. The parallel passages are 1 Chr. 18:4; 19:18.

11. Yigael Yadin, *The Art of Warfare in Biblical Lands* (New York: McGraw-Hill, 1963), 2.285.

12. See McCarter, *II Samuel*, 249, with bibliography.

business, too, and given the high costs of horses and chariots,[13] inferences can be made.

First, it will have been David's own submission, and it is the implication of the text taken alone, that no more than a hundred chariot-teams could be absorbed. These were probably incorporated into the army along with their drivers. But David would have said, and the text implies, that maintenance costs or lack of physical plant or the danger of too large a mercenary contingent from Zobah disrupting the sociology of the army prevented the integration of captured chariotry, if any, on a larger scale.

Second, the hamstrung captive horses, if not entirely fictitious, were likely put to some other, peaceable, use, probably in agriculture and haulage, but especially breeding. As it happens, a simple incision damaging a single front flexor tendon, a superficial ligament on the lower part of the horse's leg, would prevent a horse from running by making it impossible to lift the front leg: the horse would have to lift its entire side in order to advance. At the same time, the animal would be fit to walk and breed, and would retain the capacity to serve for draft work. The operation is employed today in the case of horses born with contracted flexor tendons in order to enable them to make use of the limb for stability.[14]

Chances are, in short, that David claimed to have taken some war-horses into his service, and to have sent others to pasture. The reliability of the numbers in the text is uncertain. The assertion that only a hundred units were retained may belie the claim of a bumper chariot harvest. If one could claim to have discarded chariots and horses, one could capture a hundred and claim to have captured thousands.

This text — 2 Sam. 8:4 — is the only passage recounting the appropriation of foreign chariotry or horse mounts by any Israelite king. The chariot horses are, as noted, mostly hamstrung. All the same, the text also alleges that David captured enemy horsemen, the light cavalry. In this connection, the text does not assert that he hamstrung the mounts. So, only in the case of the chariotry does he resort to this measure.[15] (The contrast between chariotry and light cav-

---

13. See Yutaka Ikeda, "Solomon's Trade in Horses and Chariots in Its International Setting," in Tomoo Ishida, *Studies in the Period of David and Solomon*, 215-38. Ikeda also links the trade to the other motifs explored above.

14. Lawrence Hutchinson, Professor of Veterinary Science at the Pennsylvania State University, in conversation.

15. The parallel in Josh. 11:6, 9 is perhaps derivative from this record, and may also be influenced by Deut. 17:16. As it is only the chariot horses *(rkb)* that David hamstrings, not the infantry mounts, the connection to Deut. 17:16 seems very indirect indeed: both Deut. 17:16 and Josh. 11:6, 9 refer to "horses" *(sws[ym])*, not specifically chariot horses. So Deu-

alry, or mounted infantry, is standard in the Iron Age, and is witnessed in the Tel Dan stela, among other inscriptions.)

The differential treatment of chariot horses and light cavalry horses speaks against the theory that David had no use for horses. Yet the hamstringing of the chariot horses also suggests that he feared their potential use, in teams, against him — by underlings, perhaps, or by people to whom the underlings might sell them. Absalom, when at the court, had his own contingent of horses. Adonijah, Solomon's rival, likewise had chariots and runners. The text mentions the fact in these two instances in order to underline its comparison of Adonijah to Absalom. But one can easily imagine that other dignitaries also gathered such private militias, or guards, around themselves.

For historiographic purposes, however, the enumeration of captured chariots and horses is a standard conceit of Middle Assyrian historiography, although the acquisition of horses and chariotry does register in the later Neo-Assyrian period.[16] The motif again puts us into contact with Mesopotamian historiographic traditions and conventions attested at the time of David and Solomon.

It is easy to overstate the weight of such parallels, particularly as the Assyrian monuments survived a considerable time. The fact that some scholars invoke parallels from the Middle Bronze Age to date the patriarchs in Genesis shows that one can always find cultural materials to compare to a text one is dating — the patriarchal narratives date hundreds of years after the events they claim to report on, and cannot be viewed as reliable unless one thinks the patriarchs kept diaries, and scribes copied them.

Another case: Josh. 12 lists the Canaanite kings whom Joshua allegedly defeated and killed, for the most part in the field. Earlier texts in Josh. 9 (vv. 1-2) and Josh. 10–11 present these kings as having confronted the Israelite invaders in coalition. The closest parallels to Josh. 12, the list of Canaanite kings Joshua defeated, appear in lists of defeated enemies in the inscriptions of Tiglath-

---

teronomy may have taken David's precedent to be an indictment of Solomon, the renowned horse trader. This dovetails with the agenda of Josiah, whose agents wrote Deuteronomy as we have it, and whose scribes blame Solomon for the loss of Israel. Deuteronomy's regulation in this instance represents an exegesis of Samuel and Kings.

The passage in Joshua refers to hamstringing horses and burning chariots, as though there were no mounted infantry. This might be thought to be archaic, but in fact reflects Samarian tactics, in which the chariotry fought without support from mounted infantry, in contrast to most Near Eastern cavalry arms of the Iron II. See the enumeration of participants in the battle of Qarqar in 853 in the Kurkh Monolith.

16. E.g., see A. G. Lie, *Inscriptions of Sargon II King of Assyria*, 1: *The Annals* (Paris: Geuthner, 1929), 4:15-16. West Semitic parallels in KAI 26A.6-7; esp. KAI 215.

Pileser I and his successors.[17] Yet Josh. 12 is certainly late in origin. It is in fact a list that apes either those found in Middle Assyrian annals or, more likely, Neo-Assyrian annals with lists of the participants in enemy coalitions — lists that are likewise heirs to the Middle Assyrian practice.

What this means is that not every parallel to historiography of a particular time — to the annals of Tiglath-Pileser I, for example — carries weight for the dating of a text. Models for the presentation of events can survive a considerable time, and later adaptations of forms can mimic earlier ones. Even given this limitation, however, it seems worthwhile to try reading 2 Sam. 8 as though it were a display inscription. In the following chapters, I will argue that the source of 2 Sam. 8 is in fact adapted from a display inscription, or the equivalent of such an inscription, left by David.

The effect of this interpretation coincides with a few previous treatments. But the assumption that the intent of the chapter or of its source is to furnish a display inscription for David is new in two senses: no previous scholar has suggested the existence or the incorporation into Samuel of such inscriptions; and, no previous scholar has suggested that a simple rule, like the Tiglath-Pileser principle, could be applied to the text. My submission is that the results — and particularly the results in light of careful attention to the language of our text — reflect a historical reality whose reconstruction validates the assumptions of the study.

17. Tiglath-Pileser I in RIMA 2.A.0.89.1(21).iv:71-83; the later kings mention coalitions (such as Shalmaneser III in the Kurkh Monolith).

Appendix: 2 Samuel 8

(1) After this

David smote Philistines and subdued them.
And David took meteg ha'ammah from the hand of the Philistines

(2) And he smote Moab
   and he measured them by the rope, stretching them out on the ground, and
   he measured two lengths to kill and a full length to let live

   And Moab were servants to David, bearers of tribute

(3) And David smote Hadadezer son of Rehob king of Zobah when he went to
erect his stela at the River

   (4) And David captured from him 1700 horsemen and 20 thousand infantry, and David hamstrung all the chariotry but left of it 100 chariots. (See
   10:6, 18 — 700 chariots, 40 thousand horse.)

   (5) And Aram-Damascus came to help Hadadezer king of Zobah and David smote Aram 22 thousand men. (See 10:18, 700 chariots, 40 thousand
   horse.)

   (6) And David placed garrisons in Aram Damascus, and Aram were servants to David, bearers of tribute.

And Yahweh saved David wherever he went

(7) And David took the gold shields which Hadadezer's servants had and brought them to Jerusalem, (8) and from Tubihi and from Berotai, the cities of Hadadezer, King David took very much bronze.

(9) And Toi, king of Hamath, heard that David had smitten all the army of Hadadezer.

(10) So Toi sent Yoram his son to the king David to sue for peace and to bless him for fighting Hadadezer and smiting him, for Hadadezer was Toi's opponent at war, and in his hand were vessels of silver and vessels of gold and vessels of bronze.

(11) These too the king David dedicated to Yahweh, with the silver and gold he dedicated from the nations he conquered.
(12) From Aram and from Moab and from the sons of Ammon and from Philistines and from Amaleq and from the spoil of Hadadezer son of Rehob king of Zobah.

(13) And David made a stela when he returned from smiting Aram, in the Salt Valley, 18 thousand (casualties/dead).

(14) He placed in Edom garrisons; in all Edom he placed garrisons; and all Edom were servants to David

And Yahweh saved David wherever he went

(15) And David reigned over all Israel, and David dispensed justice and rightness to all his people.

CHAPTER 7

Settling the Philistine Problem: 2 Samuel 8:1

And it was afterward. And David smote (the?) Philistines and subdued
them. And David took the Meteg of the Ammah from the hand of (the?)
Philistines. (2 Sam. 8:1)

The first verse of 2 Sam. 8 relates that David defeated and subdued Philistines.
At a linguistic level, it is ambiguous whether the text means that he subdued all
the Philistines or a smaller group. The text of Samuel does not say "the
Philistines," even when "the Philistines" are the subject: it almost always says,
simply, "Philistines." This means that two Philistines, or one Philistine group,
or a major city of the Philistines, or all the Philistines could be meant — at the
literal level. Naturally, were one to interpret the claim in 2 Sam. 8:1 on the lines
of the Tiglath-Pileser principle, the implication would be that David subdued
at least two Philistines, or two or three people who could be called Philistines
for his purposes, such as local Philistine vassals.

David takes Meteg Ha-Ammah from the hand of the Philistines. The term
Meteg Ha-Ammah remains obscure. It occurs in no other text. Some commentators identify it with Gittaim (Heb. *gtym*, or *gtm*, which is *mtg* spelled back-
ward); others have more complex proposals.[1] This issue is likely never to be re-

---

1. P. Kyle McCarter, Jr., reads *hmgrš*, "the common land," with LXX and reviews other
solutions; *II Samuel*, 243. My own instinct is to look for corruption in the paleo-Hebrew
script. No commentator to date claims certainty. The versional evidence is every bit as perplexing as the commentators are perplexed.

solved. The Meteg of the Ammah is not likely to be a place. The prizes numbered in 2 Sam. 8 are rarely territorial. But the Meteg of the Ammah could be a piece of booty, or even something of symbolic import, as I will suggest below (Chapter 18). The name could also be the transcription into Hebrew of a Philistine term. The Philistine language remains poorly known — probably, it was a dialect from the Aegean or northeastern Mediterranean. But a Philistine term would be alien to Israelite copyists. This would increase the likelihood that the spelling was corrupted in transmission.

The great historian Albrecht Alt argued in 1936 that 2 Sam. 8:1 was a précis of David's battles with the Philistines before the arrival of the ark in Jerusalem.[2] In other words, the victory in 2 Sam. 8:1 is identical with that in ch. 5. Alt's logic was that 2 Sam. 8:1 was a resumption of the narrative of ch. 5 after the insertion of chs. 6-7 by a later author. But another perspective can also be offered.

In 2 Sam. 5, David twice enters into contest with the Philistines in the area around Jerusalem. In the first battle, the Philistines occupy the Rephaim Valley, between Bethlehem to the south and Jerusalem (remember the story of David and Bethlehem's well in the list of his heroes!). David asks Yahweh whether he should attack "Philistines," and Yahweh promises to give them into his hand. At Baal Perazim, David then "smites" them, capturing and carrying off the icons they abandon. This achievement requites the capture of the ark by the Philistines at the time of Eli: David now repays the Philistines for their former inroads into Israel.

1 Chr. 14:12 does deny that David carried off the icons, relating instead that he burned them. The medieval commentator David Kimhi exposed the logic of the author of Chronicles. David cannot have had a use for Philistine icons. Therefore, "he carried them off" had to be reinterpreted. A different form of the verb, "to carry," means "bonfire." So the author of Chronicles simply reinterpreted "he carried them off" as "he made a bonfire of them." Lest readers fall into the trap of thinking David took idols home, the Chronicler changed the verb to the unambiguous "they were burned in fire."[3]

The second battle in 2 Sam. 5 commences with a renewed Philistine deployment in the Valley of Rephaim. Yahweh tells David to avoid a frontal assault, but to flank the enemy instead. He is, at a signal, to fall on their camp. The

---

2. Albrecht Alt, "Zu II Samuel 8,1," *ZAW* 54 (1936): 149-52.

3. Kimhi to 2 Sam. 5:21. I am not sure that the term for "bonfire" (*mś't*) is not formed by congeneric assimilation with the verb *yṣt*, "to set alight." For interchange of *ś* and *ṣ* and the reasons for it, see Richard C. Steiner, *The Case for Fricative-Laterals in Proto-Semitic.* AOS 59 (New Haven: American Oriental Society, 1977).

account ends with the following statement: "He smote the Philistines from Geba (in Chronicles, Gibeon) unto the approaches to Gezer" (2 Sam. 5:25).

Here we have the defeat of some Philistines or their agents in the passes of the central hills. This is hardly the classic, coastal territory of the Philistine Pentapolis. The five cities — the pentapolis — of the Philistines, classically, are Gaza on the southern coast, Ashkelon, to the north of it, and Ashdod, north of Ashkelon. Inland were the two centers of Eqron and Gath. Eqron was certainly located at present-day Tel Miqneh. Scholars typically locate Gath just south of Eqron at Tel eş-Şafi. More recently, Lawrence E. Stager has identified Gath with a town found further to the south, at Tel Haror, on the Wadi Besor. This is unlikely, for a variety of reasons, but it is striking that Gath, which all but disappears from the textual record after the 9th century, was a major threat to Judah in Saul's time and a reliable partner in David's and Solomon's eras.[4]

The projection of Philistine power into the hills in the neighborhood of Jerusalem would mean that these coastal elements controlled the Ayyalon Pass, north of Jerusalem, leading across the hills to the Jordan Valley and into Transjordan. The archaeological evidence for such projection is weak, but trade links certainly did exist in David's time.[5] Whether proper Philistines held the hills, or surrogates, or vassals is a question whose answer depends on how one evaluates the evidence for trade and the evidence of the text. The issue is addressed in Chapter 19.

Regardless, 2 Sam. 5 and 8 treat the Philistines as a monolithic group rather than as a collection of city-states and colonies or vassals. The language of 2 Sam. 8:1 thus implies that all the Philistines were bested. But that is merely the implication. The books of Samuel are also the only biblical texts to use the word "Philistine" as an adjective (as opposed to "Eqronite," "Gittite," etc.). For, had we the diplomatic correspondence of the time, the resemblance would be to the situation exposed by the archive at el-Amarna, during Egypt's administration of an empire in Canaan, at the time of Amenhotep III and his son Akhenaten. We would have the king of Eqron complaining about David, the king of Ashdod complaining about the king of Eqron, and so on. The image of Philistine unity in 2 Samuel and parts of Kings is nothing more than a propagandistic myth. It permits the record to imply that a victory over any Philistine element is the defeat of the Philistines as a whole.

---

4. See esp. Lawrence E. Stager, "The Impact of the Sea Peoples in Canaan (1185-1050 BCE)," in *The Archaeology of Society in the Holy Land,* ed. Thomas E. Levy (New York: Facts on File, 1995), 342-43. Against him, William M. Schniedewind, *BASOR* 309 (1998): 69-77. See further below, Chapter 18.

5. See Stager, "The Impact of the Sea Peoples."

146

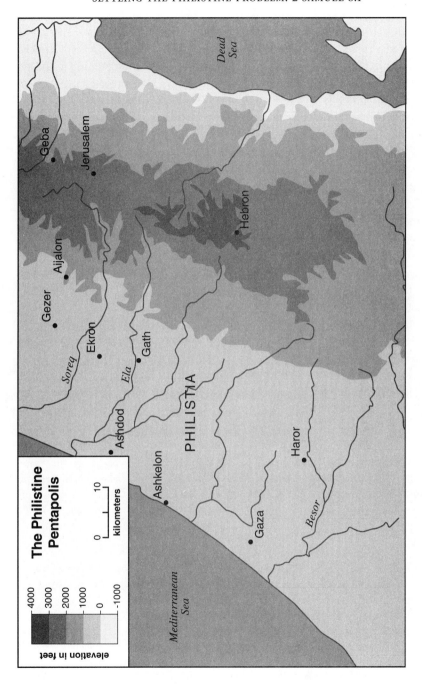

The Philistine Pentapolis

Map 7.1

We are badly informed concerning the five cities of the so-called Pentapolis in this era. No text tells us much about Gaza. Ashkelon and Ashdod are ciphers. Concerning Eqron, our texts convey no reliable information relating to the era of David and Solomon, though they do mention it. The archaeological situation is clearer, thanks to the excavation at Tel Miqneh. Some time around the era of the United Monarchy, the area occupied by habitation at the site shrinks dramatically. But it cannot be ascertained at present whether this correlates with the rise of the Israelite monarchy in Jerusalem, with the campaign of the pharaoh Shishaq after the death of Solomon, or with the ascendance of some neighboring city-state in Philistia itself, such as Gath.[6]

About the other inland Philistine center, Gath, we lack archaeological information, or even a certain archaeological identification. We do have a little textual information. Two references and one nonreference imply that the territory of Gath, including its hinterland, was beyond David's reach: first, there is only one reference to a battle at Gath, in the appendix to 2 Samuel (21:20-21), and that one makes no claim as to any conquest of the city or of any territory. The locations of other battles in 2 Sam. 21 are unsure.[7]

It was remarked earlier, in Chapters 1 and 6, that the Goliath story seems to be constructed of elements from a number of notices in 2 Sam. 21 and 23. The base text for the story, again, is 2 Sam. 21:19. Here, Elhanan, the Bethlehemite, kills Goliath of Gath, the staff of whose spear is like a weaver's beam. Elhanan is Elhanan ben-Dodo. His father's name, close to David's, and his origin in Bethlehem led storytellers to displace the contest onto David from Bethlehem.

The other major contributor to the story is 2 Sam. 23:9-10. Here, another

6. On Miqneh, see Seymour Gitin, "Tel Miqne-Ekron: A Type-Site for the Inner Coastal Plain in the Iron Age II Period," in Gitin and William G. Dever, *Recent Excavations in Israel,* 25-26, 41; Trude Dothan, "The Arrival of the Sea Peoples," 20 fig. 1.15. Gitin attributes the decline to the expansion of Solomon's kingdom "in the second quarter of the 10th century" (following Bustenay Oded, cited there) and invokes Shishaq, at least implicitly, as a factor. Conversely, the shrinkage may reflect Eqron's border status in the United Monarchy (so Lawrence E. Stager, in conversation). From other information available to us, it might seem that Shishaq was the major factor in the extreme shrinkage. This would comport with the presence of burnished red-slip pottery in Miqneh Stratum IV, which should bring its latest occupation into the late 10th century. See John S. Holladay, Jr., "Red Slip, Burnish, and the Solomonic Gateway at Gezer," *BASOR* 277/278 (1990): 23-70. For a new reconstruction, however, see below, Chapters 18 and 21.

7. This raises the question whether the location of 2 Sam. 21:20-21 at Gath is primary or secondary, possibly on the basis of the association of the site with polydactylism. Nob/Gob in other accounts (2 Sam. 21:15ff.) might be corrupt. See McCarter, *II Samuel,* 449-50, for an association of 21:19 with Gezer, which, while plausible, is not probable. In any event, the reference here as elsewhere is to the town's territory, not the city gate.

son of Dodo, Eleazar, the Ahohite, fights at Pas-Dammim (in 1 Chr. 11:13). This is Epes Dammim, the location of David's joust with Goliath, of 1 Sam. 17:1-2 — between Azekah and Socho, probably in the northward bend of the Wadi Ela. Eleazar's Philistine foe challenges Israel,[8] just as Goliath does in 1 Sam. 17. And the Israelites retreat, just as they cringe in the face of Goliath's challenge. At this juncture Eleazar takes a stand, as David does in the Goliath story. The third source of the Goliath story is 2 Sam. 23:21, in which Benaiah, armed only with a staff, faces a giant Egyptian. David too confronts Goliath "with sticks." Benaiah kills the giant with the latter's own weapon, as David does; and the giant's spear is distinctive, and in 1 Chr. 11:23 is likened to a weaver's beam. The Goliath story reads like a combination of these and other events (Chapter 6).

All this casts doubt on the Goliath story. However, at the end of the story, 1 Sam. 17:52 claims that the Israelites penetrated the territory of Eqron. The same text makes no such claim about Gath: the rout is "up to Gath" — up to the border of its hinterland, on the Tiglath-Pileser principle. This may imply that Stager is right to question the usual identification of Gath with Tell eṣ-Ṣafi, which is visible from Azekah, the location of the Goliath story. On the other hand, the text will concede a few chapters later that David entered the service of Gath: it may be that narrative logic restrains the narrator from claiming that David's earliest exploit led to inroads against Gath. Still, as we shall see, a Philistine retreat to Eqron may simply reflect conditions in David's time.

The second reference to Gath is more intriguing. It stems from a text reviewed above, in Chapter 2. David is evacuating Jerusalem in the face of Absalom's revolt. Ittay the Gittite then comes and demands the right to accompany David. Along with Ittay, 600 Gittites, who had been with David in his days at Ziklag, insist on remaining with the king. David argues against Ittay's choice: why should Ittay relocate yet again, given that he is an exile from his own land? This indicates that, in the presentation at least, Gath and Judah/Israel are not unified politically. Nor is Gath a vassal of the Israelite state, under compulsion to do service to it. On the contrary, Gath is independent of the state focused in Jerusalem, so that Gittites in the service of the king of Jerusalem are in a foreign land (2 Sam. 15:18-22).

The third text engaging Gath directly is 1 Kgs. 2:39-40. These verses relate that two slaves fled from Shimei's establishment in Jerusalem, no doubt abetted in their flight by Solomon. The slaves fled to Gath. The king there, "Achish son of Maacah" (= Achish, or Achaios, son of Ma'och), has the same name as that of David's old liege lord at Gath. But the key is that Shimei had to go to Gath in or-

---

8. See McCarter, *II Samuel*, 490.

der to arrange for the extradition of his slaves. That he was able to retrieve them suggests the existence of some sort of treaty.

But that Shimei had to go to Gath personally in order to retrieve his slaves indicates that extradition was not automatic. It again suggests that Gath was not subject to the United Monarchy. It might be submitted that Gath was in a position of vassalage and that the slaves knew no better than to flee there; moreover, that Solomon arranged the escape with the purpose of entrapping Shimei. All the same, any such claims demand a lack of sophistication on the slaves' part, or a hyper-sophistication on Solomon's part combined with Shimei's implausible gullibility, that we have no basis to hypothesize.

Gath was outside David's ambit. It may have remained an equal partner with him in diplomatic relations throughout his reign. Indeed, it is not clear exactly when he ceased to be the vassal of Achish of Gath. It is certain that Solomon was independent of Gath, and early in his reign — by the time of his marriage to the daughter of the Egyptian pharaoh, before the completion of his palace (Chapters 17, 19, 22).

What is the minimal allegation of our text on the Tiglath-Pileser principle? It is that some Philistines established or traveling between Geba or Gibeon and Gezer were overwhelmed — all three of them. Gezer was the border in David's time: "He smote the Philistines from Geba (or Gibeon, 1 Chr. 14:16) unto the approaches to Gezer" (2 Sam. 5:25). David took the territory of the town of Ayyalon, in the uplands east of Gezer.

Gezer remained the border in the reign of David's son. A pharaoh of the 21st Dynasty campaigned in Philistia — redefining relations between the Philistine cities and Jerusalem. He burned Gezer to the ground and presented the mound to Solomon as a dowry for his daughter (1 Kgs. 9:16). That is, Gezer remained outside Israel's territory until Solomon's father-in-law handed it to Solomon on a plate. Even then, Gezer's territory was the outer limit of Israel's expansion in the Shephelah, the anticline between the coastal plain and the hills of Judah. So David's expansion stopped at the edge of the hill country, at Gezer's eastern border (Ayyalon). Even Solomon controlled very little territory west of that line. The independence of Gath, to the south of Gezer, is thus again confirmed.

There are traditions of combat in the appendices to 2 Samuel (in chs. 21 and 23). Chiefly, the action takes place in sites such as Gob and Nob. Most scholars regard these place names as corruptions of Geba or Gibeon. "Nob" is also the city of the priests whom Saul eradicates in 1 Sam. 21:1(2)-22:19. These localities lie just north of Jerusalem. A further action takes place at Bethlehem, south of Jerusalem, in connection with a Philistine garrison there. One engagement is located in (E)Pes Dammim, on the fringe of the hills. Another takes place "in Gath": if this is not a corruption from "Gob," this text claims that a battle took place inside the territory, though not at the actual site, of Gath, an inland Philistine city. The battle belongs on the eastern edge of the coastal plain or, less probably, further inland.[9]

In sum, there is no evidence David fought Philistines outside of the hill country. And the only tradition of hill country conflict between David and the Philistines that mentions any standing Philistine presence (2 Sam. 23:13-17) refers to an event related to the conquest of Jerusalem: David is "in the hold" (cf. 1 Sam. 22:4-5), in a cave at Adullam. The enemy garrison is in Bethlehem, on the road from Hebron to Jerusalem. Perhaps this episode should be assigned to the time of David's conflict with the Philistines in 2 Sam. 5. The two engagements described in that chapter, like this one, place David "in the hold" and involve Philistine forces camped in the Rephaim Valley, just outside Jerusalem.[10] But it is possible that the raid on the Bethlehem cistern took place in Saul's day, or during David's time as a Philistine vassal.[11] Saul, after all, is given the credit for removing one such garrison,[12] and for recruiting David from Bethlehem. One may therefore infer that any Philistine presence at sites in Benjamin, north

9. In 2 Sam. 21:15-17, no site is mentioned; 21:18, Nob (McCarter's Gezer, with 1 Chr. 20:4); 21:19, Gob (1 Chr. 20:5, no location). 2 Sam. 21:20-21 takes place in Gath (also in 1 Chr. 20:6), though one wonders about the influence of the succeeding verse. In 2 Sam. 21:22 (1 Chr. 20:8), all the opponents in the foregoing notices are reported to have been born to the Raphah in Gath. The other appended list of engagements adds little detail to the picture: 2 Sam. 23:9-10 (1 Chr. 11:12-14), Pas Dammim (east of Azekah); 23:11, if anywhere, Lehi, which is by 'Etam in the Judahite hills (Judg. 15:9-19), but probably the term merely denotes a Philistine field camp; 2 Sam. 23:13-17 (1 Chr. 11:15-20), Adullam to Bethlehem, in the early period. The other battle vignette, 2 Sam. 23:20-23 (1 Chr. 11:22-25), is unique in that it does not involve Philistines or alleged Philistines, but an Egyptian and two Moabites with the designation "ariel."

10. It is tempting to connect the name of this valley to the term "born/dedicated to the Rapha," which describes Philistine, or more specifically, Gittite champions in 2 Sam. 21:22, and to take the term to refer to the place where these troops were permanently stationed.

11. So McCarter, II Samuel, 495. But as this text places David at Adullam, it is more likely that elements of this record, where the bravery is that of David's subordinates, and where no actual field victory is claimed, have been aggrandized in the connected narrative. That this was done in connection with the same story in the doublet in 1 Sam. 24 and 26 I have argued previously (The First Historians, 62-65). For a further case, of conflation of the appendix notices with the Goliath story, see above.

12. 1 Sam. 10:5-7; 13:2-3. On the reduction of gb'(n?) in 1 Sam. 13:3 as the fulfilment of the command to Saul to "do what comes to hand" at "gb't h'lhym, where there is a garrison of the Philistines," see Baruch Halpern, The Constitution of the Monarchy, 155-56.

of Jerusalem, such as Tell en-Naṣbeh (Mizpeh), was contemporary with or anterior to Saul's, not David's monarchy.[13]

In fact, David's collaboration with Philistines suggests that he would have had no special interest in rooting them out from the central hills. Even the text speaks of him as a net importer of them. Six hundred Gittites followed him throughout his reign (2 Sam. 15:18-22; 18:2).[14] Six hundred warriors represents a complete cohort, or brigade. In assessing the significance of the number, one need only recall that the local infantry contingent, from Hamath, at the battle of Qarqar in 853 B.C.E. numbered only 20 thousand troops, and the next largest Western contingent numbered only 10 thousand — and these are the sums provided by the Assyrian opponent whom they stymied. Six hundred Gittites would constitute a substantial component even of a large national army, let alone that of a city with so limited a hinterland. Indeed, in 1 Sam. 13:5, the entire force of the five Philistine cities amounts to 30 thousand infantrymen, or 6000 men from each town of the Pentapolis.[15]

The traditions in 2 Sam. 5 and 8 make no mention of any Philistine garrison in the vicinity of the action near Jerusalem. Whereas Saul fights the assembled forces of the pentapolis at Jezreel, David merely confronts "Philistines." In 2 Sam. 5 and 8, in sum, the subjugation of the Philistines amounted to the removal of Eqronite or Gittite filibusters or even agents from the Ayyalon Pass. There are other hints of the presence of such elements. First is the report, at the time of Saul's seizing the throne, of a Philistine garrison at Gibeah ("the hill [of God]").[16] Second is the notice mentioned above, in 2 Sam. 23:13-17, where the Philistine garrison is to the south of Jerusalem, in Bethlehem, which is another stop on Saul's itinerary en route to seizing the throne.[17]

13. And the Philistine pottery at Mizpeh is purely of the classic bichrome phase, before David's time.

14. Against McCarter, *II Samuel*, 363-64, it seems more sensible to retain "six hundred" with the Gittites: in the conflate LXX text, it is more likely the non-Gittite component of David's retinue that is apologetically augmented.

15. The number, based on standard archaeological assumptions about density of habitation, is probably too high by a factor of about two for the five cities of the Philistines. But this says nothing about its accuracy.

16. 1 Sam. 10:5. In 1 Sam. 13:2, Jonathan is in Gibeah of Benjamin, Saul's later residence. He smites a Philistine garrison at Geba (or Gibeah, or Gibeon) in 13:3.

17. The tomb of Rachel, in 1 Sam. 10:2, described there as lying inside the territory of Benjamin, in the region of Zelzah *(ṣlṣh)*. The latter term is probably used as a pun on the infusion of Yahweh's spirit into Saul — it supervenes on him *(ṣlḥ*, 1 Sam. 10:6, 10), transforming him *(nhpkt, yhpk)*, so there are further verbs denoting change in the narrative, as puns *(ḥlpt*, 10:3; *hpnt*, 10:9). In any case, the story stems from a time when Benjamin was thought to extend south of Jerusalem, before there was a separate tribe of Judah. See

The story of David's retrieval of the ark provides another index. David proceeds with the ark "belonging to Yahweh of Hosts who sits enthroned upon the cherubim" from Baale of Judah, another name for the Gibeonite town of Qiryath Yearim (1 Sam 6:21-7:2; 2 Sam 6:2). Oddly enough, when disaster halts the transfer between Baale Judah and Jerusalem, David leaves the ark not with Israelites, but at the house of Obed Edom the Gittite; in Chronicles, Obed Edom becomes the founder of a line of Levites.[18] But here he is a Gittite, resident in a Gibeonite town.

There are two traditions of conflict with Gittites in the genealogical lists of Chronicles. These are difficult to assess, to be sure, as to historical value, but are nevertheless at least suggestive. In the first, "the men of Gath who were born in the land" slew two or more descendants of Ephraim, presumably eponyms of groups, when the Ephraimites staged a raid on the Gittite cattle (1 Chr. 7:21). The son born to Ephraim after this loss is Beriah (7:22-23). Beriah reappears, with Shema, in 1 Chr. 8:13, as a Benjaminite eponym:

Beriah and Shema are the heads of the lineage groups for the inhabitants of Ayyalon. They put the inhabitants of Gath to flight.

Here, again, there is a tradition of Gittite activity in the region of the Ayyalon Pass.[19] Unfortunately, neither the date of the action nor the reliability of the tradition is evident.

All this would seem to support the notion of a Philistine thrust into that region, perhaps before Saul's seizure of power. This might mean that the 600 Gittites, including Ittay, who accompany David from the capital during Absalom's revolt (2 Sam. 15:18-22), may in fact represent a garrison unit originally from the central hill country. No Ittay the Gittite appears in the list of David's warrior chiefs in 2 Sam. 23. However, there is an Ittay son of Ribay from Gibeah of the Benjaminites (2 Sam. 23:29; 1 Chr. 11:31). That is, Ittay the Gittite is from Benjaminite Gibeah, a town that played host to a Philistine garrison until Saul's occupation of it. The Ayyalon Pass, including Bethlehem, to the south of Jerusalem, may have played host and sometimes hostage to elements that the books of Samuel would identify as Philistine.

Baruch Halpern, *The Emergence of Israel in Canaan.* SBLMS 29 (Atlanta: Scholars, 1983), 109-44.

18. 2 Sam. 6:10-11. Obed Edom becomes a son of Yeduthun, one of the guilds of singers. See 1 Chr. 13:13-14; 15:18-25; 16:38; 26:4, 8, 15; 2 Chr. 25:24.

19. For the Chronicles texts, see Manfred Oeming, *Das wahre Israel: Die "genealogische Vorhalle" 1 Chronik 1–9.* BWANT 7/8 (Stuttgart: Kohlhammer, 1990), 165, 172.

The maximal claim of 2 Sam. 5 is that David expelled Philistine elements from the Ayyalon Pass in the central hills. He pursued them to the border of Gezer's territory. In contradistinction, thus, to the Moabites and Damascenes, the text does *not* allege that the Philistines — any Philistines whatever — accepted David's sovereignty or paid him tribute. Indeed, the text does not lay claim to an inch of the coastal plain where the Philistine Pentapolis towns lay. The omission is not fortuitous.

This point has an edge to it. The text does not claim that David dominated Philistia. It discloses that throughout his reign he had Gittite allies. It admits that toward the early part of Solomon's reign Jerusalem's relations with Gath were warm enough that Shimei could expect the extradition of his runaway slaves. On the other hand, a Pharaoh campaigned on the Philistine plain and reassigned the site of Gezer to Solomon, with some or all of its hinterland as a dowry for his daughter (1 Kgs. 9:16-17). Gezer presumably belonged to the city-state that had projected its control into the Ayyalon Pass (see further below, Chapter 18). Only as a result of Solomon's marital diplomacy does Israel expand beyond the hills onto the east side of the Philistine coast. Thus, what the text does not allege about David dovetails with what it does claim for Solomon. That is precisely why 2 Sam. 8:1 doesn't stipulate where David fought the Philistines: the author hopes to insinuate that the battle took place in the plain, and traditionally readers have assumed that it did, that David conquered Philistia. This is another index of the text's early date: a late inventor of David would certainly have claimed that he did conquer Philistia: hence the interpretation of 1 Chr. 18:1 that David took the territory of Gath.

But in another arena, the text's silence raises vexing questions. It does not claim that it was David who conquered the major Canaanite fortresses of the north, including such major fortifications in the Jezreel Valley as Yoqneam, Megiddo, and Beth Shan. At the last site, the Philistines displayed trophies of their victory at Jezreel and Mount Gilboa. Yet Solomon was in control of the Jezreel fortresses, and of sites further north: the Jezreel fortresses form the centers of one of his administrative provinces (1 Kgs. 4:12), and he is said to have fortified Megiddo (9:15). His provinces include two in the Galilee, to the north of the Jezreel (1 Kgs. 4:15-16). Sometime between Saul's death and the early part of Solomon's reign, the Jezreel Valley fell under Israelite control.

What Israelite laid hold of them? The answer that we should intuitively furnish is: either Saul or Ishbaal must have subjected the great Canaanite fortresses of the interior. There is little trace of the Canaanites in the Jezreel Valley in Iron I, outside of the fortress mound sites.[20] North of the valley, at Tel Ein

20. This is the result of the 1995 and 1998 Megiddo Survey of the Jezreel Valley.

Sippori, a longstanding, wealthy Canaanite settlement seems to have made a peaceful transition to incorporation in the Israelite territorial state.[21]

At Megiddo, the situation is both slightly better illuminated and more problematic as a result of the illumination. Megiddo Stratum VIA was founded no earlier than about 1100, and was perhaps founded later. This city fell victim to a conflagration that covered the full extent of the mound, shortly after 1000. The fire may have been accidental, rather than the result of an attack. The succeeding settlement was unmistakably Israelite, including pillared houses characteristic of villages in the central hill country and the Upper Galilee. Yet it is possible that one or two such structures were already present on the site in Stratum VIA, before 1000.

Furthermore, the last phase of Stratum VIA, at the time of its destruction, contained collared-rim storage jars. This storage implement is found occasionally at lowland sites, in small quantities. But it is ubiquitous in the highlands. The frequency of the collared-rim vessel in Megiddo VIA is high, and focuses in the southern residential quadrant of the settlement. So the residential quarter looks as though it played host to a number of highlanders or Israelites, possibly through a process of connubium and the relocation of women to the establishments of their husbands' families.[22] This implies a certain sympathy, but not necessarily alliance, with the Israelites. How Megiddo VIA relates to Saul, Ishbaal, and David is thus unclear (a suggestion is made in Chapters 21-23).

In any event, the authors of Samuel neglected to mention the taking of the Jezreel fortresses. Outside Benjaminite territory, Saul captures not a single town. Ishbaal does not even capture a town *inside* Benjaminite territory, and he never engages the Philistines in battle. Yet 1 Kings opens with Solomon in possession of all of Cisjordan, except Philistia, up to Tyre and at least the outskirts of Damascus. Scholars, and most other readers, have assumed that it was David who conquered the Jezreel towns, and several centers in Transjordan. And Sam-

---

21. Excavation at Ein Sippori is ongoing, and publication is in progress. Details of the results were provided courtesy of Professor J. P. Dessel, in lecture and in correspondence.

22. See esp. Douglas L. Esse, "The Collared Pithos at Megiddo: Ceramic Distribution and Ethnicity," *JNES* 51 (1992): 81-103. Excavations at Megiddo in 1998, still unpublished, resulted in a substantial exposure of VIA on the southeastern edge of the tell (Area K). I suspect that this was an industrial establishment, though perhaps combined with residence, since the concentration of storage jars — including of the collared-rim variety, in the 2000 season — was extraordinary, and they seem to have contained a flammable liquid, such as oil. For further comment on VIA, see tentatively the summary articles by Baruch Halpern and by Israel Finkelstein and David Ussishkin in Finkelstein, Ussishkin, and Halpern, eds., *Megiddo III: The 1992-1996 Seasons* (Tel Aviv: Institute of Archaeology, 2000).

uel strives, by its description of Philistines hanging Saul's corpse at Beth Shan and displaying his armor in the Golan, to create this impression. But had David, or Solomon, had anything at all to do with the capture of Megiddo, or Beth Shan, or even Taanach or Yoqneam, their propagandists should have left us in no doubt as to the fact.

If someone from the House of Saul conquered the Jezreel, the text omits the conquests for two reasons. First, neither David nor Solomon could claim credit for them. This is another index of the antiquity of 2 Samuel. The book was not written so long after the events that authors in Jerusalem could falsify the achievement. Second, the conquests were achieved by a king of a competing dynasty, and were probably enshrined in the inscriptions of that dynasty. At any rate, the feat was widely known. *Prima facie*, it looks as though Ishbaal was the conqueror of the north (but see below). If so, the layer Ishbaal held at Megiddo was Stratum VIA.

Such an explanation comports with the treatment of Saul's dynasty throughout Samuel. Saul is denied credit for any Israelite territorial expansion. Neither he nor Ishbaal is explicitly identified with a capital city, whereas David reigns in Hebron, and he and Solomon reign in Jerusalem. Above all, the policy of silence about the achievements of others would explain the absence of Philistine interference in the Israelite civil war. Otherwise, the lacuna is difficult to explain: Philistine forces were David's allies. They were Israel's most menacing enemies. Here, however, they do not appear except as a negligible impediment to David's move to Jerusalem. This is hardly believable on the face of it.

The alternatives are far more attractive: Saul may in fact have emerged as the victor, at the cost of his life, from the battle of Jezreel — possibly betrayed and cut down by David. Or Saul may have made substantial gains in the Jezreel and north, and Ishbaal may have recouped the losses suffered at the end of Saul's life. Or Ishbaal himself may have seized control of the Jezreel and parts of Transjordan. Or another, later, member of the House of Saul may have taken them. In any of these cases, the state of the text as we have it would have a natural explanation. The traditional one — that the authors of the text merely forgot to mention the conquests — is forced in comparison (see further Chapters 21-22).

One of the primary corollaries to the Tiglath-Pileser principle is that when a king does not claim credit for positive achievements, they certainly were not his. This is the case here. The text does not prevaricate — to the extent of claiming that David took Philistine territory or the Jezreel. And yet, it gives the reader the impression that he did.

There is one difficulty with the text, which would seem to invalidate this allegation, at least in part. The opening phrase of the chapter is, "And it was afterward." The Hebrew words are, *wyhy 'ḥry kn:* the first, *way-yĕhî,* means, "it was," or "it came to pass," or "so." The other two words translate as "after" and "thus." A sympathetic reader, approaching this verse, would therefore assume that the smiting of the Philistines and their submission was after, and therefore additional to, the exploits of David in 2 Sam. 5. This has led readers to infer that David did expand beyond the territory of Gezer, in 2 Sam. 8:1.

One can rescue the veracity of this opening phrase as it is traditionally understood, by claiming that a third battle with Philistines did indeed occur after David brought the ark to Jerusalem. This would imply that the summary statement of 2 Sam. 5:25 was proleptic:

> David did so *(kn),* as Yahweh commanded him, and he smote Philistines
> from Geba unto the approach to (or "border of the territory of") Gezer.

As we have seen, David never even took the territory of Gezer, at which this verse places him. The short distance involved speaks against two successful engagements near Jerusalem, then a third (2 Sam. 8:1) to expel the Philistines from the hill country. Further, it is unlikely that there was any major permanent "Philistine" investment in the Ayyalon Pass after Saul pursued them to Ayyalon.

These considerations remind us that "It was afterward" is a part of the editorial construction of the whole book. We should probably reject Alt's conclusion. For him, 8:1 ("it was afterward that David smote Philistines") resumed 2 Sam. 5:25. This indicated that 2 Sam. 6–7 are secondary, not related in their chronological place. For this purpose, "it was afterward" is a particularly bad choice of introduction. However, Alt's instinct, as so often in the career of that superb scholar, was true. 2 Sam. 6 is probably antedated, placed by the original author of 2 Samuel out of its time; and this is almost certainly the case with 2 Sam. 7.[23] The engagements with the Philistines are identical, and the resumption of them in 2 Sam. 8:1 is deliberate. 2 Sam. 8:1, as noted, does not specify a location for the battle: this permits the reader to think of it as a third battle without the author falsifying information.

This thought opens up three possible lines of interpretation. "It was afterward" might be the product of an editor who believed that three or more battles

---

23. Royal inscriptions frequently antedate the construction of temples or shrines. See Baruch Halpern, "A Historiographic Commentary on Ezra 1–6," with bibliography. 2 Sam. 7 begins with the statement that Yahweh had accorded David respite from his enemies all about, which could even be taken to place the text after Absalom's revolt. The respite might have been temporary. But the promise that his son would build a temple creates linkage to 2 Sam. 24, where David acquires the site for the structure. And it is probably sensible to place the initiative toward temple building after the slaughter of Saul's family at Gibeon.

occurred. But this would mean that the edition was late, which is unlikely because the introductory phrase is common in Samuel. Second, "It was afterward" may refer to some, but not necessarily all, of the content of this chapter. That is, "afterward" may represent the introduction to a summation of all of David's conquests and military career. It is the sum of his accomplishments that is later, the creation of an empire, not necessarily all of the individual engagements by which the empire was constructed.

The third possibility is more subtle, and I, for one, prefer it for just that reason. The author of 2 Sam. 8, as we shall see time and again, was a highly skilled propagandist working in part on David's behalf, even if the chapter is set into a framework written under Solomon. The text may therefore be literally true, and yet deceptive. To an extent, this depends on the interpretation of the phrase itself: "And it was, afterward, (that)" + action. "Afterward" without "and it was" is reasonably common.[24] However, the sequence "and it was, after thus, (that)" + action, is rare outside Samuel. Only in two cases is it followed, as in Samuel, by "and," then by a verb describing the simple past.[25]

The phrase "and it was afterward" occurs six times in Samuel, more than in

---

24. *'ḥry kn*. In the parentheses after the next citations, the term (e) means the phrase occurs at the end of a clause; (i-f) that the succeeding verb is an imperfect with future reference *(yaqtulu)*; (p) that the following verb is a perfect with past reference; (i-d) that the succeeding verb is an imperfect with past durative reference *(yaqtulu)*. The phrase occurs in Gen. 41:31 (e); Exod. 11:1 (i-f); Josh. 10:26 (e); 1 Sam. 9:13 (i-f); 24:8 (e); 2 Sam. 21:14 (e); 24:10 (e, with 𝕲^L); Isa. 1:26 (i-f); Jer. 34:11 (e); Job 3:1 (p). After the term "and," it occurs in Gen. 15:14 (i-f); 23:19 (p); 25:26 (p); 32:21 (i-f); 45:15 (p); Exod. 3:20 (i-f); 11:8 (i-f); 34:32 (p); Lev. 16:26 (i-f), 28 (i-f); Num. 4:15 (i-f); 8:15 (i-f), 22 (i-f); 9:17 (i-d); Josh. 8:34 (p); Jer. 16:16 (i-f); 21:7 (i-f); 46:26 (i-f); 49:6 (i-f); Ezra 3:5 (no verb); 2 Chr. 20:35 (p); 33:14 (p). In all these cases, the succeeding verbs occur without "and" (w-) prefixed to them. The variant *'ḥr kn* occurs in Lev. 14:36 (i-f); Deut. 21:13 (i-f), in both cases without "and" prefixed to the verb. No short prefix-conjugation verb appears in these cases, as in the other occurrences in Samuel.

25. Judg. 16:4, "Samson loved a woman," *wyhy 'ḥry kn wy'hb 'šh*; 2 Kgs. 6:24, "Ben-Hadad gathered," *wyhy 'ḥry kn wyqbṣ* Ben-Hadad. Close is the expression of Gen. 22:1, "and it was after these things, that the God tested Abraham," *wyhy 'ḥr hdbrym h'lh wh'lhym nsh* Abraham. Note that the last text employs the perfect, not the short imperfect. The three late parallels all omit "and" before the verb. See Joel 3:1, *whyh 'ḥry kn, 'špwk*, "it will be afterward, I will pour out my spirit"; 2 Chr. 20:1, *wyhy 'ḥry kn b'w bny mw'b*, "and it was, afterward, the Moabites came"; 2 Chr. 24:4, *wyhy 'ḥry kn hyh 'm lb* Joash, "and it was, afterward, Joash had it in mind." Joel has future reference, and Chronicles uses the perfect to express the continuation of past action. These texts are all postexilic. The exilic Ezek. 16:23 is not a close parallel, and the continuation is nonverbal in any case, but the copula is missing.

the rest of the Bible. It is always followed by "and" and then the verb.[26] This is clearly the early syntax for the phrase. On the other hand, the phrase can be understood to mean "and it was (thus), afterward," in contemporary English, "and that's how it was." In that case, the phrase is a clause: the succeeding narrative then stands in a logical, not a temporal sequence following the foregoing action.

In other words, 2 Sam. 8:1, "and it was afterward thus, and David smote Philistines" may link to 2 Sam. 7. At the end of ch. 7, David prays for eternal blessing of his dynasty. 2 Sam. 8:1 says that he received it. And he smote Philistines, and others, showing that Yahweh showered him with blessing and "great repute." It is possible to take 2 Sam. 13:1 in the same way. Nathan has just condemned David to suffer for killing Uriah and taking Bathsheba. This verse introduces the rape of Tamar with the line, "And it was afterward so," possibly confirming Nathan's words. The other occurrences are uniformly temporal, and those in 2 Sam. 8 and 13 appear to be so as well. And yet, it may be that the usage is intentionally deceptive. It would be very much in keeping with the tradition of royal propaganda in the ancient Near East if the temporal clause at the start of 2 Sam. 8 was in fact an affirmation that David's dynasty was eternally blessed.

---

26. The instances are 1 Sam. 24:5, *wyhy 'ḥry kn wyk lb dwd;* 2 Sam. 2:1, *wyhy 'ḥry kn wyš'l dwd byhwh;* 2 Sam. 8:1 = 1 Chr. 18:1, under examination here; 2 Sam. 10:1 = 1 Chr. 19:1, *wyhy 'ḥry kn wymt* the king of Ammon; 13:1, *wyhy 'ḥry kn wl'bšlwm bn dwd 'ḥwt,* "Absalom had a sister"; 21:18, with a near equivalent in 1 Chr. 20:4, *wyhy 'ḥry kn wthy 'wd mlḥmh,* "there was another war." Also related is 2 Sam. 15:1, "and it was, afterward, that Absalom made himself" *(wyhy m'ḥry kn wy'ś Absalom lw).* Without "and it was," "afterward" also occurs in 1 Sam. 10:5, *'ḥr kn tbw',* "afterward you will come." "From afterward" occurs in 2 Sam. 3:28: "David heard afterward" *(wyšm' dwd m'ḥry kn).* The latter has a parallel in 2 Chr. 32:23, "[Hezekiah] was exalted in the eyes of all the nations afterward." The locution in Samuel consistently governs a *yaqtul* continuation when the reference is past, in contrast to the overwhelming preponderance of usage in later prose texts, as the previous notes detail.

159

CHAPTER 8

The Conquest of Moab: 2 Samuel 8:2

David's relations with the Philistines are the first subject in 2 Sam. 8. The choice is significant in several ways. First, David undertook few campaigns against elements that could be called Philistines. Second, his success against the Philistines was severely limited, probably by choice. He does not seem to have campaigned in Philistine territory at all. Every indication coincides on the interpretation that he more or less excluded the Philistines from the theaters of his activity.

All the same, the record forefronts this conflict, and stories of combat with Philistines dominate the appendices treating David's warriors, despite the fact that there is virtually no narrative reflex of these encounters in the body of 2 Samuel. This seeming contradiction will occupy us again in the reconstruction of David's reign. The author of the apology felt it to be of the essence that David, like Saul in the A source, earn his spurs at the Philistines' expense. Here, it indicates how careful, and attentive to detail, the reader of 2 Sam. 8 must be. While the verse about the Philistines does not overtly state an untruth, it does create an impression of David as a fighter of Philistines, which is at variance with the historical reality.

The second claim of 2 Sam. 8 is that David defeated Moab, and killed two-thirds of his captives.

> He smote Moab, and measured them out with a length of rope, laying them out on the ground. He measured out two lengths of rope to kill, and a full length of rope to let live. So Moab became servants, tribute bearers, for David.

The surviving third of the Moabites paid tribute, at least once.

This is the only one of the records of David's battles in which he executes captives. We may, however, assume that it was his standard practice. 1 Kgs. 11 describes the circumstances in which a young member of the Edomite royal family fled before Israel to Egypt:

> And it was, when David annihilated[1] Edom, when Joab, commander of the army, went up to inter the corpses, that he smote every male in Edom. For, for six months Joab dwelled there, Joab and all Israel, until he eradicated every male in Edom. (1 Kgs. 11:15-16)

This detail is absent in Samuel, and is made explicit in Kings only because it explains the flight of the Edomite prince, who was to return on David's death in order to revolt against Solomon. So the question arises, why does 2 Sam. 8 relate the slaughter of Moabite captives but not the winnowing of the Edomites?

The narrative provides no guidance as to events here. David smote Moab — as he did Philistia. Two-thirds of a group of Moabites were killed after David "smote" Moab. But in what part of his career the battle took place is not certain. No king of Moab appears in 2 Sam. 8, although one is mentioned in 1 Sam. 22:3-4 as the protector of David's family during Saul's reign. Nor is the scene of the battle identified. On the other hand, the notice in 2 Sam. 23:20 does ascribe the deaths of two Ariels of Moab to Benaiah, Solomon's executioner.

What sort of relations does the Tiglath-Pileser principle permit us to reconstruct from this text? One may presume that some Moabite force suffered an Israelite attack. It is not certain that the confrontation took place on Moabite soil. The omission of the scene of the battle suggests that the text's author was hiding one of two facts: either the battle did not take place in Moab, or it took place along the very border with Moab, that is, in a fringe corner of Moabite territory. In either case, no claim is made that David captured a major settlement, if one existed, or indeed any settlement. The text mentions nothing more than a victory in the field or brief raid.

There is an aftermath to the field victory. The Moabites paid tribute, says

---

1. Reading *bkrt* with LXX. This produces a text, translated above, with the sequence: temporal preposition + infinitive + object marker + object. The MT *bhywt* produces a text, "When David was with Edom," in which the object marker becomes a preposition, "with." The preposition in question is not commonly used without a suffix. This use of the object marker was therefore so objectionable that several versions, including the Targum and Vulgate, emended the text to replace the object marker/preposition with an unambiguous preposition, "in": "when David was *in* Edom." Further, nothing in the verse presupposes David's presence when Joab eradicated the entire male population. David, as usual, was probably not in the field.

the text. But it does not say which Moabites, or what territory they occupied. In the case of the Edomites, 2 Sam. 8 alleges that David assumed control of the entire region. In the case of Damascus, it mentions that he installed garrisons on Damascene soil. In the case of Moab, the only claim is receipt of tribute. The implication is that the defeated Moabites disgorged their personal possessions. There was no further payment, and the exaction may have come from elements on the border itself.

Can one conclude that the tribute was regularized? Based on the Tiglath-Pileser principle, the most likely scenario is of a one-time payment. That Moab resembled a productive, organized kingdom in this period seems unlikely on the basis of the archaeological remains. And, in contradistinction to Edom and Damascus, the text does *not* allege that David installed a governor or garrison in Moab. This suggests that the settled population was too sparse to support a deputation to carry tribute to the court in Jerusalem. On the other hand, it is possible that David's action strengthened one or another warlord who laid claim to the kingship and periodically did remit gifts to David or engaged in trade with him.

Taken together, this reconstruction stipulates that David's army met and defeated a contingent of Moabites. The location of the battle was either just on Moab's border or in Edom or Ammon. In the aftermath, David took goods and possessions from the defeated army, and probably from any population in the vicinity. Like Thutmosis III at the battle of Megiddo, he may then have extracted oaths of fealty from the survivors. It is not especially likely that the action led to lasting sovereignty in Moabite territory or to any regular payment of tribute.

The limited character of this accomplishment may explain why the detail about the execution of the war captives is included. In the case of the Philistines, the author claims that David wrested away the prize of the Meteg of the Ammah. In the case of the Moabites, the graphic vision of two-thirds of the captives being slaughtered is adduced in order to make the achievement seem concrete, and thus more than ephemeral, in the mind of the reader. Conversely, the campaign of eradication against the Edomites is not even mentioned. The reason? Because in Edom, David can be said to have installed his own garrisons throughout the territory (2 Sam. 8:14).

The hacking up of the Moabite captives is thus offered in the way of a consolation prize for a lack of other achievements. The same is true of the generalized statement of suzerainty over "Moab" and Moabite "tribute." The treatment of the Moabites, thus, like that of the Philistines, is far from routine. And, as in the case of the Philistines, the conquests come at the outset, early in the chapter. This leads the reader to take it in almost subliminally, allowing the implications of the words to resonate without their literal sense coming to the fore. Once the implied meanings are stripped out, however, and the literal claims identified, it can be seen that the report documents no territorial gain. The size of the Moabite army that was defeated is not recorded. However, we may infer that it consisted of at least three men, and Benaiah may have killed two of them.

CHAPTER 9

David and Hadadezer: 2 Samuel 8:3 and the History of the Ninth Century

A. David at the River

2 Sam. 8:3 relates that David defeated Hadadezer son of Rehob, king of Zobah:

> David smote Hadadezer son of Rehob, king of Zobah, when he went to erect[1] his stela (lit., "hand") at the river.

This verse is a crux, for on it, ultimately, rests the solution to the extent of David's empire. It is unclear whether it is David or Hadadezer who was erecting the stela at the river. From the language of the text alone, it is not possible

---

1. The MT has *lhšyb*, "restore," whereas the parallel in 1 Chr. 18:3 reads, correctly, *lhṣyb*. The MT locution is a product of the interchange of the letters *śin* and *ṣade*. This is rare in Biblical Hebrew, and is certainly not a product of any late period. Since the phoneme involved is Proto-Semitic *ṣade* (e.g., Aram. *nṣbʾ*), not *edh* emphatic (ẟ), differential reflection of a fricative lateral cannot be invoked. But that phenomenon is the only source of parallels to this one in antiquity — and the use of the *śin* for the purpose, as in Yoqshan (J, versus Yoqtan, P) is attested only before the 7th century. (On the phonology of JE versus P, Baruch Halpern, *A History of Israel* [in progress].) This irregular interchange involving a sibilant is of a piece with the representation of *edh* emphatic in Rezon by *zayin* (z) (see Chapter 3). On the other hand, it is also conceivable that the MT reflects a scribal error made in the paleo-Hebrew script, where the scribe interpreted the term *yad*, "hand, stela," to refer to power, and thought that David was extending his hand to the Euphrates; this can have led him to take the *ṣade* as a *šin*.

to arrive at a conclusion. The tradition identifies the author of the stela as David.

Jewish tradition also identifies the river. It preserves the unwritten version, or Qere, "when he went to erect his stela at the River Euphrates." Chronicles and various ancient versions conform to this tradition, and Chronicles may have inspired it.[2] In this view, the only logical interpretation is that David was en route to the Euphrates when he encountered Hadadezer.[3] After all, Hadadezer's kingdom lay to the north of David's, nearer to the Euphrates. If Hadadezer was on the way to the Euphrates when he and David clashed, David was heading in the same direction, behind him.

If, on the other hand, the river in question was some other river — the Yarmuk, Orontes, and Jordan have been offered as candidates[4] — then the size of David's empire diminishes markedly. However, one indication that David was probably the author of the stela comes from later in the chapter. Here is 2 Sam. 8:13:

> David made a stela (lit., "name") when he returned from his smiting Aram (or "Edom") in the Valley of Salt.

The term for the stela is different in 2 Sam. 8:3 (above). However, "when he returned" is expressed by the Hebrew verb *šwb*, and the erroneous term for the erection of the stela in v. 3 in our Hebrew text employs the same verbal root. We may have two separate references to the erection of the same stela in this chapter, as will be suggested below.

This leaves open the key question. Was the river the Euphrates, or was it some river closer to Jerusalem?

The pioneering biblical historian Abraham Malamat long ago observed that Hadadezer, David's opponent in 2 Sam. 8:3, also appears in 2 Sam. 10.[5]

2. 1 Chr. 18:3. The Qere to Samuel becomes the written text in Soncino, Brescia, Complutensian Polyglott, OG, Vulgate, Syriac, and the Targum. P. Kyle McCarter (*II Samuel*) reads with MT, but believes the gloss is correct. Note that there are MT manuscripts of Chronicles that omit the gloss, Euphrates, just as there are MT manuscripts that insert it into Samuel.

3. Note the comment of McCarter, *II Samuel*, 247; further, Hans Wilhelm Hertzberg, *I & II Samuel*. OTL (Philadelphia: Westminster, 1964 [German ed., 1960]), 291.

4. Citations are from McCarter, *II Samuel*, 248: Johan de Groot, *II Samuël*. Tekst en Uitleg (Groningen: Wolters, 1935); Adrianus van den Born, *Samuel*. De Boeken van het Oude Testament IV/1 (Roermond en Maaseik: Romen, 1956) for the Yarmuk; for the Orontes, Gösta W. Ahlström, *A History of Ancient Palestine*, 484 and n. 4.

5. Abraham Malamat, "Aspects of the Foreign Policies of David and Solomon," *JNES* 22 (1963): 1-17, esp. 2-3.

There, Hadadezer intervenes with a complex coalition in David's war on Ammon. Hadadezer's contingents in 2 Sam. 10 derive from Aram of the House of Rehob and Aram Zobah. The force is augmented by troops from Hadadezer's allies, the king of Maacah and "the man of Tob" (2 Sam. 10:6).

"The man of Tob" is a locution with resonance. It sounds as though it comes straight from the context of the Amarna archive, a set of letters from Egyptian vassals in Canaan to the pharaohs of the 14th century B.C.E. In the Amarna correspondence, the expression "the man of GN" (Geographical Name, the name of a town or region) consistently indicates vassal status. "The man of GN" is the pharaoh's representative in GN. "The man of Tob" is probably a vassal king of the region Tob under Hadadezer's sovereignty.

Hadadezer is introduced in 2 Sam. 8:3 as king of Zobah, in the Beqa' Valley. Damascus assists him. In 2 Sam. 10, kings of Maacah and Tob join Zobah and Damascus. So does the House of Rehob. But the House of Rehob has no independent king.

This complicates the interpretation of Hadadezer's name in 2 Sam. 8:3. Here he is "Hadadezer, son of Rehob, king of Zobah." The difficulty is the expression "RN (Royal Name: Hadadezer) son of RN (Royal Name: Rehob)." This sequence is ambiguous. In contemporary Assyrian inscriptions, the words "Hadadezer son of Rehob" could mean that Hadadezer is the biological son and successor of a king, Rehob. But "Hadadezer son of Rehob" could also identify Hadadezer as the reigning monarch of a dynasty founded by a king named Rehob.

The expression in 2 Sam. 8:3, again, is "Hadadezer son of Rehob king of Zobah." Does the patronym "son of Rehob" reflect filiation to a biological father by the name of Rehob, in the kingdom of Zobah? Or might it reflect Hadadezer's kingship over the dynasty, "the house of Rehob," which could be identical with or separate from Zobah? This ambiguity will be clarified in the course of the following discussion. Clearly, Rehob could be a dynastic term: 2 Sam. 10:6 speaks of "Aram of the House of Rehob." "The House of Rehob" is, like "the House of David" in biblical and extrabiblical texts,[6] a way of referring to a kingdom by naming its founder. But are the dynast, Rehob, and Hadadezer's patronym, Rehob, identical? If they were, was Zobah identical with the kingdom of Rehob, or a different kingdom?

These issues cannot be clarified from this evidence alone. However, Hadadezer appears in 2 Sam. 10:16 without any introduction or title whatsoever: 2 Sam. 10 presupposes the presence of 2 Sam. 8:3 as background. This again implies that Hadadezer was conquered early, and then rebelled. 2 Sam. 8

---

6. The Dan stela and, arguably, the Mesha stela, as noted above, Chapter 4.

belongs, thus, to the original composition of the narrative of David's, or Solomon's, apology.

B. The Northern States

1. Hadadezer, Ruler of the House of Rehob?

The identity of Hadadezer's kingdom is of considerable import for the history of the 10th-9th centuries. The following pages will show that Hadadezer's Zobah occupied the territory between Hamath and Israel in the Beqaʿ Valley. The discussion is technical, and readers more concerned with David than with geography may want to go on to Chapter 10.

In a brilliant treatment of the issue, Nadav Naʾaman has argued that Hadadezer was the son of a dynastic founder, Rehob (or Ruhubu). Rehob was, in Naʾaman's view, the creator of the state Amqi. Naʾaman locates the territory of Amqi, governed by the House of Rehob, between the northern border of Israel and Hadadezer's kingdom, Zobah.[7] So Rehob or Hadadezer united Zobah with Amqi.

The term Rehob reappears in a later Assyrian inscription. The Kurkh Monolith was written just after Shalmaneser III's sixth regnal year, in 853. The Monolith contains our most detailed account of a critical battle between Assyria and a coalition of Western allies. In the coalition, Baasha, son of Rehob, appears as the ruler of the land of Amanaya.

Naʾaman holds that "son of Ruhubu" in this inscription refers to Baasha's dynastic affiliation: Baasha was the scion of the House of Rehob, and thus a descendant of David's opponent, Hadadezer. If this were so, however, the land of Amanaya could not be the Transjordanian land of Ammon, as it has usually been understood. Instead, Naʾaman associates the House of Rehob with the Amana range, the Anti-Lebanon chain running north-south in parallel to the mountains of the Mediterranean coast, from the vicinity of Damascus up to the northern end of the River Orontes.

These suppositions position Naʾaman to hypothesize that Hazael, a usurper who seized the throne of Damascus sometime between 845 and 841, was not altogether an arriviste. Instead, Hazael stemmed from Amqi, and was descended from the House of Rehob. From this base, Hazael founded a dynasty in the neighboring and more important state of Damascus around 843.

7. Nadav Naʾaman, "Hazael of ʿAmqi and Hadadezer of Beth-rehob," *UF* 27 (1995): 381-94. See further Naʾaman, "The Historical Background of the Aramaic Inscription from Tel Dan," *ErIsr* 26 (1999): 12-18.

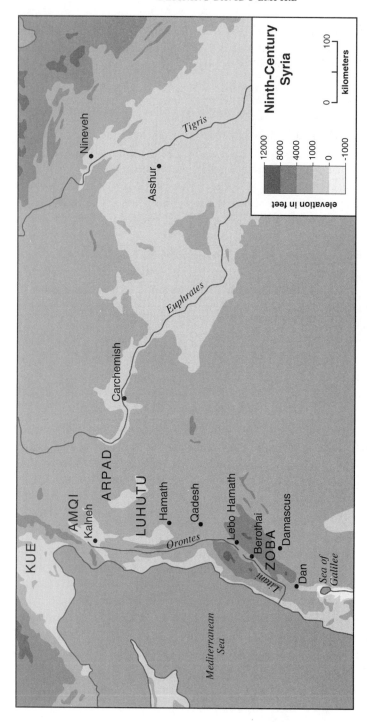

Ninth-Century Syria

elevation in feet
12000 8000 4000 1000 0 -1000

kilometers
0 100

map 9.1

This complex theory resolves a problem with an inscription. The Dan stela — sometimes referred to as the House of David stela — is an Aramaic inscription from the late 9th or very early 8th century. The stela is fragmentary, and its interpretation uncertain. However, it seems to recount the deaths of two kings, Joram of Israel and Ahaziah of Judah, who fell victim to a violent revolt in 841. The author of their deaths, according to the biblical record in 2 Kgs. 8–9, was the nativist Jehu, who requited the misdeeds of Ahab and Jezebel. (For the political circumstances, see Chapter 23.) But the author of the Dan stela claims credit for the deaths. The narrative on the stela must be about Hazael, who usurped power just before Jehu's revolt, and who was Jehu's overlord. Two versions of history, two versions of events. But most problematic is another aspect of the Dan stela: the narrator refers to inroads made by the Israelites "into the land of my father *('by)*."

Na'aman, acutely, senses the contradiction inherent in this reference. Would a usurper pretend that a king he deposed was his "father"? This could only invite snickering derision. If the reference is to the former king of Damascus, Hazael should not be the author of the Tel Dan stela. But by making Hazael the scion of the House of Rehob, in another kingdom, Amqi, Na'aman relieves the tension: Hazael was a usurper in Damascus, but his "father" was king of a neighboring state. This solution is, however, venturesome. It ties Hadadezer to a tract called Amqi, with which no evidence associates him. It hypothesizes the survival of the dynasty of Rehob in the 9th century, when no other evidence attests it. And it connects Hazael to the House of Rehob in Amqi, for which only one piece of evidence can be adduced beyond the apparent reference by the author of the Dan stela, if this is Hazael, to "the land of my father." Na'aman's construction of the one piece of evidence is discussed in the next section.

2. Hazael, King of Amqi?

The elegance and the economy of Na'aman's overture to the contradictions of the Dan stela are impressive. Still, questions remain. The first question that must be addressed is the location of Amqi.

Na'aman sets out from two inscriptions describing the collection of booty by Hazael, sometime in the second half of the 9th century. These read:

zy ntn hdd lmr'n ḥz'l mn 'mq bšnt 'dh mr'n nhr

what Hadad gave to our lord, Hazael, from Amqi in the year our lord crossed (the) river.

Na'aman takes the third word of the inscription, *hdd*, "Hadad," as the name of a person, rather than that of the god (Baal) Hadad. He correctly argues that booty would not be inscribed as a divine gift, and he cites a parallel inscription on another object delivered to Hazael, the inscription itself having been found at Arslan Tash. In this case, the name of the donor is clearly that of a human, probably a local Aramean ruler.[8]

Na'aman's analysis of the booty inscription mentioning Amqi follows from his understanding of the general picture, with Hazael being a dynast of the House of Rehob, which is located in Amqi:

TEXT	SUBJECT
That which Hadad gave::	The booty
to our lord, Hazael, from Amqi::	Hazael
in the year that our lord crossed the River	Hazael

On this reading, Hadad was a courtier of Hazael's. Hazael was the one from Amqi.

3. Hazael, Invader of Amqi?

The Amqi region first appears in Late Bronze Age texts. In the era of the Amarna archive (ca. 1360), Hittite, Canaanite, and Egyptian texts place Amqi in the northern end of the Beqa' Rift Valley. Amqi often stands on the border dividing the Egyptian from the Hittite empire. It sits north of Qadesh, on the Orontes. (It therefore falls into the territory of the Egyptian commissioner at the site of Kumidi, Kamid el-Loz, in southern Syria, in the Amarna era.) Thus, whenever Hatti invades Egyptian territory in periods when the latter controls Qadesh, the first encounter is in Amqi.[9]

Whether this kingdom extended to the far south, as Na'aman posits, all the

8. Of Hauran, possibly, or of a site to the north. See Émile Puech, "L'ivoire inscrit d'Arslan-Tash et les rois des Damas," *RB* 88 (1981): 544-62. Puech reads: [X *zy*]*br* ʿ*m*ʾ *lmrʾn ḥzʾl bšnt* [ʾ*ḥ?*]*zt ḥ*[. . .]. Na'aman renders, "the bed that Amma offered [*qrb!*] to our lord Hazael in the year of the annexation of Hauran." However, the last, fragmentary, word of the inscription may be Hazael's name, as a subjective genitive: *bšnt* ʾ*ḥzt ḥzʾl* ʾ*yt* X.

9. See for general treatment VAB 2.1112. Note further that Šuppiluliuma assaults Amqi after repulsing an Egyptian counterattack on Qadesh; Hans G. Güterbock, "The Deeds of Suppiluliuma as Told by His Son, Mursili II," *JCS* 10 (1956): 93 A ii 21-23; 94 A iii 1-6; 97 E iv 1ff. Qadesh lies east of Amqi in these texts, as Šuppiluliuma lays claim to the former, but admits that the latter belongs to the Egyptian sphere of control.

way to the vicinity of Dan, is moot. The evidence places Rehob north of Dan in the Beqaʿ Valley. But even if Zobah was between Rehob and Hamath, rather than identical with Rehob, Amqi is more likely to be found in the north.

One Amqi is known in the period of the booty inscriptions. It was a western neighbor of the kingdom of Pattina (capital: Kalneh), on the lower Orontes, in northern Syria. Ninth- and 8th-century Assyrian texts call the region Unqi (= Amqi). This must also be the Amarna region Amqi, north of Qadesh.[10] Unqi/Amqi is identical with the Syrian ʿAmuq, and lay between the northern Orontes and the coast.

This much is plain from the inscriptions of Shalmaneser III. Here, a king of the land of Pattina, Qalparunda, has his residence in the town of Unqi.[11] To reach Pattina, Shalmaneser must cross both the Amanus mountain range and the Orontes River, north of the territory of Hamath. The town Kunulua (biblical Kalneh), at Tell Taʿyinat on the northernmost stretch of the Orontes, was the capital of the district. The territory certainly extended south of the Orontes.[12] In the 8th century, Kunulua was the capital of the state of Unqi.[13] In all, Late Bronze Amqi lay north of Qadesh. Ninth-century Unqi was north of Hamath, on the north Orontes. Amqi in Hazael's booty inscriptions — from the 9th century as well — does not belong in the vicinity of Dan.

10. See, e.g., *RLA, s.v.* Hattin.

11. RIMA 3 A.0.102 1.92-95; 2.ii.18-24. The royal sequence in Pattina in the inscriptions of Shalmaneser is somewhat confusing. In RIMA 3.A.0.102 1.53-64, Sapalulme is a king of the land Pattina in 858. But in Shalmaneser's next campaign, in 857, Qalparunda of town Unqi pays tribute (1.92-95), and in subsequent texts, Qalparunda is identified as "of Pattina" — as A.0.102. 2 (Kurkh Monolith).ii.18-24, despite A.0.102 2.i.41-51, where Sapalulme is attached to a coalition of Samʾal (Hayyanu), Ahunu "son of" Adini, and Sangara of Carchemish, as second only to Hayyanu. In the report of the campaign of 848 (A.0.102 6), Qalparunda's location is not specified. However, from A.0.102 3:94-95, we learn of another king, Lubarna in Pattina, ruling there at the same time as Sapalulme. Lubarna, who submitted initially to Assurnasirpal II (RIMA 2 A.0.101 1.iii.71-77; 26:52; 28.v.5) is still in place, to be killed in 831 (RIMA 3 A.0.102 16:268-286), then as ruler of the whole area. The suggestion is that Pattina was not politically unified, and that Shalmaneser promoted the royal aspirations of Qalparunda there.

12. See RIMA 3 A.0.102. 1:64-80; 2.i.51-ii.10; 3; also, 60 (48): Qalparunda of Pattina also pays tribute while Shalmaneser is en route from Hamath — thus, north of it — in 848, as RIMA 3 A.0.102 6.iii.11-14; 8.40′-41′; possibly the depictions labeled in A.0.102 60 (48); 91, but the tribute list is closest to that for 853. For a likely land of Unqi, restored, see A.0.102 69. For Kunulua in Pattina, see RIMA 3 A.0.102 15.150-156. For Pattina extending south of the Orontes, note the description of Assurnasirpal in RIMA 2 A.0.101 1.iii.78-82.

13. See Hayim Tadmor, *The Inscriptions of Tiglath-Pileser III King of Assyria* (Jerusalem: Israel Academy of Sciences and Humanities, 1994), 56:3′–58:12′, and the note to line 11′.

There is further evidence. Around 800, a man named Zakkur identifies himself as the king of "Hamath and Lu'ash." He was in all likelihood a usurper, as he mentions no royal forebears. Hamath, as noted above, sat on the central Orontes. Lu'ash lay northeast of it, bordering Pattina to the south of the northern bend of the river, as the annals of Shalmaneser's father, Assurnasirpal II, make clear.[14]

Zakkur's capital was not Hamath, but the city of Hadrach (Hazrach), in the territory of Lu'ash. A coalition of Aramaic states invested Hadrach. At the head of this coalition was Bar-Hadad, son of Hazael, king of Damascus. Zakkur's inscription, in fact, calls him king of "Aram" at large.

Were Hazael of the royal line of Amqi (and Zobah?), his son Bar-Hadad should be king of Amqi as well as of Damascus. In the same way, David and Solomon were kings of Judah and of Israel. Zakkur too was king of two territorial entities, "king of Hamath and Lu'ash." Among his opponents, however, Zakkur numbers a king of Amqi. This king does not appear directly after Bar-Hadad, who is first and prepotent among Zakkur's foes. The king of Amqi appears instead fourth on the list. He comes after the king of Bit-Agusi and the king of Que, and before the kings of Gurgum, Sam'al, and Melid. All these states lay north or east of Hamath, in southern or central Turkey.[15]

In Zakkur's inscription, thus, Amqi has its own king and is not closely linked to Damascus, the kingdom of Bar-Hadad and Hazael. Amqi lies to the north, where the vassals Bar-Hadad activated against Hamath in the literary context are otherwise situated.[16] Certainly, locating Amqi on the northern border of Hamath is again preferable to placing it to the south. Like the Amqi of the Amarna archive, it seems likely that this one was located north of Qadesh, and even of Hamath. How a king of Amqi, then, could have reached Damascus to usurp the throne without traveling through Hamath is a question.

The formulation of the booty text also comes into question. There is no linguistic basis to determine whether the inscription says that Hazael was from Amqi. On the level of pure language, it is equally likely that the author of the inscription intended to signal that the gift, not Hazael, was from Amqi:

14. RIMA 2 A.0.101 1.iii.78-84. See Mario Liverani, *Studies on the Annals of Ashurnasirpal II, 2: Topographical Analysis* (Rome: University of Rome, 1992), 76-77.

15. Bit-Agusi was the kingdom of Arpad, in central Syria, bordering Unqi and Lu'ash on the east, north of Damascus and its hinterland in the Hauran. Adad-Nirari III establishes the Orontes as the border between Hamath, or more probably Lu'ash, and Arpad: RIMA 3 A.0.104 2:4-8. For the Hauran hinterland of Damascus, note the reports on the campaign of 841 in Shalmaneser's annals. Que was located in Cilicia, on the southwestern coast of Turkey. Gurgum was located at Marqasi (Marash) on the Ceyhan River in Turkey. Sam'al was at Zinçirli, Melid at Arslantepe near modern Malatya in Turkey.

16. KAI 202:1-7.

TEXT	SUBJECT
that which Hadad gave::	gift
to our lord, Hazael::	Hazael
from Amqi::	gift
in the year our lord crossed the river.	Hazael

But the content tips the scales: Hazael knew perfectly well where he was from, and it would be idiosyncratic, not to say impertinent, to remind him of that fact rather than of his title, such as "king of Damascus" or even better "king of Aram." Instead, this object demonstrates that Hazael exercised sovereignty over a land *not* his own — over which he could claim the title "(over)lord" (Aram. *mr'*). The title was inherited by his son: Bar-Hadad is so denominated by the Assyrian king, Adad-Nirari III. It meant more than "king of Damascus." It denoted empire over Aram, all of Syria.

The silver horse armor inscribed with the booty inscription came from a place at least nominally under Hazael's sovereignty. It commemorates the fact that he marched across "the river." This river is not in all likelihood the Euphrates — there is no evidence that Hazael ever reached that limit. Much more likely is that the river in the booty inscription is the Orontes, on which Amqi verged.

That is, Hazael crossed the river into Amqi. The gift, naturally, had to be provenanced. It is important to recall, after all, that the merchandise in question is precisely the stuff of tribute. It follows that Amqi was not under Hazael's direct rule. It was under Hadad's rule, not Hazael's, just as it had a king different from that of Damascus in Zakkur's inscription after Hazael's death. And thus it was farther to the north than any kingdom annexed by Damascus. Amqi was not Hazael's home.

4. Rehob and Zobah

Beth Rehob ("the house of Rehob") was, it is clear, Dan's northern neighbor in the southern Beqa'. In Judg. 18:28, Dan is described as lying "in the valley that belonged to the House of Rehob." A reference in Num. 13:21, in which Joshua sends his spies on the eve of the Conquest from "the wilderness of Zin to Rehob of Lebo Hamath," stems from the Priestly source (P) in the Pentateuch.[17] It sug-

---

17. For the sources of the Pentateuch, see Richard E. Friedman, *Who Wrote the Bible?* (Englewood Cliffs: Prentice-Hall, 1987). The date of P offered here will be defended in a future treatment. For P, juxtaposed with the text in Judg. 18:28, the migration of the tribe of Dan was what brought Israel into contact with Hamath's territory.

gests that "Rehob of Lebo Hamath" is just outside the reach of Israelite territory. P also understands Lebo Hamath, the southern border of the territory of the kingdom of Hamath, to be the outer limit of the Promised Land, and of Moses's vision of it, in Num. 34:7-9. Since these P texts were written late in the 7th century, they are of dubious value for understanding conditions in the 10th-9th centuries. P may even invoke Rehob in an attempt to archaize, since Zobah was the name of the region in that time. On the other hand, the phrase "Rehob of Lebo Hamath" suggests that Rehob is a town-name, not a dynasty (which is in turn dominated by Lebo Hamath, itself dominated by Hamath).

P's logic in archaizing is clear. Several texts in the Deuteronomistic History, the books of Deuteronomy through 2 Kings, suppose that David extended Israel's areas of settlement "to Lebo Hamath." Thus, Israelites whose domiciles abut the territory of Hamath attend the dedication of Solomon's temple (1 Kgs. 8:65). This view probably arose by the late 8th century, as Amos 6:14 indicates that Israel controlled that area in the early 8th century. Later texts, including the late-7th-century elements of the Deuteronomistic History, extend the borders of the Promised Land to the Euphrates.[18] But David's northernmost opponents in Samuel are the king of Zobah and the House of Rehob. And in Samuel, Israel is consistently defined as the territory extending "from Dan unto Beersheba."[19] So P thought that before David's time, it was Hamath that was the overlord of Rehob.

If P's attaching Rehob to "Lebo Hamath" did not reflect 7th-century realities, P understood 2 Sam. 8:3-8 and the narrative in 2 Sam. 10 (which will occupy us below) to represent the subjugation of Zobah up to Tubihi and Beerothai in the northern Beqa' Valley, and the town of Rehob. This extended David's ambit to embrace all the territory stretching to Lebo Hamath, Hamath's southern border. The implication for P is that Rehob is a town in the region bordering Hamath from the south. In other words, P's geography was shaped by exegetical logic: everything from Dan to Hamath had to be a single territorial unit, so that David's single victory over a power north of Dan enabled him to reach Hamath. Rehob, therefore, for P, was identical with Zobah and ran from Dan in the south to Hamath in the north.

Historically, however, the House of Rehob's geographic extent was never great, as the entity does not register outside of the Bible, except in the disputed reference in Shalmaneser III's Kurkh Monolith. It was probably a city-state. In

18. See further below, and Chapter 14. So the borders presupposed by P are not as developed as those reflected in the latest elements of the Deuteronomistic History or in the postexilic literature.

19. See below, Chapter 14.

the same way, the nearby town of Abel Beth Maacah (Abel of the House of Maacah) pertained to the dynasty of Maacah, which according to 2 Sam. 10 participated in the Ammonite war as Hadadezer's ally. Neither the House of Maacah nor, from the evidence, the House of Rehob was a significant power even in the period of atomized state formation in the Beqa' Valley and in the Hauran region that ensued on the withdrawal of Egyptian empire in the late 12th century.

The case of Zobah is different. Neo-Assyrian references in the 8th and 7th centuries to the province Zobah (Ṣubite) place this kingdom in the southern Beqa' Valley. If Rehob and Zobah were separate territories, Zobah lay north of Rehob. Thus, in the 10th century Zobah would separate Rehob from Hamath.[20] Hence the identification of Betah or Tebah in 2 Sam. 8:8 with Tubihi, in the northern Beqa' Valley south of the Orontes.[21] In the 8th-7th centuries, by contrast, when Assyria had reduced Hamath, Zobah may have extended farther north.

C. Zobah and David's Empire

Zobah bordered Hamath in the 8th and 7th centuries. It probably did so in the 10th century as well. Indeed, the claim that Zobah was subjected to David established Israelite bragging rights from the Negev to Lebo Hamath, the approach to the territory of Hamath, or the edge of Hamath's territory.[22] This

20. *ANET,* 298; Emile Forrer, *Die Provinzeinteilung des assyrischen Reiches* (Leipzig: Hinrichs, 1920), 62, 69; McCarter, *II Samuel,* 248-49.

21. Tebah's identity with Tubihi is all but certain: Shmuel Ahituv, *Canaanite Toponyms in Ancient Egyptian Documents* (Jerusalem: Magnes, 1984), 191. It (d[w]bḫ) appears with Qadesh in P.An. 19:1 and in topographic lists of Thutmosis III. In EA 179:14-29, Tubihi is connected to a revolt against Egypt by Amurru, in northern Syria, in the Late Bronze Age. The identification of Berothai in the same verse (2 Sam. 8:8) with modern Bereitan, south of Ras Baalbek, and the latter as Cun (1 Chr. 18:8, Ku-nu of Ramses III's topographic list; McCarter, *II Samuel,* 250) is less secure.

22. Lebo Hamath is not always a precise term, and P's usage, in which it extends to Dan, would imply that any expansion northward would take it in. The identification with Neo-Assyrian Lab'u is probable, as a toponymic list of Tiglath-Pileser III juxtaposes it with, but separates it from, the "cities of (the land of) Ha[math]": see Tadmor, *The Inscriptions of Tiglath-Pileser III,* 148:25 and 149 n. 25. However, related to the expression, "to *lbw'* of Hamath" are other uses of the infinitive of the verb *bw',* "come." See Gen. 24:62, and *bw'k* in Judg. 6:4; 11:33; 1 Sam. 15:7; 17:52; 27:8; 2 Sam. 5:25, etc. This is probably the origin of the name of Lab'u as well.

bragging right, though not taken up in Samuel, is in full flower in the Deuteronomistic History (1 Kgs. 8:65; Judg. 3:3; Josh. 13:5).[23]

In 1 Kgs. 4:21(5:1), Solomon receives tribute from vassals "from the river, to (MT "of") the land of the Philistines, up to the territory of Egypt." 1 Kgs. 4:24(5:4) relates that Solomon dominated all the territory "across the river, from Tiphsah unto Gaza, all the kings of 'across the river.'" The text in Kings is less forthcoming about the river than is the later book of Chronicles. Kings does not identify the river, although it implies, again, that the river is the Euphrates.[24]

The presentation in Chronicles is predicated on the assumption that Israel reached the Euphrates,[25] an assumption conditioned on 2 Sam. 8 and the texts about "the River" in Kings: in particular, the phrase "across the River" denominated the Persian super-province of Coele-Syria, the land from the Mediterranean, and Egypt, to the Euphrates. This assumption is made explicit in Gen. 15:18; Deut. 1:7; 11:24; Josh. 1:4. In these verses, Yahweh promises Israel all the land from Egypt to "the Great River, the River Euphrates." This territory is only promised. In Joshua, Judges, Samuel, and Kings, the promise is reformulated to embrace territory only up to Hamath.[26] But the effect has consistently been to mislead readers, such as the author of Chronicles and most exegetes, into thinking of "the River" in Samuel and Kings as the Euphrates.

The identification of southern Hamath as the limit of Israel's promised land continues to hold in the Priestly source of the Pentateuch (as Num. 34:8), in the 7th century, and in the book of Ezekiel, from the mid-6th century. These texts may assume that David fulfilled this promise, but they do not assert it.

---

23. For a full treatment, Halpern, "The Taking of Nothing," in *Festschrift for Paul Dion,* ed. P. M. Michèle Daviau (forthcoming). See further below, Chapter 14.

24. The choice of Tiphsah as the northern limit of Solomon's kingdom is often dismissed as a Persian-era gloss, as the town Thapsacus on the west bank of the Euphrates is known at that time. However, in 2 Kgs. 15:16 Menahem of Israel attacks a Tiphsah that may have lain in the Beqa' Valley. In the verse, the expression *mtrṣh* probably represented, originally, a term for the devastation of the site's hinterland rather than a location at Tirzah.

25. See below.

26. The revision of the promise — in Josh. 13:5; Judg. 3:3; 1 Kgs. 8:65 — is also reflected in Exod. 23:31; 1 Kgs. 4:21, 24(5:1, 4); Ps. 89:25(26); even 2 Chr. 9:26. Tellingly, P expects territory only up to Lebo Hamath: Num. 34:8. It therefore shares the view of DtrH that the maximum expansion occurred under David, not Solomon (against Chr). The same is true of Ezekiel. The view of Chronicles and of Gen. 15:18, etc. is perhaps exclusively postexilic. Not insignificantly, it is shared according to Ezra 4:20 by the Persian court of the 5th century! Chronicles takes David's prayer that Solomon outstrip him literally, and fulfills it.

However, postexilic literature, such as Chronicles and Ezra 4:20, interpreted the texts promising expansion to the Euphrates, and the texts intimating but not quite explicitly stating that David fulfilled the territorial promise, in a more positive light. It is possible that the 7th-century author of the promissory texts in Deuteronomy and Joshua had already drawn similar conclusions from 2 Sam. 8 and 1 Kgs. 5. The earliest Israelite text in which "the River," without further qualification or context, unambiguously refers to the Euphrates, and in which it is distinguished from the term for the Nile, stems from the early 6th century. Jer. 2:18 thus speaks of "the River" on the road to Assyria, as opposed to "the Shihor," in Egypt.[27] Jeremiah is close to the Deuteronomistic History on this point, as on so many others, and distinct from the Priestly source and Ezekiel.

In the postexilic era, the texts are clear. The definition of the region of Israelite settlement found in 1 Kgs. 8:65 (and its parallel text, 2 Chr. 7:8) recurs in 1 Chr. 13:5, before David's conquests. Thus, in accordance with Yahweh's promise to Joshua, Israel has settled the region up to the border of Hamath. However, in 1 Chr. 18:3 David (or Hadadezer) erects his stela on the River Euphrates.[28] Chronicles has Solomon conquer Hamath and build store-cities there (2 Chr. 8:3-4), based on a misreading: 1 Kgs. 9:18 relates that Solomon built Tamar, a small town in the Judean wilderness; Chronicles transforms this into Tadmor, the oasis of Palmyra in the Syrian desert ("discovered" by Lady Hester Lucy Stanhope in the first decade of the 19th century).

A peculiar locution, "Hamath of Zobah," occurs in 2 Chr. 8:3. Ironically, this one is not without precedent. A list of Assyrian provinces from the 7th century mentions Zobah as a dependency of Hamath.[29] The reversal of the earlier expression in Chronicles is explicable on the basis of a process of interpretation and justification similar to that which produced "Rehob of Lebo Hamath" in P (the Priestly source): David had overcome Zobah and reached the Euphrates. But the record in Samuel had Toi, king of Hamath, send gifts after that victory. So, in the rose-tinted interpretation of the author of Chronicles, the reduction of Zobah led to Hamath's submission. Chronicles construes David's relations with Hamath as that of suzerain to vassal, as the writer of 2 Sam. 8 hoped read-

27. Conversely, Isaiah uses "River" to denominate the Nile (19:5), as well as to mean the Euphrates in Isa. 7:20; 8:7. In Isa. 11:15 it may well refer to both simultaneously. Compare also Mic. 7:12, where the context indicates that the river is the Euphrates.

28. Some Massoretic texts of Chronicles omit "Euphrates" here, but see below.

29. SAA 11.1.r i.12'. This interpretation supposes that the repetition of the name Hamath is purposeful. In SAA 11.1.i.1-14, the doubling of names on a single line is also meaningful rather than accidental. Less perspicuous are the juxtapositions of names on single lines in column ii, which seem to jump about a bit.

ers would. The author of Chronicles infers that Hamath, which did not fight David, must have been the vassal of Zobah, explaining Hamath's submission. On this basis, Chronicles includes Hamath and Tadmor and the Euphrates in Solomon's ambit, in 2 Chr. 8:3-4. That Zobah ever dominated even Hamath is doubtful.

As noted, in the Deuteronomistic History the promise of expansion to the Euphrates goes unfulfilled. The ideal territory is revised in Joshua to encompass only the land up to Hamath's border, and Joshua fails to take even this much. It is David who fulfills the promise to Joshua of settlement up to the border of Hamath. And David fulfills this promise in Kings (1 Kgs 8:65), not in the book of Samuel.

Conversely, in Chronicles David reaches the Euphrates. This is concretized not just in Solomon's activities in northern Syria, cited above, but also in other texts.[30] Only in Chronicles and Ezra 4:20 does the empire reach the Euphrates in fact, rather than in prospect. It does so more under Solomon rather than under David — David set a stela on the Euphrates, but Solomon consolidated the empire. This predictable expansion of the United Monarchy reflects both the intended effect and the date of Samuel. Not only does Samuel considerably antedate Chronicles, which exaggerates David's and Solomon's achievements by exegesis of Samuel's words; Samuel antedates the interpretation of events, probably in the 8th century, which suggests that David expanded to the border of Hamath. It took David until the Persian period to penetrate to Mesopotamia.

Samuel attributes to David no town more northern than Dan. Samuel's later interpreters aggrandize David's state. In short, Samuel has led readers down the garden path without lying to them. The same is the case with Philistia, where most historians have assumed that David enjoyed uncontested supremacy. These instances should make us doubly wary of overestimating the actual extent of the kingdom of Zobah, for it was in the interest of the author of Samuel to imply that Zobah was a great prize, and that it fell into David's clutches whole. Only in this way could he be said to have reached Hamath, and through Hamath the Euphrates. Again, this is why Chronicles imagines Hamath, the dominant power in central Syria throughout the period, to have been a vassal state of Zobah, which was never more than a petty kingdom.

---

30. 1 Chr. 5:9; 18:3. See further Baruch Halpern, *ABD* 5:1120-43; "The Taking of Nothing." In Chronicles, the assumption is that Israelites exploited land and even settled individually up to the Euphrates, and through the territory of Lebo Hamath. Gen. 15:18 ("from the River of Egypt to the big river, the River Euphrates") may have been secondarily expanded with an eye to activity in Arabia.

D. The Name of Hadadezer

Two talented historians — Malamat and, following him, Na'aman — identify Hadadezer son of Rehob king of Zobah (2 Sam 8:3, 12) as Hadadezer, scion of the House of Rehob, and king of Zobah. But in Samuel and Kings, the expression RN son of RN otherwise always names a son and his father. Dynastic change in the state of Israel, after Solomon's death, is fairly regular, but no grandson or great-grandson is affiliated to the dynastic founder rather than to his biological father and predecessor. The same is true in Judah. So the first defect in the theory that Hadadezer is both a dynastic scion in Rehob and king of the separate state of Zobah is that the locution RN son of RN does not mean RN son of Dynasty Name.

Inscriptions do identify kings as "son of [Founder of Dynasty]" (see below). But no other text identifies a king as the son of a dynastic founder and then calls him king of some other kingdom. After all, why name someone as "son of" a dynastic founder from a kingdom lesser than his own, unless he was in fact the "dynastic founder's" biological offspring? If Hadadezer's pedigree means anything at all, it probably names his actual father.

But Na'aman points to a parallel, in the Kurkh Monolith of Shalmaneser III. Here, Baasha *mār Ruḫubi KUR Amanaya*, "Baasha, son of Ruhubu (Rehob), of the land of Amanaya," appears. This cannot, Na'aman submits, be Ammon. In later Assyrian inscriptions, Ammon is always "the house of Ammon." Rather, the reference must be to the northern part of the Anti-Lebanon, Mount Amana. Baasha son of Ruhubu is in fact the dynast of Beth Rehob, whose kingdom in 853 is associated with Mount Amana. This is again the Anti-Lebanon range, the Amanus.

In this text, however, Amanaya is written with a single -m-. Amanus, like Ammon, is usually written with doubled -mm-. Indeed, Ammon is not always designated as the House of Ammon: in the 8th-7th centuries, when it first appears regularly, Ammonites are at least once called *ba-an Am-ma-na-a*, "children of Ammon."[31] And a list of provinces stemming from a time after 671 names Ammon, clearly, as URU *Am-ma-a-[na]*, "the city/state of Ammon."[32] Moreover, the term for the Anti-Lebanon in the inscriptions of Tiglath-Pileser III, in the 8th century, is KUR Ammanama.[33] The writing of the name of

---

31. SAA 1.110.

32. SAA 11.1.ii: *9) KUR Melid URU Pi-l[i?]-iš?-tú 10) URU Šibartu (Sardis) URU Is-q[a- luna] (Ashkelon) 11) URU Udumi (Edom) URU [Moab] 12) URU Am-ma-a-[na] 13) KUR Ku-ú-su.*

33. For the "normal" designation of Ammon, see Riekele Borger, *Die Inschriften*

the land in Shalmaneser's Kurkh Monolith cannot be identified any more closely with the Anti-Lebanon than with Ammon.

In Shalmaneser III's annals, Baasha's patronym ("son of Rehob") might in theory reflect dynastic affiliation. This is common in Assyrian inscriptions. To take cases only from texts of Assurnasirpal II and Shalmaneser III, we have Amme-Ba'li son of Zamani (for king of Bit ["the House of"] Zamani), Ahiramu son of Yahiri (for king of Bit Yahiri), the son of Bahiani (for king of Bit Bahiani), the son of Dakkur (for king of Bit Dakkuri), the son of Adini (for king of Bit Adini), the son of Ukani (for king of Bit Amukkani), the son of Gusi (king of Bit Agusi), the son of Hanban (king of Bit Hanban), and Jehu son of Omri.[34]

Jehu is the usurper, who murdered Omri's heirs and Jezebel. Shalmaneser has no political reason to cast doubt on Jehu's legitimacy, as Jehu submitted without a fight in 841 (but see Chapter 23). So the filiation of a king (RN) to the founder of a dynasty (DF) is nothing more than an expression of his position as reigning monarch in a particular kingdom.[35] Shalmaneser affirms Jehu's legitimacy — because he can claim him as a tributary. The contrast is with Jehu's contemporary Hazael, whom Shalmaneser brands as a usurper, because he never was a tributary.

We even have a text that deliberately explains a sequence, RN the son of RF (the name of a dynasty's founder representing a territorial entity) — the dynastic name is qualified by a sign indicating that its meaning is geographic.[36] In

---

Asarhaddons, Königs von Assyrien. AfO Beiheft 9 (Graz: Weidner, 1956). Esarhaddon Nin A-F Episode 21 (p. 60): Bit Ammana.

34. Assurnasirpal II A.0.101.1 = RIMA 2.202 1.ii 12: Amme-ba'li son of Zamani = king of Bit Zamanu (possible parallels in texts 15 and 17.109; 19.85, 96); but with Ili-hite the Shubrian and (l 13) Labturu son of Tupusu of the land Nirdun; 2.203:ii 22: (tribute from) Ahiramu, son of Iahiri [= king of Bit Iahiri] ša KUR Zallaya, son of Bahiani [= king of Bit Bahiani] KUR Hattaya and from kings of Hanigalbat; Shalmaneser III: (Neuentdeckter) Text from 22nd regnal year: WO 1/6 (1952), 466: II 52: Adini son of Dakkuri; 466: Year 9: Mushallim-Marduk son of Ukani = son of Bit Amukkani; WdO 1/6 (1952), 458: Year 1: Ahuni son of Adini, the son of Gusi; Year 2: Tel Barsip, cities of Ahuni son of Adini and city Dabigi of Hatti; 460: Year 3: Ahuni son of Adini fled Tel Barsip; 462: Year 4: captures Ahuni son of Adini; Marmorplatte: Ernst Michel, WdO 2/1 (1954), 27-45: 38.4:11: Ya-a-ú son of Omri; WdO 2/2 (1955), 137-57: Black Obelisks: 140B: Yaua son of Omri; 152:95: Yanzu son of Hanban = Bit Hanban; 156:125 WdO 2/2 (1955), 137-57:(i.e., Yanzu again).

35. Against this view, see Tammi J. Schneider, "Rethinking Jehu," *Bibl* 77 (1996): 100-7; "Did King Jehu Kill His Own Family?" *BAR* 21/1 (1995): 26-33, 80, 82.

36. Ernst Michel, "Die Assur-Texte Salmanassars III. (858-824). 8. Fortsetzung," *WdO* 2/3 (1956), 221-33, *226: 154: at Kinalua, a city in central Syria (Pattina), on the death of the previous king: "Sasi son of the land Utza submitted; and I installed him as king."

West Semitic we have the case of Atarsamek son of Gush (i.e., king of Bit Agusi) in the Zakkur stela,[37] probably under Assyrian influence. Sometimes the kings in question are the direct offspring of the "dynasty founders" — this is probably the case with Aramu son of Agusi in the time of Shalmaneser III, since Gusi king of Yahanu (later, Arpad) appears in the inscriptions of Shalmaneser's father, Assurnasirpal II. But another king, Hayyanu of Sam'al, is the grandson of his "father" in Shalmaneser's annals.[38] The pattern of usage is generally clear: RN1 son of RN2 is often RN, the scion of the founder of a dynasty.

But "Hadadezer son of Rehob king of Zobah" is a more complex expression. The string "RN son of RN" does not always denote direct affiliation with the founder of the royal dynasty. The name of the king of Gath in Solomon's day, "Achish son of Maacah, king of Gath," sounds a warning: this was not a scion of the House of Maacah.[39] And Adini son of Dakkuri (king of the House of Dakkuri) may have had heirs, sons of Adini. They were not kings of the separate state, the House of Adini! Second, Rehob is a common place-name and occurs in personal names as well (Rehoboam, Rehaviahu). But the third point is the most daunting.

If Baasha the son of Ruhubi of the land Amanaya was in fact the king of Beth Rehob, Shalmaneser's scribes violated a convention of royal inscriptions. Assyrian records signal that in the string "RN son of RN," the second term represented the dynasty of a founder, by using the dynastic name and *omitting* the name of the country (GN, geographical name). Nowhere else, where Assyrians used the formula, "RN son of X king of GN," does X have any value other than the name of a king's father. Assigning it such a value would plunge readers into ambiguity, for the implication would be that RN's father's name was X. Thus right next to the mention of Amme-Ba'li son of Zamani (king of the House of Zamani), Assurnasirpal II mentions Labturu son of Tupusu of the land of Nirdun.[40] No

37. Atarsumki son of Agusi in the Assyrian record. Cf. Arame son of Agusi in Shalmaneser III's inscriptions (Michel, *WdO* 1/6 [1952], 458: 47; cf. Michel, *WdO* 2/2 [1955], 150: 86; 2/3 [1956], 221: 130; ICK 15:29-40).

38. Assurnasirpal II (Annals 3:71, 78). The case of Ahuni "son of Adini" is harder to adjudicate. Zakkur's stela is KAI 202. The case of Hayyanu son of Gabbari, in the annals of Assurnasirpal, is clarified by the Kilamuwa inscription (KAI 24), where Kilamuwa describes his ancestry as follows: "I am Kilamuwa son of Hayya. Gabbar reigned over Ya'udi, but did not act. There was Bamah, but he did not act. And there was my father Hayya and he did not act. And there was my brother Saul, but he did not act. . . ." Hayyanu son of Gabbari is thus clearly Gabbari's grandson. He is Hayyanu, scion of the dynasty founded by Gabbari.

39. 1 Kgs. 2:39; Achish son of Ma'ok king of Gath in 1 Sam. 27:2.

40. RIMA 2.202:ii 12-13.

one would dream of suggesting that Tupusu was a dynastic name. Had it been, either it or Nirdun would have been omitted. RN son of RN of the land GN means what it says.

Even more certain is a reference from Adad-Nirari III, around 800. In his Antakya stela, Adad-Nirari reports that he and his field marshal Shamshi-Ilu fixed the boundary between Zakkur, king of the land Hamath, and Atarshumki son of Adramu. In this text, the form of identification alternates. Zakkur is identified as the king of the land of Hamath, a purely territorial definition (as noted, he was a usurper). Conversely, Atarshumki is identified as the son of Adramu, his father — Shalmaneser's Aramu son of Agusi, which is to say, king of Bit Agusi.

Adad-Nirari and Semiramis, his Queen Mother, erected a boundary marker to divide the kingdoms of Ušpilulume (Šupululiuma) of Kummuh and Qalparunda son of Palalam, king of Gurgum. This inscription identifies Qalparunda in two ways: by his father's name, and by his territory. In his Pazarcik stela, Adad-Nirari relates that he fought a battle against Atarshumki son of Adramu of the city Arpad. Atarshumki is not identified as the son of Agusi, the founder of the dynasty, but as the son of his father, and king of the territory of Arpad. That is, Adad-Nirari's scribes, like Shalmaneser's, eschew the metaphoric expression, RN, son of DF, king of Land. When they provide both a father and a territory to identify a particular king, they do not introduce a dynastic name.

In two cases, the same sequence of identification (RN, father, kingdom) occurs in inscriptions from Aramaic areas, both in the 8th century. One stems from Arpad. In the Sefire treaty, the party contracting with the enigmatic Bar-Gaya of KTK is repeatedly called Matiel, son of Atarshumki, king of Arpad. Matiel is the son of the Atarshumki whom Adad-Nirari identified as the son of Adramu and king of Arpad. In addition, Zakkur identifies his chief opponent as "Bar-Hadad son of Hazael, king of Aram."[41] In all these cases, the pattern is RN + name of father + name of kingdom.

The case is the same in biblical texts where a similar string of names appears. Achish, son of Maacah, king of Gath is son of a man, Maacah (or Maoch), and king of Gath, nothing more. In 1 Kgs. 15:18-20, we read of Ben-Hadad son of Tabrimmon son of Hezyon, king of Aram who dwelt in Damascus. The name Hezyon is identical to that of the Hadyanu of Damascus later mentioned by Adad-Nirari III. Perhaps Hadyanu adopted an earlier dynastic name. His namesake may have been a usurper there,[42] after Rezin had founded

---

41. Sefire in KAI 224-226; Zakkur in KAI 202:4.

42. This would be the earliest adoption of a dynastic founder's name in the West. On the practice, see Baruch Halpern, "Sybil, or the Two Nations."

the state. In any case, the Bar-Hadad of this text, too, is identified by his biological descent, then by his territory. Even if Hezyon was a usurper, it is necessary to insert the name of the king's father in order to avoid ambiguity. One cannot simply call Bar-Hadad the son of Hezyon if one is also identifying him as king of Damascus.

Kings who do not usurp power identify themselves in the same way: as sons of a biological father and lords of a realm. "I am Mesha son of Kemosh-yet, king of Moab," Mesha's text begins. And Kemosh-yet is his father, not the founder of a dynasty. Texts of the form "RN, son of Father, of Kingdom N," routinely name the biological father, not the founder of the dynasty. In light of the potential ambiguity arising from any other use of such an expression, as well, it is predictable that the scribes should have eschewed other options.

Na'aman's thesis demands that one read "Hadadezer son of Rehob king of Zobah" and "Baasha son of Ruhubi of the land Aman" in parallel. For the latter, he proposes "Baasha king of the House of Rehob and of the Anti-Lebanon." Na'aman identifies the otherwise unattested kingdom of "Mount Amana" with Zobah, in his view north of Rehob. Na'aman further identifies Mount Amana/Zobah with Amqi, which then connects Aman(a) with Hazael, through the booty inscription.

But Zakkur, king of Hamath around 800, is not "son of GN." What is the likelihood that two traditions would produce a singleton formulary, and each about a dynast from Beth Rehob, a dynasty whose existence is otherwise unattested? Even the identification of "the land Aman" *(KUR Amanaya)* as the Anti-Lebanon is highly problematic. In the inscriptions of Shalmaneser III, from which the reference to Baasha son of Ruhubi is taken, the Anti-Lebanon is consistently referred to as Mount *(KUR-e) Ḥa-ma-na*. The first consonant of the name is *always* reflected by Assyrian /ḫa/ (a guttural, like the German "ach"). This is also true of the term Amanus (the Anti-Lebanon) in the inscriptions of Shalmaneser's father, Assurnasirpal II. The chances that the same expression was spelled differently only in representing the name of Baasha's kingdom are infinitesimal.

In each case, the more banal reading is preferable: Baasha was the son of king Ruhubu/Rehob of the land of the Ammonites. Indeed, the designation of Ammon as the land of Ammon, or of the Ammonites, rather than as the House of Ammon (Bit Amman) is typical of 9th-century annals. In these texts, as many examples cited above demonstrate, the element Bit- ("House of") was frequently dropped. Hadadezer was the son of king Rehob of the land Zobah. It is improbable that Rehob was the dynastic founder of the state. And were this wrong, if Rehob founded the dynasty of Zobah, then Rehob and Zobah were identical. More likely, Rehob was Hadadezer's father. In either case, he was not connected to Ammon (or Aman). As in the case of Achish son of Maacah, Baasha son of Rehob bore no tie to the "dynasty" of the same name elsewhere.

This reconstruction explains why the House of Rehob is mentioned only in tandem with Zobah, in 2 Sam. 10:6. Like Tob and Maʿacah, the House of Rehob never appears in 2 Sam. 8 at all. It may be included because of the coincidence with Hadadezer's patronym. The alternation of coalition partners between 2 Sam. 8 and 2 Sam. 10 is, conceivably, part of a deliberate strategy on the part of the author of 2 Samuel: the variation leads readers to think that the battles of 2 Sam. 8:3 and 2 Sam. 10 were separate engagements, when careful reflection makes it clear that they are separate reports on a single conflict.[43] As noted above (Chapter 6), the strategy implies that Ammon and Zobah were in revolt, and in the wrong, when David bested them in 2 Sam. 10–12.[44] Thus, the House of Rehob could be Hadadezer's ancestral house in Zobah, or a separate petty kingdom whose founder shared a personal name with Hadadezer's father.

But, to proceed to the most elegant part of Na'aman's edifice, the understanding of the House of Rehob as either a dynasty in Zobah or as a kingdom separate from Zobah precludes Hazael's identification with the Beth-Rehob dynasty.

To begin with, Hazael's predecessor and victim in the 9th century, Hadadezer (Shalmaneser's Adad-idri), bore precisely the same name as the Hadadezer of the 10th century. This suggests the possibility of dynastic continuity between the Zobathite overlord of the 10th century and the Damascene ruler of the 9th century. Does this mean then that Asa's contemporary, Hadadezer (Ben-Hadad), son of Tabrimmon, son of Hezyon, king of Damascus, was descended from a king of Zobah who reclaimed the throne in Damascus from the dynasty of Rezin?

Second, the Hadadezer (Adad-idri) of Shalmaneser's annals in the 9th century disposed of a coalition throughout Syria. He acted in partnership with a strong Israel to his south. The idea that a petty kingdom survived in the southern Beqaʿ without incorporation either into Damascus's sphere of influence or into that of King Ahab of Israel seems improbable. Third, and most important,

---

43. A similar logic inspires the author of 2 Sam. 8 to use two separate words to designate "stela." While the second stela (the "name") *must* be in the vicinity of Jericho, the first (the "hand") *might* be on the Euphrates, depending on what assumptions a reader brings to the text. See further below.

44. This is the conclusion of Kenneth A. Kitchen, *The Bible in Its World* (Downers Grove: InterVarsity, 1978), 101. Kitchen, assuming on the basis of 2 Chronicles that Solomon took Hamath Zobah and Tadmor, concludes that the revolt in Zobah led David to assign Zobah to Hamath. This explains the phrase, Hamath Zobah (although the phrase should indicate Hamath's subordination to Zobah). On Hamath Zobah, see further above.

Shalmaneser and Kings both report that Hazael was a usurper, in Shalmaneser's case, "son of nobody."[45] Were he in fact the ruler of Beth Rehob, some adversion to this point might have been expected, certainly from Shalmaneser.[46]

It is true that Na'aman is able to point to a putative parallel: Rezin II, in the 8th century, was not born in Damascus, but in [X]-Hadara, just as Na'aman's Hazael originates from Rehob. Still, in the Assyrian annals Rezin's relationship to his birthplace is very elaborately signaled, not resolved by styling Rezin II "son of [X]-hadara, king of Damascus."[47] The indications are fairly uniform: Hazael was a usurper, whose father's name is not furnished — yet if he could have named a royal father in Zobah or elsewhere, he could have claimed to be the conqueror of Damascus, rather than a usurper there.

It is true, too, that Shalmaneser had an interest in pointing out that Hazael was a usurper. He refrained from making the same observation about Jehu in order to privilege him. This must relate to the fact that Jehu paid him tribute. By 838, however, Shalmaneser was no longer repeating the claim. The biblical testimony, too, demonizes Hazael as a usurper. In historical perspective, Hazael's policies provoked a good deal of enmity even among those, like the Is-

45. In the case of 2 Kgs. 8:7-15, it is reasonably clear, despite recent protests, that Hazael indeed did murder his liege lord. Cf. André Lemaire, "Hazaël de Damas, roi d'Aram," in *Marchands, diplomates et empereurs*. Festschrift P. Garelli, ed. Dominique Charpin and Francis Joannès (Paris: Éditions Recherches sur les civilisations, 1991), 91-108.

46. To this critique should be added the points: (1) that it is not clear that Hazael reached the Euphrates, so that his own crossing of "the river" may in fact reflect a crossing of the Orontes; (2) that "beyond the River" insofar as it is reflected as a concept in 2 Sam. 8:3 cannot be a Mesopotamian conception, applied to the west side; (3) that, despite the inclusion of Damascus as an appendage of Zobah in 2 Sam. 10, there is no later period when a source would make the same assumption, so that, were our source on the conflict later in date, the garrisoning of Damascus by David (and its revolt under Solomon) should represent the jewel in the crown and result in a downplaying of any neighbor's role (Chapter 10B); (4) that the role of Damascus under Hazael is that of a capital of a major state, unlike its role under Hadadezer of Zobah, contrary to Na'aman's submission.

47. Tadmor, *The Inscriptions of Tiglath-Pileser III*, 80 (Ann. 23): 13'-14': [. . .]-*ha-a-da-ra É AD-šu ša* ᵐ*Ra-hi-a-ni KUR ša-ANŠE-šu-a+a [a]-~šar~ i'-al-du alme*, etc. The "house of his father . . . the place where he was born" may have borne a dynastic name, (Hadad?)-ʿadara (Hadadezer), but the key is that it is elaborately, not telegraphically, signaled that this is the relationship. Contrast Na'aman's and Malamat's views on Hadadezer, and Na'aman's on Baasha. Note that RIMA 3 A.0.102.92 speaks of a royal city of Hazael, Malaha, with a god *šeri* (probably, Syrion), who might conceivably be identical with the (moon?) god on the Beth Saida stela, on which see Monika Bernett and Othmar Keel, *Mond, Stier und Kult am Stadttor*.

raelites, whom he rescued from Assyrian domination. Still, the accusations of usurpation common to the Assyrian and biblical records are not the result of a conspiracy. Hazael truly was a usurper.

It is thus unlikely that, were Hazael the author of the Tel Dan stela, he would have referred to the "land of my father." David's opponent Hadadezer is likewise no filibuster from Rehob who claimed the kingship of Zobah. Nor was Baasha son of Ruhubi of the land Amanaya a representative of the House of Rehob in Zobah. The Tel Dan report about inroads into "the land of my father" is more probably a deliberate attempt to mislead the reader. André Lemaire suggests that the "father" of the king is in fact a predecessor addressed as a senior.[48]

If Hazael commissioned the inscription thus, he cleverly adopted a nomenclature based in kinship metaphor in order to create the impression that he had royal predecessors, without claiming to be a scion of the dynasty whose last representative he murdered. This sort of fudging on his part would invite the responses found in Shalmaneser's annals and Kings, which nowhere else insist that *any* foreign king is a usurper. Hazael inspired contempt in every court that had to deal with him, although the tradition that Yahweh commissioned him — found in 1 Kgs. 19 and 2 Kgs. 8 — reflects his long-lived sovereignty over Israel.

48. André Lemaire, "The Tel Dan Stela as a Piece of Royal Historiography," *JSOT* 81 (1998): 3-14.

CHAPTER 10

David in the North and in Transjordan: 2 Samuel 8:3-11

A. Understanding 2 Samuel 8:3-11

This background illuminates how far David expanded in the north. Scholars tend to agree that David's Aramean opponent, Hadadezer, is referred to by Shalmaneser III. In this consensus view, Hadadezer was the unnamed "king of the land of Arumu" who, in the time of Assur-rabi II, seized Pitru and Mutkinu, the latter east of the Euphrates.[1]

This hypothesis is based mainly on the description of Hadadezer's coali-

1. Abraham Malamat, "The Kingdom of David and Solomon in Its Contact with Aram Naharaim," *BA* 21 (1958): 96-102; repr. *BA Reader* 2 (Garden City: Doubleday, 1964), ed. David Noel Freedman and Edward F. Campbell, 89-98; followed by William F. Albright, "Syria, the Philistines, and Phoenicia," *CAH*[3] 2/2:533-34; P. Kyle McCarter, Jr., *II Samuel*, 248; Gösta Ahlström, *A History of Ancient Palestine*, 487, among others. The reference is from Shalmaneser III, who recovered the towns; see ARAB 1.603 = RIMA 3 A.0.102 2.ii.35-40. Both Shalmaneser, here, and his father, Assurnasirpal II (RIMA 3 A.0.101.33:11′; 40:22 Urumu), refer to the Arameans as Arumu, suggesting lengthening of */a/ to /o/ in the accented, closed second syllable of the term Aram. Contrast, on the one hand, the name Aramu, of the king of Bit Agusi under Shalmaneser (Adramu under Adad-Narari III); and, on the other, the mention of the Ahlamu by Assurnasirpal in RIMA 3 A.0.101 19:92-97. Ahlamu is a term that in early texts denotes elements that would later be designated Aramean. In between, it appears in combination with the word Aramean, so that one hears of the Ahlamu Arameans. Here, Assurnasirpal refers to the Ahlamu of the land of the Arameans, *ar-ma-a-ya*, Armaya.

tion in 2 Sam. 10. The story, again, runs as follows. On the death of Nahash, king of Ammon — Saul's old nemesis — David sends a mission to commiserate with Hanun, the son and successor to the crown. Hanun's advisers suspect David of treachery. (Who in 2 Samuel does not?) So Hanun demonstratively expels the Jerusalemite delegation, humiliating them by shaving half their beards and exposing their buttocks (2 Sam. 10:1-5).

This is a deliberate provocation. So the Ammonites engage Hadadezer's first field force — a complex coalition:

> They [the Ammonites] hired Aram of the House of Rehob and Aram of Zobah, twenty thousand foot, and the king of Maacah, one thousand men, and the Man of Tob, twelve thousand men. (10:6)

Joab and Abishai command the first expedition to Ammon, employing only David's professional army. At an unnamed walled town, which the reader is to assume was the capital, Rabbat Ammon, they confront Ammonites in front of the fortifications, and the Aramean army in the field. Here, they win a decisive field victory, and the Ammonites withdraw, unmolested, behind the walls (10:7-14).

The initial Aramean coalition having been put to rout, a new one is formed.

> Hadadezer sent and called out the Arameans who are beyond the river. (10:16)

Again, though some scholars champion another identification, most scholars follow Abraham Malamat and the tradition in identifying "the river" as the Euphrates.[2] This has been the interpretation since antiquity, when the Chronicler, the author of Ps. 60, Eupolemos, and Josephus all adopted it.[3] The interpretation is induced in part by the phrasing of the text:

---

2. For the Jordan, Johan de Groot, *II Samuël*; Adrianus van den Born, *Samuel*; Hans Joachim Stoebe, "David und der Ammoniterkrieg" *ZDPV* 93 (1977): 245. For the Leontes, Alfred Jeremias, *Das Alte Testament im Lichte des alten Orients*, 4th ed. (Leipzig: Hinrichs, 1930), 524. For an evaluation in favor of the Euphrates, and further bibliography, see McCarter, *II Samuel*, 272-73.

3. 1 Chr. 19:6; Ps. 60 Superscript (MT 2); Josephus *Ant.* 7.121 (see also 7.99ff., 127-29) read Aram Naharaim — the Arameans east of the Euphrates and west of the Tigris — for Aram Beth Rehob in 10:6. For Eupolemos, see Carl R. Holladay, *Fragments from Hellenistic Jewish Authors*, 1: *Historians*. SBLTT 20 (Chico: Scholars, 1983), 115-16 (from Eusebius). Eupolemos's tradition of a battle in Gilead against the Assyrians probably reflects exegesis of Balaam's oracles combined with the text of 2 Sam. 8 and 10.

Hadadezer . . . called out the Arameans who are beyond the river, and their forces came,[4] and Shobach, the general of Hadadezer's army, was before them. This was reported to David, and he gathered all Israel and crossed the Jordan, and their forces arrived.[5] (10:16-17)

Aram, in other words, come from "across the river," but the newly-mobilized muster of Israel cross the Jordan (in support of the professionals). The text conditions the reader to assume that the Jordan must be different from the (unnamed) river that defines Aram. Thus, the dominant view turns on the implications of the text, not the text's explicit claims. The "river" in 2 Sam. 10:16 is anonymous for the same reason that it is anonymous in 2 Sam. 8:3.

"The river" here is the "River" where David erected a stela. But, we will see, the likelihood that David reached the Euphrates is small. Indeed, "the river" will turn out to be the Jordan.

One hint is indicative. Damascus is absent from the initial confrontation in 2 Sam. 10:6. Yet it appears in 2 Sam. 8:5, as Hadadezer's ally. Damascus is the only ally of Hadadezer, other than those in the initial coalition, whose name is mentioned. So the Arameans from "across the river" could be Damascus, which entered the fray only after Hadadezer's initial rebuff. Damascus's intervention would then be very useful for suggesting that elements from across a river, here the Jordan, participated in the key battle of David's career.

Second, north of David's main foe, Zobah, sat the kingdom of Hamath, which no early account brings into conflict with David.[6] Hamath was hostile to Zobah, its neighbor to the south, as examination of the text will show. So Arameans pouring south from the Euphrates to help Zobah would presumably have been interdicted at Hamath. Of such assistance to David, or, indeed, of passivity toward Zobah on Hamath's part, we have no indication.

In purely geographic terms, the kings of Hamath, Arpad (= Bit Agusi), and, most likely of all, Bit Adini in the region of Carchemish, are the best candidates to have taken land from Assur-rabi II. Hadadezer was simply too many kingdoms removed from the Euphrates, and king of a state too limited in scope, to have been the invader of Assyria. What has happened in this instance is an un-

---

4. Usually interpreted "They came to Helam," an otherwise unattested site, thought to be the scene of the battle. See the following note.

5. Usually rendered "they arrived at Helam." The spelling in MT is ḥl'mh, the Qere (or traditional reading) ḥlmh. The final -h is taken to be a directive, indicating motion toward a location. It may, however, be an archaic variant of the third person masculine plural possessive suffix (usually -m), -mh.

6. The tradition of conflict between Hamath and Solomon (2 Chr. 8:3-4) is, as noted above, based on eisegesis.

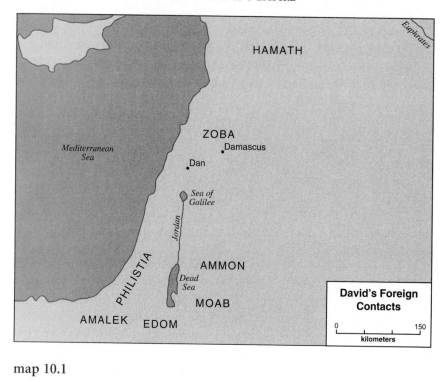

map 10.1

intended consequence of the implicit hyperbole of Samuel: Hadadezer, like David, has been magnified by association with an unnamed river, which readers are meant to assume was the Euphrates without being explicitly told it was. It is because Hadadezer summons Aram from "beyond the river" that he becomes the invader of Assyria.

David, in 2 Sam. 10:18, inflicts considerable damage on Hadadezer's second coalition:

> David slew of Aram seven hundred chariot teams and forty thousand cavalrymen, and he smote Shobach the general of his army, who died there.

Comparable is the enumeration of Hadadezer's losses in 2 Sam. 8:4:

> David captured from him one thousand, seven hundred cavalrymen, and twenty thousand infantrymen, and David hamstrung all the chariot teams, and spared one hundred chariot teams of them.

The report lists none of Hadadezer's allies. The continuation in 2 Sam. 8:5 mentions Damascus alone:

> Aram Damascus came to assist Hadadezer the king of Zobah, and David smote of Aram twenty-two thousand men.

The passage concludes (2 Sam. 8:6):

> David placed garrisons in Aram Damascus, and Aram became David's tribute-bearing servants.

There follows a coda, "Yahweh saved David wherever he went," like the codas that separate each episode in the annals of Tiglath-Pileser.

The text relates that Aram Damascus was occupied. It does not assert that the city of Damascus was garrisoned. The difference is the difference between claiming that David occupied some of the country and the assertion, not made here, that he captured the capital itself. So 2 Sam. 8:6 reports that David took some of the territory belonging to the kingdom based in Damascus.

But 2 Sam. 8 makes no such claim concerning any territory in the Beqaʿ Valley. Samuel reports no military action west of the Anti-Lebanon, north of Dan. It was Hadadezer's ally, Damascus, that suffered occupation. Zobah, Beth Rehob, Maacah, and Tob (the first three, at least, in the Beqaʿ Valley) went unmolested. This disposition comports with the fact that the real confrontation with Zobah, as the narrative in 2 Sam. 10 reports, took place in Transjordan, in connection with David's campaign against Ammon. Hadadezer meant to prevent David from gaining a hold on the Transjordanian kingdoms, and on the trade coursing through them from Arabia to the north.

In addition to prescinding, however, from any claims regarding Aramean territory north of the Bashan, 2 Sam. 8:6 engages in some delicate sleight of hand: David occupied Aram *Damascus,* but Aram became his tribute-bearers. The term "Aram" is unqualified — just like the term "Philistines." Does this mean all Aram? Not if we include Hamath or anything to the north of it, in the designation. The term is deliberately vague, and the economy of expression suggests that the tribute of Aram Damascus does literary duty for tribute from the other Aramean states. This is also true in the last half of 2 Sam. 8:5: Aram Damascus came to Hadadezer's aid, and David "smote of Aram" twenty-two thousand men. In other words, Aram Damascus and Aram may be the identical force, namely, "Aram that is beyond the river" (2 Sam. 10:16).

In the enumeration of David's extractions in 2 Sam. 8:11-12, the contributions of Hadadezer, and these alone, are referred to as "booty." There is no implication of regular tribute, just as there is no such implication when Tiglath-Pileser collects spoil but does not mention imposts. So Hadadezer did not pay tribute. That is, the text deliberately implies that David subjected all of Syria and the Aramean elements of western Mesopotamia on the upper Euphrates. It explicitly states, however, that he received tribute only from some part of the territory of Damascus. His other gains were taken somewhere in the field. The Tiglath-Pileser principle applies nowhere more clearly than here. David made no gains in Syria. But, brilliantly, the author of 2 Sam. 8 leads the uninformed reader to believe that he did.

2 Samuel intimates that David subdued all Aram in Hadadezer's double defeat in 2 Sam. 10. David retrieved, it tells us, dress military regalia from Hadadezer's vassals (enumerated in 2 Sam. 10:6)

> David took the golden shields that the servants of Hadadezer had, and brought them to Jerusalem. (2 Sam. 8:7)

He also recovered considerable quantities of bronze from two cities, Tebah, and Berotai or Kun, in the northern Beqaʿ (2 Sam. 8:8).

The text implies that David campaigned in the northern Beqaʿ Valley, where Tebah, at least, is to be found.[7] It suggests that David subdued every territory up to the border of Hamath. The goods from Tebah concretely witness to

---

7. Tebah is called Tubihi in Assyrian sources and lies to the south of Hamath, but on the northern end of the valley. See above, Chapter 9.

this assertion. Yet, he may have taken this booty from the kings relieving Rabbat Ammon, in the field.

In other words, the text leaves us with two assumptions: that Zobah was a unified nation-state rather than a territory containing various kinglets, whose existence is attested in 2 Sam. 10:19;[8] rather, it was, like the Aram of Bar-Hadad son of Hazael in the Zakkur stela, an area where a central power could compel various city-states to collaborate. The second assumption that the text intentionally conditions is that David campaigned in the vicinity of Zobah. That is why 2 Sam. 8 nowhere indicates that David fought Aram Zobah or Damascus in Transjordan. Yet in 2 Sam. 10, after the field force encounter with Aram, David's army still had unfinished business at the Ammonite capital, which it prosecuted in a succeeding year.

Indeed, at the end of the Absalom revolt, later in David's reign, Sheba ben-Bichri flees to apparent safety at Abel Beth Maacah. This is the capital, Abel, of the dynastic state, the House of Maacah. It was adjacent to Dan. As will be argued below (Chapter 20 C), Joab's negotiation at Abel represents the incorporation of that city-state into David's kingdom. Even if it was Israelite, however, it sat on Israel's northern border at the time. That is, David did not extend the border north of Dan into the Beqa' Valley. Nor does Israelite political control extend beyond Dan: the expression "from Dan to Beersheba" defines Israel at the outset of David's kingship in 2 Sam. 3:10, but also during (2 Sam. 17:11) and after (2 Sam. 24:2, 15) the Absalom revolt, and even in the older material concerning Solomon's reign (1 Kgs. 4:25[5:5]).[9]

Dan remained the border at Solomon's death, when Jeroboam led the secession of the northern tribes from Jerusalem: one of Jeroboam's state shrines stood at Dan and the other at Bethel (1 Kgs. 12:29-30). These shrines sanctified the region in which the cult they represented held the force of a legal prescription. Shortly afterward, 1 Kgs. 15:20 relates that the king of Damascus attacked Iyyun, Dan, and Abel Beth Maacah and penetrated south of the border they guarded. Dan, Abel, and Iyyun remained the border from David's day forward. In sum, there is no basis in the explicit text to hypothesize a northern campaign on David's part.[10] But it is, again, precisely the method of royal inscriptions to

---

8. As well as 1 Sam. 14:47, Saul's conflict with the "kings of Zobah." Even assuming Hadadezer had really subordinated his allies — and there is very little indication of this — the hegemony was of recent standing, subsequent to Saul's conflicts there.

9. The expression occurs elsewhere in slightly different form in Judg. 20:1, and with the terms inverted ("from Beersheba unto Dan") in 1 Chr. 21:2; 2 Chr. 30:5 (another of the themes connecting Hezekiah to Solomon in Chronicles).

10. In this particular, I part company with J. Maxwell Miller and John H. Hayes, *A*

aggrandize accomplishments in the subtext, without prevaricating at the literal level.

Having created an impression, the text hastens to reinforce it. In 2 Sam. 8:9-10, it relates that Toi, king of Hamath, sent his son to congratulate David on his victory, bearing gifts of precious metals. Here, as noted in Chapter 9, the basis is laid for a claim (made explicitly in 1 Chr. 18:3) that David's sphere of influence extended beyond Zobah, and on to the Euphrates. Hamath becomes the key to the claim that, like Hadadezer's allies from "across the river," all of Syria acknowledged David's sovereignty. Of Hadadezer's allies, at the end of 2 Sam. 10 (v. 19), we read:

> All the kings, the servants of Hadadezer, saw that they were smitten before Israel, and they made peace with Israel and served them [Israel], and Aram feared to succor the Ammonites further.

All the Arameans outside of Zobah are implicitly represented as Hadadezer's vassals, so that the defeat of Hadadezer becomes the defeat of all Syrians everywhere.

Too much has been made of the Yahwistic name of Toi's son, Yoram: it has been supposed that he altered his real name from Hadoram (1 Chr. 18:10). The name Hadoram means, "Hadad (Canaanite Haddu) is exalted." The theory runs that he changed his name to show the loyalty of Hamath's royal house to Israel, the senior partner in the alliance: thus, the variant Joram describes the god Yahweh (*yaw-*), as exalted.

Yahweh was likely a divine name indigenous to the Hamath region, as Stefanie Dalley has argued.[11] One could therefore maintain that, in Hamath, Yahweh was an epithet of Hadad. More likely, the alternation between Yoram and Hadoram is the result of scribal error.[12] In any case, it is improbable that

---

History of Ancient Israel and Judah (Philadelphia: Westminster, 1986), 185, where the possibility of an invasion of Zobah is entertained. Otherwise, their historical assessment is in large measure in agreement with this one, though they reach it by identifying what they think is hyperbole in the account, rather than by considering the difference between literally true but misleading language.

11. Hadoram in 1 Chr. 18:10; see Abraham Malamat, *JNES* 22 (1963): 6-7, with the argument for Israel's supremacy in the relationship, followed by McCarter, *II Samuel*, 250. See further Stephanie Dalley, "Yahweh in Hamath in the 8th Century BC: Cuneiform Material and Historical Deductions," *VT* 40 (1990): 21-32. Connections in Israel's territorial dreams with the Hamath region, and traditions in DtrH of Israelite settlement there (cited above), suggest that the other evidence Dalley adduces is correctly interpreted by her. See further Chapter 14.

12. It should be noted that LXX reads Hadoram as well (Iedoram). So the alternation

Hamath made any sort of formal submission to David, rather than establishing relations based on common enmity to Zobah. 2 Sam. 8:10 is explicit on the point that Toi was an enemy of Hadadezer: "a man of wars of Toi was Hadadezer." Whether the relations issued in some sort of treaty is left in the air by our account.

Toi's son brings David vessels of silver, gold, and bronze (2 Sam. 8:11-12):

> These too the king, David, dedicated to Yahweh, with the silver and the gold that he dedicated from all the nations that he vanquished. From Aram and from Moab and from the Ammonites and from (the) Philistines and from Amaleq and from the booty of Hadadezer son of Rehob king of Zobah.

By treating the gifts from Hamath, which were undoubtedly reciprocated in a friendly diplomatic exchange, on the same plane as the exactions from Aram (read: an area south of Damascus), Moab, Ammon, "the Philistines," Amaleq, and "the spoil of Hadadezer," this text reinforces the impression of Israelite sovereignty in Syria. All this betokened submission, it implies.

And yet a close reading of the text indicates the contrary. Nowhere does Samuel lay claim to territory in Syria. Most probably, the gifts and diplomatic relations stemming from Hamath were a form of alliance against the kingdom of Zobah, which lay between Hamath and Israel. And there is no indication at all that David campaigned in Zobah itself, rather than meeting the expeditionary army of Zobah in the course of his campaign in Ammon. If we take the text at its face value, rather than investing ourselves in its apparatus of implication, the picture is relatively modest.

B. David's Stela

2 Sam. 8:13 relates that David "made a name when he returned from defeating Aram," closing the segment of the text that deals with this episode.[13] The refer-

---

between *ywrm* (Joram) and *hdrm* (Hadoram) could have resulted from confusion between the letters *yodh* (y) and *he* (h) in the paleo-Hebrew script. This would have left a name, *ydrm*. Confronted with such a name in the later Aramaic script in which Hebrew Bible texts were transmitted, a scribe would naturally correct the *daleth* (d) to the very similar *waw* (w) in order to generate a name, Yoram *(ywrm)*, of a familiar form. However, there is also alternation in the name of another king of Hamath: Yaubidi, at the time of Sargon II, also appears as Ilubidi.

13. On the text of 8:13, see the treatment of McCarter, *II Samuel*, 245-46.

ence is to a monument, and it may well be the same monument referred to at the outset of the campaign against Hadadezer, in 2 Sam. 8:3.[14] If so, the second reference to the monument refers to the first as a way of closing the campaign report. If not, then the reference in 8:13 is to a monument commemorating the Edomite campaign (so the oldest Septuagint versions). The account of that campaign would then begin with a reference to a stela (8:13-14), just as the reference to a stela in 8:3 begins the account of the Ammonite-Aramean war. Regardless, twin references to monuments frame the Aramean war report. In all likelihood, the twin references are to the same monument. The alternation in the terminology for them (8:3 "hand"; 8:13 "name") is intended to obscure the fact that they are the same: the second can only have been erected near the Jordan. This leaves the naïve reader free to think that the first was on the Euphrates (see Chapter 9, n. 43).

The report of the erection of stelas is yet another theme of Middle and early Neo-Assyrian historiography: such texts lay particular stress on the location of monuments in the countryside. But the frame created by the two references to stelas, or the two references to a single stela, is augmented with a report on the subduing of the Edomites: David is said to have garrisoned their territory; they become tribute-bearing vassals. This creates yet another parallel to a passage earlier in the text, namely, the decimation of Moabites in 8:2, before the Aramean war.

The Edomite campaign combines all three elements of David's ideal policy. Heavy casualties are inflicted in the course of a victory in the field. This is also the case with Zobah and Damascus. The enemy, the Edomites, are reduced to vassalage. The same obtains in the instance of Moab. And David garrisons the countryside of Edom — the entire countryside. David otherwise installs garrisons in part of Aram Damascus. Edom is placed at the climax of the account to leave the reader with the impression that all the previous conquests were as thoroughgoing and permanent as that of the impoverished south. The direct parallel in technique is to the summary statements in the annals of Tiglath-Pileser I, which level all distinctions among the nations he harassed.

Particularly telling is one locution, in 2 Sam. 8:14:

He (David) placed garrisons in Edom. In all of Edom he placed garrisons, and all of Edom were servants to David.

14. This may also explain why MT v. 3 has the wrong verb. It might very well have had a double-reading *blktw/bšbw lhṣyb ydw bnhr*, or have originally lost the second of these verbs with the first supplying its place. The sequence *bšb(h) lhṣb* became *bšb(h) lhšb* because of or leading to haplography by homoioteleuton and subsequent correction. See Chapter 9.

Why the repetition about the garrisons?[15] It is to stress that the entire country was under David's rule. What is the contrast? It is to Aram Damascus, where David also installs garrisons. Again, the implication is that he subdued the entire territory of Damascus. But this claim is never made explicitly. In other words, in the case of Edom, David's scribes could claim the complete subjection of the countryside. This achievement could be framed to imply that David's other conquests, of Damascus and of Aram at large, were also total victories.

From this observation, two possible conclusions flow. The first is that David did take the town of Damascus itself. Were this the case, however, the conquest would have been the crowning glory of David's empire. And yet, the narrative glorifying his achievements leaves the matter in doubt. This is a sure indication that the town of Damascus was not in fact his.

Were we to assume that David did take Damascus, he must have handed it to Rezon, the son of Eliada. It is unlikely that Rezon, a breakaway vassal of Hadadezer, could have taken a royal city from a strong empire, or wrested Damascus from any king. This alternative scenario would fit with the Hebrew text of 1 Kgs. 11:23-24: when David defeated Hadadezer, Rezon and his men went to Damascus and proclaimed Rezon king.[16] Did David install Rezon in Damascus? Was Rezon in fact David's agent after the defeat of Hadadezer?

The alternative is that David did not achieve any hold over the town of Damascus itself. Again, 2 Sam. 8:5 relates that in the second encounter — the one with Aramean kings "from across the river" in ch. 10 — Damascus was secondarily enlisted in a bid to help Hadadezer.

> Aram Damascus came to assist Hadadezer king of Zobah, and David smote among Aram twenty-two thousand men. David installed garrisons in Aram Damascus, and Aram became servants, bearers of tribute, to David. . . .

The suggestion is that Damascus was independent of Zobah. In that case, the defeat of Hadadezer and his Damascene ally may have precipitated Rezon's filibuster — or his betrayal of Hadadezer. This may have led to an accommodation between Rezon and Israel. In other words, Rezon cut a deal ceding territory to

---

15. McCarter (*II Samuel,* 246) takes the text to be conflate, but the reality is that the defective variants of 1 Chr. 18:13 and some of the versions are easily explicable based on haplography by homoioteleuton, whereas the MT has a yaqtul-qatal verbal sequence that is perfectly normal, along with an inversion in word order in the second clause meant to add stress on "in all Edom."

16. It is not irrelevant that one of David's officers was from Zobah: 2 Sam. 23:36. For the problems with the Kings text, see above.

David in order to secure his dominance in Damascus. Rezon's revanchism in Solomon's day, in fact, may have represented nothing more than the attempted recovery of those territories. All the same, David dominated Damascus and occupied some of its territory.

This too fits the evidence from Kings.[17] Rezon was the tyrant of Damascus, the man who stamped his name on the foundation of the kingdom there. The impression resulted in the later appearance of a Rezin, an opponent of Tiglath-Pileser III and of Ahaz, king of Judah. And the adoption by Rezin II of the name of the king, Rezon, of David's era, attests that local tradition identified Rezon as the figure who founded the kingdom of Damascus. In the same era, there appear Jeroboam II in Israel, named after the leader of Israel's secession from the Davido-Solomonic state; Hiram II in Tyre, adopter of a name of another contemporary of David's; and, in an invocation of a truly ancient state builder, Sargon II in Assyria. The name Rezin II is a part of this pattern of kings invoking state founders in the 8th century.

The subsequent history of conflict between Aram and Israel shows that the detente between them in David's day was atypical. And yet, this does not imply that the confrontational politics of later eras between Jerusalem and Damascus were normal for the period before David's death. Damascus remained the most proximate threat to Jerusalem and Samaria down through the end of the Israelite monarchy, in the 8th century. But because it threatened Israel, Damascus was also a natural ally of Jerusalem in periods when Israel and Judah were at odds. Which was it in David's time? Most of the evidence will point to its alliance with David.

---

17. This is more or less the scenario favored by Malamat, *JNES* 22 (1963): 5.

CHAPTER 11

The Date and Reception of 2 Samuel 8

David's Display?

One strange feature of 2 Sam. 8 is that it does not mention the fall of Rabbat Ammon (2 Sam. 12:26-29) or any conflict concerning it. It is true that the chapter speaks of exactions received from the Ammonites (2 Sam. 8:12). But one might expect a review of field conflict with Ammon, or the reduction of the capital (2 Sam. 12:30).

This holds the more stringently in that 2 Sam. 12:31 lodges the claim that David impressed the population of "all the towns of the children of Ammon." The capture of the royal city would have followed, normally, from the domination of the countryside. There are sites in Ammonite territory that have been called "fortified watchtowers." But no evidence suggests their construction as far back as the early 10th century B.C.E. Thus, the "towns of the children of Ammon" were most probably unfortified in the period.

This means that the impressment of "all the towns" of Ammon is most likely a summary statement, on the Tiglath-Pileser principle.[1] It is safe to con-

---

1. Of the "fortified watchtowers," 19 have been located (one by C. R. Conder, 18 by Nelson Glueck) and dated to the Iron Age (by Glueck, and cf. George M. Landes, "The Material Civilization of the Ammonites," *BA* 24 [1961]: 72); repr. David Noel Freedman and Edward F. Campbell, *BA Reader* 2:69-88. See esp. Adam Zertal, "Three Iron Age Fortresses in the Jordan Valley and the Origin of the Ammonite Circular Towers," *IEJ* 45 (1995): 253-73, esp. 269-72. Roger S. Boraas, "A Preliminary Sounding at Rujm el-Malfuf, 1969," *ADAJ* 16 (1971): 31-46, found only Roman material in the northern tower; Henry O. Thompson, "The Ammonite Remains at Khirbet al-Hajjar," *BASOR* 227 (1977): 27-34, provided evi-

clude that David impressed some population, which then stands for all Ammonite settlements. Most of the warfare against outlying settlements will have taken place before the siege of the capital city.

Why does 2 Sam. 8, though, the summary of David's conquests, omit the fall of the capital of Ammon? Not because the campaign against Ammon would be treated in detail in 2 Sam. 10–12 and so could be passed over in ch. 8. The author of the account in chs. 10–12 felt no compunction about repeating the history of the Aramean conflict. Moreover, the details in that narrative differ from those in 2 Sam. 8. On the surface, 2 Sam. 8 has only one confrontation with Aram, to which Damascus was a party. 2 Sam. 10–12 describe two engagements with Aram, the first with Zobah, the House of Rehob, Maacah, and Tob, the second involving elements from "beyond the river." Damascus is not mentioned by name. The author of ch. 8 did not pass over the Ammonite campaign in order to avoid repetition.

A second explanation for the omission is more likely: the text reflects circumstances in which a claim of overlordship over Ammon was inappropriate. Perhaps Ammon regained something of its independence in the Absalom revolt, as a result of the service that Shobi, son of Nahash, rendered to David at the time. This will have taken place later than the fall of Rabbat Ammon — the relative sequence is a key to dating the Ammonite campaign.[2] The diplomatic circumstances permitted the author of 2 Sam. 8 to avoid mentioning Ammon while describing David's ascendance over Aram, including both Damascus and Zobah.

Neither Maacah nor Tov is mentioned in 2 Sam. 8. Neither became a vassal, despite the formulation of 2 Sam. 10:19 to the effect that Hadadezer's vassals sued for peace and served Israel: the text makes no mention of tribute.

> David slew of Aram seven hundred chariot teams and forty thousand horsemen, and he smote Shobach, commander of its army,[3] and he died

---

dence that the sites are Iron II, in at least two cases, late Iron II (cf. Thompson, "Rujm al-Malfuf South," *ADAJ* 18 [1973]: 47-50). For the plans of the fortresses, see Konrad von Rabenau, "Ammonitische Verteidigungsanlagen zwischen Ḥirbet el-Bišāra und el-Yādūde," *ZDPV* 94 (1978): 46-55; Richard Hentschke, "Ammonitische Grenzfestungen südwestlich von 'ammān," *ZDPV* 76 (1960): 103-23, esp. 111-21. What Ammon might have looked like at the end of the 11th century is still a subject waiting to be resolved, with a few exceptions only. On Rabbat Ammon (Amman) itself, see Fawzi Zayadine, "La Citadelle d'Amman: La Terre de Jordanie," *MDB* 46 (1986): 17-20: Zayadine reports that the Amman middle and upper terraces sport an acropolis with glacis and fortification walls and a Milcom temple with a 9th-century inscription.

2. See below, Chapter 13, on the relative chronology of David's reign.
3. Or: "his (Hadadezer's) army."

there. And all the kings, the vassals of Hadadezer, saw that they were defeated before Israel, so they made peace with Israel and served them, and Aram feared to succor the Ammonites any further. (2 Sam. 10:18-19)

The point of the passage is that the Arameans desisted from intervention in Transjordan to obstruct David's advance against Ammon. Thus, the continuation reads:

> At the turn of the year, when kings go forth to war, David sent Joab and his servants with him, and all Israel, and they attacked the Ammonites and laid siege to Rabbah, while David remained in Jerusalem. (2 Sam. 11:1)

Aramean servitude consists of disengagement from the conflict. Read minimally, the text claims that some Damascenes entered into vassalship. In short, 2 Sam. 8 mentions only the states from which David took booty. It was written in continuity with 2 Samuel so as to imply that David took Syria before the war with Ammon.

The Aramean submission in 2 Sam. 10:19 may reflect developments later than the writing of 2 Sam. 8. The sequence in 2 Sam. 10:18–11:1 indicates that David was deflected from campaigning in Zobah, or Syria at all, by his need to reduce Rabbah. So a third possible reason for the omission of Ammon from ch. 8 is that the source of ch. 8 was written in the interval between the conflict with Aram and the taking of Rabbah.

After all, 2 Sam. 8 does not mention Maacah. Maacah was later incorporated into the kingdom. By the time of Asa, as noted above, Ben-Hadad's idea of an attack on Israel was to strike at Iyyon, Dan, and Abel of the House of Maacah (1 Kgs. 15:18-20). Abel was not integrated into Israel under Solomon or Jeroboam. Solomon, if anything, lost territory in the north, ceding the tribe of Asher to Tyre in exchange for gold and a naval treaty to exploit the southern trade routes. He failed to quell the rise of Damascus.[4] Jeroboam, too, was occupied with establishing the independence of the Northern Kingdom of Israel. Its secession from the state administered from Jerusalem left David's heirs with the kingdom of Judah alone. After the invasion of the Egyptian pharaoh Shishaq, the founder of the 22nd Dynasty, in the fifth year of his reign, Jeroboam was surely occupied with reconstructing the centers of his kingdom. His assertion of sovereignty at Dan, by building one of his two state shrines there, indicates that he was more interested in consolidating than in expanding his borders. As

---

4. See Baruch Halpern, *JBL* 93 (1974): 519-32. Further, below, Chapter 22.

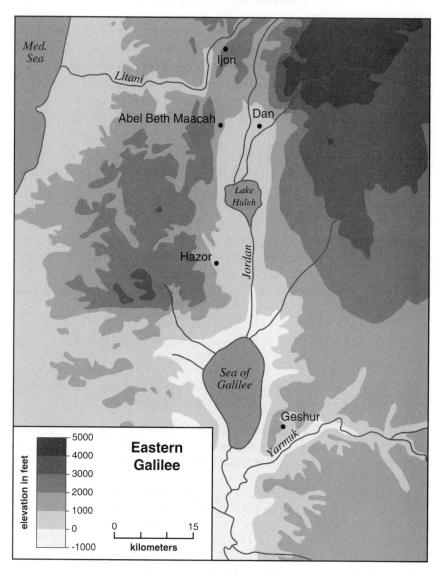

map 11.1

we have seen (Chapter 10A), Dan was the traditional boundary of David's state, before him.

Concerning Abel of the House of Maacah, we have only one explicit historical text. After the end of the Absalom revolt, it is to Abel that Sheba ben-Bichri fled. Beleaguered, Abel extradited him, or at least his head (2 Sam. 20:14-22). In the transaction, Abel is represented by a "wise woman," and the absence of a king from the narrative is more than a mere conceit of the presentation. Abel was the royal town of the House of Maacah, so the king's absence may reflect a revolution and accommodation with the state into which the town was integrated, namely, the Israel threatening it in the narrative.[5]

The sheltering of Sheba suggests Abel was extraterritorial and independent. The same is true of Joab's siege, which presupposes that the residents of the city were not in fact in revolt, but merely exercising their right to resist a foreign adversary. Yet the "wise woman" protests that Abel was an Israelite "matriclan."[6] Her words are difficult to interpret, but the speech begins as follows:

They have always said, from the start, as follows: "They will surely seek at Abel and, at Dan, be fulfilled."[7] . . . You are seeking to kill a city and

5. For the archaeological indications of 10th-century settlement, see William G. Dever, "'Abel-Beth-Ma'acah: 'Northern Gateway of Ancient Israel,'" in *The Archaeology of Jordan and Other Studies*, ed. Lawrence T. Geraty and Lawrence G. Herr (Berrien Springs: Andrews University Press, 1986), 207-22, esp. 220.

6. On "a mother and a city in Israel" see Richard S. Tomback, *A Comparative Semitic Lexicon of the Phoenician and Punic Languages*. SBLDS 32 (Missoula: Scholars, 1978), 22-23; Abraham Malamat, "UMMATUM in Old Babylonian Texts and Its Ugaritic and Biblical Counterparts," *UF* 11 (1979): 527-36.

7. See P. Kyle McCarter, Jr., *II Samuel*, 428-29. Probably, the Greek attests an omission in MT, and the original text ran more like: *š'l yš'l b'bl [wbdn ky htmw 'šr šmw 'mny yśr'l š'l yš'lw b'bl] wkn (ky?) htmw 'nky šlmy 'mny yśr'l 'th mbqš lhmyt 'yr w'm bysr'l*. The haplography, by homoioarcton *(š'l yš'l b'bl . . . š'l yš'l b'bl)*, is of most of the proverb the wise woman was citing. What follows is her reframing of Joab's appearance at Abel in terms of the proverb. The general meaning is uncertain. But like the proverb, "Is Saul (or: 'is it asked') also among the prophets?" this one probably involves a pun, and on Sheol (asking, underworld) and Abel (= mourning). "It will surely be asked in Abel" thus refers to necromancy. The continuation requires some such translation as: "and in Dan, whether those who erected the pillars/foundations of Israel have perished." Dan is adjacent to Abel, at a distance of 7 km., and was a metallurgical center at the time. The two could be considered the "pillars" between which one would pass on entering Israelite territory from the north. The wise woman continues, referring to Joab: "They certainly are asking in Abel." Without emendation, her next words would be rendered, "and indeed they have perished. I am the ally of the Craftsmen of Israel, (but) you are seeking to kill a city and mother of

mother (the matriclan) in Israel. Why should you devour the inheritance of Yahweh? (2 Sam. 20:18-19)

Probably, the proverb the wise woman cites implies that Abel is somehow in a treaty relationship with Dan and Israel, as the Targum and Josephus take it. At least, the wise woman makes it explicit that her town belongs to Israel. The extradition, then, and especially the "wise woman's" protestations that Abel was an Israelite "matriclan," indicate submission to what had formerly been a foreign power. But this development came late in David's reign, after the Absalom revolt, and not on the heels of the conflict in Transjordan. And that, or else its full-scale annexation, may explain the absence of any notice about Abel in 2 Sam. 8, despite the report in 2 Sam. 10 that Maacah participated in Hadadezer's coalition.

Thus, it is attractive to suppose that the source of 2 Sam. 8 was written early in David's reign, perhaps even before the fall of Rabbat Ammon. If so, one source suggests itself as most likely. That is the display inscription that 2 Sam. 8 refers to at least once, and possibly twice, and that David erected. The river in question is probably the river Jordan, for there is no real evidence that he ever approached the Euphrates, nor that Hadadezer recruited troops against him any further afield than Damascus (across the Jordan). Depending on the location of Helam, supposed site of the second confrontation with Hadadezer, or rather, with his general Shobach,[8] it is not clear that David penetrated far into Damascene territory. Indeed, the ongoing independence of Geshur, whose royal

---

Israel." With reasonably modest emendation, this becomes, "They certainly are asking in Abel, and indeed (whether?) those who erected the pillars/foundations of Israel have perished: you are seeking to kill a city and mother of Israel." A possible, but not likely, alternative is the one underlying the treatment of the passage in Josephus, namely that on their arrival in Canaan, the Israelites inquired at Abel of the House of Maacah before passing on to Dan, and made peace with Abel. The Targum takes the wise woman to be saying that Joab is obliged to permit the city to choose between submission on the one hand and assault and destruction on the other. In any case, the woman is certainly claiming that Abel either already is or is now willing to become Israelite de jure. In a de facto sense, its Israelite status was probably not yet established.

8. In conversation, McCarter suggests a relationship between the name of Helam and the term Ahlamu, applied in Assyrian royal inscriptions down to the 9th century to the Arameans. The spelling ḥl'm in 2 Sam. 10:17 might be adduced in support of this suggestion. No candidate for the location of Helam has been found; but, as it is the site of a field-force encounter, not of a siege, this is hardly surprising. On the other hand, as indicated above, the term may have been misinterpreted as a location, having originally meant "(military) force." As noted, Josephus interprets it to be the king of the Arameans from across the Euphrates (Ant. 7.127).

house furnished David with the mother of Absalom and later furnished Absalom with a refuge in exile, rather suggests that the small kingdoms of the north were not wholly or, with the exception of Abel, even partly overcome until Damascus expanded under Rezin and his successors in the late 10th or even 9th century.[9] Had David campaigned in Geshur, Tob, the House of Rehob, or Zobah, the text would trumpet the fact.

There is a slightly more cynical explanation for the current condition of 2 Sam. 8. It is therefore the most likely answer of all. The text as it stands decontextualizes the Aramean war by severing its political connection to the Israelite invasion of Ammon. It thus conceals the battle's location in Ammon. The decontextualization leaves the reader with the impression that David campaigned in southern Syria, on the soil of Zobah itself. It also reinforces the impression that "(the) river" of 8:3 is indeed the Euphrates. After all, having turned from the campaign against Moab *on Moabite ground* in 8:2, the text next states that David "smote Hadadezer . . . king of Zobah." The connection to the war against Ammon is altogether absent, and the succeeding action takes the reader to Damascus (8:6) and Hamath (8:9). By including Ammon only in a generalized list of those "conquered" (8:12), the author of the text further insulates the "Aramean campaign" from the Ammonite war.

And yet, the author of ch. 8 could have included in it a separate segment, after the treatment of Edom, on the capture of the Ammonite capital. What does this imply for authorship? Again, no mention is made of later conquests — the capital of Ammon, Abel of the House of Maacah. Further, it is the Succession Narrative itself (in the frame around the Bathsheba story) that enables us to recontextualize the allegations of ch. 8 concerning Aram and thus to understand that the battle against Hadadezer was fought in central Transjordan, not in the north. Traditionally, readers have assumed that the events of 2 Sam. 8, including the fight with Aram Zobah, took place before the invasion of Ammon in 2 Sam. 10 (so, e.g., the historian Flavius Josephus).[10]

In itself, 2 Sam. 8 leads the reader to infer that David's state was larger than the text of 2 Sam. 8 literally states. This is true of his victories over Philistia and Moab, at the start of the chapter. It holds for his influence over Hamath, in cen-

9. Occupations at Ein Gev and Tel Hadar indicate a continuous Aramean presence, or at least a distinctive regional culture, in this area. This is not necessarily coterminous with political sovereignty, but the textual evidence on this subject would generally seem to be consonant with the archaeological.

10. Josephus *Ant.* 7.96-129. But essentially, any claim that the empire reached the Euphrates, or any distance into Syria, also presupposes that the text in ch. 8 depicts a battle or battles different from those in 2 Sam. 10. This embraces most reconstructions of David's state.

tral Syria. It is especially true of his conflict with and ascendance over Zobah, Damascus, and Aram at large. Within the ongoing narrative in 2 Samuel, the placement of 2 Sam. 8 functions in much the same way. The broken linkage between the battles of 2 Sam. 8:3-5 and those of 2 Sam. 10 — broken mainly by the incidental narrative of 2 Sam. 9 — suggests that David campaigned in the Beqaʿ Valley in southern Syria. After that expedition, which extended his political control to the border of Hamath, and extended his influence into Hamath, the Arameans revolted in order to join Ammon in resisting him. In the second of his field fights with Aram, in Ammon, he overcame not just the Arameans of Syria but also those from "across the river" in Mesopotamia. Thus, the connected narrative in effect goes farther than 2 Sam. 8 itself. It does so by building on the materials and techniques 2 Sam. 8 affords it.

In other words, three indications show that 2 Sam. 8 comes from a source earlier than the history of David's reign. First, it presents the defeat of Hadadezer in such a way as to divorce this event from the Ammonite war, whereas the Succession Narrative, in 2 Sam. 10–12, adopts a different strategy of presentation — namely, the claim that the Arameans submitted to David directly after their field conflict, in Transjordan. Second, 2 Sam. 8 persuades readers that Hadadezer of Zobah was able to call out Arameans from beyond the Euphrates to fight against David — this is why, for example, Hadadezer, rather than a king of Hamath or of Carchemish, is often identified with the Aramean king who seized territory east of the Euphrates from Assyria.

More important is the third point. There is no logical location in the narrative of 2 Samuel for 2 Sam. 8. It could not be placed prior to David's occupation of Jerusalem, with which the fight with the Philistines was associated. Nor could it be located after the narrative of 2 Sam. 10 about the Ammonite war without exposing the fact that the only fight with Hadadezer took place in central Transjordan, rather than in the Beqaʿ Valley.

But most important of all, the current placement of 2 Sam. 8 creates an improbable sequence, by omitting the details of the Ammonite campaign. First David invades the Beqaʿ, and then the foe he vanquished there intervenes against its conqueror at Rabbat Ammon. It would surely have been the choice of an author writing without sources to place the fall of Tubihi in the northern Beqaʿ Valley after, rather than before, the battle in Ammon. However, if the account of imposts from northern Zobah was already embedded in a document, the author of the embracing narrative might hesitate to disentangle it. This seems to have been the case here.

Even if the source of 2 Sam. 8 postdates the fall of Rabbat Ammon — or particularly if it does — it still bears the look, and employs the propagandistic technology of the royal display inscription. In sum, the authors of 2 Samuel, and of its sources, deliberately employed writing techniques exhibiting a close kinship to those of Near Eastern display inscriptions. They suggested, implied, insinuated that David's achievements were a great deal more extensive than in reality they were. But they did not openly prevaricate, on this subject at least. Their method was a good deal more subtle than outright forgery, and very much at home in the historiographic traditions of the chanceries of the ancient Near East.[11] The Republic of Letters embraced, and did not stop at, the early royal court of ancient Israel.[12]

11. And this also explains why remains of any Davidic construction are absent — if John S. Holladay (*BASOR* 277/278 [1990]: 23-70) is basically right about the distribution of burnished red-slip in the 10th century, namely, that it was not present until Solomon's reconstruction of the upper gate at Gezer; then no public works antedating Solomon have been discovered in Iron Age Israel. Though some no doubt might exist, principally in respect to Jerusalem, no other building activities are attributed to David in the texts, either. Had David indeed constructed an empire reaching well into Syria and up to the Litani (as Gösta W. Ahlström proposes, *A History of Ancient Palestine*, 486 and his Map 14), a more aggressive program of fortification and display should have been expected in the archaeological record.

12. The foregoing represents an elaboration of my study, "The Construction of the Davidic State: An Exercise in Historiography," in *The Origins of the Ancient Israelite States*, ed. Volkmar Fritz and Philip R. Davies. JSOTSup 228 (Sheffield: Sheffield Academic, 1996), 44-75.

CHAPTER 12

2 Samuel 8 and the Historicity of the Davidic State

A. Propaganda and Its Implications for Historical Reality

It appears that 2 Sam. 8 takes the form of a royal inscription. Against this perspective, a number of objections might be lodged. First, no West Semitic display inscriptions are attested before the 9th century.[1] This is not a decisive point: the discovery of inscriptions depends on the accidents of secondary use and archaeological recovery, both of which differ by context. We have yet to find more than a small fragment of a royal stela from Israel or Judah in any period. Assyrian inscriptions attest Israel's importance in the 9th century. So, emphatically, does the Dan stela. Yet it is in the lesser states of Ammon and Moab that early royal inscriptions have appeared. Even around 700, a monumental inscription commemorates the building of the Siloam water tunnel in Jerusalem, but there is no royal inscription.

Most royal sites in Israel have modern occupations. Jerusalem, the only likely site for 10th-century monuments, was repeatedly torn up by ancient engineers. In such sites, royal stelas are often in re-use, as was the case with the Mesha stela and the Dan stela: inscribed stones tend to be large and squared, and so are useful in building. In the countryside, the recovery of stelae is relatively unlikely, as excavation tends to be on mounds. Thus, only something fairly massive and protected is likely to be found.

---

1. So, in conversation, Nadav Na'aman.

208

Indeed, a 10th-century stela fragment has been found in Israel — the stela belonged to Pharaoh Shishaq and was recovered, out of context, at Megiddo. The original was roughly 10 ft. high.[2] It is not as though West Semitic kings — Aramean, Phoenician, Israelite, and others — were unfamiliar with the technologies of propaganda that courts employed in Mesopotamia and in Egypt. Ambassadors and merchants traveling from or through Canaan to the Euphrates encountered the monuments of foreign courts. And Phoenician royal funerary, votive, and building monuments of the 10th century, while not themselves display inscriptions, make use of artistic motifs known from Egypt, including a mock-hieroglyphic script, and in one case the actual stela of an Egyptian pharaoh.[3]

Indeed, records of interaction in the annals of Assurnasirpal II and Shalmaneser III already indicate Assyrian contact with the southern trade in the early 9th century. This indicates that trade was already recovering in this period, corroborating the report that Solomon exploited southern trade connections in the 10th century. Texts from Suhu, including one that speaks of a holdup of a caravan from Sabaea (Sheba) at Hindanu, flesh the background out.[4] We have a similar report about the robbery of Babylonian caravaneers just north of the Jezreel Valley, by Hannaton, in the 14th-century archive from Tell el-Amarna, at another time when trade between states was flourishing.

It is plausible that a trading state, as alleged in Kings, gained ground in the 10th century. Assyrian annals attest such states south of the Euphrates. Moreover, it is precisely around 1000 that the smelting of precious metals begins a steep increase, which is consistent to about the turn of the era:[5] the opening up of a new market in exotic commodities resulted in intensified long-distance trade by royal intermediaries. It is to be recalled that the kings of the West, from eastern Syria to the Phoenician coast, were collecting animals from Africa in the late 10th century. The Egyptians themselves sent such animals directly to Assyria.[6] In addition, this is the period when trade with Cyprus resumes and

2. See Robert S. Lamon and Geoffrey M. Shipton, *Megiddo*, 1: *Seasons of 1925-34, Strata I-V.* Oriental Institute Communications 42 (Chicago: University of Chicago Press, 1939), Fig. 70.

3. For the Abibaal inscription, on the base of a statue of Shishaq I, see KAI 5. See generally the Byblian incriptions, KAI 1-7.

4. See esp. Antoine Cavigneaux and Bahija Khalil Ismail, "Die Statthalter von Suu und Mari im 8. Jh. v. Chr.," *Baghdader Mitteilungen* 21 (1990): 321-456, including 327-29, 339 and n. 61.

5. See Sungmin Hong et al., "History of Ancient Copper Smelting Pollution During Roman and Medieval Times Recorded in Greenland Ice," *Science* 272 (April 12, 1996): 246-49.

6. See above, Chapter 5B.

snowballs, as witnessed in the presence of geometric pottery in Israel, and entrepots attest the accumulation and distribution of large quantities of cash crops from agriculture.[7] The luxury exchange documents the accumulation of wealth in western Asia in this era, and jibes with our reports about the agrarian state of David and Solomon.[8]

In all, though we lack the epigraphic texts to confirm it, the 10th century presents itself as the period in which trade in precious commodities revived in western Asia, after its collapse at the start of the 12th century. The 21st Dynasty in Egypt had shifted the capital to the eastern Delta, at Tanis, to promote such trade already in the 11th century. Phoenicians were certainly plying the western Mediterranean, including Sardinia, in search mainly of rare earths.[9] The rise in trade points to the erection of royal establishments, and thus the accumulation of capital, to drive such a system of exchange. Indeed, it may have been a deliberate goal of Egyptian and of Tyrian policy to promote more efficient production and delivery in the agricultural hinterland, namely, Israel and the Beqaʿ Valley. Their encouragement, in the form of commercial opportunity, may have created the states. Where there are royal states, there can be royal inscriptions, and the reference to a monument of Absalom — that could be seen in the King's Valley (2 Sam. 18:18) — confirms the contemporary attribution of 10th-century monument-building to Israel. Tenth-century courtiers were familiar

7. For the Cypriot pottery, see Ayelet Gilboa, "New Finds at Tel Dor and the Beginning of Cypro-Geometric Pottery Import to Palestine," *IEJ* 39 (1989): 204-18; Joseph Yellin, "The Origin of Some Cypro-Geometric Pottery from Tel Dor," *IEJ* 39 (1989): 219-27. For accumulation of agricultural goods, see esp. Zvi Gal, "Khorvat Rosh Zayit — A Phoenician Fort in the Lower Galilee," *Qad* 17 (1984): 56-59, attesting, near a village named Kabul, a 10th-century ashlar fort, with three rooms brimming two stories high with containers of lentils, wheat, and wine, and featuring an inscription, *(yy)n ḥmr,* probably "strong wine."

8. And see further Alan R. Millard, "Does the Bible Exaggerate King Solomon's Golden Wealth?" *BAR* 15/3 (1989): 20-29, 31, 34; Kenneth A. Kitchen, "Where Did Solomon's Gold Go?" *BAR* 15/3 (1989): 30; and *The Bible in Its World,* 102, arguing that the 220 tons of silver and 250 tons of gold donated to gods by Osorkon I (*ARE* 4.729-37) in part reflect Shishaq's ransom for Jerusalem. For a truly able defense of the opposite view, see esp. Ernst Axel Knauf, "King Solomon's Copper Supply," in *Phoenicia and the Bible,* ed. Edward Lipínski. Studia Phoenicia 11 (Leuven: Peeters, 1991), 167-86. For the myrrh trade with Arabia in the 2nd millennium, see Kjeld Nielsen, *Incense in Ancient Israel.* VTSup 38 (Leiden: Brill, 1986).

9. See Frank Moore Cross, "The Oldest Phoenician Inscription from Sardinia: The Fragmentary Stele from Nora," in *"Working with No Data": Semitic and Egyptian Studies Presented to Thomas O. Lambdin,* ed. David M. Golomb (Winona Lake: Eisenbrauns, 1987), 65-74.

with royal monuments. Some were probably schooled in their composition. As we have seen, 2 Samuel as a whole was composed in Solomon's court. It employs just the techniques used in royal displays. This, and the structuring of 2 Sam. 8, show that at least the expertise for such creations was present in the Jerusalem of the time.

Again, a group of scholars focused around a core in Copenhagen and Sheffield (the so-called "minimalists") maintain that Jerusalem's population was insufficient for it to function as a state center until its explosion in the late 8th or early 7th century.[10] This is misleading. First, it presupposes an equation of size with the concentration of power that is occasionally belied by historical evidence. One of the earliest observations in the field of ethnoarchaeology is that of Thucydides, comparing Sparta with Athens on the eve of the Peloponnesian War. He specifically is concerned that the ancient site of Mycenae and others of that time seem too insignificant, physically, to have supported the mobilization described by Homer in the *Iliad*. However, were Sparta to fall into ruins, he suggests, future visitors would think it, too, incapable of dominating the Peloponnesian peninsula, as it did in his time. Conversely, an Athens in ruins would be adjudged to hold twice the power it did. Simply, the Spartans eschewed display, in their private as well as public conduct.[11]

It is also a fallacy to take it as axiomatic that demography is deterministic. Organization, the concentration of force, and ideology determine projection, as with Japan dominating China in the 1930s, or Russia in 1905. The victories of Alexander in Asia, and Hannibal in Italy, and of the Mongols across Asia and into Europe were won with forces dwarfed in number by the resources available to their opponents. Late Bronze Age Jerusalem was a major local power in the 14th century, as Nadav Na'aman has demonstrated, but its hegemony left little in the way of a physical imprint.[12] The simple dictum that size implies domination cannot be refuted where textual evidence is inadequate. But in the archae-

10. See for the general perspective John Van Seters, *In Search of History; Prologue to History;* Thomas L. Thompson, *Early History of the Israelite People;* Philip R. Davies, *In Search of "Ancient Israel";* and, with a grounding in archaeology, James W. Flanagan, *David's Social Drama;* David W. Jamieson-Drake, *Scribes and Schools in Monarchic Judah.*

11. See Thucydides 1.10 on the greatness of Mycenae; 1.6 on the Spartan *vs.* the Athenian attitude toward display. Sumptuary laws, banning display especially in connection with funerary rites, were introduced in Judah in the 7th century and in the Athens of the 5th century.

12. For Jerusalem, see Nadav Na'aman, "The Contribution of the Amarna Letters to the Debate on Jerusalem's Political Position in the Tenth Century B.C.E.," *BASOR* 304 (1996): 17-27; and Gabriel Barkay, "What's an Egyptian Temple Doing in Jerusalem?" *BAR* 26/3 (2000): 48-57, 67.

ology of historical periods, and in the historical record itself, it is so frequently contradicted as to be all but useless as a starting-point of analysis. Where texts can reliably be analyzed and their claims carefully and critically assessed, the results make for a far more reliable index of political relations.[13]

Another point shows the existence of a national state in the Israel of the 10th century. The earliest territorial state in Canaan/Israel maintained a deliberate policy of distancing domestic population from state centers. To show this, we must examine a little of the archaeological evidence for the period. Naturally, the interpretation of the archaeological data is controverted: it is not absolutely certain what layers at the sites, for example, of the major Israelite fortresses should be attributed to Solomon. Details supporting the association of Stratum VA-IVB at Megiddo with that king are furnished in Chapter 23. With Megiddo VA-IVB other settlements can be associated.

Stratum VA-IVB at the site of Megiddo and Strata XB-IXA at the site of Hazor are both elements of a central state structure. The city gates of both these sites exhibit a homologous character, consisting of four entryways and six chambers in the gateway, and two towers projecting outward beyond the line of the wall. That of Gezer at the time is identical. Probably slightly later, in the late 10th or early 9th century, Lachish and Ashdod adopt the same form of city gate, and in the early 8th century the gate appears at Tell el-Mudayna, in Ammon. However, the later gates of this form are based on the earlier: once the form was available, the architects of other sites were free to adopt it. At Hazor X and Gezer VIII, the fortifications too are similar, consisting in the initial phase of casemates — a row of long-rooms divided from one another by crossing walls that reinforce the exterior wall. It is possible that the same holds true for Megiddo VA-IVB, where such a line of casemates was found underneath the later city wall in the vicinity of Palace 6000, a building from Solomon's day. On the other hand, these casemates may represent the walls of a compound around the palace.[14]

---

13. Material-cultural comparison of the 20th-century Soviet Union and Eastern bloc with the United States and western Europe would, based on the bias of standard archaeological analysis, leave scholars with the impression that the eastern countries posed no threat whatever to the West.

14. This is a vexed issue, but see generally Yigael Yadin, *Hazor*. Schweich Lectures (London: British Academy, 1972), 150-64; Yadin, Yigal Shiloh, and Abraham Eitan, "Megiddo," *IEJ* 22 (1972): 161-64; David Ussishkin, "Was the 'Solomonic' City Gate at Megiddo Built by King Solomon?" *BASOR* 239 (1980): 1-18; Yigal Shiloh, "Solomon's Gate at Megiddo as Recorded by Its Excavator, R. Lamon, Chicago," *Levant* 12 (1980): 69-76, both with bibliography; more recently, David Ussishkin, "Megiddo," *ABD* 4:666-679. For the purposes of this discussion, the Solomonic attribution of the Gezer, Hazor, and

At Hazor and Gezer, as John S. Holladay has stressed, the relevant gates are associated with the first Iron Age layers in which burnished red-slipped pottery appears.[15] At Megiddo, the gate of Stratum VA-IVB follows the appearance of burnished red-slip, in Stratum VB. It is impossible to state with certainty when in the life of Stratum VB this ceramic ware was introduced, so that the gate's construction could easily follow shortly after burnished red-slip appeared. Burnished red-slip appears earlier at Tell Qasile, a Philistine center, in continuity with the ceramic tradition of the Late Bronze Age. However, again, all indications suggest the contemporaneity of the layers at the three sites — and the evidence from Qasile cannot be used to *lower* the dates of Megiddo, Hazor, and Gezer. The traditional association of the end of these layers with Shishaq's Asian campaign, ca. 927, is probably erroneous: Megiddo VA-IVB and Hazor IXA may have been destroyed slightly later than Shishaq.[16]

Megiddo VA-IVB (and the subsequent stratum, IVA) and Hazor X-IX share one specially striking feature. There have been three major expeditions to Megiddo, those of Gottlieb Schumacher at the turn to the twentieth century, of the University of Chicago's Oriental Institute from 1925 to 1939, and of Tel Aviv University, with Penn State and others, from 1994 forward. None has uncovered substantial evidence of domestic architecture in Stratum VA-IVB. At Hazor, the James Rothschild Expedition of the 1950s and a renewed effort in the 1990s by Amnon Ben-Tor have produced similar results in Strata X-IX.[17] The contemporary settlements at Hazor and Megiddo thus have the character of purely administrative centers.

Nor did Megiddo have a significant hinterland population, at least in the southern central Jezreel Valley: in the Iron II, the weight of population was

Megiddo gates-and-casemates is unimportant; but in light of the attestation of VA-IVB casemate exteriors in Palace 6000 and Palace 1723, in view of the fact that the latter was never completed, but was overlain by offset-inset wall 325, and in view of the association of these and other VA-IVB structures (including the gate) with the initial Iron Age appearance at Megiddo of burnished red-slip, I believe that the attribution is relatively secure. See further the Appendix.

15. John S. Holladay, *BASOR* 277-278 (1990): 23-70.

16. The evidence for Megiddo differs from that for other centers, for which, see the Appendix. Nadav Na'aman has argued, in my view improbably, that Shishaq did not destroy cities at all; "Shishak's Campaign to Palestine as Reflected by the Epigraphic, Biblical and Archaeological Evidence," *Zion* 63 (1998): 247-76. The evidence is that Shishaq did destroy Gezer, Rehob, and other centers.

17. See Amnon Ben-Tor and M. T. Rubbiato, "The Renewed Excavations of Tel Hazor, 1990-1995," *Qad* 29/1 = 111 (1996): 2-18; Ben-Tor and Doran Ben-Ami, "Hazor and the Archaeology of the Tenth Century B.C.E.," *IEJ* 48 (1998): 1-38. For Megiddo, see now Israel Finkelstein, David Ussishkin, and Baruch Halpern, *Megiddo III*.

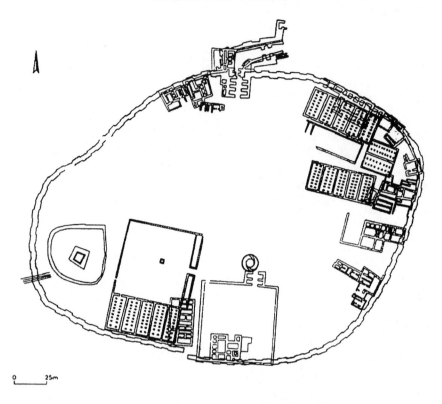

Figure 12.1   Site map of Megiddo VA-IVB + IVA

Courtesy Tel Aviv University Institute of Archaeology, Megiddo Expedition

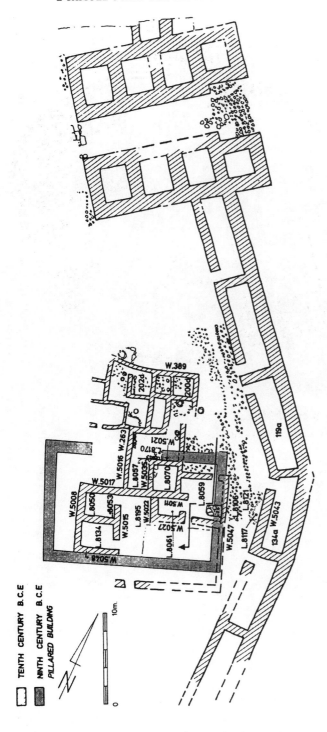

Figure 12.2 Hazor Stratum Xb

Reproduced from Amnon Ben-Tor and Doron Ben-Ami, "Hazor and the Archaeology of the Tenth Century B.C.E.,"
IEJ 48 (1998): 6, by permission of the Israel Exploration Society.

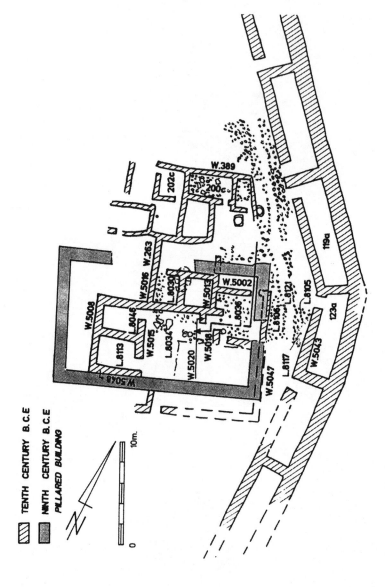

Figure 12.3   Hazor Stratum Xa

Reproduced from Amnon Ben-Tor and Doron Ben-Ami, "Hazor and the Archaeology of the Tenth Century B.C.E.," *IEJ* 48 (1998): 8, by permission of the Israel Exploration Society.

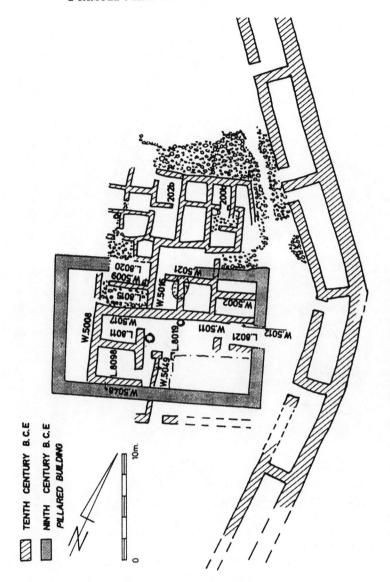

Figure 12.4 Hazor Stratum IXb

Reproduced from Amnon Ben-Tor and Doron Ben-Ami, "Hazor and the Archaeology of the Tenth Century B.C.E.," *IEJ* 48 (1998): 9, by permission of the Israel Exploration Society.

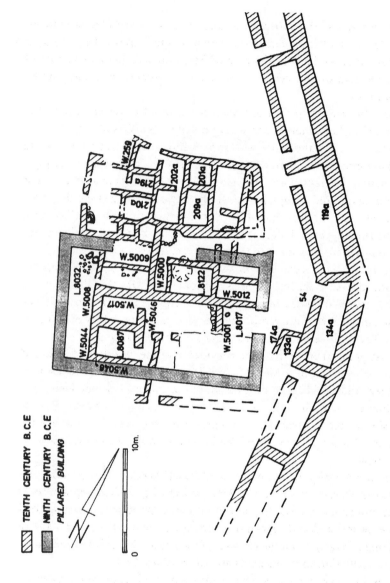

Figure 12.5   Hazor Stratum IXa

Reproduced from Amnon Ben-Tor and Doron Ben-Ami, "Hazor and the Archaeology of the Tenth Century B.C.E.," *IEJ* 48 (1998): 11, by permission of the Israel Exploration Society.

largely concentrated in the northwest sectors of the western Valley, or in major fortresses. In the southern Valley, occupation at small sites is less dense. In other words, what we have in the case of Megiddo, and perhaps in that of Hazor, is an administrative center without an immediate hinterland population to administer.

It would be strange to find one such site without evidence of a central power based elsewhere. Indeed, had we stumbled on the sites of Megiddo VA-IVB and Hazor X-IX without the assistance of textual information, we would probably have interpreted them as independent ritual centers, each servicing a rural population distributed around the site. But it surpasses imagination that two such centers should occupy prominent strategic positions: were they city-states, after all, they would concentrate population within the fortifications. They are instruments of national control, rather than independent polities. Significantly, on its incorporation into the Assyrian empire as a city-state, in Stratum III, Megiddo again becomes a population center as well as an administrative outpost: regional security problems cannot account for this alteration. At Hazor, a substantial domestic population was introduced into the town somewhat earlier, in the 9th century, probably because of the proximity of a hostile Damascus. The 10th-century evidence stands out as extraordinary.

The first point, then, is that here is evidence of the existence of a central state, under whose umbrella Megiddo and Hazor functioned. Indeed, something further can be said about the policies of that state: a disembedded capital, including a provincial capital, is something to which an elite resorts in order to be shut of the influence of prior elites and structures.[18] David's taking of Jerusalem with his private army[19] leads us to expect precisely this sort of disembedment.

The ethnic identity of the people inhabiting Megiddo before Solomon's time is unclear. The city of Stratum VIA may reflect Megiddo's incorporation as a city-state into Israel's polity. Megiddo VIA shows signs of both Canaanite and Israelite — or, lowland and highland — affiliation (and a booming trade in Egyptianizing trinkets).[20] But the removal of the population effected a distancing of historically Canaanite elements and of Israelites there.

Conceivably, Solomon's plan for Megiddo was to adopt the administrative strategy formerly employed by the Egyptian empire. The Jezreel was an impor-

18. Alexander H. Joffe, "Disembedded Capitals in Western Asian Perspective," *Comparative Studies in Society and History* 40 (1998): 549-80.

19. Gary Knoppers, in conversation.

20. Baruch Halpern, "Center and Sentry," in Finkelstein, Ussishkin, and Halpern, *Megiddo III*, 551-55. See further below, Chapter 23.

tant resource for cultivating cereals. In the southern Valley, the United Monarchy, and in its wake the monarchy of the northern kingdom, exploited it by importing population temporarily for agricultural corvée. This continued Egyptian administrative practices of the Late Bronze Age: Biridiya, king of Megiddo in the 14th century, had written the pharaoh complaining about his colleagues' failure to send labor from such sites as Jaffa for cultivating crops at Shunem, across the Valley in the northern Jezreel. The same practice of press-gang labor for the king's lands almost certainly obtained under Solomon as well.[21]

Strikingly, Solomon's district capitals (1 Kgs. 4:7-19) include a number of settlements that were not Israelite before the inception of the monarchy. Beth-Shemesh had been Philistine. Dor was a Sea-People site, associated with the Tjeker (Sikils), probably the people that lent its name to Sicily.[22] The earlier status of Arubboth is unclear. Israel first held part of the Bashan in David's time, and Gilead was perhaps first secured by Saul. And Taanach, Megiddo, and Beth Shan were previously Egyptian and Canaanite centers.

In the other districts, Solomon may have mimicked Egyptian administration again: the Egyptian commissioners of the Amarna era, for example, enjoyed the power to rove rather than being assigned to sit. Several of Solomon's governors had multiple seats of administration — multiple subordinates, that would mean.

But, as Alt observed, the urban administrative centers named are consistently associated with non-Israelite populations.[23] Insofar as recent accessions of the Israelite kingdom are concerned, then, Solomon's administration seems to have preferred to recapitulate or continue the policy David established by

21. Biridiya in EA 365. Note the parallel use of deportation/deported population in SAA 5.210; for an alternative interpretation of the text, see W. R. Gallagher, "Assyrian Deportation Propaganda," *State Archives of Assyria Bulletin* 8 (1994): 57-65. Compare also the list of deportees published for the MA period, from Kar-Tukulti-Ninurta, on which see H. Freydank, "Zur Lage der deportierten Hurriter in Assyrien," *Altorientalische Forschungen* 7 (1980): 89-117; and the lists of deportees in SAA 7; 11.

22. Ephraim Stern, *Dor, Ruler of the Seas* (Jerusalem: Israel Exploration Society, 1994), 101-11, speculates that Dor was taken from the Sea Peoples (surely the Tjeker of the Wen-Amun account) by the Phoenicians before its subjection by David. More likely, the interim phase described by Stern is that of Israelite domination at the site under Saul, Ishbaal, or David, followed by a peaceful transition to domination from Jerusalem under Solomon.

23. See Albrecht Alt, "Israels Gaue unter Salomo," *Kleine Schriften zur Geschichte des Volkes Israels* (Munich: Beck, 1953), 2:76-89. Contrast the assessment, latterly, of Paul S. Ash, "Solomon's? District? List," *JSOT* 67 (1995): 67-86. Ash underestimates the importance of arguments for the list's integrity; but his examination eminently repays close attention.

electing Jerusalem as his capital. Administrative centers were so far as possible divorced from Israelite populations.

Solomon's (and, in the 9th century, Omri's) strategy of isolating population from the major fortifications, at least of the lowlands, offered insurance against Megiddo's defection to neighboring Phoenicia or revolt against the center, on the order of the secession of Libnah in the reign of Jehoram of Judah (2 Kgs. 8:22). The policy is consistent with Solomon's general attempt to remove fiscal power from the lineages, like the system of districts itself:[24] the Israelites had probably hoped for a windfall exploiting their lowland neighbors, but the reverse was the case. Another aspect of the assault was the unification of state and cult symbolized by the construction of the Jerusalem temple in the backyard of Solomon's palace. Was Israel's participation in the Absalom revolt inspired in part by a forerunner of Solomon's policy under David, the promotion of the ark, in the capital, as a national shrine?

The policy of distancing the population from administrative centers had an economic valence as well. Research at rural sites in the Lower Galilee suggests a major change in the 10th century. Surveyors report a huge increase in the foundation of settlements in that period. Likewise, in the hill country and mountains of the western Galilee, settlement increases precipitously, while the area under occupation on the Plain of Acco recovers from a steep decline in the Iron I (the time of the United Monarchy) only later, in the Iron II. Even more impressive is the shift in distribution of the small settlements of this region: in the Late Bronze, 87.5 percent of these communities are on the plain (50%) or in the neighboring hills, whereas in Iron I, the time of the United Monarchy, 75 percent are in the hill country and mountains and only 25 percent are on the plain, a pattern that was to persist in succeeding periods. No single center in Iron I dominates the plain, whereas in Iron II the region appears from geographic analysis to have been integrated in a hierarchic pattern, subordinated to the center at Acco.[25] The population at the time of the United Monarchy was being rusticated to focus on horticulture and logging for the state's benefit.

J. P. Dessel has excavated two rural settlements: Tel Wawiyat in the Beth Netopha Valley (with Tel Hannaton at its mouth) and Tel 'Ein Zippori, some 6 km. south of Hannaton. His preliminary conclusion is that village sites in the region survived into the 10th century (in the case of Zippori) and were then

---

24. See Baruch Halpern, *JBL* 93 (1974): 519-32.

25. For the Acco Plain, G. Lehmann, "Phoenicians in Western Galilee: First Results of an Archaeological Survey in the Hinterland of Akko," forthcoming in *The Archaeology of Israel in the Period of the Monarchy,* ed. A. Mazar and M. Geller (London: Institute of Jewish Studies, University College).

perhaps supplanted by farmsteads. Whether this represents the operation of the United Monarchy, as Dessel suggests,[26] or Shishaq's legacy is unclear. But again, major social transformations mark the 10th century, as 1 Kings suggests.

The pattern of a change in the elites, as at Megiddo, indicates that Dessel's interpretation is most probable: in the Jezreel region, population was moved up and out into the Lower Galilee, where settlement was now renewed for the first time since the Late Bronze Age. The population was then subjected to conscription in order to cultivate the Valley. Cereal production in the Valley was administered through major centers such as Megiddo, Beth Shan, and Taanach. Meanwhile, at home, the relocated population was set to work on the sorts of cash-crop agriculture that produced high-cost exports for the state — viticulture and horticulture, particularly the production of olives. They also developed larger flocks of sheep and goat, as husbandry replaced cereal agriculture as their own economic emphasis. The United Monarchy looks to have focused on policies geared to enhancing economic productivity in areas formerly given over to cereal production, and in areas formerly under- or unexploited. It represented an attempt to maximize participation in the burgeoning trade of the eastern Mediterranean as a whole.

The idea that there could have been no central Israelite state until the Omride dynasty in the 9th century is contraindicated by the character of these administrative centers. It is also contradicted by Israel's possession, by the mid-9th century, of a massive chariotry arm with a distinctive tactical tradition. King Ahab's contingent of 2000 chariots was the largest at the battle of Qarqar in 853. The number comes from the annals of the Assyrian king Shalmaneser III. Whether it is correct or not, this cohort dwarfs those of Shalmaneser's other opponents. And Ahab's chariotry is not accompanied by cavalry, while Damascus and Hamath, the other major chariotry powers, field equal numbers of cavalry and chariotry. Further, whereas Damascus fields 16.7 foot soldiers per chariot, and Hamath either 14.3 or 28.6, Israel fields 5.

Later references suggest that this distinction is not arbitrary: Israelite charioteers were incorporated, uniquely, *as an intact military unit* into the Assyrian army, indicating that their tactics were both effective and distinctive.[27] And the

---

26. J. P. Dessel, in facsimile transmission, 28 April 1996. For the Lower Galilee survey, see Zvi Gal, *Lower Galilee during the Iron Age*. ASOR Dissertation Series 9 (Winona Lake: Eisenbrauns, 1992).

27. The observation is that of Stephanie Dalley, "Foreign Chariotry in the Armies of Tiglath-Pileser III and Sargon II," *Iraq* 47 (1985): 31-48, citing *ARAB*, 611; Dalley and J. N. Postgate, *The Tablets from Fort Shalmaneser*. Cuneiform Texts from Nimrud 3 (Oxford: British School of Archaeology in Iraq, 1984), no. 99, in the context of nos. 99-118. She argues persuasively that one of the officers involved was a professional stud breeder. The

numbers of chariots attributed to Ahab indicate that the creation of the Israelite state was not a recent development. Indeed, the background of the Israelite chariotry tradition is probably Egyptian. This means that the tactical doctrine was transferred during a period of intimate Israelite-Egyptian cooperation, either during the United Monarchy or just after Shishaq's conquest of the country.[28] Indeed, the author of the Tel Dan stela also attributes large quantities of chariotry to his or his father's Israelite and Judahite antagonists around 841.[29] In this case, a cavalry arm probably also appears, but as the context is a summary of multiple confrontations, including with Judah, it is not clear that the cavalry operated in concert with the Israelite chariotry.

Ahab's highly developed chariot arm, which pursued Egyptian rather than Semitic tactical doctrine, as a result of cultural, commercial, or political domination by Egypt (a more modest coalition partner at Qarqar), did not develop

---

Samarians' names are: ib-ba-da-la-a, da-la-ahu, ya-u-ga-a, a-tam-ru, ahi-id-ri, ab-di-milku, bel-duri, na-ar-me-na-a, gab-bi-e, sa-ma-a, ahi-id-ri, ba-hi-e, a-hi-ú, representing ybdly(h?) (root bdl?), dlʾḥ (cf. Delaiah), ywgʾḥ (cf. Geuel), ʾtmr (Ithamar), ʾḥyʿzr (Ahiezer), ʾbdmlk (Abdimelek), bʿldr (Baal-Dor), nrmny(h?) (?), gb/gbʿy (cf. Gabbai, Gibeah), šmʿ/ḥ (Shammah), ʾḥyʿzr (Ahiezer), bʿy (Bai) and ʾḥyw (Ahio). Of these names, two are certainly Yahwistic. Noteworthy is the rendition of the name Ahiezer, in which the Assyrian scribe employs the Aramaic orthography (d) for /ḏ/, edh. This phoneme had not yet merged in Hebrew with /z/, as later.

28. On the Israelite chariotry tradition, see esp. Dalley, *Iraq* 47 (1985): 31-48. Dalley cites George Reisner ("Tombs of the Egyptian 25th Dynasty at El Kurruw," *Sudan Notes and Records* 2 [1919]: 252-54), who observed that Egyptian horses even in the late 8th century were always attached to chariots, never ridden alone. This comports both with the Kurkh Monolith on Ahab and with Sargon's use of chariotry attached from Israel in the late 8th century (for which, see Dalley). It may be added that the 1998 results of the Megiddo Expedition cast doubt on the identification of compounds 1576 and 364 there as stables. Further testing of the hypothesis is, however, in progress. In favor of their interpretation as stables, see John S. Holladay, "The Stables of Ancient Israel: Functional Determinants of Stable Construction and the Interpretation of Pillared Building Remains of the Palestinian Iron Age," in Lawrence T. Geraty and Lawrence G. Herr, *The Archaeology of Jordan and Other Studies*, 103-65. In 1994, a pillar from the "stables," with "tether hole," was discovered covering a drain underlying Assyrian Palace 1369 in Area A. Why did the pillar go out of use? Not because there were no longer animals on the site (Stratum III had an Assyrian parade ground), but because the extent to which the site housed tethered animals was vastly reduced. If these public buildings were storehouses, there is no possibility that they functioned as markets, since there was no significant immediate hinterland population (Megiddo Expedition Survey, 1995). If storehouses, they served to stockpile the production of the Valley, as Shunem did in the Amarna era (EA 365).

29. See André Lemaire, "Chars et cavaliers dans l'ancient Israël," *Transeuphratène* 15 (1998): 165-82.

overnight. The immense wealth necessary to import the horses, purchase or build the equipment, feed the horses, train the horses and drivers, and train the accompanying infantry to fight in concert with the chariotry, all in the light of an imported tactical tradition, was not accumulated by a single feat of conquest, but represents the accretion of many harvests, much exchange, and a highly developed system of taxation administered through a central authority.

That such a state suddenly popped up in the mid-9th century is most improbable, in the absence, at least, of massive immigration from Egypt or elsewhere. That is, even on the evidence of Qarqar alone, the Israelite state must be dated to the late 10th century. And the testimony of Mesha, and of the Tel Dan stela, adds weight to that verdict.[30] Ahab's chariot arm, attested in 853, presupposes a precursor period of capital formation, territorial expansion, and long acquisition and training, conservatively, on the order of 50-100 years. Likewise, on any chronology, Israelite kings in the 9th century undertook massive building projects at Megiddo, Hazor, Samaria, Jezreel, and elsewhere. This too reflects a long period of capital accumulation. And not surprisingly, the foundation of the state shrines of the north at Dan and Bethel is attributed by Kings to Jeroboam I, Solomon's successor in the north in the 10th century. No explanation has been offered for the misattribution of the sanctuaries, and none is persuasive. The presence of a central state starting in the 10th century is confirmed, just as the mention of "the house of David" in the Tel Dan inscription should lead us to expect.

B. The Claims of Samuel and the Date of the Text

Overall, the text of 2 Samuel makes remarkably conservative claims at the literal or explicit level. The grandiose claims are all in its implications. And yet the implications are so palpable that, taken up into later biblical literature, they have resonated in the form of an extensive United Monarchy through the millennia.

The modesty of the literal claims made in early literature about David also explains why remains of any Davidic construction are absent. If John S. Holladay is basically right about the distribution of burnished red-slip in the 10th century, namely, that it was not present until Solomon's reconstruction of

---

30. I first made this point in a paper delivered in November 1997 at the Society of Biblical Literature, against the denial of a pre-9th century Israelite state. William G. Dever subsequently applied it, in conversation, in July, 1998, to a critique of the "low chronology" of Israel Finkelstein, which, he rightly remarked, lacked a stage of early state formation.

the upper gate at Gezer,[31] then no significant public works antedating Solomon have been discovered in Iron-Age Israel. Though some might exist, in Jerusalem, the text attributes no real building activity to David either. Had David indeed constructed an empire reaching well into Syria and up to the Litani,[32] a more aggressive program of fortification and display would appear in the archaeological record.

The implication of this, again, is that the text is early. Its authors did not have the license to aggrandize the accomplishments explicitly: the contrast is to some parts of the Solomon account, where claims to parts of Syria are asserted, and even more so to Chronicles. Thus 2 Samuel was only lightly edited in the 8th and 7th centuries, the period in which the history of Israel in Deuteronomy and the Former Prophets — the Deuteronomistic History — was assembled. This accounts for the differences in the claims.

Other data confirm this dating. The concern to alibi David has already been identified as evidence for an early date. Further, Rehoboam's birth a year before Solomon's accession, to a mother who was an Ammonite, dovetails with the support David received from Ammon during the Absalom revolt. Naamah the Ammonite was the daughter of Shobi, son of Nahash, and successor of David's foe, Hanun son of Nahash (below, Chapter 13). The marriage of Shobi's daughter to the son of David's wife, Bathsheba — an unlikely successor (see below, Chapter 22C) — was a reward to Shobi, for his support during the Absalom revolt (below, Chapter 21).

Likewise, Rehoboam's own marriage to a daughter of Absalom indicates an unexpected policy of reconciliation with Adonijah's supporters in the early part of Solomon's reign (see above, Chapter 4). The alliance between Solomon's son and Absalom's daughter also represents a marriage to the father's brother's daughter, the ideal union in Israel's kinship theory.[33] None of this is the invention of a later period — the connections are simply too rich, too unorthodox, including as they do not just connections to the Absalom revolt, but the anathema of the 7th-6th centuries and the Persian period, marriage to Ammonites (and without censure!).

An interesting sidelight on the same issue is present in 1 Sam. 27:6, which states that Ziklag belongs to the kings of Judah "to this very day." Patterns of settlement in the Negev being what they are, it is unlikely such a statement could be made after Shishaq's campaign. As reviewed in Chapter 3, the picture

31. Holladay, *BASOR* 277-278 (1990): 23-70.
32. So, e.g., the highly critical scholar Gösta W. Ahlström, *A History of Ancient Palestine*, 486 and Map 14.
33. See my "Sybil, or the Two Nations."

of the central Negev in Samuel fits the 10th-century evidence, but that of no later time. As to Ziklag, Shishaq very likely detached the southern plain from Judah (Chapter 23). A king of Judah did claim ownership of the western Negev in the later 7th century (Josh. 15:31; 19:5), but the plain was earlier dominated by Assyria. Whether or not Tel Haror, for example, turns out to be ancient Gath, rather than Gerar,[34] Tel Sharia, a candidate for Ziklag, could not have been held by Judah: Haror, within eyesight of Sharia, was a major Assyrian fortress. Such a claim is even less likely to stem from the Persian era, when the Negev lay outside Judah. In other words, this text, whatever its history of transmission, contains assertions that comport only with a 10th-century or a late 7th-century date (and others that exclude the 7th century). This is not to deny the existence of later elements in Samuel; but it is, again, to affirm the presence there of early elements.

Overall, the implication of the preceding chapters is that large parts of our information on the United Monarchy stem from roughly contemporary sources. Some of the information may even derive from monuments. This is the reason that, when read carefully and literally, the claims — and the silences — of the texts are so conservative. There was certainly, on the evidence of texts and of such archaeology as we have, no extensive Davidic empire in Syria. In fact, were we to find a monument of Toi of Hamath or his successors, it might even claim hegemony "unto Israel" in the south: Toi is just as likely to have asserted his own ascendancy over Zobah as is David, or David's apologists at Solomon's court.

This reading of Samuel, then, may imply a drastic reduction in traditional views of the early empire. It has two merits. It confirms that the central state did exist. It also interprets the literature about that state in light of the conventions of royal literature of the time.

34. See below, Chapter 18 (and n. 5 there), and Lawrence E. Stager, "The Impact of the Sea Peoples."

PART IV

A HISTORICAL OVERTURE
TO DAVID'S CAREER

Part IV contains the last of the technical studies that lay a foundation for the reconstruction of David's career in Part V. Readers interested in the details underlying the reconstruction are encouraged to examine the following two chapters. Those more interested in the historical reconstruction itself should move directly to Part V.

CHAPTER 13

The Relative Chronology of David's Reign

As 2 Samuel reports events out of sequence, the question of their relative chronology rears its head. The cases connected with 2 Sam. 8 have already been explored. Another instance is reasonably explicit as well. In 2 Sam. 5:13-16, the sons born to David in Jerusalem are enumerated just after his capture of the town. Among them is Solomon (2 Sam. 5:14), whose birth is narrated later (2 Sam. 12:24-25). Clearly, the list of children born in Jerusalem is not meant to imply that they were all born before the next events narrated.

Older commentators assumed that events occurred in the order of their appearance in the book. However, the murder or execution of the Saulides at Gibeon, for example, in 2 Sam. 21:1-14, is the only possible explanation of David's query, in 2 Sam. 9:1, "Is there another that remains of the House of Saul, that I may deal faithfully with him for Jonathan's sake?" Exploits related in the lists of David's warriors betray an origin nearer the beginning than the end of David's career.[1]

The details of the Goliath story, as noted above, were taken from elements of these lists. And one of the stories is set at a time when a Philistine garrison remained in Bethlehem (2 Sam. 23:14), a situation bespeaking the early period of David's career. In another notice, a threat to David's person led his troops to forbid his entering combat in the field (2 Sam. 21:17). In the Absalom revolt, reported earlier in the text, he was not even allowed to leave the confines of a fortress (2 Sam. 18:2-4). Both accounts may be attempts to put a positive face on David's physical cowardice. But the sequence is not that of the reports in the text.

---

1. 2 Sam. 21:15-22; 23:8-17. See above, Chapters 7-8.

The author of Chronicles felt likewise about Samuel. He redated David's conflicts with Philistines after the capture of Jerusalem. In 2 Sam. 5:17-25, both battles occur after Hiram's legation to David and the list of the sons born in Jerusalem, and before David attempts to bring the ark into his capital. The Chronicler, however, deduces that David first attempted to move the ark from Qiryath-Yearim (1 Chr. 13). It was during the three-month sojourn of the ark at the house of Obed-Edom that Hiram recognized David's accession, and the list of children follows (1 Chr. 14:1-7). Only then do the Philistines attack (1 Chr. 14:8-16). It is the removal of the ark from the house of Obed-Edom to Jerusalem, not the move from Qiryath-Yearim, that follows these victories. The Chronicler recognized that Samuel was narrating events out of order, and corrected the narrative sequence.[2]

Another event possibly narrated out of sequence is David's coronation in Hebron in 2 Sam. 2:1-4. The story starts, like 2 Sam. 8, "It came to pass afterward." So the reader infers David was crowned after the death of Saul (1 Sam. 31; 2 Sam. 1). Likewise, David's coronation in Hebron leads to a report that the men of Jabesh Gilead had recovered Saul's corpse. David dispatches an embassy asking that Jabesh acknowledge his kingship (2 Sam. 2:4-7). Only afterward do we read of Ishbaal's coronation — so David wooed Jabesh before it accepted Ishbaal as their sovereign. However, the text also relates that Ishbaal reigned only two years (2 Sam. 2:10), but that David reigned seven-and-a-half years in Hebron.

A sympathetic reader infers that it was five-and-a-half years after Ishbaal's assassination that David moved on Jerusalem, or that there was an interregnum in Israel after the death of Saul.[3] Neither of these scenarios commends itself. The text claims that David gained kingship over Israel while in Hebron (2 Sam. 5:1-3), at the age of 37. And it denies that Ishbaal reigned over Judah, which adhered to David at the time of his coronation (2 Sam. 2:10). Was David crowned in Hebron, at the age of 30, five years before Saul's death? The argument that David still resided in Ziklag at the time of Saul's death does not preclude his holding a crown over Judah, formally conferred in Hebron (on the model of Zakkur, king of Hamath and Luash, resident in Luash).

The whole period between the return of the ark to Qiryath-Yearim and its relocation to the house of Obed-Edom, en route to Jerusalem, is said in 1 Sam. 7:2 to have occupied only twenty years. This starts in Samuel's time, continues

---

2. See David A. Glatt, *Chronological Displacement;* Baruch Halpern, "A Historiographic Commentary on Ezra 1–6."

3. The latter is the position of J. Alberto Soggin, "Il regno di Ešbaʿal, figlio di Saul," *RSO* 40 (1965): 89-106.

through the reigns of Saul and Ishbaal, and ends after Jerusalem's capture. David takes the ark to Jerusalem at earliest in his eighth year. If David did not rule in Judah before Saul's death, Saul's entire career must be squeezed down to less than a decade. This is improbable. But all we know certainly is that no attempt was made to reconcile what seem to be conflicting figures about the lengths of David's and Ishbaal's reigns.

Indifference to sequence also characterizes the account of Solomon's reign.[4] Thus, the visit of the Queen of Sheba, related in 1 Kgs. 10:1-13 at the climax of the regnal account, probably took place early in Solomon's reign. After his 24th year, Solomon was threatened by the tide of the 22nd Dynasty in Egypt, which would invade and dominate Israel in the fifth year of his son Rehoboam.[5] On the other hand, it is possible that the visit cemented a relationship excluding Egypt from the southern trade.

More clearly out of chronological sequence are two reports in 1 Kgs. 11. This text reports that Solomon's behavior deteriorated in his dotage. His senile apostasy elicited divine retribution, in the form of two opponents. The first was Hadad, scion of the royal line in Edom. Hadad returned from his refuge in Egypt on hearing of David's death to foment a revolt in his native land (1 Kgs. 11:14-22). As note above (Chapter 5B), that it required 30 years for news of David's death to filter down to Egypt is improbable, more particularly in that Solomon wed the pharaoh's daughter while his palace remained under construction (1 Kgs. 3:1).

Solomon's other "opponent" was Rezon, who seized the kingship in Damascus around the time that David defeated Hadadezer, during the Ammonite campaign. He was probably active mainly toward the end of David's reign and during the early part of Solomon's. Kings reports that Rezon harassed Israel "all the days of Solomon" (1 Kgs. 11:23-25). So Solomon's punishment in both cases anticipates the sin of his "old age." It is not that Kings attempts to hide the chronological indications here. Rather, the thematic relationship is more important than the temporal.

How seriously are we to take the text that Rezon harried Israel "all the days of Solomon"? Did his revolt, like Hadad's in Edom, coincide with Solomon's accession? The chronology can be attacked as follows. Rezon reportedly broke with Hadadezer of Zobah to set up an independent shop in Damascus. The text indicating that he was head of a military band *at the time of Hadadezer's conflict with David* (1 Kgs. 11:24) is absent from the Old Greek translation. But the best reconstruction places Rezon at David's battles with Hadadezer. Rezon may have

4. See Baruch Halpern, *The First Historians,* chapter 8.
5. See Baruch Halpern, *JBL* 93 (1974): 519-32.

headed a "garrison" installed by David — for whose presence in Damascus David took credit. Rezon may even have relied on David's protection to wrest that territory from Hadadezer and Zobah (2 Sam. 8:5-6), making territorial concessions in return (Chapter 10B).

If David resculpted Damascus, installing Rezon, he most likely did so immediately after defeating Zobah in Transjordan. Even if Rezon's filibuster at Damascus was later, it was during David's reign, and presumably not late in it. After all, the conflict with Zobah was bound up with the early stages of the Ammonite war, which in our narrative sequence preceded both Uriah's death and the Absalom revolt.

Still, the cases in which Samuel relates events out of their true temporal sequence raise questions about the relative chronology of David's reign. The key issue is the date of the Absalom revolt. Around that episode, the rest of the reign must be organized.

In his commentary on 2 Samuel, P. Kyle McCarter places the Absalom revolt before David's battles against Aram in Transjordan and the capture of Rabbat Ammon. He argues that Ammon abetted David during the Absalom revolt. This reflects a period of alliance with Nahash, king of Ammon, and thus belongs to a time before Nahash died and David invaded the country.[6] It is likely that Nahash was David's ally, for the simple reason that Saul was Nahash's antagonist. Indeed, David reportedly entreated the Gileadites on the death of Saul to acknowledge his own, rather than Ishbaal's, sovereignty. But the latter were Saul's most fervent partisans, who recovered his decapitated corpse, and interred and mourned him. They are not said to have acceded to David's overture. The alliance between David and Nahash of Ammon suggests that David adopted a strategy that led to the subjection, rather than enlistment of Gilead.[7]

However, this does not mean that Nahash remained king at the time of the Absalom revolt. There is another possibility, presupposed by the narrative sequence in Samuel. Nahash dies in 2 Sam. 10:1, and his son Hanun succeeds him as king of Ammon. The delegation of Israelite ambassadors to Ammon then occasions the conflict with David. The campaign ends with the reduction of the population of Rabbat Ammon to forced labor, along with "all the settlements of the Ammonites" (2 Sam. 12:30-31).

This does not mean that Ammon ceased to exist as an administrative en-

---

6. P. Kyle McCarter, *II Samuel*, 274. J. Maxwell Miller and John H. Hayes, *A History of Ancient Israel and Judah*, 175, also date the Absalom revolt early in David's reign. For Ammonite abetment of David, 2 Sam. 17:27-29; for the death of Nahash, 2 Sam. 10:1.

7. The overture to the Gileadites, 2 Sam. 2:5-7; Saul's rescue of Jabesh Gilead, 1 Sam. 11; the Gileadite recovery of Saul's corpse, 31:11-13.

tity. In the normal course of events, David would appoint a successor to Hanun as king of the country. As in the case of other subjected Near Eastern states, Ammon continued to have much the same social and economic structure as before. Even if he were not the new king, Shobi, son of Nahash, was the proprietor of Ammon's most powerful establishment. This positioned him to support David during the Absalom revolt, as Samuel claims he did.

Overall, however, it seems more likely that Shobi, son of Nahash, had succeeded Hanun, his brother, as David's appointee. Overlords often appointed vassal kings from the royal family. The logic of finding a *royal* vassal is reasonably plain. The overlord could then pose as the defender of local tradition. Usually, this meant finding a half-brother of the rebel — the son of another wife of the previous king — who would promise a policy of collaboration.

This pattern appears in the appointment of Josiah's successors by Egypt and Babylon in the 7th-6th centuries, and the change of regime in Byblos after Rib-Addi in the 14th century, among others. It explains why the vassal state of Ammon, in which Shobi's position depended on David's survival, lent its support to the king during the uprising against him. And the support clearly explains how the mother of Solomon's heir might be a princess of the Ammonite royal line. Naamah the Ammonitess (1 Kgs. 14:21) was hardly a random foreigner, or a commoner.

To assess this interpretation requires a more global chronological view of David's reign. Here, the critical fact is that Absalom's maternal grandfather was Talmay, king of Geshur. No king, and no king of a city-state in the Golan, would commit a daughter in marriage to David before David was himself a king in prospect. The presumption is that the alliance took place after David proclaimed himself king of Judah, in Hebron. This is in fact also the claim of the text:

> Sons were born to David in Hebron. His firstborn was Amnon, (born) to Ahinoam the Jezreelitess, and his second-born was Kileab (Chronicles: Daniel), (born) to Abigail, the wife of Nabal the Carmelite. And the third was Absalom, son of Maacah, daughter of Talmay, king of Geshur. . . . (2 Sam. 3:2-3)[8]

---

8. The formulation changes from "born to [mother's name]" to "son of [mother's name]" after the second-born because there is no special term for a third son, whereas the first is *bkwr* (+ *-w*, "his"), and the second *mšnh* (+ *-w*, "his"). To these two terms, the Hebrew can add a possessive suffix, whereas it cannot do so with the ordinal numbers used to denominate the third through sixth sons. The mothers of the first three sons are more closely identified than the rest. The mother of the sixth son, Eglah, is called "the wife of David." But this is probably merely a form of coda for the list. Of the sons born in Jerusalem in 2 Sam. 5:14-16, no mothers are named, although Solomon appears in the list.

We may go farther: it is unlikely that the king of a Golan city-state sought an alliance with David until David threatened Geshur's foes, and in particular the neighboring kingdom of Israel, in Ishbaal's reign or late in Saul's reign. The alliance may even date as late as David's occupation of Jerusalem, if this really followed shortly on Ishbaal's death.

Absalom, again, is the third of six sons born in Hebron, but the marriage with Maacah took place at earliest toward the end of David's tenure in that settlement. Amnon, too, is supposedly born only during David's seven years in Hebron. Allow that Absalom was born a year after consummation of the marriage, before his siblings, including his sister. This places his birth sometime around the end of David's time in Hebron, after Saul's death, at earliest during Ishbaal's reign.

Tamar was Absalom's full sister. So by the time Amnon raped her, David had fathered at least two pubescent children by Maacah, Talmay's daughter. Allow that Amnon was born in, say, David's second year in Hebron. He then reached puberty no earlier than David's sixth year in Jerusalem. However, if Tamar was born a year after Absalom, and even if she was only 10 years old at the time of the rape, the text takes us about 10 years into David's (33-year) reign in Jerusalem for the time of the rape itself. The older one supposes Amnon and Tamar to have been, the later in David's reign the rape takes place. So, if Tamar was 14 at the time, and Amnon perhaps a lusty 16 or 17, the rape occurs in year 14 or so of David's reign in Jerusalem.

The internal chronology of the Absalom story dictates that two years elapsed between the rape of Tamar and Absalom's vengeance on Amnon (2 Sam. 13:23). Allow Absalom, then, to have been 15 when he killed his older brother, the probable minimum, and the rape is at earliest in year 12 or so of David's 33-year reign in Jerusalem. Allow Absalom to be older, and the rape must be later.

From Amnon's death there follow three years of Absalom's exile in Geshur (2 Sam. 13:38). After his repatriation through Joab's offices, he endures two years of house arrest in Jerusalem (2 Sam. 14:28). Thereafter, some further number of years elapse before the revolt. The actual Hebrew text of 2 Sam. 15:7 stipulates that Absalom's revolt began "at the end of forty years," which would place the uprising in David's last year as king, the 40th year representing a regnal year.

Many translations, from the oldest Septuagint evidence forward, and early commentators, including Josephus,[9] attest the existence of a different text: Absalom revolted in the fourth year after his rehabilitation and reintroduction

9. *Ant.* 7.196.

into the court. Taking this more conservative option yields a total of 11 years from rape to revolt: two from the rape to Absalom's revenge; three years of Absalom's exile; two years of house arrest; and four years for Absalom to arrange for the revolt.

In short, at least 11 years intervene between Absalom's adolescence and his revolt: at a minimum, he was in his mid-20s at the time of his death. Thus even if he were born before the conquest of Jerusalem, his revolt was after the 20th year of David's 33 years in Jerusalem. But Solomon reigned 40 years. His son Rehoboam assumed the throne at the age of 41. Rehoboam was therefore born in David's 33rd year as king in Jerusalem.[10] This has implications for Absalom's age at the time of the revolt.

The 40 years attributed to Solomon may be an approximation. Even if so, the figure is not far off. Shishaq seized the throne in Egypt no later than Solomon's 24th year. Shishaq then raided Judah and Israel in his own 21st regnal year, which was the fifth year of Solomon's successor, Rehoboam. This leaves exactly 21 years between Solomon's 24th year and Rehoboam's fifth year.[11]

And of the first 24 years of Solomon's reign, starting in his year four, 13 are occupied with the construction of a palace, seven with the temple's construction (1 Kgs. 6:1, 38; 7:1). Indeed, shortening the length of Solomon's reign merely pushes Rehoboam's birth further back into David's reign.

Rehoboam's age at accession is not likely to be an approximation, for several reasons: It stands at the head of a series in which age at accession, for kings of Judah, is consistently reported. Tyrian annals reaching back to the same period, and cited by Josephus, contain the same sort of data.[12] Unlike the round figures for the reigns of David and Solomon, Rehoboam's age is not a round figure — so if one holds that round figures represent inventions or approximations, one cannot indict this more specific figure. And it creates, rather than anneals, problems in the chronology of David's reign. It would have been more in the interest of the author to have Rehoboam ascend the throne at a more tender age.

Solomon fathered Rehoboam. If Rehoboam was born in David's last year in Jerusalem, he was conceived the year before. Solomon, in turn, must have been born at least 13 years earlier — we should probably allow 15 or more, conservatively — and conceived a year before that. Even if we accept the claim that Uriah died a month or so after Solomon's conception, Uriah must have been dead a minimum of 14 years, and probably 15 or 16 years, when Solomon's son Rehoboam was born in David's 33rd year as king in Jerusalem. Solomon can

---

10. Solomon's regnal length, 1 Kgs. 11:42; Rehoboam's age at accession, 14:21.

11. Halpern, *JBL* 93 (1974): 519-32.

12. *Ag. Ap.* 117-25.

only have been born *before* David's 20th year in Jerusalem. In the following treatment, for simplicity's sake, the year of Uriah's death is taken to be David's 17th year in Jerusalem, the latest reasonable possibility.

The siege of Ammon, and thus the clash with Aram, are connected with Uriah's death, before David's 20th year in Jerusalem (roughly, year 17). The Absalom revolt, 11 years after the rape of Tamar, must have occurred after David's 20th year in Jerusalem, on the basis of the entirely different issue of the time of David's marriage alliances. The engagements against Aram in Transjordan, therefore, must be placed before the Absalom revolt.

Finally, the birth of Solomon's heir to an Ammonite princess a year before Solomon's accession suggests the continuing importance of Ammon both to David late in his reign and to Solomon's administration of Israel. That is, the situation reflected in the account of Absalom's revolt, in which David could rely only on Ammon, elements in Gilead, and his own professional soldiery, obtained to the end of his reign. This too suggests that the Absalom revolt, when Ammon stood by David, postdates rather than antedates David's invasion of Ammon and wars with Aram. In this case, the narrative sequence in the text is accurate.

The siege at Rabbat Ammon follows the rebuff of the Aramean intervention by a year in Samuel's sequence (2 Sam. 11:1). Although some scholars have doubted that David conducted extended military operations, the temporal logic here is credible. So is the report that the field-force threat was neutralized before Joab invested the capital.

The siege itself cannot be related to chronology with certainty, as it is not patent that the rape of Tamar postdated the siege in which Uriah died. However, 2 Sam. 13:1 employs the chronographic mantra of the apology in Samuel: "and it was afterward so." This text suggests that the rape occurred after the siege. If one takes the claim seriously, then the siege took place no later than year 17 of David's reign in Jerusalem and, if the death of Bathsheba's first son is included in the mix, year 16, or the birth of Solomon, year 15. It is, however, a question whether what is "afterward" is the fulfillment of Nathan's prophecy of punishment for Uriah's murder rather than everything that led to it. Thus, Solomon's birth may be reported in a thematic, not chronological, narrative framework. So year 16 may stand for the latest date for the siege. The other chronological data concerning David's reign suggest that Absalom's vengeance on Amnon or rehabilitation may have been occurring at the same time.

If one rejects the chronological sequence from the Ammonite war to the rape, alternative paths to dating the war remain open. The Ammonite war was triggered by the death of Nahash (2 Sam. 10:1-5). David's ally was one of Saul's earliest opponents (1 Sam. 11). The later one carries Nahash's reign into David's, the more anomalous Nahash's survival becomes. The length of Nahash's reign is particularly striking if one allows for Ishbaal's two years after Saul's death and a further stretch of time before David moved from Hebron to Jerusalem (more than seven years in 2 Sam. 5:5). Still, nothing prevents our redating Saul's rescue of Jabesh to the middle or even to the latest part of his reign.

Further, Solomon's chief wife and Rehoboam's mother was Naamah from Ammon. As noted above, Naamah must have been the daughter of Shobi son of Nahash, king of Ammon, David's ally during the Absalom revolt (2 Sam. 17:27). Shobi's daughter was of marriageable age no later than year 32 of David's reign in Jerusalem. This is an upper limit, since she may have borne daughters or stillborn males before giving birth to Rehoboam. If so, her marriage to Solomon was even earlier.

Naamah's birth, therefore, can at latest be ascribed roughly to the period between years 12 and 16 of David's reign in Jerusalem. Shobi himself was an adolescent or adult by that time, and was therefore born before Jerusalem became "the city of David." Shobi was not Nahash's successor — the successor was Hanun. So, Shobi is not likely to have been the eldest son, let alone child, of Nahash. He is also unlikely to have been the son of Hanun's mother, as noted above. So the possibility exists that he was older than Hanun, though the probabilities are against it.

At a guess, Nahash, the grandfather of Solomon's wife Naamah, will have been 30 years old, or more, when Shobi was born. While we cannot stipulate that he was in reality Saul's earliest opponent in battle, some 15 or 20 (?) years before David took Jerusalem, he was fully mature by the time of Saul's death. His own death, then, is more likely to have occurred roughly mid-way through David's reign over Israel, from Jerusalem, than toward the end of David's reign, after Absalom's revolt. One could divorce Nahash's death from the Ammonite campaign by denying that David's embassy ensued directly on Nahash's death. But the text yokes them together. If false, that connection would seem to be gratuitous, rather than intelligently motivated.

Still another avenue toward the dating of events in David's reign is the data about the ages of the kings of Judah. David Noel Freedman has ably defended the reliability of the figures in Kings for regnal length and age at accession.[13] These have important implications. Rehoboam's age at accession is reported as 41. This means that he was born a year before Solomon succeeded as king, as assumed above, in year 33 of David's reign.

This brings us to the issue of standard deviation. Standard deviation is the

---

13. David Noel Freedman, "Kingly Chronologies: Then and Later," *ErIsr* 24 (1993): 41*-65*.

normal range (averaged) of variance from an average. In statistics, given a sufficiently large sample, 95 percent of cases fall within two standard deviations of the average. The ages of kings of Judah do not furnish a sufficiently large sample for this rule to hold. Still, it is worth addressing the issue in statistical terms.

Rehoboam reigned 17 years, and his successor, Abijah, three. The mean lifetime for successors of David whose age at what is reported to have been a natural death can be calculated is 53 years, but with a standard deviation of almost 13 years.[14] Abijah's age at accession is unknown. But if he reached the mean minus one standard deviation, the latest his birth can be placed is year 17 of Solomon; even at the mean minus two standard deviations, he would have been born in Solomon's year 30. An upper limit of the mean plus one standard deviation would place his birth in David's reign, which is impossible.

Taken raw, the figures suggest that the odds of Abijah's dying after the age of 50 stand at about 70 percent. Since any greater age places his birth before year 10 of Solomon, when Rehoboam was 11, it is unlikely that he was older. However, the chances that his birth occurred before year 20 of Solomon's reign rise on the raw figures to about 86 percent.[15] If we extend the data set somewhat, to include conservative figures (on the low side) for the lifetimes of three kings whose age at death is not reported, the average age at death rises to 54.15, and the standard deviation declines to 11.6 years.[16] These figures would drive Abijah's birth earlier into Solomon's reign, rather than later: at the mean minus two standard deviations, year 26 of Solomon; at the mean minus one standard deviation, year 14 or year 15; at the mean, year 3 or 4.

Rehoboam was born just before Solomon's 40-year reign. It follows that Rehoboam did not have a son before year 13 of Solomon's reign. However, Rehoboam's mother was the daughter of a foreign king. His chief wife was Maacah, Absalom's daughter. The significance of these women suggests that Solomon designated his heir rather early. This improves the odds, already strong, that Abijah was born in years 13 to 16 of Solomon's reign.

Further, Absalom did not father Maacah during Solomon's reign, and probably was not fathering children in David's last years, either. The implication is that Rehoboam's chief wife was older than he by a space of some years at least. Absalom's daughter was of marriageable age in Solomon's years 11 to 15, when Rehoboam was a young adolescent.

---

14. The sum includes the 70 years assigned to David. Removing it would reduce the mean age to 51.5 years, but also reduce the standard deviation marginally.

15. This is so if we take into account the figures for Solomon and Jehoiachin.

16. The extended data set includes Solomon, Asa, and Jehoiachin. See the appendix to this chapter.

It will be suggested below that Absalom's revolt should be dated to about year 25 of David's reign in Jerusalem. Even were we to take the semi-comic view that Maacah's mother was one of David's concubines with whom Absalom had relations, Maacah was no less than about 19 years old at the time of her marriage. By year 20 of Solomon's reign, she would have been at least 28, and possibly some years older. Again, the odds of her giving birth to her eldest male son after that age must be considered relatively low.

The early date for Abijah's birth, again, reflects the fact that Solomon, early in his reign, had fixed on a policy of reconciliation with the south, touting a marriage of his heir-apparent with Absalom's daughter. Of this policy, the Court History and Succession Narrative were integral parts, as we have seen.[17] But Absalom's daughter is more advanced in years the earlier in David's reign one puts the revolt. The later the revolt, the more likely that she was truly of marriageable age and status.

Bathsheba's son fathered a child by an Ammonite princess in David's 32nd year in Jerusalem. So he must have appeared, at least, to be destined for a position of power, and he may even have looked like an outside candidate for the throne. This was when David was already aged and the Absalom revolt was over. Solomon's age at accession is not reported. However, given the birth of Rehoboam the year before, Solomon's minimum age at the time was 14, placing his birth at latest in year 20 of David's reign in Jerusalem. The siege of Rabbat Ammon thus occurred at latest in year 19 of the reign. However, the further back one locates the siege, the more likely it is that Solomon was a plausible candidate to be put up for the succession.

The minimum chronology permits Solomon's life span to reach the mean for Davidides — 53 years. The adjusted mean would increase this by a year. Adding half of one standard deviation places his birth in years 13 to 14 of David's reign, just on the cusp of the latest likely dates (years 14 to 17) for the Ammonite war and siege.[18] These are very conservative assumptions, and it is more probable that Solomon was born earlier in David's reign, probably in the vicinity of years 8 to 12. Were there no nexus with Uriah's death, the Ammonite war could be moved to a position after Solomon's birth. But as we will see, Solomon's name as well as the testimony of 2 Samuel make this unlikely (Chapter 22).

Adding five to seven years to the minimum total makes Solomon 18 to 20 years of age at the time of his accession, and thus a more plausible candidate for

---

17. Above, Chapter 4.
18. Using the extended corpus of ages for kings of Judah, the mean plus one standard deviation would bring Solomon to the age of 65 at death, and the siege to year 8 of David.

a diplomatic marriage two years earlier. It places the siege of Rabbat Ammon in years 11 to 14 of David's reign in Jerusalem if not earlier — the span of time between Uriah's death and Solomon's birth is not determinate, but the sequence is relatively robust.

Freedman suggests that Solomon was about 25 years old when he came to the throne (the average age at accession is 22).[19] This would place his birth in David's year 8, and the siege of Rabbah in year 7. The outer limits of the siege thus seem to be years 7 and 19. One constraining factor is the question of David's age at Solomon's conception, as Freedman notes. This invites an earlier, not later date. The middle range of years 11 to 14 for the siege again seems indicated.

A similar implication can be drawn from still another chronological datum. Asa (912-872) dispatches emissaries to Ben-Hadad son of Tabrimmon son of Hezyon, king of Damascus. It is highly unusual for Samuel or Kings to provide the names of two ancestors in identifying kings in so early an era. It may therefore be supposed that the names enumerated are those of three Damascene kings. Further, the object of Asa's embassy is to provide a deterrent to Baasha of Israel, who reigned roughly 910-887. The embassy thus took place in the first half of Asa's reign.

The deterrent worked, so that we must allow at least a few years between the event and Baasha's death. In turn, this means that Ben-Hadad was on the throne by ca. 890 at latest. Assuming that his accession had occurred even within the previous few years, we still have from roughly 895 to the death of Rezon (ca. 950?) to account for the reigns of Tabrimmon, Hezyon, and perhaps other kings.[20]

This brings us back to Rezon's putative connection to the court of Hadadezer, king of Zobah. Hadadezer's intervention in Transjordan antedates the siege of Rabbah, by at least one year (2 Sam. 11:1) and possibly more. So David's victory over the Arameans belongs sometime between David's sixth and 18th years, most likely between his years 10 and 13. And this, in turn, means that Rezon was active as a leader 19 to 23 years before Solomon's accession. Even assuming that he was still young, in a career paralleling David's and Idrimi's, he will have been mature at the time of Solomon's accession, at the very minimum 40 years old, and more probably in his mid-50s. Solomon's accession would have been an opportune moment for Damascus to revolt. Solomon will have been immobilized by the need to consolidate his own coup d'etat. He lacked the support of the population at large. Solomon would have

---

19. Freedman, *ErIsr* 24 (1993): 53*.

20. 1 Kgs. 15:17-20. See also Wayne T. Pitard, *Ancient Damascus* (Winona Lake: Eisenbrauns, 1987), 101-4.

been forced to accept, and may even have encouraged, an independent force threatening the north.

It was David's policy, after all, to unite peripheral powers with a common antagonism toward the heartland of northern Israel. His primary allies were Gath, and perhaps other Philistine cities, Tyre, Geshur, and Ammon. He also extracted support from Gilead. The maintenance of Rezon in Damascus would mirror the same concerns and strategy.[21] This Davidic policy may have found its logical extension in Solomon's reign.

Solomon's allies, too, were Gath, Egypt, Tyre, and Ammon. Ammon supplied the wife whose son ascended the throne, though the queen-mother might have been Egyptian had Shishaq not seized power there. Together with the absence of any index of Solomonic sovereignty in Syria, this suggests that Damascus's independence, so long as it was coupled with hostility toward the north, was not a matter of concern in Jerusalem. Possibly, Rezon was initially a vassal of Solomon. Still, to carry Rezon's reign much further than Solomon's 20th year creates increasing improbabilities.

No specific dates, and no specific order of events, can be fixed within David's reign. Still, so far as one *can* understand the sequence, it is highly suggestive. David's persecutions of the Saulides, for example, seem long to antedate and in part to motivate the Absalom revolt. By the time of that development, certainly in the last decade of his life, his campaign in Ammon was long in the past, his successes tarnished by age, and perhaps by the other grievances that led to the great uprising. The general pattern, in all, does not suggest a happy view of David's reign.

21. See below, Chapter 21; generally, Halpern, *JBL* 93 (1974): 519-32; Jon D. Levenson and Halpern, *JBL* 99 (1980): 507-18.

Ages of Kings at Death

Ages at reportedly natural death:

	David	70	
*	Solomon	> 54	in extended data set, counted as 59
	Rehoboam	58	
	Abijah	?	not included in count
*	Asa	> 41	in extended data set, counted as 55
	Jehoshaphat	60	
	Jehoram	40	
	Uzziah	68	
	Jotham	41	
	Ahaz	36	
	Hezekiah	54	
	Manasseh	67	
	Jehoiaqim	36	
*	Jehoiachin	> 55	in extended data set, counted as 60

Unnatural deaths (not included in the reckoning of averages):

Ahaziah	(23)
Joash	(47)
Amaziah	(54)
Amon	(24)
Josiah	(39)
Jehoahaz	(??)
Zedekiah	(32)

CHAPTER 14

Geography of the Davidic State

A. The External Borders of David's State

One of the most interesting indications that the books of Samuel are antique, as noted in Chapters 9 and 12, is that their claims about the borders of the realm are so limited. Samuel lodges no claim to any territory in Philistia, until Solomon's father-in-law, the 21st Dynasty pharaoh, hands Gezer, with its hinterland, to his daughter's husband. Typically, the acquisition is not ballyhooed in 1 Kgs. 9:16, because it was not Solomon's personal achievement. Solomon also loses the "control" over Damascus that David likely never had (Chapter 10B, and below).

Solomon actually sells all or nearly all the tribe of Asher to Hiram of Tyre. The topos for presenting that loss is that Solomon extracted far more than the tract was worth: Hiram is portrayed as feeling he was bettered in a barter (1 Kgs. 9:12-13). Comparable would be presenting Thomas Jefferson as though he felt cheated in the Louisiana Purchase. A similar explanation is sometimes furnished in epigraphic and biblical texts to explain submission to a foreign suzerain.[1] The text also denominates the region not as "Asher" but as "twenty settlements in the land of the Galilee" (1 Kgs. 9:11), concealing the fact that even the "greater Israel" of the book of Joshua has only 22 settlements in Asher (Josh. 19:24-31). This subject is taken up in more detail in Chapter 22D.

---

1. Kilamuwa, KAI 24 (the king of Assyria gave a maiden for a sheep, a man for a garment); Asa, 1 Kgs. 15:17-21; Ahaz, 2 Kgs. 16:5-9. For a further parallel, see Mario Liverani, "Kilamuwa 7-8 e II Re 7," in *Storia e tradizioni di Israele*. Festschrift J. Alberto Soggin, ed. Daniele Garrone and Felice Israel (Brescia: Paideia, 1991), 177-84.

Samuel claims that David expanded in three regions. The first of these is Transjordan, where he makes inroads against Ammon, Moab, and Damascus. The second is the south, where he makes inroads against Edom, and allegedly Amaleq. The third is the Beqaʿ Valley.

Any expansion in the Beqaʿ Valley seems to be illusory, as explained in Chapter 10A. And Samuel is at best halfhearted about making such claims. It consistently defines the northern limit of Israel as Dan. It may speak of the acquisition of Abel of the House of Maacah, but speaks of nothing farther north even in this case. As we shall see, however, later sources are far less reserved about his expansion.

Likewise, the text presses no claim to more than a corner of the territory of Damascus, in Transjordan. In Transjordan, David does control Gilead, and reduces Rabbah, the capital of Ammon. However, in Moab, where nonspecific claims are made about territory, the limits of Israel even in 2 Sam. 24:5, at the very end of the story of David, remain at Aroer, the city on the border of Israel throughout the second half of the 9th century, after Jehu lost the territory.[2] Samuel alleges that part of Aroer's territory was incorporated into David's kingdom. Conversely, Mesha claims that Omri conquered all of Moab. The more modest claims in the narrative concerning David are quite believable, especially on the corner of Israelite and Ammonite territory. A text from much later would have claimed that David was the conqueror of the whole country.

Finally, the claim about the south merits review. Sometime in the 10th century, a large number of settlements appeared in the central Negev highlands. This was the first efflorescence of settlement in the region since the Early Bronze II. Most of the sites were short-lived. Their thin exterior walls suggest that they were mainly designed as caravanserais and especially as watch stations, controlling sources of water next to which they tend to be located. Their function was to direct caravan traffic in southern goods into the heartland of the Israelite state, rather than allowing it to proceed unmolested to the coast. Whether the traffic began in David's time, as I think likely, or in Solomon's, the sites were all destroyed by Shishaq. Shishaq's list of site names includes dozens in the Negev, and the only reason for his sending a battalion into the region would have been to destroy the trade connections created for Judah in the preceding decades. The evidence is assessed in more detail below, in Chapters 22-23. But here, again, the claims of the text, critically assessed, enjoy external corroboration.

This leaves, however, the most interesting case of all.

2. Mesha, KAI 181:26; 2 Kgs. 10:33.

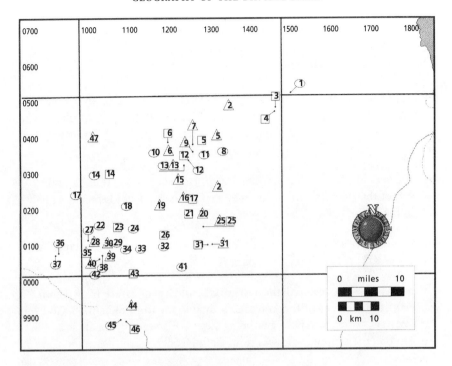

Figure 14.1   Central Negev

Courtesy David Hopkins. Reprinted from *Near Eastern Archaeologist* 61:1 (1998).

Sites marked with a square are trapezoidal forts, with an oval are oval forts, and with a triangle are decentralized settlements.

1. Ḥorvat Raḥba, str. II
2. 'Atar Har Qašqašim
3. Meṣudat Refed
4. Meṣudat Ḥatira
5. Meṣad Naḥal Boqer
6. Ḥorvat Meśora
7. Ḥorvat Ramat Boqer
8. 'Atar Haroʿah
9. Ḥorvat Ritma
10. Ḥorvat Ketef Shivta
11. Ḥorvat Ḥaluqim, str. II
12. Meṣudat Har Boqer
13. Ḥorvat Maʾgora
14. Meṣudat Har Reviv
14a. Meṣudat Nahal Rut
15. 'Atar Har Miḥya
16. Meṣad Har 'Arqov
17. Meṣad Naḥal Ṣin

17a. Meṣad Be'erotayyim
18. Meṣudat Haḥal Resisim
19. Ramat Maṭred
20. 'Atar Ramat Nafḥa
21. Meṣudat Naḥal Ṣenaʿ
22. Meṣudat Naḥal Ḥorsha
23. Meṣudat Be'er Ḥafir
24. Meṣudat Laʿana
25. Meṣudat Har Saʿad
26. Meṣad Naḥal Yeter
27. Meṣudat Sheluḥat Kadesh Barnea
28. 'Atar Naḥal Mitnan
29. Meṣudat Naḥal Sirpad
30. Naḥal Ḥorsha
31. Meṣudat Mishor Haruaḥ
31a. Meṣudat Mishor Haruaḥ East

32. Meṣudat Naḥal 'Ela
33. Meṣudat Naḥal ʿAqrab
34. Meṣad Sirpad
35. 'Atar Wadi al-ʿAsli
36. Tel Kadesh Barnea
37. Meṣudat Wadi el-Qudeirat
38. Meṣad Naḥal Ḥorsha
39. Migdal Naḥal Sirpad
40. Naḥal Ḥorsha
41. Meṣudat Har Ḥemet
42. Meṣudat ʿEin Qedeis
43. Meṣad Har Gizron
44. Borot Luṣ
45. Meṣudat Naḥal 'Ilonim
46. Meṣudat Naḥal Luṣ
47. Migdal Naḥal Qadesh Barnea

245

B. The Magnification of David's State

1. The Early Magnification

Amos 6:14 responds to those Israelites, reveling in Transjordanian triumphs in northern Ammon and in the Bashan, "who rejoice at Nothing (Lo-Debar), who say, 'did we not by our own might seize Prestige (Qarnaim)³?'" Amos's words are:

> For behold I am raising up against you, House of Israel, thus Yahweh, god of the Hosts, a nation, and they shall press you from Lebo Hamath to the Brook of the Arava.

2 Kgs. 14:25 is related to the verse in Amos. It provides the only concrete information in Kings concerning Jeroboam II:

> It was he who restored the territory/boundary of Israel from Lebo Hamath to the Sea of the Arava, according to the word of Yahweh, God of Israel, which he spoke by the agency of his servant, Jonah son of Amittai, the prophet who was from Gath Hepher.

The latter verse is of a type familiar from royal annals, and has parallels in several reliable texts in Kings.[4] Kings cites the source for its account of Jeroboam II as follows:

---

3. Lit., "two horns" (but Qarnaim as a place name). Contrast "his horn (status) will be high" in Ps. 89:24(25), and the raised horn of the anointed in 1 Sam. 2:(1), 10 (a pun on the horn of anointment, but also the status of the anointed), vs. the felled horn of Jer. 48:25; Lam. 2:3; also Ezek. 29:21 < Ps. 132:17; Zech. 1:18-21(2:1-4); Ps. 75:4-5, 10(5-6, 11); 89:17(18); 112:9; 148:14; Job 16:15; Lam. 2:17; 1 Chr. 25:5. Note Mic. 4:13, parallel to 1 Kgs. 22:11 = 2 Chr. 18:10, and influencing Ezek. 34:21. Further, Deut. 33:17, from which this last group of texts ultimately derives. Note also Num. 23:22; 24:8, "El, who produced him from Egypt, has horns like a bison's" (ktw'pt r'm lw), a phrase played on in Ps. 22:21(22); 92:10(11).

4. See James A. Montgomery, *JBL* 53 (1934): 46-52. Montgomery holds for a lapidary source for texts in Kings with "he" + suffix conjugation verb + object. The occurrences at the start of a regnal account are: 2 Kgs. 14:25; 18:4; in the middle of a regnal account, 2 Kgs. 14:7; 18:8; and after the end of a regnal account, 2 Kgs. 14:22, relating Amaziah's accomplishment in building Eilat after the death of Joash of Israel. On the texts, see further below. Montgomery may have been moved to his conclusion in part by the contrast between 14:25, which he viewed as a reliable prophecy from before 734, and 14:28, whose claims he labeled "absurd." See Montgomery, *A Critical and Exegetical Commentary on the Books of Kings*, ed. H. S. Gehman. ICC (Edinburgh: T. & T. Clark, 1951), 443-44. Rough

Source Notice

And the rest of the deeds of Jeroboam, and all that he did, and his heroism, that he fought, and that he restored *(hšyb)* Damascus and Hamath to Judah in/through *(b-)* Israel, are they not written in the book of the chronicles of the kings of Israel? (2 Kgs. 14:28)

The expression "the Brook of the Arava" occurs only in Amos 6:14. The expression in the account of Jeroboam's reign is "the Sea of the Arava" (2 Kgs. 14:25). In four other passages, the "Sea of the Arava" is the Dead Sea. All use the phrase to delineate the southern extent of Israelite land at the Arnon in Transjordan.[5] 2 Kgs. 14:25 also treats the Sea as the southern limit of the northern kingdom after the Solomonic schism. Amos is more or less similar — at least, there are Israelites there to be oppressed, as in the Deuteronomistic History, and political control extends that far south in his time. His Brook of the Arava is either the Jordan or the Wadi Arnon, emptying into it from the east.

2. Theories of the Israelite Settlement

The geographical descriptions in Amos and 2 Kgs. 14 are related. Both name Lebo Hamath as the northern border. This is common,[6] and it occurs as an element in P, from the 7th century. By way of contrast, J restricts itself to areas divided among the "tribes."[7] In such material, Dan serves as Israel's northern limit (Deut. 34:1). It does so both in the ancient catalogues of the tribes (Gen. 49; Deut. 33; Judg. 5) and in the expression, mostly in Samuel, "from Dan to Beersheba."[8] These two towns also serve as a metonym for all Israel in Amos 8:14.

---

parallels occur in the chronicle remark that Shalmaneser V ravaged Samaria and in early royal annals and captions.

5. Deut. 3:17; 4:49; Josh. 3:16; 12:3.

6. On Lebo Hamath as the northern border, see above, Chapter 9, and esp. Benjamin Mazar, "Lebo-Hamath and the Northern Border of Canaan," *Cities and Districts in the Land of Israel* (Jerusalem: Bialik, 1975), 167-81 (Heb., repr. from *Bulletin of the Jewish Palestine Exploration Society* 12 [1946]: 91-102).

7. P: Num. 34:7-9; 13:21, to Rehob of Lebo Hamath; JE: Num. 13:29; Deut. 34:1-4.

8. 1 Sam. 3:20; 2 Sam. 3:10; 17:11; 24:2, 15; 1 Kgs. 4:25(5:5). The phrase denotes all Israel. Judg. 20:1, however, restricts it to Cisjordan and adds "the land of Gilead" separately. The usage in Judges matches P's conception of Israel as Cisjordanian. Judah is described as having its southern limit at Beersheba in 2 Chr. 19:4, reaching Mount Ephraim in the north. Likewise, in 2 Kgs. 23:8 Josiah suppresses Judah's high places from Geba to Beersheba.

As noted in Chapter 9, some 7th-century texts (Deuteronomy and Josh. 1:3-4) extend the territory Yahweh promises, explicitly, to the Euphrates.[9] Deuteronomy is followed by Chronicles, which in the 5th century claims that David reached the Euphrates and that Solomon maintained a hold there.[10] The definition of territory in Chronicles is complex. Kings claims that Israelites from as far north as Lebo Hamath attended the dedication of Solomon's temple (1 Kgs. 8:65 = 2 Chr. 7:8), so Chronicles has the same group assemble under David to retrieve the ark in 1 Chr. 13:5. Still, Chronicles twice mentions an Israel stretching from Beersheba to Dan, inverting the phrase in Samuel. The first text defines the Israelite population covered in a census. The second defines the Israelite population that Hezekiah invites to celebrate Passover in Jerusalem.[11]

Chronicles thus posits three "circles" of Israel. The political circle, the Israel that is punished as a result of David's census, runs from Beersheba to Dan. The cultic community of Israel extends into the Beqaʿ Valley. Both are distinguished from the territory controlled under the United Monarchy.[12]

The Deuteronomistic History presents a similar face. Deuteronomy and Josh. 1:3-4 claim that Yahweh promised Israel the land from Canaan to the Euphrates. But Josh. 11:17 and 12:7 acknowledge that the Conquest did not result in political control north of Dan. Josh. 13:5 and Judg. 3:3 name Lebo Hamath as the northernmost extent of the promised land. Taken as a literary whole, the account of the Conquest suggests that Yahweh's original promise was never realized, and even a border abutting Hamath remained an ideal in the time of Joshua. The Beqaʿ Valley lay outside the framework of administration reflected in the allocation of tribal territories in Joshua.

Other texts name the northern extent of David's empire. Some refer to this

---

9. Deut. 1:7, against J in Num. 13:29; Deut. 11:24. So too does Gen. 15:18, often identified as J but possibly redactional. Note esp. Norbert Lohfink, "Dtn 12, 1 und Gen 15, 18: Das dem Samen Abrahams geschenkte Land als der Geltungsbereich der deuteronomischen Gesetze," in *Die Väter Israels: Beiträge zur Theologie der Patriarchenüberlieferungen im Alten Testament,* ed. Manfred Görg (Stuttgart: Katholisches Bibelwerk, 1989), 183-210, with an analysis pertinent to the discussion below. On the relationship of the Davidic empire to the patriarchal promises, Lohfink, *Die Landverheissung als Eid.* Stuttgarter Bibelstudien 28 (Stuttgart: Katholisches Bibelwerk, 1967), 73-76.

10. 1 Chr. 5:9; 18:3; cf. 2 Chr. 7:8. For Solomon, 2 Chr. 8:3-4, which is based on a willful misreading of 1 Kgs. 9:18.

11. 1 Chr. 21:2; 2 Chr. 30:5. 1 Chr. 21:2 derives from 2 Sam. 24:2.

12. This coincides with the view of Zecharia Kallai concerning the relationship to one another of the various territorial descriptions in the Pentateuch (and elsewhere). See esp. "The Patriarchal Boundaries, Canaan and the Land of Israel: Patterns and Application in Biblical Historiography," *IEJ* 47 (1997): 69-82.

as "the river," a term often taken to mean the Euphrates if deliberately inexplicit.[13] But 1 Kgs. 8:65 (= 2 Chr 7:8) has Solomon gather Israel from Lebo Hamath in the north to Egypt in the south.

Taken at face value, these texts imply that the empire at its greatest extent reached the Euphrates — or, in the case of our more careful sources in Samuel and 1 Kgs. 5, "the (unspecified) river." Israel's actual population, however, as distinct from hegemony, was restricted to the south of Lebo Hamath. Though Samuel describes no conquests by David beyond the southern territory of Damascus in Transjordan, or beyond Abel of the House of Maacah in the Beqa', this view has had an impact on P. It also programs the inference of Chronicles, which extends the empire beyond the pale of settlement, and even tells us that Reuben's pasturage extended to the Euphrates.

Yet the conception of all of Israel stretching only from Dan in the north to Beersheba in the south is not just present in Samuel, where one might regard it as evidence of a view that Israel remained so constricted until David's time. It also appears in the account of Solomon's reign (1 Kgs. 4:25[5:5]), in close proximity to the reference to Solomon's "river," and not too far from the gathering embracing all Israel up to Lebo Hamath. That this definition then vanishes is in part a function of the Solomonic schism, when Israel seceded from Jerusalem.[14] But it also reflects the distinction between the political circle of Israel (Dan to Beersheba), the cultic circle reaching from Lebo Hamath to the Brook of Egypt, and the imperial circle, reaching "the river."

Inside Samuel-Kings, thus, the promise of land to the Euphrates is realized only by implication, never explicitly: texts hint at it by not identifying "the river." But a minimal (to Dan or Abel), middle (hegemony in the Beqa' — 2 Sam. 8:8) or maximal (to the Euphrates — 2 Sam. 8:9-10) view of David's achievements does not imply the annexation of territories north of Dan. 1 Kgs. 8:65 looks to be a product of a middle reading. It places Israelite settlement in the Beqa'. This collides with the maximal promise in Deuteronomy and Joshua, but suggests that David fulfilled the middle reading — the revision of the ideal territory to reach Hamath only — in Joshua-Judges.

Conceivably, the invocation of Yahweh's name among royalty in Hamath played a role in promoting the middle reading. In the 8th century, a king there certainly bore a name evoking the Israelite god: Iaubi'di.[15] In any case, the idea

13. See above, Chapter 9. 2 Sam. 8:3 Ketib; Qere and 1 Chr. 18:3: Euphrates. 1 Kgs. 4:21(5:1) (= 2 Chr. 9:26) informs us that Solomon ruled over all the kingdoms from "the river" to the land of the Philistines, to the border of Egypt.

14. Dan and Bethel marking the north: see 2 Kgs. 23:8; 2 Chr. 19:4.

15. And conceivably Azriyau. See Stephanie Dalley, *VT* 40 (1990): 21-32. For Joram,

of settlement extending to the southern border of Hamath jibes with the enumeration of unconquered peoples only as far as Hamath in Joshua and Judges. If the authors of these texts thought that Israel under David reached the Euphrates, they would have enumerated unconquered peoples to the border of Assyria.

The extension of the empire to the Euphrates in Deuteronomy and Gen. 15, as well as in Chronicles, derives from the identification of the "river" in 2 Sam. 8:3, on which David erects his stela (and Ps. 89:25[26], where the unspecified river is under his control), as well as from the impression, deliberately given in 2 Sam. 8:10-11, that Hamath was in David's ambit. Oddly, P in the 7th century and Ezekiel in the 6th are more conservative in describing the empire than are other sources after JE. P's view can be reconciled with the view expressed in Josh. 13, namely, that the southern border of Hamath was an ideal boundary, but never in fact realized, or perhaps realized only temporarily by David. P's tribal and clan lists also omit the lands north of Dan.[16]

3. The Magnifying Lens

One catalyst in transforming David's empire from a local phenomenon to a world power may be Jeroboam II. 2 Kgs. 14:25 — the narrative statement — relates that Jeroboam II "restored" Israel's territory from Lebo Hamath down to Moab. The source notice (2 Kgs. 14:28) stipulates that he recovered Damascus and Hamath. The combination permits only two unified readings: (1) that the "territory of Israel" reached into that of Hamath; or (2) that the conquest of Hamath was hegemonic, as in David's relations with it on the maximal interpretation of 2 Sam. 8.

The source notice makes greater claims than the narrative statement, about

---

son of Toi (2 Sam. 8:10 MT, but not LXX or 1 Chr. 18:10), see above, Chapter 10. OG reads Hadoram for Joram (Iedoram). *hdrm became ywrm by scribal error. One might otherwise understand the alternation between Joram and Hadoram in reference to that between Iaubi'di and Ilubi'di later at Hamath. Nevertheless connections in Israel's territorial dreams with the Hamath region, and traditions in DtrH of Israelite settlement there (cited above), suggest that the other evidence Dalley adduces is correctly interpreted by her. On the Davidic empire as it is described in Samuel, see above, Chapters 7-10; Baruch Halpern, "The Construction of the Davidic State: An Exercise in Historiography," in *The Origins of the Ancient Israelite States*, ed. Volkmar Fritz and Philip R. Davies. JSOTSup 228 (Sheffield: Sheffield Academic, 1996), 44-75.

16. Gen. 46; Num. 26. The clan lists are in turn confirmed as accurate back into the 8th century by the Samaria ostraca. See further above, Chapter 9C.

both Hamath and Damascus. The context of the narrative statement relates that Yahweh allowed Jeroboam's conquests out of unmerited mercy (2 Kgs. 14:26-27). Thus, the narrative statement (14:25) is concessive, admitting but minimizing Jeroboam's gains: out of mercy, Yahweh might have rested content with the success of Jeroboam's father, Joash, in freeing Israel from Damascus, a success portrayed as the result of insufficient zeal.[17]

The modest narrative statement is more credible than the source notice.[18] The course of Israel's fortunes confirms the fact. In 841, when the border with Damascus stood at Ramot Gilead, Jehu ceded Transjordan to Hazael in order to secure his own putsch in Samaria.[19] Israel remained confined to Cisjordan at least until Adad-Nirari III of Assyria reduced Damascus.

Adad-Nirari's first blow fell in 805. At that time, Bar-Hadad, son of Hazael, king of Damascus, led a coalition of seven or more kings against Zakkur of Hamath, at Hazrach. Zakkur styled him "king of Aram."[20] Adad-Nirari writes that he fought a coalition of eight kings, led by one of Zakkur's enemies, Atarshumki of Arpad.[21] But, reporting his triumphal entry into the royal palace in Damascus, Adad-Nirari calls Bar-Hadad *mari'*, the title for an overlord that also appears on Hazael's booty inscriptions. Effectively, ca. 800, Bar-Hadad was king of Aram.

Conversely, in the Melqart stela of the 8th century, it is a king of Arpad who titles himself "king of Aram." The Sefire treaty of the mid-8th century treats the king of Arpad as the chief of Aram as well. This reflects the shift in power that followed the turn of the century. Thus, Hezyon (Hadianu), king of Damascus in 773, enjoys no such prestige.[22]

Kings speaks of Israel's resurgence under Joash, who reigned to ca. 790. Joash recovered territory lost to Hazael. Jeroboam II expanded from this base.[23] Amos attests Jeroboam's gains in Transjordan, but not a conquest of Damascus. Qarnaim, like the rest of Transjordan down to the Arnon, was a former territory of Damascus. Shalmaneser IV, too, reached Damascus in 773, and Assur-

---

17. 2 Kgs. 13:14-19, 22-25. Note the unlikely Moabite marauding associated with Elisha's demise in 2 Kgs. 13:20. For direct political reconstruction, the prophetic material is flimsy.

18. As Montgomery, *Kings*, 443-44, and most other commentators.

19. For the events of the 9th century, see Paul E. Dion, "Syro-Palestinian Resistance to Shalmaneser III in the Light of New Documents," *ZAW* 107 (1995): 482-89; below, Chapter 23.

20. KAI 202:4. See above, Chapter 9.

21. RIMA 3.A.0.104.3:11-13.

22. KAI 222A:5; B:3. RIMA 3.A.0.105.1:6-10.

23. Esp. 2 Kgs 13:14-19, 22-25; 14:25-28.

Dan III campaigned against Hazrach, at least, in 772 and 765, then again in 755. Resistance was apparently fierce, once again. In 754, Assur-Nirari V was back in Arpad, the major bulwark of the West against Tiglath-Pileser III at the start of his reign. Taken together, this evidence illuminates the early 8th century, and Jeroboam's sole reign (ca. 790 to ca. 750), as a time rich with opportunity for Israelite expansion because of decline at Damascus and Hamath.[24]

If Israel took the Beqaʿ as a gift from Assyria to a reliable vassal, Adad-Nirari probably transferred it. Adad-Nirari actively altered borders in the West. He extended the territory of Hazrach to include Hamath; he redefined Arpad's territory. However, Assur-Dan III's campaigns in the wake of Shalmaneser's attack on Damascus show that Hazrach had become a center of resistance. It is thus best to place Jeroboam's successes after 772. However the Beqaʿ was acquired, the text in Amos attests that the gains in Transjordan were won by force of arms, presumably against elements still loyal to Damascus. It also shows that Israel's high tide there was at Qarnaim, in the southern Bashan, not farther to the north at Damascus.

4. Is Jonah Liable?

All this bears on the character of the information that may have survived in formal records of Jeroboam's reign.

Rabbinic sources identify Jonah in Kings with the prophet who anointed Jehu to destroy the dynasty of Omri. Later tradition placed Jonah before Jeroboam II. In so doing, it expressed the concessive sense of the reports concerning the dynasty. It implied that the dynasty's longevity, and also its political success, was strictly a reward for Jehu's zeal. This is logical enough given a wooden view of prophecy as predictive, a view repudiated in the book of Jonah.

Otto Eissfeldt's reading of Amos 6:14 against the background of 2 Kgs. 14:25 typifies the scholarly view, which resembles traditional comment in this respect. For Eissfeldt, Amos reversed Jonah's original prophecy of Israelite expansion.[25]

---

24. Further André Lemaire, "Joas de Samarie, Barhadad de Damas, Zakkur de Hamat. La Syrie-Palestine vers 800 av. J.-C.," *ErIsr* 24 (1993): 148*-57*; Edward Lipiński, "Jéroboam II et la Syrie," in Garrone and Israel, *Storia e tradizioni di Israele*, 171-76, attributing the situation to the activity of Shamshi-Ilu, at Til-Barsip in Bit-Adini.

25. See Otto Eissfeldt, "Amos und Jona in volkstümlicher Überlieferung," *Kleine Schriften zum Alten Testament* (Tübingen: Mohr, 1968), 4:137-42; likewise, Hans Walter Wolff, *Joel and Amos*. Herm (Philadelphia: Fortress, 1977), 289, identifying the Brook of the Arava with the Wadi Kefren; Shalom M. Paul, *Amos*. Hermeneia (Minneapolis: Fortress, 1991), 221.

Robert Gordis, likewise, followed Qimhi in holding that Amos was mocking the claims of 2 Kgs. 14:25, and in identifying Amos's "brook of the Arava" with the "Sea of the Aravah."[26] Andersen and Freedman posit the capture of Hamath and Damascus.[27] All these readings assume that the narrative text in Kings contains information about a period earlier than the text in Amos.

Such is the effect of source citations, like the one in 2 Kgs. 14:28. But the account of Jeroboam's reign exhibits continuity with the rest of Kings in its content and formulation. All the formulas conform to models applied to other kings: the notice of the king's accession, the historian's moral judgment on the king, and the formulas relating Jeroboam's death and burial. In content, the concern with loss of territory to Hazael and its subsequent recovery lasts just as long as Jehu's dynasty, and no longer.[28] And the form of the narrative report (14:25), he + suffix-conjugation verb + object, forms part of a sequence beginning with two reports about Amaziah and concluding, after one report about Jotham, with two about Hezekiah.[29] Still, there is the peculiar syntax of the source notice (14:28) to the effect that Jeroboam restored northern possessions "to Judah by Israel."[30] There is also the problem that 14:25 fulfills a prophecy not otherwise on record, in contrast to the normal sequence, prophecy followed by fulfillment, which is otherwise especially consistent regarding the north.[31]

26. Robert Gordis, "Studies in the Relationship of Biblical and Rabbinic Hebrew," in *Louis Ginzberg Jubilee Volume* (New York: American Academy for Jewish Research, 1946), 173-99. On this interpretation, see below.

27. Francis I. Andersen and David Noel Freedman, *Amos*. AB 24A (Garden City: Doubleday, 1989), 595-96.

28. 2 Kgs. 10:32-33; 13:3-5, 15-19, 22-25; 14:25-28; also 12:18-19.

29. 2 Kgs. 14:7, 22; 15:35; 18:4, 8. See above on Montgomery's claims about the form. The closest biblical parallels stem from the lists of David's heroes (as 2 Sam. 21:20; 23:8, 10, 18). Cf. also 2 Kgs. 15:12, a supplementary notice for Zechariah, whose placement roughly parallels that of 14:22 for Amaziah. On the assignment of 14:22 to Amaziah, see Baruch Halpern and David A. Vanderhooft, *HUCA* 62 (1992): 179-244.

30. Syriac "to Israel" represents a correction of the original *lectio difficilior*. Cf. 2 Chr. 11:3, "all Israel in Judah, and Benjamin," which has also inspired correction. For another emendation Nadav Na'aman, "Azariah of Judah and Jeroboam II of Israel," *VT* 43 (1993): 227-34. Na'aman's thesis depends on identifying Uzziah as the builder of Eilat. If so, he must have done so in the reign of Amaziah, since Amaziah, not Uzziah, was the vassal of Jehoash, the king Na'aman concedes is the figure to whose death the "restoration" is linked in 2 Kgs. 14:22. See the preceding note.

31. See Gerhard von Rad, *Studies in Deuteronomy*. SBT 9 (London: SCM, 1953). There is no parallel here to the case of the Davidic covenant of conditional grant, which is related to an interpretation of 2 Sam. 7 as licensing the loss of Israel, but retention of a throne in Jerusalem, as a punishment for Solomonic apostasy. The other references to fulfillment of

And there is the question of the grudging character of the narrative description of Jeroboam's conquests.

Giving Kings precedence over Amos has appeal, the more so in that the verb Amos uses, "press, oppress," is also employed of Aramean pressure in reports about the Nimshides (2 Kgs. 13:4, 22) in proximity to our own passage. However, this is evidence of a connection, not of a direction of influence. More significant is the fact that Amos invokes the "brook of the Arava," elsewhere absent.[32] Kings refers to the "Sea of the Arava," a term used elsewhere for the Dead Sea. Amos's locution may play on the phrase "brook of Egypt," a more traditional designation of a theoretical boundary. Amos's coinage does not reflect dependence on Kings. Quite the reverse: if the texts are connected, Kings refers to Amos. Its reference to Hamath (as in Amos 6:2)[33] also connects the two.

What, then, if the author of the narrative report in 2 Kgs. 14:25 felt that Amos's prophecy of loss called for an earlier promise of gain?[34] That the Amos

---

prophecies about the northern kings — in 1 Kgs. 15:29-30; 16:12; 2 Kgs. 9:36 + 10:17; 15:12 — are all grounded in earlier narrative accounts. Formally, these texts fall into two groups: 1 Kgs. 15:29; 2 Kgs. 9:36 ("according to the word of Yahweh . . . that he spoke by the agency of his servant PN"); and 1 Kgs. 16:12; 2 Kgs. 10:17; 15:12 ("[according to/this is] the word of Yahweh that he spoke to PN [the prophet]"). In all cases, PN is the recipient of the oracle. 2 Kgs. 14:25 stands out: "according to the word of Yahweh that he spoke by the agency of his servant PN the prophet who was from GN." Whether the variation is significant remains a question.

32. For suggestions see Paul, *ad loc.*

33. With echoes in Isa. 10:9; 36:19; 37:13 > 2 Kgs. 18:34; 19:13. Amos's remarks on Kullania and Hamath refer in the first instance to Assyrian destruction or dominion. If the destruction of Gath were attributed to the same agency, then the text could not antedate 734, while Kullania falls in 738. The campaigns of Assur-Dan in the north are another possible point of reference — neither Hamath nor Kullania was a center of power after Hazael's rise (Zakkur's capital being Hazrach, which Assur-Dan attacked three times); Gath, likewise, does not appear in any other source as an independent state after Hazael. Against a relation to Tiglath-Pileser, the MT continuation in Amos may compare Israel favorably with these states, unlike the echoes. It is usually assumed that both questions must have the same implication, demanding a negative answer, as is the case in the echoes. However, even assuming that the first part of the comparison suppresses "you" (are you better than these kingdoms?), which is a question, the following might be the trope: are you better than these kingdoms, or is their territory larger than yours? Territorially, the edge probably belonged to Israel in all these cases. But then the text can be understood as the prophet's or as the prophet lampooning opponents.

34. The rough parallel is to prophecies of dynastic rise and fall, by Ahijah (twice), Jehu ben-Hanani, Elijah, and Elisha. Here, the prophecies of collapse do double duty, implying the rise of the next dynasty. That they end with the Nimshides — and without a prophecy of collapse — is characteristic.

passage is related to that in Kings is beyond question. No other text so defines Israel's borders. Moreover, on any model, Amos was written before the first compilation of Kings. And Amos 6:14 stands, prominently, at the end of the text before the Book of Amos's Visions (chapters 7–9). Amos 6:14 is attached to the prediction of an earthquake by which the book is dated (6:11; cf. 1:1). This text has more likely influenced Kings than some otherwise unattested prophecy by a Jonah. And this in turn indicates that the narrative report in Kings has displaced the prophecy of Jonah onto that figure, whose virtual juxtaposition with Amos in the Latter Prophets (albeit after Obadiah)[35] is thus explained.

Kings reused Amos in another connection. Amos furnished the model, in 1 Kgs. 13 (and 2 Kgs. 23) for the unnamed man of God who prophesied against the altar of Jeroboam (I!): in oral tradition, at least, in the late 7th century, his prophecy was antedated 150 years, and repointed just a bit to sustain the view that he predicted Josiah's actions against the Bethel high place, even announcing the king's name. This much is clear from a combination of elements in the narrative.[36] Thus the historian who wrote Kings in Josiah's time inclined to dissociate Amos from the time of Jeroboam II. Yet the citation of Amos in the Kings narrative statement is all but verbatim.

Further, the book of Jonah accurately associates his "activity" with Nineveh's heyday, although Assyria first appears in Kings after Jeroboam II. The texts on which the author relied were Hosea and Amos. Jonah's adventures, too, were in some measure suggested by the career of Amos — fleeing (Amos 7:12) to Tarshish, down into the depths of Sea/Sheol (Amos 9:2-4; 8:12), and yet being reached by Yahweh.

But Kings could not cite Amos, who prophesies the loss of territory formerly gained, as the prophet of Jeroboam's success. It had to explain Jeroboam's conquests, since it claims that the northern monarchs were guilty of apostasy. The explanation: Yahweh pitied Israel, and remembered Jehu's zeal (and this is the rabbinic view). The oracle was invented, and evinces the assumption that — as Amos (3:3-8) maintains — Yahweh would not act without first informing his prophets.

For the author of Kings, it was the stripping of Israel's possessions that was a normal divine action. What the oracle of "his servant, Jonah ben-Amittai, the

---

35. The reported activity of a character by this name in the time of Elijah (1 Kgs. 18:3-16) may explain why Obadiah is accorded precedence here. It may also partly explain Rashi's dating of Jonah.

36. Programmatically, Julius Wellhausen, in Friedrich Bleek, *Einleitung in das Alte Testament*, 244; further Baruch Halpern, *The First Historians*, 248-54; from a related perspective, Christoph Levin, "Amos und Jerobeam I," *VT* 45 (1995): 307-17. Perhaps the pun on *şywn* in 2 Kgs. 23:17 and its importance in Amos 1:2 is also related to the prophet's relocation.

prophet from Gath of Hepher" documents is the later fulfillment of Amos's prediction of Assyrian dominion down the length of Israel, a point reinforced in 1 Kgs. 15:29. Kings also confirms Amos's view of Jeroboam's gains: these were won not by Israel, but by Yahweh's will. The narrative report — in its content and in its specific wording — asserts that Amos was right. It incidentally apologizes for the success that Jehu's dynasty enjoyed.

C. Dating the Extension of David's State

What then is the relationship between the narrative statement and the source citation?

In Kings, despite external texts attesting conquests for Omri, only two kings of Israel capture foreign territory. The first is Joash, who takes Jerusalem.[37] The source citation for Joash remembers his war with Judah without mentioning the result (2 Kgs. 13:12; 14:15). The other king to take territory is Jeroboam. Here, the source citation makes more extensive claims than the narrative. Why the difference?

Further, even if Amos has influenced the narrative statement, the source cited is the same chronicle that Kings claims to rely on for northern history

---

37. 2 Kgs. 14:8-14. The placement of Joash's source notice, death and burial reports, and succession notice is unclear. In MT, they occur at 13:12-13 and at 14:15-16. OG, as represented by Lucianic miniscules differs, placing them after 13:25. Of the three locations for the concluding formulas, the first leaves a regnal account for Joash consisting entirely of formulas — unique in Kings. It also leaves the long narrative of Elisha's death and also Joash's military successes outside a regnal report framework, in parallel perhaps to the death of Elijah in 2 Kgs. 2. The location at 14:15-16 embeds Amaziah's regnal account inside of Joash's account, rather like Jehoram and Ahaziah of Judah's regnal accounts enclosed by that of Jehoram of Israel, to indicate the simultaneity of their endings. The OG alternative has on the surface much to recommend it, as it duplicates the normal course of the Kings narrative elsewhere. Elisha's death falls inside Joash's regnal account. OG makes the same alteration at the start of 2 Kgs. 2, moving Jehoram of Israel's accession formulas forward relative to MT so that his regnal account embraces the chapter. The consistency of this pattern may suggest that it is a secondary recourse. However, the original position of the formulae must have been unsatisfactory to provoke such removal, and in the circumstances 14:15-16 recommends itself as the "best," which is to say, most jarring, placement. The location fits especially with what follows (14:17). This, or 14:18, leads to the information of 14:22. But the two are spliced apart, because Kings reports assassinations of Judahite kings up to Hezekiah only after the source notice. In any case, Joash captures Amaziah, and tears down the north wall of Jerusalem. Note that even the conquest of Gibbethon is never related (1 Kgs. 15:27; 16:15-17).

throughout the period of the divided monarchy. Nonbiblical texts confirm the rough outline of the succession and the chronology from Omri forward, as well as contact with the foreign kings named in Kings from Shishaq on. So reliance on such a compilation must be granted.

But this explains the difference between the narrative report of Jeroboam's gains and the source citation. The narrative report claims only control of the Beqaʿ, whereas the source citation claims capture of Hamath and Damascus. The simplest explanation is that the narrative report, more modest, was part of an early edition of Kings, ca. 700. The source citation, however, is from the editor of the entire Former Prophets, plus Deuteronomy. Possibly, this editor had the chronicles of the kings of Israel, the source. If so, that source implied that Jeroboam conquered Hamath and Damascus. That is, it reiterated propaganda deriving from Jehu's dynasty.

How would an inscription of Jeroboam have reported his gains? It would describe any expansion as a triumph over the powers in whose territories gains were made. "I/he smote Hamath," it would report, to explain expansion in the Beqaʿ. "I defeated Damascus" would describe the taking of Qarnaim, and perhaps even Lo-Debar. And despite the fact that such words would reflect intrusions, only, into the ambit of these powers, a later reader might follow the implication of wholesale conquests.

Thus, the party concerned to rationalize the Israelite gain, in the narrative statement, to validate the prophecy of Amos, is not necessarily the interpreter of the source in the source notice. *The source notice's interpretation of the chronicle and the narrative statement have two different histories.*

In the narrative statement, Jeroboam "recovered" Israelite territory. In the source notice, he "restored" foreign territories to (Judah via) Israel. The verbs translated as "recovered" and "restored" are the same. But the source notice agrees with the strange report about Amaziah building Eilat in 2 Kgs. 14:22, as well as with usage in the Mesha stela.[38]

The source citation and the narrative report agree that the lands were "recovered." The verb places Jeroboam in the company of the northern kings Ahab and Joash, who also retrieved lost territory. He "recovered" territory, however, rather than losing it.

More important, the verb "recover" implies that someone earlier, namely David, took the same territory. The more modest narrative statement reflects the middle interpretation of David's epoch. It alleges control to, but not including, Hamath, consistent with 1 Kgs. 8:65.

---

38. See on the latter Patrick D. Miller, Jr., "A Note on the Meša' Inscription," *Or* 38 (1969): 461-64.

Jeroboam's successes may have inspired the middle view. Before his success, Judah's kings could point to David as the pinnacle of political unification. After Jeroboam's expansion, however, David's conquests had to grow. So in the 8th century, David must have expanded to the border of Hamath.

Yet the source citation, which claims that Jeroboam took Hamath and Damascus, presupposes the maximal interpretation. If Jeroboam II took these city-states, he can only have recovered them: David must have taken them first. The assumption is to be seen in the report of 1 Kgs. 11 about Rezon in Damascus — in a chapter by the historian responsible for the Former Prophets and Deuteronomy (the Deuteronomistic History). The author of the chapter understood from 2 Sam. 8 that David colonized Damascene territory. Since 1 Kgs. 11 invokes revolts to implicate Solomon in the secession of the north,[39] the assumption that Damascus was under the control of the United Monarchy can be identified as Josianic.

The source citation is most adventurous in claiming a "recovery" of Hamath. The closest Samuel comes to claiming David conquered this territory is the report that Hamath sent David gifts, modeled as tribute.[40] The same chapter yielded similar evidence for the domination of Damascus. And it also licensed the view that David had reached the Euphrates (2 Sam. 8:3), without saying so. The idea that David marched beyond Hamath makes a "recovery" of Hamath in the source citation possible. The understanding is that while Joshua assigned territory only to the Beqa', and the lands under Israelite political control stopped at Dan, David's state stretched to the Euphrates.[41] Jeroboam was not quite the man that David was.

The source citation reflects a maximal interpretation both of Jeroboam's reach and of the United Monarchy. The narrative statement is more conservative, assigning to David and Solomon only the territory south of Lebo Hamath and, correctly, land in Transjordan. Probably, the narrative statement antedates the expansive interpretation of the United Monarchy. It stems from the first edition of Kings, during Hezekiah's reign, ca. 700. The source citation belongs to a later edition — from the time of Josiah, ca. 620.

Josiah's historian took a benign view of Jehu's dynasty. The narrative report apologizes for their success. More important, Josiah's author took an expansive

---

39. Halpern, *The First Historians*, 150-57, 227-29; Gary Knoppers, *Two Nations under God*, 1.

40. 2 Sam. 8:9-10. The assertion that Toi's son bore the gifts was particularly likely to be taken as a sign of his submission to David. This is what Samuel hopes to suggest by mentioning it. Even if the son really was dispatched, however, no such relationship is likely.

41. Note that this is explicitly the understanding of Josephus, in *Ant.* 9.207, as well as, in all likelihood, of the Chronicler.

view of David's kingdom. The narrative report restricts David's conquest to the area south of Hamath. The source notice places him on the Euphrates. The more restrictive view is likely to have been earlier, slightly closer to the sources.

Overall, David took territory in Transjordan in the 10th century, and erected a stela on the Jordan. In the 8th century, he acquired the Beqa' Valley up to the border of Hamath. This is the view of the narrative report on Jeroboam, of P, and of some texts in Joshua, Judges, and Kings. The stela, then, was probably moved to the Orontes. In the late 7th century, David reached the Euphrates for the first time. The stela, now, was at "the river," the Great River, dividing eastern from western Asia Minor. These stages in the development of David's "empire" are critical to dating the exegesis of the original source in 2 Samuel. Its remarkably modest claims did not long remain the norm in Israelite royal propaganda: by the 8th century, at the latest, Samuel was already being wildly misinterpreted, as its author had always intended. By keeping the "river" anonymous in 2 Sam. 8:3, and by detaching David's stela in that verse from the same stela, near the Dead Sea at Jericho, in 2 Sam. 8:13 — even going so far as to use a different word for stela — the author of the apology insinuated that David had reached the Euphrates. In this respect, the author implied a comparison to the great Egyptian pharaohs, Thutmosis I, the first to reach the Euphrates, and especially Thutmosis III, who erected a stela on that river.[42] With the passage of the centuries, David finally acquired a reputation comparable to those of the truly great imperialists of the Apologist's world, and to those of the interpreters' worlds — of the Deuteronomistic Historian in Josiah's time, of the Chronicler in the Persian era, of Eupolemos in the Hellenistic world, and of Josephus in the Roman. The reputation has persisted ever since.

42. *ARE* 2.73, 81, 85; 2.478.

259

PART V

A LIFE OF DAVID

CHAPTER 15

David's Youth

A. The Sources

About David's youth, we have the two sources in 1 Samuel. The A source focuses the narrative spotlight first on Saul, as the man chosen by Yahweh to defeat the Philistines. It introduces David to Saul's court in the Goliath story, where he enjoys immense success as a courtier. Saul persecutes him, and he flees to the Philistines, where he does not find refuge. Saul kills those who have abetted David, the priests of Nob. This leaves David in hiding in the Judean steppe, where Saul finally reconciles with him. The narrative then relates the fateful events of the battle of Jezreel.

The B source focuses its spotlight on Samuel at the dawn of the monarchic era, portraying the change to monarchy as a freighted constitutional shift. Saul, nominated by Yahweh, designated by Samuel, and elected by the people, wins his inaugural battle against Ammon (1 Sam. 8; 10:17-27; 11). This proves his worth. In the aftermath, he crosses the Jordan River back to Gilgal, and Samuel confirms ("renews") his kingship with a lengthy speech (1 Sam. 12). But in his next confrontation, with Amaleq (1 Sam. 15), Saul earns another lengthy speech from Samuel, rejecting him from the kingship. At this juncture, the focus shifts to David (1 Sam. 16), in Bethlehem. The spotlight remains on him through his career as a songster, warrior and captain at the court, his flight into the Judean steppe, his contretemps with Nabal and acquisition of Abigail, and his life as commander of Ziklag, the underling of Achish of Gath.

The differences between the sources have been treated in Chapter 2. However, in the A source, Saul remains at the center of the action until his death. In the B source, Saul is almost never the focus of the action. In both sources, David is the protagonist. All the same, the A source incorporates a line of tradition sympathetic to Saul. He responds with appropriate humility — like that of Moses, Gideon, and Jephthah — to his anointment. He suffers even in victory, and faces a foreordained death heroically, cheating the Philistines of the glory of killing him by falling on his own sword. Such sympathy is altogether absent from the B source.[1]

These different orientations manifest themselves in other ways. In the A source, as noted in Chapter 2, Saul achieves military successes. He campaigns victoriously on all of Israel's peripheries, including in Aram. He beats down the Philistines, expelling them from the central part of the Ayyalon Pass. In the B source, by contrast, he enjoys only two successes: against Ammon, in Transjordan — this is the victory that wins him the kingship; and against Amaleq, in southern Judah, in the victory that leads to his dismissal from the kingship. He fails in his contests with the Philistines. And it is an Amaleqite, in the end, whom he begs to kill him.

Indeed, while the A source presents the Philistines as Israel's principal enemy and Saul's primary target, the B source barely brings Saul into contact with them, except for his final battle. It describes this battle only indirectly, in the report of the Amaleqite survivor to David, in 2 Sam. 1. In the same vein, the B source has no compunction about reporting that David was the lieutenant of Achish of Gath: the Philistines are only one of many enemies on Israel's borders.

The A source is much more touchy on the subject, and denies that David ever served Israel's arch-enemies:

> David rose and fled that day from Saul. He came to Achish, king of Gath. Achish's servants said to him, "Is this not David, the king of the land? Is it not of this man that they chant to flutes, saying, 'Saul has smitten his thousands, and David his myriads'?" David took these words to heart, and grew very fearful of Achish, king of Gath. So he feigned madness in their view, and acted like a madman while in their power, and scribbled on the doors of the gate and drooled his spittle on his beard.
>
> So Achish said to his servants, "Here look, the man is gone mad. Why should you bring him to me? Am I short of madmen that you brought me this one to act insane on me? Should this one enter my house?" (1 Sam. 21:10-15[11-16])

---

1. Note Walter Dietrich, *David, Saul und die Propheten,* BWANT 7/2 (Stuttgart: Kohlhammer, 1987), 151ff., for the comparable argument that traditions about Samuel and Saul were northern and those about David (and David and Saul) southern.

Better that David should simulate insanity than that he should have worked for the Philistines. There can have been no collusion between David and Achish whatever.

In this and in other particulars, the A source in its present form looks as though it is a little later than the B source. The author of the B source was in no position to deny David's Philistine links, even had he wanted to do so. And, in 2 Samuel, David's earlier links to Gath are presupposed, for example in the admission that Ittay and the Gittite troops in Jerusalem came with David from Gath and Ziklag. This is a concrete link from the B source to the history of David's reign.

Another indication comes from the great doublet in which David has Saul in his power, but spares him. The original story inspiring this account is found in 2 Sam. 23:13-17:

> Three of the thirty went down and came at the harvest to David, at the cave at Adullam,[2] while a detachment of Philistines was camping in the Valley of Rephaim. David was in his fort at the time, and the Philistine base was Bethlehem at the time. David had a craving, and said, "I wish that someone would slake me with water from the well of Bethlehem, that is in the gate!" Yet the corps of the Philistines was in Bethlehem at the time.[3] So the three heroes broke into the camp of the Philistines, drew water from the well of Bethlehem that is in the gate, and carried it off and brought it to David.[4] But he did not consent to drink it, and poured it out as a libation for Yahweh, and said, "Yahweh forfend that I should do this! Should I drink the blood of men who risked their lives?"[5] and he did not consent to drink it.

2. The cave, as in 1 Sam. 22:1, not the fort, as Julius Wellhausen, *Die Composition des Hexateuchs und der historischen Bücher des Alten Testaments,* 4th ed. (Berlin: de Gruyter, 1963), 251. Note the appearance of the term in the A source in 1 Sam. 24.

3. This sentence appears in the Greek but not the Hebrew. It clarifies the disposition of the Philistine forces: a detachment was away from the base, in the Valley of Rephaim; but the headquarters and main force remained in Bethlehem. The historicity of the point is moot, and the line may be a secondary addition, but it encapsulates the sense of the surrounding text.

4. The Greek reading is original in this verse: "they drew water from the well of Bethlehem that is in the gate," *wyš'bw mym mb'r btlḥm 'šr bš'r,* was omitted by homoioarcton — the MT copyist skipped to the following, "and they carried it," *wyš'w.*

5. The OG version omits MT "the" before "men," probably correctly. For a more radical reconstruction of this very problematic verse, based on the parallel in 1 Chr. 11:19, see P. Kyle McCarter, *II Samuel,* 481. I think the Chronicler, or his base text, has furnished an exegesis in this case, "for they brought it (the water) at the risk of their lives."

Likewise in both versions of the doublet David protests, "Yahweh forfend" that he should kill Saul (1 Sam. 24:6; 26:11), and forbears to take advantage of his power over Saul.

In the B source version (1 Sam. 26), David steals a spear and water jug from beside the sleeping Saul. The spear indicates his ability to kill Saul, but the water jug represents a connection to the account in 2 Sam. 23. In the A source version (1 Sam. 23:19–24:22[23]), David encounters Saul relieving himself in a cave, and cuts off the hem of his tunic. The A source version is slightly farther removed, in omitting the potable water and in introducing the humor of a scatological element, from the original episode.

The A source appears to be later than the B source. And yet, it preserves favorable information about Saul. Does this mean that the A source employs earlier materials than the B source in connection with Saul, at a time later than B's composition?

From a historical viewpoint, with two sources both favorable to David, we can know next to nothing about his youth. And yet, there is much we can surmise. The clues begin, if unsatisfyingly, with his name.

B. The Name of David

The meaning of David's name is uncertain. Older scholars identified it, incorrectly, with an Akkadian word that they interpreted as "leader." The root of the term is dwd (so dawid, or dawd). The most natural understanding of this root is as "(paternal) uncle" or "beloved." However, no text spells David's name dd, as "uncle" is sometimes written. It is always spelled dwd or even (later) dwyd, that is, dawíd, David.

Probably related are two other biblical names. In them, the diphthong -aw-of the name David collapses to -o-, and the /i/-vowel of the second syllable does not appear. The first is Dodo, d(w)dw. This appears as the patronym of two of David's retainers — Elazar son of Dodo the Ahohite and Elhanan son of Dodo from Bethlehem, the slayer of Goliath of Gath.[6] It also occurs as the clan name of the minor judge Tola, from Issachar south of the Jezreel Valley (Judg. 10:1).

The second name related to David is Dodaw(y)ahu. This is the father of a prophet whom Chronicles drags out to condemn a foreign alliance in Jehoshaphat's day (2 Chr. 20:37). The Chronicler consistently produces such figures wherever he understands such an alliance to be contracted, so the case is probably fictitious. And the prophet's first name is Eliezer: it is likely that

6. 2 Sam. 21:19; 23:9, 24; 1 Chr. 11:12, 26; 20:5; 27:4.

Eliezer son of Dodo is merely a recycled version of the earlier character, Elazar son of Dodo (*'l[y]'zr bn d[w]dw*). In sum, the biblical evidence associates the name with Bethlehem, there with the apparently Benjaminite clan, Ahoah, and with Issachar.

More important is a constellation of evidence from the 9th century. The king of Moab, Mesha, speaks of removing from Ataroth *'r'l dwdh*, the "Ariel" either of (Ataroth's) *dwd* or of Dodo (Dawdoh). *Dwdh* in this part of the Mesha stela contrasts with the expression *bt dwd*, "the House of David," that perhaps appears as a designation for Judah.[7] The passage runs:

> The men of Gad had dwelled in the land of Ataroth forever, but the king of Israel built (or: 'fortified') Ataroth for himself, so I waged war against the town and seized it, and slew all the people of the town as a libation for Chemosh and for Moab. I took captive (or: 'I restored') from there (the?) "Ariel of Dwdh" and dragged it before Chemosh in Qeriyyot. I settled in it the *šrn*-men and the *mḥrt*-men (heavy infantry and shock troops?).
>
> Chemosh said to me, "Go, seize Nebo from Israel." So I went in the night, and waged war against it from the break of dawn until noon, and seized it, and slew all of it, seven thousand male citizens and dependents and female citizens, dependents and "wombs" *(rḥmt)*, for I consecrated it (Nebo) as a Holy War *(hḥrmth)* to Chemosh's consort (or: 'to Ashtar-Chemosh'). I took from there the '[ ]ls of Yahweh and I dragged these before Chemosh.[8]

What an "Ariel" is is unknown, but the list of David's heroes relates that Benaiah son of Jehoiada "smote the two sons of Ariel of Moab."[9] Ariel also appears in P as the name of a clan in the Transjordanian tribe of Gad (Gen. 46:16;

---

7. Mesha line 31, with Émile Puech, "La stèle araméene de Dan: Bar Hadad II et la coalition des Omrides et la maison de David," *RB* 101 (1994): 215-41, esp. 227; André Lemaire, *BAR* 20/3 (1994): 30-37. Whether or not the *-h* appears in the context (so: *bt dwdh*) is unclear. "The House of David" *(byt dwd)* in the Dan stela is also a term for the state of Judah.

8. KAI 181:10-18. The classes of population at Nebo are *gbrn, grn, gbrt, [gr]t, rḥmt*, the last probably being included for purposes of paronomasia with *ḥrm*, "Holy War" (and the root of the term "harem, sequester"). On Chemosh's concubine, or goddess, compare Yahweh's Asherah, the terms for which are explored in Baruch Halpern, "The Baal (and the Asherah)," in *Konsequente Traditionsgeschichte: Festschrift für Klaus Baltzer*, ed. Rüdiger Bartelmus, Thomas Krüger, and Helmut Utzschneider. OBO 126 (Fribourg: Universitätsverlag, 1993), 115-54.

9. 2 Sam. 23:20 = 1 Chr. 11:22, reading with the Greek; see McCarter, *II Samuel*, 491.

Num. 26:17). P's lists of clans are clearly reliable: the Samaria Ostraca, administrative receipts from the royal court of Israel just after 800, ringingly corroborate them.

The Mesha inscription attributes the fortification of Atarot and Nebo to Omri, who founded the dynasty that was to lend Israel its own name ("the House of Omri"). But Mesha identifies "the men of Gad" as indigenous to "the land of Ataroth." Mesha does not attack Gad, but rather the town that Israel's king built in Gad's land. He treats Gad as the party intruded on by Israel (Ahab). For him, the Gadites are not allies of Israel, but its antagonists. They are Moabites.[10]

The story of Benaiah's exploit may make the same assumptions. The sons of Ariel of Moab would be two warriors belonging to the clan Ariel, identified with Gad in the P text. When the text was composed, the Gadites may have been considered Moabite by the Jerusalem court.[11] This is hardly surprising. Clans of Reuben and Judah in some lists are identical with one another, and with clans of Edom in other lists.[12] The books of Samuel, significantly, consistently use the older designation, Gilead, for Israelite areas in Transjordan.

Administrative affiliations were variable. This is why various biblical texts can ascribe Mesha's capital, Dibon, to Gad. Unfortunately, we cannot determine whether Ariel or Gad was originally independent, or non-Israelite, or became Moabite for a time, starting perhaps with Mesha. If David did not reckon Ariel or Gad as Israelite, it could have come to be regarded as Israelite late in his reign, or under Omri, or later.

We also cannot establish what the Gadite population made of its identity. The account of Benaiah's exploit against the two "sons of Ariel of Moab" is followed by two conflicts: the first is against "the lion" (h'ry), a term possibly related to Ariel; the second is against "an Egyptian man" against whom he advances with a stick, and whom he kills with the Egyptian's own spear — a weapon "like a weaver's beam" (2 Sam. 23:20-21; 1 Chr. 11:23). As noted in Chapter 6, the latter story has been appropriated for David in the Goliath account. It is possible that these were the fights with the "two sons of Ariel of Moab." More certainly, "the lion" is an image associated with Gad, possibly because of the clan name, Ariel.[13]

10. Ernst Axel Knauf, *Midian* (Wiesbaden: Harrassowitz, 1988), 162 n. 689; "Eglon and Ophrah: Two Toponymic Notes on the Book of Judges," *JSOT* 51 (1991): 26.

11. If a Gadite appears in 2 Sam. 23:36, which is a question, his position in the list of David's officers locates him adjacent to other foreigners in 23:37. The expression *bny hgdy*, "sons of the Gadites," recurs in Num. 34:14.

12. For a classic example of how scholars have attempted to exploit such material, see Roland de Vaux, *The Early History of Israel* (Philadelphia: Westminster, 1978), 579.

13. Deut. 33:20, while Dan, to the north, is "the lion's whelp" in 33:22. Note further

Two texts shed a different light on the Ariel's identity. Around 560, Ezekiel (Ezek. 43:15-16) understands it as an altar, which is a concrete object that Mesha could indeed have carried off. It is also associated with the cult, and made an appropriate dedication for Chemosh. Somewhat earlier, near 701, Isaiah calls Jerusalem, "Ariel, Ariel, the city where David encamped" (Isa. 29:1-7); the prophet's point is that he camped *against* it. But Isaiah has a reason for addressing Jerusalem as Ariel: Jerusalem will sink into the underworld, he relates, and chirp like a spirit there. The connection to the netherworld is reinforced by a cognate word in Akkadian: *arallû* denotes the underworld in Mesopotamia. Furthermore, the "paternal uncle," or *dwd,* is the relation responsible for burial when a household is without heirs.[14] He is the nearest relation to whom the incest taboo does not apply, which is the reason the term also denotes one's "beloved."

Overall, the Ariel at Ataroth has two associations: one is with a Gadite kin group, Ariel; the second is with the cult, and more particularly with the funerary cult. This Ariel, which Mesha laid before his god in another town, pertained to Dwdh or to Ataroth's (or the king of Israel's) Dwd. Conceivably, Dwdh is Mesha's spelling of David's name (Dawdoh), in which case David himself may be the Dodo who fathered Elazar and/or Elhanan. The Ariel would then be some trophy left in the town of Ataroth from the time of its founding under David. Nadav Na'aman suggests that Dwdh was a king whose dynasty was resident in Horonen in southern Moab, and if so the presence of his Ariel in Ataroth suggests that his reach extended far to the north.[15] A stronger possibility is that the Dwd(h) in question was an eponym, or the epithet of an eponym in a local ancestral cult. The Ariel was either the statue of the deified ancestor or his altar.

This is merely a possible interpretation, not a probable one. All the same, since "paternal uncle" is extremely rare as an element in Israelite personal names, the name David should probably be construed on Mesha's model. But the evidence is not strong that David — *dwd* — is in of itself an Israelite personal name. The oddness of David's name, in an Israelite setting, should be borne in mind in the discussion that follows.

---

1 Chr. 12:8. Judah appropriates the lion image in Gen. 49:9. Note the pun on Jacob in connection with Gad there. The appearance of Gad in Deut. 33 and Gen. 49 suggests that it was considered Israelite in David's or Solomon's reign.

14. Amos 6:10, *dwdw.* On the construction of the passage, see Francis I. Andersen and David Noel Freedman, *Amos,* 572. The connection to the foregoing text about the marzeaḥ, or funerary society, is not adventitious.

15. See Nadav Na'aman, "King Mesha and the Foundation of the Moabite Monarchy," *IEJ* 47 (1997): 83-92.

C. David's Daddy

David's paternity, at least, is not much in doubt. His father is Jesse. The Hebrew for Jesse, *yišay* (1 Chr 2:13 *'īšāy*), is a nickname, like Bill for William. The elements of Jesse's name were originally *yēš* ("there is") + some divine name. Thus Ishbaal, the name of one of Saul's sons, is *yēš* ("there is," in a northern form) + Baal, "the Master is (present, puissant)." No source preserves the divine name associated with *yēš* for Jesse, however. The name may have been compounded with Yahweh, with the name of some other god, or with an epithet, such as Baal.

This is an authentic patronym. Other characters in 1 and 2 Samuel, mainly Saul, call David "the son of Jesse" in direct discourse only in derogation. Saul aside, one case is Sheba's call to revolt (2 Sam. 20:1); the same cry recurs in 1 Kgs. 12:16, at the Solomonic schism: "We have no property in David, nor legacy in the son of Jesse." It is first an outcry against David, but then against his dynasty and grandson; the common misconstruction is that Sheba's revolt threatened the dynasty rather than David personally (when it threatened neither). Nevertheless, the frozen formula, however early its origin, is evidence of David's paternity.

Jesse is also invoked as the dynasty's forebear by the prophet Isaiah (Isa. 11:1, 10). This indicates that the genealogy was fixed by 700. More important, only once does a narrator's voice in Samuel denominate David as "David son of Jesse." This is 2 Sam. 23:1, in the first line of a short, archaic poem referred to as "the last words of David." The text runs as follows:

> Thus David son of Jesse,
> and thus the man whom god established,
> the anointed of the god of Jacob,
> and the beloved of the protection of Israel.[16]

Similar is the introduction of Balaam's oracles in Numbers 24:3, 15:

> Thus Balaam son of Beor, and thus the man whose eye is perfect. . . .

These rubrics lead in each case to further poetry, placed in the mouth of the character identified. The tradition of the paternity of Balaam is to some extent confirmed by the Deir 'Alla texts from the 8th century.[17] David's is not in doubt, partly because of the Balaam parallel.

---

16. David's characterization as "the beloved" may be a play on the term *dd* ("beloved"). Another play on David's name comes in Solomon's throne-name (given to him by Nathan, not his parents) Jedediah, *yddyh*.

17. For the texts, see esp. the primary edition, Jacob Hoftijzer and G. van der Kooij,

The appearance of Jesse as David's father in Chronicles implies only that the father's name was fixed by the time of that work. The author of Chronicles supplies Jesse's name to punctuate his account (1 Chr. 10:14; 29:26; in poetry, 12:18), something he would not do for Moses or Aaron. This may reflect some ideological program — the Chronicler is not telling us "*which* David" was his subject, as, like other early names (patriarchs; tribes, except for Manasseh; early kings), this one does not recur in biblical times.

Still, the preservation of David's father's name indicates that the historical Jesse possessed means and, probably, influence. Possibly, his status provoked resentment. More probably, however, the negative emphasis on David's paternity — "the son of Jesse" as it is used in 2 Samuel — reflects a set of accusations by his opponents to which we no longer enjoy direct access. One of these would be that David was a usurper, at least of the crown of Israel, so the invocation of the father's name would indicate his lack of status. However, usurpers in the ancient Near East rarely make mention of their own fathers in their literature. Is it the case that the disparaging references to David as "the son of Jesse" are of a piece with other Solomonic conciliatory strategies connected with the Absalom revolt? Or is the narrative, which has Yahweh and Samuel single Jesse out (1 Sam. 16) to have a son to be anointed as the future king, concealing something about Jesse's, or David's, status by leaving the name in full view? This inference dovetails with other information concerning David's genealogy and his rise.

D. David's Antecedents

David's genealogy crops up twice, at the end of Ruth and, identically, in 1 Chr. 2:3-17. The tradition's antiquity is moot, but P, from the late 7th century, between the time of Deuteronomy and Jeremiah, names David's ancestor Nahshon as Aaron's brother-in-law (Exod. 6:23) and Chief of Judah (Num. 1:7). This more likely reflects the genealogy than inspires it. Nor would it be surprising were the name of David's grandfather (Obed) preserved. And some see in the story of David's entrusting his parents to the king of Moab (1 Sam. 22:4) evidence of a Moabite connection commemorated in Ruth, at the time of his great-grandfather Boaz. (Could the king of Moab here belong to a House of Dwdh of Mesha's inscription? If so, is the final -h on the name short for the name of a god?)

Aramaic Texts from Deir 'Alla. DMOA 19 (Leiden: Brill, 1976); and *The Balaam Texts from Deir 'Alla Reevaluated* (Leiden: Brill, 1991).

Still, the line from David's grandfather to Nahshon, thence back to Perez and Judah, seems forced. Thus, P places Nahshon just after the exodus from Egypt. He is five generations removed from Judah. Yet David is the fifth generation after Nahshon. This symmetry is suspicious, and one might suspect that P elected Nahshon to lead "Judah" for this reason. Indeed, in David's own time there is not a hint of such a genealogy. The A source introduces David as "an Ephrathite" from Bethlehem of Judah (1 Sam. 17:12). This affiliation is absent from the genealogy. The B source — whose materials about David seem to be slightly earlier than those in the A source — does not identify David with Judah at all. It introduces him only as the son of Jesse the Bethlehemite (1 Sam. 16:1).

The contrast is to the extensive introduction of Saul. A, with the older materials about Saul, calls him the son of Kish, son of Abiel, son of Zeror, son of Bekorat, son of Aphiah, a Benjaminite (1 Sam. 9:1). In terms of the later structure of the tribe of Benjamin, this source assigns him to the clan Bichri. The B source, which takes no particular interest in Saul, identifies him as the son of Kish, of the clan of Matri, of the tribe of Benjamin (1 Sam. 10:21). The absence of such material about David in Samuel does in fact reflect his status as a usurper.

It also reflects the fact that there *was no tribe of Judah* at the time of David's birth, and perhaps for a good part of his career. Scholars have long argued on the basis of the texts alone that the tribe of Judah did not exist before the 10th century.[18] Judah does not form a part of Israel in the list of tribes furnished in the Song of Deborah (Judg. 5). Its incorporation into Israel deranged what seems formerly to have been a much more logical metaphoric national genealogy. Originally, each of the four Israelite "matriarchs" — Leah, Rachel, Zilpah, and Bilhah — probably corresponded to each of four regions: the central highlands (Ephraim, Benjamin, and Manasseh — Rachel), the southern flank of the Jezreel Valley (Zebulun, Issachar — Zilpah); parts of the Galilee (Dan, Naphtali, Asher — Bilhah); and Transjordan (Reuben, Gilead — Leah).

What is more, the Song of Deborah addresses Ephraim as follows: "After you, Benjamin, among your contingents!" Benjamin went to war under the leadership of Ephraim. The clan musters of Benjamin were integrated into those of Ephraim. Benjamin means "son of the right hand," which is, "son of the south," "the southerner," "the southernmost." By contrast, the kingdom of Sam'al, "the left hand," in southeastern Turkey, was at one time the northern-

---

18. Sigmund Mowinckel, *Von Ugarit nach Qumran.* BZAW 77 (Berlin: Töpelmann, 1958), 137-38; *Tetrateuch — Pentateuch-Hexateuch.* BZAW 90 (Berlin: Töpelmann, 1964), 66; cf. Martin A. Cohen, "The Role of the Shilonite Priesthood in the United Monarchy of Ancient Israel," *HUCA* 36 (1965): 59-98, esp. 94-98.

most Aramean state. At the time of the Song of Deborah, ca. 1100, Benjamin was thus the group of all those Israelites living south of Ephraim. It included the Israelite residents of the territory later identified with Judah.[19]

Archaeological evidence now corroborates the inference from the textual data. Surveys disclose that in the Iron I the whole region of the Judean hills was sparsely settled. There were a few settlements in the Shephelah, to be sure, and a host of 10th-century settlements in the Negev highlands in the region of Beersheba. But the spine of the hills leading from the south and the Shephelah to Hebron and then Jerusalem contained very few villages.[20] The survey data show that settlement was on the wax in this era. Previously, Jerusalem's main hinterland had been in the Ayyalon Pass. The book of Joshua assigns this territory principally to Benjamin. But then, Joshua also assigns Jerusalem to Benjamin in one tradition, yet allows that it pertained, historically, to Judah. So there is every indication that Judah was under development, and capable of supporting a certain kind of state apparatus, a sort of mafia kingdom.

On the other hand, a handful of settlements cannot possibly have permitted the embedment of the sort of complex genealogy for David reflected in Ruth and Chronicles. Even the division of Judah into clans — "sons" of the figure Judah, the eponym of the tribe — in the Priestly source of the Pentateuch is too elaborate to reflect a time in Iron I. The P (Priestly) source of the 7th century divides Judah into four parts: Shelah, Hezron, Hamul, and Zerah in Gen. 46:12 and Num. 26:19-22. Hezron and Hamul, in this taxonomy of the tribe, are the sons of the eponym Perez.[21]

The J (Yahwist) source in the Pentateuch reveals that it is earlier than P, among other things, by failing to reflect the division of Perez into Hezron and Hamul. But even J's simpler tribal structure, with two clan eponyms dropped (Er and Onan), is far more developed than the Iron I demographic evidence permits us to expect. The Davidic genealogy in Ruth 4:18-22 presupposes not just J's tripartite division of the tribe, but even the quadripartite division presented in P. This material is later than J.

19. For this view, Baruch Halpern, *The Emergence of Israel in Canaan*, 109-163. On the Song of Deborah's muster, see further Frank Moore Cross, *From Epic to Canon* (Baltimore: Johns Hopkins University Press, 1998), 54-55.

20. Avi Ofer, *The Highland of Judah during the Biblical Period* (diss., Tel Aviv University, 1993). Ofer reports 18 sites in the area, most between Jerusalem and Hebron, but it is not certain that all are permanent villages, and unlikely that all were occupied before David's accession.

21. The quadripartite division of Judah comes to expression in Josh. 15, from the 7th century, as well. It stems at least from the 8th century, when the *lmlk* stamps, on standardized jars distributed by the state, also divide Judah into four regions.

Genealogies are difficult to interpret. They can express biological relationships, but they often express other relationships as well. Sometimes these relationships are geographical; sometimes, political; sometimes, administrative. The appearance of the clans of Manasseh, for example, as P reports them, in the tax documents of the Samaria Ostraca from ca. 800, indicates that Israelite clans were administrative entities in the monarchic era.

Under these circumstances, older genealogies can be embedded into later. Thus the clan names associated with Saul in 1 Samuel are not clan names of the tribe of Benjamin in the lists of P and Joshua. Genealogical structure is not unchanging, because administrative and political realities change over time. Thus the shifts between J and P indicate a passage of time. Those between Samuel and P do likewise. Unfortunately, P is the only source that consistently provides evidence of clan names in Israel, but the coincidences with early material indicate that P's sources antedate the fall of Israel in 722.

In this light, it is possible that there is an early kernel in David's genealogy. Thus, Nahshon, for example, the ancestor whom P makes Aaron's brother-in-law (Exod. 6:23), may have lent his name to an early clan. But on such points it is impossible to rise beyond the level of speculation, to achieve a means to develop a hierarchy of probability, in place of suggestion. What we can say with relative assurance, then, is that the Davidic genealogy, beyond the name of Jesse, is not to be depended on as a source for reconstructing the history either of Judah or of the family. And, as noted in Chapter 3, the genealogical structure found in the lists of David's heroes is earlier than anything in either J or P.

E. Location in Bethlehem

David's genealogy, Ruth and 1 Samuel (16; 17:15, 58; 20:6, 28), all place David's family in Bethlehem, for several generations. Most convincing is the almost unconscious reference of 2 Sam. 2:32 to the ancestral tomb of Asahel, Joab's brother, there. Mic. 5:2(1) indicates that this tradition was entrenched by 700. Bethlehem, despite the association of Rachel's tomb with it (Gen. 35:19; 48:7; Jer. 31), was a backwater suburb an hour's march south of Jerusalem. David's affiliation with the village is hardly an invention.

Yet Bethlehem also stands in the shadow of Jerusalem. It was hardly some independent principality before David's conquest of "the city of David." Indeed, it is also singled out as the location of a Philistine base in 2 Sam. 23:13-17. Admittedly, this story presupposes that David no longer enjoyed access to the village. He longs for water from the old, hometown well. And yet, David's origins lie in a Jerusalemite dependency — a village that could not have engaged in any sort of exchange or even existed without the consent of the Jebusite center. And this dependency is also associated with a Philistine presence at some time early in David's career.

Altogether, David bears a name without a basis in Israelite nomenclature. His father is of indeterminate origin, and opponents invoke the father's name when heaping scorn on David. His genealogy is suspect. The status of his ancestral home town is in some doubt. In fact, even the text of 1 Samuel maintains that he sought refuge for his family in Moab, a tradition that programs the peculiar tradition of Ruth that he had a distant connection to a Moabite ancestor (1 Sam. 22:3-4, A source). One might follow the text: the concealment of the family relates to Saul's persecution, which was followed by a Philistine counterstrike into the region. But this is not to get at the question of why the text presents events in this fashion.

The text concedes that David's family lived for a time in Moab, during his lifetime. It concedes that his family, and his youth, were associated with the Jebusite suburb that housed a Philistine corps. These concessions are in themselves grounds for suspicion that all is not as it seems in the text. And before David's time, there is no evidence of an ethnic affiliation of a "tribe" of Judah to Israel.

Ethnicity is a notoriously complex phenomenon. It is affective in character: what makes one a member of a particular ethnic community is personal identification and acceptance. Still, there is every reason to question whether David's ancestral affiliation was Israelite. Again, there is no basis on which to decide such an issue, or even to develop a hierarchy of probabilities about it. All the same, the indications are that the connections were at best tentative, temporary, fragile, from the start. David's opponents may well have claimed he was a foreigner.

This holds the more because of the effort that the texts put into affiliating David with Israel. In the first instance, there are the late genealogies, which are artificial. In the second, David is chosen by Samuel to succeed Saul (1 Sam. 16:1-14) in a secret ceremony, rather than publicly. Third, David's primary appearance in Saul's court — and his first appearance in the A source — is to enter into contest with the Philistine Goliath.

It is certain that this account is a fabrication. Elhanan son of Dodo is credited with killing Goliath (2 Sam. 21:19). Benaiah is said to have advanced, with a stick only, against a foe armed with a spear like a weaver's beam (2 Sam. 23:20-23), and to have killed that foe with his own weapon — while Goliath mocks David for advancing against him with a staff, despite the fact that David's real weapon was a deadly sling. And it is Elazar son of Dodo who fought the Philistines — and rescued David from danger — at Epes Dammim, the site of the battle in the Goliath account (2 Sam. 23:9-10; 1 Chr. 11:13). As noted above (Chapters 1, 6), the Goliath story displaces to David, in both the A and the B sources, the accomplishments of his warriors in other contexts.

Yet this means that the two sources were at special pains to establish David's credentials as a slayer of Philistines, as a contributor to Saul's campaigns to liberate Israel from the Philistine threat. It is in light of this apologetic agenda that one must evaluate the claims about his youth.

Chart of the A and B Source
in 1 Samuel 8–2 Samuel 1

CHAPTER	A	B
8		Israelites demand kingship.
9:1–10:13	Samuel anoints Saul to fight Philistines. Jonathan takes Gibeah.	
10:14-16		[Redactor]
10:17-27		Saul chosen king by lot
11-12		Saul defeats Ammon, is confirmed at Gilgal.
13-14	Saul is rejected by Yahweh. Saul, Jonathan defeat Philistines Summary of Saul's victories	
15		Saul defeats Amaleq, is rejected by Yahweh.
16		David is elected by Yahweh, and introduced as singer to Saul's court.
17*	Goliath story, David is first introduced to Saul's army.	Goliath story
18:1-5**	David befriends Jonathan, succeeds at war.	
18:6-13		Women greet David's return with song, making Saul watchful. Saul hurls javelin at him; David escapes.

		Fearful at David's escape, Saul makes him a field commander.
18:14-19	Saul is fearful at David's success in the field and popularity. Saul offers David Merab, so that Philistines might kill him, but gives her to Adriel from Meholah.	
18:20–19:7		Saul offers David Michal for 100 Philistine foreskins, which David delivers. David fights Philistines. Saul instructs his men to kill David, but Jonathan tells David to hide, then defends David to Saul. Saul promises David will be safe, so Jonathan brings him back to court.
19:8-10	David fights Philistines. Saul hurls javelin at him; David escapes, flees court.	
19:11-24		Saul sends agents to arrest David. Michal helps David escape by lowering him from window, using teraphim and a goatskin to pretend he is still in his bed. David flees to refuge with Samuel. Saul sends agents to fetch him, unsuccessfully.
20	Abetted by Jonathan, who ferrets out Saul's intention to kill him, David hides, then flees Saul's court.	
21	David gains assistance at Nob, flees to Achish of Gath, but fears for his life and feigns madness.	
22	Saul and Doeg execute all but one of the priests of Nob. Abiathar flees to David.	
23:1-18	With oracle from Abiathar, David rescues Qeilah from Philistines, and on same authority, abandons it for fear of being betrayed to Saul. Saul pursues David. Jonathan comes and makes contract with David, recognizing David will be king of Israel.	
23:19-29	Ziphites inform on David. Saul pursues him, David escapes, as Saul must fight Philistines.	
24	Saul learns David is near Ein Gedi, comes, falls unbeknownst into Da-	

vid's power. Subordinates urge David
to kill Saul, but David refuses.

25		Samuel dies. David protects Nabal's sheep, near Carmel, takes Abigail, Nabal's wife.
26		Ziphites inform on David. Saul comes, falls unbeknownst into David's power. Subordinates urge David to kill Saul, but David refuses.
27		David joins Achish of Gath, raids pastoralists including Amaleq from base in Ziklag, tells Achish he is raiding Judah.
28:1-2		Philistines gather for war, with David as the bodyguard of Achish.
28:3-25	Samuel has died. Saul has suppressed necromancy. With Philistines camped at Shunem, Saul on Mount Gilboa, Saul consults witch of Ein-Dor, who summons Samuel. Samuel predicts Saul's death.	
29		Philistines gather at Apheq for war. The other kings refuse to have David with them, so Achish reluctantly sends him home. Philistines march to Jezreel.
30		David arrives at Ziklag, finds it has been raided. He pursues Amaleqites with oracular help from Abiathar, recovers captives, sends spoil around Judah.
31	Philistines defeat Israel, Saul begs aide to kill him, is refused, falls on sword. His corpse is sent to Beth Shan, where men of Jabesh rescue it for cremation.	
2 Sam 1		Amaleqite brings Saul's regalia to David at Ziklag, explains he killed Saul at latter's request. David kills Amaleqite, mourns Saul. David later learns men of Jabesh interred Saul.

*The division of verses in ch. 17 is uncertain, but it is clear that both A and B had some version of the Goliath story in them.
**Alternative divisions of the verses in chs. 18–19 are distinctly possible, although I believe this to be the best of the options. There is some redactional activity in these chapters.

CHAPTER 16

David and Saul

A. In Saul's Court

1 Sam. 16 introduces David as Yahweh's choice to succeed Saul. In this account, from the B source, Samuel has rejected Saul's dynasty. The narrative then takes David to Saul's court, as a musician whose skills soothe the dybbuks bedeviling Saul. The A source, conversely, introduces David into Saul's court as the son of Jesse responsible for supplying his three elder brothers; this introduction, naming David's antecedents because he has no previous introduction in the source, comes in 1 Sam. 17:12 and is the text that refers to him as an Ephrathite.

In both sources, David rises in the ranks of the court in the aftermath of his triumph over Goliath. He betroths one of Saul's daughters in each. 2 Sam. 3 continues the B strand with a story of Michal's later delivery to David from her former husband, and her subsequent sequestration and childlessness. In both sources, Saul attempts to kill David. And in both, what angers Saul in particular is a ditty, "Saul has smitten his thousands, and David his myriads."

The tradition makes David Jonathan's weapon-bearer and bosom friend. In the A source, Jonathan (and later, Saul) actually recognizes the legitimacy of David's claim on the succession — a sure sign that the literature stems from the Jerusalem court. This relationship is reinforced by David's lament over Saul and Jonathan, whose love he accounts dearer than that of women.

David preserves Jonathan's son Mephibaal when killing the rest of Saul's house. This fact is subpoenaed to support the claim that he was personally allied with Jonathan. All this reinforces the claim that David was associated with

Saul's court. Likewise, when most of Samuel was written, it would have been politic to inflate David's reputation as Saul's ally and a killer of Philistines.

The concern to assert David's credentials arises from several concerns. First, David was known to have eradicated almost the entire House of Saul, and perhaps even the majority of Saul's extended family and its relations, his clan section. One of the accusations made against him was that he colluded with the Philistines in their conflict with Saul — as we have seen, other traditions, providing David with an alibi, however flimsy, for the time of the battle of Jezreel, react against just such accusations. Second, most urgently, it was desirable to veil or to finesse the reality that David was for a critical period a Philistine vassal. The A source denies this altogether. The B source concedes it (1 Sam. 27–28:2; 29–30; 2 Sam. 1). But B affirms that it was Saul's persecution, and the collaboration of the population of Judah with him, that drove David into Achish's bosom. David calls to Saul from afar:

> Why is it that my lord should chase after his servant? For what have I done, and what wickedness is in my hand? And now, may my lord, the king, please attend to the words of his servant: if it is Yahweh who incited you against me, he will (or: 'let him') savor an offering; but if it is humans, accursed be they before Yahweh, for they have expelled me this day from attaching myself to Yahweh's lot, saying, "Go! Serve other gods!" (1 Sam. 26:18-19)

The A source adopts the same explanation for David's flight to Achish. It is because Saul tried to kill David in the royal court that David sought refuge, unsuccessfully in A, in Gath.

The third reason it was urgent for the apology in Samuel to establish David's credentials as a Philistine-fighter is that he not only started out as a Philistine agent, he remained their ally throughout his reign. At the end of his reign, the border with Philistia remained on the outskirts of Gezer, where it was in 2 Sam. 5. There was no conflict with Philistine city-states after his installation in Jerusalem. At the outset of Solomon's reign, Achish of Gath remained an ally, willing to extradite Shimei's slaves. The first sign of change came only a little later in Solomon's reign, when, as a dowry for his daughter, the pharaoh — probably Siamun, but in any case a king of the 21st Dynasty — conquered Gezer and transferred it to Israel. As Gezer lies to the north of the major Philistine cities, the implication is that Egypt conquered all of Philistia, but neutralized Israel by promising a marriage alliance, or what passed for one, and a minor territorial concession. Solomon changed David's policy, to embrace the pharaoh (see Chapter 18).

For all these reasons, and perhaps because there were questions about his Israelite ethnicity,[1] David was vulnerable to the accusation that he reversed Saul's policy of confronting the Philistines. In fact, that is just what he did. It rendered his loyalties suspect.

The account of David's time at the court therefore stresses both his relationship with Jonathan and his killing of Philistines (in the A source, 1 Sam. 18:1-5). Yet it must also stress Saul's jealousy, as in 1 Sam. 18:6-10, where women "from all the towns of Israel" greet the return of the army (in the B source, originally from the battle in which Goliath died) with song:

Saul has smitten his thousands,
And David his myriads.

The ditty works on Saul's insecurity, so that he hates David thereafter. In the combined text of the A and B sources, the episode follows on David's investiture by Jonathan and success in Saul's army. In B, it leads Saul to hurl a spear at David (18:10-11). The parallel in the A source has Saul hurl the spear on learning of a victory by David over the Philistines (1 Sam. 19:8-10). In 1 Sam. 18:11-16, Saul assigns David away from the court in order to be rid of him, only to find him the most successful of Israelite generals.

As noted, both sources claim that David was betrothed to one of Saul's daughters. The A source links him to Saul's daughter Merab in 1 Sam. 18:17-19. Saul, surprisingly, offers Merab in order to induce David to "fight the wars of Yahweh against the Philistines." Saul's logic is surprising because David's job was to fight Philistines. He hopes that the Philistines will kill David for him. Oddly, the text almost consciously casts on Saul the suspicions no doubt voiced about David's use of foreign surrogates to kill his own opponents from Saul's house. Saul, however, voids the marital arrangement and gives Merab to Adriel son of Barzillai from Meholah.

The B source reports David's betrothal to Michal (1 Sam. 18:20-24). In this source, David must furnish a hundred foreskins of the Philistines — "the uncircumcised" — as his bride-price. This is the episode in which Heller's David figures out it is easier to kill Philistines before circumcising them. David provides double Saul's price. Again, he is a fearsome enemy to the Philistines.

As in the A source, Saul asks for the bride-price in order to endanger David. The latter's success in this endeavor, too, gives Saul reason to fear David's charisma (1 Sam. 18:25-30). It is actually in David's marital bed with Michal that Saul last attempts to have him arrested for assassination (B: 1 Sam. 19:11-17).

1. See Chapters 15-21.

This part of the account stresses that David fought the Philistines, who would kill Saul and Jonathan, and that David served Jonathan. In the B source, Jonathan deflects Saul, temporarily, from killing David (1 Sam. 19:1-7). In the parallel A-source story (1 Sam. 20), Jonathan counsels David to desert Saul. Both Jonathan and Saul as much as acknowledge that David will be the future king. Jonathan makes a special covenant between his descendants and David's.

Jonathan and David are most intimate in the A source — the source more sympathetic to Saul. The B source, however, also depicts them as close comrades. This "tradition" was a powerful argument against claims that David conducted a vendetta with the house of Saul. Likewise, David's preservation of Jonathan's son Mephibaal may have been calculated. Indeed, it may be from the maintenance of Mephibaal that the authors of 1 Samuel (A and B) inferred that David enjoyed a special relationship with Jonathan. In other words, that relationship is probably invented or inferred, not recollected.

Claims that David fought the Philistines are also plainly self-serving. And, precisely because Achish *did* receive David into his court — despite the protestations of the A source — nothing suggests that the Philistines ever regarded him as a mortal foe. Even if David once served under Saul, this point is important for two reasons. First, again, his relationship with the Philistines — he tolerated them as well as being tolerated by them — is what evokes all of these stories in the apology. Second, David did not practice a politics of nativism, as did Saul and his supporters. The apology presupposes that nativism appeals to much of Solomon's constituency. Not for nothing do the texts, including the antique poetry of 2 Sam. 1, David's Lament over Saul and Jonathan, refer to the Philistines as "the uncircumcised."

It is in the interest of the apology to claim that David served at Saul's court. But none of the notices relating his men's deeds (2 Sam 21:15-22; 23:8ff.) suggests that he did. And no source claims he had followers from Saul's court, from his desertion forward.

Once we discount the traditions linking David to Jonathan, and those alleging that he killed and circumcised Philistines, his sole connection to Saul's court is his engagement to Saul's daughter. A and B differ on the identity of this daughter.[2] And, as we have seen,[3] David's alibi in 2 Sam. 4 bases itself on the allegation that Saul's daughter was his betrothed. When Ishbaal sent Abner with Michal to David, the occasion was a diplomatic marriage, involving the king's

---

2. And the Masoretic (Hebrew) text of 2 Sam. 21:8 relates that Michal bore sons to the husband identified with Merab in 1 Sam. 18:19. Michal here is, however, a copyist's error for Merab. See P. Kyle McCarter, Jr., *II Samuel,* 439. Cf. 1 Sam. 25:44.

3. See Chapter 4, on David's alibis.

sister, rather than daughter. The apology converts this into a confession, on Ishbaal's part, that David *deserved* Saul's daughter.

The whole presentation is factitious. The books of Samuel betray an anxiety to associate David with Saul's court. David's betrothal to Saul's daughter can be understood in the same light. In other words, regardless how David laid hands on Michal, it would suit the purpose of the author to insist that the betrothal took place while he was at Saul's court, because that claim shows that he was Saul's lieutenant.

The tradition of the betrothal is the strongest evidence of an affiliation between David and Saul. It is seconded by the Lament over Saul in 2 Sam. 1. The latter, again, is part of David's alibi for Saul's death. Is its attestation of contact between David and Jonathan reliable?

> It grieves me about you,
> My brother, Jonathan,
> You were so pleasing to me,
> Your love, for me, was more wondrous
> Than the love of women.
>
> (2 Sam. 1:26)

Or is it merely part of the apology, tying David to his main enemy, Saul? Whether David, the singer, is speaking of himself as Jonathan's (figurative) "brother" or posturing as a representative Israelite "comrade" is a question. Suffice it to say that we cannot rely on the view that David was Saul's courtier.

B. The Wilderness Years

In the B source, David flees from Saul to Samuel, who anointed him in 1 Sam. 16. The prophet shelters him (1 Sam. 19:18-24). But Samuel's death propels David southward (1 Sam. 25:1), into the wilderness of eastern Judah, on the authentic periphery of Israelite settlement and activity in the 11th and 10th centuries. There, David plies the "protection" racket and demands premiums from Nabal of Carmel for his vigilance with Nabal's shepherds and flocks. This is where he acquires Abigail, his second wife, who shares the name of his own sister. The first is Ahinoam, from Jezreel — who shares the name of Saul's first wife, Jonathan's mother.

In the A source, in 1 Sam. 21–22, the route is a little more circuitous. David begins by fleeing to Nob. There, a priest descended from Eli, Ahimelek, son of Ahitub, fits him out with food and Goliath's sword. Then comes David's failed defection to Achish, king of Gath. From Gath, David flees to his hold at the nearby "cave of Adullam," probably in the Shephelah near Gath, gathers a private army of desperadoes, and commits his parents to the care of a Moabite king residing in Mizpeh.[4] He returns to Judah on the advice of "Gad the prophet" and "rescues" the town of Qeilah, also in the Shephelah near Gath, from "the Philistines," as is related later.

Meanwhile, on David's escape, Saul rebukes his *Benjaminite* retainers, including his son, for conspiring against him with "the son of Jesse."[5] An Edomite named Doeg denounces Ahimelek, priest of Nob, for abetting the fugitive, so Saul summons Ahimelek "and all the house of his father, the priests that were in Nob." Though these assisted the outlaw in ignorance (which reflects poorly on their divination), Saul orders the priests slain. His retainers balk, and Doeg executes the slaughter. The sole survivor, Abiathar son of Ahimelek, flees to David at Qeilah.

This account has interesting features. The king of Moab assists David. Saul kills "the priests that were in Nob," a town that appears otherwise only in the appendices of 2 Samuel, as a locus of David's conflicts with Philistines. The killing there impels a survivor, Abiathar, who afterward serves as his oracular specialist, into David's bosom.[6] Abiathar stemmed from the line traced to Eli at Shiloh, where the ark was originally housed.[7] Further, it is an Edomite who kills the priests of Nob, and it is against Edom that David's most radical campaigns were directed.[8] The agenda is sufficiently clear: Saul massacred priests. Moab deserved clemency, and was later barely attacked. Edomites, on Judah's southern fringe, were villains.

The A source, in 1 Sam. 23, relates that David attacked "Philistines." He does so at Qeilah, a dependency of Jerusalem in the Amarna letters of the Late Bronze Age. This sole independent attack on the Philistines — only in the source that denies his affiliation with Gath — leaves David in a town in the hills above Gath. There he was joined by the only descendant of Eli, priest of Shiloh, whom Saul was unable to kill.

---

4. 1 Sam. 22. Mizpeh of Moab is not a royal town in later centuries, so its invocation here is again an index of an early date for Samuel.

5. 1 Sam. 22:6-8. Note the continuity especially with the A source in 1 Sam. 17:57–18:5, where Jonathan becomes David's partisan, and Saul's retainers look on David with favor.

6. 1 Sam. 23:6, 9; 30:7. Further, David's first oracles come in 1 Sam. 23:2-3, 4, a parallel to 2 Sam. 5:19, 23 — and probably calqued from that source. Abiathar gives him this capacity in A. Otherwise, Abiathar appears with Zadok, who seems to appear roughly at the time of the Absalom revolt — Zadoq is a creature of David's reign.

7. 1 Kgs. 2:26-27.

8. See above, Chapter 10B; 2 Sam. 8:14; 1 Kgs. 11:14-16.

Anticipating an attack by Saul, David flees to the steppe above the Dead Sea, as in the B source just after Samuel's death. This puts him in position for his final confrontation with Saul, though the A source adds a visit by Jonathan, in which Jonathan again acknowledges explicitly that David will be king.[9] The inhabitants of Ziph, in the Judean wilderness, betray David's whereabouts to Saul, and the latter gives chase. The same betrayal and pursuit appear in the B source in 1 Sam. 26. In both sources, David gains power over Saul, but declines to injure "the anointed of Yahweh." Saul, assured of David's good will, desists from pursuing him.

At this point, the A source turns to Saul's final confrontation with the Philistines. The B source now sends David to Gath, where he becomes the vassal of Achish, the king of that city-state. So the question arises, what is the nature of David's time "in the wilderness"? Did Saul in fact pursue him? Was he in fact betrayed by the people of Qeilah (A source) and Ziph (both sources)?

There are different ways to reconstruct this period in David's life. If one were to accept the allegations of the A and B sources, or if one were writing a novel, one might proceed as follows: Saul acquired Ahinoam from the Jezreel located in Judah in the 7th century. She was the relative of Nabal, a chieftain from the clan of Caleb, resident in Carmel. Nabal himself had wed Abigail, the daughter of Jesse, from Bethlehem, David's sister. After a victory over Amaleq, Saul visited Carmel, to erect a stela there. David was also present, visiting his sister, perhaps at the time of her marriage. During the festivities, David became Ahinoam's protege, and she furnished his route to the court, and to promotion. But as soon as he became engaged to one of Saul's daughters, his benefactrix precipitated his expulsion by Saul. She then arranged for his escape, and for her own with him.

But assume that the reports of David's relationship to Saul are false. Then in the B source, the wilderness experience explains why David was with the Philistines at the time of Saul's death. In the A source, it bridges the period between his expulsion from the court and his rejection by the Philistines, and Saul's death. In both cases, the texts explain how Saul persecuted David: thus, they invert the claims, contemporary with David, that David eradicated the house of Saul. In addition, the traditions place David as an independent force in the hill country of Judah before his rise to kingship in Hebron. The A source claims that he attacked the Philistines and evaded Saul. The B source claims only that he evaded Saul, and is probably the earlier account.

David, in sum, was a bandit, in both sources, before Saul's death. He led a gang of cutthroats in the sparsely-inhabited hill country and steppe of Judah.

9. 1 Sam. 23:16-18.

This tradition must have arisen no later than the 9th century, for no denizen of the much more densely settled 8th- or 7th-century countryside of Judah would imagine such successful freebooting there.[10] But in neither the A source nor the B source did David inaugurate the vendetta between two dynasties. It was Saul who according to them took the first step.

C. A Foreign Affair

And yet, coming from sources anxious to put the best face on David's career, this may be a charitable picture. The B source concedes that David was the captain of Ziklag, the head of the royal guard of Achish, king of Gath. Achish probably remained active in Solomon's reign. Moreover, a later king of Ekron, another Philistine center, assumes the same name in the 7th century, a time when the adoption of archaic names and customs was particularly rife.[11] The name is Greek: Achaios, meaning Achaean, the name for Greek ethnics in the Late Bronze Age and in Homer.[12] The information about Achish, thus, seems to reflect a time contemporary with David, or with David and Solomon.

The claim of 1 Sam. 27 is that David remained among the Philistines for 16 months. During this time David told Achish that he attacked "the south of Judah, and of the Jerahmeelite and of the Qenite." The latter two groups were on friendly terms with Israel. In fact, says the text, David attacked Geshurites, Gerizzites, and Amaleqites, all in the Negev on the border of Egypt. He left no survivors, so his overlord could not know that he was acting as a partisan of Israel.

This is the dynasty's story. It simultaneously denies that David attacked Judah and that he really, rather than ostensibly, worked for the Philistines. Yet the B source installs David as the head of Achish's bodyguard (1 Sam. 28:2). David arrives at Gath with two wives, Ahinoam the Jezreelitess and Abigail, "the wife of Nabal, the Carmelitess" (1 Sam. 27:3). It is at this juncture, says the text, that Saul ceased chasing him. In effect, this is David's first historical, as distinct from

---

10. This point on dating the origins of the A and B sources stems from Israel Finkelstein, in conversation.

11. On Achish of Ekron, see Seymour Gitin, Trude Dothan, and Joseph Naveh, *IEJ* 47 (1997): 1-16; on archaism in the 7th century, including the adoption of archaic names, Baruch Halpern, "'Sybil, or the Two Nations,'"; Achish, son of Ma'ok, in 1 Sam. 27:2. Note that in the West, the archaizing throne names are consistently of 10th-century figures: Jeroboam II, Hiram II, Rezin II, Achish. This is a function of the 10th-century date of state formation in the region.

12. Joseph Naveh, *BASOR* 310 (1998): 35-37.

literary, appearance. It is certain that he served Achish, because even the B source, which concedes the fact, is at pains to explain it away.

It is possible that David served at Saul's court. That he led a gang for hire is even probable. Moreover, only two women in the Bible bear the name Ahinoam. Saul's chief wife is one, and David's first wife is the other. Was David's first wife Saul's wife first? This pattern repeats itself: only two Abigails appear in the Bible, one of whom is David's sister, the other David's second wife. However, from the coincidence of Ahinoams — and David's Ahinoam is from Jezreel, the site of Saul's final battle — one might infer that David enjoyed relations with Saul before his time in Ziklag. Indeed, Nathan's remark in 2 Sam. 12:8 that Yahweh had given David his "overlord's women" could be construed to confirm that Ahinoam was taken from Saul in addition to Michal.[13] This would, however, be a misconstruction: nowhere does Samuel mean to imply that David's relations with Saul were less than correct: David's propriety, in relation to Saul, is of the essence to the apology.

Two points deserve consideration here. First, the presentation in 1 Samuel does not necessarily correspond to the real time sequence, such that David's first wife in Samuel may be the first wife for the purposes of the presentation only, and may in fact have been acquired after his time with the Philistines. Second, if there was in fact contact between Saul and David, such that David somehow made off with Saul's wife, the abduction could have coincided with Saul's death: the "abduction" is not, after all, reported as such. Placing it historically thus becomes impossible, and speculation about its historical place is a matter of midrashic interpretation. Further, Ishbaal inherited his father's establishment. David probably came into possession of Ishbaal's harem on the latter's demise — Nathan says, "I gave you the house of your overlord and the women of your overlord," referring to the appropriation. So Ahinoam is probably Saul's wife or descendant. David took her later than is usually assumed.

What is certain is that David's opponents accused him of taking the side of the Philistines. They probably claimed he *was* a Philistine, or other alien, himself. He came from a town, dependent for its trade on the Jebusites, which served as a "Philistine" base. He did military service for Philistines. His service so satisfied them that he earned command of his own town and the position of royal bodyguard. He was implicated in the battle of Jezreel — the one place where the books of Samuel, uncharacteristically, treat the Philistines not as a monolithic entity, but as a set of differing city-states. (The reality must have been far closer to the historical situation of Canaan in the Late Bronze Age and Iron II, with city-states in constant renegotiation of their alliances.) David

13. So Jon D. Levenson and Baruch Halpern, *JBL* 99 (1980): 507-18.

came to Judah and ultimately Jerusalem with a contingent of 600 Philistines, from Gath. Then there is the question of the icon that he brought into his capital: the "ark of the covenant of Yahweh."

The ark is the icon that Samuel and then Kings associate with the temple. These books trace it to Shiloh. It is lost on the battlefield in 1 Sam. 4. Later materials project the ark into the period of the Exodus, so that readers think of it as an authentic Israelite artifact, imbued with a hoary pedigree. It merits consideration, however, just where the ark really stems from.

In the story of the loss of the ark, Eli's sons Hophni and Phinehas (Pinchas) carry the icon from Shiloh to a battlefield at Ebenezer. Scholars have connected Eli's family with that of Moses.[14] But the arguments for this connection hang on the dynastic apology in Samuel. Furthermore, the image of Moses in biblical literature stems entirely from the royal court and the temple it constructed and operated in Jerusalem. Our information about Eli's genealogy comes almost entirely from the Priestly source in the Pentateuch, written ca. 600,[15] and from Chronicles, the first edition of which was written in the late 6th century. From Samuel, from the documentation rooted in the 10th century, indications of the family's heritage are indirect.

In the story of the battle of "Ebenezer," the Philistines encamp at Apheq. After they score an initial victory, Hophni and Phinehas bring the ark from Shiloh. When, in the following encounter, the Philistines capture the ark, killing Eli's sons, they take the icon to the temple of Dagon in Ashdod.

The story of the ark's sojourn in Ashdod in 1 Sam. 5 is amusing. First, the Ashdodites install the ark by the statue of Dagon. In the morning, they find Dagon's statue pitched forward on its face, as though doing obeisance before the ark. Dagon's head and hands are broken off, foreshadowing the dismemberment of Saul, Ishbaal, and Ishbaal's assassins.[16] Thereafter the Ashdodites suffer

14. For the most impressive treatment, see Frank Moore Cross, *Canaanite Myth and Hebrew Epic*, 195-215. It is clear that Eli's house has nothing to do with that of "Aaron" and Zadoq in Jerusalem.

15. The grounds for this idiosyncratic view remain to be defended outside of the classroom, but depend on relationships among P, D, the Deuteronomistic History and Jeremiah and Ezekiel. An important start is the work of Richard E. Friedman, *The Exile and Biblical Narrative*.

16. 1 Sam. 5:1-5. One of the peculiarities of the account is that it speaks of the statue as "Dagon" himself. Conversely, the ark is "the ark of Yahweh," not "Yahweh." This is not a practice of the 7th century, to be sure, and is probably not even witnessed in Israelite literature in the 8th century, when the conscious distinction was introduced between icons and the gods they represent. Note also the emphasis on the temple doorsill, an important element in Mesopotamian temples, and perhaps Israelite.

from "carbuncles" or some such affliction, sometimes fatal, which they attribute to Yahweh. So they send the ark to Gath, which contracts the same affliction. Then it is Eqron's turn, and the same fate ensues there. The resonance is with the story of the plagues in Egypt: this is explicit in one text.

> Why should you harden your heart as the Egyptians and Pharaoh hardened their heart? (1 Sam. 6:6)

The Philistine towns were plagued, and commentators sometimes claim that the disease was the bubonic plague.

All in all, the ark stayed seven months in the Philistine plain. To end the plague, the Philistines sent it back, from Eqron, with five gold "carbuncles" representing the Philistine city-states — Gaza, Ashkelon, Ashdod, Eqron, and Gath — and a gold mouse for each Philistine settlement. Their diviners hitched the ark to a cow-drawn cart, and stipulated that if they took it to Beth-Shemesh, it would be a sign that Yahweh had indeed visited the plague on Philistia. The cows went straight to Beth-Shemesh, a town sitting just above Eqron on the edge of the Judean hills.

Here, 1 Sam. 6 reports, local Levites took the ark down from the cart and offered sacrifice. The lords of the five Philistine towns, who had followed the cart, then returned to Eqron, in the plain below. Yet in Beth-Shemesh as well, the ark caused a slaughter.

> So they sent messengers to the inhabitants of Qiryath Yearim, saying, "The Philistines have returned the ark of Yahweh. Come down. Take it up to you." And the men of Qiryath Yearim came and took the ark of Yahweh up, and brought it to the house of Abinadab on the hill, and he consecrated Elazar his son to watch over the ark of Yahweh. And from the day of the settlement of the ark in Qiryath Yearim, the years multiplied, and it was twenty years that all the house of Israel longed after Yahweh. . . . (1 Sam. 6:21–7:2)

Thereafter, in 1 Sam. 7:5-14, Samuel wins a battle restoring Israel's border to Ebenezer, the status quo before the loss of the ark.

All this means that, in the record, the ark comes from Philistia. Specifically, it comes from Eqron, to Beth-Shemesh. Beth-Shemesh is a town whose ethnic affiliation was always a question, even in Judah's heyday. Finally, the ark winds up in Qiryath Yearim. This is a city outside of Israel, and the ark plays no part in the narrative of Saul's or Ishbaal's kingship, or David's reign in Hebron.

The ark's absence in Saul's day is significant. Either it was an essential Israelite icon or it was spurned by Saul altogether because it was alien. Since Saul spent a good deal of energy attacking the Gibeonites, and since Qiryath Yearim was a Gibeonite town, it is more than conceivable that the ark was not acknowledged, by the king at the time, as an Israelite artifact. Not coincidentally, Saul also eradicated the priests of Shiloh, to whom Samuel traces the ark, at Nob (in the A source). And this in turn means that the narrative not just of David's own life but of the introduction of the monarchy itself is conditioned by dynastic politics: one of the goals of 1 Sam. 4–6 was to present the ark as a precious pan-Israelite legacy that had slipped from Israel's grasp and was now recovered rather than introduced as a national icon for the first time.

The ark came along with an Egyptianizing cherub iconography that is associated with it from its earliest appearances,[17] and this dovetails with the Egyptian names of Eli's sons. The Jerusalem establishment, especially in Solomon's day, manifests an Egyptianizing conception of the nature of monarchy, common in Late Bronze Age Canaan's city-states and in Iron Age Phoenicia: the creation of a monumental capital city and of a huge temple in the backyard of the royal palace both project an image that apes Egyptian models, though not implying alliance with Egypt. The text does not associate any particular iconography with Saul. However, the Israelites finally liberate themselves from David's kingdom at the death of Solomon. When they do so, their leader, Jeroboam I, adopts an iconography based on the image of a calf. One suspects that this image was more authentically "Israelite" than that of the ark.[18] Indeed, even in polemicizing against it, its opponents concede to it an antiquity equivalent to that of the ark (Exod. 32). Saul, who attacked the Gibeonites and the House of Eli, probably championed the bull as an icon of Yahweh.

On the same score, the ark does not come directly to Jerusalem in David's time. From Qiryath Yearim, David deposits it at the house of Obed Edom. Obed Edom is a Gittite in 2 Sam. 6:10-11, but the founder of a clan of Levites in later texts. Plainly, Obed Edom was bound up with the Gittites of David's retinue. Later, his identity was concealed so that the sympathetic reader of the dynasty's literature no longer identified him with Gath. The presentation presupposes that David had broken with his Philistine overlords. Indeed, it is likely that the identity of the Levites in this era was so fluid as to include those whom the king commissioned as priests: Levi was a guild rather than a tribe, which explains how Barzillai's descendants could become Levites, and how David's own

---

17. 1 Sam. 4:4; 2 Sam. 6:2; and in its description in 1 Kgs. 6; 8:6-7. See Cross, *Canaanite Myth and Hebrew Epic,* 69-75, on the ark's affiliation and the competitive icon of the calf.

18. See Amihai Mazar, "The 'Bull Site' — An Iron Age I Open Cult Place," *BASOR* 247 (1982): 27-42, for argument that the bull iconography was indigenous.

sons could be made into priests — an open border-crossing into the realm of the sacred that again reflects an early date for the literature.[19]

Taken together, the stories of the ark's peregrinations in 1 Sam. 4–6 and 2 Sam. 6 make for a classic narrative of the return of a captured god.[20] David was responsible for the ark's repatriation. Was this a repatriation, or was it the invention of a tradition? David's dynasty profited from claiming that his ark was an Israelite icon. Later generations accepted this view. Their acceptance programmed the perspective, regnant now, that David was central to Yahweh's return to Judah. The Chronicler in fact attributes Saul's death in part to his failure to "seek Yahweh." So David's first act as king in Jerusalem is to recover the ark, "for we did not seek it in Saul's time."[21] This exegesis of Samuel is an accurate exposition of its implications. And yet, David reigned ruthlessly, through the imposition of terror. He created, rather than basing himself on, the tribe of Judah. And he used the ark to express his ideology of kingship. A traditional icon, if there was one, was a desideratum. But as David knitted together a coalition of non-Israelites against the Israelites whom he ruled, an icon with appeal to his real allies was particularly necessary.

If, in the end, the ark is identified with Philistine towns, and with towns allied with the Philistines, the question arises, was the ark a Philistine object? It probably was not, but on the other hand, it was not likely a purely Israelite icon either. Its strongest association in the period of David — the period for which we have near-contemporary records — is with the Gibeonites. It resides, thus, in Qiryath Yearim, a Gibeonite town, for 20 years before David retrieves it. Too, a scion of Shiloh's priestly house attends David throughout his reign, while Saul attacks the same establishment.

Related is the story of an Israelite treaty with Gibeon in Josh. 9. This treaty is invoked in 2 Sam. 21, where Saul's attack on the Gibeonites is employed as a reason for David to execute Saul's scions. At the end of the Joshua story, probably inspired by 2 Sam. 21, the Gibeonites become "hewers of wood and drawers of water for the altar of Yahweh."[22] Their affiliation with

19. 2 Sam. 8:18. Such a transition to priesthood could no longer be negotiated in the 7th century, when priesthood was strictly hereditary. Or such a transition could no longer be *reported* in the 7th century. When the priesthood became strictly hereditary is a question that deserves careful study, but is not open to direct examination.

20. See esp. Patrick D. Miller and J. J. M. Roberts, *The Hand of the Lord: A Reassessment of the "Ark Narrative" of 1 Samuel* (Baltimore: Johns Hopkins University Press, 1977).

21. 1 Chr. 10:13-14; 13:3.

22. Josh. 9:21, 23, 27. The quote here is from a passage omitted from the MT by homoioteleuton but attested in the Greek (except Codex Alexandrinus), describing the status of the Gibeonites at the time of the writing of Joshua.

the cult may have survived the exile, if they are identical with the later "Nethinim."

And, as late as the time of Solomon, Yahweh reveals himself in Gibeon:

> The king went to Gibeon, to sacrifice there, for it was the great high place. Solomon would offer a thousand burnt offerings on that altar. At Gibeon, Yahweh appeared to Solomon in a dream of the nighttime. (1 Kgs. 3:4-5)

Thus, Solomon makes his inaugural sacrifice as king at Gibeon, not in Jerusalem. The Chronicler, to rescue Solomon from the sin of sacrifice in the countryside, actually installs the tabernacle on the site.[23] The association of Gibeon with the royal cult *after* the days of David (but before Solomon's temple construction) is remarkable: the transfer of the ark, after all, must be construed as an attempt to create a royal shrine. Yet Gibeon's early sanctity has a further echo in the town's designation as a Levitical city, and in the identification of a "mountain of Yahweh" there.[24] In a sense, then, there is sufficient evidence to hold that the ark was sacred to the Gibeonites, and that David's hold on it, and then adoption of it as a state symbol, was a part of his alliance with Saul's old foes.[25]

David's primary affiliation before 2 Samuel makes him king of Judah is with Gath. His career until that point is shrouded in darkness. If he was ever pursued by Saul in the steppe of eastern Judah — and one should recollect that

23. 1 Kgs. 3:4-5; 1 Chr. 21:29; 2 Chr. 1:3, 13.

24. Gibeon is a Levitic city in Josh. 21:17; it is omitted by haplography in 1 Chr. 6:60(45) (the original, before expansion, reads, as Josh. 21:17: 't gb'wn w't mgršh 't gb' w't mgršh; this was a haplography by homoioarcton just waiting to happen; note that the total in Chronicles for Levitic cities of the Aaronides is larger than the number of cities named by one). The "mountain of Yahweh" at Gibeon appears in 2 Sam. 21:6, reading with the Old Greek. On the text, see McCarter, *II Samuel*. That may be identical with "the hill of God" in 1 Sam. 10:5, which locates a Philistine garrison at the site.

25. One final hint to the same effect is that in the B source, in 1 Sam. 26:6, David has a subordinate identified as Ahimelek "the Hittite." Ahimelek does not appear in the list of David's warriors. However, an Ahimelek is the father of Abiathar, David's oracular priest, the descendant of Eli at Shiloh. Could it be that "Hittite" is an error for "Hivvite" here? For the argument that Yahweh himself, rather than the icon of the ark, was Gibeonite in origin, and that *Saul*, not David, was a Gibeonite, see Karel van der Toorn, *Family Religion in Babylonia, Syria and Israel.* SHANE 7 (Leiden: Brill, 1996), 266-86. The proposition that Saul made Gibeon his capital is attractive (and puts Solomon's inaugural sacrifice there in a conciliatory light), but his or Yahweh's original affiliation with the town seems improbable in light of the treatment here.

this tradition is used to exonerate his betrayal of Israel by his "flight" to Gath —
it is more than likely that David was a Philistine agent at the time.

Samuel maintains that David's theater of activity as a Philistine captain at
Ziklag was in the south, and that his allies were principally concentrated in the
central Negev; there, they included pastoral elements, such as the Qenites (in
the Masoretic Hebrew versions) or Qenizzites (in the Old Greek translation)
and Jerahmeelites. It identifies his opponents as the primordial inhabitants of
the northern Sinai: Geshurites and Amaleqites.[26] As the Judean hills were
largely uninhabited, this is not improbable. But it bears note that the southern,
pastoral elements, whatever their ethnic identification, occupied districts covering the caravan traffic between Philistia and the southeast. Their economic
affiliation must have been largely with the Philistine city-states, just like David's. Their connections to Saul's kingdom, if any, can only have been distant.

All the signs thus point to a long and sincere Davidic commitment to the
Philistines of Gath. This is why the apology repeatedly asserts that he is "the
bone and flesh" of the Israelites, their kin.[27] The converse cry, "What share have
we in David, what ancestral portion in the son of Jesse?" (2 Sam. 20:1; 1 Kgs.
12:16), is precisely the Israelite denial of any kinship.[28] As we shall see, this slo-
gan reflects a consistent contention, not an extraordinary one, of David's opponents (Chapter 17). Indeed, neither on the basis of archaeology nor on that of
textual analysis is there any reason to suppose that any inhabitant of the territory of Judah was identified ethnically with Israel in the central hills, Galilee,
and Transjordan, before David's reign.

26. 1 Sam. 27:8-10; 30:26-31. In the latter text, almost every town mentioned lies in
the Negev or right on its fringe. For the Jerahmeelites, see 1 Chr. 2:9, 25-27, 33, 42. The occurrence of the name Jerahmeel as that of one of Jehoiakim's sons (Jer. 36:26) indicates the
group's kinship affiliation with Judah in the 7th century. On the text, consult P. Kyle
McCarter, *I Samuel*. AB 8 (Garden City: Doubleday, 1980).

27. 2 Sam. 5:1; 19:13-14. For the formulation, see Baruch Halpern, *The Constitution of
the Monarchy*, 229.

28. And so cannot be used in the Absalom revolt. See Abraham Malamat, "Origins of
Statecraft in the Israelite Monarchy," in *BA Reader* 3, ed. Edward F. Campbell and David
Noel Freedman (Garden City: Doubleday, 1970), 170; Giorgio Buccellati, *Cities and Nations of Ancient Syria*. Studi Semitici 26 (Rome: Istituto di Studi del Vicino Oriente, 1967),
100-101.

CHAPTER 17

On the Hot Seat in Hebron

A. From Gath to Hebron

David *was* the vassal of the Philistine king, Achish of Gath. This is an embarrassment to our authors: again, the A source denies the association altogether (1 Sam. 21:10-15[11-16]). B, however, reveals the point of the embarrassment. It alibis David extensively for the battle in which Saul perished. Though driven to the Philistines by Saul's rage, he *was* awarded a town of his own to govern. He *was* in Achish's bodyguard, at the time of the battle of Jezreel, a member of the most elite unit of the city-state's army. He *was* present at Apheq, in the muster of the Philistines for the battle of Jezreel.

But by virtue of the trust Achish placed in him, he was detailed to the rear at Apheq — a claim whose background reflects the station of the older David in the rear of Israel's army, rather than the standard practice in which the king, and especially the royal bodyguard, stationed themselves in the van of the fighting.[1] David was dismissed by the other Philistine kings: they did not trust him to be one of them, the text claims, again asserting his solidarity with the Israelites. The B source concedes, David was away from home at the time of the battle. But he was not at the battle: instead, he was chasing raiders around the south. He killed the messenger of Saul's death, who claimed to have killed the king, which explains how David came into possession of Saul's regalia: he did not receive the crown from the Philistines. Finally, David's lovely lament

---

1. On David's station in the rear of the fighting, see 2 Sam. 21:15-17; 23:11-17; and 18:1-4.

over Saul and Jonathan demonstrates the depth of his partisanship on behalf of Israel.[2]

Like all the apology of Samuel, this one is revealing. David's foes accused him of complicity in Saul's death. Given too David's enlistment in Achish's army, the report of his absence from the battle is extremely implausible. Another factor also implies his participation: he was installed as king not just of Ziklag, but afterward, allegedly, of Judah in Hebron, and was awarded Saul's royal insignia.

Just when David, the fugitive from Saul, became king in Hebron (2 Sam. 2:2-4) is disputed. The text assigns him seven years in Hebron, while Ishbaal reigns only two, and David takes Jerusalem just after his conflict with Saul's successor. Some critics posit an interregnum between Saul and Ishbaal. But according to the text (2 Sam. 2:5-9), Abner crowned Ishbaal at Mahanaim after David began electioneering for allies in Transjordan, in the vicinity of Mahanaim; implicitly, Abner's purpose was to forestall declarations for David in Gilead. If David was crowned years earlier, however, Abner's overture to Gilead can only be described as tardy. The text dates David's rise before Ishbaal's. The only reason to hypothesize the interregnum is to deny David competed with Saul during the latter's lifetime. While the impulse to exculpate David is laudable, it does appear misguided.

Other commentators suggest that David became Judah's king five years before Saul's death. Most likely, however, David did not win northern loyalties or transfer his capital to Jerusalem without delay. This explains why the first report of conflict with Philistines comes after David takes Jerusalem. In Hebron, David's kingship was unimpressive, as the poor archaeology of the site in Iron I and the scant settlement of 11th-century Judah suggest. And David continued as a Philistine vassal. There is no break with any Philistines at all until after Jerusalem's conquest. David's takeover at Jerusalem is his declaration of independence. But this is only the picture that the text *intends* to give. If the presentation conceals rather than reflects the reality, one might posit that David claimed sovereignty over Judah for a time before Saul's death, and for a time after Ishbaal's death before the Israelites acceded formally to his *de facto* ascendance over them.

B. Kingship in a Nutshell

David migrates to Hebron on receiving a favorable oracle. He takes with him his wives, Ahinoam and Abigail, "and the men who were with him, each with

---

2. 1 Sam. 27:1–28:2; 29–30; 2 Sam. 1. Above, Chapter 4.

his household" (2 Sam. 2:1-3). This signifies the invasion of the Judean hill country by the Gittite contingent supporting David. "The house of Judah" is born.

The text presents David's kingship in Judah as contractual.

> The men of Judah came and they there anointed David as king over the house of Judah. (2 Sam. 2:4)

The consent of the men of Judah is the legal basis of his kingship. Immediately, David appeals to the men of Jabesh Gilead to recognize his kingship, rather than Ishbaal's succession. After the deaths of Abner and Ishbaal, David will treat with the Israelites — at which time they too anoint him in a contractual acknowledgment of his sovereignty (2 Sam. 5:1-3).

It is a constant of Israelite constitutional theory that kingship is contractual. Thus, 2 Kgs. 11 reports an interruption in the succession. Ahaziah, king of Judah, had been murdered. His wife seized the throne, and the high priest Jehoiada staged a coup to place a child, Joash, on the throne. In order to install Joash, Jehoiada constituted an assembly at the temple, and established a "covenant," or contract, to which the parties were Joash, Yahweh, and the "people."

Jehoiada's covenant warrantied that the people accepted Joash as the successor to Ahaziah (and the replacement for the deposed queen), because the succession required renewed legitimation after an interruption. In fact, "the people of the land" regularly appear to elect kings where there is some irregularity, such as an interregnum or an assassination. Thus, "the people of the land" intervene in the cases of Joash, Josiah, and Jehoahaz, and "all the people of Judah" enthrone Uzziah.[3] The people of Judah are also instrumental in David's restoration to the throne after the Absalom revolt — as an electoral body (2 Sam. 19:41).

But whence the doctrine of a popular legitimation of a king and of his successors — where the successor's legitimacy is in question? In part, the doctrine derives from theories of kingship in early Near Eastern cultures. But such theories pertain principally to city-states, and early Israel was more of a territorial state.[4] Nor is it possible that the doctrine of popular legitimation — found also in Deut. 17:14-20 — is a fiction of the Jerusalem of the postexilic period. That

---

3. Joash: 2 Kgs. 11:14, 18-20; 2 Chr. 23:13, 20-21. Josiah: 2 Kgs. 21:24; 2 Chr. 33:25. Jehoahaz: 2 Kgs. 23:30; 2 Chr. 36:1. Uzziah: 2 Kgs. 14:21; 2 Chr. 26:1. See further Baruch Halpern, *The Constitution of the Monarchy*, 190-94. To the references there indicating that the term means simply the people who occupy Judah (as Ezra 4:4), add KAI 10:10-11.

4. The distinction was established in the key work of Giorgio Buccellati, *Cities and Nations of Ancient Syria*.

city-state had no king, and the thesis that kings must be popularly elected was hardly hatched in their absence, in a state run by priests for a Persian overlord. In the postexilic world, divine election of the temple legitimated the priestly elite, and Persian appointment legitimated the local governors. If not early, there is no period when the doctrine might logically have been introduced. Kings of Judah after David, and kings of Israel after Jeroboam, held control of the organs of governance, in particular the professional army. They had no reason to submit themselves to popular approval. This is why the kings of Israel and Judah, with the exception of Jeroboam II of Israel only, avoided adopting the names of their predecessors throughout the Iron Age. The absence of dynastic names reflects the image of a king as first citizen rather than as a deity.

It is no coincidence that British constitutional theory of the Enlightenment borrows from the biblical notion, and that Thomas Jefferson and his colleagues applied it in the Declaration of Independence. The doctrine of popular imperium is the strategy of a rebel. It must also have been deployed in the northern kingdom of Israel when it seceded from Jerusalem, and figures in the apology of Jeroboam in 1 Kgs. 12. To this source, the Josianic author of the books of Kings attached 1 Kgs. 11, explaining the loss of the north by David's son. At the same time, the text of Kings asserts that the election of kings, in Judah, must always restrict itself to candidates from the dynasty itself.

If the doctrine of popular election is early and conscious, it makes great sense as David's response to Saul's rise to power. This comports with an early date for the books of Samuel, in Solomon's day. Saul's kingdom was compact and ethnic, after all. David's was not, as we shall see. The inference that David's apologists drew was that the "whole" people must consent to be governed. This inclusiveness reflects the politics of state-building.

What we have in Samuel and Kings is a rhetoric — certainly not a reality — of popular ratification of royal sovereignty. Scholars regularly argue that abstract ideas of this sort, without concrete application, are utopian. They regularly date what they construe as utopian to late periods. But this is a strategy of desperation, like sweeping dirt under a carpet — the scholar is hoping no one will actually look. A social doctrine that is impossible at all times is, by definition, impossible at all times.

Analysis of impractical doctrines involves two questions: to what degree would an impractical doctrine have been carried into effect? And, what value did its promulgation have despite its imperfect workability? Thus, many American states long denied the vote to African Americans after their constitutional enfranchisement, and even today the American system of voter registration intentionally excludes constitutionally eligible voters by inconveniencing them, in comparison, say, to the Canadian system of voter enumeration.

Similarly, injunctions against interest-bearing loans in Israelite law are usually regarded as utopian and late. But this ignores the operation of the same principle in certain Muslim cultures today, without the catastrophic consequences that superficial reflection divulges: lenders simply become partners in an enterprise. In societies without such a prohibition, lenders either collect interest or recover their investment by taking possession of collateral. In societies governed by Muslim law, lenders purchase a share of an enterprise, which, in the case of failure, they are entitled to liquidate. In effect, the lender theoretically shares some of the risk of a venture with the borrower. The law is a primitive form of bankruptcy protection for the borrower, and whatever its date was circumvented with ease. Its function is principally rhetorical: it looks like a law protecting the indigent from debt-slavery.

The popular election of kings was not utopian, precisely because it was never more than rhetorical. What is the impact of the rhetoric of kingship by agreement of the governed? It reproduces a mythic pattern common throughout the Near Eastern world. In the Babylonian creation epic, thus, the assembly of the gods is threatened by the mother of the gods, Tiamat, who represents the salt sea. After two champions fail to defeat her, the assembly makes a contract of kingship with the storm-god Marduk. Marduk defeats her, dissects her "like a clam," founding the cosmos on her corpse. And the assembly then confirm his kingship.

This is the pattern evoked in the B source with respect to Saul — he is designated king, by Yahweh, and acclaimed, with some doubters present. Then he defeats the Ammonites, and his kingship is confirmed in Gilgal. A similar pattern appears in the A source: Saul is designated, by Yahweh, and is dispatched to fight the Philistines. However, even as he wins his victory, he forfeits the right to a dynasty. All the same, in the historiography, it is only after his initial victory that his kingship is described (1 Sam. 14:47-52).

Similarly, Yahweh's kingship over Israel, in texts that affirm it, is consistently based on some battle that he fights — either cosmogonic or in the realm of history — by which Israel is succored.[5] In the case of the Exodus, the Israelites accept his suzerainty, on the proviso that he both liberate them from Egypt and furnish them with a national territory. In relating the accomplishment of Exodus and Conquest, thus, Exod. 15, the Song of the Sea, culminates with the cry, "Let Yahweh reign forever and aye!" The victories lead to the celebratory confirmation of his kingship.

In David's case, the apology claims Yahweh designated him in "secret" in his youth, and Judah and Israel made him king in his maturity — the idea of a

---

5. Halpern, *The Constitution of the Monarchy*, chs. 3-4.

youthful designation occurs in Mesopotamia and Egypt on occasion, and is common in biblical texts, though secret designations are rare. Still, the separation between divine designation and public acknowledgment distinguishes David from Saul. Further, the covenant of kingship in Judah does *not* lead in David's case to an inaugural battle against an external enemy.

Yahweh's kingship was covenantal early — Exod. 15, for example, is from a linguistic perspective among the oldest texts in the Hebrew Bible, and almost certainly antedates David. Yet David's covenant of kingship is atypical. Even when he graduates from king of Judah to king of Israel, his inaugural battles are against a minor ethnic community in the hills — the Jebusites — and small bands of Philistines. The contrast is to Marduk fighting Tiamat; Yahweh, either the Sea or Egypt; Saul, Ammon or the Philistine city-states. Nor does the narrative record a popular confirmation of David's kingship, though he is elected in 2 Sam. 2:4 and 5:1-3. Instead, the confirmation comes in the form of an oracle from Yahweh in 2 Sam. 7. In other words, the text uses the model of elective monarchy as it is established in the B source for Saul to imply, without explicitly claiming, David's conformity to the model of popular election *and confirmation*.

Thus, the theory of kingship in Samuel is contractual. This is consonant in particular with the fact that royal literature in the Near East speaks in the first instance to an elite: the elite thought themselves the parties to the relationship with the king. On the other hand, Saul in the B source and, probably, Ishbaal assume the throne in a crossing of the Jordan River. This crossing of the river resonates with the myth of the storm-god dividing the waters, in the Babylonian creation epic. David undergoes no such ritual, until he campaigns for a renewed acceptance by the tribes after Absalom's revolt: then, he too crosses to Gilgal for a coronation. This looks to be a concession to an Israelite tradition of a ritual crossing of the Jordan at the New Year.[6]

But, again, the presentation lays claim to popular election when the evidence for it is otherwise absent. There is no accommodation to the pattern of Saul's and Ishbaal's coronations when David takes the throne in the tiny village of Hebron. There, the "men of Judah" who elected David are most likely the men of his own armed retinue, some of them from Gath. Nor is the pattern of David's dealings with the Israelites such as to suggest that he gained or maintained his royal position except through force and intimidation. So the first and only case where David contracts to be king and is then confirmed (after crossing the Jordan to Gilgal) comes when he has just soundly thrashed his electors in battle, after the Absalom revolt.

6. 1 Sam. 11:14-15; 2 Sam. 2:8-9; 19:15-43(16-44). For the "ritual conquest" involving a crossing to Gilgal, see Frank M. Cross, *Canaanite Myth and Hebrew Epic,* 99-105.

C. David across the River

David's appeal to the men of Jabesh Gilead on Saul's death in 2 Sam. 2 is an excellent example of the apology's method. David, it claims, reached out to the community that Saul had saved from the Ammonites. This same community had repaid their rescue by stealing Saul's corpse from the Philistines and according it cremation (A source) or interment (B). Thus, David can be portrayed as conciliatory toward elements that enjoyed intimate relations with Saul and his dynasty.

The text, however, does not record a response from the Gileadites. Since a positive response would ringingly confirm David's legitimacy, the silence compels us to assume his overture was rejected. What follows is Ishbaal's coronation, over all Israel — Judah is excluded — at Mahanaim, in Gilead. Presumably, Abner led Ishbaal from Mahanaim across the Jordan. In any case, the text presents Ishbaal's enthronement as the measure that prevented David's immediate recognition by Saul's most fervent partisans.

Yet the history of David's reign also indicates just why the Gileadites would have had nothing to do with him. Before the death of Nahash, the king of Ammon who opposed Saul, he was in a treaty relationship with the Ammonites. After the Ammonite campaigns of 2 Sam. 11–12, he enjoyed the support, during the Absalom revolt, of Shobi, the son of Nahash whom he installed on the throne. Yet the Ammonites were the great foes of the Gileadites, at least in the town of Jabesh. The idea that David, friend of Saul's enemy Ammon, could attract the support of Jabesh without intimidation, is preposterous. Rather, the implication of 2 Sam. 2 is that, as the vassal of Gath, he already enjoyed a cooperative relationship with Ammon. His case for Gileadite support rested on the threat he and Ammon posed in Transjordan. This occasioned Abner's strategy of shifting Ishbaal to Mahanaim, guarding the periphery David was menacing.

It was David's policy, as noted above (Chapter 13), to unite with peripheral powers in contact with northern Israel. He forged a marriage alliance with Geshur, and found allies in Tyre, Ammon, Gilead and Philistia, as well as cultivating interstitial non-Israelites, such as the Gibeonites. The scarlet thread of these initiatives was that each partnership posed a potential threat to the north, and the result was Gileadite and Ammonite abetment during the Absalom revolt. In Gilead, David installed his own elite after the subjection of Gilead and condominium with Nahash there (below, Chapter 19). But the fact that Barzillai, his supporter, did not stem from Jabesh, indicates a major change. After Saul's time, Jabesh is never again the focus of administration in Gilead, so it is even possible that David destroyed it, because it is a ritual center beforehand, and a political center in Saul's day.[7]

Barzillai's home was Rogelim, a dependency of Abel Meholah.[8] 1 Sam. 18:19 and 2 Sam. 21:8 relate that one of Barzillai's sons, Adriel, had received Merab, daughter of Saul, in marriage. (2 Sam. 3 indicates that Saul's daughter Michal was "restored" to David from Palti son of Laish.) In 2 Sam. 21, David, by extraditing Saul's children to the Gibeonites, kills Barzillai's grandchildren.[9] What induced Barzillai, after this slaughter, to join David's camp, and support him against the former constituencies of the House of Saul?

Posed in this way, the question would seem to demand an answer such as the following. The eclipse of Jabesh vastly enhanced the status of Abel Meholah in Gilead. In this sense, David's payment to Barzillai dwarfed that of a marriage alliance with Saul's house. David, one presumes, was not the only figure capable of cynical arrangements. Indeed, Saul's alliance with a non-Jabeshite family shows how important Abel Meholah was to the early monarchy, a fact also signaled by its appearance as a defining point of Solomon's Jezreel province (1 Kgs. 4:12). Further, after enjoying Barzillai's support in the Absalom revolt, David took one of Barzillai's sons to the court as his guest, and as a hostage (2 Sam. 19:31-40[32-41]).

David's alliance with Ammon, Geshur in the Golan, and important Israelite elements in Gilead mobilized Transjordan against Israel. In Cisjordan, all signs point to David's remaining an ally, or even vassal, of Achish at Gath during his tenure in Hebron. The text practically admits the fact, which probably means he remained a Philistine ally or vassal even later.

D. David's Philistine Pedigree

Every indication indeed leads to the conclusion that David remained Achish's ally throughout his tenure at Hebron. First, David engaged in warfare against Israel. During Saul's reign, he served the Philistines, perhaps after distinguishing himself as a cutthroat in the south. Throughout Ishbaal's reign, David con-

---

7. Jabesh Gilead, Judg. 21:8-14; 1 Sam. 11; 2 Sam. 2:5-7; further Judg. 11:5-11; 1 Sam. 13:7.

8. 2 Sam. 17:27; 19:32; 21:8.

9. Here, notably, David's behavior violates a rule of Deut. 24:16, according to which children should not be killed for their fathers' sins, nor the reverse. No apologist of the 7th or any later century would have included the account as it is. See Baruch Halpern, "Jerusalem and the Lineages in the Seventh Century B.C.E." (forthcoming).

ducted what the text portrays as a civil war. The continuity alone indicates that he did not divorce himself from Saul's other key enemies, in Philistia.

Second, there is no record of conflict with the Philistines during the period of the "civil war." We should not expect such a report if the Philistines took David's side, as no Near Eastern king's records gives credit to allies for their actions (though some records do enumerate vassals who serve *under* the king). Assistance from the Philistines would also be embarrassing to David and his dynasty. On the other hand, to posit Philistine indifference to a war in their hinterland — especially involving the kingdom of Israel — is a historical no-go. The reality must be the opposite. David's territorial expansion into the hills of Judah was probably a reward for his service in the battle of Jezreel. He was a proxy for the Philistines in their conflict with Israel, and must have benefitted from their activity. This is why Abner tells the elders of Israel that David would rescue them "from the hand of the Philistines" (2 Sam. 3:18): the text simultaneously portrays Saul and Ishbaal as failures at this undertaking and implies, falsely, that David succeeded at it.

The third point has to do with David's success in his conflict with Israel. The lone battle described in Samuel begins at Gibeon — a site favored by David's partisans through to the sacrifice by Solomon. It results in a rout of Israel by David's army. But it is clear from David's success that he was adept in the methods of mountain warfare. This skill was no doubt based on Philistine tactics of the late 11th century.

The development of tactics for deployment in the hill country is important. The Goliath story to an extent reflects a background in such tactics. Thus, the major divisions of ancient armies can be characterized as consisting of ballistic warriors and mobile forces — skirmishers, archers, and slingers; of heavy infantry, the shock troops; and of cavalry, in David's time, principally chariotry. The Tel Dan inscription mentions "horsemen," from Judah or Israel or both in the 9th century. In Samuel's narrative, conversely, set in the 10th century, all the Israelite riding is done on mules, not horses.

The relationship among these divisions has been reviewed above (Chapter 1). The heavy infantry lack mobility, and are vulnerable therefore to ballistic arms. The light infantry enjoy mobility, but are in turn vulnerable to the even more mobile cavalry. And the cavalry run down light infantry, but cannot form up to resist concentrations of heavy infantry. Deployed in the proper coordination, the arms can protect one another. However, in the hills, where cavalry did not operate (David takes no horse from highlanders), the light infantry are at a premium — slingers in particular. As noted, the Athenian invasion of Sicily was abortive because Sparta's allies deployed light infantry against Athenian heavy infantry in the hills.

In the case of the Near East, Assyrian annals are particularly revealing. Assyrian kings speak of how they overcame seemingly insuperable geographical obstacles in launching campaigns abroad. The key to these journeys was the engineering corps of the army, which transported the equipment, and sometimes hewed the roads through mountainous country. However, until the 12th century, these kings never pursue opponents who have taken to the hills: driving an enemy into the mountains is the mark of victory.

In the late 12th century, Tiglath-Pileser I adapted his sapper corps to provide quick passage through mountain terrain. He reorganized his troops to fight on foot in the mountains, probably using techniques developed by the sappers. This enabled him to dog and punish escapees into mountain terrain whom his predecessors were compelled to leave as refugees. Since the chariot arm was useless in these conditions, he was in theory surrendering an advantage. But the fact that on one campaign he carried with him only 30 chariots suggests that he developed an innovative tactical doctrine that differed from that of his predecessors.[10]

A superficial analyst might assume that the introduction of iron tools permitted Tiglath-Pileser to implement this change. But copper and bronze continue to be the metals of choice in Assyria for the heavy work of the sapper corps until well after Tiglath-Pileser, even as late as the 8th century. The real change comes not with the introduction of iron, but with Tiglath-Pileser, who stipulates that his sappers use copper tools and yet repeatedly scales heights to come to blows with his enemies. The presumption is that he adopted and adapted his foes' tactical systems for this terrain.

Tiglath-Pileser introduced a system of maniples, in place of the heavy brigades of earlier kings. He must also have developed tactics for defending his supply lines involving slingers and archers as projectile warriors. Heavy infantry served as the backbone that these soldiers protected. These tactics probably originated with Muršili II, in Hatti. But the organization of the army specifi-

---

10. Wolfram von Soden ("Die Assyrer und der Krieg," *Iraq* 25 [1963]: 137ff.) attributes the change to Asshur-resha-ishi, who allegedly employed iron weaponry to fight opponents in the desert or mountain, in the open or in siege-warfare (summary from *CAH* 2/2: 453). Von Soden evidently ignored the references to copper in the annals. Further, A. T. Olmstead, "Tiglath-Pileser I and His Wars," *JAOS* 37 (1917): 169-85. Cf. Ernst F. Weidner, *Die Inscriften Tukulti-Ninurtas I, und seiner Nachfolger.* AfO Beiheft 12 (Graz: Weidner, 1959), 59:71 = A. Kirk Grayson, *Assyrian and Babylonian Chronicles,* 162-64:1'-13' on his defeat of Nebuchadrezzar I at Zaqqu and Idu with a mixed force of chariots and infantry. (*CAH* also cites E. A. W. Budge and L. W. King, *Annals of the Kings of Assyria* [London: British Museum, 1902] 1:216; it is not clear to me why this is.) See also RIMA 2.A.0.87.1 ii 8-9, and Baruch Halpern, "Settlement of Canaan," *ABD* 5:1120-43.

cally to pursue foes into the mountains indicates reflection on the problem of sustaining, over time, gains that were regularly won on the plain. The systematization of the tactics is a product of the Assyrian mind.

In this light it is no coincidence that in the 11th century we have reports of Philistine garrisons in the hill country, and a subsequent mastering of the appropriate techniques of warfare by David. The spread of mountaineering tactics, which David's alleged disinterest in chariots reflects, made the Assyrian king a subject for epic poetry, spreading his renown beyond the circle of those privy to his inscriptions.[11]

In the Late Bronze Age, pitched battles consistently take place in a valley or on a coast or river plain. The elements most troublesome to Egyptian sovereignty in Canaan are consistently those in the hills. Egypt or its plains vassals stage occasional forays into the uplands against particular towns. But the hills seem to give their denizens a certain confidence to resist Egyptian demands.

In the Iron Age, first the Philistines, and then David, show themselves to be adepts in mountain warfare. The Philistines chased Saul up onto Mount Gilboa. Saul, conversely, was trying to expand onto the plain. While he likely lacked cavalry of any sort, he felt that his combination of light and heavy infantry could face the Philistines down even in the lowlands. Hence, he joined battle at Jezreel, under the shadow of the Lower Galilee. Whatever the nature of his miscalculation, he ended as prey for Philistine light infantry.

Only after David was entrained in the Philistine order of battle was an Israelite army to achieve dominance in plains settings. Curiously, this may mean that David adopted Philistine tactics in the lowlands. As to the hills, the chances are that David learned mountain combat tactics from his lowland masters, and even derived support from them. David's victory over Israel in the "civil war" owed much to his background in Gath and at Jezreel. It also owed much to his following of 600 Gittites led by Ittay. Importantly, Ittay is associated with the hill, Gibeah, in Benjamin, where the A source locates a Philistine garrison at the start of Saul's career.[12] The site itself is sometimes identified with Gibeon. Obed-Edom, David's Gittite ally who hosted the ark, lived between Qiryath-Yearim and Jerusalem as well. Thus, some of David's Gittites may also have been Gibeonites.

In Samuel, David's relocation to Hebron is occasioned by the Amaleqite — not Philistine — destruction of his former home, Ziklag. The text does not say, though it invites the reader to infer, that this event marked David's definitive

---

11. See Victor Hurowitz and Joan Goodnick Westenholz, "LKA 63: A Heroic Poem in Celebration of Tiglath-Pileser I's Muṣru-Qumanu Campaign," *JCS* 42 (1990): 1-49.

12. Ittay, 2 Sam. 15:19-22; 18:2, 5, 12; his affiliation with Gibeah, 2 Sam. 23:29; 1 Chr. 11:31. The garrison at "the hill of God" in Benjamin, 1 Sam. 10:5; 13:3.

break with his Philistine masters. This, again, represents an attempt to lead the reader to a counterfactual conclusion. There is no break with Gath or Achish down to the time of Solomon, though the nature of the relationship between David's kingdom and the Philistine city-states may palpably have altered in the interim.

E. Hebron and the Gibeonites

David, the Philistine factor, is said to have flourished in Hebron. There he begot children: Amnon, his eldest, by Ahinoam from Jezreel, perhaps the wife of Saul; Kilab (or Caleb), by Abigail, former wife of Nabal of Carmel in Judah, and possibly his own half-sister; Absalom, by Maacah, the daughter of Talmay, king of Geshur; Adonijah, by a wife identified only by name, Haggith; and two others. Some of the births may actually have antedated the move to Hebron. If so, the narrator prefers to associate them with a center in the "kingdom" of Judah rather than with "the field of the Philistines": Amnon, Absalom, and Adonijah were, after all, candidates for the succession in Israel. On the other hand, if Ahinoam really was taken from Ishbaal's harem, all the births will have come late in David's Hebron residence.

The actual time of the transition from the residence in Ziklag to that in Hebron is obscure. Perhaps the move followed the civil war between David and Ishbaal. David may even have migrated into Judah before Saul's death.

David did engage Ishbaal's forces, at some length. The story of the conflict at Gibeon, where Joab put Abner's army to rout, deserves credence even though, in the course of the rout, it retails Abner's killing of Asahel, Joab's brother (2 Sam. 2:12-32). This killing explains Joab's motive for murdering Abner, and thus furnishes the basis of David's exculpation in that episode (see Chapter 4). The result of the same battle serves in the narrative to establish that David could protect Judah against Israel's attempt to dominate it.

The location of this confrontation at Gibeon again speaks volumes. It was David's consistent policy to champion the Gibeonites against Saul's nativist persecution. The origin of the alliance between David and the Gibeonites lay in their common collusion with Philistine elements. The Gibeonites, after all, received the ark from the Philistines — possibly as the consideration, the return of their own god, for which they agreed to accept Philistine overlordship. Ittay the Gittite and Obed-Edom the Gittite are associated with the same region. Philistine garrisons are associated with Gibeon (and the hill of God in Benjamin) and its region, just as one is located in Bethlehem (see Chapter 7). And Saul made the Gibeonites the object of fierce assault.

The text also alleges that David's forces made their way from Hebron *past Jerusalem* to fight at Gibeon before David captured Jerusalem. We cannot divine what relations obtained between Gibeon and its associated centers, on the one hand, and Jerusalem, on the other. The story of Josh. 9, in which the Israelites ally with the Gibeonites, relates that the towns were neutralized before Israel's contest with Jerusalem, so that one might infer a traditional opposition between Gibeon and Jerusalem. But the story in Josh. 9 is after all merely the narrative correlative of the treaty relationship invoked by David in order to turn the Saulides over to Gibeon for execution in 2 Sam. 21. How far one should rely on it is a question.

In any case, the Gibeonite towns bestrode the Ayyalon Pass and served David, in the south, as a defilade against probes by Ishbaal.[13] To this arrangement, Jerusalem does not appear to have constituted an obstacle. As the account of the conflict at Gibeon in this sense detracts from the strategic difficulty of David's conquest of Jerusalem, however indirectly, it is likely to represent an authentic recollection.

F. The Civil War

According to 2 Sam. 3:1, the war between David at Hebron and Ishbaal was protracted and characterized by an ongoing derogation of "the house of Saul."

---

13. Gibeon is identified with el-Jib at grid reference 167 139, with settlement in the Iron I and II. Qiryath Yearim, Baalah of Judah, is reasonably solidly identified with Deir el 'Azar, 159 135, although a location further to the east would be preferable. The location of Kefireh is generally assumed to be at Khirbet el-Kefire, 160 137: but Iron I is so poorly represented there that the Benjamin survey of the Israel Antiquities Authority disclosed no Iron I sherds among 243 sherds collected, although an earlier survey did produce some. It is, admittedly, the only Gibeonite settlement first attested in the story in Josh. 9, and could conceivably be mainly an Iron II foundation. However, it was also very likely refounded in the Persian era — Ezra 2:25; Neh. 7:29 — and this period too is barely represented in the survey. For this reason, the identification is weak. Beeroth is normally identified with Khirbet el-Burj, 168 137, but the Benjamin survey turned up little Iron I there, much more Iron II; nor was there much further overburden to explain the poor representation of Iron I. Beeroth was also refounded in the Persian era, but the survey reports no early Persian ceramic there. It is also probable that Beeroth lay farther north, along the Ayyalon Pass and exposed to Saulide raids. Possible is Khirbet Badd Abu Mu'ammar or Khirbet 'Ein el-Keniseh — with the Byzantine overburden effacing most previous periods; or, assuming that the Persian refoundation did not focus on the original town, survey site 166 or 'Ein Umm esh-Sharayit. For the Benjamin survey, see Israel Finkelstein and Itzhak Magen, eds., *Archaeological Survey of the Hill Country of Benjamin* (Jerusalem: Israel Antiquities Authority, 1993).

Yet the succeeding narrative asserts that the essence of David's victory over Ishbaal was the murder of Abner by Joab. The story of Abner's contretemps with Ishbaal is contrived, a function of the apology — which claims that David had nothing to gain, and much to lose, from Abner's death. Indeed, in the story it is *Ishbaal,* not Abner, who strips Saul's daughter, Michal, from her husband, and dispatches her to Hebron. Ishbaal thus colludes in David's legitimation despite knowing — in the story — that he is conniving at his own destruction.

The meeting between Abner and David represented an attempt to cement an alliance by marital diplomacy. This was Ishbaal's strategy for prising David from the arms of his Philistine masters and posing a direct threat to the heartland of the Philistines just beyond the Shephelah — the anticline between the Judean hills and the coastal, Philistine plain. Probably, Ishbaal offered David a partnership, though on condition that David swear fealty to Ishbaal's dynasty in exchange for the preferment of marriage into the royal house.

In consideration for a permanent settlement, Abner and 20 retainers conscripted Ishbaal's sister Michal as David's wife. Abner came to Hebron with David's safe conduct. At the celebratory banquet, however, David's general Joab ambushed Abner, and doubtless his escort. 2 Sam. 3 presents this as Joab's treachery against a man traducing Ishbaal to hand David the kingdom. But in no case in which Joab kills for David (Uriah, Absalom, Amasa) does Joab suffer for his insubordination. In this case, too, Joab remained commander of the army.

Likewise, Samuel alleges that Michal was betrothed to David (1 Sam. 19:11-24) before her marriage to Palti, the Israelite husband from whom Ishbaal strips her. The unconsummated betrothal makes her extradition the grudging settlement of a just claim, avoiding any imputation that it signified alliance. Importantly, David thereafter sequestered Michal: he ruptured her former union, then refused real alliance with Saul's house.

David's ruthless slaughter of the guests at a peace conference sent the signal that his break with Saul's dynasty was unbridgeable, that his war on Israel was implacable. The contest could end only if one or the other party was brought to its knees. But despite the allegations, explicit and implicit, of the narrative, the slaughter of Abner's delegation did not lead inexorably to Israel's embrace of David's sovereignty.

Instead, two non-Israelites, from the Gibeonite town Beeroth, assassinated Ishbaal and rushed his head to Hebron — presenting it to David on a plate. David struck them down, proclaiming his innocence as usual (2 Sam. 4). The assassins had good reason to expect a heartier reception; and David had good reason for silencing them about those expectations. In punishing them with dismemberment, he mimicked the treatment "the Philistines" had accorded

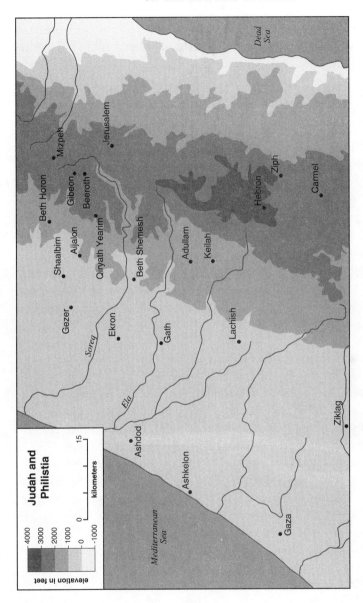

map 17.1

Saul. Contemporaries must have accused him of ordering Abner's and Ishbaal's deaths, and any historian sensible of Near Eastern political culture should incline to agree with them.

G. The Cuckoo in the Nest

It is no coincidence that Ishbaal's assassins were Gibeonites, from the town of Beeroth. Saul, the text states, had expelled the population of that town. Although David avenged the killing — of his enemy and rival — it was not much later that he allowed the Gibeonites the joy of avenging themselves on the House of Saul (2 Sam. 21).

There was no doubt something of a history behind Saul's relations with the Gibeonites. Probably, the latter acted as Philistine proxies limiting Israelite access to the regions south of Benjamin — "the son of the south," the southernmost of Israel's districts (see Chapters 7, 17F). Saul's reaction, or at least his action against them, seems to have reflected a rhetoric of ethnic rather than political opposition. The conflict carried the same sort of charge reflected in the use of "the uncircumcised" as a term of opprobrium for Philistines, with David's attendant circumcision of them. Quite possibly, "Hebrews" in the text is a term of opprobrium for the Israelites. While Saul focused on driving the Gibeonites out of the Ayyalon Pass, David incorporated them into his coalition.

The contrast between Saul and David resembles that between the Middle Assyrian empire-builders, Shalmaneser I and Tukulti-Ninurta I. Shalmaneser's inscriptions record the most barbaric war acts practiced by the Assyrians: he claims in one campaign to have burnt 180 villages and to have blinded all the captives he took from them. Tukulti-Ninurta likens himself to this glorious predecessor in claiming to burn 180 villages in the same region. In this report, Tukulti-Ninurta reports taking twice the number of Shalmaneser's captives. But he does not say that he blinded them.

Tukulti-Ninurta's policy of relative clemency reflects the conscription of the conquered as resources facilitating an advance into new territories. Its orientation is toward imperial construction, not toward the destruction of enemy populations. Such a policy had been adopted by other empires, notably the Egyptian empire in Canaan and the Hittite, and probably Mitannian, states. However, Tukulti-Ninurta seems to have introduced it in Assyria. The transition coincides with a change in the royal titulary, and with the king's construction of an isolated, disembedded capital-acropolis — much along the lines of David's innovations.

In addition, Tukulti-Ninurta instituted the annual presentation of tribute by vassals in his own homeland, in place of the former system requiring regular forays abroad to collect it. He also settled Assyria's dispute with Babylon, pillaging the latter in order to appropriate the trappings of empire. Yet the policy of domination was also one of tolerance. His empire interested itself in generating resources. Canaanites in the Amarna era, in the first half of the 14th century (Late Bronze IIA), exhibit similar concerns: the first premise of warfare in the Amarna period is the capture of population, and sometimes its ransom back to the city-states from which it was taken.

In Saul's day, thus, for the first time since the Late Bronze I, Iron Age Canaan witnessed the warfare of intentional attrition — of the destruction of significant economic assets coveted by local and more distant rulers alike. One can invoke the notion of local strife, of internecine confrontation, to explain any individual catastrophe; but the pattern is one of a form of warfare directed against populations — much as the Song of Deborah and other early Israelite poetry exhibit a marked ethnic xenophobia. It is directed, too, against installations.

Saul's vendetta against the Gibeonite towns north of Jerusalem involved the expulsion of Beeroth's population and apparently an attack on Gibeon itself (2 Sam. 4; 21). David's apologist cites these events, not long after, to explain the assassination of Saul's heir and to justify the eradication of Saul's family. The reports, therefore, reflect an authentic 10th-century perception of the nature of warfare. And this warfare is defined in ethnic terms, as warfare against competing populations. Likewise, David's conquest of Jerusalem, whatever the reality, is understood as a war in which the indigenous population was removed.

Not dissimilar is the report of Nahash of Ammon's activity in Transjordan in the period just before Saul's kingship — one of the Qumran scrolls now adds several verses indicating that Nahash's onslaught began before Saul's designation to be king, as Samuel also says in 1 Sam. 12:12.[14] This text includes the remarkable feature that Nahash made it a condition of Gileadite capitulation that his enemies' right eyes — their shooting eyes — be put out. This imposition is reminiscent of the policy of Shalmaneser I, whose (partial or complete) blinding of Hurrian captives reflects the desire to supplant the realm of Mitanni. It is precisely the sort of imposition that is inconceivable at Amarna, where the concern of the kinglets is much more focused on retaining and augmenting, and thus exploiting, their agrarian and other population than on disabling enemies of whom they have taken control. The tension is ethnic.

At Amarna, yesterday's enemy population is today's economic and military

14. See P. Kyle McCarter, Jr., *I Samuel*, 198.

asset. There is certainly an element of vengeful behavior in the Amarna materials: the king of Byblos, Rib-Addi, once expelled from his town, offers to plunder the temples of Byblos for the pharaoh; and the sons of Lab'aya, a king of Shechem killed in the Jezreel Valley, seek vengeance on the town of Gina, whose population was complicit in their father's death. But this is not a general practice: the Middle Assyrian parallel to Nahash's stance in the narrative reflects the rules of international conflict, not of fights among the vassals of an empire. The archaeological attestation of widespread destruction among Canaanite towns in the Iron I clearly marks off the situation at that time from the situation of the international age of Late Bronze II. The destruction of towns reflects the absence of a stabilizing imperial presence.

The ethnic warfare reflected in Nahash's policy in Gilead, in Saul's assault on the Gibeonites, and in the term "uncircumcised" in Samuel indicates that local leaders exploited nativism as an ideological lever for mobilization. There is such a thing, in this era, as an Israelite identity, and it is no coincidence that the antique poems, the Song of the Sea in Exod. 15 and the Song of Deborah in Judg. 5, bring Israel, "the people of Yahweh," into contrast with enemies identified with "Canaan." Despite the fact that David's apology does speak of Philistines as "the uncircumcised," however — including David's lament over Saul — there is every indication that David reversed the policy of nativism, and in fact allied with all the surrounding non-Israelite communities in order to exert pressure on Israel itself.

Indeed, the list of David's warriors in 2 Sam. 23 lists Joab's weapon-bearers as "Zeleq the Ammonite [and] Nahray the Beerothite." In modern Western categories, one might regard David as an ecumenist. But in Israelite terms, he can only have appeared to be an alien, probably a Gibeonite, or possibly a Philistine with Gibeonite connections (see above, Chapter 16C).

In fact, P. Kyle McCarter, Jr., identifies Elhanan son of Dodo the Bethlehemite, and the killer of Goliath, with the kin-group of Qiryath-Yearim. The Bethlehemite connection to the Gibeonites, and to the Philistines, if it is reliable, would form a tight circle.[15] There are, after all, Philistine garrisons in both Bethlehem and Gibeon. Accused of leading aliens, including Gittites, against Israel, David will not have escaped being tarred as an alien himself. This is the real message of the refrain, "We have no portion in David, nor ancestral lot in the son of Jesse." It denies David's assertion that he is the Israelites' "bone and flesh," their kin. His name, his father's name, his birthplace, his state icon, and his politics all jibe with the Israelites' position.

15. P. Kyle McCarter, Jr., *II Samuel*, 176-77, 449-50. Unfortunately, the text on which the inference is chiefly based, 2 Sam. 21:19, is corrupt.

No matter the fate of Ishbaal's assassins at David's hands, the implication of Gibeonites in the murder can only have confirmed the view that David's vendetta against the dynasty of Saul was an extension of the Philistine war on Israel. But David's policy regarding the Saulides was only beginning to play itself out. He had interred Abner in Hebron, rather than sending the corpse home for burial in the family crypt. He now kept possession of Ishbaal's head, leaving it in the tomb devoted to Abner (2 Sam. 4:12).

David also retained his hold on Saul's daughter Michal and relegated her to a living widowhood. Significantly, the text makes David's retrieval of the ark, and Michal's protest about it, the occasion for her lifelong sequestration (2 Sam. 6:20-23). The text claims that Michal held David's pious zeal in contempt. The historical suggestion is again that Saul's lack of interest in the ark reflected no impiety on his part, but rather a conviction that the object itself was foreign (Chapter 16C). However, Michal's confinement was no doubt planned from the first. David was bent on eradicating, not on allying with, Saul's house. Though there is no evidence that Michal was murdered, she does not appear after this episode.

At the time too, Saul's own corpse, and those of his sons, lay "beneath the [sacred] tamarisk" in Jabesh Gilead.[16] There, they were probably the objects of a local hero cult, commemorating Saul's rescue of the town from Nahash of Ammon. David was not content to leave them there. At some time before the Absalom revolt — and probably not long after he took control of Jerusalem — David discovered by a divine oracle that the only way to end a three-year famine was to appease Yahweh's anger at

> Saul and the dynasty of blood, because he killed the Gibeonites. So the king summoned the Gibeonites, and said to them — for the Gibeonites were not of the children of Israel, but of the remnant of the Amorites, and the children of Israel had sworn (an oath) to them, but Saul had sought to smite them because of his zeal for Israel and Judah — so David said to the Gibeonites, "What can I do for you, and how can I expiate (the wrong)?" in order that they should bless Yahweh's ancestral lot. (2 Sam. 21:1-3)

The Gibeonites, whose compatriots were formerly executed for murdering Ishbaal at David's instigation, demanded seven men whom they would hang "to Yahweh, in Gibeon, on the hill of Yahweh," from among the sons of

---

16. 1 Sam. 31:13; on the tamarisk as a sacred locus, note the one Abraham plants in Beersheba, Gen. 21:33. The A source in 1 Sam. 22:6 also associates Saul with a tamarisk.

the man who eradicated us, who was bent on destroying us from taking our station anywhere in Israel's territory. (2 Sam. 21:5)[17]

David turned over the sons of the concubine Abner had coveted, Rizpah daughter of Ayyah, and the five sons that Merab, Saul's daughter, had borne to Adriel, son of Barzillai, at Meholah. The dissolution of the House of Saul was the logical end of the civil war. And it was at the end of this episode that David repatriated the bones of Saul and his sons from Jabesh Gilead to the tomb of his father Kish in Benjamin (this presupposes continuity with the B source, in which they were not cremated). Whether collecting the bones from Jabesh involved only a menace to the town or the imposition of martial discipline on it is not to be discovered from the sources. However, Barzillai's support of David in the Absalom revolt, despite the execution of five of his grandchildren, suggests that the incident involved major political upheaval in Gilead.

From the general policy of exterminating Saul's descendants, then, David exempted only Jonathan's lame son Mephibaal, whom he detained as a hostage at the court. David assigned a steward, Ziba, to administer Saul's lands and thus support his master (2 Sam. 4:4; 9). After the Absalom revolt, David reassigned half the estate to the steward (2 Sam. 16:1-4; 19:24-30[25-31]). The only other relative to survive the purge was Shimei, who accused David of murdering the entire family (2 Sam. 16:5-10). Shimei was executed in the transition to Solomon's reign.

A final "Saulide," of sorts, was probably David's son by Saul's wife Ahinoam of Jezreel. Amnon, David's firstborn, was assassinated by Absalom. Unlike Joab, Absalom was actually punished for the murder: he spent three years in exile, and two more under house arrest. However, Amnon's death, presented as vengeance for his rape of Absalom's sister, removes the last vestige of Saul's house from a role in the succession. In light of the overall pattern, this is not coincidental — the more so in that the ruse to accomplish the rape is suggested to Amnon, in our narrative, by David's nephew (2 Sam. 13:1-5).

The apology in Samuel presents David's acceptance as king over Israel as the direct sequel to Ishbaal's assassination. Whether or not this reflects a political reality is a question. Certainly, from the time of Ishbaal's death, it was possible for David to allege that he was the successor to the Saulides. Equally, he will have recruited or otherwise dredged up Israelites to support his claim. How-

---

17. "Was bent on" translates Heb. *dimmâ*, "plotted, intended." This is a pun on "the house of blood" ("blood," *dāmîm*), which is in turn an inversion of the accusation leveled against David, "the man of blood," in 2 Sam. 16:8.

ever, any Israelites who went to Hebron to acclaim David king — as 2 Sam. 5:1-3 says they did — must have done so in a state of the greatest nervousness, after what had happened to Abner and Ishbaal.

There are other reasons to doubt the chronological sequence. Before Ishbaal's death, David is no more than a bandit dominating an unsettled hinterland area. His transition to kingship over Israel becomes the occasion in 2 Sam. 5 to maintain that he immediately conquered Jerusalem, earned diplomatic recognition from Hiram of Tyre, fought the Philistines, and then transferred the ark from Qiryath Yearim to his new capital. There is no doubt that all this collapses into a rapid narrative events that took place over a long period of time, some of them after the incidents recorded in succeeding chapters. Thus the apologist, organizing the material thematically, includes a list of sons born to David in Jerusalem: the list includes Solomon, whose actual birth occurs in 2 Sam. 12, near the middle of David's reign in Jerusalem.

Likewise, Hiram remained on the throne in Tyre at the least until Solomon's 24th year, and the Tyrian king-list preserved by Menander of Ephesus attributes to Hiram a reign of 34 years only.[18] In fact, one tradition has it that Solomon's fourth year was Hiram's 12th,[19] so that Hiram will have come to the throne in Tyre only eight years before Solomon's accession, hardly 33 years before it, as the sequence in Samuel implies: he did not recognize David's accession at the start of David's career. Indeed, the Chronicler changes the order of the events in 2 Sam. 5–6 to antedate David's first attempt to bring the ark into Jerusalem ahead of his recognition by Hiram and conflicts with the Philistines.[20]

In the circumstances, it is impossible to ascertain the length of time that elapsed between Ishbaal's death and David's "acclamation" as Israel's king or his taking of Jerusalem. A conservative course would be to take the difference between David's seven-and-a-half-year reign in Hebron and Ishbaal's two-year reign to signify the precise interval. Even then, as noted above (Chapter 17B), David did not execute the ritual of crossing the river for coronation at Gilgal until very late in his reign. But one thing can be said with relative assurance. David's alliance with Philistines, and the presence of Gittites in his court and in the region of the Ayyalon Pass, David's alliances with Nahash of Ammon and

---

18. Josephus *Ag. Ap.* 1.117. The regnal lengths in question appear, at least, to comport with information from non-Tyrian sources. Hiram's predecessor is Abibaal.

19. Josephus *Ag. Ap.* 1.126; *Ant.* 8.62, 11th year. The likelihood is that the datum derives by calculation from synchronisms in Judah, Israel, and Tyre, but just which were used for the purpose, and by which historian and at what time, remains unclear.

20. See David A. Glatt, *Chronological Displacement*, 57-61.

with the king of Geshur very probably at Tel Hadar in the Golan,[21] David's links to pastoral elements in the Negev — all these tell heavily on the side of the interpretation that David did not inherit the loyalty of Israel from the house of Saul. Israel was his principal conquest. He will have enforced his sovereignty there by terror in the villages and by rigid control in the towns.

21. See, e.g., Moshe Kochavi, "The Land of Geshur: History of a Region in the Biblical Period," *ErIsr* 25 (1996): 184-201.

CHAPTER 18

Rising over Zion

A. The Taking of Jerusalem

The narrative connects the proclamation of David's kingship over Israel to his immediate assault on the Jebusite fortress of Jerusalem. There is considerable controversy over Jerusalem's size and especially the density of occupation there both in the period of David and Solomon and in the period immediately preceding them. Excavators of the famous "stepped stone structure" that retains the east face of the Ophel, the ridge of the Late Bronze Age and early Iron Age town, regard the structure as a 10th-century construction: they base themselves on the dating of a small quantity of pottery found in a probe beneath the structure.

Preliminary reports from the City of David excavation conducted by Yigal Shiloh also maintain that 11th- and 10th-century pottery appeared in a number of areas, including in one case the fragment of a stand that appears to depict a "Philistine" with "feathered headdress," as on the reliefs of Ramses III.[1] Other scholars, however, hold that the exiguous character of 10th-century remains on the site — even were one to concede that the pottery in question was indeed 10th-century in date — precludes Jerusalem having functioned as the center of a regional state.[2]

---

1. Yigal Shiloh, *Excavations at the City of David* I. Qedem 19 (Jerusalem: Institute of Archaeology, Hebrew University, 1984), 4, 7, 12, 16-17, 26-27; fig. 29:2: Iron I in Areas D1 and E1, 10th century in Areas B, D1, E1, G and J, with the evidence in the latter case very unclear.

2. For 10th-century remains, see Jane M. Cahill and D. Tarler, "Excavations Directed

Archaeology in Jerusalem is complex. Architects from the Persian period forward excavated their foundations down to bedrock. Moreover, most of the Temple Mount, on the northern half of the eastern hill, is out of bounds to excavators. But it is clear that the early Israelite settlement and its predecessors were limited in extent. The town did not evolve into anything resembling a city until the second half, or perhaps the end, of the 8th century.[3] Still, the whole point of adopting a new capital is precisely to minimize the influence of a local population, so the restriction of its extent makes sense.

As a peak with springs, approachable only from the north, Jerusalem served as an almost impregnable center for the concentration of force and its projection into the surrounding countryside. This was also the situation at the time of the Amarna letters. Then, the town's king, Abdi-Hepa, entered into conflict and often into field combat with the kinglets of almost every neighboring city-state, especially Gezer. Despite this situation, tellingly, the city was never threatened from without.

According to the sources, Iron Age Jerusalem was reduced only a handful of times: by David, by Joash of Israel after he had captured the king of Jerusalem in the field, and by Nebuchadrezzar of Babylon, after a lengthy siege and the threat of submission by the inhabitants compelled the royal army to flee the town.[4] Nebuchadrezzar apart, the most impressive conquerors of Israel preferred to by-pass Jerusalem, accepting payment to do so: this was the case with the pharaoh Shishaq, the king of Damascus and lord of Aram, Hazael, and the Assyrian emperor Sennacherib.[5] Sennacherib's own annals confirm the biblical claims in this instance, while Shishaq probably omits the name of Jerusalem from his topographical list of towns captured in Israel and Judah. The omission reflects his extraction of ransom from it.

Particularly important is the willingness of Shishaq and Hazael to rest content with the payment of ransom for Jerusalem. The town that they elected not to capture, because of the difficulties involved, is, archaeologically, identical

---

by Yigal Shiloh at the City of David, 1978-1985," in *Ancient Jerusalem Revealed*, ed. Hillel Geva (Jerusalem: Israel Exploration Society, 1994), 30-45. For the lack of such remains and its implications see esp. Nadav Na'aman, *BASOR* 304 (1996): 17-27; cf. David W. Jamieson-Drake, *Scribes and Schools in Monarchic Judah;* H. J. Franken and M. L. Steiner, "Urusalim and Jebus," *ZAW* 104 (1992): 110-11. See also above, Chapter 12.

3. The basic study was that of Magen Broshi, "The Expansion of Jerusalem in the Reigns of Hezekiah and Manasseh," *IEJ* 24 (1974): 21-26. See latterly Nahman Avigad, *Discovering Jerusalem* (Nashville: Nelson, 1983), 26-60.

4. 2 Sam. 5:6-9; 2 Kgs. 14:11-14; 25:1-10.

5. 1 Kgs. 14:25-26; 2 Kgs. 12:17-18(18-19); 18:14-16. D. D. Luckenbill, *The Annals of Sennacherib.* OIP 2 (Chicago: University of Chicago Press, 1924), 32:18-34:49.

with and just as invisible as the one that has all but no reflex for David's time. This collocation has the implication that Jerusalem was much as the text of Samuel characterizes it: it was a "hold," castle, keep, a minor fortification,[6] as distinct from what is called a "fortified town."[7] The distinction was known to the author of Samuel, and the latter term is used in 2 Sam. 20:6 — not in reference to Jerusalem. 2 Sam. 5:7-9 specifically equates "the city of David" with "the keep of Zion," claiming that David dwelled in it and merely installed buildings inside it, without adding to the fortification. Not only was it difficult to overcome, it was also not a sufficiently rich repository, especially of population, to repay the investment necessary to reduce it.

The Jerusalemites' response to David's arrival confirms that this is the text's view of Jerusalem itself:

> The king and his men went to Jerusalem, to the Jebusite(s), the inhabitant(s) of the land. And (t)he(y) said to David, "You won't enter here, unless you can get rid of the blind and the lame," so as to say, "David will not enter here." (2 Sam. 5:6)

There is a dispute over the meaning of the Jebusites' remark. It most probably means that getting into Jerusalem would be the equivalent of achieving a miraculous cure of blindness and lameness.[8] It certainly implies that the Jebusites thought the fortress was untakeable. A parallel occurs in Herodotus (3.151-160), also in the tradition of challenge and counter-challenge at a siege: the Babylonians, in revolt, taunt Darius with the remark that he will capture their city only when mules foal. Here, however, the historian claims that 20 months later a mule did foal, and its owner was thereby inspired to infiltrate and then overthrow Babylon.

6. A m^eṣûdâ, 2 Sam. 5:7, 9, 17. This raises the question of whether the keep in which David is located in 2 Sam. 23:14, and derivatively, 1 Sam. 22:4-5; 24:23, is not in fact that of Jerusalem, rather than one identical with what is called the "cave of Adullam" in 2 Sam. 23:13; 1 Sam. 22:1. Contrast P. Kyle McCarter, Jr., *I Samuel*, 355. On the other hand, the report of 2 Sam. 23:13-17 may have inspired the claim that David's brothers joined him in the hold at Adullam.

7. The terms are 'îr bĕṣûrâ, 'îr mibṣār, or simply mibṣār. Note the continuum in 1 Sam. 6:18.

8. The first issue is the construction of an infinitive with a suffix followed by another noun ("the blind and the lame"). Is the suffix subjective or objective? The second issue is how to construe the phrase kî 'im, either as "unless" or as "but rather" in this syntactic context. For a treatment of the substantive issues, and comparison with the ban on access to the temple for the physically impaired, see Saul M. Olyan, *CBQ* 60 (1988): 218-27. This text probably implies an early origin of the latter practice. See further above, Chapter 2E.

Although the keep of Jerusalem was small, therefore, David's success in capturing it is magnified. The small keep constituted the entire town in his era (he built only inside it). If it lay on the Temple Mount, its archaeological recovery is unlikely. It may, however, have lain on the western hill of the later city.[9]

Just how David overcame the fortification is not described in the text (compare the much later 1 Chr. 11:6). Speculation about David's men storming the town through the water-systems carved into the Ophel is not justified. If David indeed confronted the Jerusalemites, rather than taking them by surprise, one should probably think in terms of a siege rather than an assault. The narrative is brief; but the event will have been rather protracted. Though the capital was tiny, its function was not that of a city-state, but of a stronghold from which a band of warriors could loot, terrorize, and dominate the surrounding countryside.

This situation likely continued to obtain to the end of David's life. The fact that Absalom's advance from Hebron in 2 Sam. 15:13-14 compelled David to abandon Jerusalem, thus, indicates one of two things. Either the king's eyrie was as yet unfortified, or he felt that his allies were unlikely to relieve a siege should he be caught in the city. The first seems the more likely alternative, as it is Solomon who is credited with the fortification of Jerusalem (1 Kgs. 3:1; 11:27).

B. The Philistine Wars

As we have seen (Chapters 7, 16), few texts in 2 Samuel allege that David fought the Philistines. The first comes in 2 Sam. 5:17-25, shortly after the taking of Jerusalem in the narrative. 2 Sam. 8 begins with the claim that "David smote Philistines and subdued them, and took 'Meteg Ha-'Ammah' from the hand of Philistines." This text, as we have seen, represents a reprise of the conflict reported in 2 Sam. 5.

In fact, the problematic term "Meteg Ha-'Ammah" may also have an antecedent in ch. 5: in the earlier report, David captures an icon or icons from his "Philistine" opponents (2 Sam. 5:21). "Meteg Ha-'Ammah" may well be the icon — it and the icons are the only booty, other than foreskins, that Samuel

---

9. A refined hypothesis that David's town sat on the western hill of Jerusalem was advanced by Giuseppe Pace, "Jebus sul monte e Shalem sul colle," *BeO* 20 (1978): 213-24. Excavation, however, discloses no remains on the western hill before the late 8th century. See Avigad, *Discovering Jerusalem*, 31. Pace's reasoning, basically, was sound, and might also explain the absence of Amarna-era remains on the Ophel, or eastern hill. Either the keep was quite small, and on the Western hill, or it lay on the Temple Mount.

claims David took from Philistines. In the circumstances, it is tempting to suggest that Meteg *(mtg)* is a corruption of the term *ptg-*, which appears as the name or title of the goddess of Eqron in an inscription of the early 7th century. This inscription mentions:

> The temple Achaios (Achish) . . . , official/king of Eqron, built for PTGY(H) his lady.[10]

And the letters *m* and *p (mtg, ptg)* in early Hebrew script, while distinct, are often similar in their stance and general profile. This is, admittedly, another speculative solution to a chronic conundrum. However, the identity of Meteg Ha-'Ammah with the Philistine icon of 2 Sam. 5 is probable. The different terminology used to refer to the icon, like the different words for stela in 2 Sam. 8, leads the reader to think that different actions are under discussion.

The next reports of David's confronting Philistines come in the appendices to 2 Samuel. 2 Sam. 21:15-22 reports on the achievements of four heroes: Abishai, Sibkay the Hushatite, Elhanan son of Dodo the Yearite from Bethlehem, and Jonathan son of Shimei, David's nephew. These characters each confront a Philistine, "a slave-by-birth *(yĕlîd)* of the Rapha," an expression possibly indicating their enlistment in a cult of the royal ancestors, the Rephaim.[11] These battles are located in Gezer, Gath, or "Gob" — the last possibly a cipher for Gibeon yet again.

Three further episodes are related in 2 Sam. 23:9-17. Here, the Israelites are Elazar son of Dodo, the Ahohite; Shamma son of Age, a mountain-man (Harari); and three unnamed warriors. The loci of battle are Pas-Dammim, which is the Epes Dammim of the Goliath story, and Bethlehem.

All of these conflicts might be connected with the two battles of 2 Sam. 5. The first of these takes place when the Philistines camp in the Valley of Rephaim, precisely where 2 Sam. 23:13-14 places their camp during the raid on Bethlehem. This battle, at Baal Perazim, is the subject of a reference by Isaiah (Isa. 28:21) in the late 8th century, an index of the fact that the text of Samuel was already written — and the significance of the battle wildly exaggerated — by that time. It is in this encounter that David takes the Philistine icon.

---

10. Seymour Gitin, Trude Dothan, and Joseph Naveh, *IEJ* 47 (1997): 1-16. The *-h* on the term may be a 3 m. sg. possessive suffix. To date, the expression resists explanation, in Egyptian, Semitic, or Greek. For the best effort, see Christa Schäfer-Lichtenberger, "PTGJH — Göttin und Herrin von Ekron," *BN* 91 (1998): 64-76.

11. A connection of "the Rapha" (Ha-Rapha) to Greek *harpē*, "sickle-sword" (or 'bird of prey'), or to *harpazō*, "snatch away," would be far-fetched, although the preservation of the definite article *h-* after the preposition *l-* in 2 Sam. 21:20, 22 is suspicious.

In the second conflict in 2 Sam. 5, the Philistines again aligned in the Valley of Rephaim. David stormed their camp and pursued them from Geba down the Ayyalon defile to the border of the territory of Gezer. Gezer, again, was the chief rival of Jerusalem during the Amarna era in the 14th century. It remained the border in Solomon's day. One may wonder, again, whether the association with the Valley of Rephaim in these accounts has not conditioned the description of the Philistine opponents of David's warriors as "slave-by-birth of the Rapha" in 2 Sam. 21. By the 7th century, the Rephaim were regarded as the aboriginal population of the Canaanite region whom the Hebrews — Ammon, Moab, Edom, and Israel — and the Philistines eradicated, a view certainly not in evidence in Samuel.[12]

Yet the question arises, just who were these "Philistines"? It is clear from the context that the narrative is not set in chronological order: Hiram's recognition and Solomon's birth are both mentioned before the fight with the "Philistines." But the identity of the warriors in question is also an issue.

Samuel consistently refers to "(the) Philistines" in a fashion meant to suggest to the reader that the unified forces of the Pentapolis were ranged against the Israelites. It is possible that this was on occasion the case, as perhaps at the battle of Jezreel. Yet even in this instance, there ought to be some doubt as to the character of the coalition facing Saul.

The Philistines are identified with the five towns of Gaza, Ashkelon, Ashdod, Eqron, and Gath. Of these, the first three are identified with coastal ruins. Eqron is unquestionably Tel Miqneh, at least in the Late Bronze and Iron Ages. And Gath is most likely to be located at Tell eṣ-Ṣâfi, south of Eqron on the inland coastal plain, although a more southerly location is possible.[13] These towns exhibit a dramatic shift in material culture sometime in the 12th century, when elements with a background in the Mycenean trade zone invaded and dominated them. The colonizers brought with them the artisans to manufacture

12. For this view, see Deut. 2:10-12 on Moab and Edom, 2:20-22 on Ammon and Edom, and 2:23 on the Awwim destroyed by the Philistines come from Crete; 3:11-13 on the Rephaim in the Bashan destroyed by Israel. The Awwim are the only aborigines not explicitly called Rephaim in the text. Compare further Josh. 12:4; 13:12; 17:15; Gen. 15:20. For earlier and later references to the Rephaim as spirits, see Isa. 14:9; 26:14, 19; Ps. 88:10(11); Prov. 2:18; 9:18; 21:16; Job 26:5. For another case in which ancestors become the aboriginal population when the cult of the dead is suppressed, see G. M. Berg, "The Myth of Racial Strife and Merina Kinglists: The Transformations of Texts," *History in Africa* 4 (1977): 1-29, esp. 7-8. Again, the antiquity of Samuel relative to the literature of the 7th century is in evidence.

13. See Lawrence E. Stager, "The Impact of the Sea Peoples." See further above, Chapter 7 n. 4, and below, Chapter 18.

their own fine ceramic forms, which are constructed from local clays. These forms included vessels, such as the "beer jug" (a wine decanter), and decorative elements, such as fish and birds, with no antecedents in local repertoires but ample parallels in the Aegean ecumene. Biblical sources of the 8th and 7th century impute to the Philistines a place of origin on the island of Crete (Caphtor).[14]

The Philistines occupied the city-states of the southern coast. They turned Gath and Eqron, two originally minor sites on the coastal plain, into inland centers. Other groups that the Egyptians numbered with the Philistines among "the peoples of the sea" also appeared at the time. Egyptian texts, including *The Voyage of Wen-Amun*, and archaeological soundings tend to confirm that a group called the Tjeker (Sikils) occupied the port of Dor.[15] The Sikils appear in Egyptian inscriptions, especially the famous relief at Medinet Habu, in which Ramses III claims (falsely) to have defeated the Sea Peoples. There they enjoy the company not just of the Philistines (Prst) but also of the Sherden. And just as the name of the Sherden is related to that of Sardinia, the name Sikil was somehow attached to Sicily.

The Sikils shared some features of Philistine material culture, including ceramic and cultic elements. But they constituted a different ethnic group. Egyptian texts distinguish them from Philistines. And biblical texts, including Solomon's province list, evince no sense that Dor was ever Philistine or even leagued with the Philistines, and the relative dearth of trade between Dor and Philistia seems to bear this out.[16] It is a question, thus, whether the 12th-century Sea People settlement at Tell Qasile, with ample Philistine bichrome pottery, was not a border station between the two. That is, there is no evidence of political coordination between the Philistines and other Sea Peoples after their initial settlement. Even among the Philistines themselves, there is a question as to how common such coordination was.

More puzzling still is what to make of the claim in the account of the battle

---

14. For the crucial issues of current scholarship, see the section "Philistia: Chronology and Cultural Affinities," in *Mediterranean Peoples in Transition, Thirteenth to Early Tenth Centuries B.C.E.* Festschrift Trude Dothan, ed. Seymour Gitin, Amihai Mazar, and Ephraim Stern (Jerusalem: Israel Exploration Society, 1998), 140-86. For a Cypriote in Israel, see Robert Deutsch and Michael Heltzer, *Forty New Ancient West Semitic Inscriptions*, 16-18; Frank M. Cross, *IEJ* 45 (1995): 188-89.

15. See now Ephraim Stern, *Dor, Ruler of the Seas;* "The Relations between the Sea Peoples and the Phoenicians in the Twelfth and Eleventh Centuries B.C.E.," in Gitin, Mazar, and Stern, *Mediterranean Peoples in Transition*, 345-52.

16. See Ayelet Gilboa, "Iron I-IIA Pottery Evolution at Dor — Regional Contexts and the Cypriot Connection," in Gitin, Mazar, and Stern, *Mediterranean Peoples in Transition*, 413-25.

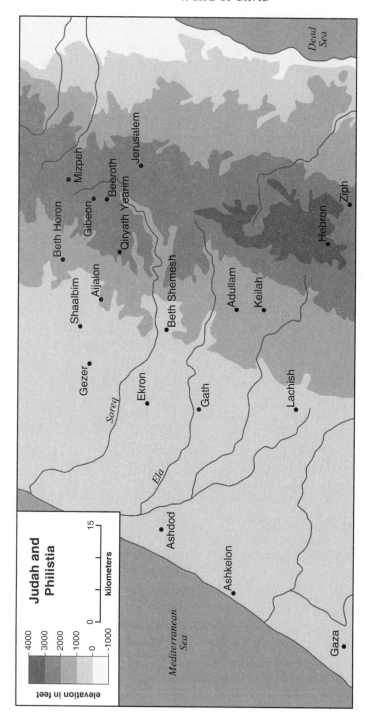

Map 18.1

of Jezreel that the Philistines exerted control over Beth Shan in Cisjordan south of the Sea of Galilee and of Ashtaroth, in the southern Golan Heights. Beth Shan has been extensively excavated, and has not disclosed a single piece of the typical sub-Mycenaean pottery of the early Philistine settlement; nor is it characterized by an abundance of the bichrome pottery of the high Philistine era, in the 11th century, the time of Saul. It is, on the other hand, not Israelite. It contains a sequence of Egyptian temples and an Egyptianizing culture.

The tradition in 1 Sam. 31:9-10 that the Philistines displayed the corpses of Saul and his sons on the wall of Beth Shan is difficult to discount, although the shipment of his weapons to "the temple of Ashtarot" (in the Bashan) is less susceptible to confirmation. The impaling of the corpses is consonant with Middle Assyrian practice.[17] Four considerations suggest the reliability of the connection with Beth Shan. First is the report that the men of Jabesh stole Saul's headless corpse and cremated or interred it, along with the corpses of his sons — in reciprocation for his succor of their settlement from Nahash of Ammon. Second is David's appeal to them, because of their relationship to Saul, to recognize his sovereignty. Third is the claim that David, after having the Gibeonites kill all but one of Saul's surviving descendants, repatriated the corpses from Jabesh to Zela in Benjamin.

The fourth consideration is more complex. David allied with Nahash, the old enemy of Jabesh, and with Nahash's son, whom he installed in Rabbah. He allied with Geshur, to which kingdom the town of Ashtarot may have belonged. And he remained allied to the Philistines to the end of his reign. The pattern of alliance, thus, is with the non-Israelite regions bordering Gilead, and into this pattern Ashtarot and Beth Shan fit well. Probably, Ashtarot, like Beth Shan, was far from being Israelite. David linked hands with just the non-Israelite elements whom Saul attacked.

Saul's opponents in the Jezreel may have been more varied in their composition than the text suggests. Whether all five Philistine city-states were represented cannot be ascertained. But other partners, such as Geshur, and Ammon, and elements from Zobah, may have participated. In other words, even Saul's final, tragic battle with "the Philistines" probably involved agencies that were not Philistine at all.

What, then, does the term "Philistines" conceal in the case of David's battles in 2 Sam. 5?[18] Battles with the Philistines had to be reported immediately

17. See for the impaling of captives RIMA 2 A.0.101 1 iii 84; 19:74-76; 21:13'-15' (Assurnasirpal II).

18. And 2 Sam. 8:1; 21:15-22; and 23:14-17, all of which may pertain to the same events.

on David's occupation of Jerusalem: immediately after he became king of Israel, the text claims, David broke explicitly with his former masters. The effect has been — among readers since the writing of the apology — to exculpate him from the charge of collaboration with the Philistines in the war on Saul's house, the civil war. Similarly, the conflicts with Philistines are presented in 2 Sam. 21:15-22 directly after the execution of all Saul's surviving descendants, save one, at Gibeon: this juxtaposition, too, indicates a certain sensitivity to the charge that David colluded with Philistines against Saul and his family. This is why the chapter stresses conflict with champions directly or indirectly associated with Gath, David's primary Philistine affiliate. In the civil war, David probably had Philistine assistance.

Two points deserve renewed emphasis here. First, David pursues the "Philistines" only as far as the border of the city-state Gezer, the western border of Israel in Solomon's day. Gezer's territory extended to the juncture where the Ayyalon Pass opened into the coastal plain. Further inland, the next towns were Ayyalon, to the south, Lower Beth Horon to the northeast, and Qiryath-Yearim to the southeast.[19] Again, Qiryath-Yearim, a Gibeonite town, figures as the westernmost political outpost of David's state. The Gibeonite town sits on a peaceful border with Philistia.

Second, neither surveys nor excavations in the hill country have divulged the presence of Philistines. Characteristic bichrome pottery has been recovered from a number of sites, including Tell en-Naṣbeh, usually identified as the biblical Mizpeh, north of Jerusalem. However, it forms a significant part of the local assemblage mainly on the plain. Inland, in the Shephelah, it occurs in quantities typifying Philistine settlement at Tell Beit Mirsim to the south and at Beth Shemesh, identified erroneously (but tellingly) in 1 Sam. 6 as Israelite, to the north. Politically, at least, Beth Shemesh was Philistine.

In sum, the "Philistines" in the Ayyalon Pass, driven by David from Geba to Gezer, did not represent a colony, and may have been Philistine agents rather than ethnic Philistines. They may, in other words, have been the forces of a kinglet whom David's apologist identified with the Philistines, based on the kinglet's political affiliations. To put the most positive face on the matter, the kinglet in question may have aligned himself with Jerusalem, against David's occupation of that town — hence the confrontation beginning in the Valley of Rephaim. Alternatively, the opponent may have been the chieftain formerly occupying Jerusalem. In either case, the opponent may have had a formal relationship with a Philistine power. He may even have been a Philistine himself, a

---

19. Assuming the identity of Ayyalon with Yalu and of Qiryath Yearim, somewhat more doubtfully, with Tel Qiryath-Yeʿarim (Deir el-ʿAzar).

filibuster like David, controlling some town with a few warriors. But the population he controlled was not Philistine.

Gezer springs to mind as a possible source of the Philistine commanders inland. But it is far more likely that the sprawling, 50-hectare city-state of Eqron, whose tendrils stretched to Beth Shemesh in the upper Shephelah, was in the position of dominating Gezer. David's action, then, would represent a strike by his master, Achish — Achaios — at Gath, against the hinterland of the more important center to the north.

Indeed, if Gath was located at Tell es-Sâfi, it too was probably nothing more than a dependency of Eqron's.[20] In that case, Gath was promoted in the text of Samuel, and in Israelite literature dependent on that text, to the status of one of the great Philistine powers in Saul's and David's eras. Thus, in archaeological terms, Eqron is at its height in the 12th to early 10th centuries, then again in the 7th. Its explosion in the 7th century came as a result of Sennacherib's campaign in 701. Following Sargon's earlier dismemberment of Ashdod, Sennacherib left a yawning vacuum in the region by depopulating Ju-

---

20. Biblical texts place Gath to the south of Eqron and inland from the coast. In the ark narrative, thus, the ark starts at Ashdod and is removed to Gath and then Eqron, before being despatched up the wadi (past Timnah) to Beth Shemesh (1 Sam. 5:8-10; 6:12-14). Furthermore, in the service of the king of Gath, David is said to have plundered southern residents either in Judah or up to the Egyptian border (1 Sam. 27:8-11). But if the Egyptian border was, as historically, the Wadi Besor, the alternative, Tel Haror, is too far south to suit the text. Chronicles also records traditions of conflict between Ephraimites (1 Chr. 7:21) and Benjaminites (8:13) on the one hand and Gittites on the other, and places Gath between Adullam and Mareshah in the list of Rehoboam's fortresses (2 Chr. 11:8). On the archaeological side, no 9th-century finds are to date reported from Haror, and yet Hazael conquered the town (2 Kgs. 12:17[18]), in the last quarter of that century. (Hazael's taking Gath before turning to Judah foreshadows Assyrian strategy in the 8th century, in which Tiglath-Pileser III and Sargon II took Philistia before dominating Judah, and Sennacherib's strategy in 701, turning the Shephelah garrisons before heading into the hills: the hill country seems always to be left for last in Assyrian military doctrine, based on the consideration that control of the lowlands is primary for logistics.) The massive fortification of the 8th century at Haror is presumably Assyrian, when Amos in mid-century refers to Gath as either a ruin or a much-reduced town (Amos 6:2). Chronicles even attributes a breach in its fortifications to Uzziah (2 Chr. 26:6), though the reliability of this claim — which might stem from a misintepretation of Amos — cannot be ascertained. The other text for which an identification of Haror with Gath creates difficulty is 1 Sam. 17:52: after routing the Philistines in the Wadi Elah, just west of Azekah, the Israelites pursue them to the gates of Eqron, quite near to the northwest, and to the territory of Gath. Haror is some 45-40 km. southwest of the site ([']Pas Dammim), which would imply pursuit in two directions at once; but perhaps the implication, the presence of Goliath of Gath notwithstanding, is simply that all of Eqron's territory was dominated.

dah and reducing Ashkelon.[21] Between these eras, however, the extent of the site shrank almost to insignificance, despite a tradition of a cult there with international repute for healing.[22]

For this reason, Eqron looms large in texts in Samuel reflecting the realities of the 11th and 10th centuries. Along with the later, even larger Ashdod, and Gath, it houses the ark in 1 Sam. 5–6. As the pentapolis site closest to Judah, it takes responsibility for the ark's transfer to Beth Shemesh (and thence to Qiryath-Yearim — to Gibeonite allies). It is the key target in the rout after the Goliath story, although in which source is not clear.[23] And it is named, with Gath, as a town that had seized towns from Israel until Samuel recovered them in 1 Sam. 7:14. The last verse manages to detract from Saul's achievements, by attributing the recovery of all Israelite territory to Samuel. It also inserts the critical claim that Israel and the Amorites had made peace — a claim that justifies the slaughter of Saul's descendants at Gibeon in 2 Sam. 21.[24]

In the literature of the late 8th and 7th centuries, Eqron is equally prominent. It appears in texts that define the extent of Philistine territory in the book of Joshua, where it forms the northern border of Philistia and the western border of Judah.[25] Joshua and Judges allege that Judah conquered it, an event that took

---

21. See Baruch Halpern, "Jerusalem and the Lineages in the Seventh Century B.C.E."

22. Baal Zebub, "lord of the fly," in 2 Kgs. 1 — often thought to be a derogatory version of Baal Zebul, "lord prince," based on the occurrence of the phrase *zbl b'l* at Ugarit. The word for the transitive verb "to heal" is *rp'*, related to the Philistine Rapha and the Rephaim. Baal Zebub is probably identical with Phoenician Eshmun, who seems to have assumed the role of Gula *(azugallatu)* in the west; hence her transmission to Greece as the son, rather than daughter, of Apollo, Asgelatas, later Asklepios. For the latter, and generally, see Baruch Halpern, "The Canine Conundrum at Ashkelon: A Classical Connection?" in *The Archaeology of Jordan and Beyond,* ed. Lawrence E. Stager, Joseph A. Greene, and Michael D. Coogan (Winona Lake: Eisenbrauns, 2000), 133-44.

23. 1 Sam. 17:52: Israel routs Philistines "to the approach to the Valley [Greek: Gath], and to Shaarayim of Eqron [Greek: Ashkelon], and Philistine casualties fell on the road of Shaarayim up to Gath and up to Eqron." In its first occurrence, Shaarayim is usually translated "gates" — but the name of the town in the northern Shephelah is being used as later in the verse, with the intention of suggesting to the reader that the pursuit reached the walls of the actual town, Eqron. Probably, Gath has been included simply because Goliath himself was a Gittite both in the story and in its source: 1 Sam. 17:4, 23 + 2 Sam. 21:19; 1 Chr. 20:5. Most likely the report stems from the B source in Samuel.

24. This is why 2 Sam. 21 stipulates that the Gibeonites were from the remnant of the Amorites. Note that the strategy of diminishing Saul's achievements is the same as in 2 Sam. 3:18, treated above, Chapter 17.

25. Josh. 13:2-3; 15:11. It is assigned to the tribe of Dan in Josh. 19:43, but does not succumb to Dan.

place in the late 8th century. The prophets Amos, before that time, and Zephaniah and Jeremiah after it, include Eqron in their imprecations against Philistines.[26]

These latter texts, however, all omit Gath. The only texts on this temporal horizon that mention it explicitly are Josh. 11:22 and 13:2-3; Mic. 1:10; and Amos. Josh. 11 places Anaqim, giants, in Gaza, Gath, and Ashdod after Joshua's conquest, presumably to lay the groundwork for traditions in Samuel about Goliath and the slaves of the Rapha, construed as aborigines. Josh. 13 simply enumerates the cities of the pentapolis, reconstructing them on the basis of tradition, and possibly of Samuel. Micah mentions Gath only because he is echoing verbatim David's threnody for Saul and Jonathan in 2 Sam. 1:20: "Do not tell it in Gath (nor proclaim it in the bazaars of Ashkelon)," which involves a pun on the name of the town. And Amos, who does not include Gath in his imprecation against Philistia, more or less explains why. In Amos 6:2, he instructs the Israelites to look to Calneh, Greater Hamath, and Gath as examples of total devastation. Gath was not a factor in the 8th or 7th centuries, which is why, in contrast to Eqron, the 7th-century book of Joshua does not lay claim to it for Judah. Nor does Sennacherib mention it in his annals, or restore territory to it from Judah, whereas all four other pentapolis cities do appear, and do receive territorial grants.[27] Conversely, in the historiography of the postexilic period, Gath is again prominent and Eqron is absent.[28]

A text in Kings may clarify the change in the towns' fortunes. In 2 Kgs. 12:18, Hazael, an Aramean king of the late 9th century, marches through the territory of his vassal state, Israel. He arrives at Gath, captures it, and turns immediately toward Jerusalem. The report is almost surely reliable. It indicates that in this period it was Gath, to the south, that was the gateway to Jerusalem, and the dominant state facing the Shephelah from the plain: its territory embraced Eqron's former land, up to the Ayyalon Pass.

This jibes with the shrinkage at Tel Miqneh in the 10th century. And Hazael's activity probably led to Gath's decline, either immediately or in the

---

26. Josh. 15:45-47; Judg. 1:18; Amos 1:6-8; Zeph. 2:4; Jer. 25:20. The oracle against Philistia in Jer. 47:1-7 mentions only Gaza and Ashkelon by name.

27. Luckenbill, *The Annals of Sennacherib*, 70:29-30; 33:30-34.

28. The Chronicler mentions Gath five times, and apart from it, only Ashdod: 1 Chr. 7:21; 8:13; 18:1; 2 Chr. 11:8; 26:6. He reconstructs a Davidic conquest of Gath (this is his interpretation of Meteg Ha-Ammah in 2 Sam. 8:1). So he has Rehoboam fortify it, and Uzziah reconquer it (and Ashdod). The other two texts — the first two — relate conflict between Israelites in the central hill country and Gittites. The only postexilic text to mention Eqron, which was abandoned at the time, is Zech. 9:5-7, which appears to be archaizing and may have been intended as a pseudepigraph. It predicts Eqron's annexation to Judah. Nehemiah (Neh. 4:7[1]; 13:23-24) mentions Ashdod only.

first half of the 8th century. That is, Gath and Eqron were alternately in the ascendant over one another's territory — in the 9th through 5th centuries. This tends to confirm the identification of Gath with Tell eṣ-Ṣâfi, not far from Eqron.[29] It also furnishes another indication that the geography reflected in the Davidic apology is earlier than that of the late 8th and 7th centuries, when Gath could hardly have been thought relevant to international politics.

The waxing of Gath's fortunes in the 10th and 9th centuries coincides with the activity of the Davidic era. Entering the 10th century, Gath was Eqron's vassal. So too were the settlements of the hinterland in the hills of Judah. After all, Eqron achieved its 7th-century extent of 50 hectares only by dint of dominating the virtually empty Judean hill country. There is every reason to suppose that the same relationship enabled it to reach 50 hectares in the 12th and 11th centuries as well.

But it is almost a certainty that the Philistines presented a united front, if at all, only rarely. A diplomatic archive, were one uncovered, would reveal that while they may on occasion have managed to collaborate, the quotidian reality was one of internecine intrigue. In the Amarna archive of the 14th century, Egyptian vassals, even erstwhile allies, consistently come into conflict over border towns and territories. During the period of Assyrian domination, the Philistine city-states consistently revolted seriatim rather than in concert. This is a symptom that their politics were fragmented: competing over their borders, they fought one another far more often than they united.

Despite the appearance of ethnic rifts, Iron I-II will have been no different. David's history with Gath and Solomon's pacific connivance with Achish, David's overlord and perhaps later partner, in the matter of Shimei's entrapment (1 Kgs. 2:39-41) are important. It is reasonable to suppose that David's irruption into Hebron and then Jerusalem and the assertion of his sovereignty over Israel represented a loss for Eqron, to Gath's benefit. The redirection of resources into a Davidic Jerusalem, rather than to Gibeon or Qiryath-Yearim, would hardly have troubled any of the Philistine polities that formerly received no direct payment from the towns in question. David likely allied not just with Gath, but also with pentapolis cities west of Eqron.

29. Against Lawrence E. Stager, "The Impact of the Sea Peoples." 1 Sam. 5, in which the ark migrates from Ashdod to Gath to Eqron, thence to Israel, indicates that Gath stood between Ashdod and Eqron, not to the south of Ashdod. Likewise, the ability of the narrator to add Gath to Eqron as an end-point in the rout of 1 Sam. 17:52 (the Goliath episode) indicates the proximity of the towns to one another. As Stager's candidate, Tel Haror, is over 45 km. distant from Eqron, one could identify Gath with Tel el-Erani, and the border with the Wadi Lachish or even the Wadi Guvrin. But Erani is small, and the Philistine ware there less well represented than publication to date indicates. It is not a prime candidate. See further William M. Schniedewind, *BASOR* 309 (1998): 69-77.

This analysis has the implication that David recruited the Gibeonites, whose towns sat to the north and the west of Jerusalem along the Ayyalon Pass, both against Israel and against Jerusalem itself in a revolt against Eqron. The revolt was sponsored by Gath, which, however, preserved deniability. A likely scenario is that Jerusalem initially supported David's war on Israel — which would explain how he was able to project his forces forward from Hebron to Gibeon. Abner and Ishbaal tried to bring David into alliance with themselves, unsuccessfully. As Israel's leaders fell victim to assassination, David was poised to turn on his former allies in Jerusalem, and to link his forces with elements from Israel, as well as Gath and Ammon.

Early in Solomon's reign, an Egyptian pharaoh, whom 1 Kgs. 3:1 portrays as Solomon's father-in-law, invaded Philistia, always the pharaoh's nominal territory. He burned Gezer, described as a Canaanite, not Philistine, town, and presented it to Solomon (1 Kgs. 9:16).[30] Given the cordial relations Solomon early enjoyed with Gath, the engineering of the relationship with Egypt might seem to represent a sudden, if effective, *volte face* on his part. However, if Gezer was a dependency of Eqron's — and ruled but not colonized by Philistines — then the pharaoh will have stripped the hinterland of a major opponent in favor of the next state over. The demolition of the megalopolis at Eqron and the rise of Gath as a dominant state in the plain were the result. The archaeology of Eqron and the texts both make sense if we jettison the assumption that "the Philistines" were monolithic, rather than in regular conflict with one another, like all other polities in the Near East. Solomon, whose chief wife was an Ammonite, continued to league with David's foreign partners at the outset of his reign. Siamun, in other words, was his great benefactor, and probably responsible at least for the start of Eqron's decline.

One other point about David's occupation of Jerusalem merits remark. Chronicles has David attempt to move the ark to Jerusalem before his confrontation with Philistia. The Chronicler was concerned to avoid the implication that David took icons from "the Philistines." Indeed, he claims that David burned the captured icons, where Samuel states that "he carried them off."[31] But this concern also reflects a paranoid thought — namely, that the icons David "carried off" were joined with the ark, moved on to Jerusalem immediately after the battle. The ark's origin may also have been an issue for the Chronicler: why did it come from Gibeonite and Gittite sources?

As we have seen (Chapter 16C), the ark may have been foreign. David's re-

30. On the authenticity of this text, see the discussion in Chapters 22D, 23E.

31. 1 Chr. 14:12. For the Chronicler's logic, see Kimhi *ad loc.*, and my treatment in "Fallacies Intentional and Canonical," forthcoming.

lations with the Gibeonites, his depending on them to eliminate Saul's house, and his integration of them into his kingdom represent signs of a thorough-going collaboration. The Gibeonites are "of the remnant of the Amorites" (2 Sam. 21:2), with whom the Israelites had come to terms (1 Sam. 7:14). The Gibeonite towns reappear at every juncture in the history of David's rise over Zion and Israel. Qiryath-Yearim forms the western boundary of the kingdom along the Ayyalon Pass. It produces the ark, which a Gittite then houses, before its translation to Jerusalem. The Gittite fathers a line of Levite temple personnel. Gittites, Gibeonites, Ammonites were David's chief allies in the war from the south against Israel. His adoption of the ark from the Gibeonites — with Gibeonite cult servants — is also a part of the pattern. The ark-shrine at Shiloh, in sum, was probably a local sanctuary formerly patronized most religiously by the Hivvite-Gibeonite denizens of the central hills. To his enemies, David was a Gibeonite.

CHAPTER 19

Bringing Home the Ark

A. Celebrating a Homecoming

Perhaps the most triumphant of many triumphant moments in the books of Samuel is the transfer of the ark from Qiryath-Yearim to Jerusalem in 2 Sam. 6–7. Though the initial attempt results in a delay and the death of one of the porters, David persists. When the ark's stay with the Gittite Obed Edom results in "blessing," David arranges a procession with a sacrifice every six steps all the way to Jerusalem. In both the initial transfer and in the second, the musical accompaniment is extensive.

In the narrative, David rejects Michal, Saul's daughter, because she has some objection to the ceremony in which he introduces the icon to the capital. Possibly, this reflects uneasiness with the ark itself among Saul's constituency, as argued above (Chapter 16). It at least takes advantage of this uneasiness — Saul's distance from the ark — to suggest that Michal was unwilling to welcome the ark on David's terms.

At the end of the narrative, David installs the ark in a tent — not a temple — and offers burnt offerings and whole-offerings. David then distributes bread and other victuals to the people, "from man to woman," a merismus, or synecdoche, that is rare but indicates the extraordinary nature of the occasion. This is David's consecration of Jerusalem as the capital of a territorial state or, in Near Eastern terms, an empire.

The parallel is to the feast laid on by the Assyrian emperor Assurnasirpal at the dedication of his own capital, Calah, in the 9th century. Assurnasirpal moved the capital from Nineveh and populated the newly-rebuilt town mainly with Aramean captives. In Calah, he constructed a palace complex and planted orchards and gardens, the use intended by Ahab for Naboth's vineyard in Jezreel. He displayed herds of exotic animals: lions and other cats, wild bulls, ostriches, monkeys, and others. He walled the town and also erected temples to various gods, including Ninurta and Enlil, gods with roots in Sumer; Adad, the (Baal) Hadad of Syria; Nabu, son of Marduk; Sin, the moon-god; and the Sibitti, or Seven.[1]

In one inscription, found in Assurnasirpal's palace, the king furnishes an abbreviated account of his campaigns, then focuses on the construction of the palace. It lists the varieties of trees he transplanted for his gardens, describes the construction of various temples, then claims that he renovated and resettled towns throughout Assyria. After a traditional celebration of the king's prowess in the hunt and annexation of foreign territory and populations, it turns to the banquet.

The banquet itself crowned the consecration of the Calah palace. To it, Assurnasirpal invited the state god, Assur, and "the gods of all the land." He sacrificed 100 fatling ("grain[-fed?]") oxen, 1000 stall-fed calves and sheep, 14 thousand sheep and 200 oxen belonging to the goddess Ishtar, plus 1000 further sheep, 1000 spring lambs, 500 (red) deer, 2000 ducks and geese, 2000 other fowl, 30 thousand smaller birds (doves, pigeons, perhaps quail), 10 thousand fish, and 10 thousand jerboa. To this he added 10 thousand of each of the following: eggs, bread loaves, beer jugs, wine-skins, and quantities of grain and sesame. The list continues with various seeds, vegetables, fruits, nuts, spices, oil, and drinks. To this feast, Assurnasirpal invited 16 thousand inhabitants of Calah, 47 thousand guests from elsewhere in his territory, and 5000 emissaries from lands as distant as the Phoenician coast or Lake Van. The total number of guests amounted almost to 70 thousand, and the feast lasted 10 days.[2]

Probably, the closest biblical parallel to Assurnasirpal's banquet is the rededication of Jerusalem, as a new capital city, under Solomon. According to the text, Solomon devoted 20 years to monumental construction on the acropolis. For 13 years, he constructed his palace, and for seven the temple of Yahweh. At the end of the process, Solomon gathered all the Israelite leaders to transfer the ark from "the city of David, that is, Zion," in the sight of "all the men of Israel" to the temple. The sacrifices of sheep and cattle on the way were so numerous

1. The planets or the Pleiades. The Sibitti appear in Israel, in the name, Elisabeth — *'ĕlîšeba'*, "my god is the Sibitti" (Exod. 6:23) — or Jehosheba(t) ("Yahweh is the Sibitti," 2 Kgs. 11:2; 2 Chr. 22:11). These names would tend to suggest that in its Israelite incarnation, at least, the Sibitti is the collocation of the planets.
2. See RIMA 2.A.0.101.30; A. Finet, "Le Banquet de Kalah."

that they "could not be counted and could not be reckoned because of their abundance." Once the ark was installed in the temple adyton, smoke filled the nave, reflecting the use of incense. Then Solomon offered up 22 thousand cattle and 120 thousand sheep. The festival lasted 14 days, but the king dismissed the people on the eighth day (1 Kgs. 6–8).

In a transmitted text, such as Kings, the numbers are always suspect. Scribes have a tendency to inflate them, to glorify figures sanctified by the tradition, such as Solomon. Even in a text contemporary with the event, such as Assurnasirpal's, the king's instinct will have been to maximize the numbers in order to demonstrate his own generosity. Yet allowing for exaggeration, the order of magnitude separating the biblical account of Solomon's feast from Assurnasirpal's inventory of comestibles is not immense. Moreover, the purpose in each case is to invite the presence of the chief god into the king's monumental construction. The contrast is to another such occasion, another local parallel to David's banquet, namely, the Passover celebrated by King Josiah.

Josiah's feast is one of rededication, like Assurnasirpal's feast, and like the feast that accompanied the dedication of Sennacherib's palace as well. Solomon's also celebrated not just the temple dedication, but that of the palace as well, although the biblical account of the feast centers on the temple rather than on the palace. However, unlike Solomon's festival, Josiah's did not involve the physical reconstruction of a temple or royal monument. And Josiah's feast is not described as a national celebration. Nor is the king's generosity underscored:

> The king commanded all the people, saying, "Make a Paschal offering to Yahweh your God as it is prescribed on this scroll of the covenant." For no such Paschal offering had been conducted since the days of the judges who judged Israel, and all the days of the kings of Israel and the kings of Judah. Only in the eighteenth year of the king, Josiah, was this Paschal offering made to Yahweh in Jerusalem. (2 Kgs. 23:21-23)

The difference between the descriptions again reflects the imbrication of the Solomon account in the cultural world of the Middle Assyrian era, in which the image of the king was different from that in the late 7th century, Josiah's time. Our literature about Josiah emphasizes piety, the restoration of allegedly ancient rites. The same emphasis characterizes Neo-Assyrian and Neo-Babylonian kings of the late 7th and 6th centuries. The emphasis for Assurnasirpal and Solomon is on the king's expansiveness and wealth, and the improvement of the kingdom.

David's dedication stands in the tradition that climaxes in the biblical text with Solomon. However, the rations distributed are almost microscopic in comparison with the parallels with Solomon or Assurnasirpal: one loaf of bread, one raisin cake, and one other item, whose translation is uncertain, to each participant. The text does state that David offered sacrifices when the ark had been set into its tent. But it does not number the animals; nor does it stipulate the types of animal involved. It does not report a length for the festival. Most of all, it does not claim that the sacrifices were shared out to the population at large.

All this suggests that David's festival at the installation of the ark was described to portray the king as a provider on a Middle Assyrian model. The god — in the instance, Yahweh — had to be invited to his new home, and propitiated with offerings, when he moved. But the poverty reflected in the description suggests that the actual celebration was nothing more than a local affair, more probably involving the Gibeonites in the region north of Jerusalem than the Israelites from the central hills. No one in the countryside can have seen the dedication as more than a onetime event. It would be a surprise if Israelites north of Gibeon thought of it as an event of any sort at all.

When was the ark transferred from the house of Abinadab in Qiryath-Yearim to the house of Obed Edom? When did it voyage to a tent pitched by David in Jerusalem? The text attaches its migration to the taking of Jerusalem, set early in David's career. However, it is a convention of Near Eastern royal literature to antedate cultic activity to the very start of a reign. So the ark's adoption as a national icon, as a vehicle for creating a state cult, cannot be dated with confidence. In the Absalom revolt, the ark is sent back to Jerusalem, in one of those vignettes that delineates David's character while advancing the plot. Uriah claims that the ark is in the field when David summons him home from the siege of Rabbat Ammon. Even without contradicting the assertions of the narrative, it is possible to date the appropriation of the ark as late as the Ammonite war.

By the same token, the story in which David acquires the threshing floor of Araunah the Jebusite is placed at the end of the account of his reign, just before his co-regency with Solomon. In the account, a census David commissioned, from Dan to Beersheba, outrages Yahweh. The grounds for the umbrage seem to be that the census displayed a lack of faith that Yahweh would continue to increase the population of Israel. The result is a plague. To placate Yahweh, however, David purchases Araunah's tract and erects an altar on it, at which he sacrifices. In theory, this is the land, extramural in David's time as threshing floors typically were, on which Solomon founded the temple.

That David conducted a census, however, only at the very end of his reign

seems unlikely. A census in premodern times is foremost a means of regulariz-
ing and checking on taxation, a concern that would have come to expression in
royal policy as early in the reign as was feasible. As it stands, the acquisition of
the ground for David's extramural altar (and Solomon's intramural palace and
temple?) is the prelude to the account of Solomon's accession and reign, including his regimen of heavy taxation. It affords David a role in laying a groundwork for the temple. This groundwork is then considerably elaborated to include all sorts of preparation and planning in 1 Chronicles. But the
arrangement of the narrative sequence is thematic, not chronological. The
same holds for the story of the ark's transfer to Zion.

B. The Dynastic Oracle

In the presentation, the transfer of the ark is the occasion for pan-Israelite celebration. If the transfer of the ark came early in his reign, such a collocation is
unlikely. Even later on, the claim of national representation will have been in
the main a pretense. Real participation in David's state was limited among Israelites to the very end of his reign. Thus, the list of his army commanders in
2 Sam. 23 mentions no one originating north of the territory abutting
Ephraim's southern border, on the northern fringe of Benjamin. And if, as in
the case of Ittay in 2 Sam. 23:29, the Benjaminites are in fact Gittites or, as in the
case of Naharay, Joab's armor-bearer, Gibeonites, the list would contain no Israelites at all. Thus, a national assembly in Jerusalem seems unlikely except under
extreme duress — before the Absalom revolt, at any rate (see below, Chapter
21).

But the transfer of the ark has to be presented as an occasion for national
celebration. It leads to David's inquiry in 2 Sam. 7 as to whether he should build
a temple. Again, the location of the story reflects Near Eastern cultural traditions: it is at the outset of his reign that a king ought to show the piety of seeking divine permission for the construction of a temple. And in fact, Yahweh's
willingness to transfer his residence to Jerusalem, the new capital, has already
been demonstrated, in the previous chapter.

The response to David's inquiry is both positive and negative. Yahweh,
through the prophet Nathan, forbids him to build a temple:

"Would *you* (presume to) build for me a house for my dwelling? For I
have not dwelled in a house since the time when I brought the Israelites
up from Egypt and until this day, but have been migratory, in a tabernacle. In all my peregrinations throughout all of Israel, have I ever spoken

an oracle regarding any of the tribes whom I charged with shepherding my people, Israel, saying, 'Why have you not built me a cedar house?'"[3]

This refusal is a disaster in the making. A god's acquiescence in a king's desire to provide permanent housing is the visible confirmation that the king's house, or dynasty, is secure. The occupation of a temple sanctions the king's line reciprocally on a permanent basis. Yet Yahweh declines David's overture here.

Still, the text continues with a promise to David. Yahweh will place David's son on the throne after him, and establish his kingship. The son is to build a temple for Yahweh, who will fix his kingdom forever. Yahweh will be his adoptive father, correcting rather than punishing him. Further, Yahweh will never withdraw his sanction from David's royal line:

> "Your House is secure, and your kingdom, forever in my presence; your throne will be fixed forever."

In other words, because David *offered* to build a permanent house for Yahweh — a temple — Yahweh reciprocated by guaranteeing a house for David — a royal dynasty.[4] He would accept the temple during David's son's reign instead of David's, so that in a sense, in 2 Sam. 7 Yahweh issues the guarantee of a dynasty on credit.

Thematically, again, this material belongs together with the transfer of the ark and Yahweh's acceptance of Jerusalem as his new residence. The real occasion of the oracle, if any, can be called into question. David could have obtained it at any time during his reign, or Solomon could have furnished it after David's death. The oracle itself was indispensable, since temples can be built, in theory,

---

3. 2 Sam. 7:5-7. For the text and bibliography, see P. Kyle McCarter, Jr., *II Samuel*, 192. He takes "tent" rather than "tabernacle" to have been the original term for Yahweh's normal dwelling. Either is possible, as is the present Masoretic reading, "in a tent and in a tabernacle." For *dbr dbr 't*, "spoken an oracle regarding," see 1 Kgs. 8:15 in contrast to 8:18; but the traditional rendering, "Have I ever spoken a word to," is certainly possible. Most scholars render *šbṭy* (usually "staves" or "tribes") as leaders of some sort. If this meaning is correct, the Hebrew term probably either reflects confusion of *p* with *b* in paleo-Hebrew script (*špty* means "judges, leaders"), or it is the source of the tradition that leaders before the kings were denominated "judge." However, it is best to take the text as it stands in the most banal sense, namely that the site of Yahweh's residence was always the tribe elected by him to lead Israel (and take the lead on the field of battle, with the ark), and it is in such a location that he would have furnished an oracle indicating his desire for a temple. That this is the interpretation of 2 Sam. 7:7 adopted in Solomon's speech in 1 Kgs. 8:16, as McCarter observes, suggests that it deserves to be taken seriously.

4. 2 Sam. 7:12-16. See Frank M. Cross, *Canaanite Myth and Hebrew Epic*, 241-64.

only if commissioned by their occupants. And since the dynasty claiming that it was eternal stemmed from David, and was called "the House of David" as in the Tel Dan and perhaps the Mesha stelas, it was most appropriate that David appear as the recipient of the dynastic guarantee tied usually to temple building.

All the same, the psychology of the narrative is complex. First, the dynastic guarantee is doubled. David, to be sure, is promised eternal kingship, through the corporation of his descendants. But so too is the successor who actually constructs the temple. In other words, the text, as it is worded, excludes from the succession those collateral descendants of David who do not trace their ancestry through the temple-builder, which is to say, Solomon. It is a striking property of Solomon's succession that it was a military coup, which disappointed the expectations of all the other sons of the king and of the nation. It is equally striking that not one of Solomon's officials, including 12 provincial governors, is a brother of his. Few of David's children long outlived Adonijah. The dynastic charter in 2 Sam. 7 made it clear that Yahweh took no stock in Solomon's brothers.

Second, the narrative furnished only one occasion on which such claims could be made. That was precisely the moment when Yahweh elected Jerusalem as his domicile and that of the ark. Yet David did not build a temple, but pitched a tent for his state icon and god. He did not build a palace that his son found suited to his international standing, or at least to his aspirations to international standing. The stories of the rape of Tamar, for example, or of the appointment of Solomon as David's successor reflect the spatial divisions of a palace type known as the Bit-Hilani. On the other hand, they could as easily be acted out in a pillared house with four rooms, the form of dwelling most commonly attested in the hill country of Iron I and Iron II Israel.[5] Probably, David's residence represented an intermediate form between the two. The capital, and the cult, were physically unprepossessing. David did not indulge in undue display.

Why did David refrain from giving himself the airs that most other Near Eastern kings, including the kings of other city-states, adopted? The usual explanation was that he stemmed from a culture that was puritanical about display, a culture of which the laws of Exod. 20:23-26 are characteristic: these forbid icons made of silver or gold, and prescribe altars consisting of earth or unworked field-stones, approached without steps — so not elevated very far above the surface of the field. Moreover, the ark, and with it Yahweh, had, in the theory of the text, never been housed in a permanent structure. David chose, in other words, to conform insofar as possible to the traditions of a premonarchic

5. Baruch Halpern, *The First Historians*, ch. 3.

Israel whose settlements reveal no evidence of significant social stratification — at least, no archaeologically visible evidence.

The highland settlements of Iron I also reveal no evidence of central government. They are characterized instead by distributed storage, especially for grain, and by food preparation facilities shared by expanded families in small housing compounds. This general prospect in fact continues in Iron II, the era of the Israelite kingdoms.[6] However, the Iron II settlements are frequently circumvallated, with impressive structures especially in the area of the gate, as for example at Tell en-Naṣbeh (Mizpeh), Tell Farʿah North (Tirzah) or Tell Beit Mirsim in Judah. These characteristics are absent from the Iron I highland settlements, along with any other sign of public works. In other words, there is no evidence of a central administration, or any agency of taxation and administration, in the Iron I highland hinterlands. David's failure to erect a temple in Jerusalem would in this light represent evidence that, on the face of things, he thought in traditional terms economically. He refrained from extensive public works, and thus from extensive taxation — precisely the issues that the Israelites would cite (1 Kgs. 12) as reasons to secede from the kingdom of Solomon on that builder's death. This is the interpretation produced by an empathetic reading of the text. Just as David abided by the rule of law, never murdering even his worst political enemies, he also refrained from decorating himself with public display and the insignia of lofty office.

But, as in the deaths of David's enemies, another explanation is more plausible. If David took Jerusalem early in his reign — and he was based there at the time of the Ammonite war — David's military reach to the north may not have extended much beyond the territory defined by the Gibeonite confederacy. His ability to press populations into corvée is unlikely to have extended even to that point, and almost certainly did not reach the heart of Ephraim. This limitation is reflected in the meagerness of the rations he distributed on installing the ark in Jerusalem. David was either destitute or frugal. Nor was his position, as a vassal or at best ally of Gath contesting with Eqron for the territory of the central hills, such as to permit him to establish an impressive state center. Indeed, if he remained a real or merely nominal vassal of a Philistine center, his masters may have prohibited his assuming the airs of a real king.

In sum, early in his reign, even assuming that he was able to attract support from Israelites north of Benjamin, David was in no position to conscript their

---

6. See esp. John S. Holladay, Jr., "The Kingdoms of Israel and Judah," in Thomas E. Levy, *The Archaeology of Society in the Holy Land,* 383-93; "House, Israelite," *ABD* 3:308-18; Lawrence E. Stager, "The Archaeology of the Family in Ancient Israel," *BASOR* 260 (1985): 1-35.

labor to construct an acropolis and a major fortification in Jerusalem. He may well have parlayed the transfer of the ark into an ideological election of his capital and dynasty. He may even have presented the relative poverty of his royal seat — really, his stronghold or den — as evidence of his modesty. And from such posturing the notion of David's unconventionality, an important part of the character witness for his alibis, may even have arisen. Still, had David enjoyed the independence, security, and wealth to undertake building projects, to project an image of gravity abroad, there is little doubt that he would have done so. Jerusalem was placed to do so only toward the end of his reign, which may in fact explain the tradition that it was he who acquired the land on which the palace and temple acropolis was later constructed.

C. The Saulide Hostage

David's earliest wars were without doubt those in the south. In the first instance, he raided what would later be southern Judah in the Negev fringe, on behalf of his patron at Gath. It is impossible to date his Edomite campaign with any confidence, and it may belong later in the reign, as Joab seems to have been the principal in it. But the one reliable tradition about David's early activity is the admission that he was the captain of Ziklag. He took an interest from the outset in the south.

David's other early conflicts have their home in the Ayyalon Pass. The conflict with Ishbaal does not pass north of the town of Gibeon, an indication of Ishbaal's offensive against David's allies (and equally an index that David made little headway at all in the civil war before Ishbaal's convenient demise). The battles with the "Philistines" end with the clearing of the western pass. These battles probably reflect a reformation of local alliances, with David attaching Benjaminites to his forces and turning on the Eqronites who had formerly supported him against Ishbaal. They thus mark the start of the more or less formal stage of Gath's wax and of Eqron's decline. David's irruption into Jerusalem did not provoke a panicked Philistine invasion. Rather, acting as an agent of Gath, he ejected elements loyal to Eqron from the hills, and possibly from Jerusalem and Bethlehem themselves.

All of this activity in southern Benjamin suggests that eradicating Saul's descendants was one of the first items of business on David's agenda after the taking of Jerusalem. The killing began well at the battle of Jezreel. It continued with the death of Abner and his retainers during the peace conference in Hebron. It was further advanced by the Gibeonites' assassination of Ishbaal in his residence. But it culminated in the consignment of Saul's descendants *en masse* to the execution at Gibeon.[7] In the last case in particular, responsibility for the slaughter, and for a policy of persecution, could not be denied. David completed the job the Philistines began at Jezreel, rooting out his masters' most implacable opponent.

The combination of these events earned David the reputation of a murderer, a "man of blood," in Shimei's immortal phrase. Naturally, the king denied having killed Saul at Jezreel. He blamed Joab for the assassination of Abner. He cited the death of Asahel as the source of a personal vendetta and of Joab's distrust of the northerners (which should lead us to ask whether Abner's involvement in Asahel's death was as direct as the text alleges). He actually executed the Gibeonites who brought him the head of Ishbaal. And he imputed the deaths of the other Saulides to Saul's violation of the treaty with Gibeon, the violation of an oath that angered Yahweh: the executions were the only way to end a famine that Yahweh brought on as a punishment. It is doubtful that any such treaty existed before David invoked it (and 1 Sam. 7:14), and it is equally doubtful that there was a famine of any serious proportions. But the effort to cover up David's prosecuting a Philistine policy about Saul bespeaks a nativist Israelite constituency.

After harvesting Saul's heirs, David attached to the court the one remaining grandson of the king (2 Sam. 9). This grandson was Mephibaal, the son of Jonathan. The text presents Mephibaal's confinement at the court as David's act of grace, reciprocating Jonathan's commitment to him. Mephibaal was lame, and David, the story of Jerusalem's capture claims, hated the lame.[8] For Jonathan, thus, David set aside his instinctual revulsion. This is again the presentation. In fact, Mephibaal was at best a hostage at the court, and sufficiently impaired to prevent his being a rallying-point for Israelites disaffected from David.

There are numerous parallels to the taking of hostages to ensure the cooperation of vassals, as early as the 2nd millennium b.c.e.. For example, Tiglath-Pileser I reports that he took one enemy king's "sons, his own issue, and his family as hostages."[9] However, such a policy uniformly applies to situations where the family of the hostages remains in power. Alternatively, states sometimes kept members of the former royal families of vassal kingdoms on tap: these served as potential threats to and replacements for kings from the subsequent ruling house.

Mephibaal, to all appearance, fulfilled neither function, though one could

7. 1 Sam. 31; 2 Sam. 1; 3; 4; 21.
8. See Shmuel Vargon, "The Blind and the Lame," *VT* 46 (1996): 498-514.
9. RIMA 2 A.0.87.1.ii:47-48.

argue he was a potential threat to Eqron. His political uselessness made him a perfect candidate to serve as David's evidence that he harbored nothing but good will toward the House of Saul. David munificently bestowed Saul's entire estate on him. However, two pieces of evidence — beyond the murders of all Saul's other heirs — give the lie to the presentation.

The first is the role of Ziba, the slave of the house of Saul. Ziba tells David where he can lay hands on Jonathan's son, in order to bring him to the court. Coincidentally, David appoints Ziba, "Saul's aide," to be the steward of Saul's estate:

> "Everything that belonged to Saul and to all his House, I give to the son
> of your lord. You will work the land for him, you and your sons and your
> slaves, and you will bring (the produce) so that the son of your lord will
> have food and will eat it, so that Mephibaal, the son of your lord, will eat
> food regularly at my table." Ziba had fifteen sons and twenty slaves.
> (2 Sam. 9:9-10)

An agricultural establishment with 35 workers is a significant holding. It should have produced enough surplus to support not just Mephibaal but a far larger group. This was, after all, the royal estate of Saul. And by enfranchising Ziba on the land, as a tenant manager rather than an owner, David positioned himself to siphon off a part of the surplus — and earned Ziba's loyalty into the bargain. After the Absalom revolt, when Israel was laid low by David's army, David would bestow half the estate on Ziba as a reward for his service. The seeming generosity to Mephibaal conceals a policy of graft and kickbacks.

The second indication that Mephibaal's confinement was part of a complex political deal is the place from which Saul's scion was extradited. He was removed "from the house of Machir, son of Ammiel, from Lo Debar," who, along with Barzillai, the grandfather of Saulides murdered at Gibeon, later lent support to David during the Absalom revolt.[10] Like Barzillai, Machir was a Gileadite. It is probably coincidental that Bathsheba's father is identified as an Ammiel in Chronicles, since Samuel identifies him as Eliam, a variant on the same name, but also as the son of Ahitophel, from Giloh on the outskirts of Jerusalem.[11] Machir's Gileadite connection, however, is striking. Again, it suggests that a power shift occurred there, away from the former highland center at Jabesh. Machir's town, Lo Debar, like Barzillai's in Meholah, lay in the Jordan Valley. Saul's former lowland allies deserted early to David's side.

For this shift, a relatively simple explanation has been suggested above

---

10. 2 Sam. 9:4-5; 17:27.
11. 1 Chr. 3:5; 2 Sam. 11:3; 23:34.

(Chapters 17C, 18B). Collusion against Gilead among David, Philistine elements, Geshur, and Nahash of Ammon is almost a certainty. The "Philistines," after all, are said in the text to have exerted political control over Beth Shan and Rehob in the northern Jordan Valley, and Ashtarot in Transjordan, at Saul's death. The Ammonites, before the death of Nahash, at least enjoyed diplomatic relations with David, and one would be justified in suspecting that their pressure on Ishbaal's seat at Mahanaim in central Transjordan redounded to David's benefit.

The wholesale Gileadite traduction of Saul's house begins with Barzillai's policy reversal, so that Saul's, and his own, grandsons die at Gibeon. It continues, however, with the extradition of Mephibaal. Both Barzillai and Machir, who extradited Mephibaal, then supported David against Absalom, for the very good reason that they expected reprisals should Absalom triumph. At the end of the Absalom revolt, Barzillai supplies yet another son as a hostage at the court (2 Sam. 19:31-40[32-41]). These relationships were built on common interests, common enmities, but hardly on mutual trust. It is not coincidental that David's other Transjordanian supporter at the time of Absalom's revolt was the son of Nahash whom he had installed as king in Ammon (see Chapter 17C).

David clearly found willing collaborators, in Transjordan, for the destruction of the house of Saul. What he offered them, beyond Ammonite and Philistine collaboration against other centers, is explored in the next chapter. But it is certain that the temptations were great. This, then, is the source of the implication — not however the claim — that the Jabeshites might have responded positively to David's overture on Saul's death, had their answer not been preempted by Abner and Ishbaal. The process of recruiting Israelites against Saul's heirs reveals a delicacy that David did not earlier show. It is in this phase of his reign, in his mobilization of Israelite resources, that he assumed for the first time the status of a king, rather than that of a brigand, a predator, the commander of a mercenary gang. The difficulty is in distinguishing just when he made that transition.

CHAPTER 20

David's Wars

A. The Ammonite War

The summary of David's conquests in 2 Sam. 8 begins with the Philistines. This text, as noted, describes his clearance of Eqronite proxies or filibusters from the western reaches of the Ayyalon Pass, and their ejection from in or near Jerusalem. It reinforces the image of David as an opponent of "the Philistines," an entity whose cohesion was infrequent. The fight with Eqron secured Jerusalem's western flank and ensured its control of its natural hinterland, the Ayyalon Pass, as in the period of the Amarna letters, in the 14th century.

The chapter then passes on to Moab. There, David extracted something he could call booty, and executed some captives. From the north, David cannot have undertaken an operation against Moabite territory without the acquiescence of Ammon. This places the foray into Moab after his Ammonite war. If, on the other hand, he entered Moab from the south, the battle with Moab will have been tied to his advance into Edom. He may have combined against southern Moab with the king the A source locates at Mizpeh of Moab.

In Edom, David pursued a policy of systematic extermination (1 Kgs. 11:15-16). He garrisoned the entire country as well (2 Sam. 8:14). This latter action may correspond to the population of the Negev highlands in the Beersheba region with regular settlements, whose presence in the 10th century is reflected in survey results (above, Chapter 14A). Three considerations place this action, possibly involving Joab's extermination campaign, late in David's reign.

First, the settlements in the central Negev, which were destroyed by the pharaoh Shishaq in the fifth year of the reign of Solomon's successor, Rehoboam, were essentially short-lived, none showing more than two archaeological phases.[1] This indicates that the earliest settlements were constructed no earlier than the very end of David's reign. Relatively few were probably erected by the time of the king's death.

Second, Solomon exploited the Negev as a route of access to the seaport he constructed at Ezion Geber, in the vicinity of modern Eilat on the Gulf of Aqaba.[2] It was the use of this seaport to reach sources of drugs, spices, and other exotica from the Arabian peninsula and the horn of Africa that led, in the end, to Shishaq's destructive detour into southern Judah. The port's construction is reported along with Solomon's construction of fortresses, in the latter part of his reign (1 Kgs. 9:26-28). The organization of the report is again thematic, so no chronological conclusions can be drawn. It is, however, clear that commercial competition with Egypt intensified in the second half of Solomon's reign. So, again, the chances are that the venture dates late in his reign and was, as portrayed, a part of the Cabul barter with Hiram of Tyre (see Chapter 22D).

Third, David's political roots lay in the Negev, so that the regularization of settlement there by a policy of extermination and colonization did not pose the urgency that taking control of Israel, to the north of Jerusalem, did. Extensive trade with Arabia was possible only once David had consolidated his hold over Israel and enjoyed the luxury of extracting, through taxation and coercion, agricultural goods, such as wine and especially oil, that could not be produced, and therefore commanded a premium value, in the south. It is true that the Negev, and especially the Sinai, offered sources of copper for metalworking industries attested up the Jordan Valley as far north as Dan. However, so long as he remained the ally of Gath, in inland Philistia, and so long as Gath enjoyed peaceful relations with Egypt, David had no need to fear loss of access to the metal. (He also enjoyed access through his partners to the abundant copper of Cyprus.) David assumed real control in Israel only late in his reign (below and Chapter 21). He probably entrenched himself all over Edom, as the text claims, only at that time.

Because he was able to colonize them, the Negev and Damascus are the last

1. For the archaeological data, see Rudolph Cohen, *The Settlement of the Central Negev in the Light of Archaeology and Literary Sources during the 4th-1st Millennia B.C.E.* (diss., Hebrew University, 1986).

2. The traditional identification of Ezion Geber with Tell el-Kheleifeh is now in doubt. See Gary D. Pratico, *Nelson Glueck's 1938-1940 Excavations at Tell el-Kheleifeh: A Reappraisal.* ASOR Archaeological Reports 3 (Atlanta: Scholars, 1993). For a more recent identification, see Alexander Flinder, "Is This Solomon's Seaport?" *BAR* 15/4 (1989): 30-43: Ezion Geber an island in the Gulf of Eilat.

opponents in the report on David's conquests. But the claim in the case of Damascus is that David garrisoned some part of its territory, not the town itself. The systematic garrisoning of the Negev reflects a form of consolidation representing the operation of a mature state. Raids in the Negev were early. But its colonization came late. Most of the sites there were probably constructed by Solomon, after Shishaq deposed the dynasty with which Solomon had been collaborating.[3]

The only other Davidic conquest reported in 2 Samuel is that of Ammon, after the death of David's friend Nahash. To support Ammon, Aram Zobah, led by King Hadadezer, intervened. At first, Zobah joined with Ammon in a field campaign. Then it led an attempt to relieve the siege of the capital, Rabbah or Rabbat Ammon ("Rabbah of Ammon"). As we have seen, the field conflict with Zobah and its allies took place, in fact, in Transjordan. In this battle, David captured booty that could be traced to towns as far north as Tubihi, which undergirded his claims to have constructed an empire. This was probably the occasion on which he essentially freed himself from Gittite impositions.

Before or after the Ammonite war, David managed to conduct one campaign that does not appear in the record. That was his greatest achievement of all — his conquest of Israel. It is plain enough that by the time of Solomon's accession, the state controlled territory in Cisjordan reaching to the border of Aram, including areas to the north of the Jezreel Valley. The very embarrassing concession that Solomon sold the Cabul — the tribe of Asher, essentially — to Tyre could not have been made if he had not somehow been in possession of it (see Chapters 22D, 23E). So Solomon's state bordered Tyre.

The same fact is attested in the list of Solomon's provinces, which include the Galilee. The list is based on a record from Solomon's own time (Chapter 22D). It reflects the politics of the court: Solomon's sons-in-law are amply represented, in sensitive districts. The other governors are closely related to Jerusalem as well.[4] Likewise, the claim that Hiram furnished Solomon's material needs in the fortification of Jerusalem and the construction of an impressive acropolis atop it implies that the kingdoms were in contact, and the line of supply was not subject to unacceptable levels of depredation. Tyre was a party to David's policy of encircling and engulfing Israel.

Where were the borders? Almost identical architecture characterizes the

---

3. The foundation of the Negev sites need not be simultaneous. It is possible that sites such as Qadesh Barnea, and even possibly Tel Ira, were settled earlier, under David, than others.

4. T. N. D. Mettinger, *Solomonic State Officials.* ConBOT 5 (Lund: Gleerup, 1971), 120-21; Baruch Halpern, *JBL* 93 (1974): 519-32.

towns of Hazor, Megiddo, and Gezer in the archaeological levels contemporary with Solomon (Appendix, Chapter 23). The levels in question at Megiddo and Hazor were also planned to serve identical, unusual functions. Given that 1 Kgs. 9:15-18 names these three towns among six that Solomon fortified, the evidence would seem to support a verdict that he was in control of the towns. And, as noted in Chapter 11, the revolt of Sheba ben-Bichri ends with the submission of Abel of the kingdom of the House of Maacah and its incorporation into the Israelite state. Abel is generally identified with Ain Ibl, just to the west of Dan, well north of Hazor in the southern Beqa' Valley. Thus, by the end of David's reign, the court in Jerusalem was in control of the lands into the Upper Galilee. Probably, Hazor, Megiddo, and Gezer were not themselves border fortifications, but the administrative capitals of *districts* on Israel's borders late in Solomon's reign. When did David overwhelm Israel?

In the Ammonite war, David performed another classic *volte face*. It is impossible to determine whether Ammon, after David's murder of Abner and Ishbaal, dominated Transjordan. After Ishbaal failed to sustain Saul's initiative, new strongmen arose in the various localities the incipient Israelite state had incorporated. In Transjordan, David found sufficiently powerful allies to turn on Ammon. His marriage alliance with the king of Geshur, in the southern Golan, pressured Gilead into collaboration, giving David's quislings the upper hand there.

On the death of Nahash, David seized an opportunity and dictated terms to Hanun, Nahash's successor. This would explain the harshness with which the Ammonite used David's emissaries, shaving the hair from half their heads and sending them home humiliated. The Ammonite provocation was the *casus belli* that the apologist wanted to present (2 Sam. 10), so that one could argue that it was a purely literary manufacture. But what could have elicited such a response? First, an unjustified demand for tribute. Second, an insolent insistence on superiority. Third, a menace the reality of which the offended successor, and his courtiers, could not accept. The Ammonite provocation was probably real enough, because it implies an imposition on David's part that the narrator is at pains to camouflage with the strange claim that the Ammonites thought David's harmless emissaries were spies. When Joab makes the same claim about Abner's visit to Hebron, after all, the narrator exposes it as a flimsy story covering up a personal vendetta. How could a ruler conduct business without receiving embassies?

The war against Ammon was probably the occasion that motivated Saul's former allies in Gilead to rally to David's side. It represented David's adoption of Saul's policy of defending Gilead, but with the aim of recovering territory held by Ammon. The naked appeal to Israelite irredentism may well have influenced the denizens of the northern hill country as well as of Transjordan. If this was the case, then the price for inducing Israelite collaborators to embrace David's leadership was merely David's betraying his former Ammonite allies.

There is one indication that the Ammonite war was not the Israelite *cause célèbre* that this scenario demands. To Gileadites who collaborated in the effort, David no doubt assigned tracts of Ammonite land and captive labor forces. Two of these continued to support him even during the Absalom revolt — Machir son of Ammiel from Lo Debar, in the north of Gilead, and Barzillai from Rogelim, in the territory of Meholah. As the town Abel, of the territory of Meholah, lay only a few miles from Jabesh Gilead, it will have been the principal beneficiary of the latter's demise, assuming importance as Jabesh vanished from the record.[5]

Barzillai, again, was the grandfather of five of Saul's grandchildren. So his defection to David suggests that his alliance with the House of Saul was a disposable product of dynastic politics. He too was willing to throw over earlier partners in the process of advancing his own interests, presumably recognizing the uselessness of ties to a dethroned dynasty. Like the Gibeonites, Barzillai's non-Saulide descendants were rewarded with a berth in the temple hierarchy.[6]

As noted in Chapter 19C, Machir from Lo Debar was the party who negotiated the surrender of Jonathan's son Mephibaal to the court in Jerusalem (2 Sam. 9:4-5).[7] Presumably, he had been sheltering Mephibaal, and yielded

---

5. For the supporters of David in Transjordan, see 2 Sam. 17:27. On Jabesh and Meholah, see above, Chapter 17C. There is some debate whether Abel Meholah was east or west of the Jordan, but the narrative of 1 Kgs. 19:15-21 has Elijah encounter Elisha at his father's field in the vicinity as he travels from Horeb to the north by way of "the steppe of Damascus," that is, in Transjordan. The other references to the site (Judg. 7:22; 1 Kgs. 4:12) are geographically ambiguous. The implication is that Solomon's Jezreel district included its natural extension in Transjordan, to the Wadi Yabis. See also P. Kyle McCarter, Jr., *II Samuel*, 442. Solomon's district system may have occasioned the attachment of the northern Gilead to Manasseh, rather than allowing it to exist, as formerly, as a distinct entity. See Baruch Halpern, *The Emergence of Israel in Canaan*, chs. 7-8, for the evolution of the early definition of Israelite "tribes."

6. The award of a priesthood to Barzillai's lineage is tempered in the texts reflecting it (Ezra 2:61; Neh. 7:63), because it is an embarrassment that non-Levites should assume priestly office. However, Samuel again antedates E, D and P, and probably J, in reflecting without censure David's non-Levitic priestly appointments (Ira the Jairite or Jethrite; David's own sons) and assignments of sacral tasks (Obed Edom the Gittite, also the ancestor of a Levitic lineage).

7. Although 1 Chr. 3:5 identifies Ammiel, the name of Machir's father, as the father of Bathsheba — such that we might contemplate whether Machir was Bathsheba's brother —

349

him to David principally in response to the latter's blandishments. It is not improbable that Machir was the beneficiary of a marriage alliance with Saul's house, as Barzillai had been. The betrayal of the House of Saul by two powerful Gileadites represented a striking turnabout.

Barzillai and Machir presumably benefited from the Ammonite war and perhaps from associated inroads into the territory of Damascus to the northeast. Yet David's other Transjordanian supporter during Absalom's revolt was Shobi, son of Nahash, no doubt the king he installed on the throne in Ammon. That is, David did not just recover territory and extract resources from Ammon. He also put himself in the position of restraining Israelite retaliation to levels that Shobi found tolerable, and that the constituents of the Absalom revolt, for example, did not. Barzillai and Machir and Shobi all believed that a victory by Absalom would be a disaster for them, as David's collaborators in exterminating the House of Saul. Their unity in adversity reflects an agreement about David's balancing act in Gilead, and perhaps a well-placed confidence in David's skills, which the Israelites did not share.

While the new order in Gilead rewarded elements later divided from the Israelites, the Ammonite war may at first have enlisted Israelite support. David captured and assumed the "crown of Milcom" or perhaps the royal crown of Ammon. He reduced the Ammonite population to corvée, to produce metal, including iron, and mudbrick (2 Sam. 12:30-31). All this can only have delighted Saul's former partisans. David may have won popularity, and subscription to his kingship, with his victory in Transjordan. If, as the text implies, the king of Hamath entered into relations with him *at this time,* his ascent over Israel to the borders of Aram in Transjordan and in Cisjordan is even likely. Whether the diplomatic contact came so early, however, is a question.

The Ammonite war, and David's installation of quislings in Gilead, was of tremendous moment, both for his kingship in Israel and for his relations with the Philistine states. In the Late Bronze Age, Transjordan south of Gilead was virtually uninhabited, according to survey evidence. But in Iron I the population of the region exploded, registering a 12-fold increase in the number of sites, from 12 to 144, some of which, like Rabbat Ammon, were probably fitted

---

2 Sam. 11:3 names Eliam as the father, and 2 Sam. 23:34 names Ahitophel as Eliam's father and his town as the Judahite village Giloh. Under the circumstances, Eliam in Samuel should not be identified with Ammiel in Chronicles (although the names are variants identifying the god as a kinsman; both versions consist of the same three elements: a possessive pronoun, "my"; the term "god"; and the term "kinsman, uncle"). The question is whether the Chronicler, who calls Bathsheba ("daughter of the Sibitti") Batshua, intended to tie her to Machir.

out with elite quarters and fortifications at the time.[8] In Gilead itself, the number of Late Bronze sites was 20, whereas 74 Iron I sites have been identified.[9]

This surge in exploitation parallels developments in the central hills of Cisjordan. In particular, it explains the crystallization of regional states — Israel, Judah, Ammon, Moab, and even Edom — in this period. It also explains the wars over Transjordan suddenly being waged, essentially for the first time. These directly involved Israelites, Judahites, Gadites, Ammonites, and perhaps Moabites. But the conflict over Gilead also attracted interest and intervention from Damascus, Zobah, and Philistia. It may also have involved Hamath, in a related struggle in a more northerly theater. The alliance with Ammon, followed by its subjection and the incorporation of Gilead into David's ambit, represented an accession of resources in manpower, production, and the control of an important trade route that positioned David to assert himself in Cisjordan north of southern Ephraim.

It is, again, unlikely that David enjoyed the power to coerce the Israelite population before or even immediately after the Ammonite war. The local rulers of the north may in fact have more or less made their peace with him by the time of the war. He and his allies in Geshur, in Gilead, and perhaps in the Galilee, offered the north some protection against the Aramean kingdoms in the Beqa' Valley. Such a league, perhaps including Gath or even Eqron, would explain the Aramean projection, probably through the territory of Damascus, to assist Ammon.

This is a moment at which David may have broken out beyond the central hills in Cisjordan. More certainly, it is a time at which he acquired a cooperative constituency in Gilead — no better than he, no doubt, but nevertheless acknowledging his sovereignty. He began now to impose a central government on the structure of the village, throughout the kingdom. The collaborators that the crown found to go about its business in the villages will have been local grandees, probably warlords in most cases, elevated in theory by association with the state. Their less tractable countrymen will have been cajoled, in some cases driven, into cooperation.

---

8. For Amman, see Fawzi Zayadine, *MDB* 46 (1986): 17-20; further, on the elite cemetery there, Wolfgang Zwickel, "I Sam 31,12f. und der Quadratbau auf dem Flughafengelände bei Amman," *ZAW* 105 (1993): 165-74, Zwickel noting also the practice of cremation there, parallel to Saul's treatment at Jabesh in the A source; Larry G. Herr, "The Amman Airport Structure and the Geopolitics of Ancient Transjordan," *BA* 46 (1983): 223-29. Further, J.-B. Humbert and Fawzi Zayadine, "Trois campagnes de fouilles à Ammân (1988-1991): Troisième Terrasse de la citadelle," *RB* 99 (1992): 214-60.

9. For the survey data, collated, and with bibliography, see Israel Finkelstein, "From Sherds to History," *IEJ* 48 (1998): 120-31.

The imposition of administration on a countryside unaccustomed to it must have been a blow. In this new situation, village resources were not being mobilized to deal with a perceived emergency — such as wars against other ethnic groups. Instead, the new royal house in Jerusalem was busying itself with imposing governance from above on a vast hinterland. This aim is reflected by the appearance, under David but not under Saul, of a class of professional government clerks.

Two lists of David's officials frame the account of the Absalom revolt. The first, in 2 Sam. 8:16-18, lists: Joab commanding the army; Jehoshaphat son of Ahilud, the royal "secretary" or herald;[10] Zadok and Abiathar, the priests; Seraiah, the scribe; Benaiah son of Jehoiada commanding the Cherethites and Pelethites; and David's sons acting as priests. The second list of officials comes in 2 Sam. 20:23-26: Joab commanding the army of Israel, Benaiah the Cherethites and Pelethites; Adoram in charge of corvée; Jehoshaphat son of Ahilud, the royal "secretary"; Shi(sh)a, the scribe; Zadoq and Abiathar, the priests; "and also Ira the Yitrite was a priest for David," possibly indicating the activity of yet another Gibeonite in the sacral realm.[11]

The development of a rudimentary bureaucracy, which was to undergo expansion under Solomon, reflects the gradual regularization of the state apparatus. It is significant that the officer in charge of forced labor does not appear until after the Absalom revolt. One can interpret the change in one of two ways. Possibly, the author of the apology used sources that reflected the reality of two different periods in David's reign. In that case, it was only after the king took complete control of Israel, in the Absalom revolt, that he was able to extract significant taxation in kind from the population.

Alternatively, the author of the apology wanted to imply that the imposition of taxes simply did not play a role in the Absalom revolt. In favor of the latter assumption is Benaiah's appearance at the head of David's Philistine mercenaries, the Cherethites and Pelethites, in 2 Sam. 8. Benaiah plays no role as a commander until Solomon's reign, when he murders Joab on Solomon's orders. In the Ammonite war in 2 Sam. 10, Joab and Abishai command the troops. In the Absalom revolt, the commanders are Joab, Abishai, and Ittay the Gittite, the last of whom would seem to occupy the post of commander of the mercenary

10. Heb. *mzkr*. See Mahmud Abu Taleb, "The Seal of *plty bn m'š*, the *mazkīr*," *ZDPV* 101 (1985): 21-29, for a seal in Moabite script, found in a tomb in Ammon, from the 8th-7th centuries. Abu Taleb argues that the term is a calque of Egyptian *wmw*, the royal herald, and thus reflects an Egyptian model of administration.

11. Read Yitrite for MT Yairite, reflecting a misreading of paleo-Hebrew *taw* (t) as an *aleph* (a glottal stop or catch), or a mis-hearing of it (as in cockney). See 2 Sam. 23:38; 1 Chr. 2:53 ties such a lineage to Qiryath-Yearim.

bodyguard (2 Sam. 15:18-22; 18:2). And in the report of Sheba's rebellion, it is Abishai who commands the professional warriors, including the Cherethites and Pelethites, and there is no mention of Benaiah in the account (2 Sam. 20:7). Thus, some scholars claim that the list of officials from the time before Absalom's revolt is an intentional literary variant of the list framing the end of that episode.[12]

There is no firm basis on which to decide this point. But the presentation in the text merits attention. On the evidence of the lists of officials, David imposed forced labor on Israel only after the Absalom revolt. This would imply that any Israelite acknowledgment of his sovereignty even after the Ammonite war was purely affective, part of a system of alliances with strongmen in various local regions in the Cisjordanian hills.

B. Edom

David's policy in Edom has been addressed earlier in the chapter. Again, he campaigned there early. But his colonization of the Negev, and the rooting out of the Edomite population, expanded Judah's hinterland, and Gath's. The colonization of the Negev enabled him to control caravan traffic through it. This strategy interposed Judah's and Gath's proxies between Eqron and the sources of southern goods in the Hejaz. In David's time, the number of foundations was probably small, but sufficed to police the major routes.

The goods being acquired in the south were principally spices, which is to say, drugs and rare earths. Exotic textiles must also have played a role. In exchange, David must have been shipping wine and oil from Israel, and possibly timber from Phoenicia. Judah, exiguously settled, could have supplied little other than textiles, though eastern Philistia and the western Ayyalon Pass will have furnished him with oil for trade.

Yet the survey of Rudolf Cohen disclosed 50 sites in the central Negev highlands on the 10th-century horizon. Most of these stem from the time of Solomon, who intensified southern trade. And several disclose the burnished, red-slipped pottery that characterizes the period from just before Shishaq's destruction forward. Like any others that survived so long, these outposts were razed by the pharaoh shortly before 925 (see Chapters 14A, 21, 22-23).

Just at the time of David, the pharaohs of the 21st Dynasty were completing their new capital at Tanis. They too were disembedding the administrative center, in this case from the old location at Avaris, (Per-) Ramses (Tell ed-

---

12. See further McCarter, *II Samuel*, 257, with bibliography.

Dabʿa). The Israelite activity in the Negev, reaching in Solomon's reign to the northern Sinai, was intensified after Solomon's break with Egypt, when Shishaq founded the 22nd Dynasty in Bubastis. However, toward the end of David's reign, Egypt acquiesced in the development of a conduit for goods from the south up to Tyre — possibly because it regarded David's Israel as an extension of its vassals in Philistia. Under these circumstances, the opportunistic creation of an Israelite state embracing the Galilee unified the Tyrian trade hinterland, and thus led to an increase in production, shipping, and exchange, not just with the west, but also with the "neo-Hittite" Aramean kingdoms of Syria and southern Turkey, and with Mesopotamia. Solomon's policy of moving earlier populations of the Galilee to the highlands to increase cash-crop production reflects the intensification of trade.

As noted in Chapter 12, the boom in trade left a mark in cores into the ice layers of Greenland. In the glacial cap, there is a steep rise in metal deposits — from smelting — starting in the vicinity of 1000.[13] At that time, the only region with an economy that could have caused such a rise in deposits, which continued all through Iron II, is the Mediterranean ecumene. No doubt the Phoenician expansion of the 10th through 8th centuries was a major contributor. But what started the Phoenician expansion? It was the introduction of southern goods through Israel to the Phoenician ports, which then shipped the goods north and westward. The demands of the Assyrian and Babylonian markets were also insatiable. But the start of the intensive trade of the Iron Age stemmed from David's knitting together of the relevant markets, and Solomon's exploitation of them.[14] This is why the territorial state, the national state, is first witnessed in Canaan rather than Syria. The territorial state is in fact a minor empire — a monopoly of trade routes — cloaked in the rhetoric of ethnic identity.

Where did David and Solomon find the population for colonizing Edom? Fifty settlements, which were in fact garrisons, presuppose a demographic investment, probably on the order of 3000 people. The basis of this estimate is not roofed space, or built-up space, but rather the numbers of people required to police such an area. Allowing just 12 grown males per settlement, on average, and thus 60 people, one arrives at the figure in question.

---

13. Sungmin Hong et al., *Science* 272 (April 12, 1996): 246-49. On iron, cf. Harold Liebowitz and Robert Folk, "The Dawn of Iron Smelting in Palestine: The Late Bronze Age Smelter at Tel Yinʾam, Preliminary Report," *Journal of Field Archaeology* 11 (1984): 265-80.

14. For decline in those markets at the time, see J. Neumann and Simo Parpola, "Climatic Change and the Eleventh-Tenth-Century Eclipse of Assyria and Babylonia," *JNES* 46 (1987): 161-82.

Judah had no well of population from which David and Solomon could have drawn for colonization. David's Negev settlers, at least, were probably drawn from conquered populations. In this connection, the Ammonites, and elements of the Israelites (Jabesh?), offer themselves as the best candidates for deportation to the south. Again, the colonization started only very late in David's reign. The bulk of this activity took place under Solomon. And it is related to the fact that Solomon claimed, at least, to have wed the daughter of a pharaoh, setting the seal on a collaboration among Egypt, Israel, and Hiram of Tyre, that Shishaq was to bring to an end, or set into a different political and logistical framework.

C. Other Regions

Ammon and Edom aside, and the "Philistines" of the Ayyalon Pass, David's only other opponents were the Aramean expeditionaries from Zobah and Damascus, and the vague group of Moabites who paid tribute to him, at least once. He advanced into territory formerly claimed by Damascus. This success is reflected in Solomon's province list. This includes portions of the Bashan and northern Transjordan.

As we have seen, David did not advance into Zobah. His exchange of embassies with King Toi of Hamath, however, indicates international status. This is why the text commemorates the contact. Late in his reign, clearly, his control extended to the vicinity of southern Zobah. David's last reported conquest, the submission of the town Abel, of the territory of the Dynasty of Maacah, brought his state into physical contact with Hadadezer's kingdom. This came on the heels of the Absalom revolt, when Amasa had in theory succeeded Joab as commander of the conscript army. It was probably what occasioned Toi's embassy.

What is absent from the lists of David's conquests is, as we have seen, as significant as what is mentioned in them. One glaring omission, other than the Philistine plain itself, is that of Amaleq. The B source in Samuel credits Saul with victory over the Amaleqites in 1 Sam. 15. It claims that David fought Amaleq while resident at Ziklag (1 Sam. 27:8). But the omission of Amaleq in 2 Sam. 8, along with that of the "Geshurites" and the "Gerizzites" David supposedly raided from Ziklag, suggests that these elements were not targets of his policy of southern expansion. Instead, they were in all likelihood the objects of a policy of rapprochement, both with Gath and with Egypt, about which the apologist prefers to remain silent. Just as the denial that David was connected with Gath is implausible, so is the claim that he fought Amaleq in the teeth of Gittite interests.

The other conquest over which the apologist imposes silence is that of the lowland regions of Cisjordan. Clearly, the major fortifications of the Jezreel, such as Megiddo, Beth Shan, and Rehob, were integrated into Solomon's monarchy. Furthermore, the coast north of Philistia, including the site of Dor, also formed a part of Solomon's kingdom. Both these regions appear in the list of Solomonic provinces in 1 Kgs. 4. How they came into Solomon's hands remains a mystery. The mystery is explicable if Saul or Ishbaal conquered the sites: no one working for David or Solomon was anxious to celebrate concrete, and impressive, achievements and territorial gains by the House of Saul. The mystery is perhaps also explicable if the destruction and refitting of the towns in question was a function of an attack on Israel or an achievement of Israelites other than David or the House of Saul. This possibility remains to be explored in the next chapter.

CHAPTER 21

Absalom's Gift

2 Samuel presents Absalom's revolt as the fulfillment of Yahweh's promise to punish David for his adultery with Bathsheba and his murder of Uriah. Someone, says Nathan in 2 Sam. 12, will rise up from David's house and sleep with his women in the sight of "this sun":

> Lo, I am raising up against you evil from your house, and I will take your women in your sight and give them to your intimate, and he will lie with your women in the sight of this sun. For you acted in secrecy, but I will do this thing before all Israel and before the sun. (2 Sam. 12:11-12)

There follows, in 2 Sam. 13, the episode in which Amnon rapes his half-sister, and Absalom's full sister, Tamar.

Amnon's motivation for violating Tamar is that he loved her, and that he sought the advice of his "intimate." The Hebrew term for "intimate," $rē^a{}^c$, is usually rendered "friend," but the real meaning in the context of a royal court is closer to counselor, adviser, or intimate. Amnon's intimate is Jonadab son of Shima, "a very wise man." It is on his advice that Amnon simulates illness and fools David into sending Tamar to his residence as an attendant nurse. He rapes her while she is feeding him.[1]

Rape is not part of Jonadab's advice. In theory, then, Jonadab was merely

---

1. Whereas David refused to take *(br')* bread while fasting for Bathsheba's doomed son (2 Sam. 12:17), Amnon asks that Tamar furnish *(brh)* nourishment *(bryh)* that he would otherwise not take (2 Sam. 13:5, 7, 10). David's sincere, if premature, mourning of the infant elicits a feigned fast on Amnon's part.

357

arranging for Amnon to be in Tamar's presence. When Amnon then forced his sister, rather than asking his father for her hand in marriage, as she suggested, he was acting on his own initiative: Jonadab's sound advice, itself a product of Amnon's moping after Tamar, had gone dreadfully amiss. Conversely, the very human motivations of Amnon and Jonadab, and the very human responses of David, Tamar, and Absalom, play out into Absalom's alienation and ultimately revolt, fulfilling Yahweh's curse on David's house. The Absalom revolt, thus, has complementary causes, both divine and human.

Why, though, does David fail to act after Tamar's ravishment?

One explanation for David's failure to punish Amnon has been advanced above, namely that it was in his character, according to the apology, to let bygones be bygone. He forgave and mourned for his dead enemies, including Saul, Abner, and Ishbaal. He gave up his ritual humiliation immediately after Bathsheba's first son had died, rather than mourn the death. He steadfastly fought Israel's enemies, such as Amaleq, even while in service in the court of Achish. And so, he did not discipline Amnon; nor did he long remember Amnon's death (2 Sam. 13:39, read with LXX).

But this is not entirely a satisfying answer. David does, after all, punish wrongdoers in the apology: he kills the killers of Saul and of Ishbaal, and publicly reviles Joab for Abner's murder. He pronounces indignant retribution on the miscreant in Nathan's parable, who turns out to be himself as the violator of Uriah's household. Another explanation of David's inaction is therefore preferable.

On its face, Amnon's action seemed to fulfill the punishment Nathan had decreed for Uriah's murder. Thus, evil arose from David's house. One of his women was ravished, and by an intimate, advised by an intimate. The rape came to public light. The logical surmise was that Amnon was Yahweh's implement of vengeance.

In this sense, Nathan's prophecy is in effect self-working. David believed, rightly, that Amnon's rape of Tamar was inspired by Yahweh. He was therefore unable to punish Amnon for the deed. Amnon was acting as Yahweh's agent. The parallel is to David's leniency during the Absalom revolt toward Shimei. Who knows, he asks, whether it is not Yahweh who inspired Shimei to curse him? And in this case too, his humiliation by Shimei is part of Yahweh's plan to chastise him. Even David's attempt to spare Absalom's life can be understood in much the same light.

David's consequent quiescence in the case of Amnon and Tamar galvanizes Absalom into action. And Absalom's murder of Amnon and flight to Geshur lead to his revolt, when Absalom would truly sleep with David's women in the sight of the sun and all Israel. The prophecy paralyzes David so as to bring an even more harrowing fulfillment of the prophecy on him. Nathan had, after all, actually called for a *cycle* of violence to dog David to his dying day.

The nearest parallel in Israelite literature to Nathan's self-working prophecy, as noted in Chapter 2G, is to the dreams or to the preferment of Joseph in Gen. 37 (JE). Dressed like Tamar in a tunic of *passîm*, "a coat of many colors" in traditional translations,[2] Joseph badmouths his brothers and reports megalomaniacal dreams. Though Jacob knows that Joseph's brothers envy him, he sends him to check on the brothers when they take their sheep up north — rather as David permits Absalom to invite his brothers to a sheep-shearing in the north.

Joseph's brothers plot his death, but Reuben (E) or Judah (J) rescues him. The rescue results in Joseph's sale into slavery in Egypt. After his removal, the brothers rub goat's blood on Joseph's tunic and present it to their father, who mourns that he will "descend to my son in Sheol."

Most readers take delight in Joseph's revenge: having risen by interpreting dreams to be vizier of Egypt, he plays a series of tricks on his brothers. He demands, for example, that Jacob part with his favorite son, Benjamin, then frames Benjamin for theft,[3] forcing Jacob to descend, though to Egypt rather than to Sheol.

Joseph is not purely good, and the brothers suffer considerable provocation. It would be one thing were they motivated solely by envy of Joseph's tunic. It is another to have him recounting dreams in which *their* sheaves bow to his, or in which the sun, moon, and stars bow to him. And it is quite the last straw to have the father, who had marked the fact that the brothers were jealous, send the little tattletale to report on their husbandry. Jacob and Joseph provoke the brothers' crime.

So were the brothers in the wrong? In a way, and in a way not. For behind the scenes, as this review shows, a providential intelligence, a bit like that of Rube Goldberg, is at work. This is explicit in the narrative: Joseph attributes his dream interpretations to God both in prison and before Pharaoh (Gen. 40:8; 41:16[4]), just as he attributes Pharaoh's dreams to divine revelation (41:25, 28, 32), and Pharaoh sees the spirit of God in Joseph (41:38-39). When the broth-

---

2. Gen. 37:3; 2 Sam. 13:18-19.

3. Theft from the palace, a crime meriting rather heavier penalties than simple theft. See, e.g., the Code of Hammurabi 6, 10.

4. There is a problem in this verse, with LXX, QR reading *bl'dy 'lhym l̲ y'nh 't šlwm pr'h*. The negative particle is probably secondary, as it represents the *lectio facilior*, "Without me, God will NOT answer for Pharaoh's welfare." The last, incidentally, is a calque of Egyptian *wḏз*. MT is more problematic, probably implying that Yahweh would answer Pharaoh without Joseph's interpreting the matter.

ers try to return the money he secretes in their sacks after their first visit, he attributes the secretion to their God (43:23). Even when Joseph springs the frame on Benjamin, Judah attributes the revelation of the theft to God (44:16).

It was to preserve life, says Joseph later on, that God sent him on ahead (45:5). It was not the brothers, but God, who sent him (45:7-9). Joseph was sold to help the children of Israel, and indirectly the Egyptians, survive the years of famine.

So the providence of Joseph's impertinence as a youth, and sale into slavery, and rise to vizier and saving both Egypt and his family from famine are the doing of Israel's God.

Yet the doing is not really supernatural: Joseph dreams. Jacob gives preferment to Rachel's son, because of Jacob's love for Rachel, which has led earlier to Jacob's being fooled by Laban. Unwittingly, each human actor in the drama plays a part for perfectly venal reasons.[5] The principle of double or complementary causation is at work here: causation at a divine level as well as at a human level; but no superhuman agency is invoked for the day-to-day operation of the relations in question. To reverse the old proverb, God proposes, Man disposes. Yahweh sets the pieces in place and the drama plays itself out as foreordained, yet with each agent in the drama acting volitionally. And it is the dream itself which causes the brothers to act in such a way as to bring about its fulfillment. The dream is a self-working prophecy.

In the Joseph and Absalom stories, good things happen to bad people, bad things turn out to be good things by misadventure. It is no coincidence that just after the sale of Joseph into slavery, Judah, David's putative ancestor, enters into ambiguous sexual relations with a Canaanite daughter-in-law, Tamar (Gen. 38).[6] This is a comment on events in Samuel, transposed into the Joseph story, but indirectly. In fact, these very stories may be the springboard for the Shakespearean worldview: scum at the bottom, scum at the top.[7]

In Greece, the case of Oedipus presents a similar face. The Pythoness at Delphi informs Oedipus's father Laius that his son will kill him.[8] Had there been no prophecy that Oedipus was to kill his father, Laius would not have

---

5. In a sense, the humans behave as though they were a form of artificial intelligence in executing God's plans — the analogy is to how colonies of social insects work.

6. See the suggestive essay of J. A. Soggin, "Judah and Tamar (Genesis 38)," in *Of Prophets' Visions and the Wisdom of Sages*, ed. Heather A. McKay and D. J. A. Clines. Festschrift R. N. Whybray. JSOTSup 163 (Sheffield: Sheffield Academic, 1993), 281-87.

7. For the literary continuum from 2 Samuel to J, see Richard E. Friedman, *The Hidden Book in the Bible*. On their relative age, see Chapters 3, 15D, 16C, among other elements of the discussion here.

8. See, e.g., Apollodoros iii.5-8.

staked him to a mountain to die, and Oedipus would not have been adopted elsewhere. Had Oedipus himself not learned that his fate was to kill his father and mate with his mother, he would not have fled the homeland that, unbeknownst to him, was adoptive. So he would not have encountered his biological parents, and fulfilled the prophecy. The Pythoness's prophecy was again self-working.

Is there something about family conflict that evokes a doctrine of complementary causation, of a god who works only through human agencies — who in Joseph's case can provide against a famine, rather than closely define its extent? Perhaps the message is this: in the most intimate of human relations, as well as in the spectacle of sun-stopping, sea-splitting miracle, even there providence is at work.[9]

The complementary causation of Samuel may thus explain David's inaction.[10] And yet, the story of Amnon's raping Tamar is the beginning of an exposition of Absalom's revolt that focuses entirely on the relationship between David and Absalom.

The sense of double entendre, or of received versus transmitted message, permeates the picture of the revolt. It reflects the way in which the author constructs double causation for the reader, though not for the actors, who act uniformly for personal reasons, rather than out of devotion to some known purpose of Yahweh. Thus, the message of complementary causation — private and providential — is delivered without overt divine action being narrated, so that the reader must divine the providential character of events.

This is the same consciousness, of reporting at two levels simultaneously, that leads to the construction of 2 Sam. 8, the list of David's conquests (see

9. For a self-working oracle in Chronicles — Josiah relying on Huldah's claim that he would die in peace as a guarantee that he could not die in battle, when "in peace" might mean something else, namely at the hands of an ally — see Baruch Halpern and David S. Vanderhooft, *HUCA* 62 (1991): 221-29; Halpern, *VT* 48 (1998): 473-514. Here, the parallel is to the claim in Herodotus that the Mede Croesus misinterpreted the Delphic prophecy that a mighty kingdom would be destroyed when he engaged Cyrus. Such explanations reflect the dual insider-outsider orientation of Near Eastern historiography, which was written always by an in-group with a view to impact on an out-group (above, Chapter 5). The cases in Herodotus and Chronicles are in terms of our ability to date the literature contemporaneous. The twinning reflects Near Eastern influence on Greece. For deliberate ambiguity in Near Eastern historiography of the 6th and 5th centuries, see Halpern, "A Historiographic Commentary on Ezra 1-6."

10. Contrast A. Shapira, "Be Silent: An Immoral Behavior?" *Beit Mikra* 39 (1994): 232-44. The idea that inaction might imply contemplation does not apply in this instance, and probably does not apply in Jacob's case, after the rape of Dinah, either. For linkage to that story, see Friedman, *The Hidden Book in the Bible.*

Chapter 5A). There, the author's object is to camouflage one level — the literal claims of the text, versus its implied meanings — from outsider readers, while revealing both levels to insider readers. And yet, in the report of the Absalom revolt, the narrator bends every effort to ensure that any reader should understand both levels of the narrative at once. In other words, in the case of royal displays, the insiders are the authors of the inscription, while the readers are the outsiders. With complementary causation in Samuel and elsewhere, the readers are insiders, and the characters in the story are the outsiders.

The text proclaims its own subtlety by exposing the mechanics of rumor, as noted in Chapter 2G. This begins with the rumor misconstruing Absalom's murder of Amnon as an attempt at revolution, as murder of all the kings' sons, in 2 Sam. 13:30-36. The rumor is quite natural: a murderer in the royal house ought to be thoroughgoing. But Jonadab son of Shima, who had suggested to Amnon the ruse by which he might lure Tamar to his quarters, scotches the rumor. In an immediate sense, Jonadab is right: Absalom murdered Amnon only. And yet, the exaggeration in the rumor was prescient: Absalom would indeed turn on David, personally, rather than merely exacting vengeance from Amnon.

Later, Hushai appeals to the exaggeration inherent in rumor as an argument against Absalom's pursuing David immediately. A rumor of an initial victory by David, he suggests, would be blown out of all proportion and dismay Israel (2 Sam. 17:9-10). Now, this bracketing with rumor indicates an understanding of the impact of news on its hearers, whose tendency is toward overreaction. This is, again, exactly the overreaction on which the writer of 2 Sam. 8 depends in recounting the litany of David's accomplishments.

In fact, more than any other character in the Bible, David relies consistently on hearsay, on words of others. Nathan fools him with a false law case, and must then inform him, "You are the man!" The Wise Woman of Tekoa fools him with a false law case. He discounts the rumor of all his sons' death only when he actually hears the living sons (2 Sam. 13:36). He is fooled by Amnon's pretense of illness, by Absalom's festival of sheep-shearing. He believes Ziba's claim that Mephibaal had deserted to Absalom's cause. He must even be told, by Bathsheba and Nathan, that he promised the throne to Solomon. Much of this is a part of the strategy of apology. It also goes to create a character for David that fits with his alibis, and to alert the reader that hidden agendas, including that of Yahweh, underlie speech, actions, and events.

The presentation of the Absalom revolt employs the same strategy, of selective silence and selective reportage, to create its effects. The first silence concerns the aspirations of the Israelite rebels. The real causes of the revolt are shrouded in mists of generalization. Thus, the text claims that Absalom "stole the hearts" — in biblical thought, the minds — of the men of Israel: he "brainwashed" them. His appearance was prepossessing; he was without blemish from head to toe, and blessed with a luxurious head of hair.

Absalom's natural gravity and extensive retinue were augmented by a promise to award judgment to every man bringing a lawsuit to Jerusalem. He promised, the text claims, everything to everyone. He offered a hearing — more, a favorable verdict — to all (2 Sam. 15:1-6). "You have a just cause, but no *hearer* from the king," he says. Ironically enough, in the text, David has just given hearings to two petitioners — Nathan, and Joab's Wise Woman of Tekoa — whose cases cloaked their real purposes. "If only someone would make me judge . . . to vindicate everyone with a just case." That is, he wishes to fulfill the king's angelic function as a hearer, a point made by the Wise Woman of Tekoa in 2 Sam. 14:17, 20. And, indeed, he is the Judge, as Yahweh's agent, avenging Uriah. The issue of jurisprudence was very much in the mind of the apology's author.

The apologist's picture enjoys a degree of verisimilitude. Alienated by Amnon's escaping punishment, Absalom avenged his sister's violation and the insult to himself, and went into exile. On his return, he remained unreconciled, and remade himself from an impulsive youth into a consummate deceiver, a crafty politician. When the moment was ripe, he unveiled his plan and, supported by all Cisjordanian Israel and Judah, instantly occupied Jerusalem. Even at this moment, when Ahitophel counseled immediate pursuit of David, Absalom elected the more cautious course urged on him by David's agent, Hushai: he gathered the entire national army so as to confront his father with overwhelming force rather than press his immediate, and still compelling, advantage.

Historically, it seems more likely that the trustworthiness of Absalom's supporters was in some doubt: the text itself admits to Hushai's activity on David's behalf — stressing that it is the activity of "the king's intimate" (2 Sam. 15:37; 16:16), as opposed to the "intimate" fulfilling the curse against him. The text also admits to partisanship for David against Absalom on the part of the priests, Zadoq and Abiathar and their families, who remained with Absalom. Absalom's camp was thoroughly penetrated — no doubt long before the evacuation of Jerusalem. It was, if anything, the question of reliability among the courtiers and court soldiers who had gone over to Absalom's side that made it advisable to muster the entire nation of Israel in order to fight David: the presence of the tribal musters made defection in the field, among the courtiers, more dangerous to the traducers. Given the outcome, one might almost suspect David instigated the alliance of Absalom with Israel.[11]

11. David Noel Freedman observes, in correspondence, that Napoleon's express military ambition was to fight against his allies.

But this incident does provide a clue as to what our text is concealing about the nature of the revolt. In the story, Absalom enjoyed the support of those who had gathered with him in Hebron, which can only have been, in the main, denizens of the south. The cry sent round Israel, "Absalom reigns in Hebron" (2 Sam. 15:10-12), is meant to imply to the reader that the Israelites too supported Absalom's kingship as a substitute for David's kingship over them. Yet the only indication that David actually exercised kingship in Israel is the claim in the text that Israelite elders acknowledged his sovereignty before the conquest of Jerusalem in 2 Sam. 5:1-3.

We have seen that some Israelites recognized David, colluded with him, affectively. Elements in particular settlements — Barzillai in Meholah — collaborated at the expense of local rivals, such as the town of Jabesh. But the introduction of governance, taxation, and corvée into the villages was at best in its embryonic stage by the time of the uprising. The imposition no doubt involved a certain level of violence, a higher level of resistance, and, where taxation was regularized, resentment. A census, if undertaken before the Absalom revolt, will have contributed to the general unease even in the most distant quarters of Israelite settlement. Taxation, or the prospect of it, was no doubt one of the causes of the revolt.

In addition, the text relates that Absalom campaigned against the judicial process in Jerusalem. Traditionally, tort settlements were negotiated at the local level — within the lineage group, or among competing lineage groups. David's royal claims left him poised to overturn local negotiated verdicts. New mechanisms of conflict resolution, and a new layer of appeal, offered the king an opportunity to meddle in the governance of Israel, to interfere on behalf of his own partisans. Aggrieved Israelites could attempt to summon help from David in Jerusalem, no doubt at the price of acknowledging his sovereignty. Again, the process was part of the creeping centralization of authority in Jerusalem, upsetting traditional balancing mechanisms among the countryside lineages, and probably involving intervention in vendettas.

The apologist insists that David exercised sovereignty before Absalom's coup, to legitimate Solomon's impositions. On this assumption, the Israelites, like the Judahites, can only have meant to exchange David's kingship for that of his son. It is a commonplace of Near Eastern royal literature for kings to claim legitimate sovereignty over independent foreign powers, and to insist that resistance to any demand at all, however preposterous, represents a revolt.

This is an extension of the king's tendency to cast any exchange as a form of tribute. That is, if Israelites came to terms or treated with David after Ishbaal's murder, as for example asking him to decide cases at law, David will have taken whatever their delegation delivered to him as tribute, remaining silent on whatever he delivered in exchange. Just such a rhetorical strategy underlies 2 Sam. 8, the list of his conquests. Indeed, the text makes no mention of his reciprocation of Hamath's diplomatic overture, leading later readers to believe that he achieved suzerainty over Hamath (and to the Euphrates). In all likelihood, the situation was similar with Israel, and David ratcheted up his demands after the Ammonite war, with the help of his collaborators in Gilead and elsewhere.

Second, Absalom declines to pursue David until he can execute Hushai's plan:

> Let all Israel be gathered unto you from Dan unto Beersheba, like the sand that is by the sea in number, and, your presence proceeding in their midst, let us encounter him in one of the places where he is found, and camp against him as the dew falls on the soil, so that not even one will remain of him and of all the men who are with him. And should he be gathered into a town, then let all Israel bear ropes to that town and drag it up to the wadi, until not even a stone can be found there. (2 Sam. 17:11-13)

But Absalom has enjoyed communications with the elements south of Jerusalem, as well as the defectors to his cause from his father's court. His field commander is Amasa, Joab's cousin and thus David's nephew, and possibly even David's step-son.[12] The appointment of a kinsman as commander, with links to southern Judah, indicates that Absalom's primary orientation was toward Judah, and that his real constituency was there. Indeed, he mustered his real army in Hebron, to the south, before marching on Jerusalem. It is thus the mobilization of the Israelites for which he is waiting in the account. These are the elements whom he expects to keep his Judahite supporters in their alignments during the confrontation with his father.

This furnishes yet another hint as to the nature of the revolt: the Israelites joined Absalom's forces as Israelites, not necessarily as subjects of the king of Judah. The very cry, "Absalom reigns in Hebron," the proclamation of the revolt, can be understood in one sense as a renunciation by Absalom of the claim

---

12. 2 Sam. 17:25. Amasa's mother is Abigail, again the name of David's sister, and his father is "an Israelite." His father's name is Yitra in this account, but this may be the Nabal (lit., "fool") of the B source in 1 Sam. 25. See Jon D. Levenson and Baruch Halpern, *JBL* 99 (1980): 507-18. Note that Josephus lists Amasa as one of David's sons in *Ant.* 7.70, in a passage drawing on 2 Sam. 5:14. Amasa's inclusion reflects the fact that his mother was Abigail, identified in the tradition with David's wife. Coincidentally, and curiously, rabbinic tradition has it that Kileab (Chronicles: Daniel), David's second son, by Abigail, in Hebron, was in fact the son of Nabal, and was simply born after David married Abigail. The purpose of the midrash is to explain why Kileab plays no role in the succession narrative.

to kingship over Israel. It is not from the capital of the "unified" state that he reigns, but from the former seat of the territory of Judah.

The Israelites may have fought not as rebels, but as foreign allies of Absalom, intervening in a neighboring kingdom to put an ally on the throne. They thus understood the conspiracy as a chance to worm free from David's darkening shadow. The Israelites hoped for their own king, for independence. They joined forces with the upstart from a foreign dynasty to which they were otherwise hostile, precisely to rid themselves of the dynasty. It was this very relationship that made them the perfect partners for keeping Absalom's southern troops in line: the Israelites would not betray Absalom because his success would represent riddance of the dynasty.

One other indication comports with this scenario. In the course of evacuating Jerusalem and fleeing to Gilead, David meets Ziba, the steward of Saul's estate at Bahurim. Ziba brings David donkeys laden with bread, raisins, summer fruit, and wine. At the time, David is descending the Mount of Mashhit, a part of the Mount of Olives,[13] to the east. This is before David arrives at Bahurim, where Saul's kinsman, Shimei, curses him. Ziba relates that Mephibaal, the lone surviving scion of Saul,

> is dwelling in Jerusalem, for he says, "Today the House of Israel will restore to me the kingship of my father." (2 Sam. 16:3)

David's response is to transfer the estate of Saul to Ziba's possession.

In other words, in the apology, David finds Mephibaal's reported expectations believable. In the context of Absalom's revolt, Mephibaal might realistically think that he was about to inherit his grandfather's crown. This means that one possible outcome of the insurrection was a division of the kingdom of Israel from that of Judah. Though no sentient analyst would take this as Absalom's true intention, he probably promised to let the Israelites go.

Indeed, in the aftermath of the revolt, in 2 Sam. 20, Sheba son of Bichri allegedly calls on Israel to secede from the Davidic state. In response, David pronounces the danger greater than that posed by Absalom. The thought of a kingdom of Israel independent of Judah, which was to be realized after Solomon's death, was current at the latest by the time the apology was written — shortly after Absalom's revolt, not long into the reign of Solomon. Indeed, Sheba, a Benjaminite, may have been the leader of the Israelite contingent that lent support to Absalom. His lonely flight to the House of Maacah, then, would have been a logical outcome of David's victory.

13. See P. Kyle McCarter, Jr., *II Samuel*, ad 15:30.

The presentation of the Absalom revolt veils Israel's independence as a force in the coup. Yet what had Absalom, David's own son after all, to offer an independent Israel? One possibility is the promise that he would reverse David's policy of collusion with the Philistines against Israel. The state of Judah (with 18 settlements identified in Iron I) would join the Israelites in turning on populations outside the highlands, and on their Gibeonite collaborators inside the hill country. Indeed, the tableau of Absalom's campaigning begins with his asking the origin of "any man" bringing a lawsuit to the king. It is only when his interlocutor declares that he is Israelite that Absalom makes his unconditional promise of support. The implicit premise is that Absalom, while being depicted as a political Pollyanna, in fact promised to settle all conflicts between Israelites and non-Israelites — conflicts that could not be resolved through traditional kinship-system mechanisms — in favor of the Israelites involved.

Two properties of the report on Absalom's revolt are particularly suggestive. The first of these is the extraordinary admission of dynastic bloodguilt — David murdered Uriah and suffered for it. Notably, the focus of this bloodguilt, Uriah, has neither a natural following nor children according to the account in 2 Samuel.

So, Saul's kinsman, Shimei, taunts David, as the latter reaches Bahurim after his flight from Jerusalem:

> Leave, leave, Man of Blood, and man of wantonness. Yahweh has turned against you all the blood of the House of Saul, in whose stead you became king, and Yahweh has placed the kingship in the hand of Absalom, your son. Now you find yourself in your troubles, because you are a man of blood. (2 Sam. 16:7-8)

When Abishai offers to decapitate Shimei, David reflects that it is impossible to determine whether Yahweh inspired the curse.

David, in the narrative, is correct in his assumption. Shimei's curse is part of his humiliation by Yahweh. Shimei too is right, though not about the House of Saul: David's punishment as a man of blood has arrived; Absalom will be sleeping with his women in public, in sight of all Israel. And the punishment is deserved: David had ordered up Uriah's murder.

By this expedient, however, the partisans of Absalom, and of Saul, are conciliated. Again, the text presents the revolt as Yahweh's will — which means that the participants in it were blameless. What the text denies, over and over again, is David's implication in the murders and executions of Saul's lawful heirs. It certifies his innocence not just by the alibis for Saul's, Abner's, and Ishbaal's killings, but also by having the Israelite elders accept David's sovereignty and by having the Israelites reelect him king after Absalom's death. Central, too, to the apology's purpose is the report of 2 Sam. 21, namely, that an oracle from Yahweh compelled David to allow the Gibeonites to hang Saul's heirs: *Saul's* was the House of Blood, whose misdeeds in attacking legal allies precipitated a famine. In Shimei's case, *again*, David shows mercy to a kinsman of Saul in the face of extreme provocation.

In the supersession of Saul's dynastic claim on the throne of Israel, the apology furthers David's policy. The figures to whom the apology appeals to confirm David's authority against the House of Saul are: Samuel, Jonathan, Saul, the witch of Ein Dor, and Nathan. Samuel rejects Saul, and in the B source elects David as future king. Saul and Jonathan acknowledge David's election in the A source. The witch of Ein Dor raises Samuel's spirit to reject and condemn Saul one last time. And Nathan promises the dynasty. More specifically, he warranties the succession of David's son to the throne over Israel. He is the harbinger of the Absalom revolt, and Solomon's prophetic supporter. In the B source, a prophet condemns the priests descended from Eli, for their ancestors' corruption: Solomon then expels Abiathar, the last scion of Eli, from the temple.[14] Among the priests of Shiloh, Samuel — the adoptee, the cuckoo in Eli's nest — is the only one worth a hang. All this goes to show that Yahweh has abandoned the previous dynasties — Eli's, which came into conflict with Saul, but especially Saul's — in favor of David, and Solomon.

Another feature of the text is related to the first. It is the treatment of the rebels after the war. Again, up to the time of David's accession as king of Israel in 2 Sam. 5, the apology expends much energy denying David's assault on Saul and his heirs. It also relates his kindness in taking Jonathan's son Mephibaal into the court.

During the revolt, David forbears to kill Shimei, as the latter curses him at Bahurim. After the revolt, Shimei hastens from Bahurim to the Jordan with a thousand other Benjaminites to join the Judahite contingent leading David's progress across to Gilgal, and David promises him safety despite Abishai's renewed urging that Shimei be executed.[15] The policy of clemency toward all his enemies, of the House of Saul — a part of the alibi for their murders — continues.

At the same time, Mephibaal turns up and denies that he remained in Jerusalem during the retreat because he hoped to win back his kingdom:

14. 1 Sam. 2:12-36; 3:11-18; 4; 1 Kgs. 2:26-27.

15. 2 Sam. 19:21-22(22-23): Abishai urges the killing, but David rebukes both him and his brother, painting Joab again as a fanatic enemy of the House of Saul.

My servant tricked me, for your servant said to him, "Saddle me a donkey, and I will ride on it, so I can go with the king," for your servant is lame. But he denounced your servant to my lord, the king. Now, my lord the king is like an angel of god, so do what is right in your eyes. For all the house of my father were nothing but capital criminals against my lord the king, but you placed your servant among those who eat at your table. So what justification have I to cry out further against the king?[16]

David has, as noted, already reassigned Mephibaal's holdings to the faithful steward, Ziba. But at this juncture, he revises the arrangement, depriving Mephibaal of only half the estate instead. This Solomonic verdict represents a correction by the "angel of god" of an earlier failure to see through the question of loyalties in the matter. Again, David is compared to an angel in a juridical context.[17]

Mephibaal admits that, as a descendant of Saul, he is legally liable to the death penalty — for the attack on Gibeon, again, validating David's policy. He describes David's actions toward him as graciously generous, and then accepts the division of his estate with the remark that Ziba might have it all, so great is his joy at the king's safe return. Mephibaal had after all committed the faux pas of remaining in the capital at the time of Absalom's occupation. He had at best allowed himself to become Absalom's rather than David's hostage. David's decision, in hindsight, looks lenient indeed.

All this seeming generosity toward Saul's clan is probably historical, though David's motives in the text are chimerical. The policy programmed the orientation of the apology. What with Shimei's abasement before David, and Mephibaal's admission that he was well-treated despite deserving death, the Davidic apology must be addressing an audience favorably disposed toward Saul. Abiathar, who fled from Nob as a refugee to David on Saul's attack, and Abiathar's ancestor, Eli, portrayed as the last Israelite proprietor of the ark before David, can be minor players. (The ark connects Abiathar to the Gibeonites.) There is no need to soften the judgments on them, given their opposition to the House of Saul.

But like Saul, Absalom is treated with seeming sympathy. Neither Saul, who must fall on his sword, nor Absalom, whose hair catches in a tree bough, dies a very dignified death.[18] Yet the conciliation of the partisans of the House of Saul

---

16. 2 Sam. 19:24-28(25-29). For the text, see McCarter, *II Samuel.*

17. As 2 Sam. 14:17, 20. But compare 1 Sam. 29:9, in contrast to 29:4. See T. N. D. Mettinger, *King and Messiah,* 268-75; on the angelic aspects of kings, see above, Chapter 2 n. 44.

18. On Saul's death, see W. Boyd Barrick, "Saul's Demise, David's Lament, and

resonates with those of Absalom. David bewails Absalom, as he does all his enemies. He appoints Amasa, Absalom's general, as his chief-of-staff. He campaigns for reelection in Judah and Israel — separately — after the revolt.

All the grudges are in some sense combined. The rejection of Saul focuses on his cultic trespasses, and yet there is no narrative of his attack on the Gibeonites (except the priests of Nob in the A source), which is the justification invoked for exterminating the king's descendants *en masse*. The reason that this alleged treaty violation is not cited as a cause of Saul's own death is that the Gibeonites were allied with David and the Philistines. The Gibeonites also furnished the ark, as well as providing David's preferred site for fighting the civil war and for the murder of Amasa. The resentment both of Judah and of Israel thus reduces to a form of nativism. No wonder David's Gittites stood by him when all others deserted him. This is the reason for the repeated insistence that David is the Israelites' "bone and flesh."

Samuel admits that David turned Saul's brood over to Gibeon. But it moves that episode out of chronological sequence, and hides it behind the account of Absalom's rebellion. Resentment of these murders represented a huge political deficit. Shimei's taunt, though now occurring before the eradication of Saul's house, the apology's converse appeal to the bloodguilt of Saul's house, and Joab's execution in 1 Kgs. 2 for killing a blood enemy — Abner — all this follows from that open wound. And this is why David's one admitted murder is of a foreigner, albeit in his service — especially in his service. It is not just that Uriah had no following, politically: he is identified, despite his Yahwistic name, a name indicating a family commitment to the Israelite state god, as a Hittite. Good for David: he killed that foreigner! All this is a part of the apology. Nativism was a flash point of resistance to David's expanding administration.

More and more, after the Ammonite war, the coercion of Israelites had accompanied a reaching out from Jerusalem for their recognition of David's authority. Toadies and quislings in the north collected taxes, perhaps at some points imposed corvée. The king centralized ultimate juridical authority, sup-

---

Custer's Last Stand," *JSOT* 73 (1997): 25-41. Barrick argues that the death is shameful, and the Lament in 2 Sam. 1 more favorable to Saul than the narrative. Of this, I am not certain: though the sword of the Lament *is* tainted by its role in the suicide, the phrase applied to Saul and Jonathan, "slain on your backs" (2 Sam. 1:19, 25), and the loss of their renowned weaponry (1:21, 22, 24, 27) suggest either subtle disdain or, more likely, a sense of tragedy that does affect readers of 1 Sam. 31, rather like the syndrome of "the nobility of failure" in Japan and in peasant societies. On "slain on your backs," note Raymond C. Van Leeuwen, "Isaiah 14:12, *ḥôlēš ʿal gwym* and Gilgamesh XI,6," *JBL* 99 (1980): 173-84. The reference to "backs" in 2 Sam. 1 is, however, to high places *(bmt)*, and the implication one of nearness to Yahweh.

planting the old structures of conflict resolution within the lineage systems of the countryside and depersonalizing the administration of justice. The imposition of governmental structures, the use of force against the population, the creeping aggrandizement of the administration in Israel were doubtless the real causes of the revolt. But it was nativism that Absalom and, explicitly, his northern counterpart, Sheba, used to ignite the uprising. Even in the text of the apology, Sheba denies that David was an Israelite (see above, Chapter 16C).

How did Absalom propose, explicitly or implicitly, to heal the wounds in which David had rubbed the salt of ecumenism? What were Absalom's campaign promises? Vengeance for Michal and all the House of Saul. An acknowledgment of Israelite autonomy. Most likely of all, rescission of the concessions made by David to non-Israelite populations: to the Hivvites of the hills north of Jerusalem; to the Ammonites; arguably, to the Canaanites in the valleys; especially, to the Philistines, or at least the Gittites. Judah would fight these peoples, as Israel under Saul had done. Absalom may also have promised to administer the countryside under his sovereignty through, rather than across, lineage lines.

This, again, is why David is presented as a Philistine-fighter. It is why there are stories of his vengeance on an Amaleqite who killed Saul, on Gibeonites who killed Ishbaal. It is also why he preserved Shimei and Mephibaal, and treated the latter with undeserved clemency. And under Solomon, the placation of the Israelites continued, at least for a time. Joab was executed, for his assassination of Abner, Saul's general, and of Amasa, the military leader of the Absalom revolt. (Still, David was no doubt wise to rid himself of Amasa, the architect of Absalom's catastrophic final battle.)

Again, David is exculpated, for killing a retainer of Saul and another of Absalom. But it is Solomon who gets the credit for avenging Abner and Amasa by killing Joab. Solomon also banished Abiathar, the scion of Eli and associate of the ark, from the temple — a man attacked by Saul in the latter's war on Nob and on Gibeon. Solomon's son Rehoboam was wedded to Maacah, daughter of Absalom (1 Kgs. 15:2, 10), in the most unambiguous accommodation of Absalom's partisans imaginable. And, in the main body of the account of Solomon's reign, in 1 Kgs. 1–10, the Gittites, Cherethites (Cretans?) and Pelethites, David's 600 men from Gath, disappear.

All of this hangs together with the claim, in the account of Solomon's reign, that the Israelites helped to build the temple, but that thereafter only Canaanites performed forced labor. In the Near East, citizen participation in temple construction often led to tax remission. The technical term for the policy, in Mesopotamia, was *kidinnūtu*. Thus, in 1 Kgs. 5:13-16(27-30), Solomon dispatches Israelites to obtain the materials for his projects in the capital. In

1 Kgs. 9:20-22, after the temple dedication, he is said to have subjected only non-Israelite populations — those dreaded foreigners, again — to corvée.

This contrast, obscured in 9:15, 25, reflects the historian's assumption and implicit assertion that after the temple was finished, its builders were no longer liable to corvée.[19] The fact that the claim is implicit, however, is an indication that the state did not honor the promise that it held out to the temple builders. This in turn shows that the claim is nearly contemporary with the reign: a later text would have omitted the claim, or made it explicit. But the very claim — and again this shows that the text had a source close to Solomon — reflects an urge to conciliate the Israelites. This seems to have been, on paper more than in reality, an abiding theme of Solomon's policy.

There were exceptions. Solomon's regnal account admits to one — the execution of Shimei for violating his house arrest by traveling to and collaborating with Gath; tying Shimei, Saul's kinsman, to Gath was a master stroke on Solomon's part. One might imagine this as a trade-off for the execution of Joab. In addition, the fact that Adonijah can say, in the text, that "all Israel" looked to him to take the throne also suggests that the policy of reconciliation undertaken by Solomon was in fact a continuation of that planned by David — albeit a continuation adopted after Solomon seized the throne by force. Until Solomon's coup, "all Israel" had a role in the succession.

Solomon, in his early policies, and in producing David's apology, actively campaigned for the loyalty of his subject Israelites. By the latter part of his reign, this had ceased to be the case. He had returned to the politics of the early David — making an Ammonitess his heir's queen-mother, for example, and thus appealing to a foreign power for support; allying with Hiram of Tyre, and selling to him the tribe of Asher; and, especially, reconstructing and outfitting northern fortifications purely as government outposts (see below, Chapters 22-23).

19. This movement is absent in the OG, which lacks 1 Kgs. 9:15-25, leaving Israelites building the temple only. The effect is to suppress the implicit claim of *kidinnūtu,* and thus to free Solomon from the contrary allegation of having exploited Israelite labor for any other purpose, which it is clear from 1 Kgs. 11–12 that he did. The effect is that the OG implies that the Israelite motive for secession in 1 Kgs. 12 was resentment for the labor demanded for the construction of the temple: it implies natural Israelite impiety, on which Yahweh drew for his own purposes. The theology of the OG, while complex, comes to expression in significant pluses, minuses, and changes in the order of the text throughout 1 Kgs. 1–11. Despite the fact that the loss of 1 Kgs. 9:15-25 could be explained as a haplography conditioned by homoioarcton (*w* to *w*; so David Noel Freedman, in correspondence), the version of Solomon's regnal account underlying the OG is secondary and apologetic.

One more aspect of the report on Absalom's revolt claims our attention. It is the report's silence about the activity of Philistines.

A common convention of Near Eastern royal inscriptions is that they pass over foreign military assistance except when the ally becomes an overlord. Sometimes they remain silent even then. The king takes credit for the victory the inscription claims, or assigns it to his god. Thus, Mesha, the king of Moab who claims to have freed his country from Israelite domination ca. 841, does not mention that it was his overlord, Hazael, king of Damascus, who subjugated Israel and compelled it to withdraw from Transjordan (Chapter 23). Zakkur, king of Hamath, was rescued by Adad-Nirari III of Assyria ca. 800 from a group of western kings led by Hazael's son Bar-Hadad. He attributes his rescue to his god, never mentioning the Assyrian. Likewise, among biblical texts, the story of Jehu's coup in Israel in 841 omits mention of Jehu's alliance with Hazael against the ruling house of Omri. Around 800, King Joash of Judah is rescued from Bar-Hadad, Hazael's son, by "a savior," not by Adad-Nirari III, who liberated him by defeating Bar-Hadad. In 701, King Hezekiah of Judah is miraculously saved from the Assyrians by a plague in the Assyrian camp, rather than by the effect of an Egyptian intervention. The same holds true for the Absalom story.

David enjoyed the support both of his cronies in Gilead and of his vassal, the king of Ammon. Yet their contributions to his field force are never mentioned in the account. Moreover, the battle in the "forest of Ephraim" is described as an overwhelming victory. In particular, the narrator expects the reader to understand that terrain played a key role:

> The army went out to the field to meet Israel, and the battle took place in the Forest of Ephraim. The army of Israel was defeated there by David's servants, and the casualties were great there on that day, twenty thousand. For the battle there was distributed across the whole theater, and the forest consumed more of the army than the sword consumed on that day. (2 Sam. 18:6-8)

The professional soldiery, with David, was able to maintain communications and command control, and thus coordinate its maneuvers, despite fighting in various, scattered parts of the theater of combat. The citizen army, composed of occasional soldiers, was at a disadvantage when line-of-sight contact was lost. The result was a smashing victory, says the text.

The text's scenario is certainly possible. But one should certainly assume that Ammon and Gilead reinforced David's professionals. That omission is in itself an index that the account of David's victory deliberately avoids mentioning the collusion of Transjordanians against the Israelites. It follows that one should ask, with revolution afoot in their backyard, what role did the Philistines and other denizens of Canaan play in these momentous events?

Again, one of the components of David's royal bodyguard was a cohort from Gath, led by Ittay. Though originating in a Gibeonite center, Ittay's ethnic identification with Gath is invariable in 2 Samuel. He is the third field commander, after Joab and Abishai, against Absalom's force. In this light, and in the absence of any contrary indication, we may assume that Gath and David continued to make common cause.

But what was going on in the Philistine plain during the Absalom episode? David did not expand to the west as a consequence of the encounter. Gezer remained on Solomon's western border until his father-in-law, the pharaoh, presented it to him, burnt. But if David's kingdom in the hinterland was an extension of Gath in opposition to Eqron, it would be logical to expect the two to take sides in a struggle, particularly a struggle involving Eqron's dependencies — former or current — in the central hill country.

A number of destruction layers, on more or less the same chronological horizon, have previously been attributed to David, or simply been treated in isolation. These layers are found, among other places, at Megiddo VIA, Dan V, Yoqneam XVII, Beth Shan Upper VI, Tel Hadar IV, Tell el-Oreime V, Qasile X, and Dor.[20] At least some of them probably should be linked together. If the cause was not an earthquake, the Absalom revolt presents perhaps the only plausible moment for the burning of these towns (Chapters 22-23). Absalom's revolt was, at a minimum, the moment when David seized uncontested, naked power over the territory of Israel off the Philistine plain. Joab and Abishai murdered Amasa, intimidated the army of Judah as it arrived at Gibeon into accepting the killing, and pursued Sheba son of Bichri, possibly Israel's field commander under Absalom, to Abel of the House of Maacah. Their actions indicate that David enjoyed unrestricted freedom of maneuver all the way to Israel's border with Zobah after the revolt. The professional army had established its supremacy by smashing the citizen-soldiers of the tribal muster.

But there were also upheavals in the lowlands. Solomon's kingdom com-

20. For Dan, see Avraham Biran, *Biblical Dan* (Jerusalem: Israel Exploration Society, 1994), 135-38, 155; for Dor, Ephraim Stern, *Dor, Ruler of the Seas*, 92, 98; for Hadar, Moshe Kochavi, "The Eleventh Century BCE Tripartite Pillar Building at Tel Hadar," in Seymour Gitin, Amahai Mazar, and Ephraim Stern, *Mediterranean Peoples in Transition*, 468-78; for Oreime, Volkmar Fritz, "Kinneret: A Biblical City on the Sea of Galilee," *Archaeology* 40/4 (1987): 42-49; for Qasile, Amihai Mazar, *Excavations at Tell Qasile, Part Two.* Qedem 20 (Jerusalem: Hebrew University, Institute of Archaeology, 1985), 123, 125. Mazar links the fall of Beth Shemesh III and Masos II to the same horizon.

prehended the coast from Jaffa to the north, including Dor. Megiddo, Taanach, and Beth Shan had by the time of his accession passed into Jerusalem's possession. Material culture of a recognizably Israelite cast appears for the first time in the relevant strata — Gezer VIII, Megiddo VB and VA-IVB, Hazor X, Beth Shan Lower V. In the region of Dor, ceramic affinities swing in the direction of Phoenicia.[21] At the same time, the distinctive "Philistine" motifs vanish from the pottery repertoire. This need not signal a change of political or ethnic affiliation, but it certainly indicates a cultural shift.

Close to Philistia proper, the picture is more complex. Tell Qasile, at the ancient mouth of the Yarkon River, passes into the same cultural horizon with the destruction of Stratum X. However, it exhibits important elements of the ceramic profile of the Solomonic era already in Strata XII-XI. Qasile was probably early in introducing the diagnostic ceramic elements, because of Phoenician contact, which was probably a factor at Eqron as well.[22] On the other hand, Qasile may have been incorporated intact into the Israelite kingdom (Stratum X), as distinct from towns that suffered a destruction roughly contemporary with that of Dor or of Megiddo VIA, such as Beth Shan Upper VI.

Tel Miqneh, the proud 50-acre metropolis of ancient Eqron, discloses a similar picture. The city roughly contemporary with David (Stratum V), like Qasile, had burnished red slip pottery earlier than other sites. Eqron V metamorphosed into a different town before the onset of a phase (Stratum IV) with the pottery profile of the early Iron II, in Solomon's time. The city of the Solomonic era was shortly thereafter destroyed and rebuilt as a town (III) of only 10 acres.

Even then, some cultural continuity was maintained. The 7th-century temple built by the Eqronite king Achish (Achaios) to the goddess Ptgy(h) contained objects curated from the time of the Philistine colonization, including cartouches of the pharaohs Merneptah and Ramses VIII. Given the interest in anthropoids in the Middle Assyrian period, a baboon statuette also found in the temple may also stem from the same era.[23] The archaeological evidence

21. For a general discussion, Stern, *Dor, Ruler of the Seas*, 97-111.
22. See Amihai Mazar, "On the Appearance of Red Slip in the Iron Age I Period in Israel," in Gitin, Mazar, and Stern, *Mediterranean Peoples in Transition*, 368-78. As Gezer lies between Qasile and Eqron, the appearance of the red-slip there only in Stratum VIII seems anomalous.
23. For the finds, see Seymour Gitin, Trude Dothan, and Joseph Naveh, *IEJ* 47 (1997): 1-18. The authors conclude that these objects reflect Egyptian control of Eqron in the 7th century, after the Assyrian withdrawal ca. 623, following Nadav Na'aman, "The Kingdom of Judah under Josiah," *TA* 18 (1991): 34-41; "Chronology and History in the Late Assyrian Empire (631-619 B.C.)," *ZA* 81 (1991): 243-67. However, both the ivories stem from the

from Eqron and the textual evidence in general indicate that Eqron was on its way to becoming a dependency of Gath at this time. That development, however, would seem to be a product of events late in David's reign, when Gath wriggled free of Eqron's dominance and, with real finality, of events at the time of Shishaq's raid, five years after Solomon's death. In Shishaq's list of towns conquered, Eqron is the only Philistine city to appear, and it does so as an after-thought.

It is impossible on the basis of archaeology to determine which destructions were caused by campaigning at the time of the Absalom revolt, and which were occasioned by the invasion of Solomon's father-in-law, within a decade or two thereafter, which by Shishaq, and which by other upheavals (Megiddo VIA may have burned accidentally). And the Israelite texts furnish no details. However, it is easy enough to imagine that the war between a David in refuge in Transjordan, on the one hand, and Absalom and Israel, on the other, involved more than a single battle. This was an opportunity both for the Israelites and for David's allies to strike, and the chances are that both sides availed themselves of it.

A key to the course of the war is Megiddo. Megiddo VIA appears to have met its end around the start of the 10th century.[24] It was a town of mixed culture: late "Philistine" bichrome characterizes the layer, and houses of typical Canaanite form. Too, as noted in Chapter 7, there is a particularly heavy representation of collared-rim store jars, which are almost exclusively confined to hinterland regions of central Canaan and Transjordan. This led one scholar, Douglas Esse, to the conclusion that the storage jars were being constructed on the site, and that the potters were Israelite females active in domestic industry. The implication is of connubium between the residents of Megiddo VIA and the contemporary inhabitants of Manasseh or Ephraim, just to the south of the site. We may go farther: possibly, the site was in part populated by elements identical with those of the hills to the south.

Megiddo VIA is peculiar in several respects. The luxury goods of previous layers had been concentrated in the great palaces on the northern edge of the upper city. They included jewelry, precious metals, and exquisitely carved ivories. The city of VIA contained no real palace, and it is doubtful whether it even contained a temple. The housing stock was of mudbrick. The luxury goods

---

13th-12th centuries, and the odds that a Saite pharaoh would export them to Philistia seem low.

24. This is true both in terms of the ceramic repertoire, which is characteristic of the transition from the 11th to the 10th centuries, and in terms of the carbon dates, which tend to fall in the early 10th century.

were mainly trinkets, and they were distributed across the site.[25] Indications of social stratification are minimal, although two relatively large structures were present in the earlier palace area, suggesting the existence of a modest local elite.

Megiddo VIA shows every sign, then, of being a mixed settlement consisting of Canaanites and Israelites, possibly with some admixture of "Sea People." It may have been incorporated into Israel by Saul or Ishbaal.[26] If so, and if it remained loyal during the Absalom revolt, Megiddo may have been destroyed by David or his Philistine allies. Conversely, Megiddo may have been exploited by the Eqronites, and subsequently perhaps by David, as a brake on Israel's independence and communications across the Jezreel Valley. In that case, the Israelite "rebels" may have turned on it before coming to grief at the hands of David at the Jordan and possibly at the hands of the Philistines in the west.

In favor of the latter scenario are two considerations. First, given the mixed ethnic or political character of Megiddo, and of other sites destroyed or taken over at roughly this time, such as Keisan in the Plain of Akko and Beth Shan (Upper VI, or S-2) and Yoqneam in the Jordan Valley, we should expect a certain tension between them and Saul's nativist appeal. These sites would — on their archaeological face — make apt collaborators with Philistia and with David against Israel. Indeed, another site leveled on the same temporal horizon is Tel Hadar, possibly the royal seat of Geshur. Geshur's king was David's ally, the alliance sealed by a royal marriage; he also warehoused Absalom before his revolt.

Such sites may have provided some of the "Israelite" petitioners who acknowledged David's sovereignty over the north. But a resurgent nativism attaching itself to Absalom, grandson of Israel's neighbor in Geshur, might well deal harshly with the settlements. A post-Saul Israel is more likely than David to have destroyed or endangered them. While, as noted above, the catastrophe at Megiddo VIA may have resulted from a sudden fire, the pattern of destructions in the early 10th century may reflect Absalom's allies' activity.

Second, until the 10th century, on the northern side of the Jezreel Valley, there remain settlements in territories like the Lower Galilee whose continuity

25. For discussion and bibliography, along with treatment of VIA on the lower terrace at Megiddo, see Baruch Halpern, "Center and Sentry." For the collared-rim store jar outside the central hills and Transjordan, at Dan and elsewhere, see Joseph Yellin and Jan Gunneweg, "Instrumental Neutron Activation Analysis and the Origin of Iron Age I Collared-rim Jars and Pithoi from Tel Dan," *AASOR* 49 (1989): 133-41. Note their assumption that local manufacture of collared-rim jars confirms Danite migration from the central hills (Judg. 17–18).

26. For the possibility that Megiddo VI was Israelite, see Graham I. Davies, "Megiddo in the Period of the Judges," *OTS* 24 (1986): 34-53; above, Chapter 7.

with the Canaanite past was unbroken. The premier example is Tel Ein Sippori, where the indigenous elite lost its hold in the early 10th century. Tel Yin'am seems also to have lost its function at this time, despite continuity in function from the Late Bronze Age into David's era.[27] The elimination of the Canaanite villages on the border of the Jezreel, in favor of Israelite settlements in their place or in the vicinity, also bespeaks the conversion of the urban, or settled, population to the state culture that David or Solomon introduced.

In sum, Absalom's allies probably destroyed any such settlement that remained. It is less likely that David did so. The settlements in question were his natural allies against Israel. Even if the House of Saul had controlled them, it is unlikely that Saul or Ishbaal enfranchised them rather than treating them as aliens. In fact, it is possible that Ishbaal's successors, led perhaps by Sheba son of Bichri, together with the citizen army of Israel, were active and reducing fortresses up to the time of the Ammonite war, or even that of the Absalom revolt.

An alternative is that Gath and Eqron fought to a standstill at the same time. Whatever the interest of the other Philistine cities, there was no clear winner in the struggle between Eqron and Gath before Eqron's dismantlement. But Gath may have won independence from Eqron late in David's reign, weakening Eqron to the point at which Israel took control of the northern coast. Siamun, Solomon's father-in-law, raided the coast, to be sure, probably securing Gaza, Ashkelon, and Ashdod. He reduced Eqron's territory, shearing Gezer off to attach it to Solomon's realm. This gave Solomon a buffer between Eqron, on the inner plain, and the coastal regions to the north that were under Israelite control. These events may correlate to the revision of Eqron's site plan after Stratum V there.

Late in his reign, Solomon could have leagued with Eqron, against Egypt. Another turnabout in Jerusalem's policy after the accession of Shishaq and the change in dynasty is even likely. On the other hand, Eqron IV, the last great city there before the 7th century, may have been destroyed as early as the time of Siamun's raid on Gezer. The Philistine pottery in the layer is the same as that in Megiddo VIA. But strata have different lengths, and certain styles of pottery enjoy earlier and later vogues in different sites. Correlating layers chronologically

27. For Sippori, J. P. Dessel, "Tel 'Ein Zippori and the Lower Galilee in the Late Bronze and Iron Ages: A Village Perspective," in *Galilee through the Centuries: Confluence of Cultures,* ed. Eric M. Meyers. Duke Judaic Studies 1 (Winona Lake: Eisenbrauns, 1999), 1-32. For Yin'am, Harold Liebowitz, "Excavations at Tel Yin'am: The 1976 and 1977 Seasons: Preliminary Report," *BASOR* 243 (1981): 79-94; Liebowitz and Robert Folk, "The Dawn of Iron Smelting in Palestine: The Late Bronze Age Smelter at Tel Yin'am, Preliminary Report," *Journal of Field Archaeology* 11 (1984): 265-80. Smelting at Yenoam begins in LB II (VIB), but then resumes after the destruction of that layer in VIA, Iron I.

across sites with any real specificity, purely on the basis of their pottery, is in part an aesthetic, not scientific, enterprise. The ceramic evidence, thus, is ambiguous.

At the end of David's reign, assuming Absalom's allies were as nativist as the dynasty to which they seem to have adhered, a number of northern towns lay in ruins. Those on the coast were casualties in a formerly non-Israelite zone, suggesting that the Israelites were simultaneously at war with David and with powers on their flank. Eqron or Gath, or both, should be numbered among the enemies they encountered. This was the time when David enlisted Tyrian assistance: while Israelite hills settlers off the Tyrian coast posed a threat to Tyre's interests in its hinterlands, David may have offered to restrain and discipline them as a *quid pro quo* for Hiram's intervention to the south. The evidence from Dor, at least, would seem to indicate that the establishment in Jerusalem peacefully picked up the pieces after the revolt. The texts — not just Kings, but also the course of Shishaq's campaign, as he reports it in his Karnak itinerary — indicate that the coasts and lowlands were indeed a part of Solomon's kingdom (below, Chapter 23).

Overall, the best explanation for our sources' silence about Davidic expansion on the plain is that the Israelites leveled the towns in question. Sites that had resisted Israel probably experienced increased pressure during Absalom's uprising. Whether Eqron sided with the Israelites against David and Gath is uncertain, but the transitions from Strata V-III in the town, roughly in the period in question, suggest that it suffered either at the hands of Gath during the Absalom revolt, or shortly after, at Siamun's, and possibly both. Meanwhile, David inherited the coastal regions, probably because the conflict between Eqron and Gath left both exhausted.

David did not make direct inroads into Eqronite territory. Gezer remained the border, after all. And yet, he or his son came up the winner in the Jezreel Valley and on the coast after the revolt. It is not just that they were in control of the lowlands: they were able to project power through to the Upper Galilee, as in the case of Hazor and Dan, and the sale of the tribe of Asher. This indicates that the Israelites, distinct from Judah, conquered these regions. The same circumstance explains why David and Solomon get no credit for the accessions to the Israelite realm.

In general, the great tension was between the Cisjordanian Israelites, on the one hand, and the populations of Transjordan, Judah, and Philistia, on the other. The destructions of towns on the coast identified with Sea Peoples and of other towns in the Jezreel signify Israelite successes. Even where the Israelites had dominated under the House of Saul, matters probably came to a head in the latter half of David's reign.

Representative Archaeological Layers
in the Time of David and Solomon

Site	David	Solomon	Shishaq
Megiddo	VIA, VB	VB*, VA-IVB	VA-IVB
Hazor	XI	XB*, XA	-
Gezer	IX	IX-VIII*	VIII-VII transition
		IX burnt by Siamun	
Beth Shan	Upper VI	Lower V*	Lower V
Taanach	IIA?	IIA-IIB*	IIB
Eqron	V*(-IV?)	(V?-)IV(-III?)	IV-III transition, or III
Ashdod	X*	X-IX	IX
Dan	V	IVA*	-
Hadar	IV	III	-
Oreime	V	IV	-
Beth Shemesh	III	IIA*	IIA-B transition?
Timnah (Batash)	V	IV*	IV abandoned
Yoqneam	XVII-XVI	XVI-XIV	XIV-XIII transition
Qasile	X	IX	IX

*First appearance of quantities of burnished, red-slipped pottery

David's professionals, in the end, were more than a counterweight to the forces ranged against him. The tribes of Israel remained independent until the Ammonite war. They fitfully developed ties to David thereafter, with elements here and there embracing his leadership. But as David extended his tentacles into their society, the Israelites grew nervous about the regime in Jerusalem. They joined with Absalom in Hebron to be rid of the regime in Jerusalem. They lost their ability to resist Jerusalem in the course of the revolt. This is why David does not repeat Saul's coronation pattern until Absalom's revolt. He gains election, crosses to Gilgal, and is then re-elected by the Israelites (see Chapter 17D). It was only after Absalom's revolt that David became the legitimate king of all Israel.

The Absalom revolt could not have turned out better if David had planned it. How he might have done so is obscure. But since he profited from it, one ought to wonder. Did David — and Joab — rehabilitate Absalom to be the rallying point of a planned "popular" uprising? In other words, were they luring the army of Israel into a trap, only to crush them, centralize taxation, and build a modern state? If so, Hushai's advice to Absalom was crucial: it was by this ruse that the combined armies of the Israelite tribes, in their entirety, were induced to roll the dice against David's mercenaries in terrain that favored David. A true paranoiac would suggest that David's nephew, and perhaps step-son, Amasa was another of David's deep penetration agents in Absalom's hierarchy: Amasa's murder then will, like those especially of the Gibeonite killers of Ishbaal, have served to ensure that the conspiracy was never exposed.[28]

28. This last suggestion was inspired by a comment of David Noel Freedman, in correspondence.

CHAPTER 22

The Aftermath of Absalom's Revolt

A. The Aftermath: David's Policies for Expansion

After the Absalom revolt, David allegedly campaigned for reelection by Israel and Judah (2 Sam. 19). To Israel he made the concession of sparing Shimei and his Benjaminite cohorts. He continued to maintain Mephibaal, Jonathan's son, at the court. In Judah, he appointed Amasa, Absalom's field commander, as his army chief. Joab rescinded this appointment with his sword at Gibeon. The embarrassing admission that Amasa was appointed suggests that David did campaign for office.

David's kingdom seems to have exploded in the aftermath of the revolt. Joab was able to follow the Israelite schismatic, Sheba son of Bichri, to the very northern border of the ethnic arena. Joab bent Abel of the House of Maacah to David's will. David assumed real control of the whole area previously dominated by Israel.

Several policies flowed from Absalom's defeat. Joab's census through the length and breadth of the land, from Dan to Beersheba, probably started before Absalom's time. But his activity in the far north — to Dan — more likely came after Absalom's revolt than before (2 Sam. 24). The crown stood in a position to impose a real reckoning of population and resources in the far north. If the Israelites resented David's politics before the war, they certainly experienced reasons to hate him afterward. The textual link between the census and the acquisition of the temple plot foreshadows the conscription of Israelite labor for the temple's construction.

A second innovation at the end of David's reign is his collaboration with

Hiram of Tyre. Though reported just after Jerusalem's conquest in 2 Sam. 5, Hiram's collaboration cannot have been won before the Ammonite war, and possibly came much later. Hiram stood to gain particularly when David's state was able to direct southern goods through Israelite territory. That is, Hiram will have become an active partner when David's control over the north was complete. The victory over Zobah in Ammon may have sparked a correspondence between David and Hamath. But the creation of trade links to Tyre, and David's reaching the border of Zobah, more than the Ammonite war, triggered the delegation of the son of Hamath's king. Hamath and Tyre tended to remain closely aligned in other periods, including the 9th century, as well.

The other arena of expansion was in the Negev. The colonization of the south must have accelerated after the Absalom revolt, when the state stretched from Tyre to Edom. The 50 sites in the central highlands uniformly stem from the 10th century, and all were destroyed by Shishaq after 930 (see Chapter 23E). Because the settlements are almost all mere houses or small enclosures, rather than fortifications, it has been suggested that they represent sedentarization by local nomads.

Still, their density alone indicates that the sites served as a combination of police stations and caravanserai on the trade route from the Arabian peninsula, directing traffic toward the Israelite heartland, and perhaps to Gath. The sites were within signaling distance of one another. Animal bone samples are not available from most of them. But one Negev site, at least, Tel Masos, on the border of Philistia, specialized in cattle production. So the economy of the region was not undifferentiated: the locale was exploited in order to maximize resources and perhaps spread risk. Still, the appearance and maintenance of the stations in the Negev reflect the activity of the state in Jerusalem in Solomon's reign, starting, as noted in Chapter 20, late in David's.[1]

---

1. For discussion of the Negev settlements, see Israel Finkelstein, "The Iron Age 'Fortresses' of the Negev Highlands: Sendentarization [sic] of the Nomads," *TA* 11 (1984): 189-209 (dating Masos early and placing the region under Israelite control); "Arabian Trade and Socio-Political Conditions in the Negev in the Twelfth-Eleventh Centuries B.C.E.," *JNES* 47 (1988): 241-52 (sedentarization preceding Israelite control, which produced renomadization); Diana Edelman, "Tel Masos, Geshur, and David," *JNES* 47 (1988): 253-58 (identifying Masos with the Geshur that produced Absalom's mother, incorrectly). On Arad XII, to be dated roughly to this time, see Ze'ev Herzog, Miriam Aharoni, Anson F. Rainey and Shmuel Moshkovitz, "The Israelite Fortress at Arad," *BASOR* 254 (1984): 1-34. On Ein Hazeva, see Rudolph Cohen and Y. Yisrael, "The Excavations at 'Ein Ḥazeva/Israelite and Roman Tamar," *Qad* 29/112 (1996): 78-92. A leading candidate for a Davidic foundation is Beersheba V. Notably, some of the ceramic forms in the Negev sites relate to the horizon represented by Megiddo VIA, which may imply age or may imply activity under

The colonization of the Negev was a key step in the development of the countryside of Judah itself. As noted in Chapter 15, there was effectively no hinterland population in Judah before David's time. By Solomon's death, however, the state there was at least able to retain its autonomy relative to Eqron and Gath on the one hand and Israel on the other. Judah's population, like David, was probably distinct from that of Israel.

Indeed, even today, oriental and occidental Jewish populations are characterized by different genetic diseases, which may reflect the ancient distinction. Sephardic (oriental) populations suffer from Familial Mediterranean Fever and glucose-6-phosphate dehydrogenase deficiency. Ashkenazic (western) populations have high occurrences of Tay-Sachs and Gaucher's diseases. It may be that the Sephardic populations predominantly reflect the genetics of the Israelites, which are related to those of other Mediterranean peoples. The Ashkenazic profile is distinct from that of European populations among which the Jews lived, and may reflect the genetics of the population of Judah.[2] Eventually, the Human Genome Project may shed definitive light on the subject, particularly if Israel reverses its medieval interdiction on invasive analysis of ancient human remains.

The settlement of the Negev facilitated the rise in trade that led western Asia out of the economic doldrums of Iron I. This was in part occasioned by poor harvests, probably induced by a long cycle of droughts ending in the late 11th or early 10th century.[3] But it was also exacerbated by a political economy that militated against the construction of wider zones of trade. Unifying most of Cisjordan from the north to the Negev, from Dan to Beersheba, permitted the king in Jerusalem to mediate trade from Arabia to Tyre and Hamath. The rise in trade lifted the economy throughout the region, leading to an economic floruit in the late 10th and 9th centuries (see Chapters 12A, 20).

B. After Absalom: David and Israel

The garrisoning of the Negev, and the six months spent by Joab in Edom, thus probably belong to the stages just after the Absalom revolt. The population of the region with colonists probably also reflects the deportation of Israelites

---

David, though it may also imply conservatism in the potting tradition: the surface treatment is often that first witnessed, outside of Philistia, in the latter part of Solomon's reign.

2. See J. J. Groen, "Historical and Genetic Studies on the Twelve Tribes of Israel and Their Relation to the Present Ethnic Composition of the Jewish People," *JQR* 58 (1967): 1-13.

3. J. Neumann and Simo Parpola, "Climatic Change and the Eleventh-Tenth-Century Eclipse of Assyria and Babylonia," *JNES* 46 (1987): 161-82.

there. Occasional northern ceramic forms turn up in the Negev settlements. Though these could be relics of exchange, they include open forms such as bowls that did not serve as containers for transport. Since the majority of the open forms found at the Negev sites were handmade, the northern tableware suggests affinities with the population of Israel.

As noted earlier, David's major strike against his former allies in the south succeeded rather than preceded his reduction of Israel. If the Ammonite war represents his first policy reversal in the direction of recruiting support from Israelites, especially in Gilead, the southern campaign involved wholesale betrayal of allies useful in penning in the southern highland populations of Judah in particular. The prize was control of the overland traffic, of which he deprived the former allies.

Roughly in David's time, surveys disclose 18 settlements in Judah, a small but still considerable presence in addition to the professional army in Jerusalem. The extension of the king's reach to the caravan routes placed him to improve his standing with Gath, and Gath's with the coastal Philistine centers to whom southern goods were to be delivered for transshipping. With the proceeds, David might in theory have kept the level of taxation in Israel relatively low, while supporting his army and modest royal establishment.

Yet it remains a question how far David conciliated the Israelites at the end of his reign. Certainly, the apology, from Solomon's scribes, executes a strategy geared to proselytization and co-option in the north, as we have repeatedly seen. And this continued David's later politics. But was it a reversal of David's actual policies?

David had, after all, smashed all resistance in the course of the Absalom revolt. Israel lay prostrate at his feet. He did appoint Amasa, Judah's rebel general, as his chief-of-staff. Yet the murder of Amasa is the most immediate and most cynical of all his assassinations: Joab simply lay in wait for Amasa and dispatched him without ceremony. The apology — which makes Amasa's murder, along with Abner's, the basis for Joab's execution by Solomon — describes the victim rolling in his own gore as the men of Judah came to join the expedition against Sheba son of Bichri (2 Sam. 20:11-13). And immediately afterward, Joab took up the reins of the army once again (see 20:23). David made a concession, principally to the Judahites, then immediately withdrew it, violently.

Nor is it likely that Amasa was his only victim after the revolt. He is merely the victim who was awarded a high government post as the price of David's re-enthronement. There will have been a purge attendant on David's return to power, particularly if, in the cases of Zadoq, Abiathar, Hushai, and perhaps even the silenced Amasa (Chapter 21), he had spies and informers in Absalom's inner circle of advisers.

385

In this light, the report that Ahitophel, Absalom's chief adviser, went home to Giloh and hanged himself reflects the reality of what such figures could expect of a David returned to power. In the narrative, Ahitophel hangs himself immediately on the rejection of his advice that Absalom dispatch him forthwith in pursuit of the retreating David (2 Sam. 17:23). However, the exact timing of the suicide is implied, not stipulated. Even so, the text presupposes that Ahitophel foresaw David's victory and Absalom's undoing. Whenever he did see this, he did David's work for him, preferring to die by his own hand than by a method of David's choosing. Even assuming that David had the man assassinated, the treatment in the story alone is suggestive.[4]

Another combination of texts relates to Absalom's children. 2 Sam. 14:27 reveals that Absalom had three sons and a daughter, Tamar, who bore the name of Absalom's ravished sister.[5] But during the report on the revolt, the apologist explains that

Absalom had taken and erected for himself during his life the pillar that is in the Valley of the King, for he said, "I have no son for the proclaiming of my name."[6] So he named the stela after himself, so it is called the Monument of Absalom until this day. (2 Sam. 18:18)

Did Absalom have sons, or did he not? Most commentators have, again, assumed that the two passages contradict one another.[7] Yet Absalom had a daughter, whom he named Maacah, after the founder of the dynasty that gave

4. On the dignity of suicide in Samuel (Saul and Ahitophel), see above, Chapter 21 n. 18. Only these texts seem to reflect and respect an ethic of preferring death to capture and torment. Somewhat different is Samson's suicide, which involves killing a Philistine multitude.

5. Jack Sasson has suggested, in passing conversation, the possibility that Amnon ravished not Absalom's sister, but his daughter. This would explain why she could suggest that he ask David for her hand, since a marriage between uncle and niece would be licit. At the same time, the author of the apology will then have changed the daughter into a sister in order to increase the repulsiveness of Amnon's behavior. I have refrained from adopting the suggestion only because the implication would be to place the rape, and Absalom's revolt, even later in the reign than is usually done: this would go to reinforce the positions adopted above, Chapter 13.

6. The proclamation of the name is a part of the ancestral cult, representing a form of immortality. It is related to the ordinance of Exod. 20:24, which urges the Israelites to erect altars consisting of earth: "In every place where I proclaim my name I will come upon you and bless you." The wording of the Exodus text is probably later than the text in Samuel. This is an example of the state god attempting to co-opt the ancestral cult, to become, so to speak, the national ancestor. The parallel is to imperial China.

7. See P. Kyle McCarter, Jr., *II Samuel*, 407-8.

him refuge. Maacah was the wife of Rehoboam and mother of his heir, Abijah. And she remained queen-mother, chief priestess of the kingdom, into the reign of Asa, Abijah's successor.[8]

Assuming that Maacah's descent from Absalom was not an imposture perpetrated by Solomon, Absalom's daughter, at least, survived. What of the boys? The most probable solution is that David attainted Absalom's family — that is, having convicted Absalom of treason, David executed his male heirs and confiscated all his properties. This is how Ahab handled the family of Naboth (1 Kgs. 21; 2 Kgs. 9:26). It is also how Joshua treated the treason of Achan (Josh. 7). And the Ten Commandments proclaim that Yahweh, too, roots out the sons of "those that hate me," which is, traitors, to the third and fourth generation.

When Absalom's sons were subject to attainder is a question. One possibility is that the unreported executions came on his flight to Geshur, and occasioned his resentment of David. Most likely, David killed his grandsons on learning of the revolt, and Absalom accordingly constructed a monument. If David failed to take action, Solomon will not have allowed Absalom's sons to survive. David probably also banished Absalom from remembrance in the royal funerary cult.[9] The women, however, survived. It would be intriguing indeed to have Maacah's reflections on the events of her lifetime.

All this suggests that David dealt harshly with Absalom's family. It explains why Absalom's helpers, such as Ahitophel, preferred suicide to falling into David's hands. This may have been a means to avoid attainder: David spared both the daughter and the grandson of Ahitophel — Bathsheba and Solomon — though killing his own grandsons by Absalom. The purge following on David's victory was in all likelihood a great deal more widespread than limited to immediate circles. Blood will have flowed in the villages of Judah, among the real partisans of Absalom. It will have flowed in Israelite villages as well, among those who regarded the war as an opportunity for vengeance on David for the deaths of the sons and grandsons of Saul.

---

8. 1 Kgs. 15:2, 10. The first passage names Maacah as Abijah's queen-mother, which is striking, but not surprising. The second names her as Asa's queen-mother. Chances are, she outlived her son, and so remained in the position past the time of Asa's succession and the recording of it in what were probably annual lists. For the queen-mother as the earthly surrogate of Yahweh's consort (his Asherah), Ashtoret, see Susan Ackerman, "The Queen Mother and the Cult in Ancient Israel," *JBL* 112 (1993): 385-401.

9. See for a parallel in the Hittite Old Kingdom, Michael C. Astour, *Hittite History*, 27. Note that attainder was practiced in Britain into the 18th century and remained legal into the 19th century. Attainder was excluded by Article 1, Section 9, Paragraph 3 of the United States Constitution. It is also forbidden in Deut. 24:16, again indicating the antiquity of Samuel relative to Judah's literature of the 7th century.

On the other hand, the scale of the reprisals and the subsequent repression was probably limited. There is no indication that David pressed the Israelite population into forced labor for grandiose building projects. The only report of movement toward the construction of a temple in Jerusalem comes in the story of 2 Sam. 24, where he acquires the threshing floor of Araunah. Neither the fortification of Jerusalem nor the undertaking of temple construction is attributed to him. As noted, he is excused from the duty of temple construction by the peculiar explanation that it was an Israelite tradition never to have a temple — so Yahweh would commission his successor to build one, rather than David.

There is a pattern to events in David's reign. He does not commit murder, of political opponents, openly. He consistently denies responsibility for the deaths of his enemies, going so far as to mourn them, bury them, and, in two cases, kill those foreigners he blames for their deaths. He does not, according to our text, subject Israelites to forced labor. He does not reorganize the kingdom.

Some of this is probably true. But David remained politically active after the Absalom revolt. On the other hand, he did not decide the succession. The text claims that he chose Solomon as his successor. But as we shall see (below, Chapter 22C), all the evidence is against his designation of Solomon as prince regent and heir. This may indicate what policies he pursued in his last years. If he supported Adonijah's claim on the throne, then an argument might be mounted that he dealt relatively harshly with Cisjordanian Israel, and clung to the alliances he had formed with Gath and elements in Gilead. After all, the army's support for Solomon suggests that Solomon's policies were different from what Adonijah's would have been.

Still, the archaeological evidence is ambiguous. At Megiddo, the city whose culture is neither classically Israelite nor classically Canaanite, Stratum VIA was destroyed sometime toward the end of David's reign. The later (VA/IVB) full-blown state center there reflects activity from the second half of Solomon's reign and thereafter. Between the two is Stratum VB, which seems to have been incorporated into a central state. It has some public architecture. There is no palace, but there is also little in the way of domestic population. There may be a local shrine, but there is no dominant temple. The layer could date from the end of David's or the start of Solomon's reign. But the population that covered the mound in Stratum VIA was removed. Much of that population was not ethnically identified with Israel. A similar transitional phase characterizes Dor at roughly the same time. Conversely, there seems to be no intermediate phase between the Canaanite city at Beth Shan and the Israelite administrative center there.[10]

10. On Beth Shan, see Amihai Mazar, "Beth Shean in the Iron Age: Preliminary Re-

When did these centers come under Israelite control? Possibly, Saul or Ishbaal emptied the towns in question, enslaving their inhabitants. Possibly, David sacked them. And yet, as argued in Chapter 21, it is most likely that an Israelite successor of Ishbaal and ally of Absalom destroyed them during or just before Absalom's revolt. Still, the permutations are complex.

As an example, Saul or Ishbaal may have taken Megiddo and Beth Shan by siege or storm, or the sites may have allied with one of them against the Philistines. If they took it and destroyed it, they simply left it abandoned. Conversely, they may have accepted such sites as strategic partners, or simply failed to overcome them. In the Absalom revolt, either the Israelite allies of Absalom or David and his Philistine allies then would have devastated the site, and perhaps Dor, and Rehob and Beth Shan. We have seen (Chapter 21) that the likeliest scenario is that Absalom's allies destroyed the sites in question: it is entirely possible that Israelite forces did so before Absalom's revolt, not during it. But capitulation during the revolt is also possible. David, after all, abandoned Cisjordan to his opponents.

In either case, reconstruction at Megiddo, starting in Stratum VB, clearly occurred under Jerusalem's direction. And it was sparse. David, late in his reign, or Solomon withheld possession of the fortress from the people of the local hinterland: the spoils went to the state, not to the inhabitants of the region. In the latter part of Solomon's reign, this policy would be redoubled, such that Megiddo was virtually devoid of any domestic population whatever. It was disembedded from the local economy and region and, like Hazor in the same period, entirely devoted to governmental activities.

The policy of rebuilding major tells without their local populations — if inaugurated by David or by Solomon — represents a compromise. Canaanite populations were not reintroduced into the sites that David inherited from the Israelites. On the other hand, the Israelites did not inherit the strategic cruxes such as Megiddo. Such sites were the most valuable properties that countryside leaders could hope to gain. They were reserved for a central elite instead.

This decision resembles David's policy in Transjordan. There, he reduced the influence of Ammon, but retained it as an ally. He found Israelite collaborators willing to accommodate him on the basis of a limited reduction of Ammon's territory and power. David even married off Solomon, son of a royal consort, if not the heir designate, to an Ammonite princess, to cement the

---

port and Conclusions of the 1990-1991 Excavations," *IEJ* 43 (1993): 201-29; "The Excavations at Tel Beth Shean during the Years 1989-94," in *The Archaeology of Israel: Constructing the Past/Interpreting the Present*, ed. Neil A. Silberman and David B. Small. JSOTSup 237 (Sheffield: Sheffield Academic, 1997), 144-64.

Ammonite alliance.[11] In the south, David maintained relations with Gath throughout his reign and posed no threat to Gezer, in the territory of Eqron. He remained leagued with the Gibeonites, yet through threats and blandishments, found willing collaborators among the Israelites in Benjamin and Judahites in the hill country and Negev. His politics were pusillanimous. Despite allying with every peripheral power, he maintained the pretense of not having murdered everyone in Saul's house, and a lot of others besides, to the end of his career. David, it would seem, never wrote off a single possible constituency.

Solomon, likewise, appealed to the northern population and especially the population of Judah. He denied David's murders of the Saulides, and of Absalom and Amasa. He married his heir off to Absalom's daughter. But Solomon also retained an Ammonite bride as his first wife and eventually as the mother of his heir. He divided the country into districts, imposing a real administration controlled by the central court on the countryside, rather than dealing with the lineage heads.[12] And he introduced the principle of massive public works, constructing an enormous acropolis in the capital, including an extensive palace, a large temple, the Millo — possibly the "stepped stone structure" of the City of David excavations — and a city wall.[13]

Conversely, it is the implicit claim of the text that Solomon offered his Israelite laborers freedom from further forced labor — *kidinnūtu* — in exchange for their work on the capital (above, Chapter 21). The claim is the more believable because it *is* implicit, and the promise was probably never fulfilled. That is, Solomon's imposts were heavy, but were presented as an avenue to privilege. This is why the issue of who is *permitted* to build a temple is of moment in reports on the temple's reconstruction after the Babylonian exile (Ezra 4:1-3; contrast Zech. 7:2-3). Based on these elements, it might be argued that, even early in his reign, Solomon's policies represented more radical inroads on Israelite resources than David's. But the spin on those policies, in the promise of tax remission, in the production of the royal apology, was uniformly conciliatory.

It seems unlikely that David's straddling was much different in the wake of his triumph over Absalom. Enjoying uncontested power, he probably posed as the vindicator of the oppressed and the liberator of Israel from Philistia, in particular Eqron. This view comes to expression in the apology, both in the ab-

11. Bathsheba's status as a "wife" of David is reported in the text. The text, however, has Bathsheba's footprints all over it. She may have been a concubine. See below.
12. 1 Kgs. 4:7-19; Mettinger, *Solomonic State Officials*, 120-22; Halpern, *JBL* 93 (1974): 519-32.
13. Solomon's early public works, 1 Kgs. 6–7; 9:16-28; 12; for the stepped stone structure, see above, Chapter 18.

sence of any claim that Saul expanded Israelite territory or controlled the Jezreel, and in the words of Abner to the Israelite elders:

> Both yesterday and earlier you were yearning for David as king over you. So now, act! For Yahweh has spoken regarding David, saying, "By the hand of my servant, David, will I rescue my people Israel from the hand of the Philistines and from the hand of all their enemies." (2 Sam. 3:17-18)

The fulfilment of the promise comes in the form of David's conflict with the Philistines in the Valley of Rephaim, in 2 Sam. 5, and its reprise in 2 Sam. 8:1, at the very head of the list of his conquests. Yet David remained tied to Gath, the Gibeonites, the Ammonites, Tyre, to all the powers on Israel's periphery who were, or were probably, connected to one another. The story of David's reign is that of the encirclement of his principal conquest, Israel. And the presentation of David's reign is the concealment of his conquest of Israel.

There is even some archaeological evidence for the contrast between David's territory and that of Israel: the latest phase of Philistine bichrome pottery registers regularly in the territory of Judah, including Beersheba and Beth Zur. It has also been found in Transjordan, where David found estimable allies. It does not occur with any frequency in Israelite territories, even in towns just north of Jerusalem, such as Tell en-Naṣbeh and Bethel, where an earlier bichrome phase is represented. As is documented in the Appendix, late ("debased") bichrome coincides with much of David's reign. At the time of its production, exchange between Judah and Philistia was ongoing, probably including the exchange of people. Exchange between Israel and Philistia was evidently rare.

C. Solomon's Succession

The most suggestive moment in David's career is his leaving of it. The text claims that Solomon was his designated heir and dutiful successor. The two were coregents for a time. Solomon's reign began roughly 975-970 (best: 971), based on the regnal data in Kings and a synchronism between Jehu of Israel and the absolute dating of Assyrian kings that places Jehu's *coup d'état* in 841. But it is impossible to tell when David took the city of Jerusalem, or to calculate how far back his own regime should be dated. Was it six weeks or six years into Solomon's reign that David died? Or did he die before appointing Solomon his heir? All we know is that David came to the throne up to 33 years before his death.

David's heir dreamed of transforming the den — David's hole in the wall — into a capital. This scenario perhaps exaggerates the reality. David accumulated resources that astonished local populations, and Solomon exploited them to the point of bankrupting himself. Solomon overspent the capital that David frugally amassed. How long did the two overlap? Did the overlap, if any, affect Solomon's policy?

The politics of the succession are even more perplexing than its implications for the chronology of David's reign. Of central importance is understanding the structure of the account. The narrative sequence in 1 Kgs. 1 begins as follows:

David was old and could not "be warmed." So his servants found him the lovely Abishag, from Shunem, on the north side of the Jezreel Valley, to nurse him. The two did not have intercourse.

Meanwhile, Adonijah son of Haggith "raised himself up, saying, 'I will be king.'" Like Absalom, he assembled chariotry, horsemen, and runners to herald him.

> His father had not reproved him from his birth, saying, "Why did you do that?" He, also, was very attractive [implied: like Absalom], and him she [Haggith, not Absalom's mother] bore after Absalom.

The implied connection to Absalom is deliberately forefronted. Adonijah is staging a coup. Having recruited Joab and Abiathar as his supporters, Adonijah invited all his brothers, and all the men of Judah, to a feast celebrating his coronation, at the Spring of Rogel by Jerusalem. Not invited were "Zadoq, the priest, and Benaiah son of Jehoiada, and Nathan the prophet, and Shimei and his fellows, the professional warriors," and Solomon.[14]

Nathan therefore contacted Bathsheba. He urged her to confront David. (Note the inversion of the logical chain of communication here.) She was to claim that David had promised that Solomon, Bathsheba's son, would be king. No such promise is recorded, but Nathan all the same offered to confirm that

---

14. 1 Kgs. 1:8 (with the OG *wr'yw hgbwrym*), 10. Solomon's name appears only in the latter verse. The text names these as Adonijah's opponents, but leaves open the possibility that Adonijah invited Zadoq to the banquet. On Shimei, note the governor, Shimei son of Ela, of 1 Kgs. 4:18, conceivably identical with the warrior, Shammah son of Ega, of 2 Sam. 23:11, 25, 33. Shammah is the only one of David's warriors to appear both in one of the stories heading the list of warriors in 2 Sam. 23 and in the list itself. If Benaiah son of Jehoiada from Qabzeel and Benaiah the Pirathonite were identical, Benaiah would constitute the other example. Elhanan son of Dodo is named in the list, and appears in a story illustrating David's struggle with Philistia in 2 Sam. 21.

the commitment had been made. Bathsheba duly gained an audience with David. She told him that he had sworn to her by Yahweh "that Solomon, your son, will be king after me." She and Nathan shared the view that should Adonijah take the throne, she and Solomon would be counted as traitors, and sentenced to death (1 Kgs. 1:12, 21). Nathan then arrived and reported that Adonijah had convened Joab, Abiathar, and all the sons of the king for a coronation feast, without himself, Zadoq, Benaiah, and Solomon.

David sprang, creaking, into action. He ordered the conspirators, Bathsheba aside, to take Solomon to another local spring, Gihon, and anoint him the future king. Expressing the hope that Yahweh would make Solomon's throne greater than David's, Zadoq, Nathan, and Benaiah carried out the order, at the head of the Cherethites and Pelethites, the last time that this phrase denotes the professional army (1 Kgs. 1:32-40).

On hearing the news, Adonijah and his guests fled, Adonijah taking refuge by grasping the horns of the altar. Solomon enticed Adonijah from his sanctuary with a promise to parole him so long as he abstained from politics. Adonijah did obeisance at Solomon's feet and went to his home.

David then imparted to Solomon his final instructions. Solomon was to kill Joab, for the murders of Abner and Amasa. He was to maintain the sons of Barzillai the Gileadite at his table, for their service during David's flight from Absalom. And he was to kill Shimei son of Gera from Bahurim, for cursing David at that time.

David expired. Adonijah begged an audience with Bathsheba, at which he asked for her intercession in securing for him the hand of Abishag, from Shunem.

> "You know that the kingship was mine, and that all Israel had set their faces on me to be king, but the kingship turned and became my brother's, for it was his from Yahweh." (1 Kgs. 2:15)

Bathsheba relayed the request to Solomon, who answered,

> "Why are you asking for Abishag the Shunamite for Adonijah, when you should ask for the kingship for him — for he is my brother, who is older than I — and he has Abiathar the priest and Joab son of Zeruiah?" (1 Kgs. 2:22)

Solomon immediately dispatched Benaiah, who dispatched Adonijah.

Solomon declared Abiathar under a death sentence, but spared his life, since he had borne the ark for David. In removing him from priestly office, however, he fulfilled Yahweh's curse on the house of Eli, from the time before the loss of the ark and the introduction of the kingship. Solomon banished Abiathar to his own field, in Anathoth, just north of Jerusalem.

Joab, who "inclined after Adonijah, though after Absalom he had not inclined," seized the horns of the altar in "the tent of Yahweh," claiming sanctuary. When ordered by Benaiah to come out, Joab refused. "No, I will die here." "Do as he said," said Solomon, so Benaiah violated the sanctuary of the tent and killed Joab there (1 Kgs. 2:28-35). This outcome would seem to make nonsense of Solomon's fear that Adonijah, with Joab's support, might yet come to power. In fact, the flight to the altar was occasioned, in the narrative, by Adonijah's execution.

Solomon then appointed Benaiah chief-of-staff in Joab's place, and Zadoq priest in Abiathar's place.

So far, Solomon's executions of his own enemies and of David's final instructions seem to intertwine. However, the last killing is that of Shimei. Solomon ordered that worthy to build a house in Jerusalem, and adjured him to remain within the city:

> "When you go out and cross the Wadi Qidron, know with assurance that you will surely die. Your blood will be on your head." (1 Kgs. 2:37)

Three years later, Shimei went to extradite his fugitive slaves from Achish, son of Maacah, king of Gath. On his return, Solomon ordered Benaiah to strike him down.

This presentation is the climax of the apology, which extends in large measure to 1 Kgs. 10, furnishing a view of Solomon's as well as David's career.[15] It leaves David alive just long enough to reverse the election of Adonijah, and justifies both Solomon's accession and the purge that followed it. Whether or not David survived Solomon's coup, he had endorsed the succession of Adonijah, and never changed his mind.

The story told by the apologist reveals several crucial facts. First, Joab stood behind the candidacy of Adonijah. This, not his service to David, really occasioned his execution. Yet Joab was David's most loyal retainer, his chief-of-staff. He had been with David from the earliest stages of his career right through to the aftermath of the Absalom revolt, and took the blame for several of David's

---

15. For the verisimilitude of Solomon's correspondence with Hiram, where "all your heart desires" (*'rš*) coincides with a term for trade goods, *mereštu*, see P. E. Dion, in *Handbook of Ancient Hebrew Letters*, ed. Dennis Pardee, SBLSBS (Chico: Scholars, 1982). For the cultural background of the portrait of Solomon as natural philosopher and a collector of exotic animals and products in Middle Assyrian royal propaganda, see above, Chapters 5B, 12A.

murders — probably more than we read about. And he remained in high office even after the assassination of Amasa. The list of officials furnished after the Absalom revolt, in 2 Sam. 20, makes Benaiah his subordinate. Joab's position alone is a strong indication that Adonijah was David's choice for the throne.

The second key is the fact that all the men of Judah are said to have been celebrating Adonijah's election to be king. As reviewed above, the theory of kingship in Israel was contractual (Chapter 17), and this is the theory that repeatedly comes to expression in Samuel. But what is perhaps even more surprising is that Adonijah's plea to Bathsheba asserts that "all Israel" looked to him to be king. Likewise, when Bathsheba confronts David, she states that "all Israel" had turned their eyes toward him to learn whom he would designate as his successor.

The invitees to Adonijah's banquet are "all the men of Judah, the servants of the king" (1 Kgs. 1:9). Israel is omitted, as a subject people, from the royal contract. But the invitation to all the men of Judah, the servants of the king, gives the lie to the claim that David knew nothing of the celebration. It again insinuates a comparison of Adonijah to Absalom. But in contrast to Absalom, who staged a secret coup in Hebron, Adonijah celebrated openly, in the capital.

The texts describing Israel's expectations link Adonijah, like Absalom, to Israel's support. But it is only the men of Judah who attend his banquet. All the men of Judah would seem to denote both David's professional soldiers from Judah — like Joab — and the general population of the region. The text's diction indicates that conciliation was David's policy at most in the south, and not in the north. It also shows that the real royal electorate did stand behind Adonijah's candidacy.

Moreover, it is not just the men of Judah, but all of Adonijah's brothers, who join in the sacrifice. Given Solomon's methods of dealing with Adonijah's supporters, this suggests an explanation for why none of Solomon's brothers appears as one of his officers: none of them long survived his accession. But, given David's methods of dealing with those who opposed him, the brothers' public presence in support of Adonijah is yet another index that David, at least, stood behind Adonijah's candidacy. In fact, the convening of the brothers, if Absalom's invitation of them in 2 Sam. 13:26-27 is a guide, demanded David's active assent.

Still another important point is the fact that Bathsheba acts on Solomon's behalf because she is convinced that she and her son will be killed if Adonijah assumes the throne. Implicit, again, is a comparison of Adonijah to Absalom, who also invited all his brothers to a banquet in order to kill just one. But the literary conceit veils a more important consideration: all of Adonijah's brothers attended the banquet. Adonijah had no intention of killing them. It is therefore as highly suggestive that Solomon was not invited, if this was the case, as it is that he might have been executed by Adonijah. Either Adonijah was implacably dedicated to Solomon's death or he did not reckon Solomon a political force at all.

In the story, David's designation of Solomon as heir takes place in relative privacy. Bathsheba does not address him in a hall, but in his private chamber. Ordinarily, in Israelite court protocol, the king receives only one visitor in his chamber at a time. Thus, Nathan enters, and when the king wants to speak with Bathsheba again, he must have her summoned. And after her second audience, Nathan too must be summoned again.[16] The group instructed to crown Solomon, thus — Zadoq, Nathan, and Benaiah together — hear the king's wishes in privacy. The fact that the apology sets David's appointment of Solomon in the private chamber rather than in an audience hall is testimony that the conspirators could not claim that David endorsed Solomon's succession publicly.

The apology concedes that Judah, and the royal house, regarded Adonijah as David's heir. This is why Adonijah himself is permitted to say that the nation expected him to rule. In the same breath, he confesses that the diversion of the kingship to Solomon was Yahweh's work. But this admission is the work of the apologist: Adonijah does not mean what he says, since he is plotting to regain the throne by taking Abishag, his father's nurse-concubine; at the same time, his words, unwittingly, are true. Yet, as Tomoo Ishida has observed, as heir apparent, or possibly co-regent, Adonijah had no cause to stage a coup of his own. The text portrays him as a second Absalom — attractive in appearance, with runners to herald him, coddled by his father (as was Amnon). And the text repeatedly mentions or alludes to Absalom.[17] To put matters in their right sequence, David's failure to discipline Amnon and haste to rehabilitate Absalom are features of the history because the apologist wanted to draw a parallel to the arrogance of Adonijah. The truth of such claims about David's family relations is consistently questionable.

Again, the apology hardly conceals the fact that Solomon's accession was a *coup d'état.* The idea is Nathan's, in the text, rather than Bathsheba's, as in reality. The text's most important silence concerns David's promise to Bathsheba: the text does not claim that he designated Solomon before Nathan and Bathsheba insist that he had sworn to do so. It portrays their importunity as a

---

16. 1 Kgs. 1:15, 28, 32. For the protocol, Baruch Halpern, *The First Historians.* ch. 3.

17. See the excellent discussion by Tomoo Ishida, *History and Historical Writing in Ancient Israel.* Studies in the History and Culture of the Ancient Near East 16 (Leiden: Brill, 1999), 114-17. Much of the analysis of the succession generally here follows Ishida's treatment.

stratagem for saving Bathsheba's and Solomon's lives. Again, David relies on hearsay, this time about what he himself had formerly sworn. There is no assertion that Bathsheba and Nathan were telling the truth.

A priest, Zadoq, and a prophet, Nathan, sanctify Solomon's succession to the throne.[18] The aged — and forgetful — David commands it, in private. But the only constituency for it is the professional army. This is the logical outcome of the Absalom uprising: the professional soldiery, all of them far younger than Joab, were in a position to install their own candidate on the throne, to impose the policy they chose on the country. Which professional soldiers install Solomon on the throne? The ones who, along with Solomon, were not invited to participate in the sacred occasion — for Judahites — of Adonijah's banquet. The Cherethites and Pelethites (1 Kgs. 1:38, 44), David's Philistine or Gibeonite mercenary corps, were not "men of Judah." This is why they were excluded from Adonijah's festivities.

All this leads to the question, who was Solomon? His conciliation of Israel and of Absalom's partisans in Judah, in his apology, has been reviewed above. While he finally made an Ammonite princess his chief wife, he also married his heir off to Absalom's daughter Maacah.[19] This suggests that in the earlier part of his reign, when the marriage took place, Solomon attempted to recruit Absalom's partisans, at least with symbolic acts and publications. He murdered Joab, for siding with Adonijah, but ostensibly for murdering a Saulide figure and Amasa, Absalom's general. Absalom's followers will have recalled that Joab also executed their leader.

But Solomon did not break definitively, at least in his first years, with Gath. And at some time before the completion of his acropolis, and perhaps of his palace, he wed the daughter of the king of Egypt, and received Gezer as a prize from that king's campaign.[20] This represented, as seen above, an attack on Eqron, probably to Gath's advantage as well as Jerusalem's. And Solomon also imposed an imperial administration on the north. This does not mean that Solomon was an equal partner of the Egyptian king. Solomon himself, after all, was also wedded to the daughter of David's vassal. He was probably an Egyp-

18. Suspiciously, Nathan is the name of the son of David who is listed just before Solomon in 2 Sam. 5:14; 1 Chr. 14:4, and who is assigned to Bathsheba (Batshua), but probably by midrash, in 1 Chr. 3:5. No one on Solomon's team is actually active before the Absalom revolt, allowing that 2 Sam. 7 is not placed in correct chronological order.

19. 1 Kgs. 15:10, 13, with 15:2; 2 Chr. 11:20; also 2 Chr. 11:18, evincing a sense for royal policy. In 2 Sam. 14:27, Absalom's daughter Tamar appears as Maacah in some versions; compare Josephus Ant. 7.190.

20. 1 Kgs. 3:1 places the marriage before the completion of the temple (perhaps in year 11 of Solomon's reign) and palace (in Solomon's year 24); 9:16 reports the gift of Gezer.

tian vassal and protégé, given to emulating his overlord's culture.[21] But the rising status of subordinate administrators in the 21st Dynasty makes the claim of marriage at least possible, even plausible. It would not have been so under the pharaohs of the New Kingdom.

Solomon's early policy involved turning on David's allies at the court. He murdered Joab, and probably most or all of David's sons. He supplanted Abiathar as chief priest, with the newcomer, Zadoq. While Abiathar was connected to the house of Eli, and to the Gibeonites, Zadoq had no such ties. He installed Benaiah, the ambitious colonel from Qabzeel in southern Judah, in charge of the army, in place of Joab.[22] He installed his own sons-in-law, and other representatives of the court — including offspring of Hushai and of Zadoq — as the governors of his Israelite provinces. And over the governors he appointed a son of Nathan, the alleged architect of his coup, while adopting another son of Nathan as his priest and intimate (1 Kgs. 4). He rewarded his co-conspirators with power.

The treatment of Shimei also sheds light on Solomon's early policy.

Solomon has no hesitation in framing Adonijah. It is not believable that Adonijah solicited Bathsheba to request that Solomon turn Abishag over to him. The text stresses that David did not have intercourse with Abishag, clouding her status as a consort to make the request credible. But the apology repeatedly underscores the lethal role of women in the succession, leaving the reader in no doubt as to the proper outcome of Adonijah's alleged entreaty.

Thus, Abigail treats with David, and her husband dies. Her son Amasa joins Absalom, and dies. Rizpah, daughter of Ayyah, occasions a rupture between Abner and Ishbaal. David actually receives Michal, Saul's daughter. On that occasion, Abner is murdered, and Michal is shortly after sequestered for life. David is compelled to murder Uriah in order to cover up his adultery with Bathsheba. Bathsheba's grandfather Ahitophel becomes Absalom's chief counselor. The rape of Tamar leads to Amnon's murder, and to Absalom's expulsion

21. So, e.g., Solomon's apology depicts him as reacting to provocation, not taking the initiative against his enemies, in his purge. This is a characteristic of the Egyptian "Königsnovelle," or royal apology. Likewise, despite the clear Phoenician connections of the temple itself, the closest parallel to the House of the Forest of Lebanon that Solomon constructed on the Jerusalem acropolis is Karnak's hypostyle hall: 45 ft. high on its sides, 65 ft. in the center, with 124 pillars, a forest of columns, consisting of open and closed papyrus and lotus shapes.

22. For an origin of Zadoq in southern Judah, and ties to Jehoiada, father of Benaiah, see Saul M. Olyan, "Zadok's Origins and the Tribal Politics of David," *JBL* 101 (1982): 177-93. Olyan refutes the "Jebusite hypothesis" that Zadok was an aboriginal Jerusalemite priest, with Frank M. Cross, *Canaanite Myth and Hebrew Epic*, 209ff.

and revolt. Absalom's intercourse with David's concubines signals his assumption of the crown. And while David is in Abishag's care, Bathsheba plays a leading role in Solomon's rise to power. Possession of the harem, as stressed above, signaled a claim on the throne. Frank M. Cross writes that if Adonijah did ask for Abishag, he deserved to die — for stupidity.[23]

Solomon's procedure in the death of Adonijah is transparent, no less than David's in the murder of Amasa. Solomon maintains at least a semblance of juridical propriety: the enemy is not innocent, like Abner, Amasa, and, to an extent at least, Saul and Ishbaal. Nor does Solomon deny responsibility for the death. Rather, each killing represents a legal execution, for cause. Adonijah dies because he was the rightful heir and was conspiring to retake the throne, if a little obviously, and through the wrong channel, namely, Solomon's mother.

The case of Joab is similar. Essentially, Solomon declares Joab guilty of murder, rather than of supporting Adonijah's claim on the throne. So in the cause of justice for Abner and Amasa, he sends Benaiah as an executioner. He even goes so far as to disregard the tradition of sanctuary, openly. Curiously, an ordinance in the so-called Covenant Code in Exodus directly addresses just this case.

> One who smites a man, and he dies, shall be put to death. But for him who did not hunt [a victim], but God chanced to deliver him [the victim] into his hand, I will make a sacred place to which he can flee. But should a man scheme against his fellow, to slay him guilefully, from my [very] altar you shall take him to die. (Exod. 21:12-14)[24]

A more direct validation of Solomon's action against Joab can hardly be imagined, as Joab's guile and guilt in the slayings of Abner and Amasa could not be more vividly drawn. Given that Solomon does not appeal to the principle it em-

---

23. Cross, *Canaanite Myth and Hebrew Epic*, 237. Another female role in 2 Samuel is to rescue males: the nurse who lamed Mephibaal disqualified him from the succession, and thus in some sense saved his life. More clearly, a handmaiden at Ein Rogel gave a message to Jonathan and Ahimaaz, and a woman of Bahurim — no doubt related to Ziba — hid Abiathar's and Zadoq's sons in her cistern during David's flight from Absalom. For the role of royal women in the succession, see Michael C. Astour, *Hittite History*, 21-24.

24. For the translation of *māqôm*, "sacred place," see latterly in connection with 2 Samuel, David S. Vanderhooft, *JBL* 118 (1999): 625-33. For intentionality in the law of refuge here, see A. Schenker, "Die Analyse der Intentionalität im Bundesbuch (Ex 21-23)," *ZABR* 4 (1998): 209-17, esp. 210-11, with bibliography. Schenker's analysis, and comparison to the Middle Assyrian Laws, show, against his conclusion, that the ordinance is unitary — the logic is unitary, despite an apodictic introduction. As Schenker points out, the final version is clearly pre-Deuteronomistic.

bodies, one might suspect that the law in question derives ultimately from the Jerusalem court at roughly Solomon's time (see Chapter 4C). In any case, whether creating a precedent or not, Solomon acts, again, swiftly and openly.

The same holds for Solomon's banishment of Abiathar. The action was swift and unceremonious. In this instance, only, Solomon acted with restraint. If Abiathar's closest relations had already been killed (by Saul's Edomite agent in 1 Sam. 22) or died out, the reason for this restraint is not to be found in direct family connections. Perhaps Solomon spared Abiathar's life, as he claims in the text, out of a certain piety. But it is just as likely that he was currying favor with a constituency, namely the Gibeonites, in southern Benjamin. If the Cherethites and Pelethites were related to the Gibeonites (as in the case of Ittay), if the ark was a Gibeonite icon, if Shiloh was a Gibeonite shrine, Solomon's policies cohere.

What stands out, therefore, is the case of Shimei. Though the consequences are fatal in the end, in this instance, Solomon treads lightly. Solomon does not order Shimei's immediate execution. Instead, he plays an elaborate game. Shimei must relocate from Bahurim to Jerusalem, and it is three years, according to the text, before he violates the terms of his parole. Why this delicacy? Again, the object of the prosecution is a Benjaminite, and this time, from the House of Saul. As we have seen, Solomon's apologist went to some lengths to appease pro-Saul, as well as pro-Absalom, sentiment.

Why Solomon actually killed Shimei, his hostage in Jerusalem, is not so clear. Perhaps Shimei was no longer needed, because Solomon successfully co-opted other elements connected to Saul's house, or because he abolished it altogether. Perhaps the detention did not have the desired effect on Saul's former partisans. Or perhaps, after three years, Solomon inaugurated negotiations with Egypt, and his foreign policy shift affected domestic priorities. But the comparative delicacy with which Solomon handled Shimei's case — setting limits that Shimei eventually violated, however he was induced to do so — is suggestive. For Shimei's murder, Solomon required a palpable rather than surface justification.

In treating with the parties to the Absalom revolt, Solomon dealt delicately at first. In some sense, his politics reversed David's, but without a total break with Gath. Certainly the gift of Gezer came at Eqron's expense. Yet Solomon relied on the professional army, chiefly, and attempted to recruit some Benjaminites and Ephraimites, and elements in Judah, probably including the populations of towns such as Hebron, which had been marginalized under his father. Political logic dictated that he broaden his constituency beyond the Philistine mercenary corps.

How is it, though, that Solomon could be so distinct from the rest of the royal brood, from his brothers? How did he suddenly become the darling of the professional army? The clues go back to the time of his birth.

As explained in Chapter 2, the death of David's and Bathsheba's first, bastard, son has been poorly understood. The death was not reported to protect Solomon from the allegation that he was the product of an adulterous relationship. Instead, the son's death proves beyond doubt that Solomon was really David's, not Uriah's, child.[25] But the very fact that the narrative takes the trouble to combat the allegation is a reason to ask whether Solomon *was* really David's son.

The first indication that Solomon was not David's son are his names. His divine name, mediated to him by Nathan, is Jedidiah (2 Sam. 12:25). The narrative does not indicate when this name was bestowed on him. It is quite possible that it was his throne-name. It means "the beloved of Yahweh," and implies, not too subtly, that he was the love-child of David, *dwd*, "the beloved." But Solomon's birth-name tells another story. The narrative clearly indicates that it is Solomon: this was the name bestowed on him by his parents, and probably more specifically by his mother.[26] Solomon's name means "his replacement." Assume Solomon was the son of a father who died before his birth, and the name makes perfect sense. But follow the story in Samuel, and the explanation of the name violates the natural sensibilities of ancient Near Eastern cultures: Solomon's name in the existing narrative sequence implies that he was a replacement for the first son, who died; but it is unlikely that an infant who died nameless would have drawn such attention.[27] The death of the first son of David and Bathsheba has long drawn a wink and a nod from scholars. It would ap-

---

25. See the very suggestive treatment of Ishida, *History and Historical Writing*, 151-57, which observes the stress on Yahweh's adoption of Solomon in 2 Sam. 7 as well as Solomon's legitimation in the birth narrative, and wrestles with the report on David's adultery.

26. 2 Sam. 12:24. While the Masoretic text reads *wyqr'*, "he (David) named" (the child, 'Solomon'), the Qere, a number of Hebrew manuscripts, and the Targum and Syriac all agree on *wtqr'*, "she (Bathsheba) named." As these are the chief witnesses to the gender of verbs, and as the practice of mothers naming children is prevalent in older biblical texts, including 1 Sam. 1:20; 4:21 and JE, but absent from 7th-century texts, this is the preferred reading.

27. See esp. Timo Veijola, *VTSup* 30 (197): 235-37. Veijola believes that the name was an attempt to pretend that Solomon was Uriah's child, and his view is followed in modified form below. See above, Chapter 2F, on the name. Its vocalization precludes a connection to the god Shalem. It is possible to construe the name as the noun in construct to a divine name, "God's compensation." Compare Gideon's altar, named Yahweh Shalom, in Judg. 6:24. But see J. J. Stamm, "Hebräische Ersatznamen," in *Studies in Honor of Benno Landsberger*. AS 16 (Chicago: University of Chicago Press, 1965), 413-24, for the name type.

pear that they have been right, and that Solomon was Bathsheba's first son after Uriah's death.

If Solomon was thought to be named for a posthumous father lost in battle, the chances of his being anyone else's son are minimal. The irony of his name would be too rich, and this seems to exclude David's paternity. In other words, the name Solomon ties him to the dead hero, Uriah. Bathsheba may later have claimed otherwise. The throne-name Jedidiah explicitly reinforced her allegation. But for all the world knew, as he was growing up, Solomon was not David's child.

The second indication that Solomon was not David's child is his exclusion from Adonijah's banquet. Granted, it is necessary to the narrative that Solomon be excluded; but a story of a botched attempt on him, or a plot against him, would have helped sustain the claim that Bathsheba staged her coup — and it was *her* coup — in self-defense. The others who are excluded from the banquet are foreigners, Gibeonites and Gittites. A foreign ancestry, say from a Hittite, would also explain why Solomon was not invited.

The third indication that Solomon was not David's son is the activity of Ahitophel, Solomon's great-grandfather. Ahitophel defected from David and supported Absalom's attempt to seize the crown. Yet he was the grandfather of Bathsheba. Ahitophel had nothing to gain from an upheaval if Solomon had a natural claim on the throne. After all, Solomon was more likely to attract preferment from a royal father than from a half-brother. Absalom, as a rebel, would need to kill his brothers, so it is impossible to suppose that Ahitophel delivered Solomon to him, if Solomon was David's child. Solomon's great-grandfather joined Absalom's cause in order to advance the family fortunes.

But how did his granddaughter, Bathsheba, end up as David's wife, and especially as the woman who commanded the loyalty of the royal bodyguard?

Two explanations suggest themselves. The first is that Solomon was really Absalom's own posthumous son. This scenario might imply a marriage alliance between Absalom and Ahitophel, with David taking Absalom's women on his return to power. Or, it might imply that Bathsheba was already in David's harem when Absalom captured Jerusalem, and that she was one of the concubines (though the text portrays her as a wife) with whom he had relations. In either case, the name Solomon, "his replacement," would then refer to the dead Absalom, and the actual birth would be narrated out of sequence.

Against this scenario, however, are two considerations. First, Absalom's revolt came toward the end of David's reign, so that Solomon would have been too young to have produced a son, Rehoboam, a year before his accession (see above, Chapter 13). Second, David seems to have made it his business to root out the males descended from Absalom, and while Solomon might have borne the name Jedidiah from his birth to his accession as a sort of mask of his true identity, we should not be in a hurry to suppose that David was remiss in policing the harem or in pursuing the leads from that quarter.

The other, more likely, scenario, is simply that Solomon was Uriah's son. His name indicates that he was presented as Uriah's son in the court. If Bathsheba's son did not stand in line for the succession, Ahitophel's role in the Absalom revolt makes a good deal more sense: With three sons of his own, Absalom was unlikely to advance a half-brother, Solomon, to a position of power. But if Solomon was the posthumous son of Uriah, then Solomon's great-grandfather, and perhaps his grandfather Eliam (2 Sam. 23:34), had good reason to join in the uprising. Eliam's and Solomon's preferment was the price of Ahitophel's support.[28]

Solomon, then, was named for Uriah, not for the rapidly-doomed but probably fictitious love-child of David and Bathsheba.

Did David order Uriah to be killed? The narrative concedes that the only parties to the order were David, Joab, and the unwitting victim. The actual killing was undertaken by an enemy in battle. So only Yahweh can detect the "murder." To defend the apology's version, one would have to assume that Bathsheba's entry into the royal harem after Uriah's mourning laid the groundwork for the apologist's conclusion that David wanted Uriah dead.

The real question in any case is not whether David killed Uriah. Rather, why does the narrative *relate* that David killed Uriah? It is striking that the only crime of which Samuel convicts David is the murder, not of Solomon's father, but of the first husband of Solomon's mother. It convicts David of the undetectable murder of one of his own royal bodyguard, a man whose name, suspiciously enough, appears at the end of the list of warriors in 2 Sam. 23:39. And David deliberately accepted other casualties in order to get to Uriah.

Here we have a sign, perhaps, of Bathsheba's own attempt to ingratiate herself with and advance her son's case with the professional soldiery in Jerusalem. The allegation of Uriah's murder may have been an ideological tool for mobilizing support for Solomon's coup. It could conveniently be tied to another falsehood, namely, that Solomon was David's son.

Along the same lines, the narrative makes Uriah's murder the true, concealed cause of the Absalom revolt. Any sin, even a cultic one, could have been turned into the occasion for that episode. And, Shimei, at least, is permitted to

---

28. David Noel Freedman, in correspondence, offers a third possibility: citing the detachment of Monica Lewinsky's abortion from the charges of impeachment against Bill Clinton, he suggests that were the apology a contemporary Washington thriller, it would turn out that Nathan was Solomon's father.

give voice to the conviction that David was suffering for the deaths of Saul's descendants.

But the narrator chooses to connect the event to the death of Bathsheba's first husband instead. It is because David took Uriah's wife, and then his life, that his own wives were to be violated in sight of all Israel. Even assuming that the apologist believed that David truly did murder Uriah, Uriah's importance in death far exceeded his importance in life.

Attaching that significance to Uriah makes Solomon's accession the end of the curse that had plagued David's house. The child who came to the throne and purged David's establishment was the product of the liaison that caused the struggle for the succession. Solomon heals the tear in the moral fabric of the universe caused by David's and Bathsheba's infidelity. He closes the circle on the cycle of violence set off by their affair, by David's remaining in Jerusalem at the time "when kings go out to war."[29]

But that child was named for Uriah, "his replacement." His name, Adonijah's failure to invite him, and his grandfather's politics all indicate that he was not David's son. Only Yahweh and Solomon's supporter, Nathan, in the apology in Samuel, penetrate this surface presentation. Even if Solomon *were* the product of a liaison between David and Bathsheba, his name would imply that Bathsheba and David presented him as a boy that Uriah had fathered. In other words, there was considerable doubt as to his royal ancestry — because he had none. Ironically, in Matthew, as distinct from Luke, Jesus' lineage descends through Solomon, the beneficiary of Yahweh's dynastic promise to David in 2 Sam. 7. A cloud on Solomon's paternity affects Jesus's genealogical claim to be the Davidic messiah.

The brilliant story of David's adultery and Uriah's murder might contain a grain of truth. But it is more likely that it was a fabrication. It is a large part of the apologist's purpose in weaving the tale to show beyond a shadow of a doubt that Solomon was David's son. The reason for the insistence, for the graphic detail in which Uriah's perfectly ordinary death is reported, before the birth of the child who died, for Bathsheba's nearly immediate removal to the palace, for the form of Solomon's throne-name and its apparent bestowal at his birth, is to dispel the view that Solomon was Uriah's child. It is because he was known to be Uriah's son that Adonijah did not invite him to the coronation banquet. It is because Solomon was the grandson of the rebel, Ahitophel, that he stood in danger of capital reprisal. Adonijah, perhaps even more than David, may have been bent on rooting out Absalom's allies.

The linkage between Bathsheba and the Absalom revolt is more complex,

29. 2 Sam. 11:1. See Veijola, *VTSup* 30 (1979): 240.

and difficult to analyze. Bathsheba will have remained in Jerusalem with David's harem, if she was in it during that episode. She will have been treated well, because of her grandfather's position, and probably her father's, in the ranks of Absalom's supporters. After the collapse of Absalom's coalition, she evidently set to work conspiring to set her son, and Uriah's, on the throne, as a measure of vengeance for her grandfather's death and, again, probably her father's. She may even have imagined that her husband's death at Rabbat Ammon was engineered by David.

The claim, though, that David murdered Uriah because of Bathsheba's charms seems more flattering to her vanity than plausible. Even the idea that David wanted to cover up the fact that he was the one who impregnated Bathsheba seems weak. After all, Bathsheba would have her child whether Uriah lived or died. Once Uriah, in the story, had refused to go home during the campaign, the game was up. All that Uriah's death would accomplish would be to call suspicion down on David's head.

If David wanted to cover up his infidelity with a married woman, it is Bathsheba that he logically should have killed. And had he wanted to take Bathsheba as a wife, he would have done better to bribe Uriah, or post him to duty in a lonely spot, and induce a divorce. The idea that David could have been held legally liable for his liaison with Bathsheba is charming and indicates, as other texts do, that the king attempted to appear to remain within the law.[30] Given David's other escapades, however, it will not in reality have applied to him.[31]

In the apology of Samuel, the standard view of the Absalom revolt is expressed by Shimei. Israel's support for the change of kings, though not of dynasties, in Jerusalem arose from resentment of David's persecution of the House of Saul. The apology explicitly denies that view. Instead, it asserts that the Absalom revolt was David's punishment for spawning first Solomon's brother and then Solomon himself. The rape of Tamar, the murder of Amnon, and the Absalom revolt itself are now presented as the evidence that Solomon was David's son. But all the indirect indications — Solomon's name, his great-grandfather's support for Absalom's revolt, Bathsheba's and Nathan's manufacture of David's earlier oath that Solomon would take power, Solomon's palace coup — speak against the direct assertion of the text. So too does the fact that Solomon's wife was the daughter of a vassal-king, rather than an ally — such as we might imagine Adonijah's wife to have been. Solomon was not a

---

30. Baruch Halpern, *The Constitution of the Monarchy*.

31. See Reuven Yaron, "Social Problems and Policies in the Ancient Near East," in Baruch Halpern and Deborah W. Hobson, *Law, Politics and Society*, 19-41.

high flier, until the foreign troops in the king's guard propelled him onto the throne.

Overall, the link between Uriah's death and the Absalom revolt is a part of the presentation of Solomon as the king who would rebuild burnt bridges and reclaim the allegiances alienated by David. It is riskier, but still reasonable, to suggest that it reflects Bathsheba's view of things. Doubtless, she transmitted her version of events to her son. In it she incurs no blame at all: David sends for her on his own initiative. In Nathan's parable she is the lamb, with whom the poor man slept, before the rich neighbor stole and ate her, although in the actual narrative she wound up sleeping with the rich neighbor instead. At the time of the succession, when she reappears, it is Nathan who has to suggest she speak to David in order to save her own life. Nowhere does the text indicate why she should be in fear for her life. And finally, it was Adonijah, not Bathsheba, who requested that Solomon give him David's nurse. Bathsheba merely served as the innocent conduit of the request, which precipitated Adonijah's execution. Bathsheba is insulated from blame even more seamlessly than are David and Solomon.[32]

Solomon's accession was Bathsheba's revenge for her grandfather and father and for Absalom. In the apology of Samuel, it is Bathsheba's voice that we hear, though the hand be the hand of Solomon.

D. Solomon's Politics

The text presents Solomon's accession as fulfilling David's unreported vow that Solomon would be his heir. It does not conceal the fact that the professional army placed Solomon on the throne by force. But it prescinds from the claim that counts: Solomon's enthronement was revolutionary; it realized Absalom's aims.

Solomon's accession reflects Absalom's agenda most clearly in the deaths of David and his real heir. Solomon's politics were an extension of David's in roughly the measure that Solomon's real descent was. Consider the apology: where David never owned up to a murder, Solomon transformed all his murders into executions. And the apology also makes Joab into David's nemesis, truly a thug, to justify one of Solomon's executions. Solomon also executed Absalom's program by betraying his northern allies. He exploited the northern parts of Israel, particularly the Galilee, as conquered territory. The rebuilding of Megiddo and Hazor, as cities with no domestic population, precluded the local Israelites from taking advantage of these strategic positions for commerce.

32. Much of this paragraph derives from David Noel Freedman, in correspondence.

One of the things Judah expected from Absalom was a reduction in royal demands. This meant more intensive exploitation of the Israelite hinterland to their advantage. The Israelites, conversely, expected to be liberated from that exploitation. Their ambition was the short-sighted hope of exploiting and pillaging their Canaanite neighbors rather than being themselves the object of a predatory state's ambitions. This pillaging they very likely accomplished during the revolt — at Dor, Yoqneam, Beth Shan, and Megiddo, for example (see Chapters 21, 23). Though the revolt did not accomplish territorial gains in the Philistine heartland, it reduced the weight of David's Canaanite allies, a fact of which Solomon was not insensible.

So far as the residents of Jerusalem's natural hinterlands were concerned, Solomon's *Realpolitik* meant freedom from forced labor after the construction of the temple. But for this concession, Solomon was compelled to compensate. As we shall see, he divided the north into provinces that often cut across traditional tribal lines (to be fair, Israel had probably never digested the lowlands before). He treated with the pharaoh to hamstring Eqron. He expanded the network of settlements in the Negev, in part using northern populations displaced from the lowlands, and received a queen from the Arabian peninsula in his capital. He built the capital as such, fitted it out for display, created and consumed immense wealth.

Solomon in this sense was a modernizer, like the Shah in Iran. Judah at the end of Iron I had something on the order of 18 settlements in it. But in the early Iron II, as a result of Solomon's activity, it was growing, with the characteristic ceramic assemblage of the Israelite-Phoenician axis supplanting that of its Philistine-Canaanite predecessor. Lands formerly controlled by Philistine powers — especially in the eastern dependencies of Eqron around Beth Shemesh and even Timnah, but perhaps also Tell Beit Mirsim — were claimed by Israel.[33] This resulted from the pharaoh's strike in Philistia, to limit what had continued to seem, throughout David's time, ongoing Philistine expansion into the hinterlands of Canaan.

Solomon thus seemingly adopted the anti-Philistine platform of the Absa-

---

33. Beth Shemesh IIa, Timnah IV. On the latter, Amihai Mazar, *Timnah (Tel Batash)*, 1: *Stratigraphy and Architecture*. Qedem 37 (Jerusalem: Hebrew University, 1997), with a summary on 255. On Iron I Tell Beit Mirsim, see Raphael Greenberg, "New Light on the Early Iron Age at Tell Beit Mirsim," *BASOR* 265 (1987): 55-80. At Eqron, there is increasing representation of the non-Philistine ceramic repertoire in Stratum IV, either after the Absalom revolt or after Siamun's raid revised the state's hinterland. See Neil Bierling, *Report on the 1995-1996 Excavations in Field XNW: Areas 77, 78, 79, 89, 90, 101, 102 Iron Age I Text and Data Base (Plates, Sections, Plans)* (Jerusalem: Albright Institute and Hebrew University Institute of Archaeology, 1998), 20-27 for Strata VIIB-V.

lom revolt, one of the strongest reasons for Israel's enlistment on Absalom's behalf. And, assuming that the expedition came after the extradition of Shimei's slaves, probably in Solomon's third year, the change in policy may have been genuine, explaining the detachment of Tell Beit Mirsim from Gath. Conversely, Solomon may have retained that old alliance, violating the trust of Absalom's partisans, but rewarding that of the Gittite mercenaries who installed the son of Uriah as David's legitimate heir.

The Philistine city-states will have been Egyptian vassals through most of Solomon's reign. If the assertion that he *claimed* to be wed to the daughter of the pharaoh is true, Solomon compounded his partnership with Gath against Eqron by allying with Egypt to contain all the Philistines. The text concedes that he came into possession of Gezer by the pharaoh's gift, and nowhere suggests he exercised his military prowess. Solomon was, if an Egyptian ally, in a subordinate relationship with the king in Tanis. In this period, then, Gath may have taken its place as the leading city of the Philistine interior, and perhaps even inherited much of Eqron's former holdings, but it was no longer in the ascendant over Jerusalem. None of the Philistine city-states retained the power now to threaten the kingdom unified by Absalom's revolt.

The accession of Shishaq in Egypt signaled the onset of a new era, and more particularly the rise of a new dynasty. Shishaq would invade Israel and Judah in his 21st year, five years after Solomon's death. His foreign policy involved competition with Solomon's Israel from the start.

Shishaq assumed power in Egypt in Solomon's 24th year. It is to this period, after the completion of the acropolis, that 1 Kgs. 9:10-14 assigns the sale of the tribe of Asher to Tyre. This episode is of central import to understanding Solomon's reign.[34] The story runs, Solomon started building his temple and palace in his fourth year, with the support of Hiram of Tyre. After 20 years of building, Solomon gave Hiram "twenty towns in the land of the Galilee." Hiram evaluated the settlements as insufficient, and called them "the land of Cabul to this day," signifying that he had been cheated — Cabul means "hobbled (land)." But Hiram remitted 120 talents, roughly 3600 kg., of gold in exchange (the purity of the gold is not recorded, but we may assume Solomon complained about it).

34. The fact that the text refers to years of building rather than of Solomon's reign has confused commentators, who often date the Cabul purchase to Solomon's 20th year. The reason the text veils this date is unclear. It may be to break the link with Shishaq's accession, or it may be to antedate the building, by implication, to Solomon's first year. The former seems more likely, and the impulse is that of dual chronology, familiar from display inscriptions.

The presentation, as previously noted, suggests that Solomon got the better of the deal, as readers through the ages have understood. He came off with a bargain. The trope for encrypting the alienation of sovereignty is the same one adopted by Kilamuwa of Sam'al for his submission to Assyria. A later king of Sam'al, Bar-Rakib, explains that his father had to submit to Assyria in order to restore security and prosperity to the land.[35] Likewise, Kings adopts this rhetorical strategy to justify appeals to foreign overlords, notably by Asa and Ahaz.[36] That is, the trope is apologetic, masking loss as a bargain. The use of such a device suggests the reliability of the report: if he once held it, Solomon sold the tribe of Asher to Tyre.[37] What is more, in Near Eastern texts, and in biblical his-

---

35. See Halpern, *The First Historians*, 231; Bar-Rakib in KAI 215:2-10, regarding Panamuwa's submission to Tiglath-Pileser. Kilamuwa probably submitted to Shalmaneser III, but possibly to Shamshi-Adad V or even Adad-Nirari III. For the inscription, see KAI 24, esp. lines 5-8. Kilamuwa son of Hayya is the great-grandson of the founder of the dynasty, Gbr, and Shalmaneser refers to his father as "Hayyanu the son of Gabbari," meaning king "of the House of Gabbari." Hayyanu appears (as does Sam'al) in the annals only in reports of Shalmaneser's early campaigns, in 858-857. Hayyanu was therefore on the throne already at the time of Shalmaneser's accession, so that his son was probably on the throne by the end of Shalmaneser's career. The coalition against which Kilamuwa claims to have fought included the kingdom of Danuna (Adana), but Sam'al later joined the anti-Assyrian coalition, led by Damascus, whose members are enumerated by Zakkur of Hamath and Luash and by Adad-Nirari, at the end of the century. Kilamuwa's inscription could thus antedate the high tide of Damascene power in the 810s, or it could follow on Adad-Nirari III's demolition of Damascus's hegemony.

36. Mordecai Cogan and Hayim Tadmor, *II Kings*. AB 11 (Garden City: Doubleday, 1988), 188, take the term "bribe" applied to Asa and Ahaz as an editorial criticism of their actions. This is possible, but it is on the taking, not the giving, of bribes that Near Eastern censure focuses, especially in the Bible. Their most important observation on this subject is the fact that no Assyrian king would have described himself as taking a bribe, as distinct from receiving a vassal's submission and tribute. This principle can be extended to embrace all kings. So the giver of the bribe can be understood as achieving a success, in fact: the word "bribe" puts the best possible face on what both parties understand to be tribute.

37. The difficulty in maintaining that Solomon never held Asher inheres in the fact that the report hides its loss. However, one might argue that it aggrandized David in some earlier form and that a subsequent apologist reframed it to salvage Solomon's reputation. The problem is, there is no conquest of Asher by David in the text, so he earns no credit from the supposed fraud. Further, the idea that someone reframed a report that damned Solomon for losing Asher is unlikely: the final layers of the Deuteronomistic History are extremely hostile to Solomon (Halpern, *The First Historians*, 144-80, 220-28). An author concerned to salvage Solomon's reputation would have done what the Chronicler does, and misinterpret the source to imply that it was Hiram who gave 20 cities to Solomon (2 Chr. 8:1-2).

toriography, loss of territory is uniformly a sign of divine disfavor, which is why kings who give up territory must put a positive spin on their "strategic retreat." 2 Kgs. 18:8, for example, mentions that Hezekiah conquered Philistia up to Gaza, without explicitly stating that he lost all of it, and nearly all of Judah, to Sennacherib in 701.

It is unlikely that the text would claim falsely that Solomon held the tribe of Asher, only to lose it later, unless its aim were to assail Solomon. But the text does not indict Solomon. It defends him: it calls the "Cabul" part of "the land of Galilee," instead of "Asher," which would underscore the alienation of Israelites from the national state. It uses the name of the northernmost town in eastern Asher (Josh. 19:27) to designate the region, in order to minimize the sense of the area sold. And it speaks merely of 20 towns, concealing the size of the territorial concession, so that readers have tended to neglect the import of the transaction. But the tribe of Asher even in the record of the book of Joshua consists of 22 towns. The sale of 20, seven of which Judg. 1 names as never conquered, looks very much as though it represents the sale of Asher in its entirety.

Solomon retained two towns in Asher to demonstrate the falsity of claims that he sold the whole tribe. Likewise, Jordanian negotiators in 1949 consistently drew the ceasefire line with Israel between villages, on the Jordanian side, and their fields, on the Israeli side, rather than ceding some villages in exchange for others. When taxed by their Israeli counterparts, the Jordanians explained that the whole Arab world would hear of it if they surrendered settlements, but conceding farmland would carry no political price.[38]

Indirectly linked to the loss of the Cabul is Solomon's construction of a port at Ezion Geber on the Red Sea. This drew on the expertise of Hiram's navy, and resulted in an expedition to Ophir that brought 120 talents of gold to Jerusalem.[39] Yet 120 gold talents is the price Hiram paid for the tribe of Asher. Thus, in exchange for the Cabul, Hiram undertook to outfit Solomon to conduct the southern trade, bringing drugs and other goods through Israel to Tyre for shipment. The construction of the port belongs to the period of commercial and political competition with Egypt that dawned with Shishaq's rise. So, therefore, does the visit of the queen of Sabaea (Sheba). And the colonization of the Negev, though it had earlier beginnings, will have been completed in this era.

The text of Kings does coordinate the sale of the tribe of Asher with the fortification of Jerusalem and of Solomon's fortresses, including Megiddo, Hazor, and Gezer, at all of which six-chambered gates with projecting towers

38. Yigael Yadin, in conversation, 1983.
39. 1 Kgs. 9:26-28. The sum is from the OG version, as opposed to the Hebrew text's 420 talents.

appear shortly after the introduction of burnished pottery with a red slip (see Chapter 23). Solomon's other reported fortification projects are at Baalat, or Qiryath Yearim, and Lower Beth Horon, both just to the east of his second province, in the Ayyalon Pass from the coast to Jerusalem, and at Tamar, in the Judean desert.[40] As noted, the fortresses at Megiddo and Hazor, at least, were almost devoid of domestic populations, and functioned in the relevant layers purely as administrative centers.

The policy of emptying the fortifications may have begun, as noted, in the preceding layer at Megiddo (VB). Imposing forced labor on the noncitizens, but freeing the citizenry from it after the temple construction, a contrast implicit in Judg. 1 as well as in Kings, would have delighted Absalom's xenophobic constituency. Notably, the claim in Judg. 1 is that when Israel gained control of the regions in question, it imposed corvée on the Canaanites (Amorites). "Israel's" control means David's, and the corvée was probably Solomon's innovation, since David counted on the Canaanites as a counterweight to the Israelites he was conquering and digesting. Whether the Israelites, as distinct from the population of Judah, were really exempted from forced labor, as 1 Kgs. 9:22 claims, seems doubtful. Taxation was the major issue in Israel's secession from the regime in Jerusalem after Solomon's death.

Judg. 1 claims that Jerusalem imposed corvée on the Canaanites in the Jezreel Valley, the coast at Dor, parts of Zebulun, and the western Ayyalon Pass.[41] These are the areas of Solomon's greatest activity. He perhaps built and certainly dismantled Megiddo Stratum VB in the Jezreel, and installed a governor there and in the other Jezreel towns named in Judg. 1. He installed another province head at Dor. The Ayyalon Pass is also the location of two of Solomon's fortresses, to the east of the centers of non-Israelite population mentioned by Judg. 1 and in the description of Solomon's second province.

By way of contrast, there is no claim that the "Canaanite" population of Gezer was reduced to forced labor, which is the more interesting in that the town came into Solomon's hands in ruins (1 Kgs. 9:16). Nor are the Canaanites resident in the territory of Asher reduced to forced labor — because Solomon divested himself of the territory before his most intensive building efforts began. There is no mention of such labor in Judah, Benjamin, or Ephraim, suggesting that the Gibeonites were not press-ganged, since they were cult servants. Conversely, the fortification of Qiryath Yearim may have involved its

---

40. For a recent identification of Tamar as a 10th-century fortress site, see Cohen and Yisrael, *Qad* 29/112 (1996): 78-92.

41. For the implication of *kidinnūtu* in 1 Kgs. 5:13-14(27-28); 9:15, 21, see above, Chapter 21. The corvée appears in Judg. 1:28, 30, 33, 35; and Josh. 17:13.

expropriation from the Gibeonites. And there is no mention of corvée in Transjordan: Rehoboam's Ammonite mother and the priestly sinecure of Barzillai's sons suggest that Solomon continued David's policies there; Gilead was probably treated much like Judah. Judg. 1 reads as though a source from the time of Solomon informs it.[42] But 1 Kings alone — confirmed by Judg. 1 — indicates that he fulfilled Absalom's program even in the taxation policy he adopted.

The delineation of Solomon's provinces in 1 Kgs. 4:7-19 dovetails with this perspective. The province list overlaps significantly with Judg. 1. The list, at least, is old. The officials in charge of the more sensitive districts are tied closely to Solomon's court. Two are sons-in-law of the king. One of these is either the son or grandson of Zadoq, the priest who survived Solomon's purges. A third governor with close ties to the court is a son of Hushai, David's counselor, and a hero, in our text, of the Absalom revolt. And a fourth is the son of Ahilud, and thus the brother of the highest civilian official in Solomon's court, the herald.[43] Ahilud's son, and Hushai's, share the same name, Baana, which is also the name of one of Ishbaal's Gibeonite assassins.

The governor of Benjamin, Shimei, was linked to Solomon as the otherwise enigmatic officer of 1 Kgs. 1:8 who was "not with Adonijah."[44] Abinadab, the governor of Dor and Solomon's son-in-law, may in fact be the son of Abinadab (see below). In that case, Solomon's uncle, the second son of Jesse, is a candidate to have been the governor's father. So is the host of the ark in Qiryath Yearim before its removal to the house of Obed Edom the Gittite. Or, given David's Gibeonite connections, these two may be one and the same person.[45] Geber son of Uri, governor in Gilead reaching up to the Bashan, may well be the father of "the son of Geber" who was posted to Ramoth Gilead in order to police the "camp-sites of Yair" and the Argob region of the Bashan.

A second element of the list is the form of the governors' names. The only

42. On similar grounds, Baruch Halpern, *The Emergence of Israel in Canaan*, 179-82. For corvée at Gezer, see the Greek of Judg. 1:29; and Josh. 16:10, which are probably supplying an element some tradent felt to be lacking.

43. 1 Kgs. 4:3; 2 Sam. 8:16; 20:24.

44. See also the similar name in 2 Sam. 23:11. Note that two governors' father's names — the patronyms, Hur (Horus) and Uri — are combined in the genealogy of Judah in 1 Chr. 2:20, and in the genealogy of the workman responsible in P for the regalia of the tabernacle shrine: Exod. 31:2; 35:30; 38:22, and derivatively, 2 Chr. 1:5. Hur also appears as the name of a son of Aaron in Exod. 17:10, 12; 24:14. Uri bears a variant on the name Uriah. His son, Geber, may have been Solomon's full brother.

45. 1 Sam. 7:1; 16:8; 17:13; 2 Sam. 6:3, 4; 1 Chr. 2:13; 13:7. A third, unlikely candidate is Saul's son Abinadab, mentioned in 1 Sam. 31:2; 1 Chr. 8:33; 9:39; 10:2.

other character in the Former Prophets referred to only by patronym is David. And when David is called only "the son of Jesse," the tone is uniformly derisory. Yet the first four governors in Solomon's province list, plus the sixth, are referred to as "the son of [father's name]": "the son of Hur," "the son of Deqer," "the son of Hesed," "the son of Abinadab," and "the son of Geber." One of these is even Solomon's son-in-law.[46] Furthermore, the governor of the eighth province is not assigned a father's name at all, though he himself was son of Zadoq the priest and eventually succeeded to the high priesthood, probably rather early under Solomon.[47]

Most of Solomon's other officials, named in 1 Kgs. 4 just before the province list, are identified by personal name and their father's name, including a son and successor of Zadoq, who was the brother of Ahimaaz. The only exceptions are Abiathar, whom Solomon expelled, and the royal steward, Ahishar.[48]

So why is the province list itself so peculiar? A suggestion that has enjoyed widespread circulation in the scholarly discussion is that the list was originally written on a sheet of papyrus or a clay tablet, and that the right-hand side of the original text was already effaced when the list was inserted into the account of Solomon's reign in Kings. Thus the list originally ran:

46. "The son of Abinadab" in 1 Kgs. 4:11. If Abinadab was Solomon's uncle, Abinadab's son will have married his father's brother's daughter, the most desirable form of endogamy in Israelite kinship theory.

47. 2 Sam. 15:27, 36; 18:19, 22-29; 1 Chr. 6:53(38), which ends Aaron's genealogy with Ahimaaz son of Zadoq; 1 Chr. 6:8(5:34). The fact that the genealogy of 1 Chr. 6:53(38) ends at Ahimaaz might be taken to support the view, expressed by a number of scholars, that the Levitical cities, a list of which follows, were instituted early in Solomon's reign. On the other hand, in the absence of reference to such an institution in any text older than Josh. 21, it is difficult to achieve any certainty on the subject. If Solomon did institute them, he intended the Levitical cities to be centers for collecting taxes, and the Levites served essentially as clerical tax farmers for his regime. This would explain Jeroboam's "non-Levitic" priesthoods at Dan and Bethel. If, on the other hand, the Levitical cities are a product of a later time, the institution is altogether imaginary or, rather, programmatic, and probably bound up with Josiah's plans (and thus to an extent reflected in Ezekiel's temple vision).

48. The OG of 1 Kgs. 4:6 reflects a Hebrew text: "Ahi was officer (variant: 'Ahishar was') over the house, and Eliah was (officer?) over the house, and Eliab son of Saph was over the army (variant: 'ancestral spirits'), and Adoniram son of Abda was over the levies." Notably, the second steward is also named without a patronym. Scott C. Layton has argued ("The Steward in Ancient Israel: A Study of Hebrew ('ăšer) 'al habbayit in Its Near Eastern Setting," *JBL* 109 [1990]: 633-49) that the office of steward originates in a Canaanite office. However, Mesopotamian texts also attest it, e.g., in the title of a witness in Sargon's era: Balawat BT 101 from 710 B.C.E., cited in Stephanie Dalley, *Iraq* 47 (1985): 31-48.

[First name] son of Hur in Mount Ephraim

[First name] son of Deqer in Maqaz and . . .

[First name] son of Hesed in Arubbot

[First name] son of Abinadab in all the coast of Dor

Baana son of Ahilud in Taanach and Megiddo and . . .

[First name] son of Geber in Ramoth Gilead

Ahinadab son of Iddo at Mahanaim

[First name of son of] Ahimaaz in Naphtali

Baana son of Hushai in Asher and in Alot (eastern Upper Galilee?)

Jehoshaphat son of Paruah in Issachar

Shimei son of Ela in Benjamin

Geber son of Uri in the land of Gilead. . . .

That is, the top of the list was less well preserved than the bottom. The pattern suggests fraying of an original list on papyrus. This, like the court connections of the governors, would indicate that the author of Solomon's regnal account (in 1 Kgs. 3–10) used a source for the names of that king's officials.[49] Given the other considerations outlined above, it is fair to conclude that the list derived from Solomon's court.

A final index of the antiquity of the province list comes from the geographic names it contains. The term "Mount (or: 'hill country of') Ephraim" is the first province. This term is sometimes used to describe purely Ephraimite

---

49. For the theory of an effaced list, see esp. George Ernest Wright, "The Provinces of Solomon," *ErIsr* 8 (1967): 58*-68*. Solomon's regnal account in 1 Kgs. 3–10 was composed no later than the reign of Hezekiah, when the first edition of Kings was written. See latterly Erik Eynikel, *The Reform of King Josiah,* 1-135, with bibliography. It may, however, antedate the composition of Kings as a whole, as it contains elements such as the image of the king as natural philosopher and the collection of exotic animals, which are not a part of the propagation of the royal image in the 8th or later centuries and are not repeated elsewhere in Kings. It is clear that written records from Solomon's time were available to the author of the segment, just as Shishaq's campaign is accurately placed shortly after Solomon's death, in the late 10th century. From there, a string of accurate recollections of foreign monarchs begins. For details, see Baruch Halpern, "The State of Israelite History," in *Reconsidering Israel and Judah: Recent Studies on the Deuteronomistic History,* ed. Gary N. Knoppers and J. Gordon McConville. Sources for Biblical and Theological Study 8 (Winona Lake: Eisenbrauns, 2000), 540-65. The use of 10th-century sources, whether monumental or archival, could explain the preservation of the antique elements in 1 Kgs. 3–10, as well as the fact of Shishaq's campaign. In any case, Solomon's coup is justified in 1 Kgs. 1–2 as it would be in a royal inscription — as in the case of Idrimi and Bar-Rakib (KAI 215:2-7). The regnal account is thus based on a source, probably a relatively laconic one. Further, the legitimation of Solomon's reign by the temple construction bespeaks concerns contemporary with him.

territory. But in various texts it refers to a larger entity than the territory of the tribe Ephraim: it can mean the undifferentiated territory of "Joseph," which is, the tribes of Manasseh and Ephraim taken together; or it can designate the whole of the central hills, between Jerusalem and the Jezreel Valley.[50] This last is its most probable reference in 1 and 2 Samuel, and perhaps in general. But the province list distinguishes between "the hill country of Ephraim" and Benjamin's tribal territory. The "hill country of Ephraim" stretches from the Jezreel Valley in the north to Benjamin's border, which is not the pattern in later texts.

More important are the towns mentioned in the province list. "The son of Deqer" was "in Maqaz," a center not attested in any other text. His other centers are Shaalbim, Beth Shemesh, and Ayyalon of Beth Hanan. Shaalbim appears as Shaalbin in the lists of Joshua, which thus employ a later form of the name.[51] Beth Shemesh was, as noted, a town in Eqron's hinterland until Solomon's era, at the start of Iron II, though it also remained Israelite later. Ayyalon plays a role in 1 Sam. 14:31, where Saul clears the central pass to its border, meaning that it remained outside Israel; and, with Shaalbim, Ayyalon is regarded as Amorite in Judg. 1:35. It continued to exist in the monarchic era, but, with the attachment of Gezer, fell within, not on the edge of, Israel's holdings and thus does not appear in any narratives or texts.

The cities mentioned in Solomon's Jezreel district are Taanach, Megiddo, Beth Shan near Zarethan, below Jezreel, and Abel Meholah across the river from Yoqmeam. Taanach, Megiddo, and Beth Shan were all occupied in the late 10th century, in the years leading to Shishaq's invasion. Megiddo and Beth Shan were major fortifications, Taanach a smaller center. Taanach was effectively not settled after the 10th century. It may have served as some sort of official outpost, but was certainly minor in importance. Thus a later author would not have included it in an invented list, but would probably have named Jenin (Beth Haggan, as in 2 Kgs. 9:27) instead.

Abel Meholah appears as a geographic marker in Judg. 7:22, and is named as the home of the prophet Elisha, but does not appear in Joshua's later lists of

---

50. Minimally, Ephraim itself (or some indeterminate more extensive meaning): Josh. 19:50; 20:7; 21:21; 24:30, 33; Judg. 2:9; 10:1; 17:1, 8; 18:2, 13; 19:1; 1 Kgs. 12:25; 2 Kgs. 5:22; cf. Judg. 12:15, "land of Ephraim". Minimally, Ephraim and Manasseh: Josh. 17:15. Including Benjamin and thus the whole central hill country: Judg. 3:27; 4:5; 19:16, 18; 1 Sam. 1:1; 9:4; 14:22; 2 Sam. 20:21; Jer. 4:15; 31:5; 50:19; 2 Chr. 13:4; 15:8 (vs. "land of Ephraim," 30:10).

51. Shaalbim in 1 Kgs. 4:9 and Judg. 1:35 makes the gentilic Shaalboni in 2 Sam. 23:32; 1 Chr. 11:33. It is by back-formation from the gentilic that the version Shaalbin reached the author of Josh. 19:42. On the character of Judg. 1, see above, Chapter 22D.

Israelite settlements, possibly because it was in Transjordan. Jezreel was certainly occupied in the 10th century (and was the home of one of Saul's wives in the 11th century). It was, however, not occupied after the mid-9th century. Neither of these towns would have appeared on a list invented after the 9th century.

Yoqmeam is a Levitical city in Chronicles, but does not otherwise appear, despite being in Ephraim, where Joshua enumerates important towns of the 8th century. And Zarethan was the home of Jeroboam, as well as the neighborhood of some of Solomon's foundries. However, it appears in a late text, so its location was not forgotten.[52] If its identification with Tell es-Saʿīdîyeh is correct, then some form of occupation continued there from David's or Solomon's time through the end of the Iron Age.

Most of the other administrative districts are unrevealing. Mahanaim appears in Samuel, and as a Levitical city in Joshua, but also as a marker of borders in Josh. 13:26, 30. Further districts are tribal names: Naphtali, Issachar, and Benjamin. But the Asher district is qualified: "in Asher and in Alot." The latter could represent the Upper Galilee east of the Plain of Akko and to the north, and the distinction between it and Asher may reflect the sale of the Cabul, but not the uplands.[53] The provinces in Gilead are also revealing: the region is not yet divided between Manasseh and Gad; a later writer would have referred to the tribes, as did the author of 2 Kgs. 10:33. Nor is there any indication of government activity south of the Mahanaim region, in Gad and Reuben. The contrast is to the list of Levitical cities, which includes those tribes. Any Jerusalem scribe composing the province list in the 8th or any later century would have included these southern areas in it.

Overall, there is every indication that the list of Solomon's administrative

---

52. Zarethan, Josh. 3:16; with Solomon's foundries, 1 Kgs. 7:46. In another form, it occurs in Judg. 7:22 (where *resh* replaces *daleth* as the third radical of the name, by scribal error), on a line of march, and as Jeroboam's home in 1 Kgs. 11:26, a text whose incidental information appears to be reliable. 2 Chr. 4:17 duplicates 1 Kgs. 7:46, but reproduces the place name as it appears in 1 Kgs. 11:26 — a 7th-century (Josianic) text. The phonetic variation chiefly reflects the expression of a dental combination. Thus: /ṣaridatu/ and /ṣaridatānu/ are the original bi-forms. In the former case, *-atu becomes -â, hence Zaredah. However, the second form is reduced to /ṣaridtanu/, which generates Zarethan instead of the expected Zarethon. The older form is that in 1 Kgs. 7:46, which locution speaks to the date of the account of Solomon's reign.

53. For an archaeological reflex of the sale of the Cabul, see Zvi Gal, "Ḥurbat Rosh Zayit and the Early Phoenician Pottery," *Levant* 24 (1992): 173-86. The finds reflect the fact that Israel had been supplying olive oil to Tyre, and the fact that Tyre took possession of the site. Oil, wine, and grain were all separated by jar type, though the last was transported in sacks.

districts stems from his time. And this makes the list invaluable. It illuminates Solomon's approach to the organization of the country.

In the provincial system, up to five provinces may reflect traditional organization. The first is that of "[ ] son of Hur" in Mount Ephraim (reflecting the invention, in the United Monarchy, of a super-tribe, Joseph, consisting of Ephraim and Manasseh).[54] The second is that of Ahinadab, centered on Mahanaim. The third is that of Jehoshaphat in Issachar, the fourth that of Shimei in Benjamin. The fifth is the territory of Geber son of Uri in Gilead, identical with the later Transjordanian section of the tribe of Manasseh. These are the regions where corvée was probably enforced unevenly.

The other provinces in 1 Kgs. 4 were liable to corvée. The first four provinces named after the hill country of Ephraim (Joseph) in the list are regions detached from it, or not yet attached to it. Thus Mount Ephraim heads the list in 1 Kgs. 4:8. The next four provinces appear in 1 Kgs. 4:9, 10, 11, and 12. The first is the western end of the Ayyalon Pass, the territory of the original tribe of "Dan" as it is defined in the book of Joshua. Here were the populations that Judg. 1 alleges were subject to corvée. Solomon's governor, "son of Deqer," had a special purchase on Maqaz, Shaalbim, Beth Shemesh, and Ayyalon of Beth Hanan. Judg. 1 includes Shaalbim and Ayyalon in the corvée from Dan's territory. Shaalbim plays no role in any other narrative. Ayyalon is the western extent of Saul's expansion. To judge from the treatment of Megiddo and Hazor, Solomon rusticated the local Canaanite population from the major centers and taxed it in its villages.

The second region detached from Ephraim, under "son of Hesed," is Arubboth, containing Sochoh in the Sharon, and the land of Hepher — which a P text shows was characterized by matrilinear succession, in contrast to all other Israelite regions (Num. 26:32-33; 27; cf. Josh. 17:2-3). In addition, Josh. 12:17 claims that a king of Hepher was killed during the conquest — Hepher, in other words, was thought to be a site that lent its name to the region, "the land of Hepher." It is a prime candidate, in sum, for the presence of Canaanites in the transition to Solomon's reign.[55]

The third region on the periphery of Ephraim is Dor, under "son of Abinadab." Again, here was a former Sea People center in which there was a sudden change — probably reflecting the Absalom revolt — to a more indigenous culture. The excavator, Ephraim Stern, characterizes the culture as Phoenician, and this may represent the collusion between David or Solomon and

---

54. For the invention, Halpern, *The Emergence of Israel in Canaan*, 109-63.

55. For the archaeology of the region, see Adam Zertal, *Arubboth, Hepher and Solomon's Third District* (M.A. thesis, Tel Aviv University, 1984).

Tyre that followed the Absalom revolt, or merely cultural influence from Tyre. In any case, the region was a lowland area, and therefore populated more by Canaanites and Sea People (Sikils) than by Israelites. It is not coincidental that Abinadab's son, in this border region, is Solomon's son-in-law.

The fourth province bordering Ephraim begins to complete the circle about it. The earlier provinces embrace the territory from the western Ayyalon Pass in the south up through the Sharon to Dor, on the northern coast. Now, from Dor, through the pass to Megiddo, we enter the Jezreel Valley, extending to Transjordan. The Jezreel was host to the great tells, with a predominantly Canaanite population, on which David relied for controlling the Israelites. Solomon evidently subjected them to heavy imposts. His governor was Baana, son of Ahilud, and brother of a high court official.

The list of provinces next moves to Transjordan. In 1 Kgs. 4:13, the sixth province is centered at Ramoth Gilead, under "son of Geber." The province covered northernmost Gilead and the Bashan. The son of Geber's district included the territory of Damascus that David had held. Imposing taxation there will have been a high priority both of David and of Solomon. The son of Geber was probably the son, as noted, of the governor of the rest of Gilead. But on the southern end of Israel's holdings in Transjordan, Solomon posted an official, "Ahinadab son of Iddo at Mahanaim." Ahinadab's province stretched at least to Ammon, where a native king descended from Nahash ruled a vassal state. Thus the two appointees on the peripheries of Transjordan were responsible to monitor foreign territories there.

The ninth governor is "[ ] Ahimaaz" in Naphtali. Ahimaaz was the son of Zadoq, Solomon's high priest. As the first names of so many governors are missing, it is probable that Ahimaaz's son was the governor, not Ahimaaz himself. This governor was another of Solomon's sons-in-law. In Asher, the next governor was a son of Hushai.

These two Galilean provinces cover the northernmost extent of Solomon's realm. They are also the areas whose interests he sacrificed, not coincidentally. Both appear in Judg. 1, with no corvée, but many Canaanites, in Asher and some corvée in Naphtali. Naphtali also included Dan, a small area at the headwaters of the Jordan. Solomon sold Asher to Tyre. He permitted Damascus to aggrandize itself, endangering Naphtali and especially Dan, which fell at least once and possibly even twice in the next century.[56] Small wonder that proven

56. Asa's ally, "Bar-Hadad" (I), is said to have sacked Dan in 1 Kgs. 15. Hazael also took it, as the Dan stela attests. That it reverted to Israel in the interim is actually likely: this would explain the claim of the Dan stela that the king of Israel "advanced against the land of my father." When the Dan stela was erected toward the end of the 9th century, then,

courtiers with impeccable political genealogies were installed in the far north, since this was the region where the tax regimen was probably most merciless.

The next governors enumerated are those of Issachar, Benjamin, and most of Transjordan, between Mahanaim and the Golan. Possibly, the text then goes on to say that there was a province of Judah as well, though it names no governor for it. Overall, the province list looks as though it faithfully respects the distinction between Solomon's two political economies. The first was aimed at protecting the heartland. The other was based on the exploitation and even the sacrifice of the northern peripheries. The intact tribal areas, allowing for sales and threats from abroad, were Judah, Benjamin, and Issachar, the last in the Lower Galilee.

It looks, in short, as though Solomon imposed a heavy tax burden on much of the population. The text claims that the burden fell disproportionately on the Canaanites, and spared the Israelites themselves. Even were this true, the extraction of resources from the Canaanites would have depressed exchange with their Israelite neighbors. The more heavily Solomon relied on the Canaanites as a source of labor, the more his fiscal needs demanded imposts from Israelites as well.

Among Solomon's imposts, the sale of Asher must be counted. This sale, together with Solomon's imperial administration of the north and his ineffectiveness in controlling Rezin, the filibuster in Damascus, triggered the coup of Jeroboam. Conversely, in the south Solomon dealt effectively with a revolt in Edom, holding on to his possessions there, including the Red Sea port of Ezion Geber. Solomon's willingness to strip the north in order to protect and coddle the south reflects a sectional favoritism that was not lost on the Israelites, and led to their eventual secession on his death.[57]

Jeroboam, who was to lead that secession, made an attempt on Solomon's life, then fled to Shishaq's court in or just after Solomon's 24th year. But Solomon's 24th year was the year of Shishaq's accession, which occasioned the sale of Asher to Tyre. The timing of Jeroboam's attempt on Solomon marks it as a reaction against Solomon's sectionalism, and marks Jeroboam as Shishaq's creature. Shishaq identified Egypt's chief competitor, for the Arabian trade and for influence in Phoenicia, as the Solomonic state, reversing his predecessors' policy of containing the Philistines. He made it a special object of his campaign

---

the kings of Damascus had probably been reckoning Dan an Aramean town for something on the order of 70 years. Naturally, of Dan's recovery by Ahab or probably Omri, the Bible relates nothing, just as it is silent about Omri's conquest of Moab, attested in the Mesha stela.

57. Halpern, *JBL* 93 (1974): 519-32.

to destroy the Negev settlements, which comprise about half the sites enumerated in his topographic list.

Shishaq also made it a point to establish himself on the border of Tyre. He confined his campaigning to the territory of Solomon's kingdom, devastating the region that had become such a successful counterweight to Philistia (below, Chapter 23).

When Israel seceded from the House of David, after Solomon's death, they rejected state symbols to return to traditional views. Jeroboam's adoption of the antique iconography of the bull-calf was a return to local tradition, as opposed to the Egyptianizing iconography of the ark and cherubim. Cherub iconography is found only in extremely elite contexts, whereas the bull appears in village or countryside settings as well.

Jeroboam separated the state cult from the state capital — a situation also characterizing Saul's realm. He ruled from Tirzah in the central hills of Ephraim, and had a second royal center in Penuel, in Transjordan, supplanting the old center of Mahanaim. He located the national shrines on the borders of his kingdom, at Bethel and Dan, trumpeting their pertinence to the nation rather than the crown. The same strategy was aimed at pacifying sectional concerns. Jeroboam thus distinguished himself from Solomon, who incorporated the single central shrine of his state into the royal acropolis. Solomon, like the kings of most Near Eastern city-states, built the temple in the backyard of his palace.

Yet, Jeroboam was an ally of Shishaq, a beneficiary of that king's sanctuary. He administered Israel as an Egyptian vassal. He defended Israel against taxation, which fell heaviest on former Canaanites. If the Samaria ostraca of the early 8th century reflect earlier policies, Jeroboam's tax regimen was administered through the traditional kinship structures, rather than by the imposition of a parallel system of royal officials across those structures, as under Solomon.

Did Jeroboam introduce a policy of pluralism in regard to the former Canaanites? He did not reenfranchise them in the fortresses of the Jezreel, which remained empty of domestic population. It is possible that he did not lighten the "Canaanites'" corvée, and gave vent to the xenophobia that had characterized Saul's and Absalom's politics. But the "Canaanites," now dispersed to village sites from the fortresses, had sufficiently assimilated into the local economy to have receded as an ethnic lightning rod for Israelite resentment. That resentment was directed more outward, against Jerusalem, to be sure, against the Aramean state of Damascus, against Ammon and Moab in Transjordan, and against the northern Philistine states of Ashdod and Gath.

Under Jeroboam, there was probably an early break with Tyre. The northern kingdom, Israel, had no real tradition of orderly succession. It experienced repeated *coups d'état* before achieving stability under Omri and his descendants. Omri fashioned a marriage alliance between his son and the royal house of Tyre. He or his son Ahab also concluded an alliance with the kingdom of Judah. Together, these parties re-created the trade network from Arabia to Tyre first fashioned by Solomon after Shishaq's accession. It was to interrupt traffic along this coastal corridor that Shishaq erupted into Asia. While Egyptian oversight continued, during and beyond Jeroboam's reign, the flow was undoubtedly interdicted, the border a hostile one.

If Solomon's program embodied the external politics of Absalom, Jeroboam's recapitulated those of Saul. His revolt left Israel surrounded by enemies, on all sides. The rhetoric of the dynasty was very likely nativist. And the wars of Israel with Judah and Philistia continued until the rise of Omri. Omri's resurrection of Solomon's policies placed Israel among the leading powers west of the Euphrates. It laid a foundation for economic expansion that went unrealized until Assyria removed the threat from Damascus at the start of the 8th century. By mid-century, Assyria had replaced Damascus as an invader attracted by Israel's prosperity. Solomon's policies were no doubt enforced with the ruthlessness for which his father was renowned. But in their orientation, they were farsighted, linking Israel and Tyre in a condominium, sometimes with Egypt, in the long-distance trade in southern drugs and spices.

Only in the 7th century, when Assyria made Eqron the processing center for the olive production of Judah, did Judah achieve a similar economic pattern — under King Manasseh — by resurrecting its control and colonization of the south. The trade route of the time with the Phoenicians and the West ran through southern Judah to Eqron, and then to whichever Philistine port Assyrian interest favored at the time. Goods destined for Assyria, meanwhile, flowed through Judah to the Assyrian provinces of Samaria and Damascus.

As Assyria withdrew its aegis, the arrangement continued. It again led to conflict with Egypt, during the course of Egypt's attempt to shore Assyria up against the Babylonians and Medes. The pharaoh in question, Neco, even dug a canal from the Delta out the Wadi Tumeilat to the Gulf of Suez in an attempt to control the flow of southern goods. A few decades later, in the 550s, the Babylonian king Nabonidus removed his royal residence to Arabia again in quest after exotica from the south.

Solomon's external policies were thus programmatic for subsequent kings of Israel and of Judah. They were, however, too far advanced, too cosmopolitan in their implications, for the inhabitants of the hill country of Cisjordan. These citizens, accustomed to a relative lack of social stratification, lived mainly in villages without defensive walls or any other sign of public works. Though they lived consensually, they were probably at one another's throats on a regular basis. They stored their grain in their own houses, and in small pits pertaining to the compound housing the extended family, where processing and cooking facilities, and storage, of food and water, were shared.

With the introduction of administration, particularly in the wake of the Absalom revolt, the conquered territory of Israel was honeycombed with lowland fortifications. Not just Megiddo, Hazor, and Gezer, but other major sites came under Jerusalem's control. Beth Shan, Taanach, and Dor are representative for the lowlands, but Shaalbim and Beth Shemesh, on the edge of the hill country, and Mahanaim in Transjordan, Ishbaal's Transjordanian residence and David's walled refuge from Absalom, with an inner and an outer gate, will also have been impressive sites at the time.[58]

At roughly this time, circumvallations appear in the hill country for the first time, including at the northern capital, Tirzah. Architectural elements reflecting the installation of public administration appear by city gates, at Tirzah and at Tell Beit Mirsim in Judah.[59] And social stratification becomes archaeologically transparent, as at the site of 'Izbet Ṣarṭah, where Stratum II, with pottery of the late 10th century, consists of a huge manor house and outlying shanties. Similarly, a manor house appears at Tell es-Sa'îdîyeh in Strata X-IXA, with late-10th-century pottery, after a more modest structure in the preceding stratum, XIA. Another appears at Ein Sippori in the lower Galilee.[60] The proliferation of arrowheads inscribed with an official's name, whether for archery contests, for belomancy, or for purposes of making awards, is another index of stratification, at least at the political-military level.[61] But not one arrowhead to

58. For a fort at Kinrot in this era, see Volkmar Fritz, "Kinneret: Excavations at Tell el-'Oreimeh (Tel Kinrot), 1982-1985 Seasons," *TA* 20 (1993): 187-215. Its identification as an Israelite site at the time is, however, not certain, and it is a question as well when the kingdom of Geshur vanished. On the latter, see Moshe Kochavi, "The Land of Geshur Project," *IEJ* 39 (1989): 1-17.

59. See William F. Albright, *The Excavation of Tell Beit Mirsim III. The Iron Age.* AASOR 21-22 (New Haven: ASOR, 1943): 12-14, for an assignment of the thickened casemate wall adjoining the West Tower and Gate to Stratum A1, and comparison to the wall of Beth Shemesh IIa; and 40-47, for the identification of the thickening with the aftermath of Shishaq's campaign. The pottery associated with the thickening, however, belongs to the late 10th century. The earliest phase of the West Tower and Gate takes the form of a *bīt hilāni*.

60. For the archaeological record, see esp. John S. Holladay, "The Kingdoms of Israel and Judah"; and on individual sites the entries in *NEAEHL*. For Beth Shemesh in this period, see Shlomo Bunimowitz and Zvi Lederman, "Beth-Shemesh: Culture Conflict on Judah's Frontier," *BAR* 23/1 (1997): 42-49, 75-77.

61. See esp. Benjamin Sass, "Inscribed Babylonian Arrowheads of the Turn of the Second Millennium and Their Phoenician Counterparts," *UF* 21 (1989): 349-56. For the ar-

date is inscribed with a clearly Israelite name (with the element Yahweh as a part of it), and it is therefore not possible to link them to Israel with certainty. (One cache, at el-Khadr, was found near Bethlehem.)

When stratification is evident in the archaeological record, the implication is that it was open. The level of display at Megiddo was extraordinary. Two palaces dominated the site, behind the enormous gate. Their lower courses consisted of carefully worked stone blocks, and they no doubt contained treasures, looted by Shishaq. The center of the site was largely devoid of construction at all — in a walled city at the entrance to the Jezreel Valley, the most expensive real estate in Israel. All this display was intended to impress the local population, to be sure, but it was especially meant to impress travelers from abroad whose paths led them through Hazor, in the north of the kingdom, through Megiddo, at the key pass in the kingdom, and en route to Jerusalem, through Gezer. Solomon claimed, both in his literature and in his architecture, to be a "great king," almost the equal of the pharaoh or of the king of Assyria.

This display, writ large in the palaces at Megiddo and Jerusalem, meant prestige and wealth for the state, enriching the population. Solomon's trade network opened lucrative foreign markets for wine, oil, and cereals from the heartland. For these, for land, and for goods from southern markets, he received wood and precious and base metals from Phoenicia and Cyprus.[62] The network was constructed on alliances abroad, and its effectiveness depended in part on display. And yet that very display, while creating wealth, occasioned resentment among those who benefited from a prosperous expansion. Stratification was a reminder of the regimen in Canaan under David and the Philistines, where the distribution of wealth concentrated in lowlands centers. Worse, Solomon's display at administrative centers, at least in the second part of his reign, was unrestrained.

To the Israelites, Solomon was the king of a city-state, and no more. Solomon's town, its temple, was meant to inspire awe. Only for a disembedded center, inherited from David, without Israelite population, does Solomon's province scheme make sense. Solomon's fortress towns — and the fortresses that served as administrative centers housed palaces and shrines, but no temples in

---

rowheads, see further Robert Deutsch and Michael Heltzer, *Windows to the Past* (Tel Aviv-Jaffa: Archaeological Center, 1997). These have ordinarily been dated a bit earlier on typological grounds, but a 10th-century date is far from excluded.

62. See Gal, *Levant* 24 (1992): 173-86, for evidence of transmission of crops from Israel to Tyre. On the exchange, see Volkmar Fritz, "Salomo," *MDOG* 117 (1985): 47-67; and for ties to the southern trade, see above on the Negev caravanserais, and Yohanan Aharoni, "Forerunners of the Limes: Iron Age Fortresses in the Negev," *IEJ* 17 (1967): 1-17; Rudolph Cohen, "The Iron Age Fortresses in the Central Negev," *BASOR* 236 (1979): 61-79.

the classical sense — were meant to intimidate locals as well as to concentrate the wealth pouring into the country through trade. He was an emperor, if of a backwater. He gave himself the airs of an international player.

The Israelites were right to complain that Solomon was sacrificing the far north in order to protect his state. The losses of territory around Damascus and of Asher were clear enough signals of Solomon's real orientation. But their refusal to endorse Rehoboam, Solomon's son, as king (in 1 Kgs. 12) indicates that, in Solomon's time, they were less effectively beaten down than immediately after Absalom's revolt. They had the power to secede. With Egyptian help, they ejected Jerusalem's garrisons and brought their revolt to fruition. This power explains why Solomon's literature so stressed the innocence of the dynasty in Jerusalem of charges of exterminating the House of Saul.

Perhaps enlightened minds in Israel, such as Jeroboam, thought that secession would lead to long-term gains. When Omri and his descendants held power, and re-created the trade links, Israel expanded, certainly in Transjordan, and perhaps to the north. Ahab reunited the palace with a state shrine in the capital. The Israelites may have hoped for the same successes with less centralization.

Thus, in some sense, the creation of an Israelite state, independent of Jerusalem, was an attempt to permit the north to blossom, to enjoy the full trade value of its produce, to prosper in a way that could not be imagined under the dynasty of David. It was only later that Omri's dynasty made it clear that the nexus worked best in combination with an alliance with Jerusalem, and in combination with display at a level that registers in the archaeological record. Omri came to the throne roughly 50 years after Solomon's demise. The implication is, Solomon was roughly half a century too far out in front of his countrymen.

APPENDIX

CHAPTER 23

The Archaeology of David's Reign

A. Introduction

The following discussion is confined to an appendix because it is technical. It employs standard scholarly jargon in treating the archaeology of the United Monarchy. Readers brave of heart but unfamiliar with the history of the archaeology should consult a standard archaeological reference work before venturing into this treatment. Recommended are Amihai Mazar's *Archaeology of the Land of the Bible, 10,000-586 B.C.E.* (Anchor Bible Reference Library [New York: Doubleday, 1990]), Amnon Ben-Tor's collection, *The Archaeology of Ancient Israel* (New Haven: Yale University Press, 1992), or, in German, Helga Weippert's *Palästina in vorhellenistischer Zeit* (Handbuch der Archäologie [Munich: Beck, 1988]). More specialized discussion is available in John S. Holladay, "The Kingdoms of Israel and Judah: Political and Economic Centralization in the Iron IIa-b (ca 1000-750 B.C.)," and on individual sites, the entries in *NEAEHL*. The periods about which to read are Iron I and early Iron II.

In recent years, as we have seen, the United Monarchy has been the site of a symbolic battle over the reliability of biblical historiography. Three elements of evidence relate to this subject: first, historical texts particularly in the books of Samuel and 1 Kings, and references in prophecy, liturgy, and historiography; second, the archaeological record especially in Judah and Israel and, to a lesser extent, in southern Phoenicia, Philistia, and Transjordan; and, third, germane epigraphs, such as the Karnak list of the pharaoh Shishaq and Assyrian records of Aramean incursions across the Euphrates in the 11th/10th centuries and Assyrian counterstrikes in the 9th century.

External writings, including various West Semitic epigraphs of the 9th/8th centuries, also illuminate the historical realities of the time of the United Monarchy (11th-10th centuries). They condition our expectations about the conventions employed in royal records likely compiled at the time — and these records were used as sources for larger works, such as Samuel as a whole or the Deuteronomistic History. They sharpen our understanding of the political and social processes that evoked contemporary historiography. Equally, they attune us to the royal ideologies that Israel's literate elite absorbed from abroad as features of governance and of royal propaganda.

No complex cultural manifestation, such as literary composition, is identical from place to place. Our texts, thus, only imperfectly reflect the ideologies of surrounding cultures. The differences from text to text, and indeed in the encodement of ideology in architecture and material culture from place to place, are as important as the similarities in the reconstruction of the culture.

On any objective measure, the most reliable textual data concerning biblical kings after Solomon are their ages at accession and the length of their reigns. Synchronisms of Ahab and Jehu with Shalmaneser III in 853 and 841 are undisputed. Biblical data make it clear that 853 was Ahab's last year on the throne, and 841 Jehu's first. A synchronism between Rehoboam and Shishaq obtains toward the end of the latter's reign. This places the end of the United Monarchy in the neighborhood of 930, probably in 931.

As noted above, Jerusalem shows few signs of having been a capital city during the period (Iron IB/IIA). There are indications, however, of its occupation and of the introduction of monumental structures at least on the eastern slope of the City of David in the 10th century.[1] Admittedly, the remains are sufficiently exiguous to have elicited claims on the one hand that the town could not have been an administrative center, and on the other that one cannot judge from the vagaries of material survival and recovery alone.[2] The latter submission is the more compelling in a site such as Jerusalem, where monumental construction especially in the Persian through Herodian periods was repeatedly carried down to bedrock, and where the overburden of modern settlement and political constraints prohibit extensive soundings.

In the main, therefore, the archaeology of the United Monarchy has been investigated at sites outside Jerusalem. Significant is the settlement pattern during the period in question, ascertained through survey evidence. The difficulty

---

1. See Jane M. Cahill and D. Tarler, "Excavations at the City of David." See further above, Chapter 18 and n. 2.

2. See esp. Nadav Na'aman, *BASOR* 304 (1996): 17-27; cf. David W. Jamieson-Drake, *Scribes and Schools in Monarchic Judah.*

here is that ceramic typology alone is a highly labile tool for dating: local tastes and materials and the conservatism of local suppliers all affect the repertoire at a particular site. Periods of occupation do not necessarily coincide at two sites even with similar pottery, and often vary widely even within a site. And critical forms or wares may not penetrate political, ethnic, and economic boundaries at all times. So while surveys paint an overall picture of occupation in the long term, their results are best understood as a sort of rolling average of occupation, rather than a series of period-long snapshots.

Surveys suggest that Israelite population burgeoned at the transition from Iron I to Iron II, and increased again in the 9th-8th centuries, while that of Judah reached a peak at the end of the 8th century and then a lesser one at the end of the 7th century. But the latter datum is best known from the comparison of stratified with survey remains; the extent of the 8th-century settlement efflorescence in Israel is as yet unknown from the ground, primarily because the hill country there is barely excavated.[3]

Direct textual intersections with the archaeology remain fairly limited. As we have seen, the books of Samuel make modest claims about the kingdoms of Saul, Ishbaal, and David. Saul is said to have barely held any ground at all, progressing only to Ayyalon. David's borders reach into the Negev, and encompass parts of Moab and Ammon, and some territory south of Damascus. They never cross the Philistine plain, while in Phoenicia no clear delineation can be found (though the cession by Solomon of the Cabul implies its possession at the end of David's reign, on which see above, Chapter 22D). Samuel claims neither that David took any territory north of Abel (of Maacah), nor that he exercised sovereignty over so near a major center as Damascus. Even his diplomatic relations extend only as far as Hamath and Tyre, and those are late in his reign.

Just what one might expect in the way of archaeological reflexes of such a state remains a question — not yet addressed in the literature. The reconstruction offered above suggests that it was only late in his reign, for the most part after the Absalom revolt, that David was even capable of imposing abiding structures of national governance on Israel. Earlier, he was principally a Philistine filibuster in Jerusalem and the south, allied with the Gibeonite confederates, a Hivvite population, against the Israelites north of his political

---

3. Important is the fortified center at Marjameh, on which see Amihai Mazar, "Excavations at the Israelite Town at Khirbet Marjameh in the Hills of Ephraim," *IEJ* 45 (1995): 85-117. The fortification of the terminus of the fairly insignificant Wadi Ujah system reflects an economic interest in controlling the steppe that suggests, in turn, exploitation of the steppe region for pastoralism.

catchment. Although he probably accumulated surplus wealth in Jerusalem, there is no indication that he was spending it on display, rather than soldiers, or hoarding it.

About Solomon, the claims are more elaborate, stipulating trade relations with Arabia, Egypt, Cilicia (Que), and the kings of "the Hittites" (1 Kgs. 10:29), as opposed to those of Aram, who are often mentioned later (see Chapter 22D and below). Later texts make similar claims about David, who never trades even with Egypt in Samuel (or before Eupolemos), and extend the claims about Solomon, attributing to him activity in Palmyra. Solomon's relations with Hamath, thus, and his activity on its borders are amplified in Chronicles. Later texts also assert (as 2 Kgs. 14:28?) the extension of Israel's borders to this arena, or even to the Euphrates during the United Monarchy. These aggrandized claims were not, however, contemporary with the kings in question, as the relative reticence of 2 Samuel and 1 Kgs. 1–11 attests (see Chapters 9, 14B2-C). Silence reigns on the contacts of either David or Solomon with Cyprus, perhaps because of sensitivity about mercenary forces from that island. And no later king is reported to have received diplomatic recognition from afar, with the exception of Hezekiah, the ally of Babylon.

The early documents made limited claims, couched so as to imply larger gains; the later texts followed the implications. But little of the later interpretation was imposed upon the earlier. Both Chronicles (1 Chr. 5:9; 18:3) and Ezra (4:20) reflect the later view of a United Monarchic Israel extending to the Euphrates. As a historical accomplishment, however, this is elsewhere never attributed to David or Solomon, being instead expressed as an ideal for fulfillment in Deut. 1:7; 11:24; Josh. 1:4. The one related passage in Kings (1 Kgs. 4:21, 24[5:1, 4]) claims that Solomon was sovereign over "all the kings across the river" (this is the text echoed in Ezra; cf. 2 Sam. 10:16), but *which* river is not stipulated, as elsewhere in Samuel and 1 Kgs. 1–11, where the implication is that the empire reached the Euphrates, but no explicit reference much overshoots the upper Jordan. Even the Greek of Kings, which tends to extend Solomon's influence into Syria (as 1 Kgs. 2:46d Lucianic), is less than explicit in this respect (1 Kgs. 2:46f, k; 4:24).

The United Monarchy "grows." It expands across the Jordan in 2 Samuel and 1 Kgs. 1–11. It reaches central Syria in Amos 6:14 (cf. v. 2), P (Num. 13:21; 34:8) and parts of DtrH (Josh. 13:5; Judg. 3:3; 1 Kgs. 8:65, speaking of Israelite settlers, not political control; 2 Kgs. 14:25, 28) and Ezekiel (47:15-20; 48:1). This reflects the same extension of sovereignty instantiated in Chronicles (1 Chr. 13:5; 18:3; 2 Chr. 7:8; 8:3-4) on the basis of a misreading of Samuel.[4]

4. See above, Chapter 14.

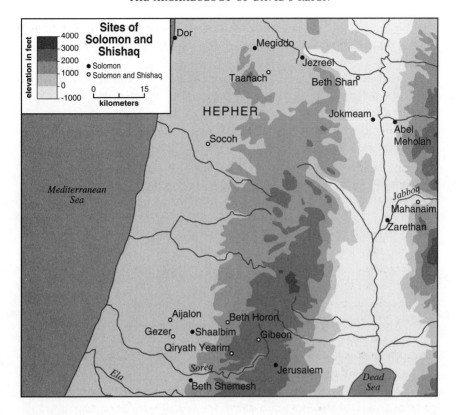

Map 23.1

This misreading, along with the claim that David or Solomon reached the Euphrates in Ezra, Chronicles, and all subsequent literature, suggests a progressive extension of the idealized boundaries of the Davidic state over time. The limited borders of 2 Samuel, thus, cannot be those of the postexilic period. Nor are the idealized boundaries of the 8th to 6th centuries, usually reaching to Hamath and perhaps in some cases from the late 7th century to the Euphrates, compatible with the view either of Samuel or, when they reach to Hamath, Chronicles. The diachronic development is plain, and refutes any notion of wholesale creation of the literature in the postexilic era. It has at the same time the implication that the "empire" of the later United Monarchy was too limited to pour surplus funds into monumental capital projects without straining the social and economic fiber of the country.

Yet some texts make claims that, critically regarded, should have archaeological correlates. For example, the decline of Eqron, and commensurate rise of Gath, comports with the textual indications, as we have seen. Inside Israel, setting aside the issue of Jerusalem, there should, on the record, have been a *relative* influx of capital in the United Monarchic period, from such peripheries as Edom, Moab, and perhaps Ammon. The regularization of administration in Cisjordanian Canaan — under Solomon — facilitated government extraction of capital in kind and in labor. The state should have derived commercial advantage from bestriding conduits of exchange from the south (Arabia, Babylonia, and Egypt) to the west. The garrisoning of the Negev, late in David's reign, and especially in the second half of Solomon's reign, should and does yield archaeological correlates.

The text's claims about Solomon's trade are commensurate (1 Kgs. 3:1; 5:9-11[23-25]; 9:26-28; 10). The cargoes of 1 Kgs. 10:22 are typical of those that attract contemporary Middle Assyrian concern. The reports about David's incipient bureaucracy and about Solomon's reorganization of the kingdom into districts fit the same mold.[5] As noted, the presentation in Kings claims implicitly and falsely — as is usually the case with implicit claims in royal literature — that participation in the building of the temple led to tax remission for the Israelites. This view is falsified by 1 Kgs. 11–12, where Jeroboam, formerly head of forced labor for "the House of Joseph," leads a secession motivated by the hope of tax relief.

But this view of Solomon implies that the kingdom could, if the king was so inclined, concentrate resources for public construction. The list of Solomon's provinces demonstrates the same thing, as does the list of building proj-

---

5. See H. Michael Niemann, *Herrschaft, Königtum und Staat,* for evolution in the sequence of officials from Saul and David forward.

ects in 1 Kgs. 9:15-25. As 1 Kgs. 14:25-26 maintains that Rehoboam bribed Shishaq not to destroy Jerusalem, and implies that Shishaq controlled the rest of the countryside, one might logically look both for building projects in Judah and Israel and for evidence of Shishaq's advent.

B. Megiddo, Gezer, and Hazor

This evidence comes in two forms. The first is the construction of a Judah in the 10th century. The Negev settlements have been mentioned above. They, in and of themselves, represent a major investment from some other center — there being no true center among them. Tel Masos was probably the dominant regional site of the period, where, as John S. Holladay has argued, tolls were collected.[6] Likewise, Judahite sites arise at the start of Iron II, as at Beth Shemesh, Timnah, and Tell Beit Mirsim, on the backs of sites that previously participated in the culture of Judah's lowlands surroundings. This same transition went on all over Israel — it is the transition between Megiddo VIA and VB, to which changes at Dor, Rehob, Beth Shan, Sa'idiyeh, Taanach, and other sites are compared. The question of dating that transition is the only issue that raises its head in this regard.

The second form in which Solomon's kingdom is attested is the one that has historically been cited in the field. A list of Solomonic fortification projects appears in 1 Kgs. 9:15, 17-19. Among these are Jerusalem, Hazor, Megiddo, Gezer, Lower Beth Horon, Baalat (Qiryath Yearim), Tamar and store- and army-towns. As is well known, in 1960, the discovery of a six-chambered gate attached to a casemate fortification wall at Hazor (X-IX) inspired Yigael Yadin to reinvestigate the stratification of the six- and subsequent four- and two-chambered Iron Age gates at Megiddo. After a brief sounding at Megiddo, he linked the six-chambered gate there to Stratum VA-IVB, the "Solomonic" stratum comparable to Hazor X. He further interpreted a "Hasmonean castle" found by R. A. S. Macalister at Gezer near the turn of the century as half of another such gate, also tied to a casemate town wall. In the absence of excavations at Beth Horon, Baalath, and Tamar (if the latter are correctly identified), he linked the homologous fortification elements at Megiddo, Hazor, and Gezer to the text of Kings, and thus to the building program of Solomon. This furnished an archaeological baseline for the late United Monarchy. Yadin's conclusions as to the nature of the material evidence

---

6. John S. Holladay, "The Kingdoms of Israel and Judah," n. 62.

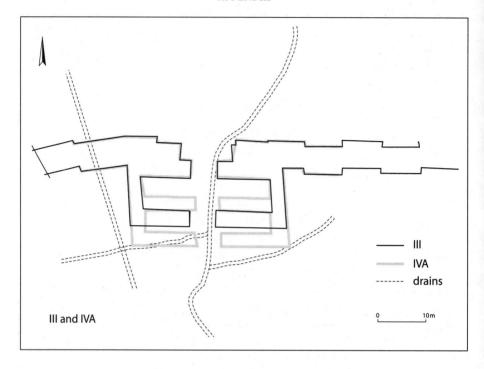

Figure 23.1   Megiddo gates in III and IVA
Courtesy Judith Dekel

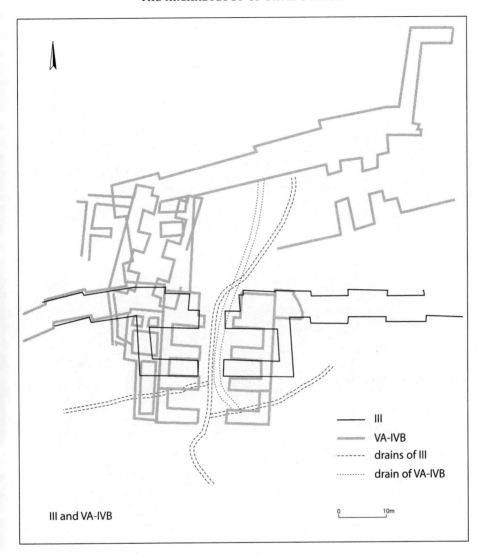

III and VA-IVB

       III
       VA-IVB
       drains of III
       drain of VA-IVB

0   10m

Figure 23.2   Megiddo gates in III and VA-IVB
Courtesy Judith Dekel

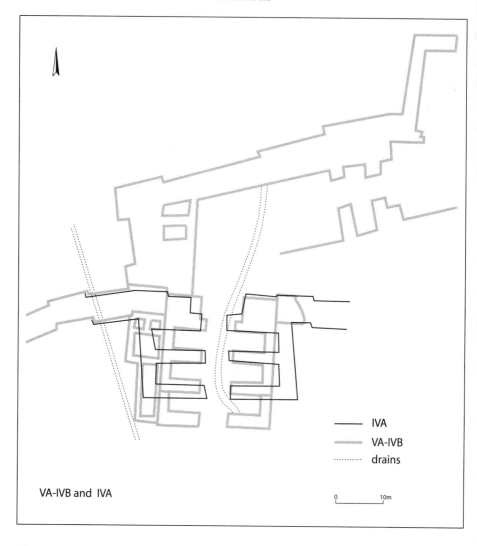

IVA

VA-IVB

drains

VA-IVB and IVA

0   10m

Figure 23.3   Megiddo gates in VA-IVB and IVA
Courtesy Judith Dekel

at Gezer were borne out both by excavations in the 1970s and later under the direction of William G. Dever.[7]

Yadin's baseline embraced concrete remains of the United Monarchy. Two of these were palaces attributed to Megiddo VA-IVB (the northern palace, 6000, by the gate, and the southern, 1723). Included were other public and elite structures both at Megiddo and at Hazor. In addition, Yadin's correlation established a ceramic horizon by which other sites could be dated relative to the United Monarchy. For example, the pottery assemblage of Ashdod X bears a resemblance to that of Megiddo VA-IVB, Hazor X, or, more proximately, Gezer VIII. As a result, the excavators, laboring under the conviction that David must have subjected Philistia, dated the end of that stratum to the first half of the 10th century. The result was to bring the gate of Ashdod IX, also six-chambered, into conformity with those of Gezer, Hazor, and Megiddo in date — or at least nominally so. It was also the result that the "degenerate Philistine ware" of Ashdod X[8] was distanced in date from the late United Monarchy.

But the largely "degenerate" Philistine bichrome of Ashdod X is witnessed at Megiddo VIA, not VB or VA-IVB. That is, either Ashdod X is earlier than Megiddo VB, or pottery of this style was preserved longer at Ashdod than in centers to which this pottery spread by exchange. Assume David did not subject Philistia, and the anomaly disappears. Ashdod X persisted after the destruction of Megiddo VIA, into the time of Solomon, and was thus at least partly contemporary with Megiddo VA-IVB as well as with Megiddo VIA. Ashdod IX may or may not be later than the Solomonic fortification program: it was not a part of the same state, in any case. The dating of the layer depends on pottery from its final occupation. This is no index of the time of its construction. Indeed, the most likely time of the transition from Ashdod X to Ashdod IX is the same as that from Eqron V to Eqron IV. So it is possible that both belong to the period of Siamun (see the Table in Chapter 21).[9]

Of these sites, the only one with an independent chronological "anchor"

7. Not as to the gates all being built from one blueprint, however. See David Milson, "The Design of the Royal Gates at Megiddo, Hazor, and Gezer," *ZDPV* 102 (1986): 87-92. Milson concludes that all the gates were built on the basis of the same basic cubit, corresponding to the Egyptian royal cubit of ca. .5235 m. For the gate at Gezer, and its relation to the other gates in question, see esp. William G. Dever, *Recent Archaeological Discoveries and Biblical Research* (Seattle: University of Washington Press, 1990), 87-117.

8. See esp. Moshe Dothan and Yehoshua Porath, *Ashdod, 5: The Fourth-Sixth Seasons of Excavations, 1968-1970.* Atiqot 23 (Jerusalem: Israel Antiquities Authority, 1993).

9. For the destruction of Ashdod X, see Moshe Dothan, *Ashdod, 2-3: The Second and Third Seasons of Excavations, 1963, 1965, Soundings in 1967.* Atiqot 9-10 (Jerusalem: Department of Antiquities, 1971), 31-34, 136, attributed there to Davidic expansion.

was Megiddo, where a fragment of a stela of the pharaoh Shishaq was discovered, out of context.[10] As Megiddo appears on Shishaq's list of towns taken, one of the strata there had to be assigned to his conquest, and the destruction of VA-IVB seemed to fill the bill. Moreover, Gezer later disgorged evidence, in the form of the construction and destruction of its upper, six-chambered gate over a lower gate, of the sequence: destruction (by Siamun, for Solomon, 1 Kgs. 9:15-17); rebuilding (by Solomon); destruction (by Shishaq), with the latter pottery horizon correlating to Hazor X and Megiddo VA-IVB.

The Shishaq destruction seemed at all these sites to succeed — not by many decades — the widespread popularization of a burnished red-slip as a surface treatment on the interior of bowls, for example, for the first time in the Iron Age.[11] Were one to take it, therefore, that Ashdod X was destroyed in Shishaq's campaign, both degenerate Philistine ware and burnished red-slip would simultaneously be represented, though it remains possible that the latter might have been introduced after the former had gone out of production and distribution (but not out of use, or at least out of deposition). The same is true at Eqron, where classic bichrome is represented in a layer (V, with an earlier example in VIA) with burnished red-slip, but where the red-slip is found largely on forms that are discontinued in the succeeding stratum. There, burnished red-slip seems to be more or less coeval with the degenerate Philistine wares.[12] As we will see, with the exception of Eqron, it is unlikely that Shishaq campaigned against Philistine towns.

The differential chronological distribution of these wares from site to site is clear. Thus, at Qasile XII, burnished red-slip appears in the company of classic Philistine bichrome. The same is true at Eqron V. The degenerate bichrome of Ashdod X is later, in theory. Further, at Megiddo, burnished red-slip certainly appears in VB, just before VA-IVB. It may perhaps appear in VIA, which, like Ashdod X, contains degenerate Philistine vessels and perhaps small quantities of classic bichrome. Megiddo VIA certainly contained a large number of collared-rim store jars and a "Philistine anchor seal," a counterpart to which appears in Ashdod Stratum XII.[13] But if the few examples from VIA (none from the 1992-1998 excavations at Megiddo) were correctly stratified, they remain extremely rare, and the slip seems to be of a different character than in the later periods.

10. In a Gottlieb Schumacher dump: Clarence S. Fisher, *The Excavation of Armageddon*. Oriental Institute Communications 4 (Chicago: University of Chicago Press, 1929), 12-13.
11. John S. Holladay, *BASOR* 277/278 (1990): 23-70.
12. Seymour Gitin, in conversation.
13. For the anchor seals, Othmar Keel, "Philistine 'Anchor' Seals," *IEJ* 44 (1994): 21-35.

THE ARCHAEOLOGY OF DAVID'S REIGN

There are two issues here. Whether the red-slips of Qasile XII and Megiddo VB are identical with those of the towns traditionally identified as Solomonic is a question. But Holladay is surely right that the real issue is when they became common enough to take on statistical value, as in the Solomonic layers, and, indeed, Qasile X. It may be that at some sites the tradition of red-slip was never in fact lost after Late Bronze (especially where, as at Megiddo, the Late Bronze culture continued to the early 10th century, or in parts of Philistia). Still, the soundness of the earlier consensus does not turn on purely ceramic considerations.

Second, pottery can easily survive to the end of a layer after having been introduced toward its beginning. This is especially true of elite and imported wares. The presence of red-slip together with bichrome does not imply their contemporary production. So Qasile XII may have been occupied during the early period of Eqron V. And Megiddo VIA, possibly constructed during the life of Qasile XII, may have burned during the life of Eqron V or, if the red-slip had not yet spread, early in the life of Eqron IV. Ashdod X is most probably contemporary with Eqron V, and, depending on the relationships between Eqron and other sites, Megiddo VIA or VA/IVB. But Ashdod X might also be earlier or later.

Absolute chronological anchors are also in question. Since 1980, two elements of the absolute dating at Megiddo have been debated. The first is the stratification of the six-chambered gate. David Ussishkin, a director of the Megiddo Expedition starting in the 1990s, refitted the Chicago excavators' argument that the six-chambered gate was not related to Stratum VA-IVB at all, but to IVA, a city of the late 10th or (Ussishkin) 9th through 8th centuries. Ussishkin's points were, typically, incisive and deserve detailed treatment.

First, there are six-chambered gates that do not belong to the 10th century. In support of this position, Ussishkin subpoenaed his later dating of the similar gates of Ashdod IX (possibly 10th-century, but Ussishkin convincingly indicts its stratification), Lachish IV-III, and possibly Tel Baṭash III. Today, we can add the early 8th-century gate of Khirbet Mudayna in Jordan, whose final date of use is assured by carbon analysis of a reed mat in one of the chambers and whose final (re)construction is dated by the radiocarbon of a critical beam in the structure.[14] The similar gate of Tel 'Ira in the Negev has also been attributed to the late 8th or 7th century, though Holladay suggests it represents reuse of a structure from the 10th century, when 'Ira was also occupied.[15]

---

14. Michèle Daviau, in conversation, August 1998.

15. Holladay, "The Kingdoms of Israel and Judah," 384-85. If Holladay's insight is correct, Ira would make a better candidate for Solomon's Tamar than does 'Ein Ḥazeba. For Ira, see Itzhak Beit-Arieh, "Tel 'Ira — a Fortified City from the Judean Monarchy Period," *Qad* 18 (1985): 17-25.

Even if one attributed Lachish IV and Ashdod IX to a period earlier than Ussishkin maintains, Ashdod remained in any case outside of Solomon's ambit, which is to say, outside the realm in which such gates could be expected to be built by royal command and under the guidance of Israelite architects. This is probably true at Mudayna as well. (At Mudayna one would have to posit that the 8th-century beam in the gate was installed during a rebuilding of it.) On this point, Ussishkin is in the right: the gate at Megiddo cannot be imputed to the 10th century or to Solomon simply on the grounds that it consists of six chambers and four entryways.

Still, the gates whose dating Ussishkin lowers are not in towns attributed to Solomon. Lachish, Ashdod, and Mudayna do not appear in 1 Kgs. 9:15-18. Nor does Tel 'Ira, if it is not identical with Tamar. Ussishkin's argument forecloses on a facile dating by architectural parallels. Once a particular style of architecture appears, it can be copied or adapted again and again. But conversely, the appearance of late copies is not an argument for downdating their parallels: were it, archaeologists would enjoy the liberty of indulging in an infinite regress of downdating. Nothing here affects the *correlation to the text* set out by Yadin. Indeed, given the imprecision of Chicago's stratification of the Megiddo gateways, the correlation might yet be our best evidence for the dating.

Second, Ussishkin argued that the six-chambered Megiddo gate was nothing but a foundation. Under it, no other foundation was found. But not every structure had a foundation, still less an upper city gate, enclosed by an outer gateway, as at Megiddo (and Gezer).[16] Above the six-chambered structure was a four-chambered gate, tied to Wall 325 of Stratum IVA (as was the two-chambered gate, 500, of Stratum III). The outer sides of its facing halves, in Israelite terminology the "shoulders" of the gate, correspond to a part of the (VA-IVB) "foundation." But the internal dividing walls, the entryway portals, do not conform to those of the "foundation" shoulders. This required that the central chamber of the six-chambered structure be secondarily filled in to support construction above it. The VA-IVB Gate 2156, in sum, was not the foundation for the structure now overlying it.

Chicago, which also took Gate 2156 to be a foundation, nevertheless found no sign of a superstructure above it and below the four-chambered gate. Fur-

---

16. The LB gate of Stratum VIII had only one foundation course, .45 m. high and only .10-.15 m. thick, with carbonized wood between upper courses (the third and fourth), as more or less with the six-chamber gate. See Gordon Loud, *Megiddo, 2: Seasons of 1935-1939.* OIP 62 (Chicago: University of Chicago Press, 1948), 16-25, 47. It would not be surprising were the first course of the six-chamber gate to have served as its foundation.

THE ARCHAEOLOGY OF DAVID'S REIGN

ther, Gate 2156 is constructed with dressed ashlar on its inner and outer faces, and its top. For so deep a foundation, this would make no sense.

After its construction (most likely, when it went into disuse), Gate 2156 was filled with stone chips (see below).[17] The blocking walls to retain this fill were made of unworked stones ("heavy rubble walls"). Admittedly, the stones of the gate were not fully dressed in all cases, but most were characterized by marginal drafting. Even so, the nature of their finished presentation is not clear, and the effort devoted to the drafting included evening out the bosses. Neither drafting nor dressing is replicated in the blocking walls. Yet if Gate 2156 was a foundation only, the blocking walls were an integral part of the original structure — they held the fill.[18] Still, Ussishkin here was extending the logic of the early excavators, who also thought the six-chambered gate the substructure of a missing Stratum IVA brick gate.

Similar arguments apply against the submission that the gate connected to Wall 325, the defensive perimeter defining Stratum IVA at Megiddo. Only the projecting towers of the gate are joined to 325. But even those were not bonded — although the sections of six-chambered Gate 2156 were bonded top to bottom in the northern three piers.[19]

The construction also leaves the towers inset into the line of the outer wall (325). The inset is at variance with the standard (offset) disposition of gate towers at other sites. But towers must project outward to be useful for directing missile weapons at attackers. The juxtaposition with Wall 325 is thus secondary. Even if Gate 2156 and Wall 325 once stood together, the builders of the wall must have decided that thickening it outward beyond the line of the gate entrance and towers was more important than allowing the gate towers to retain their defensive function. But this is a peculiar decision: the builders of Wall 325 could even more easily have added thickness on its inner side, allowing the gate towers to fulfill their function. Thus, the juxtaposition of Wall 325 with Gate 2156 is simply artificial — an artifact of the construction of the four-chambered gate atop the filled structure of Gate 2156, which *did* then serve as a foundation.

Possibly, the builders of Wall 325 built over and thickened the line of an earlier fortification wall bonded to Gate 2156. Yet Chicago reports that the

---

17. Loud, *Megiddo* 2:48.

18. For the blocking walls, see Loud, *Megiddo* 2: fig. 112. For the drafting, fig. 95. An argument regarding the bosses is made by Ze'ev Herzog, *The City-Gate in Eretz-Israel and Its Neighboring Countries* (Tel Aviv: Institute of Archaeology, 1976), 113-14, but it assumes that the marginal drafting was the extent of the finishing of the stones.

19. See Loud, *Megiddo* 2:46.

outer gate, too, was (inexcusably, in their word) not bonded into 325: it was integrated into the IVA fortification system (and cobbled approach road) as an intact structure. That is, the approach to the gate and the wall beside Gate 2156 may well have been breached at some time in the duration of Stratum VA-IVB.

It is in fact the upper gate (500), identified by P. L. O. Guy as that of Stratum III, which was bonded into Wall 325.[20] As Guy failed to distinguish the four-chambered gate of IVA from the two-chambered gate of III (below), it is not impossible that the four-chambered gate between Gate 500 and Gate 2156 was originally bonded to the solid wall. In any case, the bonding of the upper structure to 325 again indicates that Gate 2156, the six-chambered gate, predated the wall.[21]

Third, Ussishkin denied that Shishaq would have destroyed Megiddo. His argument was that the presence of Shishaq's stela there, 10 ft. high, argued against a destruction. He further argued that there was no textual evidence, from Shishaq's inscriptions, that Shishaq destroyed Gezer. As we shall see, these inferences are probably correct. The implication is that there is no need to assign the obliteration of Megiddo VA-IVB or Gezer VIII to the king. Israel Finkelstein, Ussishkin's other co-director in the Megiddo Expedition of the 1990s, argues for a destruction of Megiddo by Shishaq, and links it to Stratum VIA (see below). But the end of Stratum VA-IVB could easily carry into the later 10th or even the early 9th century on the basis of Ussishkin's observation alone. The removal of the link between its destruction and Shishaq opens up the possibility, embraced on other grounds by Finkelstein, that Stratum VA-IVB might even postdate Solomon.

Fourth, and most important, Ussishkin argued that the six-chambered gate at Megiddo stood above the floor level of Stratum VA at its foot: the floor of Stratum VA in the gate's passageway is several centimeters below the bottom of the lowest stone layer of the gate at the inside of its eastern half. This heavily in-

20. P. L. O. Guy, *New Light from Armageddon.* Oriental Institute Communications 9 (Chicago: University of Chicago Press, 1931), 25ff.; Robert S. Lamon and Geoffrey M. Shipton, *Megiddo,* 1:74.

21. Note that the "VA" buildings near the gate, according to Chicago, were oriented to the line of the city wall (325), while those of VA to the south of the gate area and those of IVA were not oriented to 325, but lined up north-south: Loud, *Megiddo* 2:45-46. This says little about the sequence of the strata in the gate area, but a great deal about the planning of the town, namely, that the IVA town was built within Wall 325, the VA-IVB town having been built *to* the earlier wall, if any. While there may be some ideological significance to the choice, the IVA strategy was less exacting. The planners and builders of VA-IVB had to reckon with changes in orientation from building to building inside the town.

fluenced Chicago's team;[22] as Ussishkin notes, the VA surface met the top of a now-uncovered drain through the center of the gateway. This put the drain in VA(-IVB), and the gate in a later layer, namely, IVA.

But the drain remained uncovered as it passed beneath the innermost or southeastern pier of the gate. Indeed, the ends of two stones of the lowest course of the gate, on the northern (inner) face of the southern pier, meet right over the opening of the drain. As a result, the two stones partially collapsed into the drain. Only the weight of the higher courses on them outside the drain prevented a total collapse. Ussishkin concluded that the drain had been filled with earth, out of use, when the gate was constructed, and that the collapse came later, as erosion set in after construction.[23]

This argument is the stratigraphic crux. However, were Gate 2156 part of the IVA town, then the VA-IVB town would be lacking a gate. And the VA drain runs through the dead center of the gate passage. If Ussishkin is right to think that Gate 2156 belongs to Stratum IVA, and the drain at the foot of Gate 2156 belongs to the earlier Stratum VA-IVB, then the drain must also have belonged to some structure, probably a gate itself, under which it directed water off the tell. In other words, the logic of Ussishkin's position is that another gate, under the existing gate, is the entryway of Stratum VA-IVB.

But there is no such underlying structure. The Oriental Institute excavations in the western half of the gate did not unearth a gate of Stratum VB, just the entryway to a gate which the excavators assigned to VA, but which could as

---

22. Loud, *Megiddo* 2:45, on the drain under the southeastern pier of the IVA gate.

23. For discussion on the gate, see generally Yigael Yadin, "Hazor, Gezer and Megiddo in Solomon's Time," in *The Kingdoms of Israel and Judah*, ed. Abraham Malamat (Jerusalem: Israel Exploration Society, 1961), 66-109; *Hazor — The Head of All Those Kingdoms*. Schweich Lectures, 1970 (London: British Academy, 1972), 147-64; "Solomon's City Wall and Gate at Gezer," *IEJ* 8 (1958): 80-86; "A Rejoinder," *BASOR* 239 (1980): 19-23; Yohanan Aharoni, "The Stratification of Israelite Megiddo," *JNES* 31 (1972): 302-11; *The Archaeology of the Land of Israel* (Philadelphia: Westminster, 1972), 200-11; William G. Dever, "Further Excavations at Gezer," *BA* 34 (1971): 112-20; "Gezer Revisited: New Excavations of the Solomonic and Assyrian Period Defences," *BA* 47 (1984): 206-18; "Solomonic and Assyrian Period 'Palaces' at Gezer," *IEJ* 35 (1985): 217-30; "Late Bronze Age and Solomonic Defenses at Gezer: New Evidence," *BASOR* 262 (1986): 9-34; Israel Finkelstein, "The Date of Gezer's Outer Wall," *TA* 8 (1981): 136-45; "Penelope's Shroud Unravelled: Iron II Date of Gezer's Outer Wall Established," *TA* 21 (1994): 276-82; Adam Zertal, "The Gates of Gezer," *ErIsr* 15 (1981): 222-28; Yigal Shiloh, *Levant* 12 (1980): 69-76; esp. David Ussishkin, *BASOR* 239 (1980): 1-18; "Notes on Megiddo, Gezer, Ashdod, and Tel Batash in the Tenth to Ninth Centuries B.C.," *BASOR* 277/278 (1990): 71-91; *ABD* 4:666-79; Amihai Mazar, *Timnah (Tel Batash)*, 1:256-57. For the collapse in the drain, see Loud, *Megiddo* 2: fig. 94.

easily belong to VB. The VA drain would not run through the center of this earlier entryway, as it does through Gate 2156.

Understanding Gate 2156 as a IVA structure thus involves positing two missing gates. The superstructure to Gate 2156 is entirely missing. And the earlier gate, of Stratum VA-IVB, is also missing. All that is left of the missing VA-IVB gate is a drain. The drain coincidentally runs dead center through Gate 2156.

This evidence is of a piece with the relationship between the stones in the southern pier of the gate and the drain that runs below it. The southeastern pier sits directly atop the sides of the open drain, with nothing between them. So if there was a gate under the rear pier of Gate 2156, it must have been torn out in its entirety. Alternately, a hypothetical earlier gate may not have extended so far to the south. But then it is a question why the drain extended so far, and especially why it has no cover.

The drain was uncovered all along the length of the gate when Chicago unearthed it. Yet outside the gate, the covering stones were in place. Where Gate 2156 sits on top of the drain, the gate has partly collapsed into it. Yet the drain must have been visible on the surface if a IVA gate was built right atop it. Indeed, Gate 2156 was placed so that the drain runs right through the center of the gate passage. So the builders knew that the drain was there, or that they were going to install it. If the six-chambered gate structure was a foundation only, perhaps its builders did not reckon the drain as an engineering obstacle. But even underground, one would normally check the foundation's underpinnings. It would have been easy enough to cover the drain with heavy flagstone, preventing the collapse of the rear pier into it.

It is also strange that the builders chose to set a seam between stones of a first course so that it stood exactly above the open drain. They could, instead, have ensured that a single stone of the rear pier covered the drain's area, preventing the collapse. If the drain was, as Ussishkin claims, out of use, then they could have filled it with stone instead of dirt, preventing the collapse.

This is the more puzzling since the builders knew the drain was there, and centered the gate passage on it. Given that they also snapped off a chalk line to assure themselves that the third course of the gate was level (below), the builders' insouciance with the drain is surprising. And all this is still more perplexing if Gate 2156 was not all a foundation, for its integrity then depended even more heavily on the stability of the lower course.

Another feature of the gate requires attention. The top of the existing structure, when it went out of use, served as a base for the four-chambered gate. At the top of the base, the stones facing the passageway on the end of each pier were deliberately carved to produce an inset facing the passageway. The Chicago excavators identified the inset as a device for locating a setback super-structure.[24] However, in laying a foundation, one would not go to the trouble of carving the stones: instead, one would leave the foundation course extending beyond the first course of the superstructure, and set the first course of the superstructure back. Just such a setback distinguished the foundation from the superstructure of Palace 1723 on the southern end of the tell. Indeed, inside the gate side-chambers, the third through fifth courses are slightly set back, probably in order to provide for decorative inserts or tenons. Noting the point, the Chicago excavators contemplated the possibility that the side-chambers were floored below the third course, at what would be a subterranean level in Stratum IVA.[25] They understood that such inserts would not be placed underground, in a foundation. Yet they also placed the side-chamber floors *above* the top course of Gate 2156, without reconciling the contradiction.

The carved inset atop the gate would serve no functional purpose in a foundation. It, like the inset in the chambers, also looks as though it was made to support wood. In this case, the wood took the form of beams running across the fronts of the side-chambers at the height of the surrounding first-story walls of the side-chambers (the parallel is to Mudayna). This would have permitted the installation of second-story flooring over the top of the gate passage itself, flush with the other floors of the story, above the shoulder side-chambers.

In either case, the carved inset supported a wooden beam. The elevation of this inset is 156.26 m. Less than 25 m. south of the gate, the University of Chicago excavators left a high baulk standing, in which a good deal of Iron Age stratification can be identified. Noteworthy in particular is a wall beneath Assyrian (Stratum III) Palace 1052, connected to a floor. The latter is a typical, thick lime floor of Stratum IVA, and its elevation (156.5) is approximately that of the inset (156.3). Both conform with the elevation of the Stratum IVA monumental building found by Chicago in the area of the gate, at Locus 2066 (156.4).[26] Normally, one would expect a slope from the town down to the gate (the elevations of the loci west of 2066 rise rapidly). This is necessary for any drainage system to carry water out from, rather than into, the town (and, indeed, the VA-IVB drain inclines downward from south to north).

Too, Stratum IVA, at least on the mound peripheries, was a planned town,

24. Loud, *Megiddo* 2:47. The data from the excavation of the gate is given on 45-57.

25. Loud, *Megiddo* 2:46-47. The construction of the gate parallels that of Gate 1567 of the compound around 1723, which also has a gap between the second and third courses, and floors running to the second or third course; further, the setback on the foundation is witnessed in 1723 itself. See Lamon and Shipton, *Megiddo* 1:15, 17-20. That is, the lowest course of Gate 2156 is in fact its foundation.

26. Loud, *Megiddo* 2:46.

whose interior space was extensively raised, so that one would expect higher inner than gate-passage levels. The presence of a drain in the gate indicates that this was so in Stratum VA-IVB, as in Stratum III.[27] But if the six-chamber structure was all a IVA foundation, the wooden beam in the carved inset sat just above the ground, where it would not long survive (and where wood is not otherwise found in Canaan). Indeed, in 1999, two members of the Megiddo Expedition, Norma Franklin and Jennifer Peersman, cleaned the baulk where it meets the gate, and traced the line of the Stratum IVA floor. It meets the inner face of the gate not far from its top.[28] At the inner entrance to the gate, the inset is a mere 20 cm. above the Stratum IVA roadway surface.[29] Furthermore, a Stratum IVA doorsocket was found *in situ* atop the gate structure at the front, above the inset for the wood beams.[30] The road inside the gate was evidently lower than the outer part of the gate passage itself.[31]

The inset, the uniform, unnecessarily expensive ashlar facing and construction of the six-chamber gate, the absence of an underlying gate to go with the VA drain, the absence of any sign of an original superstructure and the need for adaptation to support the overlying four-chamber gate all speak against the theory that Gate 2156 was a foundation. So, too, does the insertion of a layer, between its second and third masonry courses, of small stone chinks: these more nearly correspond to allowance made for lower decorative insets of other gates[32] than to anything incorporated into a foundation structure.

Inside the gate chambers, this inset layer marks the second course as superstructure: the red chalk leveling line was found along the third inner masonry course, and the side-chamber setbacks, from the third course up, correspond roughly to it. After the layer of chinks, thus, the masons had again to level the

27. For the latter, see Lamon and Shipton, *Megiddo* 1:79 (the drain from 1066 through courtyard 500 and over outer gate 1855), 69 (the drain of Palace 1052 running from Room 483 out over the four-chambered gate — there, IIIB).

28. The same surface is visible in Loud, *Megiddo* 2: fig. 114.

29. 156.04: Loud, *Megiddo* 2: fig. 389.

30. The doorsocket is visible and labeled in Loud, *Megiddo* 2: fig. 112. It cannot be tied to Stratum III.

31. See Loud, *Megiddo* 2: fig. 389.

32. For an enumeration, see Yigal Shiloh, *Levant* 12 (1980): 69-76. Note that Gate 1567, to courtyard 1693 of Palace 1723, is fitted out similarly. Shiloh also maintains that the floor of one chamber of the six-chamber gate was not trenched out away from the wall, as it would have been had the structure been laid down through an existing floor as a foundation, but extends to the ashlar courses themselves. Loud, *Megiddo* 2:47, stipulates that the side-chamber floors were higher than the top of Gate 2156, and above the level of the gate passageway. So any lower floors would, as Shiloh held, pertain to an earlier stratum, presumably VA-IVB.

next course. The side-chamber setback was initially above floor level (for a wood insert), which might then be level with that in the passageway (preservation of the chalk line was best on the passageway jambs, suggesting ramping into the side-chambers); alternatively, the bottom of the setback may have been faced with plaster.

No answer to these problems is self-evident. But linking Gate 2156 to Stratum VA-IVB avoids the hypothesis of a VA-IVB drain without a gate and a IVA gate without interior drainage. It presents an alternative to the prospect of a VA-IVB gate butted to the fortification wall with which it was built and a later gate (500A of Stratum III) bonded to the wall that was built before it. It alleviates the embarrassment of supposing that the towers outside Gate 2156 did not project even up to the line of the city wall.

Wall 325 is bonded to a later gate because it was built with a later gate (the four-chambered Gate 500B). It is butted to Gate 2156 because Gate 2156 was already there when it was erected. And Wall 325 protrudes beyond the projecting towers of Gate 2156 because the towers were out of use when the wall was built. Wall 325 served as a retaining wall for the entire top of the mound — it is a massive structure, as both Schumacher's excavations and those of Chicago revealed. In the area of the gate, it permitted an expansion of the mound's surface, along with the "hand of the gate," the outer wall leading to the outer gate, in part to retain the pathway leading up the slope. To the east, it also permitted the retention and reuse of Palace 6000 as a foundation for the northern "stables."

Why was the southeastern pier collapsed into the drain? Why was the drain lower than the bottom course of the gate? The explanation must be this: the drain was secondarily installed. That is, after the construction of the gate, drainage problems to the southeast required that it be fitted out with a sewer, to prevent erosion. This meant that the drain had to be dug down, below the original level of the gate floor, in order to pass under the southeastern pier. The drain had then to continue downward through the passage. At the front, the drain runs more than a meter under the surface of the passageway. It must have been covered to support the fill on top of it, through the whole of the gate passage as well as outside it.

The results of a secondary drain would be three. First, starting under the southeastern pier, from the site south of the gate toward the gate passageway, the drain could be brought in from the south (inner) face under a single stone. But because it curved to the west as it progressed northward, it had to pass, at some point, under the seam of two stones of the bottom course. Second, the drain could not be covered underneath the pier. And third, the surface associated with the drain was necessarily lower than the bottom of the lowest gate masonry as the drain moved north and out through the passage, even though the lowest course of the structure initially served as a foundation. That is, the new gate configuration, at the lowest point in the upper tell, required new, albeit unanticipated, drainage arrangements.[33] In sum, the six-chamber gate is, as Yadin argued, an element of Stratum VA-IVB.

Another point corroborates this reconstruction. The Chicago excavators found the six-chamber gate filled to the top with lime chips, fragments, and powder, and next to no soil, held in by secondary rubble walls. The lime was not rounded by weathering: it was all quarry waste that was never exposed to the elements. So, if the six-chamber gate (2156) was a foundation, the builders dug a hole large enough to contain the entire structure. Then they built the six-chamber gate in the hole, leaving a pointless chalk line around its third course at a maximum variance in elevation of 3 cm. and adding a pointless layer of chinking to receive an inset. Then they built the secondary blocking walls, which they inexplicably omitted from the original construction. They built these walls both in the entrances to the side-chambers and at the ends of the passageway. And then, instead of using the dirt from the hole as backfill, they fetched freshly-quarried lime and used it to fill the elaborate structure they were now burying.[34]

This is an extraordinary procedure. Normally, one digs a foundation where required, and sets in the requisite stones. One minimizes the work of excavating the foundation trench. One minimizes further labor by backfilling the trench with some of the dirt removed to insert the foundation courses. Inside the outlines of the foundations, one leaves the original dirt undisturbed. The situation with the six-chamber gate clearly indicates that an existing structure was put out of use and deliberately filled up to serve as the foundation for a later structure.

Another Stratum IVA structure also involved a massive fill, namely, the courtyard extending north from the southern "stable" complex. At the northern end of the courtyard, there are 7 m. of earthen fill, according to the Chicago report, all under a thick lime pavement. The high ground under the southern

33. On the levels of the gate and its surroundings, Herzog, *The City-Gate in Eretz-Israel*, 117, and the figures in Loud, *Megiddo* 2, esp. fig. 389. Cf. Lamon and Shipton, *Megiddo* 1:79, for the elaborate water management systems required when the gate orientation altered in Stratum III. Note that the failure to bond the southern, innermost piers of Gate 2156 to the outer gate walls is duplicated in the case of Gate 500A, the two-chambered structure of Stratum III. In the interior of the site, bonding is less crucial than at the front of the gate. At the same time, the lack of bonding is somewhat puzzling.

34. Herzog, *The City-Gate in Eretz-Israel*, 114, focuses on the secondary insertion of what he regards as doorsills at the level of the top of the IVA fill of the gate. It is not the doorsills, but the blocking walls and general fill that show that the gate was not planned as a foundation. See just below.

"stables" themselves was not cut down in order to facilitate the leveling, but the earth and then lime brought in and spread out to even the complex.

Conceivably, earth and lime were brought from outside the site to level the courtyard, and limestone chips were quarried to fill up the six-chamber gate. But there is a water system on the southeastern edge of the tell, just by the 7-m. fill of the southern "stables." The water system consists of a huge shaft cutting down through the tell and then a tunnel leading outward through limestone bedrock to a spring in the southwest. This water system was probably hewn out of the tell when Stratum IVA was founded. Most likely, the fill below the courtyard of the southern "stables" and the fill in the six-chamber gate were both products of the work on the water system.

The excavation of the water system made massive amounts of earth and of unweathered lime waste available to the builders of Stratum IVA. They could have hauled this waste off the site for disposal, or could have used it more efficiently for leveling buildings and courtyards. Clearly, the site's engineers chose the latter option.[35] Indeed, another large buildup of lime fill (1.6 m.) is present above an ash layer separating the original Stratum VA-IVB courtyard (1693) of Palace 1723 and the associated phase of Building 1482 from the main use phase of Stratum IVA as represented by Wall 325. In addition, the thick lime floors ubiquitous in Stratum IVA — and especially in the "stables" of IVA — also required masses of material.[36] In sum, the fill in the gate reflects a taphonomic event that embraces the mound almost as a whole, in Stratum IVA. This fill is a leveling fill, not an artificial platform in an anomalous, gaping foundation hole.

This interpretation explains another problem as well. Gordon Loud, who excavated it, never located the floor of the Stratum VA-IVB gate (2156) passage because it had already been dug through down to the level of its foundations in order to insert the drain, and was dug out again in order to uncover the drain (see below). The passageway floor (2150) was recovered only outside the gate, in the passage between the inner and outer gates. It ran to the bottom course of stones of the front of the six-chambered gate, but was cut by the secondary blocking walls, indicating that the blocking walls were later than the gate itself.[37]

35. Thus Lamon and Shipton, *Megiddo* 1:32.

36. See Lamon and Shipton, *Megiddo* 1:17-32. The excavators drew the connection between the earth fill (1674) in the courtyard of the southern stables (1576) and the "reexcavation" of the water shaft (925): the latest pottery in both was related, in their view, to Stratum IV.

37. Herzog (*The City-Gate in Eretz-Israel*, 115) claims that Loud, *Megiddo* 2: fig. 97, shows that the gate itself was dug into surface 2150, but fig. 93 indicates that this is not so. The Chicago excavators would not have missed such an obvious index of stratification.

This surface, passageway 2150, was connected to a bench outside the gate, over which another bench was erected in a later phase of the gate. The upper bench structure thus belongs to Stratum IVA, and, diagnostically, it was butted to but not bonded with Gate 2156, rendering the tower of 2156 that it meets even less useful. The lower bench structure may belong to Stratum VB, with the upper part of the Stratum VIB/A gate, as the excavators themselves conceded.[38] Or surface 2150 may have been produced after the secondary installation of the drain through Gate 2156. The drain empties out over the slope of the mound under surface 2150. This would fit with the fact that surface 2150 met the lowest course of Gate 2156 on the outside. The VA drain runs just under its level.

Chicago's team misidentified the four-chambered Stratum IVA gate (500B) as a mere false start of the Stratum III gate (500A), though drainage of Stratum III ran over the top of its remains. On their theory, the final Stratum III gate plan remedied an earlier planning error that called for unavailable 9-m.-long beams.[39] But misjudging the dimensions of materials that can be supplied is not a typical architect's error: the average builder would procure required materials even at heightened cost. And the superimposition of the Stratum III gate on that of IVA is clear from the fact that the foundations for the III piers cut into IVA (Chicago's IIIB) floors.

With the exception of Drain 2093 to the west, no IVA drainage was associated with the IVA gate (500B). Further, the Stratum IVA floor in Locus 2066 (and in the baulk south of the gate) is just below the level of the IVA gate passage. The implication is that the unlocated gateway drainage of IVA was below the top of the six-chamber structure. This drainage is in fact in evidence: having been filled up with lime chips rather than dirt, the disused Gate 2156 served as a foundation (where the fill was contained by walls) for the four-chambered gate. In the central passageway, it served as an enormous French drain, a trench filled to the surface with rock, taking water down to the original (and now open) drain below: in other words, it was a function of the engineering of the Stratum IVA fortification that the drain coursing through the center of the VA-IVB gateway *had* to be uncovered, and this is why neither the floor nor any of the covering stones — which must have been present to support the VA-IVB passage floor — have ever been located. The builders of the IVA gate reopened the drain of Gate 2156 before filling the whole structure with limestone from the water system.

38. Loud, *Megiddo* 2:44.

39. See Lamon and Shipton, *Megiddo* 1:77-78; for the Stratum III drainage over the remains of the IVA gate, 69 (from 1052), 73 (from 490), 79 (over outer gate 1855).

C. Downdating the Solomonic Layers

In all, the six-chamber gate (like the structures beneath the southern "stables") is a feature of Stratum VA-IVB. However, in recent years, Israel Finkelstein has challenged the traditional association of that stratum with the 10th century, arguing instead that it belongs in the 9th. Finkelstein's arguments proceed from several important observations.

The only evidence for dating the arrival of the Philistines on Canaan's littoral, and thus for dating Philistine Mycenaean IIIC:1b monochrome pottery, is the Medinet Habu inscription of Ramses III. On that temple's wall, the pharaoh claims, ca. 1175, to have repulsed the invaders and settled them in fortresses some years earlier. Leaving the question of the pharaoh's victory to one side, it is not clear where these fortresses were located. Finkelstein claims that the text places the captives in the Delta.

Moreover, 20th-Dynasty materials, especially inscriptional materials, appear in the southern reaches of Canaan in some number. But nowhere do they appear *together* with Philistine monochrome. In other words, the evidence can support a reconstruction of Egyptian domination followed by a Philistine invasion rather than a reconstruction of simultaneous Egyptian and Philistine presence.[40] In addition, Finkelstein argues that Ashdod XIV may have survived into the 20th Dynasty (it may have produced a Ramses III scarab; but such objects can also be curated). The succeeding layer, Ashdod XIIIB, contains the first monochrome on the site. The Late Bronze layer, Miqneh VIIIA, claims Finkelstein, is earlier than the monochrome settlement in another part of the tell, VII. Imported, rather than local, Mycenaean ware of the IIIC:1b variety at Beth Shan, in a layer contemporary with Egyptian materials, is conversely understood as a different phenomenon from the locally-manufactured material farther south on the coast, possibly representing an earlier phase of trade relations.

Finkelstein's revision of the received ceramic sequence places Philistine monochrome after 20th-Dynasty materials. As the Egyptians seem to have re-

---

40. For the Philistine settlement, Israel Finkelstein, "The Date of the Settlement of the Philistines in Canaan," *TA* 22 (1995): 213-39; for the implications, "The Stratigraphy and Chronology of Megiddo and Beth-shan in the 12th-11th Centuries B.C.E.," *TA* 23 (1996): 170-84; "The Archaeology of the United Monarchy: An Alternative View," *Levant* 28 (1996): 177-87; "Bible Archaeology or Archaeology of Palestine in the Iron Age? A Rejoinder," *Levant* 30 (1998): 167-74. The last of these is a response to Amihai Mazar, "Iron Age Chronology: A Reply to I. Finkelstein," *Levant* 29 (1997): 157-67. Further, Finkelstein, "Hazor and the North in the Iron Age: A Low Chronology Perspective," *BASOR* 314 (1999): 55-70.

mained in southern Canaan until at least 1140, the effect is to lower the dates of monochrome, and of the succeeding bichrome phase, by 50-100 years. This means that the latest bichrome phases, as in the Pentapolis sites that have been excavated and in their neighboring communities (including, for example, Qasile X, Eqron V, and Gezer XI), can be downdated from the 11th century into the 10th.

This has ramifications for the dating of the strata at Megiddo and Hazor. Finkelstein maintains that Megiddo VIA, in particular, may belong to the 10th century and VA-IVB in the 9th, irrespective of the stratigraphic connection of the six-chamber gate (which he, however, links to Megiddo IVA). His 1998 treatment of the subject denies the presence of Philistine bichrome and collared-rim store jars in VIA in Area F of the contemporary Megiddo Expedition and in Chicago's VIA, although Douglas Esse has documented the presence of collared-rims in the stratum in Area CC.[41]

Ongoing excavation in the production zone of Area K in 1998 divulged the presence of "degenerate" bichrome wares and possible body fragments of collared-rim store jars in VIA (both of which Finkelstein in fact assumed in his 1996 treatment). Probably, VIA and VIB are temporally inseparable — VIA in parts of the site is contemporary with the VIB-VIA sequence in others. This would mean that the confinement of "true" bichrome to VIB in earlier studies is probably illusory.[42] The conflagration that ended VIA, on the other hand, is one of the markers of the site, and Area K of the new excavations is replete with evidence for its onset — an onset far more sudden and widespread than an ordinary military assault of the time.

Finkelstein supports his lower dates by arguing that Megiddo VA-IVB pottery is identical to that in the enclosure casemates at Jezreel.[43] As biblical texts date the enclosure to the time of the Omrides, the comparison would tend to confirm the downdating of the Megiddo stratum into the 9th century. However, there are three difficulties here. First, the Jezreel sample and the 10th-9th-century seriation may not support much weight in differentiating 75 years across sites. Second, the Jezreel contexts producing pottery comparable to that of Megiddo VA-IVB include not just the enclosure, but also the pre-enclosure

---

41. Douglas L. Esse, *JNES* 51 (1992): 81-103.

42. This idea stems from Finkelstein, in discussion on site, in 1998. Even should the differential distribution prove out, it might imply spatial rather than temporal distinctions. This is now clearly the case for the absence of bichrome and collared-rim ware on the terrace (Area F) in VIA.

43. For the data, Orna Zimhoni, "The Iron Age Pottery from Tel Jezreel — An Interim Report," *TA* 19 (1992): 57-70; "Clues from the Enclosure-fills: Pre-Omride Settlement at Tel Jezreel," *TA* 24 (1997): 83-109.

fills, some of which may well have risen into the overlying levels.[44] This fact is compounded by the third difficulty, namely, that the pottery is not univocal: one scholar argues that the Jezreel enclosure assemblage has later elements than does Megiddo VA-IVB.[45]

Even more basic is the fact that, like Samaria, Jezreel was occupied before the Omride era. It was allegedly the site of Saul's last stand against a Philistine army that ran him to ground on nearby Mt. Gilboa (as 1 Sam. 29:1, 11; 2 Sam. 1:4-6; compare 1 Sam. 28:4; 31:1); more important, it was the home town of Saul's wife Ahinoam, and is a prominent dependency of Beth Shan in Solomon's district list (1 Kgs. 4:12, on the date of which see above, Chapter 22). The village thus existed from the 11th century or earlier. The enclosure itself might be a rebuild of some Solomonic structure.

Even were one sure that Jehu destroyed Jezreel, this would not reveal much about the time when the ceramic types recovered in the excavation (of a site mostly robbed to the foundations) were introduced on the site, let alone into the repertoire of the region.[46] In any case, the presence of collared-rim sherds and late bichrome in Megiddo VI (B and A) and three calibrated radiocarbon dates (so, too, the corresponding date at Beth Shan Upper VI or S-2) place Megiddo VI in the late 11th or early 10th century. Jezreel's pre-enclosure fills, too, could preserve early 10th- or even 11th-century material.

And finally, Megiddo VA-IVB may have survived into the 9th century, as is argued below. The same may be true of Hazor X-IX. Nothing on the regional screen stands in the way of dating the construction of Megiddo VA-IVB to the 10th century and, along with it, Hazor X and Gezer VIII.

44. On the stratification and comparison, see Zimhoni, *TA* 19 (1992): 57-70; *TA* 24 (1997): 83-109; and David Ussishkin and John Woodhead, "Excavations at Tel Jezreel 1990-1991: Preliminary Report," *TA* 19 (1992): 3-55; "Excavations at Tel Jezreel 1992-1993: Second Preliminary Report," *Levant* 26 (1994): 1-48; "Excavations at Tel Jezreel 1994-1996: Third Preliminary Report," *TA* 24 (1997): 6-72.

45. See Anahel Zarzeki-Peleg, "Hazor, Joqneam and Megiddo in the Tenth Century B.C.E.," *TA* 24 (1997): 258-88; Amnon Ben-Tor and Doran Ben-Ami, *IEJ* 48 (1998): 1-38. Finkelstein's response to Zarzeki-Peleg is *BASOR* 314 (1999): 55-70, which denies the significance of the appearance on the Jezreel enclosure floors, but not in the fills, of the particular sub-forms to which she points, on the basis of the presence of the overarching types in the Megiddo, Jezreel, and Hazor assemblages.

46. In this light, the caution of H. G. M. Williamson, "Jezreel in the Biblical Texts," *TA* 18 (1991): 72-92, is much to be commended. As to the destruction of Jezreel, 2 Kgs. 10:11 no more implies this than 10:17, 18-27 does a destruction of Samaria, on which cf. 10:35-36; 13:1. To attribute the destruction, if any, to Damascus is equally speculative.

D. Ramses III and the Sea Peoples

On the earlier end of the spectrum, Finkelstein's reading breaks the correlation between the Ramses III inscriptions and the arrival of the Philistines. Finkelstein presupposes that the only contact at the time was in Egypt. Ramses is, however, explicit that Canaanites appealed to him for help, and that the Philistines and Tjeker (Sikils) had been active to the north of Egypt.[47] On Finkelstein's reading, too, Ramses III really did win a decisive victory over the Sea Peoples, who were therefore unable to begin the colonization of Canaan until after Egypt's withdrawal, around the time of Ramses VI. It is a logical step, on this scenario, to connect the withdrawal with the Sea Peoples' arrival. Finkelstein therefore places the coming of the Philistines in the last third of the 12th century.

This position is certainly possible. There are, however, historiographic indications against it. First, Ramses III speaks of Philistine towns in Canaan after the Sea Peoples wreaked havoc on Hatti, including Carchemish on the Euphrates, Arwad on the northern Lebanese coast, and Cyprus. He identifies the place of the land battle as Asia.[48] Finkelstein places the sea battle in the Delta, and this is possible, though the Medinet Habu inscription clearly implies that the harbors in which the battle was fought lay in Canaan, by referring to the frontier there as the place where Ramses equipped his harbors.[49] Further, for Finkelstein, the settlement of the Sea Peoples in strongholds cannot refer to the Philistine pentapolis but only to fortresses in Egypt, possibly in the western Delta or Nubia.[50]

But what becomes of the evidence when we apply the Tiglath-Pileser principle to Ramses's inscriptions? What are the minimal objective correlatives of Ramses's artful claims at Medinet Habu and in Papyrus Harris regarding this conflict? He was able to assert that he enjoyed sovereignty over lands his predecessors did not hold ("I extended the territory of Egypt"). Such sovereignty could be real, nominal, or partial, a mix of both. He claims to have won the surrender of his Philistine and Tjeker (Sikil) opponents. And he claims to have taken captives and resettled them in his own strongholds. Only the last claim is concrete.

47. *ARE* 4.39, 44, 64, the last with a "camp" in Canaan.
48. *ARE* 4.64, 71-73. The advance of the Sea Peoples (Philistines, Sikils, Shekeresh, Danaeans, and Weshesh) "against" Egypt (4.64) is parallel to that of Israel's king in the Dan stela against *(qdm)* the land of the author's father. It might refer to a threat to imperial, not home, territory, as the outfitting of the "border" in Djahi (4.65) indicates.
49. *ARE* 4.65-66.
50. *ARE* 4.74-77, 403.

In fact, the crucial omission at Medinet Habu is the name of the towns or places where the land and sea battles took place. This is highly suspicious. In 845, Shalmaneser III would also omit the location of his campaign — a campaign in which he achieved nothing at all — and for good reason. The logical inference in both cases is that the battle took place either on home territory or so close to it that the advance into foreign land was embarrassingly paltry. Thus, at Medinet Habu, Ramses sets out for Djahi, Asia — in the instance, for southern Canaan. But it is not clear how far he went. Nor does he enumerate either enemy casualties or captives, as he does in the case of both his Libyan wars.

Only in the depiction of his campaign in Canaan, after his 11th year, does Ramses III name particular settlements. Other than those possibly taken from the Karnak toponym list of Ramses II, these are few. Here, however, he does depict seven captives, whom he labels as "the wretched ruler of Hatti as a living captive; the wretched ruler of Amurru; chieftain of the enemy, Tjeker (Sikil); Sherden (Sardinian) of the Sea; chieftain of the enemy, Shasu; Teresh of the Sea; chieftain of the Ph[ilistines?]." In Papyrus Harris, he claims to have campaigned in and taken Shasu captives from Seir, Edom: "I destroyed the people of Seir of the tribes of the Shasu; I plundered the tents of their people. . . . They were pinioned and brought as captives, as tribute of Egypt."[51] It is reasonably clear that he was able to fight in Canaan in his 11th year.

Whether Ramses ever really campaigned in the far north or not, he certainly maintained control of Megiddo, and seems to have held Ashkelon — though whether only at the outset of his reign is a question. This is clear from the inscription of the "temple singer of Ptah" on the ivory found at Megiddo with Ramses's cartouche, and the suggestion is of a connection to Memphis.[52] But the inclusion of the Tjeker, who settled Dor, and Sherden, and very probably Philistines in the account of his Canaanite war is a sure indication that those ethnic groups were already established in Canaan at the time. Thus, Finkelstein's date for the Philistine settlement is decades too late. Ramses's 11th year was 1172 on the low chronology, 1188 on the higher. Philistine monochrome should therefore be dated to the 1190s or 1180s.

Ramses maintains in Papyrus Harris that he built a temple in Asia, specially in "the Canaan," to which Asiatics came to worship and make donations.[53] But

---

51. *ARE* 4.129-31, 217, 404.

52. See Baruch Halpern, "Center and Sentry."

53. One is reminded of the funerary stela of Ramses II found 2.5 km. outside Ashdod: a funerary monument might be tucked away from any important settlement. See Dothan and Porath, *Ashdod* 5:111-14.

he dedicates to the gods of Thebes only nine towns in both Syria and Nubia, captives from which he installed in Theban temples. Only 19 bovids are claimed as an Asian impost, although Canaan does contribute a great deal of oil and a few cedars, its most valuable trade goods at the time.[54] At Heliopolis, Ramses mentions the consecration to Re of some ʿApiru, a number of Asiatics and Nubians, and imposts of indeterminate size collected from unnamed places along the coast of Canaan, eight cedar planks, and a little over five bushels of Canaanite barley.[55] And in the list of his gifts to the gods, Ramses again mentions Canaanite oil and a large quantity of cedar.[56]

In all this, there is little indication of control over Canaan. In the historical section of Papyrus Harris, the only ventures into Asia are the campaign against Shasu in Seir, and probably an expedition into the Sinai for copper.[57] The logical inference is that Ramses's confrontation with the Sea Peoples ended in a sort of stalemate, in which the one success that one can, charitably, attribute to him is holding on to the Delta. Still, the texts attest that in his time the Philistines and Tjeker were established on the Mediterranean coast. It is possible that they never directed an assault against Egypt itself, but advanced successfully into Canaan despite Egyptian attempts to defend the Asian empire. It is this failure that Ramses's inscriptions mask.

Finkelstein is quite right to argue that it is improbable that the Philistine settlement, and its associated Mycenaean IIIC:1b pottery, could coexist for any significant length of time side-by-side with Egyptian outposts, like those at Lachish or Tel Sharia, without some exchange of goods flowing out from Philistia. These outposts and the Canaanite centers associated with them contain objects attesting relations with Ramses III, IV, and VI, spanning a period, from the end of the reign of Ramses III to the start of that of Ramses VI, of at least 10, and not more than about 25, years. Most contemporary scholars restrict the period to 10 years only.[58] But this interval is sufficiently short, after all, to permit the hypothesis of a *cordon sanitaire* containing the Philistines, and indeed a sort of Egyptian embargo on commerce with hated newcomers to the empire. The boycott resulted not in the containment of the Philistines, but in the end of Egypt's control of Canaan. The Sea-Peoples bridgehead was simply

54. *ARE* 4.219, 384, 225, 226, 229, 233, 235.

55. *ARE* 4.281, 338, 328, 341, 344. Cedar also appears in 4.355. The barley is mentioned again in 4.391.

56. *ARE* 4.376, 379. The cedar reappears in the total of the gods' estates in 4.385.

57. *ARE* 4.408.

58. For the chronological data, see *ARE* 4.415. On the high chronology, Ramses III dates to 1198-1166, Ramses VI 1156-1148. On the lower chronology, Ramses III reigned from 1182 to 1151 and Ramses VI from 1141 to 1133.

too broad and successful, and the empire too fragile to withstand the collapse of the coastal trade.

For a time, before Ramses III, as he himself relates, Egypt was no longer in a condition to project power beyond its borders. According to his autobiography, it was even dominated by a Canaanite chieftain, probably in the Delta. This is a logical time for the first Sea-Peoples strikes on the Canaanite coast. The first Egyptian counterstrike came later, with Ramses.

The arrival of the Sea Peoples was a defining event for ethnic consciousness in Canaan itself. One marker here is foodways, often reflecting ethnic consciousness. Prior to and during the Sea-Peoples settlement, Canaanite sites reveal low levels — but real levels — of pig consumption. The early Philistine layers conversely indicate a very high level of pig consumption. But the Israelite sites of the highlands disclose an almost complete absence of pig, showing in addition a general preference for sheep over goat. A site such as Eqron, in the 11th century, was in fact importing its sheep.[59]

Likewise, the Philistines were the first newcomers to Canaan who did not practice circumcision, normally a ritual marking adolescence for agecomplements (though individualized and practiced in infancy in later Israel). This contrast occasioned frequent references in Samuel, and in early Israelite poetry, to "the uncircumcised," namely, the Philistines. Later literature does not stress the point. The difference inhibited connubium: for a community that practices circumcision to deliver its females into the hands of a community that does not is perhaps conceivable, but females unaccustomed to circumcision must regard it as a mutilation, so that a mutual exchange is difficult.

The socialization of Israelite identity in the hill country thus responded in part to Philistine characteristics: contrasting practices took on ideological charge in the definition of ethnicity. It may have had a similar impact on the local populations who did not identify with the Israelites. In fact, the cries for help that Ramses III claims to have heard from Canaan suggest that it did, as

59. See Brian Hesse, "Animal Use at Tel Miqne-Eqron in the Bronze Age and Iron Age," *BASOR* 264 (1986): 17-27; "Pig Lovers and Pig Haters: Patterns of Palestinian Pork Production," *Journal of Ethnobiology* 10 (1990): 195-225; "Husbandry, Dietary Taboos, and the Bones of the Ancient Near East: Zooarchaeology in the Post-processual World," in David B. Small, *Methods in the Mediterranean*, 197-232; Paula Wapnish, "Archaeozoology: The Integration of Faunal Data with Biblical Archaeology," in *Biblical Archaeology Today, 1990*, ed. Avraham Biran and Joseph Aviram (Jerusalem: Israel Exploration Society, 1993), 426-42; Hesse and Wapnish, "Can Pig Remains Be Used for Ethnic Diagnosis in the Ancient Near East?" in Neil A. Silberman and David B. Small, *The Archaeology of Israel*, 238-70. For the development of pig consumption into an ethnic marker, based on the work of Wapnish and Hesse, see Baruch Halpern, *ABD* 5.1130.

does the distribution of Egyptian artifacts, which are far more widespread than Philistine monochrome.[60]

It is possible to model the arrival and early history of the Philistines in Canaan in various ways. Locally manufactured monochrome is essentially confined to the coastal region, from Ashdod south to Gaza (Akko being the exception), reaching inland only as far as Eqron in the north and Tel Haror, near the Egyptian residency at Shariah. The contrast is to the succeeding phase of ceramic production in the pentapolis. Philistine bichrome is attested all over the region of modern Israel, and into Transjordan. However one understands it, the Philistine monochrome culture was relatively contained, enjoying little economic interaction with the neighboring regions.

A general enlistment of the Canaanites, along with the Israelites, against the Philistines and other Sea Peoples would have had this effect, particularly with encouragement from Egypt. Biblical texts suggesting an accommodation between the Israelites and the Amorites in the period just before the introduction of the kingship (Josh. 9; Judg. 1; 1 Sam. 7:14) should not be taken as direct reflections of the time, but of the general ethnic opposition between the circumcised and the uncircumcised that grew out of the Philistine colonization. But one element of Solomon's apology does reflect Egyptian influence. The taking of those Philistine foreskins mirrors Egyptian policy in the 12th century in regard to Libyans, and perhaps Sea Peoples. The application of the policy in Samuel expresses the same xenophobic hostility as the Egyptian practice.[61] More important, it shows that attitudes toward the Philistines among the intended audience of the A source in Samuel remained hardened even in the late 10th century, and perhaps later.[62] A Solomonic state, colluding with

60. See Lawrence E. Stager, "The Impact of the Sea Peoples"; and Carolyn R. Higginbotham, *Egyptianization and Elite Emulation in Ramesside Palestine.* Culture and History of the Ancient Near East 2 (Leiden: Brill, 2000).

61. See *ARE* 4.42, 52, 54 and 44 n.e.

62. Another parallel between Ramses III and David is, oddly enough, the harem conspiracy at the end of the life of each. For Ramses, see *ARE* 4.416-56. Queen Tiy solicited the assistance of harem officials, royal butlers, scribes, a treasury official, and ranking army officers to kill the pharaoh and place her son on the throne. The conspirators were uniformly Egyptian, whereas the tribunal that investigated the plot and pronounced judgment on the conspirators after Ramses's death was in part composed of foreigners. The rebels apparently hoped to incite the people against Ramses (4.427). They also attempted to attain their end by magical means (4.454-56). The difference seems to be that in the case of Ramses the harem conspiracy was discovered and frustrated. The periodic usage in Kings, "he" and perfect verb (3 m. sg.) and object, is also paralleled throughout Ramses III's inscriptions: *ARE* 4.3.

Egypt against the Philistines, might have made good use of such a general disposition.

It is reasonable to posit Canaanite opposition to the Philistines. At Ashdod, a heavy destruction layer separates the production center of Mycenaean IIIC:1b pottery (Stratum XIIIb) from the next phase of Philistine occupation, characterized by bichrome as well as monochrome.[63] At Eqron, the monochrome (IIIC:1b) dominates in Stratum VII, bichrome becoming abundant in Stratum VI.[64] To date, monochrome is not published from the same occupational context — a single floor of a house, for example — as the succeeding bichrome ware. But both appear in Eqron VI.

The apparent discontinuity between monochrome and bichrome was the original inspiration for the "two wave theory," according to which monochrome came with one set, bichrome with a second set of Philistine colonizers.[65] While the situation at Eqron bespeaks continuity, Ashdod in the succeeding century grew to a size of 100 acres. Given the absence of Philistine monochrome at Gezer, it would appear that it was only in the stage of the bichrome phase when monochrome had gone out of general production that the Philistines were able to dominate that site. The same is true of other sites, such as Tell Beit Mirsim B2 and Beth Shemesh III. All of this suggests that the violent end of the monochrome phase at Ashdod may have coincided with an Egyptian-led counterstrike into Philistia that shortly after led to Egypt's disappearance from Canaan, in the mid- to late 12th century. It is likely that other layers coming to an end roughly at this time, like Megiddo VIIA and Lachish Level VI, fell victim to related upheavals.

It is in the full-blown bichrome phase, when the Philistines expanded northward to the Yarqon River in the northern suburbs of modern Tel Aviv, and eastward into the Shephelah of Judah, that a lack of exchange would be inexplicable. By this time, the Philistines had recovered from whatever pressure Egypt had brought to bear against them, and were unrestricted by Egyptian opposition. In other words, the best historical date for the transition to bichrome comes in the last third of the 12th century, not later — and the historical argument is the only basis for achieving an absolute date for the pottery. Monochrome characterized the time of Ramses III, and imported monochrome is in

63. Trude Dothan, *The Philistines and Their Material Culture* (New Haven: Yale University Press, 1982), 37-41. Monochrome persists into Stratum XII there, though this is again the time of its deposition, not production.

64. Seymour Gitin and Trude Dothan, "The Rise and Fall of Ekron of the Philistines: Recent Excavations at an Urban Border Site," *BA* 50 (1987): 197-222.

65. See Dothan, *The Philistines and Their Material Culture*, 295-96.

fact found in Beth Shan Lower VI, a city that probably produced a statue of Ramses III. But bichrome had already appeared before the destruction of Megiddo VIIA, after the accession of Ramses VI. The part of the bichrome phase after monochrome had gone out of production, on the other hand, post-dated the irredentism of Ramses VI.

E. The Dating of the Tenth-Century Strata: Positive Evidence

A statue of Ramses VI at Megiddo was not just removed from its original, no doubt prominent location, but was broken up, like the later stela of Shishaq. In both cases, the purpose of the defacement was more than simple resentment. Thomas Babington Macaulay, in his life of Robert Clive, re-creates the thinking:

> On the road lay the City of the Victory of Dupleix, and the stately monument which was designed to commemorate the triumphs of France in the east. Clive ordered both the city and the monument to be rased to the ground. He was induced, we believe, to take this step, not by personal or national malevolence, but by a just and profound policy. The town, and its pompous name, the pillar, and its vaunting inscription, were among the devices by which Dupleix had laid the public mind of India under a spell. This spell it was Clive's business to break. The natives had been taught that France was the first power in Europe, and that the English did not presume to dispute her supremacy. No measure could be more effectual for the removal of this delusion than a public and solemn demolition of the French trophies.

The point of a monument is to establish an atmosphere of stability and supremacy, and the same is true of the use of a town name as a monument (Shishaq's *ywdhmrk* at Megiddo?), as in the case of Kar-Tukulti-Ninurta, Kar-Shalmaneser or Kar-Esarhaddon. Monuments are erected in remote locations, away from settlement areas, at the sources of rivers or in inaccessible mountains, to discourage their demolition, their symbolic rejection, until they have accumulated the mana of antiquity. This is also the reason for the inscription of curses on personal monuments. Such curses were the more common because control was evanescent in ancient empires, and enforcement even of uncontested suzerainty sporadic, until the time of Tiglath-Pileser III.

But by destroying monuments, an upstart or resurgent power proclaims its contempt for its predecessor and opponent. Egypt was the traditional hegemon of the Canaanite littoral, and this is the reason for the socialization of the Exodus myth in the Israelite state as well as for the shattering of monuments. Since

Canaan and Israel stood always in the pharaoh's shadow, the Israelite national government that controlled Megiddo IVA needed to make a statement such as the one Macaulay attributes to Clive.

Just such a situation also obtained at Megiddo in the period of Stratum VIA. Not only the novel organization of Megiddo VIA but also its treatment of Ramses VI's monument indicates a change in orientation, away from association with an imperial, or pseudo-imperial, organization. The reconstruction of Megiddo after the destruction of Stratum VIIA reflects local initiative in the absence of Egyptian control. Still more, the destruction of the palace and stela reflects Megiddo's integration into a wider polity, controlled by Saul and Ishbaal, or by Dor or Ashdod. It was probably the larger state that condemned the stela to destruction, with the intention, à la Clive, of impressing it on the inhabitants that Egypt would not be returning to take control of the region.

Late Bronze Megiddo was a palatial town, with gold and ivory luxury goods, concentrated in the palace. The mudbrick town, VIA, divulged base metals and elite trinkets, such as stone stamps inscribed with imitation Egyptian cartouches. These were distributed throughout the town, as was storage, including masses of collared-rim store jars in Area CC, which suggest connubium with Israelites, as noted above. And fish imported from Egypt are found in contexts indicating household industry, perhaps including manufacture of fish oil. The town had neither a real palace nor a real temple, suggesting a relative lack of internal hierarchy and very likely subordination to some power based elsewhere. This merchant town, heavily dependent on mediating trade to the Jezreel region from the coast, perished in a fierce and sudden conflagration.

In the real successor layer, VA-IVB, palaces stand alongside pillared buildings typical of the highlands. As we have seen, most scholars rightly ascribe to this layer the six-chambered ashlar gate that resembles gates at contemporary Gezer and Hazor, with all three sites linked to Solomon in Kings.

But VA-IVB, and IVA, as noted in Chapter 22, are poor in domestic architecture. The population was deliberately distanced from the fortification and distributed into the site's hinterland. The same obtains at the contemporary Hazor X.

These layers attest a state strategy, disembedding administrative centers from the population. Comparable are David's adopting a foreign city as his capital and Omri's construction of Samaria. Unlike Egyptian or Assyrian policy, which incorporated Megiddo as a city-state into the imperial ecumene, the policy of the Iron Age broke down the autonomy of the walled center.

Archaeologically, Megiddo VIA is a city-state, peripheral to a larger polity, with a low degree of visible social stratification. The succeeding towns are dedicated, elite administrative outposts of a larger state. Naturally enough, scholars have understood the end of VIA as the point of Megiddo's incorporation in the Israelite kingdom, and attributed its destruction to David. They likewise assign the end of VA-IVB to Shishaq, before 925. The alternative mooted by Finkelstein is that Shishaq destroyed VIA and that Hazael destroyed VA-IVB.

Shishaq's topographic list is a key to establishing the archaeological reality of the 10th century. Too little attention has been focused on the periods of occupation, witnessed by excavation, by survey and by texts, of the sites named in that epigraph. However, the Egyptian itinerary involved a substantial divagation through the Negev, and in particular through its central highlands, whose intensive occupation in the Iron Age was restricted to a single period only.[66] In other words, there is only one possible correlation of Shishaq's record with archaeological remains, namely, those of the central Negev highlands. This is the key to identifying the ceramic horizon of the mid- to late 10th century.

The Negev as a whole was more extensively marked with permanent habitations in the 10th century than in any later period until the 7th century (when the principal emphasis was on the Arava). The previous phase of Negev exploitation was in Early Bronze II-III. Yet Shishaq names over 50 sites in the region, and there is considerable overlap in the names with biblical toponyms in the Negev. Indeed, a large number of sites are termed *ḥqr* or *ḥgr* in the toponym list, followed by a personal name, a pattern common among place names in southern Judah. The tendency among scholars has been to identify this with the Arabic *hijr*, "fort." But equally possible is that the Egyptian text reflects informants' pronunciation of Heb. *ḥṣr*, where the middle radical, *edh* emphatic, was realized differently in different dialects (thus, *qlʿ* in 1 Kgs. 6:34 is *ṣlʿ* in normal Hebrew usage).[67] This word is common in Negev place-names in the Bible, and Hazer Gaddah, attested in Josh. 15:27, seems to appear on Shishaq's list as

---

66. For the Shishaq text, see Kenneth A. Kitchen, *The Third Intermediate Period in Egypt (1100-630 BC)*, 2nd ed. (Warminster: Aris & Phillips, 1986); for the central highlands survey, see Yohanan Aharoni, *IEJ* 17 (1967): 1-17; Rudolph Cohen, *BASOR* 236 (1979): 61-79; "Qadesh — L'Archéologie," *MDB* 39/5-7 (1985): 9-23, for the sequence of fortresses there; *The Settlement of the Central Negev*. Further to the point, Baruch Halpern, "Research Design in Archaeology: The Interdisciplinary Perspective," *NEA* 61 (1998): 53-65; Mordecai Haiman, "The Iron Age II Sites of the Western Negev Highlands," *IEJ* 44 (1994): 36-61.

67. Further Exod. 27:9-15; 35:17; 38:9-18; 39:40; 1 Kgs. 6:18-35; 7:31. See further Baruch Halpern, "Dialect Distribution in Canaan and the Deir Alla Inscriptions," in D. Golomb, *"Working with No Data,"* 121-26, citing also Judg. 5:26 *mḥq*, a variant of *mḥṣ*. Note that a *q* = /δ/ equivalence, while unattested in loanwords, is possible, at least in toponyms, particularly those unattested in previous lists. Note Pap. An. I 22:8 *trqʾl. < trδ*.

Haqr-el-gad.[68] Arad, which Shishaq names as one of his conquests, was first settled in the mid-10th century.[69] There are other cases of overlap with towns in southern Judah named in 7th-century texts.

The pottery repertoire of the 10th-century Negev sites included the burnished red-slipped surface treatment of Iron IIA, albeit on vessel forms that are sometimes more conservative, including open vessels that did not figure in transport of goods. That the surface treatment came early to so peripheral a zone is unlikely. Conversely, the conservative shapes of the pottery may reflect local manufacture by populations now isolated from the heartland of Israelite culture. Local potters familiar with older styles in the north — such as deportees from lowland fortress centers — copied the surface treatment of more recent pottery without altering their throwing techniques to mimic the new forms. So, the Negev sites were destroyed no later than was Gezer VIII, the first stratum at that site to disclose burnished red-slip, and the corresponding strata elsewhere, such as Hazor X and Megiddo VA-IVB (though the ware was present in VB, as in Qasile XII, Ashdod X, and Eqron V, earlier than at the other sites in question).[70]

Shishaq therefore arrived in Canaan before the destruction of Gezer VIII and Hazor X, correlating to Megiddo VA-IVB. Under the circumstances, it is difficult to downdate the start or even the main use phase of Megiddo VA-IVB into the 9th century, or to assign the destruction of an earlier layer to Shishaq there. If Shishaq destroyed Megiddo VIA, then at the time of his raid there was burnished red-slip all around the central Negev highlands but the same avant garde ware had yet to arrive at Megiddo, Hazor or Gezer. And it is the Negev that is without the Late Bronze pottery tradition in which burnished red-slip persists, yet produces it — on such a scenario — ahead of other major centers with a prior history of its production. Megiddo VIA is therefore highly problematic as a candidate for Shishaq's attack.

68. See generally Kitchen, *The Third Intermediate Period in Egypt*, 439-42.

69. See esp. Miriam Aharoni, "Preliminary Ceramic Report on Strata 12-11 in the Arad Fortress," *ErIsr* 15 (1981): 181-204; Ze'ev Herzog, Miriam Aharoni, Anson F. Rainey, and Shlomo Moshkovitz, *BASOR* 254 (1984): 1-34; Herzog, M. Aharoni, and Rainey, "Arad — An Ancient Fortress with a Temple to Yahweh," *BAR* 13/2 (1987): 16-35; Amihai Mazar and Ehud Netzer, "On the Israelite Fortress at Arad," *BASOR* 263 (1986): 87-91. Shishaq's "Greater Arad" is probably identical with the enclosed Stratum XI there, but the fortification may have followed his accession, so that the foundation of Stratum XII cannot with confidence be placed in David's time.

70. See above, Chapter 23B. On the introduction of burnished red-slip and its value for dating across sites see John S. Holladay, *BASOR* 277/278 (1990): 23-70; Amihai Mazar, "On the Appearance of Red Slip," 368-78.

Conversely, as Orna Zimhoni showed, the pottery of Megiddo VA-IVB does resemble that of the Jezreel enclosure. On the basis of biblical texts, which do not report its construction, scholars *assume* the enclosure is Omride.[71] So VA-IVB is also not an ideal candidate for destruction by Shishaq 80 years earlier. Even forgoing this argument, there is a presumption that Shishaq left Megiddo intact. First, as Ussishkin observes, the pharaoh left a 10-ft.-high stela there. Kings do erect monuments in the absence of habitation. However, with rare exceptions,[72] they do so in mountains, or at river sources, not in ruined towns. The installation of the memorial at Megiddo, not in the Pass behind the site, suggests that Shishaq intended the town to operate under his sovereignty.[73]

Furthermore, we have seen above (Chapter 22) that Solomon peddled the tribe of Asher, down to the Akko Plain, to Hiram of Tyre. As noted there, 1 Kgs. 9:10-28 is sufficiently apologetic, sufficiently concerned to put a positive spin on Solomon's sale of the tribe of Asher, to warrant historical reliance. Moreover, the 7th-century (Josianic) author of 1 Kgs. 11 was disposed to find evidence, in the loss of or in threats to territory (Rezin, Hadad), of Solomon's apostasy. The marks of this apostasy were put right, the same author writes, by Josiah.[74]

But even with 1 Kgs. 9 standing in his source, this Josianic author did not penetrate the apology to recognize the loss of the Cabul as anything but a Solomonic triumph, rather than as a further index of deserved adversity. In other words, in antiquity, as well as among modern readers, 1 Kgs. 9 successfully effected its purpose. Its apology was inherited as early as the 7th century, and can have had no other intended function than to protect Solomon's reputation, a concern not pressing much beyond the time of Solomon's reign (and then again in the postexilic period). The apology places Asher in Hiram's hands in the second half of Solomon's reign.

So, Shishaq's stela sat on the border with Tyre. Scholars have suggested that Shishaq sent raiding parties from Megiddo north, but there is no hard basis for

71. Orna Zimhoni, *Studies in the Iron Age Pottery of Israel: Typological, Archaeological and Chronological Aspects* (Tel Aviv: Institute of Archaeology, 1997), 29-56. Note that Jezreel appears in the description of Solomon's fifth province in 1 Kgs. 4:12 as well as lends its name to the valley in 2 Sam. 2:9 and produces a wife for Saul. The royal enclosure there could conceivably stem from the 10th century.

72. Only in the early Middle Assyrian era, so far as I know, and perhaps in the case of Late Bronze Egyptian funerary temples abroad. For Tiglath-Pileser I inscribing a town with a warning that it was not to be rebuilt, see RIMA 2 A.0.87 1.vi.15-21.

73. David Ussishkin, *ABD* 4:666-79; *BASOR* 277/278 (1990): 71-91.

74. For the connection between Solomon's apostasy and the Josianic edition of the Former Prophets, see Baruch Halpern, *The First Historians*, 154-55, 220-28, 249-53, followed by Gary R. Knoppers, *Two Nations Under God*, 1.

this view.[75] Megiddo and the stela represent the high-water mark of Shishaq's expansion. This is why it is only at Megiddo that a stela has been found. It projected menace to the Tyrians, to induce them to collaborate with Egypt. Early 22nd Dynasty stelae were also imported to Byblos. Thus, the pharaoh's influence and collaborators reached up the coast, crowding in on the Tyrians from the opposite direction. Megiddo had to be maintained as an outpost of Egyptian power in order to apply the pressure of a pincer.

The pharaoh's primary targets lay in the Negev, the one place where David's conquest is described in unadulterated terms and confirmed archaeologically, and where Solomon was actively engaged. Shishaq's second targets were the central hills and Jordan Valley. He proceeded directly from Gaza to Judah and Israel, and *confined himself* to their territory, of which Megiddo was thus part.[76] Philistia, Eqron alone aside, is omitted. Shishaq's strategic target, in sum, was the kingdom of the United Monarchy. In particular, Shishaq's concern was to interdict the long-distance trade running from the Hejaz to Tyre and points west, and a Karnak stela may place him at the Red Sea.[77] Yet at Megiddo he stopped.

At Karnak, Shishaq addresses the list of Thutmosis III iconically.[78] He makes Megiddo the turning point in his text.[79] The campaign, too, was de-

75. The items in the itinerary between Megiddo and Aruna, the latter in the Wadi Ara leading southwest to the coastal plain, are *3dr, ydmrk*, [ ]*rt*, and *nm*. The first two could be interpreted as Heb. *'addîr*, possibly the citadel of Megiddo or an adjective describing it; and as a mention of the erection of Shishaq's stela at the site. The third is unclear, and the fourth obscure. There is, however, no reason to think that they are north of the site. In fact, the most likely index of more northerly campaigning is the entry that could be read "House of Zobah," which appears near an entry, "Abel," in Row 4 of the inscription. As the context is extremely fragmentary, however, it would be an error to draw any conclusions on this basis.

76. The coincidence between Shishaq's topographic list and the list of Solomonic government centers in 1 Kgs. 4 is reasonably extensive, especially when one adds the fortifications of 1 Kgs. 9 to the mix. Some of the overlap: Beth Horon, Mahanaim (Sukkot, Penuel, Tirzah), Rehob, Beth Shan, Taanach, Megiddo. Qiryath Yearim may also be included, as is Gibeon. "The Valley" at the end of Row 5 of the list may be the town of Jezreel itself.

77. ARE 4.724A. I owe this reference to my colleague, Donald B. Redford. On the other hand, that *šbrt n gbry* on the stela refers to Ezion Geber seems doubtful. More likely to bear some relation to that toponym or region is Row 7's *ngb 'dnt*.

78. The cords of the captives, the extensive topographic list, the figure of Amun completing the action he is in the midst of all resonate with Thutmosis III.

79. Geographically, in that it is from Megiddo that he turns back south; but also in that Megiddo is the first toponym in Row III (of five rows in the first section). I have wondered whether the principle for ordering the text was not intended to place Megiddo at the focus of the campaign report.

signed to evoke the earlier king: by taking Megiddo, Shishaq likened himself to Thutmosis.[80] This is why, for example, scarabs of Shishaq were collected in later Israel, along with those of Thutmosis and Ramses II. Megiddo was central to Shishaq's ideological scheme of the campaign and, again, the right place for a stela.

All these considerations tell against a Shishaq destruction at Megiddo, as distinct from Rehob, Beth Shan, and Taanach. Nor did the town have reason to resist after the pharaoh had gutted the vicinity. But if Shishaq did not destroy VIA, or VA-IVB, he also did not destroy Hazor X: unless Row IV of the Karnak text contained it, that entire region is omitted from his itinerary.[81] In other words, the only candidate for a contemporaneous destruction of Megiddo VA-IVB and Hazor IX is Hazael, the figure favored by Finkelstein.

Yet there are difficulties here as well. By 880, Omri ruled an Israelite state already outfitted for expansion. He colonized Moab, dominated Ammon, and disembedded a capital. He integrated into a network of local alliances, gaining a daughter of a king of Tyre for his son. Omri's kingdom was not of recent and dubious vintage. He stamped his name on the state ever after, but the kingdom had a history before him.[82]

Ahab's highly developed chariot arm, which pursued Egyptian rather than Semitic tactical doctrine, possibly as a result of cultural, commercial, or political domination by Egypt (a more modest coalition partner at Qarqar), reflects a long period of development and adaptation (above, Chapter 12A and n. 24). The immense wealth needed to import the horses and erect the necessary framework for their maintenance and integration with other arms was not accumulated by a single feat of conquest. It represented the fruit of many harvests, much carriage and exchange, and a highly developed system of taxation

80. Hence Shishaq's inscription does not mention Judah or Israel, but does mention Mitanni, the latter long since defunct. The absence of Jerusalem may be due to one of the lacunae in the text, as James H. Breasted suggested. Or it may reflect the fact that the capital was ransomed. In any case, the omission of Judah and Israel permits Shishaq to portray his assault on Canaan in Thutmoside, rather than Ramesside, terms.

81. See above, n. 75. If Row IV does contain a reference to "the House of Zobah," Shishaq may have explored the limit of the Israelite kingdom in the northeast as well as the northwest. If "the House of Zobah" is a dynastic denomination, however, Zobah cannot have been "the House of Rehob," for the latter term presupposes that Zobah was the territory, as in Neo-Assyrian texts, not the dynasty.

82. Kings suppresses Israelite conquests except for those of Nimshides, as noted in Chapter 14. So, Kings devotes all of five verses to Omri's reign. No Israelite except Joash and Jeroboam II, both descendants of Jehu, conquers anything, and here we learn one reason why — it didn't get reported.

administered through a central authority. This alone renders the idea that the Omride state suddenly popped up in the mid-9th century improbable. At a minimum, 40 years of state-building should be posited as a precursor to the phenomenon; in reality, more are probably indicated. That is, even on the evidence of Qarqar alone, the Israelite state must be dated to the end of the 10th century. And the testimony of Mesha, and of the Tel Dan stela, adds weight to that verdict, and time to the chronology, if Omri really did colonize Moab. The colonization indicates that a mature state was already in existence. Thus, the United Monarchy was real enough to impose such structures as those at Megiddo VA-IVB on the countryside.[83]

Ahab succeeded to the throne in 874. He completed the construction of Omri's sprawling acropolis, accumulated still more chariotry, and expanded his trade network by a diplomatic marriage with Judah — confirmed by the Dan stela — before 863.[84] In 853, Ahab joined Hadadezer of Damascus and Irhuleni of Hamath, along with nine other Western kings, in a confrontation with Shalmaneser III at Qarqar. Ahab died in that same year.

Shalmaneser licked his wounds for a year after the battle of Qarqar, marching east of the Euphrates to the source of the Tigris. For two further years, he intervened in a civil war in Babylonia. Only in 849 did he again cross the Euphrates, but by this time the states lying on the west bank of the river had been absorbed into the Western coalition. Assyria's closest neighbors had thus concluded that the West had stemmed the Assyrian tide.

Shalmaneser evidently weakened the states on the bank of the Euphrates. In 848, he cut a swath through them and raided northern Hamath (Luhuti or Luʻsh), again claiming to have conquered Pattina, north of the Orontes. However, in 847 and 846 he again chose soft targets for the army, suggesting that he suffered another reverse at Hamath.

In 845, Shalmaneser crossed the Euphrates against the same Western opponents, and he boasts repeatedly of having raised an army of 120 thousand men. He doesn't claim to have traversed further obstacles — this is unusual in Assyrian annals, whose authors revel in describing difficult travel conditions. He doesn't

---

83. This point was first made in a paper delivered at the Society of Biblical Literature in November 1997 as an argument against the denial of a pre-9th-century Israelite state. William G. Dever subsequently applied it, in conversation, in July, 1998, to a critique of Israel Finkelstein's "low chronology," which, he remarked, lacked at the time a stage of early state formation. But see now Finkelstein, "State Formation in Israel and Judah: A Contrast in Context, a Contrast in Trajectory," *NEA* 62 (1999): 35-52.

84. 2 Kgs. 8:26: Ahazyahu of Judah dies in 841, his single year of reign, at the age of 22. He was therefore born in 863. His mother was Athalyah, probably Ahab's young daughter as she continued to bear children until 842/841 according to the claims of 2 Kgs. 11.

claim to have captured territory or taken booty. He claims to have taken prisoners and equipment from the battlefield only. Most of all, he doesn't say where the battle took place! He does not ford the Euphrates for another four years. An army of 120 thousand, and nothing to boast of but its size (which suggests that the magnitude is relatively reliable). Yet four years later, the usurpers Hazael and Jehu appear, and Hadadezer, the descendants of Omri, Irhuleni, and Hamath vanish. The world was turned upside down — in Shalmaneser's absence.

On this year, 841, biblical, Assyrian, and Damascene claims coincide. Shalmaneser claims to have contained Hazael in Damascus, and to have received the submission of Jehu in Israel. The Dan stela claims that the kings of Israel and Judah were killed, although it claims, against the report in Kings, that it was the king of Damascus, not Jehu, who killed them. Kings claims that Jehu killed Jehoram of Israel and Ahaziah, king of Judah, and seized power. Mesha, in Moab, commemorates the same events: "I outlasted [the son of Omri] and all his dynasty."[85]

The regnant view is that Jehu revolted against the House of Omri to ally with Assyria against Damascus.[86] Yet Israel and Damascus were at war *before* Jehu's coup, at Ramoth Gilead, where Joram of Israel was wounded: the rift came earlier.[87] Further, Jehu sundered relations with Judah and Tyre, and suffered 40

---

85. *w'r'h bh.* "Son of Omri" here means Ahab at one level, and the king of the House of Omri at another. See esp. André Lemaire, "La stèle de Mésha et l'histoire d'Israel," in Daniele Garrone and Felice Israel, *Storia e tradizioni di Israele,* 143-76; 157-60 elaborated in "Les territoires d'Ammon, Moab et Edom dans la deuxième moitié du IX-e s. avant notre ère," *Studies in the History and Archaeology of Jordan* 4 (1992): 209-14.

86. The programmatic study is that of Michael C. Astour, "841 B.C.: The First Assyrian Invasion of Israel," *JAOS* 91 (1971): 383-89.

87. The Dan stela now attests Hazael's accession in advance of Jehu's, confirming the sequence in Kings. The wounding of Joram of Israel at Ramoth Gilead is Hazael's justification for claiming that Jehu merely completed the killing he began.

The story of Joram's wounding at Ramoth Gilead is certainly the origin of the story in 1 Kgs. 22, of Ahab's alleged death in battle. 1 Kgs. 22 is later than the account of Jehu's coup, and therefore than the Nimshide apology, but how much later is a question. It is also first inserted into the history in the Josianic edition of Kings.

The death in battle is contradicted by 1 Kgs. 22:40, which tells us that Ahab died in peace. See Baruch Halpern and David S. Vanderhooft, *HUCA* 62 (1991): 179-244, on the expression, and on the literary and literary-historical issues. Note that if Ahab had a marriageable daughter in say 865, who could bear a child in 863, then if she was no younger than 15 at the time of the birth, he was no younger than about 15 or 16, and perhaps a good deal older, in 878. This places his birth before 892, and probably a good deal earlier, so that his death "in peace" in the original edition of Kings, which presupposes perhaps a birth ca. 908-903, makes sense. Certainly, Omri in 885, at the start of the civil war, was no

years of Aramean domination; so on the hypothesis, he grossly miscalculated Assyria's potency, the power of the very nation Israel had recently been defeating. Most of all, the standard view does not reckon with the collapse of Hamath.

Famously, in the story "Silver Blaize,"[88] Mr. Sherlock Holmes recommends to a policeman's attention "the curious incident of the dog in the night-time." "But the dog did nothing in the night-time," comes the reply. "That was the curious incident." In royal inscriptions, as we have repeatedly seen, silence is meaningful: if the king does not claim an accomplishment, he *cannot* take credit for it; this is the contrapositive of the principle that royal inscriptions exaggerate the king's achievements to the limits of verisimilitude, if rarely beyond. The principle continues to apply to communiqués today. Our record is filled with things that are curiously absent from it.

The taking of Hamath was the dog in the night-time of the 9th century. It left no mark on the record, until a Sargonic reference, a century later, to Irḫuleni's submission. In 841, Shalmaneser appeared at the gates of Damascus, but he remains silent about Hamath. The silence is unbroken in 838, Shalmaneser's last trip south of the northern Orontes. In 831, Shalmaneser sent a field marshal to deal with a revolt in Pattina, north of the Orontes.

Again, the same ground rules for interpretation apply to Assyrian royal propaganda as to Egyptian or Israelite. Any action that can be construed as an achievement is maximized. Thus, if the Assyrian king survives a battle in which an enemy soldier suffered so much as a fractured nail, he has smitten his enemies. The corollary is that what the text does not say is just as important as what it does. If the Assyrian king actually achieved anything, it would be narrated, in maximized form.

Shalmaneser's annals do not claim that he conquered Hamath. They do not claim that Hamath submitted to him. They do not even claim that Hamath sent him gifts. The silence about Hamath's submission indicates that its disappearance has nothing to do with Shalmaneser, and may even redound to his discredit. Shalmaneser's reports about the campaigns of 841 and 838 enumerate all the other Western vassals and report his ravaging the territory of refractory Damascus, but pass over Hamath in silence.

Hazael's booty inscriptions celebrate his inroads across "the river," Orontes, to dominate Unqi. By 831, his northward expansion occasioned a revolt in Pattina, which Dayan-Assur suppressed. Revolt in Assyria followed in the 820s. On the basis of the booty inscriptions, some scholars posit that Hazael

---

spring chicken, but as commander of a royal army certainly in his 30s, perhaps in his 40s or even 50s, which also explains his death "in peace" in 874.

88. *Strand,* December 1892; collected in *The Memoirs of Sherlock Holmes.*

forded the Euphrates. But the accounts of the revolt in Assyria indicate that the contenders for Shalmaneser's throne continued to maintain control of regions west of the Euphrates. So Hazael's crossing of the Euphrates is the product of scholars being duped by the rhetorical strategy of the booty inscriptions — which do not name the "river" Hazael crossed. Still, Hazael's expansion into Hamath, and the defection of Unqi and Pattina to him, explain the titulature of his son Bar-Hadad — king of Aram. Along with Shalmaneser's silence, the revolt in Pattina by 831 dates the submersion of Hamath early.

What happened must be this. The Western allies thrashed Shalmaneser in 845, possibly having initiated the conflict by crossing or at least reaching the Euphrates itself. This would explain Shalmaneser's reluctance to name the battlefield. It also explains the huge size of his army, which would have taxed Assyria's logistics had it been sent far afield as an expeditionary force. Shalmaneser's 120-thousand-man force reflects mobilization of the home guard. Likewise, a year later, in 844, as in 852, the year after his defeat at Qarqar, Shalmaneser chose to exercise his army in a march to the sources of the Tigris rather than take on a serious military opponent. He received "tribute" from Melid, far to the north, but without engaging in battle. This may represent a mere exchange of gifts. Even in 843 Shalmaneser campaigned in the populated but impoverished Zagros range. The year, 845, was disastrous for Assyrian arms.

Shortly after the war of 845, Hazael murdered his predecessor. His coup prompted a nasty description in Kings, and a reference of unusual asperity — he is "the son of nobody" — in Shalmaneser's annals. His plan was that Damascus, not Hamath, should lead the West's revanche. The origins of Mesha's revolt thus date to ca. 845, though Mesha conceals both this and the fact that he ruled at Hazael's pleasure. This is also the setting of Edom's revolt against Jehoram of Judah. With Mesha diverting Israel, Hazael reduced Hamath, perhaps pretending to join it in a march on the east.[89] The next year, Hazael turned on Israel, his other local rival. As late as 841, Ramoth Gilead was the border between them. The Jezreel was secure: during Jehu's murderous putsch, Ahazyahu flees wounded from Jezreel to a fortified safe haven, Megiddo.[90] Thus, before Jehu,

89. For an alternative construction of the events, and a superb treatment of Shalmaneser's annals, see Shigeo Yamada, *The Construction of the Assyrian Empire: A Historical Study of the Inscriptions of Shalmaneser III (859-824 B.C.) Relating to His Campaigns to the West.* Culture and History of the Ancient Near East 3 (Leiden: Brill, 2000).

90. Only two strata come into question here: IVA and VA/IVB. If the Chicago excavators are right, however, that VA/IVB was not completed in Palace 1723 in the south, this would leave a vulnerable point insufficiently guarded. It may also be that the original fortification wall of the stratum was never completed. IVA is thus the Omride stratum, and Ahazyahu huddled behind Wall 325.

the north remained intact. Even Kings, whose loathing for the House of Omri knows no limits, admits that the Omrides lost no territory.

Jehu, however, ceded Transjordan all the way to "Aroer on the Arnon," Mesha's northernmost fortification: "I built Aroer, and I made the highway on the Arnon."[91] He abandoned Moab, and lost control over Ammon.[92] He killed a Tyrian princess, a king of Judah, and his own king and royal family, and did so as Hazael's cat's paw — hence the Dan stela, in which Hazael claims to have defeated, and implies that he killed, Jehoram of Israel and Ahaziah of Judah.[93] Later that spring, while Hazael was still securing his new accessions, Shalmaneser turned up, shutting Hazael into Damascus. Shalmaneser lacked the logistical network to sustain a long stay, and departed, with much of Hazael's chariotry, which could not be sheltered in the fortification. Jehu, however, found himself in the uncomfortable position of paying Shalmaneser, only to remain Hazael's vassal. In 838 there was a recurrence, but Hazael merely huddled in Damascus until Shalmaneser's forces lost interest and wandered off home.

Jehu represents Israel's collapse under Damascene pressure. His apology, taken up whole in Kings, asserts that he was a religious reformer, filled with zeal for Yahweh and disgust at the Phoenician connections, display, and acropolis temple of the House of Omri. But this is an old story: reform, said Roscoe Conklin, is the final refuge of a scoundrel. Opponents of Jehu's dynasty, such as Hosea, saw his patriotism and reform as mere window-dressing for the bloody massacre that left the royal family dismembered, and the heads of 70 Omride princes mounded up in a pile outside Samaria's gate.

Jehu sold the country into servitude as the price of personal power. Like Mesha, Jehu was Hazael's creature, and held the throne as a dependent. Later in Kings, Hazael reaches Gath and Jerusalem (2 Kgs. 12:17-18[18-19]). We have no report of a campaign in Israel because he enjoyed a right of way: as Jehu's overlord, he likely enlisted Jehu's army in the attack.[94]

91. 2 Kgs. 10:32-33. Mesha: *'nk bnty 'r'r w'nk 'śty hmslt b'rnn*, KAI 181:26. For a different perspective on the term "highway," see N. L. Tidwell, "Mesha's *hmslt b'rnn*: what and where?" *VT* 46 (1996): 490-97.

92. For the king of Ammon, Baasha son of Ruhubi, see above, Chapter 9D. For an alternative, see Yamada, *The Construction of the Assyrian Empire.*

93. The Dan stela furnishes a parallel to Shalmaneser's claim about Giammu in 853, thus, in the one annals edition where he implies that he himself killed Giammu, which, indirectly, is true, as here; Hazael knew and may have imitated his annals when he or his son inscribed the Tel Dan stone. See Chapter 5, n. 12.

94. Thus, Adad-Nirari III is the first Assyrian king to mention Judah or Edom. He names Joash, who accepted the Assyrian yoke in hopes of escaping the domination of Damascus. Hazael controlled the whole region under Jehu and his heirs. And our author in

While it is possible that Hazael demolished fortifications, such as Hazor, Jehu's betrayal of Israel without a fight made such a policy unnecessary. And a fortification on the Tyrian border would be useful both for staging campaigns to the south and for securing the lines of trade. In the circumstances, Hazael makes no more plausible a candidate than Shishaq for the destruction of Megiddo VA-IVB.

For Megiddo VIA, David makes no better a destroyer: our texts attribute no such conquest to him — so we have an Israelite dog in the night-time. Saul and Ishbaal are possible conquerors, since they conducted warfare against local populations — a practice rare in Canaan. But other scenarios are as likely: the site succumbed to a disaster unconnected with war; or it was destroyed by Philistines after it leagued with Saul or Ishbaal; or it fell in a conflict between Ashdod or Eqron and Dor. Of the possibilities, the most likely is that Megiddo VIA was destroyed by the Israelite partisans of Absalom.[95]

There is a possible explanation for the destruction of Hazor IX. 1 Kgs. 15:17-21 relates that Asa bribed the king of Damascus to attack Israel. "Ben-Hadad," king of Aram, in Damascus, "smote Iyyun, Dan, and Abel of the House of Maacah, and all of Kinrot, in addition to the land of Naphtali." A narrative set at least a decade later, 1 Kgs. 20, relates that Ahab won back the towns lost previously to Damascus. The Dan stela then relates that the king of Israel had advanced against the land of the author's father. It is possible that stela refers to the territory captured in the campaign of 1 Kgs. 15 and restored to Israel in that of 1 Kgs. 20. The campaign of 1 Kgs. 15 is probably historical, insofar as the presentation, again, uses a standard strategy of apology for the alienation of territory to which Jerusalem staked a theoretical claim.[96] The campaign of 1 Kgs. 20 makes sense between that of "Ben-Hadad" and of the author of the Dan stela.

But this conclusion is speculative. 1 Kgs. 20 is not from an archival source. Moreover, the theory cannot account for the fall of Megiddo VA-IVB. The cause of the latter is to be sought in one of the upheavals within Israel, from Jero-

---

Kings, dependent on the Nimshide apology, has no inkling that Jehu participated in Hazael's attack on Jerusalem, or, favoring Jehu, does not care to relate the fact.

95. See above on the destruction of the statue of Ramses VI probably in Stratum VI or VII (it was under a VIA floor, but Chicago also located it, improbably, under a VIIB wall), and the destruction of Shishaq's stela, presumably in Stratum IVA but possibly in VA-IVB, both reflecting the operation of a larger state. See further Chapter 21 on the destruction of Megiddo VIA. Because what was going on in Cisjordanian Israel until the Absalom revolt is not reported in any source, it may be that Megiddo VIA was in fact destroyed during David's reign but before that uprising.

96. For this argument, and the accuracy of the political framework in 1 Kgs. 20, see Yamada, *The Construction of the Assyrian Empire.*

boam's reign to that of Jehu. Or possibly, the change from Megiddo VA-IVB to Megiddo IVA was occasioned by a king's desire — possibly Omri's or Ahab's — to replace the city of palaces with a city of industry. There is probably no way to achieve certainty on this question.

The point here is the same one that scholars widely accept about the destructions marking the end of the Late Bronze Age in Canaan. We lack the basis in critical history for assigning Megiddo's destruction layers to particular kings. What we could correlate to historical processes — were we only in agreement as to their dates — are changes in the function of the site.

Thus, Megiddo VIA is a bustling mercantile center mediating highland produce to the plain. VB marks the transition to highland architecture, and is the short-lived precursor of VA-IVB. VA-IVB is an Israelite layer that presents Tyrians and other traders with the formal facade of display. International exchange and claims of prestige were of central moment to the state in this period. The utilitarian layout of Stratum IVA, with its reuse of VA-IVB ashlar and VA-IVB palace space for the industry of the "stables," reflects a concern less with display than with maximizing income.[97] Like Hazor VIII, with its own tripartite building, Megiddo IVA sat on a border and did service as an entrepot for the state. Of these sites, only the last layers' destroyers can be fixed: they were the Assyrians of the late 8th century, who repopulated Megiddo as a city-state regulating a province. However, the early structures of Megiddo IVA — Building 338 and the southern stables — are more formal than the later structures, which may include domestic quarters. The layer may have been more impressive at the time of its construction than at the end.

The transition from Megiddo VB to Megiddo VA-IVB was such that the latter may peaceably have been imposed over the former. All the same, VA-IVB is a town certainly affording residence to a highly prestigious governor (the palaces; note 1 Kgs. 4:12). The rustication of the population to the margins of the surrounding valley here and at Hazor X, reflecting the policy of a territorial state, did not take place in the 9th century, when Hazor was under pressure (witness the conquest of Dan by Aram Damascus). Rather, the policy reveals greater concern with the secession or defection of the city-state than with an immediate prospect of invasion. It belongs to a time of secure borders, such as that of the United Monarchy. Megiddo VA-IVB and Hazor X fit historically, as well as ceramically, into the kingdom of Solomon.

---

97. The "stables" may be stables. However, preliminary indications from soil samples taken by myself or under my direction, in consultation with Israel Finkelstein and David Ussishkin, in 1998, and augmented by further sampling in October 1999 with Steven Weiner of the Weizmann Institute, have been inconclusive.

Yet the same policy bespeaks a fixation on display, on the creation of "new" cities, like those of Assyrian monarchs on the borders of their own realms, that comports with a policy of emptying the public purse into public works. This ill suits Megiddo VIA or corresponding strata at Hazor or Gezer: no one bankrupted the state building Megiddo VIA, or mortgaged large tracts of land to finance it. Megiddo VA-IVB was the fancy facade on an empty husk, a triumph of desperate hope and avaricious expectation over a realistic view of the state's place in its world. It belongs to Solomon's world, not that of Omri.

In addition, neither Hazor X nor Megiddo VA-IVB, nor either town in the succeeding period, boasts anything on the order of a traditional temple (shrines, to be sure, even in Megiddo VA-IVB, at Building 2081; and, in IVA, perhaps at 338, but in each case as part of a larger administrative complex). These are not, thus, independent city-states, not royal centers, but nodes in a national administrative network. Megiddo VA-IVB and Hazor X are in this sense new strata at each of these sites — they reflect the operation of an invasive national administration. If such an administration comes only in the mid-9th century, however, it is problematic to explain the extent of the Israelite contingent at Qarqar, or Omri's marriage alliance with Tyre.

Not least, the invention of the collocation of Megiddo, Hazor, and Gezer in 1 Kgs. 9:15 would be a remarkable coincidence. At a textual level only, Shishaq's preoccupation with the Negev settlements establishes, yet again, that the central Negev settlement pattern reflected in the accounts of David's reign (1 Sam. 27:6, 10; 30:27-31; 2 Sam. 8:13-14; 23:20) and made a central element of Solomon's activity (Ezion Geber, Tyrian alliance, queen of Sabaea) is an authentic 10th-century artifact. The organization of Solomon's provinces (1 Kgs. 4:7-19) consistently reflects 10th-century realities (above, Chapter 22D). The towns in 1 Kgs. 9:15-18 do not duplicate the province list, in which neither Hazor nor Gezer appears. And the province list includes, as an independent district, the tribe of Asher that was dismantled in the Cabul purchase.

The refitting of Hazor and Megiddo also squares with a late Solomonic concern with pressure from Damascus and the newly relocated border of Tyre. Tyre was some 75 km. from Megiddo, but the border was far closer. Gezer remained the border with Philistia, and perhaps with Egypt. It was the threat of commercial competition from Ezion Geber that drove Shishaq to efface the regularization of occupation and thus of travel in the Negev, after all, to relegate the populations there once again to the status of bandits, rather than extensions of a Canaanite state.

Likewise, it was the threat from Shishaq that most exigently drove Solomon to renew his construction activity after the completion of the capital and temple, and that occasioned his concession of Asher to Tyre. In other words, the historical geography of the fortification program fits into a continuum of reliable historical geographic contexts, and makes sense within the overall strategic picture emerging from but carefully concealed by the Solomon narrative. Again, the concern of the narrative is to glorify Solomon's achievements by minimizing the contraction of his kingdom, so the fortification scheme becomes a major achievement. This indicates that these data are reliable, and that it is the tropes in which the data are presented that require deconstruction.

Archaeologically, the conjunction of Megiddo with Hazor and Gezer in 1 Kgs. 9:15 must be taken in three contexts:

1. Shishaq left his footprint over the passes, lowlands, and highlands of Israel. Its presence in the Negev is marked. Other possible traces are at such Shephelah or lowland sites as Khirbet Rabûd, Tell Beit Mirsim B3, Tel Ḥalif VII, Beth Shemesh IIA, Tel Baṭashi IV, Gezer VIII, Qasile X, ʿIzbet Ṣarṭah II, and, less probably, Ashdod X and Tel Miqneh IV. In the Jezreel, Yoqneam XIV, Taanach IIB, ʿEin Ṣippori, Rehob lower city Stratum 2 (and E-2 and C-2), and Beth Shan S-1 (Lower V); in Manasseh, Tell el-Fârʿah VIIB; and in the Jordan Valley, Tell el-Ḥammah were all destroyed along the same pottery horizon as that of Hazor X and Megiddo VA-IVB. There are differences in the assemblages from site to site, but the materials are comparable — the latest elements belong to the same ceramic period.[98] Conversely, the destructions associated with that of Megiddo VIA, if any, are more restricted, comprising chiefly Yoqneam XVII and perhaps Beth Shan S-2, Gezer IX, and Yarmut.[99] The Megiddo VA-IVB horizon is intrinsically more likely to have been that of Shishaq's time.

2. If Megiddo VIA, a settlement avoiding display, was Solomon's town, the contemporary layer at Hazor, Stratum XI, was a village. This means jettisoning the text of 1 Kgs. 9:15, which reports public works *(bnh)* at these sites. Again, the text presents the construction as a royal achievement while masking the

---

98. The survival of early forms in a site, or part of a site, says nothing about the *terminus ante quem* of its disuse. The presence of "degenerate" Philistine forms, e.g., is meaningless beside the introduction of later materials alongside them. The introduction of later forms is not simultaneous across space, but it is in any case a far more sensitive index of end-use than is the overall assemblage. For the horizon, see Holladay, *BASOR* 277/278 (1990): 23-70. For Hammah, see Jane M. Cahill, Gary Lipton and David Tarler, "Tell el-Hammah," *IEJ* 38 (1988): 191-94.

99. For a possible destruction at Tel Yarmut, see P. de Miroschedji, "Tel Yarmut, 1987," *IEJ* 38 (1988): 199. Most likely, Yarmut was a casualty of the conflict between David and Gath, on the one hand, and Israel on the other, during Absalom's revolt. Note also the slightly later abandonment of Dawwara: Israel Finkelstein, "Kh. Ed-Dawwar, 1985-86," *IEJ* 38 (1988): 79-80; "Excavations at Khirbet ed-Dawwara: An Iron Age Site Northeast of Jerusalem," *TA* 17 (1990): 163-208.

pressing strategic concerns that demanded it despite a high cost in territory and prestige. The absence of expensive architecture in Megiddo VIA (and before Stratum X at Hazor) speaks against the comparison. Likewise, Kings reports that Jeroboam made Tirzah (Tell Fârʿah) his capital in Cisjordan. There, the 10th-century Stratum VIIb is the first circumvallated town. It is possible, of course, that the [Ti]rzah in Shishaq's list is another town, or that it was unwalled. But it is most likely that Jeroboam chose a town with an existing fortification, and that Shishaq encountered it. Fârʿah VIIb is on the horizon of Megiddo VA-IVA. Shishaq may not have destroyed it, presenting it instead to his protégé. But it is far more likely to be the town of his time than is the unwalled VIIa, with pottery from the horizon of Megiddo VIA.

3. With Yadin and Dever, Hazor, Megiddo, and Gezer had similar gates on one pottery horizon. The gates at Gezer and Hazor connected to casemate defensive walls. Megiddo had exterior casemates running out from the palaces, but possibly had a wall formed from a mix of structures atop the mound.[100] Like Hazor (VIII),[101] Megiddo (IVA) was subsequently fitted with a solid wall (325). Like Dor, it had a four-chambered gate. It lacked a recognizable palace. The town dominated by palaces in VA-IVB gave way to one dominated by industry (the "stables") in IVA. Similarly, in Hazor VIII, an imposing commercial building was imposed over a large public complex of Stratum X-IX. Domestic architecture is introduced at Hazor in some quantity in Stratum VIII and at Megiddo at some point in the occupation of Stratum IVA.[102] The two sites develop more or less in lockstep over Iron IIA-B, reflecting central planning based elsewhere.

The comparison with Gezer in the later era is not clear, although inside the Gezer gate some sort of palace (10,000) does appear, as at Megiddo. And the introduction of similar gates, for example at Lachish IV and Ashdod, makes it improbable that a later historian would guess that it was precisely Gezer, Hazor, and Megiddo that Solomon built, that had contemporary 10th-century six-chambered gates. Later, the construction of a four-chambered gate at Dor

---

100. So the critique in Herzog, *The City-Gate in Eretz-Israel*.

101. See now Ben-Tor and Ben-Ami, *IEJ* 48 (1998): 12.

102. The Chicago reports support a phasing of IVA into at least two stages, e.g., the additions to the northern stables (403, 404), for which Lamon and Shipton, *Megiddo* 1:44, and the likelihood that Building 1616 was based on Palace 1723, but belonged to a phase after 1444, thus, to a second phase of IVA (68-69). The difference in their construction, including the heights and quality of the troughs, the courtyard space, location, and paving all suggest that the northern and southern "stables" do not themselves belong to the same construction phase. This would imply in turn that the additions to the northern stables in fact represent a subphase of a phase.

Site	Ramses III-Myc	VI Bichrome	Saul David	Siamun Solomon	Hiram Shishaq
Megiddo	-	VIIA/VI	VIA/VB	VB*, VA-IVB	VA-IVB
Hazor		XII	XI	XB*, XA	-
Gezer	-	XIII-XI	XI-IX	IX-VIII* IX burnt by Siamun	VIII-VII transition
Beth Shan	Lower VI	Upper VI		Lower V*	Lower V
Taanach			IIA? IIA-IIB*	IIB	
Eqron	VII-VI	VI-V*	V(-IV)	IV(-III?)	IV-III transition, or III
Ashdod	XIIIb-XII	XIIIa-XI	X*	X-IX	IX
Dan		V?	V	IVA*	-
Hadar			IV	III	-
'Oreime			V	IV	-
Beth Shemesh		III	III	IIA*	IIA-B transition?
Timnah (Banash)			V	V	IV* IV abandoned
Yoqneam		(XIX-XVIII)	XVII/XVI	XVI-XIV	XIV-XIII transition
Qasile	-	XII-XI*	X	IX	IX
Masos	-	IIIa	II		
Shari'a			VIII		
'Izbet Sartah		II*	II	II-I	
Beersheba		IX	VIII	VIII-VII*	VII/VI transition

*First appearance of quantities of burnished, red-slipped pottery

should have led to the claim that *it* was "built" by Solomon, particularly if the historian's aim was sheer glorification.

The probability is thus that Stratum VA-IVB at Megiddo survived Shishaq by an indefinite number of years. The occasion for its destruction may have had something to do with the destruction of Shishaq's stela. The town, generally, was not really destroyed. The palaces were burned, but otherwise the town was for the most part simply remade along the lines of a new and less hierarchical urban plan. Palace 6000, at least, may have served as a stronghold for the local garrison, explaining its surgical destruction, perhaps by Shishaq. Megiddo VA-IVB may have fallen victim to the Israelite state after Egypt lost its capacity to maintain, or interest in maintaining, a forward base there.

But the end of the stratum, toward the end of the 10th century or the start of the 9th, says nothing about the time of its construction. There is some evidence, in the Chicago report, that VA-IVB was never completed, and this may be confirmed by the absence of a completed circumvallation. So its construction may shortly antedate Shishaq's campaign — by about 14 years on the biblical account. But in any case, Megiddo VA-IVB has all the marks that we should expect of a Solomonic construction. It, and Hazor X, and Gezer VIII are like the Negev settlements chronological markers of the 10th century.

Overall, the archaeological evidence for the United Monarchy coincides with the historical evidence. The state was far from impressive, but it was real.[103]

103. Much of the foregoing chapter represents an adptation of my essay, "The Gate at Megiddo and the Debate over the Tenth Century," in *Congress Volume, Oslo 1998*, ed. A. Lemaire and M. Sæbø. VTSup 80 (Leiden: Brill, 2000): 79-121.

Afterword

The preceding investigations indicate that David's enemies regarded him as a non-Israelite. Specifically, they thought of him as the Gibeonite agent of Philistine masters. They accused him of importing a foreign icon, the ark, as his state symbol. He consistently allied with foreign powers to suppress the Israelites whom he dominated. He spent most of his career as a brigand-king, and, where he ruled, he did so by employing murder and mayhem as tools of statecraft. In fact, the only murder in the books of Samuel of which he was probably innocent is the one murder of which he stands accused in the apology. His enemies considered him a mass murderer.

David's empire, such as it was, was first confined to Judah, then extended into Transjordan. In the latter sphere, he brokered a balance between Israelites in the north and Ammon in the south, and as his price extracted all the heirs of the House of Saul to kill at Gibeon. He did not achieve full control over Israel until the end of the Absalom revolt.

At the end of his life, David was certainly betrayed by one of his harem women, Bathsheba, and his foreign mercenary bodyguard. Instead of his heir, Adonijah, they installed Solomon, hitherto known as the son not of David but of Uriah the Hittite, on the throne. Quite as homicidal as his predecessor, but more punctilious and self-righteous about it, this second king of Judah quickly cleaned house, erasing his rivals, and probably all of David's sons, from the scene. He gave his kingdom the airs of a great power, and incidentally gave us the portrait of a flawed but heroic, then finally pathetic, David. Through him, his mother speaks with stunning artfulness.

The real David was not someone whom it would be wise to invite to dinner.

And you certainly would not be happy to discover he was marrying your daughter, or even a casual acquaintance. But he did have one virtue. His achievement in creating Judah and conquering Israel left, through his wife and through his successor, if not his son, a legacy of hope and of aspiration. If that legacy has little to do with the real David, if later imaginings of his empire magnify a small, sanitize a corrupt, and beautify an ugly reality, a reality there nevertheless was. The biblical story of David is indeed mythic in nature. But the myth was made necessary, though not by his glory, by his gore.

General Index of Select Topics

481

Index of Scholars Cited

488